ENVIRONMENTAL POLICY

ENVIRONMENTAL POLICY

NEW DIRECTIONS FOR THE TWENTY-FIRST CENTURY

Fourth Edition

Edited by

Norman J. Vig
Carleton College

Michael E. Kraft
University of Wisconsin–Green Bay

CQ PRESS

A Division of Congressional Quarterly Inc.
Washington, D.C.

CQ Press
A Division of Congressional Quarterly Inc.
1414 22nd Street, N.W.
Washington, D.C. 20037

(202) 822-1475; (800) 638-1710

http://books.cq.com

Printed in the United States of America

Cover design: Naylor Design Inc.

Library of Congress Cataloging-in-Publication Data

Environmental policy : new directions for the twenty-first century /
    edited by Norman J. Vig and Michael E. Kraft. — 4th ed.
        p.   cm.
    Originally published: Environmental policy in the 1990s. 3rd ed. Washington, D.C. :
CQ Press, 1997.
    Includes bibliographical references and index.
    ISBN 1-56802-520-3 (cloth : alk. paper). — ISBN 1-56802-341-3 (pbk. : alk. paper)
    1. Environmental policy—United States.   I. Vig, Norman J.   II. Kraft, Michael E.
GE180.E586   1999
363.7'056'0973—dc21
                                                                                99-35420

For
Carol, Ted, Jesse, and Peter
Sandy, Steve, and Dave

Contents

Preface

As we enter the twenty-first century, environmental policy is being challenged as never before. New demands worldwide for dealing with the risks of climate change, threats to biological diversity, and similar issues will force governments everywhere to rethink policy strategies and find new ways to reconcile environmental and economic goals. Within the United States, a conservative Republican Congress elected in 1994 brought a markedly higher level of criticism of environmental programs and the agencies that implement them. That criticism continued through the 105th Congress (1997–1998), although it was somewhat more subdued. The resulting legislative gridlock prevented Congress from revising the major environmental laws, an action that serious students of environmental policy believe is essential to address contemporary challenges. The struggle to redefine policy goals and means for the next century has been equally evident at state and local levels as policymakers, business leaders, and environmentalists have searched for new approaches that might better address concerns over the efficiency, effectiveness, and equity of environmental programs. As much as the debate over the environment has shifted in important ways in the 1990s, however, government and politics will continue to play crucial roles in shaping our environmental future.

When the first environmental decade was launched thirty years ago, protecting our air, water, and other natural resources seemed a relatively simple proposition. The polluters and exploiters of nature would be brought to heel by tough laws requiring them to clean up or get out of business within five or ten years. The sense of urgency that swept Congress in 1969 and 1970 as it passed the National Environmental Policy Act and Clean Air Act with scarcely a dissenting voice reflected the rise of one of the most dramatic popular movements in American history. Since then, despite ebbs and flows, the tide of public opinion favoring environmental protection has entered the mainstream of political life. But preserving the life-support systems of the planet now appears a more daunting task than anyone imagined three decades ago. Not only are problems such as global climate change more complex than controlling earlier sources of pollution, but the success of American policies is now more than ever tied to the actions of other nations.

Events during the 1990s demonstrated the new demands and difficulties for environmentalism. In 1992 the largest international diplomatic conference ever held was convened in Río de Janeiro, Brazil, to address an enormous range of global environmental issues. That same year, Bill Clinton's election as president promised a renewed commitment to environmental protection in the United States. Yet the president was largely unsuccessful in implementing his agenda, and in 1995 the Republican Congress proposed major revisions to most of our national environmental legislation. Congress has also threatened to block ratification of the 1997 Kyoto Protocol that for the first time establishes binding national limits on greenhouse gas emissions.

Translating symbolic commitments into effective action is no easy task. The making of public policy often resembles an awkward dance between idealistic ends and deficient means. The history of environmental protection is no exception. Implementing the major legislation of the 1970s on air and water pollution, hazardous waste, and preservation of public lands and other resources proved to be difficult and frustrating. Although genuine progress was made, few deadlines were met and results have fallen considerably short of expectations. At the same time, environmental protection has turned out to be a moving target. What appeared to be a relatively straightforward job of controlling a few key pollutants by mandating corrective technologies at the "end of the pipe" has become a much larger and more difficult task that may require fundamental changes in human behavior.

By the end of the 1970s it was evident that many of the most serious environmental problems had their origins in the massive use and careless disposal of industrial chemicals whose cumulative health and environmental effects were largely unknown. These second-generation problems required cleanup of thousands of abandoned dumps, leaking toxic waste sites, and military bases and weapons-production facilities under Superfund and other programs. By the end of the decade, these programs were plagued by growing controversy over the slow pace and escalating costs of cleanups. But by then a third generation of even more challenging ecological issues captured public attention: global climate change, deterioration of the ozone layer, tropical deforestation, extinction of species, and ocean and coastal pollution. The agenda for the twenty-first century is already crowded with issues that will take the greatest human ingenuity to resolve.

This book seeks to explain the most important developments in environmental policy and politics since the 1960s and to analyze the central issues that face us in the early twenty-first century. Like the previous editions, it focuses on the underlying trends, institutional shortcomings, and policy dilemmas that all policy actors face in attempting to resolve environmental controversies. This edition contains two new chapters, and all other chapters have been revised and updated. We have also attempted to place the Clinton administration and the congressional agenda in the context of the ongoing debate over the cost and effectiveness of past environmental policies, as well as the search for ways to reconcile and integrate economic, environmental, and social goals through sustainable development. As such, the book has broad relevance for the environmental community and for all concerned with the difficulties and complexities of finding solutions to our worsening environmental conditions.

Part I provides a retrospective view of policy development as well as a framework for analyzing policy change in the United States. Chapter 1 serves as an introduction to the book by outlining the basic issues in U.S. environmental policy over the past three decades, the development of institutional capabilities for addressing them, and the successes and failures in implementing policies. The evolving role of the states in implementing federal policies and developing their own innovative approaches is considered by Barry G. Rabe in chapter 2. The states' capabilities have become a more urgent question, he says, as Congress seeks to devolve responsibilities from Washington. In chapter 3 Christopher J. Bosso examines public opinion trends and the emergence of environmental opposition groups as well as new grassroots environmental movements. One of his most important conclusions is that environmental groups in the 1990s are becoming more fragmented, decentralized, and diversified in their concerns and modes of action. Part I concludes with a perceptive essay by Robert C. Paehlke that discusses the core values of environmentalism and proposes a variety of ways in which environmental ethics may be incorporated into environmental, social, and economic policies.

Part II analyzes the role of federal institutions in environmental policymaking. Chapter 5, by Norman J. Vig, discusses the role of recent presidents as environmental actors, focusing on the varying approaches of the Reagan, Bush, and Clinton administrations. In chapter 6 Michael E. Kraft examines the causes and consequences of policy gridlock in Congress, especially in light of the new Republican agenda. Chapter 7, by Lettie McSpadden, explores the evolving role of the federal courts in interpreting environmental laws, reviewing administrative decisionmaking, and ultimately resolving many environmental disputes. She also discusses new legal trends such as the growing controversy over private property rights and legislative "takings." In chapter 8 Walter A. Rosenbaum takes a hard and critical look at the Environmental Protection Agency, the nation's chief environmental institution, and discusses recent efforts to "reinvent" its regulatory functions. As he notes, other federal bureaucracies face similar problems of institutional reform as they attempt to implement the far-reaching environmental policies enacted by Congress.

Some of the broader dilemmas in environmental policy formulation and implementation are examined in Part III. The first two chapters focus on approaches that are increasingly being advocated to improve the efficiency and effectiveness of environmental regulation. Economist A. Myrick Freeman III discusses the potential for more rational economic decisionmaking, including the use of cost-benefit analysis, in chapter 9. He also asks how market incentives such as pollution taxes and tradable discharge permits could be introduced to achieve better results at less cost. Chapter 10, by Richard N. L. Andrews, takes up a parallel set of questions regarding scientific risk assessment: how well can environmental risks be measured given the technical obstacles and human judgments involved? And should comparative risk assessment be used to set environmental priorities? The last two chapters in Part III consider broader social responsibilities that are becoming recognized as central to environmental health and progress. In chapter 11 Evan J. Ringquist analyzes the emergence of the environmental justice movement in response to growing awareness of racial and social inequities in the distribution of environmental burdens. He presents new empirical evidence regarding these inequities and discusses potential remedies. Chapter 12 moves the spotlight to evolving business practices. Daniel Press and Daniel A. Mazmanian examine the transition to a sustainable economy, in part through the "greening of business" and the use of market-based initiatives such as voluntary pollution prevention and reduction. They find the transition from command-and-control regulation to greening to be well advanced, but with mixed results to date.

Part IV shifts attention to selected issues and controversies, both globally and domestically. In chapter 13 Lamont C. Hempel surveys the key scientific evidence and major disputes over climate change, as well as the evolution of the issue, especially since the late 1980s. He also assesses government responses to the problem of climate change, and the outlook for public policy actions in the twenty-first century. Chapter 14, by William R. Lowry, considers the "new era" in natural resource policies. He reviews the history of U.S. natural resource policies and agencies, the lively debates that have arisen over them in recent years, and a range of proposals for institutional change—from privatization and devolution to ecosystem management and collaborative planning. Richard J. Tobin, in chapter 15, examines the plights of developing nations that are struggling with a formidable array of threats brought about by rapid population growth and resource exploitation. He surveys the pertinent evidence, recounts cases of policy success and failure, and also indicates the remaining barriers (including insufficient commitment by rich countries) to achieving sustainable development in these nations. The last chapter in Part IV, by David Vogel, discusses the effects, actual and potential, of new international trade agreements such as the North American Free Trade Agreement (NAFTA) and the General Agreement on Tariffs and Trade (GATT) on national policies for resource preservation and environmental protection.

The final chapter, by the editors, draws on the contributions to the book and on other current research to define an agenda of major environmental issues and new policymaking approaches that have been the focus of contention during the 1990s and that are critical if we are to move toward sustainable development in the twenty-first century. We discuss recent initiatives of the Clinton administration and its nemesis in Congress in offering some suggestions for a more constructive policy dialogue in the future.

We thank the contributing authors for their generosity, cooperative spirit, and patience in response to our seemingly ruthless editorial requests. It is a pleasure to work with such a conscientious and punctual group of scholars. Special thanks are also due to Brenda Carter, Gwenda Larsen, Tracy Villano, Chris Karlsten, Talia Greenberg, and the rest of the staff at CQ for their customarily splendid editorial work. We also gratefully acknowledge support from the Department of Political Science and the Environmental and Technology Studies Program at Carleton College and the Department of Public and Environmental Affairs at the University of Wisconsin–Green Bay. Finally, we thank our students at Carleton and UW–Green Bay for forcing us to rethink our assumptions about what really matters. As always, any remaining errors and omissions are our own responsibility.

Norman J. Vig
Michael E. Kraft

Contributors

Richard N. L. Andrews is professor of environmental policy in the Department of Environmental Sciences and Engineering and in the Curriculum in Public Policy Analysis, University of North Carolina at Chapel Hill. He is the author of *Managing the Environment, Managing Ourselves: A History of American Environmental Policy* (1999) and of many articles and other publications on environmental policy.

Christopher J. Bosso is associate professor of political science and department chair at Northeastern University, where he specializes in American politics and public policy. He is the author of *Pesticides and Politics: The Life Cycle of a Public Issue* (1987)—winner of the 1988 Policy Studies Organization award for the best book in policy studies. He also has written on the intersection of environmental values and American democratic institutions, on trends within the environmental community, and on public policymaking dynamics.

A. Myrick Freeman III is William D. Shipman Professor of Economics at Bowdoin College. He also has held appointments as senior fellow at Resources for the Future, visiting college professor at the University of Washington, and Robert M. La Follette Visiting Distinguished Professor at the University of Wisconsin–Madison. He is the author of *The Measurement of Environmental and Resource Values: Theory and Methods* (1993) and *Air and Water Pollution Control: A Benefit-Cost Assessment* (1982). He is currently a member of the Science Advisory Board of the U.S. Environmental Protection Agency.

Lamont C. Hempel is Hedco Chair of Environmental Studies and Director of Environmental Programs at the University of Redlands. He specializes in U.S. and international environmental policy, with emphasis on issues of climate change, sustainable community development, air pollution, and coral reef protection. His recent publications include *Environmental Governance: The Global Challenge* (1996) and *Sustainable Communities: From Vision to Action* (1998).

Michael E. Kraft is professor of political science and public affairs and Herbert Fisk Johnson Professor of Environmental Studies at the University of Wisconsin–Green Bay. He is the author of, among other works, *Environmental Policy and Politics* (1996) and coeditor of *Public Reactions to Nuclear Waste* (1993), *Environmental Policy in the 1990s* (1997), and *Technology and Politics* (1988)—the last two with Norman J. Vig, and, with Daniel A. Mazmanian, *Toward Sustainable Communities: Transition and Transformations in Environmental Policy* (1999).

William R. Lowry is associate professor of political science at Washington University in St. Louis. He has published numerous articles and three books: *The Dimensions of Federalism: State Governments and Pollution Control Policies* (1992), *The Capacity for Wonder: Preserving National Parks* (1994), and *Preserving Public Lands for the Future: The Politics of Intergenerational Goods* (1998). His current research involves the politics of restoration of ecosystems on the Missouri and Colorado Rivers.

Daniel A. Mazmanian is dean of the School of Natural Resources and Environment at the University of Michigan. He served as director of the Center for Politics and Economics at the Claremont Graduate School from 1986 to 1996, and has written numerous articles and books. Among them are *Can Organizations Change? Environmental Protection, Citizen Participation, and the Corps of Engineers* (with Jeanne Nienaber, 1979), *Implementation and Public Policy* (1983, 1989), and *Beyond Superfailure: America's Toxics Policy for the 1990s* (with David Morell, 1992). He is coeditor (with Michael E. Kraft) of *Toward Sustainable Communities: Transition and Transformations in Environmental Policy* (1999).

Lettie McSpadden teaches public law and public policy in the Department of Political Science at Northern Illinois University. She is the author of *One Environment under Law* (1976), *The Environmental Decade in Court* (1982), and *U.S. Energy and Environmental Groups* (1990). She has written numerous articles and book chapters on air and water pollution, natural resources conservation, and other environmental issues. She has a special interest in how federal courts oversee administrative discretion in environmental policy.

Robert C. Paehlke is professor of political studies and environmental and resource studies at Trent University, Peterborough, Ontario. He is the author of *Environmentalism and the Future of Progressive Politics* (1989), coeditor of *Managing Leviathan: Environmental Politics and the Administrative State* (1990), and editor of *Conservation and Environmentalism: An Encyclopedia* (1995). He is a founding editor of the Canadian journal *Alternatives: Perspectives on Society, Technology, and Environment.*

Daniel Press is associate professor of environmental studies at the University of California, Santa Cruz, where he teaches environmental politics and policy. He is the author of *Democratic Dilemmas in the Age of Ecology* (1994) and is currently studying local open-space preservation in California.

Barry G. Rabe is professor of environmental politics at the School of Natural Resources and Environment at the University of Michigan. He is the author of, among other works, *Beyond NIMBY: Hazardous Waste Siting in*

Canada and the United States (1994) and *Fragmentation and Integration in State Environmental Management* (1986). He is coauthor of *When Federalism Works* (1986). His current research examines pollution prevention, environmental regulatory integration, and subnational capacity to devise policy to address global climate change in Canada and the United States.

Evan J. Ringquist is associate professor of political science at Florida State University, where he teaches courses on environmental and energy policy as well as American government and public policy. He is the author of, among other works, *Environmental Protection at the State Level: Politics and Progress in Controlling Pollution* (1993) and coauthor of *Contemporary Regulatory Policy* (forthcoming 1999). He is completing a new book on environmental justice: *Green Justice for All? The Influence of Race and Class in Environmental Protection.*

Walter A. Rosenbaum is professor of political science at the University of Florida in Gainesville, where he specializes in environmental and energy policy. During the academic year 1990–1991 he served as a senior analyst in the Office of the Assistant Administrator for Policy, Planning, and Evaluation at the Environmental Protection Agency. Among his many published works are *Environmental Politics and Policy*, 4th ed. (1998), and *Energy, Politics, and Public Policy* (1987).

Richard J. Tobin is principal research scientist at the American Institutes for Research in Arlington, Virginia. In this capacity he provides technical assistance to governments in developing countries in Asia, Latin America, and sub-Saharan Africa on issues related to education, environment, and natural resources management. His book *The Expendable Future: U.S. Politics and the Protection of Biological Diversity* received the Policy Studies Organization's Outstanding Book Award.

Norman J. Vig is professor of political science and the Winifred and Atherton Bean Professor of Science, Technology, and Society at Carleton College. He has written extensively on environmental policy, science and technology policy, and comparative politics, and is coeditor (with Michael E. Kraft) of *Environmental Policy in the 1990s* and *Technology and Politics*. His most recent books are *The Global Environment: Institutions, Law, and Policy* (1999), coedited with Regina Axelrod, and *Parliaments and Technology: The Development of Technology Assessment in Europe* (1999), coedited with Herbert Paschen.

David Vogel is professor of business and public policy at the Haas School of Business at the University of California, Berkeley. He has written extensively on business-government relations and government regulation in the United States, the European Union, and Japan. He is the author of *National Styles of Regulation: Environmental Policy in Great Britain and the United States* (1986) and *Trading Up: Consumer and Environmental Regulation in a Global Economy* (1995).

1

Environmental Policy from the 1970s to 2000: An Overview

Michael E. Kraft and Norman J. Vig

Environmental issues soared to a prominent place on the political agenda in the United States and other industrial nations in the early 1990s. The new visibility was accompanied by abundant evidence domestically and internationally of heightened public concern over environmental problems.[1] Reflecting such worries, policymakers around the world pledged to deal with a range of important environmental challenges, from protection of biological diversity to air and water pollution control. Such commitments were particularly evident at the 1992 United Nations Conference on Environment and Development (the Earth summit), held in Río de Janeiro, which approved an ambitious agenda for redirecting the world's economies toward sustainable development, and in Kyoto, Japan, in December 1997 where delegates agreed to a landmark treaty on global warming.

Equally evident throughout the 1990s, however, were rising criticism of environmental programs and a multiplicity of efforts to chart new policy directions. Intense opposition to environmental and natural resource policies arose in the 104th Congress (1995–96). The Republican Party took control of both the House and Senate for the first time in forty years and mounted a concerted campaign to reduce the scope of governmental activities, including environmental regulation (see chap. 6). It was the most direct and forceful attack on environmental policies since the early 1980s during Ronald Reagan's presidency, although like the effort by the Reagan administration, ultimately it failed to gain public support.[2] Nonetheless, increasing dissatisfaction with the effectiveness, efficiency, and equity of environmental policies could be found among a much broader array of interests, including the business community, environmental policy analysts, environmental justice groups, and state and local government officials.[3]

The last half of the 1990s has been a period in which governments at all levels have struggled to redesign environmental policy for the next century. The U.S. Environmental Protection Agency (EPA) has tried to "reinvent" environmental regulation through use of community-based environmental protection, collaborative decisionmaking, public-private partnerships, and enhanced flexibility in rulemaking and enforcement (see chap. 8).[4] New emphases within the EPA and other federal agencies and departments on ecosystem management and sustainable development have sought to foster comprehensive and long-term strategies for environmental protection.[5] As Barry Rabe notes (see chap. 2), state and local governments have pursued similar goals, with adoption of a wide range of innovative policies that promise to address some of the most important criticisms directed at contemporary environmental policy.

The precise way in which Congress, the states, and local governments will change environmental policies over the next few years remains unclear. The outcomes will depend on how environmental issues are defined by the various policy actors, the role of the media in covering the disputes, the state of the economy, the relative influence of opposing interest groups, and political leadership. One thing is certain, however. Political conflict over the environment is not going to vanish any time soon. It will likely increase as the United States and other nations struggle to define how they will respond to the latest generation of environmental problems.

Another conclusion is inescapable. The heightened antienvironmental rhetoric and political backlash during the 1990s—in the states as well as in Congress—plainly indicate that environmental policy is at an important crossroads. More than ever we need to learn what works and what does not, and how best to refashion environmental policy for the demands of the twenty-first century. We also need to sort out the genuine efforts to reform environmental policies and programs by improving their effectiveness and efficiency from those actions that would compromise the broadly supported commitment to environmental protection goals that the public and policy-makers have made over the past thirty years.

In this chapter we examine the continuities and changes in environmental politics and policy over more than three decades and discuss their implications for the early twenty-first century. We review the policy-making process in the United States and we assess the performance of government institutions and political leadership. We give special attention to the major programs adopted in the 1970s, their achievements to date, their costs, and the need for policy redesign and priority setting in light of the limited budgetary resources likely to be available in the years ahead. The chapters that follow address in greater detail many of the questions we explore in this introduction.

The Role of Government and Politics

The greater political salience of environmental protection efforts in the 1990s underscores the important role government plays in devising solutions to the nation's and the world's mounting environmental ills. Global climate change, population growth, the spread of toxic and hazardous chemicals, loss of biological diversity, and air and water pollution each requires diverse actions by individuals and institutions at all levels of society and in both the public and private sectors. These range from scientific research and technological innovation to improved environmental education and significant changes in corporate and consumer behavior. As political scientists, we believe government has an indispensable role to play in environmental protection and improvement. The essays in this volume thus focus on environmental policies and the governmental institutions and political processes that affect them. Our goal is to illuminate that role and to suggest needed changes and strategies for achieving them.

The government plays a preeminent role in this policy area because most environmental threats represent public or collective goods problems. They cannot be resolved through purely private actions. There is no question that individuals and nongovernmental organizations can do much to protect environmental quality and promote public health. The potential for such action is demonstrated by the impressive growth of grassroots environmental groups over the past decade and the diversified efforts by business and industry to prevent pollution through development of "greener" products and services (see chaps. 3 and 12).

Yet such actions are often insufficient without the backing of public policy—for example, laws mandating control of toxic chemicals that are supported by the authority of government. The justification for governmental intervention lies partly in the inherent limits of the market system and the nature of human behavior. Self-interested individuals and a relatively unfettered economic marketplace guided mainly by a concern for short-term profits tend to create spillover effects, or "externalities," such as pollution. Collective action is needed to correct such market failures. In addition, the scope and urgency of environmental problems typically exceed the capacity of private markets and individual efforts to deal with them effectively. For these reasons among others, the United States and other nations have relied on governmental policies—at local, state, national, and international levels—to address those problems.

Adopting public policies does not imply, of course, that voluntary and cooperative actions by citizens in their communities cannot be the primary vehicle of change in many instances. Nor does it suggest that governments should not consider a full range of policy approaches—including use of market-based incentives, public-private partnerships, and provision of information to the public—to supplement or even replace conventional regulatory policies where needed. In an era of profound skepticism about governmental performance and deep citizen distrust of the political process, it is imperative to consider alternative ways of dealing with environmental and other public problems. The guiding principle should be to use those approaches that work best—those that bring about the desired improvements in environmental quality, reduce health and ecological risks to a minimum, and help to integrate and balance environmental and economic goals.

Political Institutions and Public Policy

Public policy is a course of governmental action or inaction in response to social problems. It is expressed in goals articulated by political leaders; in formal statutes, rules, and regulations; and in the practices of administrative agencies and courts charged with implementing or overseeing programs. Policy states an intent to achieve certain goals and objectives through a conscious choice of means, usually within some specified period of time. In a constitutional democracy like the United States, policymaking is distinctive in several respects: it must take place through constitutional processes, it requires the sanction of law, and it is binding on all members of society. Normally, the process is open to public scrutiny and debate, although secrecy may be justified in matters involving national security and diplomatic relations.

The constitutional requirements for policymaking were established more than two hundred years ago, and they remain much the same today. The U.S. political system is based on a division of authority among three branches of government and between the federal government and the states. Originally intended to limit government power and to protect individual liberty, this division of power may impede the ability of government to adopt timely and coherent environmental policy. Dedication to principles of federalism means that environmental policy responsibilities are distributed among the federal government, the fifty states, and thousands of local governments (see chap. 2).

Responsibility for the environment is divided within the branches of the federal government as well, most notably in the U.S. Congress, with power shared between the House and Senate, and jurisdiction over environmental policies scattered among dozens of committees and subcommittees (see table 1-1). One recent study, for example, found that thirteen committees and thirty-one subcommittees in Congress had some jurisdiction over EPA activities.[6] The executive branch is also institutionally fragmented, with at least some responsibility for the environment and natural resources located in eleven cabinet departments and in the EPA, the Nuclear Regulatory Commission, and other agencies (see fig. 1-1). Although most environmental policies are concentrated in the EPA and in the Interior and Agriculture Departments, the Departments of Energy (DOE), Defense, and State are increasingly important actors as well. Finally, the more than one hundred federal trial and appellate courts play key roles in interpreting environmental legislation and adjudicating disputes over administrative and regulatory actions (see chap. 7).

The implications of this constitutional arrangement were evident in the early 1980s as Congress and the courts checked and balanced the Reagan administration's efforts to reverse environmental policies of the previous decade. They were equally clear during the 1990s when the Clinton administration vigorously opposed efforts in both the 104th and 105th Congresses (1995 to 1998) to weaken environmental programs. More generally, divided authority produces slow and incremental alterations in policy, typically after broad consultation and agreement among diverse interests both within and

Table 1-1   Major Congressional Committees with Environmental Responsibilities

Committee	Environmental Policy Jurisdiction
House	
Agriculture	agriculture in general; forestry and private forest reserves; soil conservation; human nutrition; rural development; water conservation related to Department of Agriculture; groundwater; pesticides and food safety
Appropriations[a]	appropriations for all programs
Commerce (formerly Energy and Commerce)	air pollution; national energy policy and issues related to the Department of Energy; exploration, production, storage, marketing, pricing, and regulation of energy sources, including all fossil fuels and solar and renewable energy; energy conservation; regulation of the nuclear energy industry and disposal of nuclear waste; safe drinking water; pesticide control; Superfund and hazardous waste disposal; toxic substances control; noise control
Resources (formerly Natural Resources)	public lands and natural resources in general; national parks, forests, and wilderness areas; irrigation and reclamation; mines and mining; grazing; energy and nuclear waste disposal; oceanography, fisheries, international fishing agreements, and coastal zone management; wildlife, marine mammals, and endangered species; Geological Survey
Science (formerly Science, Space, and Technology)	environmental research and development; energy research and development; research in national laboratories; global climate change; NASA, NOAA, and National Science Foundation
Transportation and Infrastructure (formerly Public Works and Transportation)	Clean Water Act, pollution of navigable waters; water resources and flood control; rivers and harbors; dams and hydroelectric power; surface transportation; management of emergencies and natural disasters; Superfund and hazardous waste cleanup
Senate	
Agriculture, Nutrition and Forestry	agriculture in general, soil conservation and groundwater; forestry and private forest reserves; human nutrition; rural development; pesticides and food safety; global change
Appropriations[a]	appropriations for all programs

(Continued on next page)

Table 1-1   *(Continued)*

Committee	Environmental Policy Jurisdiction
Commerce, Science and Transportation	interstate commerce and transportation in general; coastal zone management; inland waterways and marine fisheries; oceans, weather, and atmospheric activities; outer continental shelf lands; technology research and development; surface transportation; global change
Energy and Natural Resources	energy policy in general; conservation research and development; oil and gas production and distribution; nuclear waste policy; solar energy systems; mining; national parks and recreation areas; wilderness; wild and scenic rivers; public lands and forests; global change
Environment and Public Works	environmental policy and research in general; air, water, and noise pollution; construction and maintenance of highways; safe drinking water; environmental aspects of outer continental shelf and ocean dumping; toxic substances other than pesticides; Superfund and hazardous wastes; solid waste disposal and recycling; nuclear waste policy; fisheries, wildlife, and Endangered Species Act; water resources, flood control, and dams; improvements of rivers and harbors; global change

Source: Compiled from descriptions of committee jurisdictions reported in *Congressional Quarterly, Players, Politics, and Turf of the 105th Congress* (Washington, D.C.: Congressional Quarterly, March 22, 1997).

[a] Both the House and Senate Appropriations Committees have Interior subcommittees that handle all Interior Department agencies as well as the Forest Service. In both houses a subcommittee on VA, HUD, and Independent Agencies is responsible for EPA appropriations. The Energy Department, Army Corps of Engineers, and Nuclear Regulatory Commission fall under the jurisdiction of the subcommittees on Energy and Water Development. Tax policy affects many environmental, energy, and natural resources policies, and is governed by the Senate Finance Committee and the House Ways and Means Committee.

outside of government. Such political interaction and accommodation of interests enhance the overall legitimacy of the resulting public policies. Over time, however, the cumulative effect has been disjointed policies that fall short of the ecological or holistic principles of policy design so often touted by environmental scientists and activists.

Nonetheless, when issues are highly visible, the public is supportive, and political leaders act cohesively, the American political system has proved flexible enough to permit substantial policy innovations.[7] As we shall see, this was the case in the early to mid 1970s, when Congress enacted major changes in U.S. environmental policy, and in the mid 1980s, when Congress overrode objections of the Reagan administration and greatly strengthened policies on hazardous waste and water quality, among others. Passage of the monumental

Figure 1-1 Executive Branch Agencies with Environmental Responsibilities

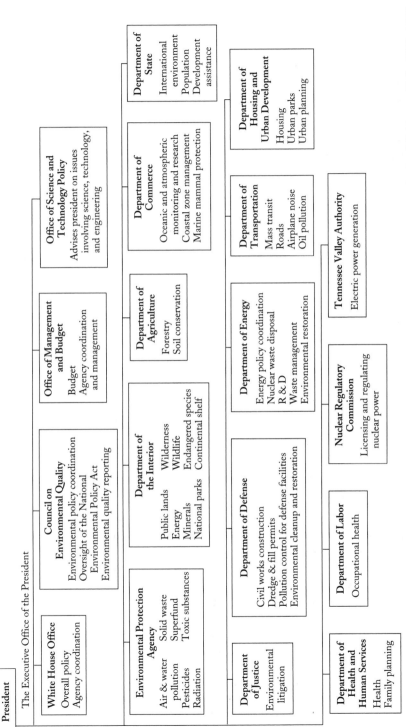

Sources: Council on Environmental Quality, *Environmental Quality: Sixteenth Annual Report of the Council on Environmental Quality* (Washington, D.C.: GPO, 1987); *United States Government Manual 1997/98* (Washington, D.C.: GPO, 1997), and authors.

Clean Air Act Amendments of 1990 was a more recent example of the same alignment of forces. With bipartisan support, Congress adopted the act by a margin of 401 to 25 in the House and 89 to 10 in the Senate.

Policy Processes: Agendas, Streams, and Cycles

Policy scholars have proposed several models for analyzing how issues get on the political agenda and move through the policy processes of government. These theoretical frameworks help us to understand both long-term policy trends and short-term cycles of progressive action and political reaction. One set of essential questions concerns *agenda setting:* how do new problems emerge as political issues that demand the government's attention, if they do achieve such recognition? For example, why did the federal government initiate controls on industrial pollution in the 1960s and early 1970s but do little about national energy issues until well into the 1970s, and even then only to a very limited extent?

There are some hurdles to overcome in an issue's rise to prominence: it must first gain societal recognition as a problem, often in response to demographic, technological, or other social changes. Then it must get on the docket of governmental institutions, usually through the exercise of organized group pressure. Finally it must receive enough attention by governmental policymakers to reach the stage of decisional or policy action.[8] An issue is not likely to reach this latter stage unless conditions are ripe (for example, a "triggering event" that focuses public opinion sharply, as occurred with the Exxon *Valdez* oil spill in 1989). One model analyzes agenda setting according to the convergence of three "streams" that can be said to flow through the political system at any time: (1) evidence of the existence of problems; (2) available policies to deal with them; and (3) the political climate or willingness to act. Although largely independent of one another, these problem, policy, and political streams can be brought together at critical times when "policy entrepreneurs" are able to take advantage of the moment and make the case for policy action.[9]

Once an issue is on the agenda, it must pass through several more stages in the policy process. These stages are often referred to as the *policy cycle.* Although terminology varies, most students of public policy delineate at least five stages of policy development beyond *agenda setting*: these are (1) *policy formulation* (the actual design and drafting of policy goals and strategies for achieving them—which may involve extensive use of environmental science and policy analysis); (2) *policy legitimation* (mobilization of political support and formal enactment by law or other means); (3) *policy implementation* (provision of institutional resources and detailed administration of policy); (4) *policy evaluation* (measurement of results in relation to goals and costs); and (5) *policy change,* including termination (modification of goals and/or means).[10]

The policy cycle model is useful because it emphasizes all phases of policymaking. For example, how well a law is implemented is as important as the goals and motivations of those who drafted and enacted the legislation. The model also suggests the continuous nature of the policy process. No policy decision or solution is "final" because changing conditions, new information, and shifting opinions will require policy reevaluation and revision. Other short-term forces and events, such as presidential or congressional elections or environmental accidents, can also profoundly affect the course of policy over its life-cycle. Thus, policy at any given time is shaped by the interaction of long-term social, economic, technological, and political forces and short-term fluctuations in the political climate. All of these factors are manifest in the development of environmental policy.

The Development of Environmental Policy from the 1970s to 2000

As implied in the policy cycle model, the history of environmental policy in the United States is not one of steady improvement in human relations with the natural environment. Rather, it has been highly uneven, with significant discontinuities, particularly since the late 1960s. It can be understood, to borrow from the concept of agenda setting, as the product of the convergence or divergence of two political currents, one that is deep and long term and the other shallow and short term.

Social Values and Environmental Policy Commitments

The deep political current consists of fundamental changes in American values that began after World War II and accelerated as the nation shifted from an industrial to a postindustrial (or postmaterialist) society. Preoccupation with the economy (and national security) has gradually given way to a new set of concerns that includes quality-of-life issues like the environment.[11] These changes suggest that in the coming decades ecological issues will replace, or be integrated with, many traditional political, economic, and social issues, both domestically and internationally. This integration was evident at the 1992 Earth summit and its concern about sustainable development. It is also championed in *Our Common Future,* an influential report by the World Commission on Environment and Development that helped to shape the Earth summit's agenda.[12] Historian Samuel Hays describes these changes as a social evolutionary process affecting all segments of American society. Political scientist Robert Paehlke, the author of chapter 4 in this volume, characterizes environmentalism as a new ideology with the potential to alter conventional political alignments.[13] These long-term social forces are setting a new direction for the political agenda.

The shallow political current consists of shorter-term political and economic forces—elections, economic cycles, and energy supply shocks—that may alter the salience of environmental issues. These short-term developments may either reinforce or weaken the long-term trends in society that support environmental protection. For example, in the early 1970s the deep and shallow currents converged to produce an enormous outpouring of federal environmental legislation. Yet later in the decade energy shortages and high inflation rates led the Carter administration to pull back from some of its environmental commitments. The election of Ronald Reagan in 1980 shifted the environmental policy agenda sharply to the right for much of the 1980s. The two currents joined once again in the early 1990s at the beginning of the Clinton administration. However, the 1994 and 1996 congressional elections blunted that particular convergence (see chap. 6). At the same time, these elections and comparable developments at the state level reinforced the search for new directions in environmental policy to which we referred above.

Thus the interaction of these two currents helps to explain the fluctuations in environmental policy commitments from one year, or decade, to the next. Over time, however, one can see the continuity of strong public support for environmental protection, expanding government authority, and increasingly effective, if often controversial, policy implementation—even if scarce resources and sometimes poor agency management limit success. The near-term discontinuities, such as environmental policy opposition in the 104th and 105th Congresses, capture our attention, yet they can be misleading. The longer-term transitions and transformations in American values and environmental behavior arguably are more important. We focus here on the major changes from 1970 to the late 1990s. We discuss the future agenda for environmental politics and policy in the conclusion of the book.

Policies Prior to 1970

Until about 1970 the federal government played a sharply limited role in environmental policymaking—public land management being a major exception. For nearly a century Congress had set aside portions of the public domain for preservation as national parks, forests, grazing lands, recreation areas, and wildlife refuges. The "multiple use" and "sustained yield" doctrines that grew out of the conservation movement at the turn of the century ensured that this national trust would contribute to economic growth under the stewardship of the Interior and Agriculture Departments. Steady progress was also made, however, in managing the lands in the public interest and protecting them from development.[14] After several years of debate, Congress passed the Wilderness Act of 1964 to preserve some of the remaining forest lands in pristine condition, "untrammeled by man's presence." At the same time it approved the Land and Water Conservation Fund Act of 1964 to fund federal purchases of land for conservation purposes, and the Wild and Scenic Rivers Act of 1968 to protect selected rivers with "outstandingly remarkable features," including biological, scenic, and cultural value.[15]

During the mid 1960s the United States also began a major effort to reduce world population growth in developing nations through financial aid for foreign population programs, chiefly family planning and population research. President Lyndon B. Johnson and congressional sponsors of the programs tied them explicitly to a concern for "growing scarcity in world resources."[16]

Despite this longtime concern for resource conservation and land management, and the new interest in population issues, federal environmental policy was only slowly extended to control of industrial pollution and human waste. Air and water pollution were long considered a strictly local matter, and they were not high on the national agenda until around 1970. In a very early federal action the Refuse Act of 1899 required individuals who wanted to dump refuse into navigable waters to obtain a permit from the Army Corps of Engineers; however, the corps largely ignored the pollution aspects of the act.[17] After World War II policies to control the most obvious forms of pollution were gradually developed at the local, state, and federal levels. With passage of the Water Pollution Control Act of 1948, the federal government began assisting local authorities in building sewage treatment plants, and it initiated a limited program for air pollution research in 1955. Following the Clean Air Act of 1963 and amendments to the water pollution law, Washington began prodding the states to set pollution abatement standards and to formulate implementation plans based on federal guidelines.[18]

Agenda Setting for the 1970s

The first Earth Day was April 22, 1970. Nationwide "teach-ins" about environmental problems demonstrated ecology's new place on the nation's social and political agendas. With an increasingly affluent and well-educated society placing new emphasis on the quality of life, concern for environmental protection grew apace and was evident across all groups in the population, if not necessarily to the same degree.[19] The effect was a broadly based public demand for more vigorous and comprehensive federal action to prevent environmental degradation. In an almost unprecedented fashion a new environmental policy agenda rapidly emerged. Policymakers viewed the newly visible environmental issues as politically attractive and they eagerly supported tough new measures, even when their full impacts and costs were unknown. As a result, laws were quickly enacted and implemented throughout the 1970s, but with a growing concern over their costs and effects on the economy, and an increasing realization that administrative agencies at all levels of government often lacked the capacity to assume their new responsibilities.

Congress set the stage for the spurt in policy innovation at the end of 1969 when it passed the National Environmental Policy Act (NEPA). The act declared that

> it is the continuing policy of the Federal Government, in cooperation with State and local governments, and other concerned public and private organizations, to use all practicable means and measures, including financial and technical assistance, in a manner calculated to foster and promote the general welfare, to create and maintain conditions under which man and nature can exist in productive harmony, and fulfill the social, economic, and other requirements of present and future generations of Americans.[20]

The law required detailed environmental impact statements for all major federal actions and established the Council on Environmental Quality (CEQ) to advise the president and Congress on environmental issues. President Richard Nixon then seized the initiative by signing NEPA as his first official act of 1970 and proclaiming the 1970s as the "environmental decade." In February 1970 he sent a special message to Congress calling for a new law to control air pollution. The race was on as the White House and congressional leaders vied for environmentalists' support.

Policy Escalation in the 1970s

By the spring of 1970 rising public concern about the environment galvanized the Ninety-first Congress to action. Sen. Edmund Muskie, D-Maine, then the leading Democratic hopeful for the presidential nomination in 1972, emerged as the dominant policy entrepreneur for environmental protection issues. As chair of the Senate Public Works Committee, he formulated proposals that went well beyond those favored by the president. Following a process of policy escalation, both houses of Congress approved the stronger measures and set the tone for environmental policymaking for much of the 1970s. Congress had frequently played a more dominant role than the president in initiating environmental policies, and that pattern continued in the 1970s, particularly because the Democratic Party controlled Congress during the Nixon and Ford presidencies. Although support for environmental protection was bipartisan, Democrats provided more leadership on the issue in Congress and were more likely to vote for strong environmental policy provisions than were Republicans.[21]

The increase in new federal legislation in the next decade was truly remarkable, especially since, as we noted above, policymaking in American politics is normally incremental. Appendix 1 lists the major environmental protection and natural resource policies enacted between 1969 and 1998. They are arranged by presidential administration primarily to show a pattern of significant policy development throughout the period, not to attribute chief responsibility for the various laws to the particular presidents. These landmark measures covered air and water pollution control (the latter enacted in 1972 over a presidential veto), pesticide regulation, endangered species protection, control of hazardous and toxic chemicals, ocean and coastline protection, better stewardship of public lands, requirements for restoration of strip-mined lands, the setting aside of more than 100 million acres of Alaskan wilderness for varying degrees of protection, and the creation of a "Superfund" (in the Comprehensive Environmental Response, Compensation, and Liability Act, or CERCLA) for cleaning up toxic waste sites.

There were other signs of commitment to environmental policy goals as Congress and a succession of presidential administrations through Jimmy Carter's cooperated on conservation issues. For example, the area designated as national wilderness (excluding Alaska) more than doubled, from 10 million acres in 1970 to more than 23 million acres in 1980. Seventy-five units, totaling some 2.5 million acres, were added to the National Park Service in the same period. The National Wildlife Refuge System grew similarly. Throughout the 1970s the Land and Water Conservation Fund, financed primarily through royalties from offshore oil and gas leasing, was used to purchase additional private land for park development, wildlife refuges, and national forests.

The government's enthusiasm for environmental and conservation policy did not extend to all issues on the environmentalists' agenda. Two noteworthy cases are population policy and energy policy. The Commission on Population Growth and the American Future recommended in 1972 that the nation should "welcome and plan for a stabilized population," but its advice was ignored. Birth rates in the United States were declining and population issues were politically controversial. Despite occasional reports that highlighted the effect of population growth on the environment, such as the *Global 2000 Report to the President* in 1980, the issue remained more or less dormant over the next two decades.[22]

For energy issues the dominant pattern was not neglect but policy gridlock. Here the connection to environmental policy was clearer to policymakers than it had been on population growth. Indeed, opposition to pollution control programs as well as land preservation came primarily from conflicting demands for energy production in the aftermath of the Arab oil embargo in 1973. The Nixon, Ford, and Carter administrations all attempted to formulate national policies for achieving "energy independence" by increasing energy supplies, with President Carter's efforts by far the most sustained and comprehensive. President Carter also emphasized conservation and environmental safeguards. For the most part, however, their efforts were unsuccessful. No consensus on national energy policy emerged among the public or in Congress, and presidential leadership was insufficient to overcome these political constraints.[23]

Congress maintained its strong commitment to environmental policy throughout the 1970s, even as the salience of these issues for the public seemed to wane. For example, it strengthened the Clean Air Act of 1970 and the Clean Water Act of 1972 through amendments approved in 1977. Yet concerns over the impact of environmental regulation on the economy and specific objections to implementation of the new laws, particularly the Clean Air Act, began creating a backlash by the end of the Carter administration.

Political Reaction in the 1980s: The Reagan and Bush Administrations

The Reagan presidency brought to the federal government a very different environmental policy agenda (see chap. 5). Virtually all environmental protection and resource policies enacted during the 1970s were reevaluated in light of the president's desire to reduce the scope of government regulation, shift responsibilities to the states, and rely more on the private sector. Confidence in the efficacy of "environmental deregulation" was predicated on the questionable assumption that enforcement of environmental laws had a major adverse impact on the economy.[24] Whatever the merits of President Reagan's new policy agenda, it was put into effect through a risky strategy that relied on ideologically committed presidential appointees to the EPA and the Agriculture, Interior, and Energy Departments, and on sharp cutbacks in budgets for environmental programs.

Congress initially cooperated with President Reagan, particularly in approving budget cuts, but it soon reverted to its accustomed defense of existing environmental policy, frequently criticizing the president's management of the EPA and the Interior Department under Anne Gorsuch Burford and James Watt, respectively; both Burford and Watt were forced to resign by the end of 1983. Among Congress's most notable achievements of the 1980s were its strengthening of the Resource Conservation and Recovery Act (1984) and enactment of the Superfund Amendments and Reauthorization Act (SARA) (1986), the Safe Drinking Water Act (1986), and the Clean Water Act (1987) (see app. 1). It was less successful in overcoming policy gridlock on acid rain legislation, the Clean Air Act, and the nation's pesticides law. Only in the late 1980s did energy policy issues reappear on the congressional agenda, as concern mounted over the threat of global climate change. The same pattern of policy neglect and rediscovery characterized many other international environmental issues.

As we will show, budget cuts and loss of capacity in environmental institutions took a serious toll in the 1980s. Yet even the determined efforts of a popular president could not halt the advance of environmental policy. Public support for environmental improvement, the driving force for policy development in the 1970s, increased markedly during the Reagan presidency and represented a stunning rejection of the president's agenda by the American public.[25]

Paradoxically, Reagan actually strengthened environmental forces in the nation. Through his lax enforcement of pollution laws and prodevelopment resource policies, he created political issues around which national and grassroots environmental groups could organize. They appealed successfully to a public that was increasingly disturbed by the health and environmental risks of industrial society and by threats to ecological stability. As a result, membership in national environmental groups soared and new grassroots organizations developed, creating further political incentives for environmental activism at all levels of government (see chap. 3).

By the fall of 1989 there was little mistaking congressional enthusiasm for continuing the advance of environmental policy into the 1990s. Especially in his first two years, President George Bush was eager as well to adopt a more positive environmental policy agenda than his predecessor. Bush's White House, however, was deeply divided on the issue for both ideological and economic reasons. The EPA under Bush's appointee, William K. Reilly, fought continuously with the president's conservative advisers in the White House over the pace and stringency of environmental regulations. By 1992 Bush had lost much of the support of environmentalists he had courted in 1989 and 1990 (see chap. 5).

The Greening of the White House? The Clinton Administration

Environmental issues received considerable attention during the 1992 presidential election campaign. Bush, running for reelection, criticized environmentalists as extremists who were putting Americans out of work. The Democratic candidate, Bill Clinton, took a far more supportive stance on the environment, symbolized by his selection of Sen. Al Gore, D-Tenn., as his running mate. The leading environmentalist in the U.S. Congress, Senator Gore was also author of the best-selling *Earth in the Balance,* in which he argued for making the "rescue of the environment the central organizing principle for civilization." [26]

Much to the disappointment of environmentalists, President Clinton exerted little visible leadership on the environment during his first two years in office. However, he and Vice President Gore quietly pushed an extensive agenda of environmental policy reform as part of their broader effort to "reinvent government," making it more efficient and responsive to public concerns.[27] Clinton was also generally praised for his environmental appointments, most notably Bruce Babbitt as secretary of the interior, and for his administration's support for initiatives such as restoration of the Florida Everglades and other actions based on new approaches to ecosystem management. Clinton reversed many of the Reagan- and Bush-era executive actions that were widely criticized by environmentalists, and he favored increased spending on environmental programs, alternative energy and conservation research, and international population policy.

Clinton also earned praise from environmental groups when he began speaking out forcefully against antienvironmental policy decisions of the 104th and 105th Congresses (see chaps. 5 and 6), for his support in 1997 of controversial new EPA clean air standards for ozone and fine particulates, and for his strong backing of international action on climate change (see chap. 13). His administration's efforts through the President's Council on Sustainable Development to encourage ways to reconcile environmental protection and economic development were also well received in the environmental community.[28] Yet Clinton displeased environmentalists as often as he gratified them, particularly with his support for the North American Free Trade Agreement and for signing a "timber salvaging" measure in 1995 that shielded timber companies from having to comply with environmental laws in their logging operations in federal forests (an action Clinton later called a "mistake").

Institutional Development and Policy Implementation

Aside from the enactment of landmark environmental policies in the 1970s and 1980s, some important institutional developments greatly affected implementation of those policies. A brief review of the most important of them is instructive given continuing opposition in Congress and the states to many environmental programs.

Institutionalizing Environmental Protection in the 1970s

The most notable institutional development in the 1970s was the establishment of the EPA by President Nixon in December 1970. Created as an independent agency that would report directly to the president, it brought together environmental responsibilities that had previously been scattered among dozens of offices and programs. Under its first administrator, William Ruckelshaus, the agency's legislative mandate grew rapidly as a consequence of the policy process summarized earlier, and it acquired many new programs, offices, and staffs. The EPA's operating budget (the funds available to implement its programs) grew from about $500 million in 1973 to $1.3 billion in 1980. Full-time employees increased from about 7,000 in 1971 to nearly 13,000 by 1980 (see apps. 3 and 4), with two-thirds of them in the agency's ten regional offices and other facilities outside of Washington, D.C. Even with its expanded budget and staff, however, the nation's leading environmental agency found it increasingly difficult by 1980 to meet new program obligations.

During the 1970s virtually every federal agency was forced to develop some capabilities for environmental analysis under NEPA, which required that environmental impact statements (EISs) be prepared for all "major federal actions significantly affecting the quality of the human environment." Detailed requirements for the statements were set out by the Council on Environmental Quality and enforced in the courts. Provisions for public hearings and citizen participation allowed environmental and community groups to challenge administrative decisions, often by filing legal suits questioning the adequacy of the impact statements. In response to these potential objections, agencies changed their project designs—sometimes dramatically. Even the Army Corps of Engineers, which had often been castigated by environmentalists, learned to adapt.[29] Although the EIS process was roundly criticized (indeed, it was revised in 1979 to focus more sharply on crucial issues), most studies show that it forced greater environmental awareness and more careful planning in many agencies; moreover, such success led to extension of this kind of impact analysis to other policy areas.[30]

Established natural resource agencies, such as Agriculture's Forest Service and Interior's Bureau of Land Management, generally made the transition to better environmental analysis and planning more easily. Long-standing doctrines of multiple use and strong professional norms of land management were gradually adapted to serve new environmental goals and interests. Wilderness preservation, never a dominant purpose of these agencies, came to be accepted as part of their mission, as did the new and comprehensive approach called ecosystem management (see chap. 14).[31]

Both in their compliance with new environmental laws and in their adjustment to democratic norms of open decisionmaking and citizen participation in the 1970s, some agencies and departments lagged seriously behind others. Perhaps the most striking case is the Department of Energy (DOE), which for years had neglected changing standards and demands with respect to environmental protection, safety, and health. The price the nation pays for such environmental neglect and mismanagement can be seen in the enormous cost of cleaning up the department's seventeen principal weapons plants and laboratories—more than $200 billion over the next thirty years.[32] For fiscal 1998 alone, DOE and Department of Defense budgets for environmental management and cleanup of federal facilities totaled about $10 billion, or more than the entire budget of the EPA.

Successive administrations also gave modest support to the development of international environmental institutions. The United States played an active role in convening the U.N. Conference on the Human Environment held in Stockholm, Sweden, in June 1972. This conference, attended by delegations from 113 countries and 400 other organizations, addressed for the first time the environmental problems of developing nations. The result was the creation of the U.N. Environment Programme (UNEP), headquartered in Nairobi, Kenya. Although it disagreed with some of UNEP's initiatives, the United States provided the largest share (36 percent) of its budget between 1972 and 1980.[33]

Environmental Relief and Reform in the 1980s

By the time President Reagan assumed office in 1981, the effort to improve environmental quality at federal and state levels had been institutionalized, though not without a good many problems that required both statutory change and administrative reform. Implementation often lagged years behind schedule because much of the legislation of the 1970s overestimated the speed with which new technologies could be developed and applied. The laws also underestimated compliance costs and the difficulty of writing standards for hundreds of major industries. As regulated industries sought to block implementation and environmental organizations tried to speed it up, frequent legal challenges compounded the backlog. Other delays were caused by personnel and budgetary shortages, scientific and technical uncertainties, and the need for extensive consultation with other federal agencies, Congress, and state governments.[34]

As a result of these difficulties, an extensive agenda for reforming environmental policies and improving administrative capabilities emerged by 1980. It was, however, largely unaddressed by the Reagan administration, which was more concerned with providing short-term regulatory relief to industry.[35] The president's neglect of policy reform was exacerbated by his reliance on an administrative strategy that J. Clarence Davies described as "designed largely to reverse the institutionalization process" begun in the 1970s. This was accomplished through sharp budgetary reductions, weakening of the authority of experienced professionals in environmental agencies, and elimination or restructuring of many offices, particularly at the EPA.[36] Staff morale and EPA credibility suffered under the leadership of Anne Burford, although both improved to some extent under administrators William Ruckelshaus and Lee Thomas in the Reagan administration, and

William Reilly in the Bush administration. Nevertheless, the damage done to administrative capacity in the early 1980s was considerable and long lasting. At the end of the Reagan presidency in January 1989, environmentalists still complained that there was no policy leadership at the EPA and that little had been done to "restore the momentum of environmental protection."[37]

They also criticized President Reagan for failing to pursue regulatory reform, saying he "blew the chance to streamline regulations and use marketplace incentives in an honest way to speed up environmental progress, lower regulatory costs, and foster economic growth." Business groups remained dissatisfied with what they believed was still an unnecessarily expensive and rigid system of federal environmental regulation. And even conservative critics expressed disappointment with what the Heritage Foundation termed a "squandered" opportunity to reform environmental protection laws and reduce their cost.[38] Many of the same reform issues, such as risk-based priority setting and use of market incentives to supplement regulation, continued to be widely discussed throughout the 1990s, and they emerged as major issues in congressional debates (see chaps. 6, 8, 9, and 10).

Institutional Capacity: Environmental Agency Budgets and Policy Implementation

As we try to assess the degree to which environmental quality might improve as a result of present laws and to consider the ability of government to meet the ecological and public health challenges of the early twenty-first century, there is little that is more important than budgets. Although spending more public money does not guarantee policy success, substantial cuts can undermine established programs. It is apparent that the massive reductions in environmental funding during the early 1980s had long-term adverse effects on the government's ability to implement environmental policies. Equally sharp budget cuts proposed by Congress in 1995 and 1996 raised the same prospect, although they failed to win approval in the face of opposition by the American public and the Clinton White House. The numbers merit a brief review.

In constant dollars (that is, adjusting for inflation), the total authorized by the federal government for natural resource and environmental programs remained about the same between 1980 and 1998 (see app. 2). However, in some areas, such as pollution control and abatement, spending actually declined (17 percent) over this eighteen-year period. For most budget categories, spending decreased substantially during the 1980s before recovering under the Bush and Clinton administrations. An exception is spending on water resources, where the phase-out of water infrastructure programs resulted in a sharp drop in spending (37 percent) from 1980 to 1998. In other areas, such as conservation and land management, the same period witnessed a significant increase in spending (over 100 percent).

Looking across an even longer span of time, overall spending on environmental programs increased significantly between the early 1970s and the late 1990s. Yet the same period saw the enactment of virtually all the federal environmental laws. Thus, despite improving budgets over the past three decades, many agencies continue to find themselves with insufficient resources to implement federal policies and to achieve the environmental quality goals they embody.

These constraints can be seen in the budgets and staffs of selected environmental and natural resource agencies (see apps. 3 and 4). For example, in constant dollars, the EPA's operating budget as we calculate it (the EPA determines it differently) grew by only 6 percent between FY 1975 and FY 1998, despite the many new responsibilities given to the agency by Congress over this period. The picture would be far bleaker if Presidents Bush and Clinton had not favored large increases in the agency's budget during the late 1980s and 1990s. The EPA's staff increased by a greater percentage than its budget, rising from a little less than 13,000 in 1980, the last year of the Carter administration, to nearly 18,000 by 1998.

The picture is mixed for the natural resource agencies. The Bureau of Land Management, the Army Corps of Engineers (civilian programs), the Office of Surface Mining, and the Forest Service all suffered stagnant or declining budgets (in constant dollars) during the 1980s and 1990s (see app. 3). In contrast, the Fish and Wildlife Service and the National Park Service enjoyed budget increases over the same period, although much less than each of them needed given their responsibilities (see chap. 14). There is little question that limited budgets and staff have affected the ability of many agencies to implement environmental policy over the past two decades. They are likely to be equally significant constraints over the next decade as well.

Improvements in Environmental Quality and Their Cost

It is difficult, both conceptually and empirically, to measure the success or failure of environmental policies.[39] Yet one of the most important tests of any public policy is whether it achieves its stated objectives. For environmental policies, we should ask if air and water quality are improving, hazardous waste sites are being cleaned up, and wilderness areas are adequately protected. There is no simple way to answer those questions, and it is important to understand why that is so even if some limited responses are possible.[40]

Measuring Environmental Conditions and Trends

Environmental policies entail long-term commitments to broad social values and goals that are not easily quantified. Short-term and highly visible costs are easier to measure than long-term, diffuse, and intangible benefits, and these differences often lead to intense debates over the value of environmental programs.

Variable and often unreliable monitoring of environmental conditions and inconsistent collection of data over time also make it difficult to assess environmental trends. The time period selected for a given analysis also can seriously affect the results, and many scholars discount some data collected prior to the mid 1970s as unreliable. To improve monitoring, data collection, and analysis, some have proposed a new and independent Bureau of Environmental Statistics to supplement such activities now handled by the EPA and the Council on Environmental Quality, as well as other federal agencies.[41]

Despite these limitations on measuring environmental conditions and trends, it is nevertheless useful to review selected indicators of environmental quality. They tell us at least something about what we have achieved or failed to achieve after almost three decades of national environmental protection policy.

Air Quality. Perhaps the best data on changes in the environment can be found for air quality, even if disagreement exists over which measures and time periods are most appropriate. The EPA reports that between 1970 and 1996, total emissions of the six principal or "criteria" air pollutants decreased by some 32 percent even while the nation's population grew by 29 percent, the gross domestic product (GDP) rose by 104 percent, and vehicle miles traveled increased by 121 percent. The only criteria pollutant emissions increase was for nitrogen oxides, which contribute to the formation of ozone or smog. Emissions increased by 8 percent over this period—a major reason for EPA's approval in 1997 of a rule to reduce emissions of nitrogen oxides in twenty-two eastern states and thus reduce generation of ozone in the region.

Looking at the most recent period where data are firmer, between 1987 and 1996 the nation experienced a reduction in ambient levels (concentrations in the atmosphere) of 75 percent for lead, 37 percent for carbon monoxide, 37 percent for sulfur dioxide, 25 percent for particulate matter, 15 percent for ozone, and 10 percent for nitrogen dioxide. The 1996 air quality levels were the best on record for all six criteria pollutants. Toxic air emissions from sources such as oil refineries, dry cleaning facilities, and chemical plants are beginning to decrease as new federal regulations on air toxics take effect. The same is true for production and release of ozone-depleting chlorofluorocarbons (CFCs), which began moving downward by the end of 1994, largely as a consequence of actions taken under the Montreal protocol.[42]

Despite these impressive gains in air quality, in 1996 some 46 million people lived in counties that failed to meet at least one of the national air quality standards for the six major pollutants covered by the Clean Air Act. Approximately 39 million people resided in counties where pollution levels in 1996 exceeded federal standards for ozone, the chief ingredient of urban smog. Such figures vary from year to year, reflecting changing economic activity and weather patterns. In 1995, 70 million Americans lived in counties that did not meet the ozone standard.[43]

One of most significant remaining problems is toxic or hazardous air pollutants, which have been associated with cancer, respiratory diseases, and other chronic and acute illnesses. The EPA was extremely slow to regulate these pollutants, and it had set federal standards for only seven of them by mid 1989. Public and congressional concern over toxic emissions led Congress to mandate more aggressive action in the 1986 Superfund amendments. That law required manufacturers of more than three hundred different chemicals (later doubled by the EPA) to report annually to the agency and the states in which they operate the amounts of those substances released to the air, water, or land. The EPA's Toxics Release Inventory (TRI) indicated that in 1989 some 22,000 companies released 5.7 billion pounds of hazardous substances to the environment, including 2.4 billion pounds of toxic chemicals emitted into the air. By 1996 (the latest year for which data are available), total on-site releases dropped to 2.14 billion pounds and emitted air toxics had declined to 1.45 billion pounds, significantly lower but still substantial.[44] These figures tell only part of the story, however, because not all sources of air toxics participate in the TRI program. In the 1990 Clean Air Act Amendments Congress stiffened regulation of toxic air pollutants, so the downward trend in air toxics should continue.

Water Quality. The nation's water quality also has improved since passage of the Clean Water Act of 1972, although more slowly and more unevenly than air quality. Monitoring data are less adequate for water quality than for air quality. For example, the best evidence for the present state of water quality can be found in the EPA's biennial National Water Quality Inventory, which compiles data reported by each state. But in 1996 the states surveyed only 19 percent of all the nation's rivers and streams (although the report included 53 percent of those rivers and streams that flow year round), and only 40 percent of lakes, ponds, and reservoirs.

Based on those inventories, for the nation as a whole 64 percent of the surveyed river and stream miles fully support all uses set by states and tribes, and 36 percent were found to be impaired to some degree, as were 39 percent of lakes, ponds, and reservoirs. A classification as impaired means that water bodies are not meeting or fully meeting the national minimum water quality criteria for "designated beneficial uses" such as swimming, fishing, drinking-water supply, and support of aquatic life. These numbers show some improvement over previous years, yet they also indicate that many problems remain. The same survey found that 38 percent of the nation's estuaries were impaired, as were fully 94 percent of Great Lakes nearshore waters (generally because of persistent toxic pollutants in the food web and habitat degradation and destruction).[45] Prevention of further degradation of water quality in the face of a growing population and strong economic growth could be considered an important achievement. At the same time water quality clearly falls short of the goals of federal clean water acts.

Further evidence can be seen in the data on wetland loss. Between 1982 and 1992 the United States lost an estimated 70,000 to 90,000 acres a year of marshes, swamps, and other ecologically important wetlands to commercial and residential development, agriculture, road construction, and modification of hydrologic conditions, although this was well below the estimated 458,000 acres a year lost from the mid 1950s to the mid 1970s. The rate of loss seems to have slowed over the past decade, yet it is still unacceptably high, particularly in light of the valuable ecological functions of wetlands.[46]

Most of the huge financial investment in clean water since 1972 (more than $700 billion in public and private sector funds through 1996) has been expended on conventional "point" sources of water pollutants (where a particular source is identifiable), and most industries and municipalities have greatly reduced their discharges consistent with the intent of the Clean Water Act. Increasing emphasis on toxic pollutants and nonpoint sources such as agricultural runoff (the regulation of which is required by the Clean Water Act Amendments of 1987) is likely in the future.

To date little progress has been made in halting groundwater contamination despite passage of the Safe Drinking Water Act of 1974 and the Resource Conservation and Recovery Act of 1976 and their later amendments. In its 1998 Water Quality Inventory EPA reported that groundwater is of good quality overall, but that "contaminant problems are being reported throughout the country." With some 51 percent of the nation's population relying on groundwater for drinking water, far more remains to be done. Indeed, the Natural Resources Defense Council released a study in 1995 that concluded some 53 million Americans drank water that violated EPA standards under the Clean Water Act; it estimated that nearly 1,000 deaths a year and at least 400,000 cases of waterborne illness may be attributed to contaminated water.[47]

Toxic and Hazardous Wastes. Progress in dealing with hazardous wastes and other toxic chemicals has been the least satisfactory of all pollution control programs. Implementation of the major laws has been extraordinarily slow due to the extent and complexity of the problems, scientific uncertainty, litigation by industry, public fear of siting treatment and storage facilities nearby, budgetary limitations, and poor management and lax enforcement by the EPA. As a result, gains have been modest to date when judged by the most common measures, particularly for the Superfund program. By the late 1990s, however, the pace of action appeared to be improving. By February 1998, for example, the EPA reported that 509 sites had been fully cleaned up out of the 1,400 on the Superfund National Priorities List (NPL) and remediation was actively under way at more than 90 percent of the remaining sites.[48] These achievements come at a high price. The EPA in recent years has spent about $30 million per NPL site remediated, sometimes with unclear and disputed benefits. Realistic estimates for cleanup of the tens of thousands of hazardous waste sites nationwide range from $484 billion to more than $1 trillion, with the job expected to take three to five decades to complete.[49]

The EPA has also set a sluggish pace in the related area of testing toxic chemicals. For example, under a 1972 law mandating control of pesticides and herbicides, only a handful of chemicals used to manufacture the fifty thousand pesticides in use in the United States has received full testing or retesting. The inadequate progress is especially worrisome in light of new evidence that some of those chemicals may disrupt human immune and reproductive systems and cause neurotoxic disorders.[50]

The track record over the past fifteen years on these programs clearly suggests the need for reevaluation of federal policy. Congress partially addressed that need in its revision of the Superfund program in 1986, and in passage of amendments in 1996 to the nation's pesticides control and drinking water policies. Regrettably, Congress found itself mired in gridlock on overhaul of Superfund through the end of 1998 (see chap. 6).

Natural Resources. Comparable indicators of environmental progress can be found for natural resource use. As is the case with pollution control, however, interpretation of the data is problematic. We have few good measures of ecosystem health, and much of the usual information in government reports concerns land set aside chiefly for recreational and esthetic purposes rather than for protection of ecosystem functions.[51] Nonetheless, the trends in land conservation and wilderness protection suggest important progress over three decades and more of modern environmental policies.

For example, the National Park System grew from about 26 million acres in 1960 to over 83 million acres by 1995, and the number of units in the system nearly doubled. In 1997, over 270 million people visited at least one of the 376 units (including 54 parks) in the system, and the number of visitors increased by 5 percent a year in the late 1990s. Unfortunately, increased visitation also has created serious problems in an overcrowded park system that has been chronically underfunded. Since adoption of the 1964 Wilderness Act, Congress also has set aside 104 million acres of wilderness through the National Wilderness Preservation System. Since 1968 it has designated over 150 Wild and Scenic Rivers with more than ten thousand protected miles. By 1993 the National Forest System consisted of 187 million acres, of which more than 32 million acres were protected as wilderness. The Fish and Wildlife Service manages more than 92 million acres in about five hundred units of the National Wildlife Refuge System—triple the land area of 1970.[52]

Protection of biological diversity through the Endangered Species Act (ESA) has produced some success as well, although far less than its supporters believe essential. Through 1995, twenty-two years after passage of the act, only about 960 U.S. species had been listed as either endangered or threatened. Scores of critical habitats have been designated, and a number of recovery plans have been put into effect, yet only a few endangered species have fully recovered. Still, the Fish and Wildlife Service reports that more than 41 percent of listed species are stable or improving.[53]

Insufficient budgets and staffs greatly slow the process of listing and recovery of species, as does conflict over property rights near affected habitats. Largely because of financial constraints, the Fish and Wildlife Service failed to protect hundreds of species even where substantial evidence existed to document threats to their existence. Over three thousand species are candidates for inclusion on the list, but at the current pace of review, it would take decades to resolve their status. Moreover, development of recovery plans to protect all of those species would vastly exceed the annual budget of the agency.[54] The Interior Department's National Biological Service has been building an inventory of the nation's biological diversity, and the department is beginning to emphasize an ecosystem approach to protection of biodiversity. The future of these programs depends, however, on congressional willingness to reauthorize the much-criticized ESA.

Assessing Environmental Progress

As the data reviewed above suggest, the nation made impressive gains between 1970 and 1998 in controlling many conventional pollutants and in expanding parks, wilderness areas, and other protected public lands. Despite some setbacks in the 1980s, progress on environmental quality continues, even if it is highly uneven from one period to the next. In the future, however, further advances will be more difficult, costly, and controversial. This is largely because the easy problems have already been addressed, and at this point marginal gains in air and water quality will cost more per unit of improvement than in the past (see chap. 9). Moreover, second-generation environmental threats such as toxic chemicals, hazardous wastes, and nuclear wastes are proving to be even more difficult than regulating "bulk" air and water pollutants in the 1970s. In these cases substantial progress may not be evident for years to come, and it will be expensive.

The same is true for the third generation of ecological problems, such as global climate change and protection of biodiversity. Solutions require an unprecedented degree of cooperation among nations and substantial improvement in institutional capacity for research, data collection, and analysis as well as policy development and implementation. Hence, success is likely to come slowly as national and international commitments to environmental protection grow and capabilities improve. Some long-standing problems, such as population growth, will continue to be addressed primarily within nation states, even though the staggering effects on natural resources and environmental quality are felt worldwide. By late 1998 the Earth's population of 5.9 billion was increasing at an estimated 1.3 percent (or about 78 million people) per year, with continued growth expected for another hundred years or more (see chap. 15).

The Costs and Benefits of Environmental Protection

The costs and benefits of environmental protection have been vigorously debated over the past two decades. Critics argue that the kinds of improvements cited above are often not worth the considerable costs, particularly if they believe regulations adversely affect economic growth and employment or unduly restrict technological development. Environmentalists and other policy supporters point, however, to the improvements in public health, the protection of "priceless" natural amenities such as wilderness areas and clean lakes, and the preservation of biological diversity. They remain convinced that these benefits are well worth the investment of governmental and private funds. They also question assertions about adverse economic impacts of such policies, for which evidence is slim.[55] Some business leaders agree, and the evidence can be found in their determination to promote greening of their enterprises both for the economic gains they anticipate and to appeal to an environmentally concerned public (see chap. 12).

Skepticism about environmental policies led to several attempts in the 1980s and early 1990s under Presidents Reagan and Bush to impose regulatory oversight by the White House. It was hoped that costs could be limited by subjecting proposed regulations to cost-benefit analysis (see chaps. 5 and 9). The imposition of these controls, particularly by Bush's White House Council on Competitiveness under Vice President Dan Quayle, sharpened debate over the costs and benefits of environmental policies. The council had become a "back door" for business interests seeking to overturn what they saw as excessively costly environmental and other regulations. In January 1993 President Clinton abolished the council by executive order two days after taking office. Clinton signed a new executive order calling for economic impact studies of proposed regulations that were to inform decisionmaking and ensure cost effectiveness. The benefits of regulation would have to justify the costs though not necessarily outweigh them as required under the Reagan-Bush executive order (see chap. 5).

The impetus for these kinds of centralized control efforts, and the intensity of the conflict over them, can be seen in the amount of money now spent on environmental protection by the federal government, as well as by state and local governments and the private sector. In 1998 the federal government was spending about $24 billion per year for all environmental and natural resource programs as calculated in the official budget category for these programs. These totals are only a small part, however, of the country's annual investment in environmental protection. The EPA estimated in 1994 that the nation's overall spending on the environmental programs that the agency administers was about $140 billion per year, or about 2.2 percent of the GDP. By one calculation, private industry bears about 57 percent of that amount, local governments 24 percent, the federal government 15 percent, and state governments 4 percent.[56]

The benefits of environmental programs are more difficult to calculate and are often omitted entirely from reports on the costs or burdens of environmental policies. Should one measure only public health benefits of pollution control? What about esthetic values? Or the value of conserving ecosystems—water, soil, forests, wetlands—or of preventing disastrous climate change? These kinds of questions have led to a broad reexamination of the way in which nations account for the value of natural resources.

Making rough comparisons of the benefits and costs of environmental policies, one could fairly conclude that many programs can be justified through standard economic analysis. That is, they produce measurable benefits that exceed the costs. This was true of the original Clean Air Act as it is for efforts to phase out the CFCs that destroy the Earth's protective ozone layer. Energy conservation also makes good economic sense given the costs and environmental impacts of new power plants. Some environmental programs, such as thorough cleanup of all hazardous waste sites, however, are so expensive that they would be far more difficult to justify on economic grounds alone (see chap. 9).[57]

Debates over the costs and benefits of environmental policies will continue over the next few years, but with several new twists. Government spending on natural resources and the environment, which rose sharply in the 1970s, is unlikely to increase much in the near term for several reasons: persistent concern about federal expenditures and a determination by Congress and the White House to avoid budget deficits; widespread resistance to raising taxes; competing budgetary priorities, particularly from federal entitlement programs; and opposition to regulatory programs by powerful interest groups and elected officials.

The burden of raising additional funds for environmental programs may be shouldered by the states, but some of them are more able and willing to do so than others (see chap. 2). These new conditions mean that more of the additional cost of environmental protection will be borne by the private sector: by industry and, eventually, by the consumer. Another implication is that the federal government as well as the states will have to seek innovative policies that promise improvements in environmental quality without adding substantially to their budgets. A third conclusion is that some form of risk-based priority setting is essential if environmental regulation is to make economic as well as environmental sense. This argument was advanced regularly by EPA administrator William Reilly in the early 1990s as well as by his successor, Carol Browner, and it is widely endorsed by students of environmental policy (see chaps. 8 and 10).[58]

Recent policy developments reflect these concerns—for example, the passage of the Pollution Prevention Act of 1990, which puts a premium on preventing, rather than cleaning up, pollution. Industry is already actively seeking ways to reduce the generation of waste and to promote sustainable development (see chap. 12). A parallel development among environmental groups, particularly the Nature Conservancy, is a successful venture into private purchase of ecologically important land for preservation. Private efforts to save endangered lands have recently been extended to financially strapped developing nations in so-called debt-for-nature swaps.

At another level the question of whether environmental programs are "worth it" must be answered with another question: what are the costs of inaction? In some cases the risks to the environment and to society's well-being are so great that it would be imprudent to delay development of public policy. This is particularly so when modest measures taken at an early enough date might forestall the enormous costs of remedial efforts in the future, whether paid for by governments or the private sector. That was clearly the lesson of environmental contamination at DOE nuclear weapons facilities, as noted above. It is also apparent that such a precautionary policy response is called for in the cases of global climate change and deterioration of the ozone layer, where there is the potential for significant impacts on the environment, human health, and the economy. Much the same argument could be made for preserving biological diversity, investing in family planning programs, and responding to other compelling global environmental problems likely to be high on the agenda in the early twenty-first century.

Conclusion

Over the past three decades, public concern and support for environmental protection have risen significantly, spurring the development of an expansive array of new policies that substantially increased the government's responsibilities for the environment and natural resources, both domestically and internationally.

The implementation of these policies, however, has been far more difficult and controversial than their supporters ever imagined. Moreover, the policies have not been entirely successful, particularly when measured by tangible improvements in environmental quality. Given the country's persistent and severe budgetary constraints, further progress requires that the nation search for more efficient and effective ways to achieve these goals, including the use of alternatives to conventional "command and control" regulation.[59] Despite these qualifications, the record of the past thirty years demonstrates convincingly that the U.S. government is able to produce significant environmental gains through public policies. Unquestionably, the environment would be worse today if the policies enacted during the 1970s and 1980s had not been in place.

Emerging environmental threats on the national and international agenda are even more formidable than the first generation of problems addressed by government in the 1970s and the second generation that dominated political debate in the 1980s. Responding to them will require creative new efforts to improve the performance of government and other social institutions, and effective leadership to design appropriate strategies both within government and in society itself. We discuss this new policy agenda in chapter 17.

Government is an important player in the environmental arena, but it cannot pursue forceful initiatives unless the public supports such action. Ultimately, society's values will fuel the government's response to a rapidly changing world environment that, in all probability, will involve severe economic and social dislocations over the coming decades.

Notes

1. See the survey data reviewed in chapter 3. On global opinions as of 1992, see Riley E. Dunlap, George H. Gallup Jr., and Alec M. Gallup, "Of Global Concern: Results of the Health of the Planet Survey," *Environment* 35, no. 9 (1993): 7–15, 33–40.
2. Norman J. Vig and Michael E. Kraft, eds., *Environmental Policy in the 1980s: Reagan's New Agenda* (Washington, D.C.: CQ Press, 1984).
3. J. Clarence Davies and Jan Mazurek, *Pollution Control in the United States: Evaluating the System* (Washington, D.C.: Resources for the Future, 1998); National Academy of Public Administration (NAPA), *Setting Priorities, Getting Results: A New Direction for*

EPA (Washington, D.C.: NAPA, 1995); and Ken Sexton, Alfred A. Marcus, K. William Easter, and Timothy D. Burkhardt, eds., *Better Environmental Decisions: Strategies for Governments, Businesses and Communities* (Washington, D.C.: Island Press, 1998). See also chapters 8, 10, and 11 in this volume.

4. Michael E. Kraft and Denise Scheberle, "Environmental Federalism at Decade's End: New Approaches and Strategies," *Publius: The Journal of Federalism* 28, no. 1 (Winter 1998): 131–146; and Daniel A. Mazmanian and Michael E. Kraft, eds., *Toward Sustainable Communities: Transition and Transformations in Environmental Policy* (Cambridge, Mass.: MIT Press, forthcoming 1999).

5. U.S. Environmental Protection Agency (EPA), Office of the Chief Financial Officer, *EPA Strategic Plan*, EPA/190-R-97-002 (Washington, D.C.: EPA, 1997); Marian R. Chertow and Daniel C. Esty, eds., *Thinking Ecologically: The Next Generation of Environmental Policy* (New Haven, Conn.: Yale University Press, 1997); and President's Council on Sustainable Development, *Sustainable America: A New Consensus for Prosperity, Opportunity, and a Healthy Environment* (Washington, D.C.: President's Council on Sustainable Development, 1996). The many official reports and task force recommendations of the council have been consolidated in Daniel Sitarz, ed., *Sustainable America: America's Environment, Economy and Society in the 21st Century* (Carbondale, Ill.: EarthPress, 1998).

6. NAPA, *Setting Priorities*, 124–125.

7. John W. Kingdon, *Agendas, Alternatives, and Public Policies*, 2d ed. (New York: HarperCollins, 1995).

8. Roger W. Cobb and Charles D. Elder, *Participation in American Politics: The Dynamics of Agenda-Building* (Boston: Allyn and Bacon, 1972).

9. Kingdon, *Agendas*.

10. For a more thorough discussion of how the policy cycle model applies to environmental issues, see Michael E. Kraft, *Environmental Policy and Politics* (New York: HarperCollins, 1996), chap. 3. The general model is discussed at length in James E. Anderson, *Public Policymaking: An Introduction*, 3d ed. (Boston: Houghton Mifflin, 1997).

11. Ronald Inglehart, *The Silent Revolution: Changing Values and Political Styles among Western Publics* (Princeton, N.J.: Princeton University Press, 1977), and *Culture Shift in Advanced Industrial Society* (Princeton, N.J.: Princeton University Press, 1990).

12. World Commission on Environment and Development, *Our Common Future* (New York: Oxford University Press, 1987).

13. Samuel P. Hays, *Beauty, Health, and Permanence: Environmental Politics in the United States, 1955–1985* (New York: Cambridge University Press, 1987); and Robert C. Paehlke, *Environmentalism and the Future of Progressive Politics* (New Haven, Conn.: Yale University Press, 1989). For a comprehensive review of public opinion surveys on the environment and the evolution of the environmental movement, see Riley E. Dunlap and Angela G. Mertig, eds., *American Environmentalism: The U.S. Environmental Movement, 1970–1990* (Philadelphia: Taylor and Francis, 1992); and Riley E. Dunlap, "Public Opinion and Environmental Policy," in *Environmental Politics and Policy: Theories and Evidence*, 2d ed., ed. James P. Lester (Durham, N.C.: Duke University Press, 1995).

14. Paul J. Culhane, *Public Lands Politics: Interest Group Influence on the Forest Service and the Bureau of Land Management* (Baltimore: The Johns Hopkins University Press, 1981), esp. chap. 1.

15. See Kraft, *Environmental Policy and Politics*; and Walter A. Rosenbaum, *Environmental Politics and Policy*, 4th ed. (Washington, D.C.: CQ Press, 1998).

16. Michael E. Kraft, "Population Policy," in *Encyclopedia of Policy Studies*, 2d ed., ed. Stuart S. Nagel (New York: Marcel Dekker, 1994).

17. J. Clarence Davies III and Barbara S. Davies, *The Politics of Pollution*, 2d ed. (Indianapolis: Bobbs-Merrill, 1975).

18. Evan J. Ringquist, *Environmental Protection at the State Level: Politics and Progress in Controlling Pollution* (Armonk, N.Y.: M. E. Sharpe, 1993), chap. 2; and Davies and

Davies, *Politics of Pollution*, chap. 2. A much fuller history of the origins and development of modern environmental policy than is provided here can be found in Michael J. Lacey, ed., *Government and Environmental Politics: Essays on Historical Developments since World War Two* (Baltimore: The Johns Hopkins University Press, 1989).

19. Hays, *Beauty, Health, and Permanence*. See also Dunlap, "Public Opinion and Environmental Policy," and Robert Cameron Mitchell, "Public Opinion and Environmental Politics in the 1970s and 1980s," in *Environmental Policy in the 1980s*, ed. Vig and Kraft.

20. Public Law 91-90 (42 USC 4321–4347), sec. 101. See Lynton K. Caldwell, *Science and the National Environmental Policy Act: Redirecting Policy through Procedural Reform* (Tuscaloosa: University of Alabama Press, 1982).

21. Michael E. Kraft, "Congress and Environmental Policy," and Sheldon Kamieniecki, "Political Parties and Environmental Policy," in *Environmental Politics and Policy*, ed. Lester.

22. Kraft, "Population Policy"; Council on Environmental Quality (CEQ) and Department of State, *The Global 2000 Report to the President* (Washington, D.C.: GPO, 1980).

23. James Everett Katz, *Congress and National Energy Policy* (New Brunswick, N.J.: Transaction, 1984); and David Lewis Feldman, ed., *The Energy Crisis: Unresolved Issues and Enduring Legacies* (Baltimore: The Johns Hopkins University Press, 1996). For a discussion of the politics surrounding passage of the 1992 act and an outline of the provisions, see Kraft, *Environmental Politics and Policy*, chap. 5.

24. See, for example, Edwin H. Clark II, "Reaganomics and the Environment: An Evaluation," in *Environmental Policy in the 1980s*, ed. Vig and Kraft.

25. See Riley E. Dunlap, "Public Opinion on the Environment in the Reagan Era," *Environment* 29 (July–August 1987): 6–11, 32–37; and Mitchell, "Public Opinion and Environmental Politics."

26. Keith Schneider, "For Clinton and Gore, Contradictions in Balancing Jobs and Conservation," *New York Times*, October 13, 1992, A12; and Al Gore, *Earth in the Balance: Ecology and the Human Spirit* (Boston: Houghton Mifflin, 1992), 269.

27. See EPA, *EPA Strategic Plan*. The EPA's many reinvention activities and initiatives to foster community-based environmental protection are discussed in some detail on its Web page. See especially *www.epa.gov/reinvent/* and *www.epa.gov/ecosystems/osecbak/*.

28. President's Council on Sustainable Development, *Sustainable America*. The President's Council on Sustainable Development held a National Town Meeting for a Sustainable America in May 1999 in Detroit, Michigan, and in other cities across the nation to further promote sustainable development.

29. Daniel A. Mazmanian and Jeanne Nienaber, *Can Organizations Change? Environmental Protection, Citizen Participation, and the Corps of Engineers* (Washington, D.C.: Brookings, 1979).

30. Richard N. L. Andrews, *Environmental Policy and Administrative Change: Implementation of the National Environmental Policy Act* (Lexington, Mass.: Lexington, 1976); Caldwell, *Science and the National Environmental Policy Act*; and Robert V. Bartlett, *Policy through Impact Assessment: Institutionalized Analysis as a Policy Strategy* (New York: Greenwood, 1989).

31. See Jeanne Nienaber Clarke and Daniel C. McCool, *Staking Out the Terrain: Power and Performance Among Natural Resource Agencies*, 2d ed. (Albany: State University of New York Press, 1996); and Hanna J. Cortner and Margaret A. Moote, *The Politics of Ecosystem Management* (Washington, D.C.: Island Press, 1998).

32. Michael E. Kraft, "Searching for Policy Success: Reinventing the Politics of Site Remediation," *Environmental Professional* 16 (September 1994): 245–253; and Milton E. Russell, William Colglazier, and Bruce E. Tonn, "The U.S. Hazardous Waste Legacy," *Environment* 34 (1992): 12–15, 34–39.

33. John McCormick, *Reclaiming Paradise: The Global Environmental Movement* (Bloomington: Indiana University Press, 1989), 110. McCormick provides a useful overview

of international developments during this period. See also Lamont C. Hempel, *Environmental Governance: The Global Challenge* (Washington, D.C.: Island Press, 1996); and Norman J. Vig and Regina S. Axelrod, eds., *The Global Environment: Institutions, Law, and Policy* (Washington, D.C.: CQ Press, 1999).

34. Alfred A. Marcus, *Promise and Performance: Choosing and Implementing Environmental Policy* (Westport, Conn.: Greenwood, 1980); Lettie McSpadden Wenner, *The Environmental Decade in Court* (Bloomington: Indiana University Press, 1982); Rosemary O'Leary, *Environmental Change: Federal Courts and the EPA* (Philadelphia: Temple University Press, 1993); Ringquist, *Environmental Protection at the State Level*; and Marc K. Landy, Marc J. Roberts, and Stephen R. Thomas, *The Environmental Protection Agency: Asking the Wrong Questions*, 2d ed. (New York: Oxford University Press, 1994).

35. George C. Eads and Michael Fix, *Relief or Reform? Reagan's Regulatory Dilemma* (Washington, D.C.: Urban Institute Press, 1984).

36. J. Clarence Davies III, "Environmental Institutions and the Reagan Administration," and Richard N. L. Andrews, "Deregulation: The Failure at EPA," in *Environmental Policy in the 1980s*, ed. Vig and Kraft.

37. See Philip Shabecoff, "Reagan and Environment: To Many a Stalemate," *New York Times*, January 2, 1989, 1, 8.

38. Ibid., 8.

39. Robert V. Bartlett, "Evaluating Environmental Policy," in *Environmental Policy in the 1990s*, 2d ed., ed. Vig and Kraft; Evan J. Ringquist, "Evaluating Environmental Policy Outcomes," in *Environmental Politics and Policy*, ed. Lester; and Gerrit J. Knaap and Tschangho John Kim, eds., *Environmental Program Evaluation: A Primer* (Champaign: University of Illinois Press, 1998).

40. The most thorough evaluation of environmental protection policies of this kind can be found in Davies and Mazurek, *Pollution Control in the United States*.

41. See Paul R. Portney, "Needed: A Bureau of Environmental Statistics," *Resources* 90 (Winter 1988): 12–15; and Clifford S. Russell, "Monitoring and Enforcement," in *Public Policies for Environmental Protection*, ed. Paul R. Portney (Washington, D.C.: Resources for the Future, 1990). The most convenient compendium of trend data on U.S. environmental quality can be found in the Council on Environmental Quality's *Environmental Quality: Twenty-fifth Anniversary Report* (Washington, D.C.: CEQ, 1997). For other nations, see *World Resources*, a comprehensive biennial report of the World Resources Institute.

42. EPA, *National Air Quality and Emissions Trends Report* (Research Triangle Park, N.C.: Office of Air Quality Planning and Standards, January 1998); and Richard A. Kerr, "Ozone-Destroying Chlorine Tops Out," *Science*, January 5, 1996, 32. For a broader discussion of air quality trends and policies, see Paul R. Portney, "Air Pollution Policy," in *Public Policies for Environmental Protection*, ed. Portney; and Gary C. Bryner, *Blue Skies, Green Politics: The Clean Air Act of 1990*, 2d ed. (Washington, D.C.: CQ Press, 1996).

43. EPA, *National Air Quality and Emissions Trends Report*.

44. Ibid.; CEQ, *Environmental Quality*; and EPA, *1996 Toxics Release Inventory* (Washington, D.C.: EPA, May 1998).

45. EPA, *National Water Quality Inventory: 1996 Report to Congress* (Washington, D.C.: Office of Water, April 1998). See also Debra S. Knopman and Richard A. Smith, "Twenty Years of the Clean Water Act," *Environment* 35 (January–February 1993): 17–20, 34–41; and CEQ, *Environmental Quality*, chap. 13.

46. EPA, *National Water Quality Inventory*.

47. Ibid., and Erik Olsen and Diane Cameron, "The Dirty Little Secret about Our Drinking Water" (Washington, D.C.: National Resources Defense Council, February 1995).

48. CEQ, *Environmental Quality*, and EPA Web page at *www.epa.gov/superfund/* (November 19, 1998). For a more positive assessment of the Superfund program than is usually found, see Charles De Saillan, "In Praise of Superfund," *Environment* 35

(October 1993): 42–44. For critical overviews of the Superfund program, see Daniel Mazmanian and David Morell, *Beyond Superfailure: America's Toxics Policy for the 1990s* (Boulder, Colo.: Westview, 1992); and John A. Hird, *Superfund: The Political Economy of Risk* (Baltimore: The Johns Hopkins University Press, 1994).

49. Russell, Colglazier, and Tonn, "U.S. Hazardous Waste Legacy," and Kraft, "Searching for Policy Success."

50. Theo Colborn, Dianne Dumanoski, and John Peterson Myers, *Our Stolen Future* (New York: Dutton, 1996).

51. Hallett J. Harris and Denise Scheberle, "Ode to the Miner's Canary: The Search for Environmental Indicators," in *Environmental Program Evaluation*, ed. Knaap and Kim.

52. CEQ, *Environmental Quality*, 411–417. See also Charles Pope, "National Parks, Private Funds: Trouble in Paradise?," *CQ Weekly*, October 31, 1998, 2938–2941; and William R. Lowry, *The Capacity for Wonder: Preserving National Parks* (Washington, D.C.: Brookings, 1994).

53. CEQ, *Environmental Quality*, chaps. 7 and 8, and Table 26, p. 429.

54. See Richard J. Tobin, *The Expendable Future: U. S. Politics and the Protection of Biological Diversity* (Durham, N.C.: Duke University Press, 1990); and Steven Lewis Yaffee, *The Wisdom of the Spotted Owl: Policy Lessons for a New Century* (Washington, D.C.: Island Press, 1994).

55. See, for example, Portney, *Public Policies for Environmental Protection;* and Tom Tietenberg, *Environmental Economics and Policy,* 2d ed. (Reading, Mass.: Addison-Wesley, 1998). Estimates of economic impacts show a wide variance, depending on the methods and models used, and on the economic indicators selected, but generally they are small. A number of studies indicate that at the state level environmental protection and economic prosperity go hand in hand. See Stephen M. Meyer, *Environmentalism and Economic Prosperity* (Cambridge, Mass.: MIT Press, forthcoming). The same is true at the international level. See, for example, Roger H. Bezdek, "Environment and Economy: What's the Bottom Line," *Environment* 35 (September 1993): 7–11, 25–32; and Michael E. Porter and Claas van der Linde, "Green and Competitive: Ending the Stalemate," *Harvard Business Review* (September–October 1995): 120–134.

56. See the budget tables in appendixes 2 and 3. The Commerce Department's estimates of total national spending on pollution abatement and control are lower than the EPA's. Commerce reports a total of $117.6 billion for 1994 (current dollars). See CEQ, *Environmental Quality*, 402. For the estimates of who pays for these amounts, see Paul Portney and Katherine N. Probst, "Cleaning Up Superfund," *Resources* 114 (Winter 1994): 2–5.

57. Portney, *Public Policies for Environmental Protection.*

58. See NAPA, *Setting Priorities;* and J. Clarence Davies, ed., *Comparing Environmental Risks: Tools for Setting Government Priorities* (Washington, D.C.: Resources for the Future, 1996).

59. See Mazmanian and Kraft, eds., *Toward Sustainable Communities.*

2

Power to the States:
The Promise and Pitfalls of Decentralization

Barry G. Rabe

The problem which all federalized nations have to solve is how to secure an efficient central government and preserve national unity, while allowing free scope for the diversities, and free play to the . . . members of the federation. It is . . . to keep the centrifugal and centripetal forces in equilibrium, so that neither the planet States shall fly off into space, nor the sun of the Central government draw them into its consuming fires.

—Lord James Bryce
The American Commonwealth

Thirty years ago the conventional wisdom on federalism viewed "the planet States" as sufficiently lethargic to require a powerful "Central government" in many areas of environmental policy. States were widely derided as mired in corruption, hostile to innovation, and unable to take a serious role in environmental policy out of fear of alienating key economic constituencies. In more recent years, the tables have turned—so much so that the conventional wisdom now berates an overheated federal government that squelches state creativity and capability to tailor environmental policies to local realities. The decentralization mantra of the 1990s calls for the extended transfer of environmental policy resources and regulatory authority from Washington, D.C., to states and localities. Such a transfer would pose a potentially formidable test of the thesis that more localized units know best.

What accounts for this sea-change in our understanding of the role of states in environmental policy? How have states evolved in recent decades and what sorts of functions do they assume most comfortably and effectively? Despite state resurgence, are there areas in which states fall short? If so, should they defer authority to their federal counterparts? Looking ahead, should regulatory authority devolve to the states, or are there better ways to sort out national and state responsibilities?

This chapter will address these questions, relying heavily on evidence of state performance in environmental policy. This will involve both an overview of state evolution and a set of brief case studies that explore state strengths and limitations. These state-specific accounts will be interwoven with assessments of the federal government's role, for good or ill, in the development of state environmental policy.

The States as "New Heroes" of American Federalism

Political scientists and policy analysts are generally most adept at analyzing institutional foibles and policy failures. Indeed, much of the literature on environmental policy follows this pattern, with criticisms becoming particularly voluminous and potent when directed toward federal efforts in this area. By contrast, states have received much more generous treatment. Many influential books on state government and federalism, in addition to journals, think tanks, and professional associations, portray states as highly dynamic and effective. Environmental policy is often depicted as a prime example of this general pattern of state effectiveness. Some analysts go so far as to characterize states as the "new heroes" of American federalism, having long since eclipsed a doddering federal government. According to this line of argument, states are consistently at the cutting edge of policy innovation, eager to find creative solutions to environmental problems. When the states fall short, an overzealous federal partner is often said to be at fault.

Such commentary has considerable empirical support. The vast majority of state governments have undergone fundamental changes since the first Earth Day in 1970. Many have drafted new constitutions and gained access to unprecedented revenues through expanded taxing powers. Substantial amounts of federal transfer dollars have further swelled state coffers, allowing them to pursue policy commitments that would previously have been unthinkable. In turn, state bureaucracies have expanded and become more professionalized, as have the staffs serving governors and legislatures.[1] This activity has been further stimulated by increasingly competitive two-party systems in many regions, intensifying pressure on elected officials to deliver desired services. Expanded use of direct democracy provisions, such as the initiative and referendum, and increasing activism by state courts have further contributed to this new era. Studies of this resurgent "statehouse democracy" show that policymaking at the state level has proven highly responsive to dominant public opinion within each state.[2] On the whole, citizens are thought to be a good deal more satisfied with the package of public services and regulations dispensed from their state capitals than with those from Washington.

This transformed state role is evident in virtually every area of environmental policy. States collectively spent more than $12.5 billion on environmental and related natural resource concerns in fiscal year 1996, with only slightly more than 20 percent of that funding coming from federal grant programs. The Council of State Governments has estimated that about 70 percent of all significant environmental legislation enacted by states has little or nothing to do with federal policy.[3] Many areas of environmental policy are clearly dominated by states, including most aspects of waste management, groundwater protection, and coastal zone management. And even in those areas of policy that bear a firm federal imprint, such as air pollution control and pesticides regulation, states have considerable opportunity to oversee implementation and move beyond federal standards if they so choose. Political scientist DeWitt John speaks for a wide range of policy analysts in noting that "states are willing to spend their own dollars and enact their own policies, without being forced by the federal government to do so. Virtually all states have taken some steps to go beyond federally imposed requirements, and some have taken the lead in several areas."[4]

That growing commitment is further reflected in the institutional arrangements established by states to address environmental problems. Many states have long since moved beyond their traditional placement of environmental programs in public health departments in favor of comprehensive agencies that gather most environmental responsibilities under a single organizational umbrella.[5] These agencies have sweeping, cross-programmatic responsibilities and have continually grown in staff and complexity over the past three decades. Ironically, many mirror the organizational framework of the much-maligned U.S. Environmental Protection Agency (EPA), dividing regulatory activity by environmental media of air, land, and water and thereby increasing the likelihood of shifting environmental contamination back and forth across medium boundaries. Despite this fragmentation, such institutions do provide states with a firm institutional foundation for addressing a wide array of environmental concerns.

This expanded state commitment to environmental policy may be accelerated not only by the broader factors introduced above but also by features somewhat unique to this policy area. First, a growing number of scholars contend that broad public support for environmental protection provides much impetus for bottom-up policy development. Such "civic environmentalism" stimulates numerous state and local stakeholders to take creative collective action independent of federal intervention.[6] In turn, game-theoretic analyses of efforts to protect "common-pool resources" such as river basins side decisively with local or regional approaches to resource protection as opposed to top-down controls. Many such analyses go so far as to argue that any central government intervention in such settings is often unnecessary at best and downright destructive at worst.[7]

Second, the proliferation of environmental policy professionals, representing industry, advocacy groups, and particularly state agencies, has created a sizable base of talent and ideas for policy innovation. Contrary to conventional depictions of agency officials as shackled by elected "principals," an alternative view finds considerable policy entrepreneurship in state and local policy-making circles. This pattern is especially evident in environmental policy, where numerous areas of specialization place a premium on expert ideas and allow for considerable innovation below the level of agency head.[8]

Third, environmental policy in many states is further stimulated by direct democracy, facilitating initiatives, referendums, and recall of elected officials not allowed at the federal level. State constitutional amendments must be approved by voters via referendum in every state except Delaware.

Thirty-one states and Washington, D.C., also have some form of direct democracy for approving legislation, representing well over half the U.S. population. Moreover, several states are currently considering the addition of such provisions, and thousands of localities employ some direct democracy form of their own. Use of this policy tool has grown at an exponential rate to consider a wide array of state environmental policy options, including nuclear plant closure, mandatory deposits on beverage containers, mandatory disclosure of commercial product toxicity, and public land acquisition, among others. Some nineteen states held one or more environment-related ballot propositions in the November 1996 elections.[9] In addition, numerous such policies first launched in a single state have become models for other states.[10]

The Cutting Edge of Policy: Cases of State Innovation

The convergence of these various political forces has served to unleash substantial new environmental policy at the state level. Scholars have attempted to analyze some of this activity through various ranking schemes that determine which states are most active and innovative. They consistently conclude that certain states tend to take the lead in most areas of policy innovation, followed by an often uneven pattern of innovation diffusion across state and regional boundaries. Somewhat related studies attempt to examine which economic and political factors are most likely to influence the rigor of state policy or the level of resources devoted to it.[11] An important but less-examined question concerns recent developments in state environmental policy and whether or not they constitute a marked improvement over conventional approaches. Evidence from select states suggests that a number of state innovations offer worthy alternatives to prevailing approaches. Indeed, many of these innovations constituted direct responses to shortcomings in existing regulatory design. A series of brief case studies offers some indication of the breadth and potential effectiveness of state innovation.

Pollution Prevention

One of the greatest challenges facing U.S. environmental policy is the need to shift from a pollution control mode to one of prevention. Historically speaking, both federal and state policies have performed poorly in the prevention area, but growing evidence suggests that some states are pursuing prevention in an increasingly systematic and effective way. All fifty states now have at least one formal pollution prevention program, with the oldest and most common of these involving technical assistance to industries and networking services that link potential collaborators. A smaller but growing set of state programs, however, is redefining pollution prevention in larger terms, cutting across conventional programmatic boundaries with a series of mandates and incentives for pursuit of prevention opportunities.[12]

Among these, Minnesota may now have the most multifaceted program to date. The state dramatically increased its traditional technical assistance efforts in 1990 with passage of the Minnesota Toxic Pollution Prevention Act. This legislation calls on approximately three hundred and fifty Minnesota firms to submit annual toxic pollution prevention plans. These plans must outline each firm's current use and release of a long list of toxic pollutants and establish formal goals for their reduction or elimination over a specified period of time. Firms have considerable latitude in determining how to attain these goals, contrary to the technology-forcing character of much federal regulation. But they must meet state-established reduction timetables and pay fees on releases. Overall releases of these substances have dropped consistently during the 1990s.[13]

In both these instances, firms often relied not on expensive technological solutions but on equipment modification; substitution of less-dangerous chemicals; manufacturing-process adjustments; and improved training, housekeeping, and equipment maintenance. Minnesota officials have supplemented these efforts with ongoing training and conferences, awards for pollution prevention excellence, and grants to local governments. In addition, the state created an Interagency Pollution Prevention Advisory Team with representatives of twenty agencies to implement an aggressive gubernatorial executive order to pursue pollution prevention opportunities in all state-sponsored activities.

Regulatory Integration

Both federal and state environmental protection efforts have long been suspect owing to their reliance on medium-based strategies to control pollution. This approach is unsatisfactory not only because it reacts to pollution after it is created but also because it tends to shift pollutants to the medium least regulated at a given moment. Few states showed much awareness of this problem, much less addressed it, prior to the mid 1980s.[14] But there is growing evidence that some states are beginning to look systematically at various regulatory areas—such as permitting, monitoring, inspection, and enforcement—to find more integrative ways to approach environmental problems, thereby minimizing pollutant transfer across medium boundaries.

Permitting may be the regulatory tool most in need of integration. Permits are used to limit specific pollutant releases into individual environmental media but often target narrow concerns without any consideration of possible impact on other programs or media. Many states have attempted to streamline their administration of permit programs, although these have generally served to accelerate the process of permit issuance rather than explore integration prospects. More recently, states such as New Jersey and Minnesota have taken particularly bold steps toward integration. New Jersey, for example, is using data from its Minnesota-like pollution prevention planning requirements to attempt to transform its approach to permitting. Eighteen manufacturing facilities around the state have been selected for a project whereby each of their disparate permits are eliminated in favor of a single document that outlines a unified environmental protection strategy. As in the Minnesota prevention case, firms are given considerable flexibility in determining how to reach state-established emissions reduction goals. They are nevertheless expected to achieve significant environmental improvements and refrain from cross-media transfers.

In the first case completed under this program, state officials found a major pharmaceutical firm mired in a typical maze of permits administered by different officials with distinct program orientations at separate times. In all, the facility had 897 separate permits for air quality alone, in concert with dozens of additional permits for other areas such as water quality and solid and hazardous waste management. Upon review of the entire facility through integrated inspection and permit review, state officials discovered numerous instances of inadvertent cross-media transfer and pollution prevention opportunities waiting to be seized. They compressed all permits into a single document with individual chapters for each of the thirty-one separate parts of the facility. This comprehensive permit establishes significant emissions-reduction goals for the facility. The success of this approach has been heralded as a model for regulatory innovation.[15] Eight additional cases in New Jersey have subsequently been completed with comparable outcomes, although the future of this program has been jeopardized by state budget cuts and partisan divisions.

Such integrative activity is not confined to permitting, as select states are reviewing other cornerstones of the traditional regulatory process. Idaho, Massachusetts, and Minnesota have taken particularly prominent roles in reworking inspection and enforcement efforts to better consider cross-media concerns. In turn, states such as California, Maine, Massachusetts, New Jersey, and Wisconsin have pursued reorganizational options that might better foster integration—and prevention—strategies. These range from wholesale reorganization of agencies into divisions that merge single-medium programs to issue-specific efforts to pull together officials from diverse programs to secure a unified focus on a particular problem.

Economic Incentives

Economic analysts of environmental policy have long lamented the U.S. system's penchant for command-and-control rules and regulations. They would prefer to see a more economically sensitive set of policies, such as fees on emissions and incentives to reward good environmental performance. Neither federal nor state governments have escaped such critical scrutiny, although a number of states have attempted to respond in recent years. In all, the states have enacted more than two hundred and fifty measures that can be characterized as "green taxes," including environmentally related charges and tax incentives.[16] Many states have become increasingly reliant on emission or waste fees, to provide both an economic disincentive to pollute and a source of funds for program management.

A growing number of states are also revising their tax policies for environmental purposes. For example, Iowa exempts all pollution-control equipment purchased for use in the state from taxation, while Louisiana exempts such equipment from the state sales tax. Other states, such as New Jersey and Oregon, offer a series of tax credits for purchase of recycling equipment or capital investments necessary to facilitate recycling or reuse of a particular product. Minnesota began to levy sizable sales taxes on nonrecycled municipal solid waste in 1989, which may well have contributed to the increase in the state's solid waste recycling rate from 9 percent in 1989 to more than 40 percent in 1998. The scope of this tax was expanded through legislation approved in 1997. States are also exploring use of market mechanisms to protect threatened habitat and endangered species. Florida, for example, has established a program for "wetlands mitigation banking," whereby state and local water districts may license wetland owners as mitigation bankers. They may sell mitigation credits to other developers and use portions of the proceeds to improve their wetlands.[17]

Perhaps the most visible economic incentive programs involve refundable taxes on beverage containers. Ten states, covering 30 percent of the population, have such programs in place. Particular provisions of these programs vary somewhat, although most operate with limited direct involvement by state officials. Deposits are passed along a system that includes consumers, container redemption facilities such as grocery stores, and firms that actually reuse or recycle the containers.

Michigan's program is widely regarded as among the most successful of these state efforts and, like a number of others, is a product of direct democracy. Nearly two-thirds of Michigan voters endorsed a ballot proposal for the deposit program in 1976, despite the fact that forces opposing the program outspent proponents by a ten-to-one margin during the campaign. All subsequent polling has indicated continuing high levels of public support for the program, and it clearly influenced comparable action in a few other states in the years immediately following enactment. The state's program is alone in placing a dime deposit on containers—double the more conventional nickel—which may contribute to its unusually high compliance rate. Whereas most states achieve a return rate of 79 to 83 percent, Michigan has consistently reached a rate of 95 percent or higher. Various studies have concluded that the program has contributed to significant declines in litter and the volumes of solid waste requiring disposal, as well as generated energy savings and reduced injuries from container-caused lacerations.[18]

The diffusion of this innovation to other states has not been as extensive as might be expected, in large part due to strong opposition from beverage manufacturers and distributors in states where proposals have been advanced. But while no additional states have imposed deposit requirements on beverages since 1983, a growing number of them are using this method to promote recycling of such items as lead-acid batteries, motor oil, pesticide containers, and appliances. In turn, Florida has eschewed the Michigan deposit strategy but has imposed a two-cent advance-disposal fee on containers that are not recycled at a rate of at least 50 percent.[19]

One particularly effective spin-off of this approach involves efforts by Oregon, Minnesota, Virginia, and Wisconsin to address the problem of used tires. The proliferation of such tires, due to the growth in number of automobiles in use and miles driven as well as the glacial pace of used tire decomposition, has led to serious environmental problems in many regions of the nation. Tire piles are notorious breeding grounds for insects and have been shown to facilitate the spread of diseases such as encephalitis; some piles have caught fire, leading to significant release of unrestricted toxic air emissions.

Oregon pioneered the use of economic incentives for waste tires with legislation enacted in 1987 intended to address a substantial backlog of used tires and to facilitate reuse of the approximately two million tires removed from active use in the state each year. The state banned disposal of whole waste tires unless recycling proved unworkable and established a $1 fee on retail sale of new tires for use in a waste tire-recycling account. This account was intended to provide partial reimbursement to firms that made use of waste tires. It provided a penny per pound of material used (reaching $20 per ton) for new products such as doormats, benches, buoys, and artificial reefs and also set aside funds to clean up existing tire piles. The program proved so successful, it began to phase out in 1991 and was closed entirely in 1993. Tire piles have disappeared in Oregon, and markets have now emerged to handle the ongoing supply of used tires without the reimbursement subsidies. In the event the problem recurs, the state has kept $1.5 million from the fund as a contingency and retains legislative authority to reactivate its efforts.[20] It continues to operate a permitting program that oversees collection, transport, and storage of waste tires.

Disclosure Mandates

California has also played a prominent role in developing policy that places essential information concerning potential risk posed by chemicals directly in the hands of the citizenry. As in the Michigan deposit program, California's Safe Drinking Water and Toxic Enforcement Act of 1986 was a direct democracy measure passed with overwhelming voter support. Better known as Proposition 65, this legislation supplements existing right-to-know programs through mandatory disclosure of exposure to chemicals known by the state to cause cancer or reproductive toxicity. The state must update this list annually, and firms may not "knowingly and intentionally" expose any person to listed chemicals without providing "clear and reasonable warning." Exemptions from the list require evidence that exposure will pose "no significant risk."

California's warning list now contains approximately five hundred chemicals, including pharmaceutical products and others with an array of commercial uses. More than two hundred and fifty numeric standards have been established to set a clear line for implementing the "no significant risk" provisions. Whereas such standards are imposed at a halting pace at the federal level, this legislation gives companies an incentive to move apace with risk assessment in order to establish clear guidelines on what substances require warning procedures. To assure compliance, the legislation imposes stiff penalties for violations and allows "any person in the public interest" to bring suit against violations sixty days after notice. There are stiff penalties for violations, 25 percent of which can be used as "bounty" rewards for individuals who successfully bring suit. A report by a Proposition 65 review panel concluded that "by federal standards, Proposition 65 has resulted in 100 years of progress in the areas of hazard identification, risk assessment, and exposure assessment." Industry evaluations are less enthusiastic, although many leaders confirm the burden has not been as onerous as anticipated. Interestingly, no other state has followed California's path in this area to date, although others have experimented with various forms of environmental information disclosure to the public.[21]

State Limits

Such a promising set of innovations would seem to augur well for the states' involvement in environmental policy. Any such enthusiasm must be tempered, however, with an enduring concern over how evenly that innovative vigor extends over the entire nation. One of the long-standing rationales for giving the federal government so much authority in environmental policy is that states face inherent limitations in environmental policy. Rather than a consistent, across-the-board pattern of dynamism, we shall see a more uneven pattern of performance than the current conventional wisdom might anticipate. This imbalance becomes particularly evident when environmental problems are not confined to the boundaries of a specific state. Many environmental issues are by definition transboundary, raising enduring questions of interstate and interregional equity in allocating responsibility for the burden of environmental protection.

Uneven State Performance

Many of the efforts to rank states according to their environmental regulatory rigor, institutional capacity, or general innovativeness find the same subset of states on the top rungs year after year. By contrast, a significant number of states consistently tend to fall much further down the list, raising questions as to their overall regulatory capacity and commitment. As political scientist William Lowry has noted, "not all states are responding appropriately to policy needs within their borders. . . . If matching between need and response were always high and weak programs existed only where pollution was low, this would not be a problem. However, this is not the case."[22] Interestingly, given all the hoopla surrounding the newfound dynamism of states in environmental policy, and public policy more generally, there has been remarkably little analysis of the performance of those states that not only fail to crack "top ten" rankings but also consistently lag below the median.

What we do know about such states should surely give one pause over the extent to which state dynamism is truly cross-cutting. Despite considerable economic growth in formerly poor regions, such as the Southeast, substantial variation endures among state governments in their rates of public expenditure, with no demonstrable change in the amount of interstate expenditure variation over the past quarter-century.[23] Similar fiscal patterns are evident in environmental and natural resource spending. State expenditures in fiscal year 1996 ranged from more than $80 per capita in nine states to less than $40 per capita in eighteen others. Similar variation is evident when viewing such spending as a percentage of total state expenditures, in dollars per manufacturer, or as number of state environmental officials per capita, and it has remained relatively stable over time.[24] Cost of living differences among states account for only a small portion of this variation in state expenditure levels. In turn, efforts to classify states by other measures reveal similarly discordant patterns. A growing number of states in recent years have enacted legislation that prohibits their environmental agencies from exceeding any federal regulatory standards, whereas some others continue to view federal standards as establishing minimum levels that they frequently elect to exceed. Such disparities are consistent with studies of state political culture and social capital, which indicate vast differences in likely state receptivity to governmental efforts to foster environmental improvement.[25]

While some states are unveiling exciting new programs, there is growing reason to worry about how effectively states in general handle core functions either delegated to them under federal programs or left exclusively to their oversight. Studies of water quality program implementation undertaken by the U.S. General Accounting Office and the Natural Resources Defense Council in the 1990s have found enormous variation in the methods used by states to determine water quality and the frequency with which they undertake enforcement actions when violations are discovered.[26] States also employ highly variable water quality standards in areas such as sewage contamination, groundwater protection, nonpoint water pollution, wetland preservation, fish advisories, and beach closures. Inconsistencies abound in reporting accuracy, suggesting that national assessments of water quality trends that rely on data from state reports may be highly suspect. Moreover, many major water bodies receive remarkably minimal monitoring attention of any sort from state authorities. States such as Alabama and Texas, for example, conduct no regular monitoring of their extensive marine beaches, yet report consistently that all estuaries and coastal waters meet the swimmability goals of the Clean Water Act. Ironically, large percentages of these same waters have been closed for fishing over extended periods due to high levels of bacteriological pollution. Insufficient drinking-water monitoring by state and local officials has led to a number of disease outbreaks in recent years, perhaps most notably the 1993 Milwaukee-area contamination of drinking water by livestock runoff that caused an estimated 370,000 citizens to become ill with cryptosporidiosis, a gastrointestinal illness.[27]

Comparable problems have emerged in state enforcement of air quality and waste management programs, where officially reported numbers on regulatory actions, emission levels, waste disposal capacity, and waste reduction levels are of similarly questionable utility[28] Despite efforts in some states to integrate and streamline permitting, many states have extensive backlogs in the permit programs they operate and thereby have no real indication of facility compliance with various regulatory standards. Nationally in the mid 1990s, more than half of all water pollution permits had expired, reaching rates of up to 94 percent in Virginia and 93 percent in New Mexico.[29] In 1996 and 1997, serious federal allegations of state negligence in tending to regulatory enforcement responsibilities in Pennsylvania, Virginia, and other states underscored this enduring issue.[30] In turn, a two-year examination of state enforcement and inspection practices by the EPA inspector general resulted in a series of 1998 reports that offered a scathing assessment of basic environmental program implementation in a number of states.[31]

Enduring Federal Dependency

More sweeping assertions of state resurgence are further undermined by the penchant of many states to cling to organizational design and program priorities set in Washington, D.C. While some states have indicated that it is possible to pursue far-reaching agency reorganization and other integrative policies without significant opposition—or grant reduction—from the federal government, the vast majority continue to adhere to a medium-based, pollution control framework for agency organization that contributes to enduring programmatic fragmentation. Although a growing number of state officials speak favorably and knowledgeably about shifting toward integrative approaches, many remain hard-pressed to give any concrete illustration of how their states have begun to move in that direction. Thus far, many Clinton-era federal initiatives to give states more freedom to innovate have been used to streamline operations rather than foster prevention or integration.[32]

In fact, a good deal of the most innovative state-level activity has been at least partially stimulated—and underwritten—through federal grants. Indeed, in Canada, where central government grant assistance—and regulatory presence—is extremely limited, provinces have proven far less innovative than their American state counterparts.[33] Although a number of states have developed fee systems to cover a growing portion of their costs, many states rely heavily on federal grants to fund pollution prevention activities. In the 1990s more than one-third of all state pollution prevention expenditures have come from federal sources, with some states completely reliant on federal dollars for their prevention efforts.[34] Similarly, states have continued to be recipients of other important sources of federal support, including grants and technical assistance for twenty-six state comparative risk assessment and reduction projects.[35] On the whole, states receive slightly more than 20 percent of their total environmental program funding from federal grants, although a few states rely on Washington for as much as 40 to 50 percent of their total funding.

Furthermore, for all the opprobrium heaped on the federal government in environmental policy, Washington has provided states with at least four other forms of valuable assistance, some of which has directly contributed to the resurgence and innovation of state environmental policy. First, federal development of a Toxics Release Inventory, modeled in 1986 after a program initially attempted in New Jersey, has emerged as a vital component of many of the most promising pollution prevention and cross-media integration initiatives. This program has generated unprecedented information concerning toxic releases and provided states an essential data source for exploring alternative regulatory approaches. Current pollution prevention programs in states such as New Jersey, Minnesota, New York, and elsewhere would be unthinkable without such an annual information source. Second, states remain almost totally dependent on the federal government for the essential insights gained through research and development. Each year the federal government outspends the states in environmental research and development by more than twenty to one, and states have shown little indication of wanting to pick up this burden in search of research programs tailored to their particular technological and informational needs.

Third, the most successful efforts to coordinate environmental protection on a multistate, regional basis have received a great deal of federal input and support. A series of initiatives in the Chesapeake Bay and Great Lakes Basin has received much acclaim for tackling difficult issues and forging regional partnerships; federal participation—through grants, technical assistance, coordination, and efforts to unify regional standards—has proven useful in both cases.[36] By contrast, other major bioregions, including the Puget Sound, Gulf of Mexico, Columbia River system, and Mississippi Basin, have lacked comparable federal participation and have generally not experienced creative interstate partnerships.[37] Their experience contradicts the popular thesis that regional coordination improves when central authority is minimal or nonexistent.

Fourth, the hamhandedness of regulatory actions by EPA headquarters is legendary, but the federal role in overseeing state-level program implementation looks a good deal more constructive when examining the role played by the agency's ten regional offices. Most state-level interaction with the EPA involves such regional offices, which employ approximately two-thirds of the total EPA workforce. Relations between state and regional officials are generally more cordial and constructive than those between state and central EPA officials, and may even be, in some instances, characterized by high levels of mutual involvement and trust.[38] In fact, regional offices have played a central role in many of the most promising state-level innovations, including those in Minnesota and New Jersey discussed above. Their involvement may include formal advocacy on behalf of the state with central headquarters, direct collaboration on meshing state initiatives with federal requirements, and special grant support or technical assistance. In recent years, at least two regional offices have completed major reorganizations, intended in part to transcend medium program divides in favor of a more integrated, functional approach.[39]

The Interstate Environmental Balance-of-Trade

States may be structurally ill-equipped to handle a large range of environmental concerns. In particular, states may be reluctant to invest significant energies to tackle those problems that literally might migrate to another state in the absence of intervention. The days of state agencies captured securely in the hip pockets of major industries are probably long gone, but state regulatory dynamism does appear to diminish when faced with such cross-boundary issues.

The state imperative of economic development clearly contributes to this phenomenon. As states increasingly devise development strategies that resemble the industrial policies of western European nations, a range of scholars have concluded they are far more deeply committed to strategies that promote "investment" or "development" than those that involve social service provision or public health promotion.[40] In 1995 alone, states enacted one hundred and fifty new business tax incentive programs and a number of states now offer incentives in excess of $50,000 per new job to prospective developers.[41] Environmental protection can be eminently compatible with economic development goals, promoting overall quality of life and general environmental attractiveness that entices private investment. In many states, the tourism industry has played an active role in seeking strong environmental programs designed to maintain natural assets. Even in New Jersey, widely known as an industrial and chemical behemoth, tourism is the state's fourth-largest industry, and it has lobbied assiduously to secure state support for environmental protection likely to benefit popular natural areas. On the whole, the limited formal linkage between environmental protection and economic development remains evident in the very tenuous, slow development of state "sustainable development" programs. But the linkage is increasingly evident and influential in certain environmental areas.[42] Such convergence clearly sustains support for many state environmental programs.

But much of what a state might undertake in environmental policy may largely serve to benefit other states or regions, thereby reducing an individual state's incentive to take meaningful action. In fact, there are many instances in which states continue to pursue a "we make it, you take it" strategy. As political scientist William Gormley, Jr., has noted, there are cases in which "states can readily export their problems to other states," resulting in potentially serious environmental "balance of trade" problems.[43] In such situations, states may be inclined to export environmental contaminants to other states while enjoying any economic benefits to be derived from the activity that generated the contamination.

Such cross-boundary transfer takes many forms, and may be particularly prevalent in those environmental policy areas where long-distance migration of pollutants is most likely. Air quality policy has long fit this pattern. States such as Ohio and Pennsylvania, for example, have depended heavily on burning massive quantities of high-sulfur coal to meet energy demands. Prevailing winds invariably transfer pollutants from this activity to other regions, particularly New England, leading to serious concern over acid deposition and related contamination threats. In turn, states around the nation have relied heavily on so-called dispersion enhancement to improve local air quality. Average industrial stack height in the United States soared from 243 feet in 1960 to 730 feet in 1980.[44] Although this resulted in significant air quality improvement in many areas near elevated stacks, it generally served to disperse air pollution problems elsewhere. It has also contributed to the growing problem of airborne toxics that ultimately pollute water or land in other regions; between 80 to 90 percent of many of the most dangerous toxic substances found in Lake Superior, for example, stem from air deposition, much of which is generated outside of the Great Lakes Basin.

Growing interstate conflicts, often becoming protracted battles in the federal courts, have emerged in recent decades as states allege they are recipients of such unwanted "imports." Midwestern states such as Illinois, Indiana, Michigan, Ohio, and Wisconsin and Eastern states such as Connecticut, Delaware, Massachusetts, New Jersey, New York, and Rhode Island, among others, continue to be mired in such disputes. Even a multi-year effort funded by EPA to encourage thirty-seven states to find a collective solution to the transport of ground-level ozone has not resulted in agreements on core recommendations. The so-called Ozone Transport Assessment Group (OTAG) received considerable national attention as a possible model of intergovernmental problem-solving and did reach some important agreements among most of its members. But five states formally opposed OTAG's July 1997 recommendations to EPA and five others have joined this group in challenging EPA's proposed rule that draws on those recommendations, reflecting a serious schism between Midwestern and Northeastern states.[45]

States have also facilitated cross-boundary movement of their environmental problems by erecting such high standards that contaminants must invariably be shipped elsewhere for disposal. This allows state officials to "claim credit" for taking bold environmental protection steps while enabling them to "avoid blame" for concentrating contaminants anywhere within state boundaries. The disposal of sludge generated by wastewater treatment plants illustrates this pattern, as states have been largely left free to set their own standards. Many states, including those usually ranking atop innovation lists, tend to set the toughest standards. But for many of them, such as New York, criteria are set so high that in-state sludge generators uniformly turn to states with lower standards for disposal.

Perhaps nowhere is this type of interstate transfer more evident than in disposal of solid, hazardous, biomedical, and low-level radioactive wastes. Each type of waste features some degree of federal regulatory oversight and legitimate challenges can be made concerning the effectiveness of guiding federal legislation. But in many respects this area has offered a test of decentralization, as states have been given enormous latitude to devise their own systems of waste management and facility siting, either working independently or in concert with other states. In the area of low-level radioactive waste, in fact, federal legislation enacted in 1980 and 1985 was virtually dictated to Congress by the demands of state gubernatorial and legislative associations.[46]

This test of state capacity to take effective collective action has had its triumphs, including some of the efforts to promote waste reduction and prevention discussed above. Moreover, many states have moved to close their most environmentally suspect waste disposal facilities, particularly unlined landfills. Louisiana and New Jersey have closed nearly one thousand solid waste dumps apiece, allowing only the most technically sophisticated firms to stay in business. But many other aspects of waste management policy at the state level have involved a disconcerting pattern of interstate and interregional transfer of waste. Many states, including a number of those usually deemed among the most innovative and committed environmentally, continue to generate massive quantities of waste and have been hugely unsuccessful in siting modern treatment, storage, and disposal facilities. Instead, out-of-state (and region) export has been an increasingly common pattern, with wastes often shipped to facilities opened before concern over hazardous waste and facility siting became widespread. In fact, many of the largest of these facilities are located in states widely derided as least innovative and active on environmental issues, making them the dumping ground for wastes generated in states thought to be more environmentally responsible. At its worst, the system resembles a shell game in which waste is ultimately deposited in the least resistant state or facility at a given moment.

Many states have banded together to devise regional strategies to share the waste management burden. But these have been little more than mechanisms to assure a steady flow of federal grant dollars and to delay the larger questions of long-term waste management and distributional fairness. A few states—and Canadian provinces—have made some progress in developing comprehensive systems of waste management, although these remain exceptional cases.[47]

While planning efforts generally languish, the conflict between states endures, occasionally becoming quite nasty. Nearly two dozen other states responded to the waste import problem in the 1980s by erecting a wide array of barriers to further imports, ranging from differential regulatory standards and fees—in some cases tripling charges for disposal of out-of-state wastes—to a South Carolina effort to use its militia to turn away low-level radioactive waste shipments heading toward its aging disposal facility.[48] Many of these state barriers have since been ruled unconstitutional by state and federal courts, most commonly because of perceived violation of the Commerce Clause of the U.S. Constitution.[49] As a result, the pattern of export continues unabated.

Waste transfer may constitute an extreme type of intergovernmental environmental problem. Yet it suggests that certain issues may not be best addressed through decentralized units. Policy analysts should be examining policy options for states with an eye to whether burden shifting across state boundaries is likely to be an option. If not, the case for decentralization becomes considerably stronger.

Looking Ahead

Determining the most appropriate role for states to play in environmental policy becomes all the more important given political developments set in motion by the November 1994 elections and the shift to Republican control of both the House and Senate in the 104th and 105th Congresses. Many prominent legislative proposals could have considerable impact on states if enacted, in many instances transferring to them greater authority for program design, funding, and implementation. However, subsequent changes in state environmental policy appear more closely linked to intra-state political developments than devolution triggered by Washington.

Perhaps the most visible early step taken by the 104th Congress involved passage of the Unfunded Mandates Reform Act (UMRA), signed into law by President Bill Clinton in March 1995, that banned any new legislation that imposes new regulatory mandates on states or localities if they lack sufficient federal funding to cover compliance costs. This represented a response to a growing chorus of state and local complaints about so-called unfunded mandates, whereby Congress utters detailed marching orders to states and localities but provides little if any financial support necessary for implementation. Environmental regulations, such as those imposed by federal air, surface water, and drinking-water quality legislation, are frequently cited as among the most burdensome. The mayor of Columbus, Ohio, for example, has estimated that his city will have to provide well over $1 billion to comply with fourteen major environmental mandates between 1991 and 2000, representing an average payment of $856 per Columbus family per year.[50] The new federal legislation received broad acclaim but thus far has had limited actual impact. It is loaded with exclusionary loopholes, does not apply to any mandate already in existence, and can be nullified by any future act of Congress. Indeed, no sooner had the ink dried on UMRA than new federal legislation appeared that imposed a wide range of new mandates, largely by changing the technical ways in which they were to be implemented.[51] Similar limitations have been evident in the seventeen states that have either passed legislation or amended their constitutions to limit the ability of states to impose mandates on local governments.[52]

Some subsequent federal attempts to transfer substantial regulatory authority to the states have generally failed in the face of industry resistance to the possible loss of national regulatory consistency. In fact, in some instances, such as regulation of pesticides in the production, distribution, and handling of food, frustration with state-by-state regulatory differences prompted industry to prod the 104th Congress into enacting new legislation that imposes uniform federal standards and preempts states from setting tougher standards. A proposed Conference of the States, which promised to rally support for regulatory devolution, was scheduled to convene in 1997. Actively supported by Utah Republican governor Michael Leavitt and endorsed by one or both legislative chambers in thirty-five states, the Conference intended to petition Congress for possible constitutional amendments to expand states' rights. One such provision called for a "People's Legislative Recall," whereby a majority of states could veto any federal law or regulation. But the conference was never held, following a withering set of attacks from conservative interest groups who contended that it might undermine the Constitution and foster international control of American institutions.

Ironically, the most significant environmental decentralization initiatives since the 1994 elections have emerged from the Clinton administration rather than Congress. In May 1995, the administration unveiled a National Environmental Performance Partnership System (NEPPS), a multifaceted approach designed to give states considerably more flexibility in their management of federal environmental programs in exchange for state capacity to demonstrate "actual performance in improving the environment."[53] The Clinton EPA also developed "pollution partnership grants" (PPG) to give states more flexibility in grant usage and to encourage state innovation and established Regulatory Reinvention Pilot Projects, such as Project XL, to allow individual firms and state agencies to pursue innovative regulatory ideas. Forty of the states had signed NEPPS and PPG agreements with EPA by early 1999.

This added flexibility has served to somewhat mitigate continuing uncertainties over federal funding of transfer grants to states, although even the emergence of an unexpectedly large federal budget surplus in 1998 and 1999 has not translated into major increases in federal grants or resolved the long-term issue of federal financial support for state environmental policy efforts. If the experience of the Reagan era's new federalism is any guide, most states will prove unwilling or unable to generate their own revenues to replace federal program cuts.[54] Most states enjoyed generally robust fiscal health in the 1997 and 1998 fiscal years, with overall tax revenues growing and swelling both annual surpluses and rainy-day funds. However, intensifying pressures to boost state expenditures for medical care, elementary and secondary education, and criminal justice continue to crowd out claims for increasing environmental funding.[55] Thus, the states may continue to rely significantly on federal transfer dollars in the years ahead.

This fiscal pinch may be particularly evident in states with elected leaders firmly committed to substantial reduction of overall tax burden, state spending, and regulatory activity. These policy shifts, in many states, stem from tremendous Republican successes in the 1994 elections, when Republicans enjoyed a net gain of twelve governorships and eighteen state legislative chambers. After the 1998 elections, this redistribution of power was holding firm, with Republican governors at the helm in thirty-one states and Republican majorities in nearly half of the nation's statehouses. In many states, these partisan gains have translated into strong attacks on existing environmental programs. Ironically, those states promoting the most far-reaching reductions of taxation, spending, and regulatory rigor include a number of those historically ranked among the most innovative and fiscally supportive of environmental programs, such as Michigan, New Jersey, New York, and Wisconsin. In Michigan, for example, Republican control resulted in a reorganization of state environmental and natural resource agencies widely seen as an effort to rein in environmental policy. The move prompted the resignations of many veteran state environmental officials and coincided with a major reduction in state environmental and natural resource department staff in the wake of a massive early retirement plan for state personnel. In New Jersey, major cuts in state spending have eliminated one-fifth of the positions in the state Department of Environmental Protection, jeopardizing continued operation of many of the innovative programs previously noted. In such cases, there is little indication of a creative effort to make state environmental policy more effective. Instead, the predominant theme appears to be rolling back as much regulatory activity as quickly as possible, with scant consideration of innovative alternative approaches.

The future role of states in environmental policy may be further shaped by three additional developments. First, intensified debate at the federal level over the meaning of the so-called takings clause of the U.S. Constitution has been supplemented by a flurry of state legislative proposals that call on state or local governments to compensate landowners for any property value decline that can be attributed to environmental regulation. Twenty-six states enacted thirty-nine "property rights" laws between 1991 and 1996, although these laws vary enormously and are only just beginning to be implemented by agencies and reviewed by courts.[56] Such legislation has already received consideration under direct democracy, as Arizona voters rejected a takings proposal in 1993 and Washington voters repealed state legislation in 1995. Some of the more far-reaching laws, including measures in Florida, Louisiana, Mississippi, North Carolina, and Texas that hold out promise of considerable economic compensation, could profoundly alter the way states approach environmental policy, particularly in such controversial areas as wetlands, habitat, and groundwater protection.

Second, the era of term limits is beginning to unfold. As of 1999 forty-one states had imposed some form of term limits on governors, and twenty-one states had placed them on legislators. Many of these restrictions were established during the 1990s and are only just beginning to take effect. Some remain under constitutional challenge in the state courts. Gubernatorial term limits most commonly involve a pair of four-year terms whereas legislative term limits range from six to twelve years. Even before they formally took hold, the threat of these limits contributed to considerable legislative turnover. Only 28 percent of state senators and 16 percent of state house members serving in 1997 held the same positions a decade earlier.[57] In many states, veteran legislators who championed the environmental programs that have given states such a dynamic image have either left office in recent years or will soon be forced to step down. It is anyone's guess as to what long-term impact the arrival of cascades of new elected officials, all allowed to stay in specific offices for limited periods, will have on environmental policy.

Third, Republican successes in the 1994 elections further contributed to a pattern of divided, joint-party control of state government that shows no signs of abating. In 1999, twenty-five states, including many of the most populous, featured formally divided power between Republicans and Democrats. This may explain the increasingly acrimonious atmosphere of policy-making at the state level and could conceivably facilitate gridlocks analogous to those long lamented in Washington. In any event, environmental policy will require the support of both parties in a great many states in order to move forward productively.

Amid the continued squabbling over the proper role of the federal government vis-à-vis the states in environmental policy in recent decades, there has been remarkably little effort to sort out which functions might best be concentrated in Washington or transferred to state capitals. Some current and retired federal legislators of both parties have offered useful proposals over the past decade that might allocate such responsibilities more reasonably than at present. These have been supplemented by thoughtful scholarly works by political scientist Paul Peterson, policy analyst John Donahue, and economists Alice Rivlin, Henry Butler, and Jonathan Macey.[58] Interestingly, many of these experts concur that environmental protection policy defies easy designation as warranting extreme centralization or decentralization. Instead, they consistently call for a process of selective decentralization, one leading to an appropriately balanced set of responsibilities across governmental levels. In moving toward a more functional environmental federalism, certain broad design principles might be useful to consider.

A more discerning environmental federalism might begin by concentrating federal regulatory energies on those problems that are clearly national in character. Many air and water pollution problems, for example, are by definition cross-boundary concerns unlikely to be resolved by a series of unilateral state actions. In contrast, problems such as protecting indoor air quality and clean up of abandoned hazardous waste dumps may present more geographically confinable challenges; they are perhaps best handled through substantial delegation of authority to states. As Donahue has noted, "most waste sites are situated within a single state, and stay there," yet are governed by highly centralized Superfund legislation, in direct contrast to more decentralized programs in environmental areas where cross-boundary transfers are prevalent.[59] Under a more rational system, the federal regulatory presence might intensify as the likelihood of cross-boundary contaminant transfer escalates. Such an initial attempt to sort out functions might be reinforced by federal policy efforts to encourage states or regions to take responsibility for internally generated environmental problems rather than tacitly allow exportation to occur. In the area of waste management, for example, federal per mile fees on waste shipment might provide a disincentive for long-distance transfer, instead encouraging states, regions, and waste generators to either develop their own capacity or pursue waste reduction options more aggressively. The growing use of economic approaches to environmental policy at both state and federal levels provides numerous models that might be used to encourage states to be more responsible environmental citizens in the federal system.

There are, of course, many areas in which some shared federal and state role remains appropriate, reflecting the inherent complexity of many environmental problems. Effective intergovernmental partnerships may already be well established in certain areas. Even a 1995 National Academy of Public Administration study that excoriates many aspects of federal environmental policy concedes that the existing partnership between federal and state governments "is basically sound, and major structural changes are not warranted. The system has worked."[60] But even if essentially sound, the partnership could clearly benefit from further maturation. Alongside the sorting-out activities discussed above, both federal and state governments could do much more to promote creative sharing of policy ideas and environmental data. There is remarkably little dissemination of such information across state and regional boundaries and potentially considerable advantage to be gained from increasing such activity. More broadly, the federal government might also explore other ways to encourage states to work cooperatively, especially on common-boundary problems. State capacity to find creative solutions to pressing environmental problems is on the ascendance, as we have seen. But as Lord Bryce concluded many decades ago, cooperation among states does not arise automatically.

Notes

1. Alan Rosenthal, *The Decline of Representative Democracy: Process, Participation, and Power in State Legislatures* (Washington, D.C.: CQ Press, 1998); and Rosenthal, *Governors and Legislatures: Contending Powers* (Washington, D.C.: CQ Press, 1990).
2. Robert S. Erikson, Gerald C. Wright, and John P. McIver, *Statehouse Democracy: Public Opinion and Policy in the American States* (New York: Cambridge University Press, 1993).
3. R. Steven Brown et al., *Resource Guide to State Environmental Management*, 3d ed. (Lexington, Ky.: Council of State Governments, 1993), 4–102.
4. DeWitt John, *Civic Environmentalism: Alternatives to Regulation in States and Communities* (Washington, D.C.: Congressional Quarterly, 1994), 80.
5. Deborah Hitchcock Jessup, *Guide to State Environmental Programs*, 3d ed. (Washington, D.C.: Bureau of National Affairs, 1994).
6. John, *Civic Environmentalism*.
7. Elinor Ostrom, *Governing the Commons: The Evolution of Institutions for Collective Action* (New York: Cambridge University Press, 1990); and Elinor Ostrom, Roy Gardner, and James Walker, *Rules, Games, and Common-Pool Resources* (Ann Arbor: University of Michigan Press, 1994). For a contrary view, see Edward P. Schwartz and Michael R. Tomz, "The Long-Run Advantages of Centralization for Collective Action," *American Political Science Review* 93, no. 3 (September 1997).
8. Sandford Borins, *Innovating with Integrity* (Washington, D.C.: Georgetown University Press, 1998); Mark Schneider and Paul Teske with Michael Mintrom, *Public Entrepreneurs: Agents for Change in American Government* (Princeton, N.J.: Princeton University Press, 1995); Dennis O'Grady and Keon S. Chi, "Innovators in State Government," in *The Book of the States, 1994–95* (Lexington, Ky.: Council of State Governments, 1994), 496–507; and Barry G. Rabe and Janet B. Zimmerman, "Beyond Environmental Regulatory Fragmentation: Signs of Integration in the Case of the Great Lakes Basin," *Governance* 8 (January 1995): 58–77.
9. David M. Hedge, *Governance and the Changing American States* (Boulder, Colo.: Westview, 1998), 35.

10. Thomas E. Cronin, *Direct Democracy: The Politics of Initiative, Referendum, and Recall* (Cambridge, Mass.: Harvard University Press, 1989).
11. Evan J. Ringquist, *Environmental Protection at the State Level: Politics and Progress in Controlling Pollution* (Armonk, N.Y.: M. E. Sharpe, 1993); and James P. Lester, "A New Federalism? Environmental Policy in the States," in *Environmental Policy in the 1990s*, ed. Norman J. Vig and Michael E. Kraft (Washington, D.C.: CQ Press, 1994), 51–68.
12. David H. Folz and Jean M. Peretz, "Evaluating State Hazardous Waste Reduction Policy," *State and Local Government Review* 29 (Fall 1997): 134–146.
13. Minnesota Office of Environmental Assistance, *1998 Pollution Prevention Evaluation Report* (St. Paul: Minnesota Office of Environmental Assistance, 1998).
14. Barry G. Rabe, *Fragmentation and Integration in State Environmental Management* (Washington, D.C.: Conservation Foundation, 1986).
15. Barry G. Rabe, "Integrated Environmental Permitting: Experience and Innovation at the State Level," *State and Local Government Review* 27 (Fall 1995): 209–220.
16. J. Andrew Hoerner, "Life and Taxes," *The Amicus Journal* (Summer 1995): 14–17.
17. William Fulton, "The Big Green Bazaar," *Governing* (June 1996): 38–42.
18. National Academy of Public Administration (NAPA), *The Environment Goes to Market: The Implementation of Economic Incentives for Pollution Control* (Washington, D.C.: NAPA, 1994), 138–159.
19. Betsy Fishbein, "Extended Product Responsibility for Consumers and Producers" (Paper prepared for President's Commission on Sustainable Development, January 30, 1995, 4).
20. Interview with Terence Hollins, Oregon Department of Environmental Quality (July 6, 1995).
21. Daniel Mazmanian and David Morell, *Beyond Superfailure: America's Toxics Policy for the 1990s* (Boulder, Colo.: Westview, 1992), 169–174; and "California's Prop 65: Lessons for the National Risk Debate?" *Risk Policy Report* (January 20, 1995): 24–25.
22. William R. Lowry, *The Dimensions of Federalism: State Governments and Pollution Control Policies* (Durham, N.C.: Duke University Press, 1992), 125.
23. Paul E. Peterson, *The Price of Federalism* (Washington, D.C.: Brookings, 1995), chap. 4.
24. Council of State Governments, *Resource Guide to State Environmental Management*, 5th ed. (Lexington, Ky.: Council of State Governments, 1999).
25. Tom W. Rice and Alexander F. Sumberg, "Civic Culture and Government Performance in the American States," *Publius: The Journal of Federalism* 27 (Winter 1997): 99–114.
26. U.S. General Accounting Office (GAO), "Water Pollution: Greater EPA Leadership Needed to Reduce Nonpoint Source Pollution" (Washington, D.C.: GAO, 1990); GAO, "Water Pollution: Stronger Efforts Needed by EPA to Control Toxic Water Pollution" (Washington, D.C.: GAO, 1991); GAO, "Water Pollution: Differences Among the States in Issuing Permits Limiting the Discharge of Pollutants" (Washington, D.C.: GAO, 1996); and Robert W. Adler, Jessica C. Landman, and Diane M. Cameron, *The Clean Water Act 20 Years Later* (Washington, D.C.: Island Press, 1993).
27. Christopher H. Foreman, Jr., *Plagues, Products & Politics: Emergent Public Health Hazards and National Policymaking* (Washington, D.C.: Brookings, 1994), 141–142.
28. Ringquist, *Environmental Protection at the State Level;* and Mazmanian and Morell, *Beyond Superfailure,* 107–110.
29. GAO, "EPA and the States: Environmental Challenges Require a Better Working Relationship" (Washington, D.C.: GAO, 1995); and "Expired Permits," *Detroit Free Press,* February 20, 1995, 6A.
30. John H. Cushman, Jr., "States Neglecting Pollution Rules, White House Says," *New York Times,* December 15, 1996, 1; and Cushman, "Virginia Seen as Undercutting U.S. Environmental Rules," *New York Times,* January 19, 1997, 11.
31. John H. Cushman, Jr., "E.P.A. and States Found to be Lax on Pollution Law," *New York Times,* June 7, 1998, 1.
32. J. Clarence Davies and Jan Mazurek, *Pollution Control in the United States: Evaluating the System* (Washington, D.C.: Resources for the Future, 1998), 41–42.

33. Barry G. Rabe, "Federalism and Entrepreneurship: Explaining American and Canadian Innovation in Pollution Prevention and Regulatory Integration," *Policy Studies Journal* 27 (Spring 1999); and Rabe, "The Politics of Sustainable Development: Impediments to Pollution Prevention and Policy Integration in Canada," *Canadian Public Administration* 40, no. 3 (Fall 1997): 415–435.

34. Laura L. Barnes, ed., *The Pollution Prevention Yellow Pages* (Washington, D.C.: National Pollution Prevention Roundtable, 1994); GAO, "Pollution Prevention: EPA Should Reexamine the Objectives and Sustainability of State Programs" (Washington, D.C.: GAO, 1994).

35. NAPA, *Setting Priorities, Getting Results: A New Direction for EPA* (Washington, D.C.: NAPA, 1995), 140–144; and Christopher J. Paterson and Richard N. L. Andrews, "Procedural and Substantive Fairness in Risk Decisions: Comparative Risk Assessment Procedures," *Policy Studies Journal* 23 (Spring 1995): 85–95.

36. Tom Horton and William M. Eichbaum, *Turning the Tide: Saving the Chesapeake Bay* (Washington, D.C.: Island Press, 1991); Barry G. Rabe, "Sustainability in a Regional Context: The Case of the Great Lakes Basin," in *Toward Sustainable Communities: Transition and Transformations in Environmental Policy,* ed. Daniel A. Mazmanian and Michael E. Kraft (Cambridge, Mass.: MIT Press, forthcoming 1999).

37. Adler, Landman, and Cameron, *The Clean Water Act 20 Years Later,* 221–224, 251.

38. Denise Scheberle, *Federalism and Environmental Policy: Trust and the Politics of Implementation* (Washington, D.C.: Georgetown University Press, 1997).

39. Davies and Mazurek, *Pollution Control in the United States,* 43.

40. John D. Donahue, *Disunited States: What's at Stake as Washington Fades and the States Take the Lead* (New York: Basic Books, 1997); Peterson, *The Price of Federalism;* Peter K. Eisinger, *The Rise of the Entrepreneurial State: States and Local Economic Development Policy in the United States* (Madison: University of Wisconsin Press, 1988); and Frank R. Baumgartner and Bryan D. Jones, *Agendas and Instability in American Politics* (Chicago: University of Chicago Press, 1993), chap 11.

41. Donahue, *Disunited States,* chap. 6.

42. Brown, "Emerging Models for Environmental Management," 539–540.

43. William T. Gormley, Jr., "Intergovernmental Conflict on Environmental Policy: The Attitudinal Connection," *Western Political Quarterly* 40 (1987): 298–299.

44. Lowry, *The Dimensions of Federalism,* 45.

45. Kay Jones and Joel Bucher, "Will Reducing Transported Ozone Improve Regulatory Compliance?" *EM* (July 1998): 11–16; Inger Weibust, "Green Giant: The Need for a Federal Environmental Leviathan" (Paper presented at the annual meeting of the American Political Science Association, 1998, Boston); and Diahanna Lynch, "The Ozone Transport Assessment Group: A New Effort at Regional Environmental Policymaking" (Unpublished paper, University of Michigan, April 29, 1998).

46. Mary R. English, *Siting Low-Level Radioactive Waste Disposal Facilities* (New York: Quorum, 1992); and Richard C. Kearney, "Low-Level Radioactive Waste Management: Environmental Policy, Federalism, and New York," *Publius: The Journal of Federalism* 23 (Summer 1993): 57–73.

47. Barry G. Rabe, *Beyond NIMBY: Hazardous Waste Siting in Canada and the United States* (Washington, D.C.: Brookings, 1994).

48. David H. Feldman, Jean H. Peretz, and Barbara D. Jendrucko, "Policy Gridlock in Waste Management: Balancing Federal and State Concerns," *Policy Studies Journal* 22 (Winter 1994): 589–603.

49. Rosemary O'Leary, "Trash Talk: The Supreme Court and the Interstate Transportation of Waste," *Public Administration Review* 57 (July–August 1997): 281–284.

50. Gregory S. Lashutka, "Risk Policy—A Mayor's Perspective," *Risk Policy Report* (January 20, 1995): 20–21.

51. Paul L. Posner, "Unfunded Mandates Reform Act: 1996 and Beyond," *Publius: The Journal of Federalism* 27 (Spring 1997): 53–71; and Timothy J. Conlan, James D. Riggle, and Donna E. Schwartz, "Deregulating Federalism? The Politics of Mandate Reform in the 104th Congress," *Publius: The Journal of Federalism* 25 (Summer 1995): 23–39.

52. Keith Schneider, "Many States Are Limiting the Power to Pass the Bucks," *New York Times*, February 5, 1995.

53. Davies and Mazurek, *Pollution Control in the United States*, 41–42.

54. James P. Lester, "New Federalism and Environmental Policy," *Publius: The Journal of Federalism* 16 (Winter 1986): 149–165; and Charles E. Davis and James P. Lester, "Decentralizing Federal Environmental Policy," *Western Political Quarterly* 40, no. 2 (1987): 555–565.

55. John E. Brandl, *Money and Good Intentions Are Not Enough Or Why a Liberal Democrat Thinks States Need Both Competition and Community* (Washington, D.C.: Brookings, 1998), chap. 2. Also see Steven D. Gold, ed., *The Fiscal Crisis of the States: Lessons for the Future* (Washington, D.C.: Georgetown University Press, 1995).

56. Kirk Emerson and Charles R. Wise, "Statutory Approaches to Regulatory Takings: State Property Rights Legislation Issues and Implications for Public Administration," *Public Administration Review* 57, no. 5 (September–October 1997): 411–422.

57. Rosenthal, *The Decline of Representative Democracy*, 72–74.

58. Alice M. Rivlin, *Reviving the American Dream: The Economy, the States, and the Federal Government* (Washington, D.C.: Brookings, 1992); Peterson, *The Price of Federalism*; Donahue, *Disunited States*, chap. 4; and Henry N. Butler and Jonathon R. Macey, *Using Federalism to Improve Environmental Policy* (Washington, D.C.: American Enterprise Institute, 1996).

59. Donahue, *Disunited States*, 65.

60. NAPA, *Setting Priorities, Getting Results*, 71.

3

Environmental Groups and
the New Political Landscape

Christopher J. Bosso

From Earth Day 1970 to January 1995, when Republicans gained control of Congress for the first time in forty years, American environmental groups worked within a surprisingly predictable political landscape: Democrats ran Congress, controlled most state legislatures, and held most of the nation's governorships; Republicans typically occupied the White House. Environmental groups adapted their strategies and tactics to these contours, particularly to a Congress where the Democrats' almost unbroken control gave them policy influence regardless of the occupant of the White House. This legislative landscape, combined with a muscular array of federal environmental statutes and regulatory mechanisms, also assured a Washington-focused environmental community. The action was in the nation's capital.

The new political landscape is very different. In it the presidency probably will rotate between moderate-to-conservative candidates of either party, ensuring an environmental agenda rooted in largely consensual goals and constrained by budgetary politics. Republicans, having broken the Democratic monopoly in the South, are likely to control at least one chamber of Congress. As such, environmental groups can no longer assume access to key committees and staffs. Beyond Washington, Republicans now control over thirty governorships and almost half of all state legislative bodies, a matter of note since conservative Republicans initiated most of the state laws and referenda opposed by environmentalists in the 1990s.

These macrolevel political changes are forcing environmental organizations of all types to examine their goals, strategies, and tactics. This is partly a variation on an old theme, since environmentalists have constantly adapted to broad shifts in the political terrain.[1] However, the current political landscape poses unprecedented challenges that may fundamentally reorder the character and shape of environmental advocacy in the United States. A decade from now much of what we consider familiar about the environmental "movement" may look very different.

In this chapter I will view American environmental advocacy from three points of reference. First, I will look at the effects of public opinion on environmental agendas; next, I will examine the struggles at the grassroots between environmental advocates and their foes; finally, I will highlight the challenges faced by the nation's environmental groups in trying to adapt to current realities.

Public Opinion and Policy

The environmental record of the 105th Congress is discussed by Michael Kraft in chapter 6, but it is a good place to begin any discussion of public opinion and its effects on public policy. If nothing else, it reveals how Republicans learned from their experiences in the 104th Congress (1995–96), where they mounted a direct assault on federal environmental laws.[2] By contrast, in the 105th Congress (1997–98) the actions of conservative Republicans were indirect, focused on riders contained in congressional spending bills. To environmentalists these tactics were more dangerous because they were largely hidden from public scrutiny, leading major environmental groups to warn of a Republican "stealth attack" on federal environmental policies.[3]

Eluding the Salience Trap

A July 1998 *Washington Post*–ABC News Poll asked respondents to list the most important issues facing the nation as it neared the midterm elections. Education was first, followed by Social Security, tax reform, crime, and health care. Environmental issues were nowhere among these priorities.[4] Similarly, an April 1998 Gallup Poll asked respondents to cite the most important issues facing the country; only 2 percent listed the environment.[5]

A political novice studying these data might conclude that Americans had little concern about the environment. But that novice would be mistaken, as were Republicans in 1995 who equated similar opinion data with weak public support for environmental protection. In polling parlance, they fell into a "salience trap," a common error in that "most important issue" polls are headline-sensitive. As such, Robert Mitchell argues, they are "an untrustworthy guide to how the public will respond to policy changes in apparently non-salient issues."[6] In short, low issue salience should not be interpreted as weak concern, especially when actions by policymakers themselves can reawaken issue salience.

Connecting public opinion to policy outcomes is easier under conditions of high issue salience.[7] Disasters such as the core meltdown at the Chernobyl nuclear power plant undoubtedly prompted George Bush to promise to be "the environmental president" and in 1990 helped to break a decade-long impasse on revising the Clean Air Act. But issue salience ebbed in the 1990s in the absence of agenda-setting disasters, the primacy of other issues (for example, the Persian Gulf War), perceptions of a proenvironment Clinton administration, and, for many, the success of environmentalism when embodied in the revival of endangered species such as the bald eagle. So it was within a low-salience environmental issue context that Republicans regained control over Congress in 1995.

What is more, the Republican agenda reflected widespread but diffuse public demands for leaner and less intrusive government, attitudes that party leaders interpreted as supporting major revisions in federal environmental policies. Indeed, Americans in 1995 seemed to show little interest in environmental issues. Only 1 percent of respondents in a January 1995 Gallup Poll mentioned the environment as the "most important problem" facing the nation, down dramatically from 11 percent in 1992.[8] More persuasive to Republicans, 29 percent of Americans in a May 1995 Times-Mirror study felt that environmental laws had struck "about the right balance," up from 17 percent in 1992, while those believing that the laws had gone "too far" increased from 10 percent to 22 percent. By contrast, those who thought the laws "have not gone far enough" decreased from 63 percent to 43 percent.[9] With such data one might conclude that for most Americans, as Karlyn Bowman and Everett Carll Ladd noted, "the urgency has been removed, and the battle to protect the environment is being waged satisfactorily."[10] The new majority thought it had voters' permission to extend its deregulatory agenda to the environment.

They were wrong. Republicans found that Americans still worried about environmental progress even if their preferences were not clearly expressed. For one thing, if respondents in the Times-Mirror study evinced little urgency about environmental issues, 72 percent still did *not* feel that environmental laws and regulations had gone "too far." The Gallup Poll at the time found that 83 percent believed the nation needed to take "some additional" actions to address environmental problems.[11] Voters may have expressed theoretical support for less government and a streamlining of bureaucratic rules, but they also wanted a strong federal role in protecting the environment.

That same picture emerged in 1998. Despite its apparently low standing in open-ended "most important issue" polls, environmental protection still enjoyed strong support when respondents were asked directly about it. A January 1998 Pew Charitable Trust poll asked respondents to indicate the level of priority the nation should give to protecting the environment. Given a forced-choice option, 53 percent said it should be a top priority, while another 37 percent said it should be a lower but still important priority. More telling, when these respondents were asked to pick among alternative uses for a federal budget surplus, the single greatest option (33 percent) was "for increased spending on domestic programs such as health, education, and the environment." Only 11 percent wanted a tax cut.[12]

What do these data say? First, as Riley Dunlap argues, issue salience fluctuates but overall public concern endures "to the point that support for environmental protection can be regarded as a 'consensual' issue which generates little open opposition."[13] Second, there is an active core constituency for the environment, the roughly one-third of Americans who consider themselves "strong" environmentalists regardless of issue salience. Such self-identification is notably high among the young, the college-educated, liberals, and Democrats, all of whom are likely to be suspicious of major changes in environmental programs.[14] Finally, even those who don't consider themselves strong environmentalists are concerned about the health of future generations. For example, 53 percent of Americans in a March 1998 CBS poll believed that the environment will worsen in the next century; only 15 percent thought it will get better.[15] Given these data, politicians seen as hostile to the environment risk igniting latent concern and transforming it into active outrage.

However, broad support for the environment does not preclude initiatives promoted as preserving individual freedom or "traditional ways of life." Most Americans are "Lite Greens," that is, while they may recycle and buy "green goods" they are wary of making major life-style changes in the name of the environment. The boom in gas-guzzling sport utility vehicles is just one indication of Americans' reluctance to significantly alter their ways.[16] Strong general support for the environment does not keep local constituencies from siding with economic interests in defense of jobs, or from voting for candidates with weak environmental records. If, as Dunlap observes, relatively few candidates want to be painted as openly antienvironment, "there is as yet little evidence of a 'green bloc' of single-issue voters comparable to the anti-abortion or anti-gun control blocs."[17] The environment competes with other priorities. Absent major crises, public concern for environmental protection does not translate automatically into support for specific policies. It translates only into *opportunities* to transform attitudes into action.

The Republican "Stealth Campaign"

In an earlier version of this chapter, composed in 1996 after Republicans retreated from their efforts to reshape federal environmental policies, I predicted that party leaders would moderate the language and substance of the party's environmental agenda to keep from alienating voters in upcoming elections. Republican candidates also would make at least symbolic commitments to environmental progress, if for no other reason than that almost twice as many Americans trust Democrats over Republicans to do a better job in protecting the environment.[18]

These predictions proved accurate. The strategy pursued by Republicans in the 105th Congress relied mostly on low salience budget riders and quiet "holds" by conservative senators on judicial and administrative nominees whose environmental records were not to their liking.[19] The rhetoric of revolution also evaporated as Republican candidates avoided language that made them sound like defenders of big business, talked about "sensible" environmental policy, and muted their attacks on the U.S. Environmental Protection Agency (EPA). "Remember," Republican pollster Frank Luntz counseled his clients, "even Republicans have limited faith in your ability to keep their air clean and their water clean. You have a lot to prove."[20]

Even hard-core conservatives played a more subtle game. In June 1998 a group of Republicans formed the Coalition of Republican Environmental Advocates (CREA) to promote free-market approaches to environmental problems. Two-thirds of the Senate Republicans who signed up had earned a "zero" environmental support rating from the League of Conservation Voters during the 104th Congress,[21] and the group's steering committee included lobbyists for the petroleum, mining, and automobile industries.[22] Formation of CREA nettled members of Republicans for Environmental Protection, a group formed in 1995 by Republicans with stronger environmental records who regarded their intra-party competitor as neither grassroots nor proenvironment.[23]

The "stealth campaign" largely failed, and Republicans suffered surprising losses in the 1998 elections. But environmentalists were left knowing that their foes still controlled the congressional venues for policy formation and budget allocation, not to mention a majority of governorships. These realities are sobering given the fundamental truth that the American system tends to favor parochial economic interests such as those of loggers and ranchers over more diffuse national interests. These core traits of the policy-making system were palatable to environmentalists as long as they were certain of friendly voices and helping hands in positions of policy leverage. The new political landscape puts all assumptions into play.

Battling at the Grassroots

In October 1997 members of the "radical" environmental group Earth First! ransacked the district office of Rep. Frank Riggs, R-Calif., located in the heart of the northern California redwood country. The protesters, who targeted Riggs because of his support for logging in old-growth forests, then chained themselves to the door of his office. They remained there until police applied pepper spray directly into demonstrators' eyes and forcibly removed them.

Such instances of environmental "direct action," including arson at a controversial ski resort in Colorado, spurred conservatives to demand congressional hearings into what they called "ecoterrorism." They got their wish at a June 9, 1998, hearing of the House Judiciary Committee Subcommittee on Crime. The only subcommittee member present was Rep. Riggs, fresh from losing a Senate primary election contest. In attendance was a regular "Who's Who" of conservative activists led by Ron Arnold, director of industry-backed Center for the Defense of Free Enterprise and longtime scourge of environmental groups, who demanded that "resource care takers" such as logging companies be able to pursue federal felony charges against protesters. Riggs even wanted to extend federal antiracketeering statutes to groups like Earth First!, but his suggestion went nowhere.[24]

The Conservative Backlash

Conservative antipathy to environmentalism may be refracted in Congress, particularly among western Republicans, but its depth and range are manifest among the often well-organized and well-funded groups allied loosely under "property rights" and "Wise Use" banners. In 1994 these groups mobilized the voters who decided a number of tight congressional races that contributed to the Republican takeover, while generous campaign contributions from industries such as timber and mining aided sympathetic, mostly

Republican candidates. If Republicans after 1995 adopted a lower profile on environmental issues, these groups have not, and their influence with Republican conservatives remains important.

"Property rights" groups agitate for compensating property owners whenever government regulations adversely affect a property's "fair market" value, such as when a wetlands designation precludes commercial development. Some groups, such as the Chicago-based Environmental Conservation Organization, are essentially staff operations representing major real estate or development interests, but others (for example, the Maryland-based Fairness to Land Owners Coalition) are comprised of small property holders genuinely worried about governmental restrictions on the use of their land.

The same distinctions hold true for the possibly hundreds of "Wise Use" groups, clustered largely in the West, that promote local (and presumably more development-friendly) control over the vast federal lands in the region. Some, such as the off-road vehicle industry-financed Sahara Club, are little more than industry fronts. Even so, their resources enable them to wield clout in the battle for the hearts and minds of average Americans. For example, in August 1998 the off-road industry, led by its Web-zine *Off-Road.com*, launched an e-mail campaign against the Internet search engine company Lycos over its contract with EnviroLink, an Internet service provider for environmental and other progressive groups. EnviroLink (*www.envirolink. org*) was accused of being a "radical environmental web haven" because among its hundreds of sites were "direct action" groups like Earth First! and the Animal Liberation Front. Lycos eventually caved in to demands that it cancel its contract with EnviroLink, saying that it did not want to work with organizations that might "mislead" users seeking environmental information. *Off-Road.com* itself is easily found through Lycos even though its columnists rail against "enviro-Nazis" and "eco-terrorists."[25] EnviroLink suffered "a major budget shortfall" as a result of the Lycos action.[26]

Other Wise Use groups reflect the latest iteration of the real grassroots conservative populism that has long flourished in the West.[27] These groups share a staunch faith in use of federal lands for grazing, mining, logging, and recreation, and a hostility to what they see as misanthropic attempts by suburbanites to end traditional rural ways of life. Such self-labeled Wise Users consider themselves *real* conservationists, lovers of the outdoors who hunt and fish and who oppose locking up public lands from resource use. In some ways their complaints about environmentalism echo the traditional if oversimplified tensions between Gifford Pinchot's emphasis on the "managed use" of natural resources and the arguably more absolutist dictates of John Muir's preservationism.[28]

Wise Users come in several flavors. The "moderates" are property owners near national parks or residents of towns dependent on industries such as logging, who worry that both the federal government and environmentalists are insensitive to their basic economic needs. The more zealous Wise Users, especially in the Rocky Mountain states, reflect conservative populism's strident defense of private property, its suspicion of the federal government, and its occasional xenophobia. Many are veterans of the 1970s Sagebrush Rebellion that spawned Reagan administration officials such as Interior Secretary James Watt. Others have links to the Young Americans for Freedom, the National Rifle Association, and other conservative groups that oppose most restrictions on the use of private property. These activists seek to open all federal lands to resource development and campaign against the Endangered Species Act because they believe it unconstitutionally restricts what citizens can do with their property.

At the farthest fringes are the John Birch Society, the Reverend Sung Yung Moon's Unification Church, followers of Lyndon LaRouche, and others on the reactionary right who see environmentalism as a threat to core American values and ways of life. Some Wise Users are reputed to support, or are themselves members of, antifederal "militias" that gained much national attention in the mid 1990s.[29] These activists believe, for example, that environmental laws are part of a conspiracy to restrict property rights that will eventually enable the United Nations to take over the country. These groups adopted lower profiles after self-styled militia members bombed the Murrah Federal Building in Oklahoma City in April 1995, killing 168 people. Other groups promoted a "county supremacy" movement in which they and county officials in some western states argued that the Tenth Amendment properly gives control over federal lands to local governments. Those claims sparked occasional confrontations with federal authorities but did not seem to gain broad public support.

The overall dimensions of this conservative cohort are hard to gauge. Its proponents claim tens of thousands of members at the grassroots, with the mining-industry backed People for the West! (PFW) alone claiming 23,000 members.[30] Its critics counter that it is no more than a few hundred hardcore activists backed by an interlocking phalanx of professional organizers and conservative foundations and promoted by allies in industry, libertarian think tanks, and conservative media personalities. However, there is no argument that this coalition is organized, has considerable financial support, and has helped to shape the debate on environmental policies in the 1990s. They have had successes especially in western state legislatures, in federal courts populated by Reagan and Bush appointees, and in federal bureaucracies traditionally sympathetic to producer interests, such as the Bureau of Land Management. Six years of the Clinton/Gore administration have not entirely changed these realities.

In Congress these groups enjoy considerable support among conservative western Republicans. In the 105th Congress, for example, five western Republicans on the House Committee on Resources were PFW members; another hired a former PFW official as his senior staff aide.[31] Such members have blocked environmental legislation and have made life miserable for federal officials such as Secretary of the Interior Bruce Babbitt. Wise Use ties to congressional Republicans also give them clout in setting the legislative agenda, crafting statutory language, and shaping the federal budget—riders and all. None of this would surprise any student of Capitol Hill, but it has disconcerted environmentalists accustomed to a more receptive Democratic Congress.

Overall, David Helvarg concludes, these groups comprise "a new and militant force on the political Right that has the power to impede and occasionally sidetrack attempts at environmental protection," but they have yet to generate broad public support.[32] This is an accurate assessment. For example, in the 1990s property rights advocates won passage of various kinds of "takings" bills in the cozy confines of state legislatures, where development interests wield influence, but could not get voters to approve "takings" ballot initiatives even in western states where Wise Use groups proliferate. In most cases the initiatives were defeated by strong grassroots opposition uniting environmentalists and more traditional conservationists, including those who hunt and fish.[33]

In addition, the Wise Use rebellion has not always panned out exactly as expected. In California, where Earth Firsters ransacked the office of former representative Riggs, and where one protester was killed by a falling tree in 1998 during a demonstration against logging, local residents, property owners, and even loggers have begun to express misgivings about timber company clear-cutting practices. Residents harmed by mudslides from slopes cleared of trees have filed lawsuits against one timber company; two even copied Earth First! tactics by occupying trees to protest against the practice. "Loggers want their kids to continue on in the woods," said one local official, "but they're starting to see the environmental impacts of clear-cutting. They don't like the Earth Firsters and never will, but they're worried about their jobs. If all the trees are cut, they'll be out of work just as easily as if the environmentalists shut down logging."[34]

This change of heart notwithstanding, the Wise Use–conservative alliance remains a potent one. It wields leverage in Congress and acts as a rallying point for those alienated from major institutions, a category into which major environmental groups get lumped.[35] Regardless of short-term defeats, Republican control of Congress, any number of governorships, and more than a few state legislatures give the Wise Use–conservative alliance valuable points of access and leverage.

Extending the Environmental Grassroots

In October 1998, Defenders of Wildlife announced a State Biodiversity Project designed to "create a nationwide grassroots network of conservation and wildlife advocates with the goal of strengthening state wildlife and wildlands legislation." The project is based in the organization's Grassroots Environmental Effectiveness Network, long used to mobilize members on national policy issues, and is designed to keep members up to date on state-level environmental efforts and political activities, train local activists, and provide technical support.[36]

This is but one aspect of an expanding campaign by national environmental groups to counter the Wise Use agenda at the grassroots level. Political reality has forced groups long reliant on Washington lobbying and passive, dues-paying memberships to focus more energy and resources on mobilizing grassroots constituencies. Such efforts, as noted above, enabled these groups to defeat virtually every "takings" measure put on the ballot in the 1990s. Beyond referenda, national environmental groups find themselves spending more time and resources working with state and local groups to build stronger grassroots connections to members of Congress and state legislators. There is also intense pressure within the major national groups to reverse years of organizational centralization and devolve more authority and resources to local chapters, which for many groups revives a style of organizational governance that predated the contemporary, Washington-centered environmental era.[37]

The renewed emphasis on grassroots organizing and focus on local issues has had a notable impact. For example, as table 3-1 shows, organizations with strong local chapters have had more stable memberships in recent years than those with a more global focus or centralized structure. In particular, the National Audubon Society and National Wildlife Federation have fared better than organizations such as Greenpeace, with its global orientation and emphasis on "direct action," or Friends of the Earth, which is better known outside the United States. When asked about it, one National Wildlife Federation official said that members "want the organization to help them solve the problems facing their own communities, not demonstrate against plants a thousand miles away."[38]

Accompanying this shift of emphasis is a debate over what an environmental grassroots should look like. On one hand, the "deep greens" found in groups like Earth First! are too radical for most Americans, a cultural gap conservatives are happy to exploit in recruiting alienated working-class voters. On the other hand, the major national groups are fueled by the membership dues of middle-class suburbanites, for whom an activist environmentalism is tempered by a libertarian streak on most other social and economic issues. Any green grassroots worth discussing by necessity will have to include constituencies not traditionally regarded as part of either kind of environmentalism, whether the loggers in northern California or the less affluent, often minority residents who live closest to industrial sites or waste dumps. The former are worried about their jobs and communities, the latter about human health issues.[39] Greater sensitivity to local economic issues may put off some middle-class members, while a strong focus on human health may alienate the more biocentric "deep ecology" activists, but this type of outreach is imperative if environmentalists are to expand their base.

Other outreach efforts mesh conservation's emphasis on managed resources with environmentalism's focus on ecosystems and biological diversity. One unusual example involves the Wilderness Society and the National Rifle Association (NRA), which worked together to increase congressional funding for National Wildlife Refuges. In this case the wildlife preservation interests of environmentalists merged with those of NRA members, who would be able to hunt on half of the refuges. Some environmentalists also have be-

Table 3-1 Membership Trends Among Selected National Groups, 1970–1998

Group	Year Founded	1970	1980	1990	1995	1998
Sierra Club	1892	113,000	181,000	630,000	570,000	555,000
National Audubon Society	1905	148,000	400,000	600,000	570,000	575,000
National Parks and Conservation Assoc.	1919	45,000	31,000	100,000	450,000	500,000
Izaak Walton League	1922	54,000	52,000	50,000	54,000	50,000
Wilderness Society	1935	54,000	45,000	350,000	310,000	350,000
National Wildlife Federation[a]	1936	540,000	818,000	997,000	1.8 million	4.0 million
Defenders of Wildlife	1947	13,000	50,000	80,000	122,000	243,000
Nature Conservancy	1951	22,000	NA	600,000	806,000	901,000
World Wildlife Fund	1961	NA	NA	400,000	800,000	1.2 million
Environmental Defense Fund	1967	11,000	46,000	200,000	300,000	300,000
Friends of the Earth[b]	1969	6,000	NA	9,000	35,000	12,000
Environmental Action	1970	10,000	20,000	23,000	10,000	Defunct
League of Conservation Voters	1970	NA	35,000	55,000	NA	NA
Natural Resources Defense Council	1970	NA	40,000	150,000	185,000	400,000
Greenpeace USA	1971	NA	NA	2.35 million	1.6 million	350,000

Sources: Annual reports; personal calls; *Public Interest Profiles, 1992–1993,* (Washington, D.C.: CQ Press, 1993); *Encyclopedia of Associations* (Detroit: Gale Research, various years); *Outside,* v. 19, n. 3 (March 1994), 65–73; *Buzzworm: The Environmental Journal,* v. 2, n. 3 (May/June 1990), 65–77; *National Journal,* July 28, 1990, 1828; *Congressional Quarterly Weekly Report,* v. 48, n. 3 (January 20, 1990), 144; Congressional Research Service, *Selected Environmental and Related Interest Groups,* CRS Report 91-295 ENR (March 22, 1991), *passim; National Journal,* January 4, 1992, 30; *Chronicle of Philanthropy,* v. 4, n. 11 (March 24, 1992), 31.

Note: Figures are rounded and often approximations based on conflicting data, definitions, or reporting dates. NA = not available.

[a] Figures through 1995 are for full members only and do not count affiliated memberships (e.g., schoolchildren) of around 4.4 million in 1995. For 1998, figure is aggregate, as the NWF no longer releases data on full versus affiliated memberships.

[b] Merged in 1990 with the 30,000-member Oceanic Society and the nonmember Environmental Policy Institute.

gun to work with "life-style conservatives" whose suspicion of government is matched only by their fear of corporate capitalism and its corrosive impact on their health and hometowns. These views are in step with environmentalism's core faith in decentralized decisionmaking and small institutions.[40] Potentially far-reaching efforts now link major environmental groups with conservative interests ranging from budget cutters seeking to eliminate subsidies for mining companies to evangelical Christians in favor of renewing the Endangered Species Act because they believe, as the director of the Evangelical Environmental Network put it, "that every creature—every slug, every salamander—is a gift from the hand of the Creator."[41]

Not all environmentalists are comfortable with these alliances, and the cultural differences between the camps still matter. The typical environment group member is white collar, younger, suburban, and more liberal, while the typical NRA member or logger is blue collar, older, rural, and more conservative. Divisive issues such as abortion, immigration, and economic growth will continue to divide them, but emerging commonalities of interest on such issues as endangered species and ecosystem preservation raise tantalizing possibilities for a new breed of American environmental populism.

The Challenge Ahead:
Green Electoral Politics and the Environmental Lobby

If environmentalists learned nothing else in 1994, they learned that elections matter. Before 1994, too many of them believed that it really didn't matter who was elected to Congress, the presidency, or any other office. After all, "they" were all alike, and there wasn't a dime's worth of difference between the two major parties. This attitude about politics and politicians, while typical among issue purists, is less entrenched today than in years past.

Green Electoral Politics

The 1998 elections produced two relevant story lines for environmentalists. The first was their apparent success in helping to defeat candidates deemed hostile to environmental goals. Indeed, environmentalists took credit for helping Democrats pick up a net gain of House seats, something no party in the White House had achieved in over sixty years. Republicans still controlled Congress, but the outcome in 1998 was a contrast to only four years earlier when Wise Use groups claimed credit for helping to elect the new GOP majority.

Two environmental groups were especially active during the elections. The League of Conservation Voters (LCV) claimed credit for defeating nine conservative Republicans from its "Dirty Dozen" list of antienvironmental candidates. Its political action committee, the LCV Action Fund, spent $2.3 million in television ads, direct mail and telephone campaigns, leaflets, and media releases about the Dirty Dozen, and spent another $350,000 to support proenvironment candidates locked in tight campaigns.[42] For its part, the

Sierra Club's political action committee contributed $500,000 in direct and in-kind contributions to proenvironmental candidates and conducted a get-out-the-vote effort to mobilize its members. In-kind contributions included television and radio ads in forty markets describing the records of twenty-five incumbents, volunteers and staff loaned to Senate and House races, as well as "nonpartisan" voter guides detailing candidates' stands on environmental issues. The Sierra Club claimed that its efforts "contributed to the victories of pro-environment candidates in 38 out of 43 (88 percent) priority races."[43] How much the LCV and Sierra Club contributed to the electoral outcome in 1998 is hard to know, but they certainly helped.

The second story concerns the impact of self-labeled Green Party candidates on House races. Few garnered more than a few percentage points in votes, but in three cases those votes affected outcomes. In California's Thirty-sixth District, Republican Steve Kuykendall beat Democrat Janice Hahn by two percentage points, equal to the vote percentage of Green Party candidate Robin Barrett. In New Mexico's First District, incumbent Republican Heather Wilson defeated Democrat Phillip J. Maloof by six points, while Green Party candidate Robert Anderson picked up ten percent of the vote—repeating the outcome of a June special election. In a 1997 special election to fill a vacant seat in New Mexico's Third District, Republican Bill Redmond—who had strong ties to Wise Use groups—beat Democrat Eric Serna, largely because Green Party candidate Carol Miller took 17 percent of the vote. In 1998 Redmond lost his bid for reelection against Democrat Tom Udall, son of the former secretary of the interior, by a 52 to 43 percent margin. This time Miller received only 5 percent of the vote, abandoned even by fellow Greens who decided to back a Democrat with a good record rather than risk reelecting Redmond.[44]

Such results prompt the question: Are environmentalists better off running Green Party candidates or, alternatively, becoming a major force within the two party system? On its face, a vibrant Green Party challenges two party orthodoxy and forces the major parties to respond to new ideas. Certainly, the recent experience of German Greens highlights the potential for their American cousins. Green candidates in the former West Germany, Anna Bramwell argues, fell on hard times in the early 1990s as "established political parties, together with international agencies, took on board those environmental programmes and criticisms that could be incorporated into established, institutionalized forms of political life."[45] Mainstream parties co-opted the most popular Green ideas, often leaving the more purist Greens to promote less politically palatable "fringe" goals.

German Greens learned these lessons, and made a stunning comeback in 1998 when they became a key minority partner in the new Social Democrat government that replaced the sixteen-year hold of the Christian Democrat government of Chancellor Helmut Kohl. They did so by emphasizing a pragmatic agenda of economic and health issues, coupled with a determination to play a role in coalition politics. In return, the Greens were given key cabinet appointments, as well as pledges to close Germany's nuclear power plants and raise energy taxes to foster greater conservation.[46] The message: Greens win only when they form strategic alliances with a major party in systems that allow coalition governments.

But American Greens looking to Europe for lessons forget that the winner-take-all nature of the U.S. electoral system and the resulting two party system do not offer the kinds of postelection coalitional opportunities found in parliamentary systems. Indeed, it is a system of governance that fractures parties even as it creates incentives to form interest groups.[47] Thus, American Greens are unlikely to win seats in Congress unless they are able to displace one of the major parties. While individual Greens might win local elections, at the state and national levels they are more likely to siphon away Democratic votes and thus actually help Republicans win, as happened in New Mexico. Such leverage might compel Democrats to adopt stronger green platforms to forestall similar outcomes elsewhere. Most important, the Green Party can influence issue debate and encourage people to use environmental concerns as voting cues. It may be unable to forge the coalitions necessary to win statewide or national office, but it can help to define the ideas that become part of the nation's public discourse.

Today the major environmental groups act as the nation's quasi-green parties, playing the kind of policy roles typical of green parties in parliamentary systems.[48] Mainstream environmentalists, for their part, are left with two practical approaches to fighting their foes in the electoral arena. One is to work more openly within the Democratic Party, which of the two major parties today offers more ecologically sensitive candidates and party platforms. The nature of pre-election coalitional politics in the American system guarantees that environmental values will be balanced against other, sometimes more immediate, social and economic concerns; but at least the Democratic coalition is responsive to environmental values. The Wise Use forces within the Republican Party and the libertarian strain of conservatism that currently dominates its policy agenda give environmentalists who want to play party politics little real choice.

Being a part of the Democratic Party coalition can force environmentalists to pull their punches for the sake of party unity. Environmental groups were criticized sharply for doing exactly this in Bill Clinton's first term during the bitter fight over the North American Free Trade Agreement. On the other hand, Clinton veered left on environmental issues during the 1996 campaign to bring green voters back into the fold, and the Democratic Party made sure that green goals were stressed in the 1998 elections. Clinton's support for the 1997 Kyoto Protocol was also good green politics, especially given congressional Republican opposition to the treaty.

Still, working openly as Democrats involves political risks that many mainstream groups are unwilling to take given that Republicans still control Congress and might possibly regain the White House in 2000. As Earth First!'s David Foreman, a former Goldwater Republican, argues, "when conservation groups engage in electoral politics, they should be single-issue proponents" not tied to any one party.[49] Most major environmental groups adhere to this view and are trying to rouse constituent pressure on suspect candidates of both parties. For example, conservative House Democrat Charlie Stenholm of Texas made it onto the LCV's 1998 "Dirty Dozen" because he "has the worst lifetime environmental record of any non-freshman Democrat in Congress."[50] Stenholm squeaked by, but the message to Democrats was not to take environmentalists for granted.

Environmentalists cannot match the campaign donations of their corporate foes, but like labor unions, the Christian Coalition, or the National Rifle Association they have sophisticated national operations and faithful grassroots activists that can keep the heat on legislators and, when the time comes, get out the vote. A number of losing candidates found that out in the two most recent elections. If candidates were as sensitive to a politically potent green grassroots as they were to senior citizens on Social Security, it may matter less to environmentalists which party is in control.

Remaking the Environmental Lobby

If a Republican Congress gives environmentalists insomnia, it is also an asset for environmental groups seeking to reverse the stagnant memberships and soft revenues of the early 1990s.[51] Indeed, Republicans such as former Speaker Newt Gingrich of Georgia, House Majority Whip and former pest exterminator Tom DeLay of Texas, and Senators Ted Stevens and Frank Murkowski of Alaska have been convenient foils against which environmentalists could rally the faithful and build their resources (see tables 3-1 and 3-2).

Beneath the improving membership and revenue figures, however, lie serious tensions over organizational goals and tactics. The Republican takeover sparked rebellion within the ranks of the major groups, typified by an extraordinarily public dispute over the future direction of the Sierra Club and by forced resignations of longtime leaders at the National Wildlife Federation and the National Audubon Society.[52] More recently, leadership changes have occurred at the Wilderness Society, the League of Conservation Voters, and, again, at the Sierra Club. At these last two the new leaders are self-identified Republicans, suggesting that some environmental groups are looking for leaders with potentially greater access to the congressional majority.

As always, the major groups struggle to balance the practical need to be active "players" in Washington with the idealism essential to motivating committed members. The "corporate environmentalism" tag hung on these professionalized organizations hits close to home insofar as they rely heavily on direct mail and other tools to maintain the huge memberships and big budgets needed to play the conventional lobbying game. Yet organizational "success" creates pressures to weigh the budgetary effects of issue positions and tactics and, to some degree, to stay "respectable" so that their middle-class supporters feel that their dues are wisely spent. Size by itself also creates pressures toward "efficiency" and "rational" decisionmaking, organizational virtues that conflict with powerful core values of decentralization and democratic governance.[53]

Table 3-2   Operating Budgets Among Selected National Groups, 1980–1998

Group	1980	1985	1990	1995	1998
Sierra Club	9.5	22.0	40.0	35.0	47.0
National Audubon Society	10.0	24.0	36.0	46.0	47.4
National Parks and Conservation Assoc.	NA	1.7	6.0	13.0	14.0
Wilderness Society	1.5	6.5	17.7	14.5	15.0
National Wildlife Federation	34.5	46.0	89.5	97.2	100.0
Defenders of Wildlife	NA	3.0	4.3	6.6	10.4
Nature Conservancy	NA	NA	111.3	141.7	187.0
Environmental Defense Fund	1.9	3.3	15.8	24.6	23.4
Friends of the Earth	1.0	1.0	3.4	3.4	NA
Environmental Action	.5	.6	1.1	1.0	Defunct
League of Conservation Voters	.5	1.6	1.4	2.0	NA
Natural Resources Defense Council	3.5	7.0	16.0	17.5	27.0
Greenpeace USA	NA	24.0	40.0	26.0	21.0

Sources: See Table 3-1.

Note: In millions of dollars. Figures are rounded and often are approximations based on disparate data, reporting dates, and fiscal years. Totals do not include nonrecurring capital expenditures, such as for land, (see esp. the Nature Conservancy).

These tensions are old news to such groups as the Audubon Society or the Sierra Club, yet in some respects the struggles seem more pronounced. Leaders selected in the early 1980s to build powerful national environmental lobbies in response to the Reagan juggernaut were now attacked for alienating their most faithful grassroots activists. While those leaders were replaced, the tensions remained. These groups face an ongoing struggle over the extent to which they should put resources into their Washington operations even as their members demand greater attention to local concerns and strategies. The major groups cannot abandon Washington to their opponents, yet the disappointing track record of the "green lobby" in the 1990s underscores the limitations inherent in an "inside" strategy.[54]

The green lobby is strong enough to repulse legislative efforts it opposes, but has had little success in building support for its own reforms or policy ideas.[55] This sense of futility is all the more telling because the environmental lobby is well-established, respected, and sophisticated. From extensive use of free and paid media, telephone banks, and direct mail to "fax trees" and Web sites, environmentalists have copied and even perfected techniques used by every advocacy group, including their Wise Use foes. However, as critic Mark Dowie argues, their cultivated image of insider clout belies the sobering reality that environmentalists are constantly outgunned by resource-rich industry lobbyists and by the millions in campaign contributions that flow into Congress from corporate political action committees.[56] The green lobby may be necessary, but it is expensive.

Progressive public interest groups that challenge corporate power and question dominant social and economic values always face a struggle in becoming "respected" members of the mainstream lobbying community. Making some commitment to work within the political system forces them to become, as Kirkpatrick Sale says, a "reformist citizens' lobby, pressured on the fringes by more radical groups but for the most part willing to work within the system and reap the victories, and rewards, therein."[57] By doing so these groups succumb to what Robert Mitchell and his colleagues portray as the "inherently conservatizing pressure to play by the 'rules of the game' in the compromise world of Washington, D.C."[58]

For many environmental groups growing accustomed to, even comfortable with, the world of Washington was a natural result of decades of attention to and reliance on federal policy, especially given the tremendous variability of state government capacities and intentions. It also was part of a natural tendency for successful movements to spin off lobby groups, law firms, think tanks, and other institutions that together help to give a movement's ideas respectability in the halls of power. But, Dowie argues, there are pitfalls to this kind of institution-building.[59] First, their focus on the federal government exposed environmentalists to the full force of the post–cold war collapse in public faith in the federal establishment. To many citizens "environmentalism" was synonymous with "big government"—remote, professionalized, and arcane. Second, the focus on Washington to some degree came at the expense of grassroots organizing, which critics accused the major groups of ignoring as they poured attention and resources into their national lobbies. Worse, national environmental leaders often seemed to pursue agendas contrary to the needs of poor and minority residents, a perception that sparked the emerging "environmental justice" movement (see chap. 11). Finally, environmentalists convinced of the goodness and popularity of their cause seemed to discount the Wise Use backlash at the local level, leaving many who might otherwise be natural allies—especially working-class voters—to fall in with their foes.

Similar struggles over organizational focus and tactics have emerged within virtually every other progressive movement (for example, women's rights) of the past three decades. The major environmental groups in fact are playing roles that one expects of mature organizations within a political context that forces groups to grow and professionalize or die. They are the key players in what has become, to use a term coined by Grant Jordan and William Maloney, the American environmental "protest business."[60] As such they can be like the Sierra Club and juggle idealism with a need to be a major player in the policy game, or they can be like Environmental Action, the perpetually underfunded organizer of the first Earth Day that refused to abandon its ideals and nonhierarchical mode of organizational management.

The Sierra Club thrives despite endless internal disputes over its mission and organizational management; Environmental Action folded in 1996.[61]

The story of Greenpeace underscores these dilemmas. Greenpeace was the most visible of all environmental groups in the early 1990s, its swashbuckling activists pursuing highly publicized nonviolent protests against polluting corporations and nations. Greenpeace was bold, pure, action-oriented. Its membership rolls and revenues exploded, enabling it to establish regional offices and subsidize the global activities of its parent organization, Greenpeace International. By 1997, however, Greenpeace was in bad shape: it closed most regional offices, slashed its staff from four hundred to sixty-five, and cut its subsidies to Greenpeace International.[62] It suffered, some analysts argue, because of real successes in saving whales (a signature Greenpeace campaign), because Americans saw the Clinton administration as proenvironment, and, perhaps more important, because groups such as the Environmental Defense Fund (EDF) and Defenders of Wildlife were better at showing supporters how their dues produced tangible results. Greenpeace had always faced criticism (tinged with envy) from other environmental groups that it cared more about self-promotion than actually getting things done. Fair or not, such perceptions eroded the willingness of many Americans to continue to subsidize Greenpeace when so many other groups were competing for the always tight environmental dollar.

Greenpeace's experience underscores the political reality faced by the major American environmental groups. Despite criticisms from activists, the major national groups are still environmentalism's flagships, professional organizations able to go toe-to-toe with entrenched interests; pursue complex lawsuits in the federal courts; offer financial and technical assistance to activists in local, state, and, increasingly, international arenas; and even to stand up against governments. *Someone* has to play these roles because that is the way the system works. In this sense the national groups are guilty of being normal Washington lobbies, thereby facing the usual perils of bureaucratic stagnation, staff careerism, routinized issue advocacy, and passive "checkbook memberships."[63] Smaller groups such as Environmental Action play an important role as the conscience of the community, but they will have briefer, if more incandescent, lifespans.

At the same time, if a Greenpeace flags another group will emerge to occupy some niche in the policy domain. A good example is the San Francisco-based Rainforest Action Network (RAN), spun off from the Earth Island Institute in 1985 to focus on issues of tropical rain forest depletion. Today RAN has over 30,000 dues-paying supporters, but doesn't work like the major groups. Instead, RAN is almost a "virtual group" with a staff of twenty that relies on the Web and other information technology to educate and mobilize local activists who, in turn, form autonomous Rainforest Action Groups to educate local citizens, raise funds for programs in countries containing rain forests, or organize boycotts against companies whose practices threaten the forests. It works on a far smaller scale than the Sierra Club or

Selected Environmental Group Web Sites

Major Organizations

Defenders of Wildlife	*www.defenders.org*
Environmental Defense Fund	*www.edf.org*
Friends of the Earth	*www.foe.org*
Greenpeace International	*www.greenpeace.org*
Izaak Walton League of America	*www.iwla.org*
League of Conservation Voters	*www.lcv.org*
National Audubon Society	*www.audubon.org*
National Parks and Conservation Association	*www.npca.org*
National Wildlife Federation	*www.nwf.org*
Nature Conservancy	*www.tnc.org*
Natural Resources Defense Council	*www.nrdc.org*
Sierra Club	*www.sierraclub.org*
Wilderness Society	*www.tws.org*
World Wildlife Federation	*www.panda.org*

Other Organizations

American Farmland Trust	*www.farmland.org*
American Rivers	*www.amrivers.org*
Conservation International	*www.conservation.org*
Ducks Unlimited Inc	*www.ducks.org*
Earth First!	*www.enviroweb.org/ef/*
Rainforest Action Network	*www.ran.org*
Surfrider Foundation	*www.surfrider.org*

Note: A good index of "Wise Use" sites is maintained by the Alliance for America at *http://home.navisoft.com/alliance/afaweb/mutual.htm.*

Friends of the Earth, but it occupies a focused niche within the overall environmental community.

Finally, environmental activism went truly global during the 1990s, with environmental nongovernmental organizations sprouting up everywhere and major American organizations joining already internationalized groups such as Greenpeace, Friends of the Earth, and the World Wildlife Fund in campaigns on an array of transnational problems. But such groups as Audubon or the Natural Resources Defense Council (NRDC) haven't really gone international. In fact, if some truly international groups such as Greenpeace have run into hard fiscal times despite a generally healthy world economy (at least prior to 1998), it may be because many Americans have concentrated their attention and dues in organizations with a sharper local focus and more pragmatic outlook. Groups such as Sierra Club and Audubon may have strengthened their grassroots and focused on local issues not only to respond to domestic political realities but also to generate the resources necessary to extend their reach beyond the United States. The Nature Conservancy may focus largely on preserving important domestic ecosystems, but its success at home allows it to spread its efforts to Latin

America and Asia. If Americans are reluctant to directly subsidize international efforts, they don't seem to mind if their groups range afar, so long as the home fires are tended first.

Into the Future

I once argued that the notion of a "movement" is useless in describing the vast array of organizations and efforts dedicated to protecting, saving, or fixing some part of the environment.[64] That statement is truer than ever.

So what do we have? What we see today, and what we will see a decade from now, is a vast and inchoate community of organizations dedicated to the environment in one way or another. We will see a community where a handful of major national groups such as the Sierra Club or NRDC fulfill their roles as the quasi-green parties of American politics, fueled by the dues of hundreds of thousands of supporters and branching out into a broad spectrum of issues and tactics. In fact, we will probably have fewer such groups a decade out, since some that overlap may well decide that a strategic merger is the best way to maximize their clout, if not simply to survive within a highly competitive market. After all, if Exxon can merge with Mobil, or Netscape with America Online, why not Defenders of Wildlife and the Wilderness Society? Why not NRDC and EDF? Bigger may be better for some in the environmental "protest business," particularly if they want to go toe-to-toe with political parties, corporations, or governments.

But environmentalism will be more than a few big groups. To expect otherwise is to deny the realities of interest group formation and mobilization in the United States. The Sierra Club, to use one example, will continue to beget splinter groups as activists decide to pursue their own paths. Sierra begat the Friends of the Earth, which begat the Earth Island Institute, which begat the Rainforest Action Network, and so on into the future. Local groups tied together through organizations like RAN and services like EcoNet will fill niches left open by the major groups. Instead of one "environmental movement" we have its progeny: animal rights, rain forests, local right-to-know, and so on. In effect, the Movement is dead: long live all the movements.

The environmental community also will develop more clearly defined ideological wings, particularly as conservatives accept the reality that environmentalism is now at the core of the American political culture. On the right, free-market groups such as the Competitive Enterprise Institute will jostle with social conservative groups such as the Evangelical Environmental Network, reflecting a broader struggle within American conservatism. On the left, Friends of the Earth will challenge the larger Sierra Club, but both will express the belief that progressive environmentalism may well be the sole remaining critique to triumphant corporate capitalism.[65] At the center will be groups such as the Nature Conservancy, NRDC, and EDF, wary about the heart of the Right but skeptical about the head of the Left. All will share a core belief in the importance of the environment, but differ in priorities, strategies, and tactics.

The environmental movement has become a mature and very typical American interest group community, albeit one with a greater than average array of policy niches and potential forms of activism. That sheer variety will be its lifeblood and its salvation, for within every major group resides tomorrow's rebels, frustrated believers determined to challenge the status quo by starting their own groups. There are no guarantees that any particular group will be around in a decade—the environmental activism market is as competitive as any—but there will be a vibrant community of groups dedicated to saving the environment both here and around the world. The dimensions of that community are before us right now.

Notes

1. Christopher J. Bosso, "Adaptation and Change in the Environmental Movement," in *Interest Group Politics*, 3d ed., ed. Allan J. Cigler and Burdett A. Loomis (Washington, D.C.: CQ Press, 1991), 152–176.
2. Christopher J. Bosso, "Seizing Back the Day: The Challenge to Environmental Activism in the 1990s," in *Environmental Policy in the 1990s*, 3d ed., ed. Norman J. Vig and Michael E. Kraft (Washington, D.C.: CQ Press, 1997), 53–74.
3. "Conservationists Warn Interior Appropriations Bill Loaded with 'Worst-Ever' Anti-environmental Riders," *U.S. Newswire,* June 25, 1998.
4. Dan Balz and Claudia Deane, "Education Is First in Voter Priorities," *Washington Post*, July 14, 1998, A1.
5. *Gallup Poll* at *http://www.gallup.com/Gallup_Poll_Data/mood/problem.htm* (April 1998).
6. Robert C. Mitchell, "Public Opinion and the Green Lobby: Poised for the 1990s?" in *Environmental Policy in the 1990s*, ed. Norman J. Vig and Michael E. Kraft (Washington, D.C.: CQ Press, 1990), 84.
7. Anthony Downs, "Up and Down with Ecology: The Issue-Attention Cycle," *Public Interest* 28 (1972): 38–50.
8. Lydia Saad, "Welfare, Federal Deficit Emerge as Public Concerns," *Gallup Poll Monthly* (January 1995): 6–8.
9. Times-Mirror Organization, *The Environmental Two-Step: Looking Back, Moving Forward* (Washington, D.C.: Roper Starch Worldwide, May 1995), 2.
10. Karlyn H. Bowman and Everett Carll Ladd, *Attitudes toward the Environment* (Washington, D.C.: American Enterprise Institute, 1995), as cited in Margaret Kriz, "Drawing a Green Line in the Sand," *National Journal*, August 8, 1995, 2976.
11. David W. Moore, "Public Sense of Urgency About Environment Wanes," *Gallup Poll Monthly* (April 1995): 17–20.
12. Pew Research Center, "Education, Crime, Social Security Top National Priorities Spending Favored Over Tax Cuts or Debt Reduction," *National Issues Index* at *http://www.people-press.org/jan98que.htm* (January 1998).
13. Riley E. Dunlap, "Public Opinion and the Environment (U.S.)," in *Conservation and Environmentalism: An Encyclopedia,* ed. Robert Paehlke (New York: Garland, 1995), 536.
14. Kriz, "Drawing a Green Line," 2976; and Moore, "Public Sense of Urgency," 20.
15. CBS News, "Environment A Worry," at *http://www.cbs.com/prd1/now/display?p_section=215* (March 1–2, 1998).
16. Kriz, "Drawing a Green Line," 2976.
17. Riley E. Dunlap, "Public Opinion in the 1980s: Clear Consensus, Ambiguous Commitment," *Environment* 33 (October 1991): 33.
18. Dan Balz, "Education Is First in Voter Priorities," *Washington Post*, July 14, 1998, A1.
19. Paul Rauber, "Frontier Justice," *Sierra* 83, no. 1 (January 1998): 18–19.
20. Paul Rauber, "Republican Charm School," *Sierra* 83, no. 1 (January 1998): 20.

21. GOP Green Group," *Chemical Week*, June 24, 1998, 44.
22. "GOP Feuds over What It Means to Be 'Green'," *Christian Science Monitor*, July 31, 1998.
23. Clearinghouse on Environmental Advocacy and Research, "The Green GOP?" *A CLEAR View* 5, no. 11 (September 1, 1998) at *http://www.ewg.org/pub/home/clear/view/latest.html#F1*.
24. Clearinghouse on Environmental Advocacy and Research, "Antienvironmental Leaders Testify at 'Eco-terrorism' hearings," *A CLEAR View* 5, no. 8 (June 3, 1998) at *http://www.ewg.org/pub/home/clear/view/CV_Vol5_No9.html#F1*.
25. Clearinghouse on Environmental Advocacy and Research, "Off-Road.com Declares Slam a Success, Lycos Cancels EnviroLink Contract," *A CLEAR View* 5, no. 11 (September 1, 1998) at *http://www.ewg.org/pub/home/clear/view/latest.html#F1*.
26. "Internet Firm Drops Oakland Service," *Oakland Tribune-Review*, August 18, 1998.
27. See David Helvarg, *The War against the West* (San Francisco: Sierra Club Books, 1994), and Jacqueline Switzer, *Green Backlash: The History and Politics of Environmental Opposition in the United States* (Boulder, Colo.: Lynne Reinner, 1997).
28. Samuel P. Hays, *Conservation and the Gospel of Efficiency* (Cambridge, Mass.: Harvard University Press, 1958).
29. For a report on one self-described Montana militia member, see "Trochmann in Washington State," *A CLEAR View* 3, no. 2 (January 1996) at *http://www.ewg.org/pub/home/CLEAR/View/CV_Vol3_No2.html*.
30. Barbara Ferry, "New Mexico Congressman Linked to 'Wise Use' Movement," *States News Service*, June 5, 1997.
31. "Enviros Blast Rep for Joining Land Use Group," *Greenwire*, August 27, 1997.
32. David Helvarg, "Grassroots for Sale: The Inside Scoop on (un)Wise Use," *Amicus Journal* 16, no. 3 (Fall 1994): 24.
33. Andrew Branan, "Going against the Greens," *Ripon Forum* 30 (July 1995): 10.
34. Yvonne Daley, "In California, Cause of Saving Redwoods Gaining," *Boston Globe*, November 8, 1998, A10.
35. Brian Tokar, "The 'Wise Use' Backlash: Responding to Militant Antienvironmentalism," *Ecologist* 25 (July 1995): 150.
36. Defenders of Wildlife, "State Network Launched to Help Local Environmental Activists," Press Release, October 29, 1998, at *http://www.defenders.org/pr102998.html*.
37. Frank Graham, Jr., *The Audubon Ark: A History of the National Audubon Society* (New York: Knopf, 1990).
38. Hearst News Service, "National Environmental Groups Find More Success Locally," *Baltimore Sun*, October 12, 1997, 20A.
39. Robert Gottleib, *Forcing the Spring: The Transformation of the American Environmental Movement* (Washington, D.C.: Island Press, 1993).
40. Margaret Kriz, "The Greening of a Conservative," *National Journal*, June 6, 1995, 1419.
41. Erin Kelly, "Environmentalists Finding Nontraditional Allies," *Gannett News Service*, October 11, 1997.
42. League of Conservation Voters, "Conservationists Claim Victory for the Environment in Key Congressional Races," *U.S. Newswire*, November 4, 1998, at *http://www.lcv.org/dirtydozen/pr_1104.htm*.
43. Sierra Club, "Environment a Winning Issue from Sea to Shining Sea," *U.S. Newswire*, November 4, 1998, at *http://www.sierraclub.org/media/1998_elections.htm*; see also Richard Berke, "Sierra Club Ads in Political Races Offer a Case Study of 'Issue Advocacy'," *New York Times*, October 24, 1998, A12.
44. "Green Party Painting Democrats into a Corner," *USA Today*, July 22, 1998, 1; and Michael Coleman, "Grass-Roots Prowess Lifts Green's Miller," *Albuquerque Journal*, September 11, 1998, 1.
45. Anna Bramwell, *The Fading of the Greens: The Decline of Environmental Politics in the West* (New Haven, Conn.: Yale University Press, 1994), 203.

46. William Drozdiak, "Schroeder Takes Office, Vows Swift Modernization of Economy," *Washington Post*, October 28, 1998, A26.
47. R. Kent Weaver and Bert A. Rockman, eds., *Do Institutions Matter? Government Capabilities in the United States and Abroad* (Washington, D.C.: Brookings, 1993).
48. Bramwell, *Fading of the Greens*, 56.
49. David Foreman, "Around the Campfire," *Wild Earth* 5 (Spring 1995): 2.
50. League of Conservation Voters, "Conservation Group Pegs Anti-Environment Congressional Candidates for Defeat," *U.S. Newswire*, June 23, 1998.
51. John Lancaster, "War and Recession Taking Toll on National Environmental Organizations," *Washington Post*, February 15, 1991, A3.
52. "Enviro Groups: Money, Management Woes Paralyze Greens," *Greenwire*, July 18, 1995.
53. See Bosso, "Color of Money," 110–117
54. Richard E. Cohen, *Washington at Work: Back Rooms and Clean Air*, 2d ed. (Boston: Allyn and Bacon, 1995).
55. Michael McCloskey, "Twenty Years of Change in the Environmental Movement," in *American Environmentalism: The U.S. Environmental Movement, 1970–1990*, ed. Riley E. Dunlap and Angela G. Mertig (Philadelphia: Taylor and Francis, 1993), 83.
56. Mark Dowie, *Losing Ground: American Environmentalism at the Close of the Twentieth Century* (Cambridge, Mass.: MIT Press, 1995), 192–195.
57. Kirkpatrick Sale, "The U.S. Green Movement Today," *The Nation*, July 19, 1993, 94.
58. Robert C. Mitchell, Angela G. Mertig, and Riley E. Dunlap, "Twenty Years of Environmental Mobilization: Trends among National Environmental Organizations," in *American Environmentalism*, ed. Dunlap and Mertig, 24.
59. Dowie, *Losing Ground*, xiii.
60. Grant Jordan and William Maloney, *The Protest Business? Mobilising Campaign Groups* (Manchester, England: Manchester University Press, 1997).
61. "Environmental Action Closes Up Shop," *Greenwire*, December 10, 1996.
62. Carey Goldberg, "Downsizing Activism: Greenpeace Is Cutting Back," *New York Times*, September 17, 1997, A1.
63. Michael T. Hayes, "The New Group Universe," *Interest Group Politics*, 2d ed., ed. Allan J. Cigler and Burdett A. Loomis (Washington, D.C.: CQ Press, 1986), 133–145.
64. See Bosso, "Adaptation and Change," 174.
65. See Robert Paehlke, *Environmentalism and the Future of Progressive Politics* (New Haven, Conn.: Yale University Press, 1990).

4

Environmental Values and Public Policy

Robert C. Paehlke

This chapter is about how environmental politics and policy result from the ongoing and effective expression of environmental values by environmentalists, environmental organizations, political leaders, civil servants, and ordinary citizens. Understanding the history of this process confirms David Easton's definition of politics as the authoritative allocation of values.[1] The chapter sets out the value dimensions of contemporary environmentalism and identifies some of the difficult issues that the acceptance of these values has helped to urge onto the political agenda.[2] It also develops a framework for integrating these values with other prominent politically relevant values. This framework might be called a "triple E" perspective, for environment, economy, and equity.

From the nineteenth century to the middle of the twentieth century, politics centered on the struggles between economic values (capital accumulation, enhanced trade, economic growth) and equity values (wages, working conditions, social welfare, public health, and public education). Although these issues have not been resolved, it might be argued that since the 1970s, other issues and tensions have gained in relative prominence. Two sets of issues are of particular concern to us here—those that arise between environment and economy on the one hand, and environment and equity on the other. Points of mutual support as well as of conflict occur in both cases, but many contemporary political issues can be better understood within this wider framework. In effect, environmental values (among others) have been added to, and complicate, the old debates between left and right, rich and poor.

The Principal Dimensions of Contemporary Environmental Values

Historians as well as philosophers have observed that the contemporary environmental movement is based on a transformation of human social values. The historian Samuel Hays noted that new values, rooted in the advances in prosperity and educational levels following World War II, have emerged in virtually all wealthy societies.[3] Others have suggested that these recent value shifts run deeper than those that sustained the earlier conservation movement. The philosopher George Sessions has concluded that the ecological "revolution" is fundamentally religious and philosophical and involves "a radical critique of the basic assumptions of modern Western society."[4] More recently, some analysts have suggested that the churches must take an important role in environmental politics if they wish to remain the leading nongovernmental institution within which values are considered.[5]

Using opinion survey instruments, Ronald Inglehart and other social scientists have measured related shifts in popular attitudes, postulating a "silent revolution" that entails the spread of "postmaterialist" values.[6] Riley Dunlap, Lester Milbrath, and others have identified a "new environmental paradigm."[7] Whatever name one attaches to the change, the environmental movement and the responses to it are the political manifestation of significant turmoil in societal values.

Recently, and in the early 1980s, the forceful assertion of environmental values has provoked a strong reaction from the political right—even from some who would accept relatively "shallow" environmental values. In chapter 1, Michael Kraft and Norman Vig distinguish between "deep" and "shallow" currents of environmentalism. They suggest that environmental values have moved into the mainstream of American political culture but that short-term political currents often conflict with these underlying trends.[8] Such conflict has seldom been more apparent than in the recent debates in the U. S. Congress and many state legislatures. This raises the question of which values are central to the environmental movement, how they relate to other values and to policymaking, and whether they are strong enough to withstand present challenges.

But what values constitute the essential core of an environmental perspective? In an earlier work, I set out a list of thirteen central environmental values, and others have developed lists similar to this one:

1. An appreciation of all life forms and a view that the complexities of the ecological web of life are politically salient.
2. A sense of humility regarding the human species in relation to other species and to the global ecosystem.
3. A concern with the quality of human life and health, including an emphasis on the importance of preventive medicine, diet, and exercise to the maintenance and enhancement of human health.
4. A global rather than a nationalist or isolationist view.
5. Some preference for political and/or population decentralization.
6. An extended time horizon—a concern about the long-term future of the world and its life.
7. A sense of urgency regarding the survival of life on Earth, both long term and short term.
8. A belief that human societies ought to be reestablished on a more sustainable technical and physical basis. An appreciation that many aspects of our present way of life are fundamentally transitory.
9. A revulsion toward waste in the face of human need (in more extreme forms, this may appear as asceticism).
10. A love of simplicity, although this does not include rejection of technology or "modernity."

11. An esthetic appreciation for season, setting, climate, and natural materials.
12. A measurement of esteem, including self-esteem and social merit, in terms of such nonmaterial values as skill, artistry, effort, or integrity.
13. An attraction to autonomy and self-management in human endeavors and, generally, an inclination to more democratic and participatory political processes and administrative structures.[9]

This list and others like it can be distilled to three core items: (1) the protection of biodiversity, ecological systems, and wilderness; (2) the minimization of negative impacts on human health; and (3) the establishment of sustainable patterns of resource use. These core items are relatively new as significant actors on the stage of political ideas. They are all ideas with an extended history, but were for at least a century swamped by the larger ideological battles of left and right—the struggles over and between economy and equity. Throughout the 1990s a growing response to each of these three core items came to the fore.

Ecology as a Core Value

The first of the three core environmental values is captured to a large extent in the concept of ecology. All life forms are bound up each with the other in a complex, and frequently little understood, web of life. Fruit bats are essential to the propagation of many tropical trees and numerous other plant species in other climatic zones. Forests, in turn, help to determine the climate of the planet as a whole. The transformation of forest to agriculture in Latin America can dramatically affect migratory songbird populations in North America. The web of life ties all species together inextricably.

Human well-being, and indeed human survival, depends on the success of an almost endless list of plant and animal species, often in ways we barely understand. Our global food reserves would endure for but a matter of months should our food production capabilities suddenly decline. That capability is determined in turn by rainfall and temperature, by the activities of many insect species such as bees, and by microbiological life within the soils of the planet. All of these in turn are affected by both plants and animals. Our well-being is determined by other species in other ways as well, not the least of which is our deep need for contact with, or awareness of the existence of, wild nature. The significant place of wild nature in human history has been captured by Max Oelschlaeger, who writes:

> By abandoning the view that nature is no more than an ecomachine or a stockpile of resources to fuel the human project, preservationists tend not to be bulls in an ecological china shop. They typically reject a strictly economic approach to valuing wilderness, and entertain other considerations such as rarity, species diversity, and even beauty. And by adopting a holistic view, preservationists are attentive to the pervasive linkages and interactions essential to any concept of a wilderness ecosystem.[10]

The deep ecologists, who express biocentric or ecocentric values, go further than this. They see preservationism (as distinct from the mere conservation of "resources") as itself anthropocentric and therefore suspect. In other words, biocentrism and ecocentrism go beyond strict preservationism by questioning "speciesism": the idea that humankind is somehow superior to, and therefore entitled to impose its values on, nature.[11] Deep ecology is a philosophical perspective that sees humans as no higher or lower than other life forms. All life forms are equally valued, and the ecological whole that they comprise cannot and should not be "managed" in the interests of any particular species.[12] Human interference in the natural processes of the living planet should be kept to a minimum. For some, animal rights and vegetarianism follow logically from a deep ecology perspective.

Consider some of the political and policy implications of a deep ecology perspective (or even a strict preservationist perspective). Should we continue to permit the cutting of our few remaining virgin forests? Forests, after all, from the perspective of other species, are home and indeed the source of life. Should we not, for example, strictly control the number of humans and the character of their transportation within wilderness areas, including national parks? Should we not disallow the testing of toxic substances on animals, and, indeed, all animal experimentation?[13] Should farmers be allowed to fill in hedgerows on their lands given that these provide corridors essential to the local survival of many animal species? What of filling in wetlands for shopping malls? And what of ultimate situations where humans and other species both require use of the same land for survival?

The way we understand and value ecology clearly has very important political implications, and each of the questions posed above has gained in political salience in recent years. As Oelschlaeger put it in the preface to his book: "*The Idea of Wilderness* . . . is . . . subversive, for I have assumed that what the members of a democratic society think ultimately makes a difference." [14] Ideas and values, if widely shared, can establish a new political agenda. They can also provoke a strong political response.

Recent actions in U. S. courts and Congress seem to raise questions about how broadly ecological values are shared. Numerous cases have been heard in the courts regarding environmental policy "takings" from property rights (reductions in property value owing to restrictions on the use of that property). Some of these cases regarding interpretation of the provisions of the Fifth Amendment have been heard by the Supreme Court, and many other cases are in the courts seeking compensation to property owners, for example, for restrictions on the transformation of wetlands or requirements that endangered species be protected.[15] These cases have been supported by leading conservative legal foundations and by a significant, antienvironmentalist, property rights movement. Such views are fueled by the assertions of some prominent business figures, such as Richard Lester of the U. S. Chamber of Commerce, who wrote: "I believe that the existence of 'antienvironmentalism' is, like so many alleged environmental hazards, a figment of the fevered imagination of a few zealots who have permitted their fanaticism to subvert their thought processes." [16]

Health as a Core Value

Health, the second core belief of environmentalism, is widely supported, but nonetheless also at times controversial. The present era is highly health conscious, and many Americans are concerned about their exposure to toxic chemicals. Strong parallels also exist between an increased interest in outdoor recreational activities and public concern regarding wilderness protection. Concerns regarding diet, food additives, and "natural" foods are often linked to environmental concerns regarding pesticides and herbicides. Keeping fit often produces an increased concern for air and water quality. Health is more than the absence of illness, and physical well-being is very hard to separate from environmental well-being.

Nonetheless, the minimization of impacts on human health can also be politically contentious. Here one might consider the opposing views of two noted social scientists. Aaron Wildavsky argues that in a clash between health values and wealth values the latter should be encouraged by public policy. Wealth, in his view, largely determines health.[17] That is, the wealthier the nation, the healthier it is. Wildavsky thus would never expend more public funds on health than the calculable value of the lives saved, or improved, by such expenditures. A contrasting view is put forward by Mark Sagoff. As he sees it, health and environmental protection must sometimes come first, economics second. In Sagoff's words:

> Since the New Deal, environmental law and policy have evolved as a continuous compromise between those who approach the protection of public health, safety, and the environment primarily in ethical terms and those who conceive it primarily in economic terms. The first attitude is moral: It regards hazardous pollution and environmental degradation as evils society must eliminate if it is to live up to its ideals and aspirations. The second attitude is prudential or practical. It argues that the benefits of social regulation should be balanced more realistically against the costs.[18]

Since the early 1980s the views of those who would balance economic costs and environmental benefits on a dollar basis have usually prevailed, both in the executive branch (through President Ronald Reagan's Executive Order 12291) and in the courts (in, for example, the decisions on the exposure standards for benzene and cotton dust). In Sagoff's view this trend has run counter to the historic intent of most environmental health legislation. Sagoff would prefer a balance between economic costs and benefits and an ethical assertion of the right to health protection. In effect, Wildavsky might be asked if additional wealth automatically produces increments of health. His view does not account for the inferior health performance in some very wealthy nations, including the United States. Nor for the enormous health costs of the single-minded (if ineffective) drive for economic growth in eastern Europe and the former Soviet Union.

There is agreement that environmental health is an important societal value. There is disagreement as to how to maximize health outcomes and as to how large a risk we might simply accept as the price of (economic) prosperity. Should we emphasize the avoidance of risks, or should we take chances in the name of increased wealth and assume that health improvements will follow? Wildavsky draws an analogy with a jogger who must run a greater short-term risk of a heart attack while running in order to achieve a lower long-term risk of heart disease. If automobiles, toxic chemicals, or nuclear power advance our economy significantly while adding a small increment to overall health risks, these are risks worth taking. Most environmentalists would disagree, both on moral grounds (the risks are mostly involuntary) and on practical grounds (the risks are large, the economic gains minimal).

The political battle on this issue has been joined in the Congress around bills to require risk analysis and/or cost-benefit analysis prior to the passage of some or all environmental and health regulations. In this debate Rep. John D. Dingell, D-Mich., was compelled to ask: "What is the cost-benefit analysis that is going to determine the price of a healthy child?"[19] Science is a part of these procedures, but neither risk assessment nor cost-benefit analysis are "pure" or "certain"—the former often requires highly uncertain estimates, the latter requires value assumptions. This is not to say that such procedures do not have a place; it is to say that science cannot decide whether we wish to err on the side of prudence or on the side of cost-effectiveness when human health and human lives are clearly involved.

Sustainability as a Core Value

The third core belief of environmentalism, sustainability, has perhaps received less attention recently, but may be the most important dimension of environmentalism because it, even more than ecology and health, implies a thoroughgoing transformation of industrial society. As a goal, sustainability suggests a radically reduced dependence on nonrenewable resources, a commitment to extract renewable resources no more rapidly than they are restored in nature, and a minimization of all human impacts on natural ecosystems. In sum, sustainability sets the economic opportunities and ecological foundation of future generations on the same ethical level as those of present generations. Those who promote sustainability assume that now is the time to acknowledge how finite and fragile Earth is.

Perhaps the most important aspect of sustainability is the recognition that fossil fuels are not renewable. There is no obvious substitute that can supply comparable amounts of energy at a comparable cost. Nor can humankind continue to extract wood from forests or fish from the seas at present rates; they are not being replenished at those rates. Nor can we continue to burn combustible fuels at present rates lest we significantly alter the global climate, if we have not already done so. Sustainability, then, shifts the focus of societal concern from the present to the future and presumes a fundamental obligation to future generations.

Lester Milbrath, a political scientist, argues that the need to focus public policy on sustainability is an urgent one. Our "entire social system is in jeopardy," he writes, and "we cannot continue on our present trajectory." He argues that "open-minded recognition of the deep systemic nature of our problem would allow a planned gradual transition, with minimal dislocation and pain."[20] Milbrath and many others come to this view in a consideration of human population trends and the long-term potential for food supply and adequate resources, global climate change, and numerous other patterns and trends. Joel Kassiola entitles his inquiry *The Death of Industrial Civilization* and argues that future economic growth is fundamentally limited by ecological and resource constraints.[21] Indeed, there is a widespread sense that the Western standard of living, or anything like it, cannot ultimately be enjoyed by humankind as a whole, nor even indefinitely by those who enjoy it now. Yet human numbers continue to grow, as does the rate at which we extract nonrenewable resources (or remove renewable resources too rapidly for recovery). At the same time, a variety of possible futures are attainable that are both less resource dependent and profoundly comfortable. Advocates of sustainable development are seeking a viable future for postindustrial society.[22]

The fundamental question is which, if any, people within the wealthy economies would consider any upper limit to economic well-being or convenience to help achieve sustainability and other environmental values. To what extent are our economic and environmental values fundamentally in conflict? Willett Kempton, James Boster, and Jennifer Hartley take us part of the way to a better understanding of these tensions. Most Americans, they find, accept many environmental values, but some flinch when it comes to making some specific economic sacrifices to achieve them.[23] However, in this study even a group of sawmill workers, in majority, would allow that life-style changes should sometimes be forced for the sake of the environment. This group would resist fuel taxes and, understandably, job losses—but a strong majority of all participants in the survey would favor, for example, taxing products depending on their environmental effects.

Competing Values and an Environmental Ethic

The three core values of the environmental movement are clearly important, but they must compete with other values (especially those of economy and equity). To complicate matters further, they also sometimes conflict with each other. For example, high-yield, sustainable forests may lack the diversity that would otherwise provide habitats for many animal species. Similarly, even the act of protecting human health, and thereby ensuring that human population will rise, reduces resource sustainability and virtually guarantees the diminution of nonhuman habitat. Such dilemmas do not absolve us of the task of sorting out difficult value questions; indeed politics, as the authoritative allocator of values, requires it. Technical solutions to some environmental problems exist, but they are usually partial solutions that sometimes create their own problems.

There is in the end no avoiding hard questions. An environmental ethic helps us to establish priorities. Acknowledging that all nonhuman species have a right to a wild existence carries implications, as we have seen, for the meaning and character of property rights. Similarly, if all humans are to have a right to a healthy environment, some industries must spend moneys that they would prefer to put to other uses. A societal commitment to sustainability—as we will see—suggests that we may all need to adjust many dimensions of our everyday behavior, including what we buy, what we throw away, and which mode of transportation we select in various circumstances.

Environmental values, then, involve much more than just concern for attractive animals and the protection of scenic beauty. The core values of environmentalism, if taken seriously, challenge nothing less than how we organize our society and how we live our lives. These values provoke policy dilemmas and can lead to choices so hard as to be almost impossible to make. Yet we must make them. The following three sections focus on the tough questions in the hope that considering challenging cases will deepen our understanding of the political significance of environmentalism. These cases arise out of each of the three core values of environmentalism: ecology, health, and sustainability. I also discuss one case that arises out of all three simultaneously.

The Ethical Challenge of Ecology

Throughout the developing world humans and other large animals compete for space. In the wealthy nations this competition has largely been resolved in favor of the human species. Lions and bears no longer roam the forests of Europe. Few bison populate the vast prairies of North America; gone, too, are the nonhuman predator populations they once supported. Now much of the wild habitat of the elephant is threatened, and the rhino, and the cheetah, and the tiger, and a long list of other creatures less grand. So too are the tropical rain forests as a whole—as well as the nontropical rain forests of the Pacific Northwest. These are popular issues in part because it was one thing for humankind to appropriate some of the planet, another thing to appropriate nearly all of it. Few would disagree with the assertion that the lives of future humans would be profoundly less rich should we humans appropriate most of the space required by other species. Yet here is the dilemma: both the animals and humans now need the same land. Who will decide what to do? And how?

Particularly perplexing issues include how best to protect the spotted owl, the tiger, and the elephant. The case of the spotted owl is familiar to most North Americans. Its protection under the U.S. Endangered Species Act blocked the logging of some old-growth forests, its habitat. Intense political conflict erupted in the Pacific Northwest following this decision, conflict that gave further impetus to the property rights movement. Loggers, industry, small businesses, and the local media rallied against both the decision and the owl. In the process, some environmental positions have been widely misunderstood. The owl itself, however deserving of protection, has been seen by environmentalists as but one species under threat. In their view, the ancient forest itself deserves protection. As Patrick Mazza put it, "the spotted owl is a 'canary in a coal mine,' whose troubles signal a warning for the entire old growth ecosystem."[24] The jobs are soon to be lost in any case because little old-growth forest remains. The larger question is, should humankind remove and replace all the forests of the world? The replacement forest may be vastly different ecologically. The issue for most environmentalists is not the economic value of forests, but whether all the world exists simply for our benefit. Jobs that might have existed for a few years more must, in this view, come to an end a few years sooner.

The "spotted owl" dilemma is difficult—very difficult if one's life is directly affected—but it is not nearly so tough as the case of tigers and elephants, both of which require vast wilderness habitats. The land the tiger needs is also coveted by Indian peasants who would hope to grow crops there and nearby. Given the numbers of humans in India, and their present rate of growth, it is only a matter of time before this is literally a matter of human lives versus tiger lives. Additionally, as humans encroach on tiger populations, fatalities are inevitable.

Laura Westra and others provide important ethical arguments to help resolve these enormous moral dilemmas. As she puts it, "just as all individual and group interests need to start with the preservation of their existence, so too all our moral doctrines prescribing appropriate principles for human interaction should be preceded by a principle aimed at preserving life in general, in and through ecosystems."[25] There is no doubt that sometimes, and increasingly, these values will carry a very high price.

In East Africa humans who hunt elephants are now themselves hunted and killed regularly by protection authorities. Something near to a state of war exists. Most African nations are cooperating in seeking an end to trade in ivory worldwide. Other African nations with more stable elephant populations (Zimbabwe, Botswana, and South Africa) issue permits to hunt elephants. This strategy has been partially successful against poaching, and elephant populations appear, for now, to be secure in these countries.[26] But should the existence of elephants in the wild depend on the desire of some humans to kill them? Do not both tigers and elephants have an absolute right to a safe habitat somewhere on the planet?

Most people—if unaffected personally—would answer the last question affirmatively. But the implications may be far more radical than most understand. As George Sessions has stated:

> Population biologists have argued that 1 to 2 billion people living lightly on the planet would be sustainable given the ecological requirements of maintaining carrying capacity for all species. A human population decrease from its present level to that level (by humane means such as steady low birth rates) would also be good for humans and for the diversity of human cultures, as well as for wild species and ecosystems.[27]

The individual policy dilemmas, however difficult, pale to insignificance if one accepts the profound nature of the challenge posed by this view. Those human numbers may be optimal, but that conclusion hardly provides our species with a means of humanely achieving a significant population reduction (see chap. 15). There is, further, no general agreement that such a goal is either feasible or desirable.[28] Some feel, however, that it is possible in the long run, and from this perspective our zoos and parks are seen as arks for a very different planetary future.

The Ethical Challenge of Health

Cost-benefit analysis regarding health matters requires placing a price on human lives, an ethical dilemma if ever there was one. The cost of changing an industrial process is calculated and compared to the additional health costs of continued human exposures at present levels. Environmental exposures of other species are usually ignored. Indeed, calculations are usually for either human occupational exposures or human environmental exposures, but not both.[29] Typically, a small number of human fatalities is set against an estimate by industry of the cost of cleaning up. The costs of nonfatal illnesses are often underestimated or ignored and so too are some nonhealth gains to industry associated with most retooling of industrial processes. Thus, the price assigned to the estimate of human lives lost is a significant part of the overall calculation.

What is important here is seeing that all of the above objections are technical objections. The ethical objection is, simply put, that a human life is beyond price. If a life can be saved, it should be saved. Yet if that were literally true governments might be expected to set speed limits at 10 miles per hour (mph) or to close down all oil refineries and uranium mines. One is drawn back to Sagoff's view that what is appropriate is some compromise, some balancing, between the two approaches to matters of environmental and occupational health. Cost-benefit calculations can be made, but governments should not imagine that they are utterly bound by them. Other factors must be considered. Do technologies exist that would ameliorate or eliminate the problem? How deep are the polluters' pockets relative to the cost of cleaning up? How important to society is the product associated with the imposed risk? Regarding this latter question, consider that it is possible that some human lives may be lost to achieve dandelion-free suburban lawns. Does that make ethical sense even if risking those lives generates millions of dollars in economic activity? In the case of asbestos (a known potent carcinogen), does it not matter if the substance is used in protective garments for fire fighters or for a more trivial purpose? Should we not also ask whether or not substitutes are readily available?

Releases of chemicals into the wider environment raise additional important questions. In particular, one must consider the likely duration of the environmental impact. If a risk will exist in perpetuity, the price is infinite regardless of the value one assigns to any one life. But in practice, we more frequently err in an opposite way. We site toxic chemical dumps, or municipal solid waste containing hazardous chemicals, on clay soils because they delay movement through the ground. But ultimately those chemicals will reach larger bodies of water. Arguably, it makes more sense to bury toxic wastes in sand, but to bury them in an amount and form that will release no more than we can tolerate in nearby aquifers. Otherwise all we are doing is assigning a toxic world to distant future generations. We are unable, it seems, to reason morally beyond our own grandchildren.

The Ethical Challenge of Sustainability

Any number of policy complexities arise from sustainability values as well. In the mid 1970s and again in the early 1980s North Americans were acutely aware of the long-term nonsustainability of fossil fuel supplies. This reality remains, though it has slipped for the present from public consciousness. Acutely in the public mind at present, however, are the limits of future lumber supplies from old-growth sites. So, too, in many locations are acceptable sites for the disposal of municipal solid waste. But lest all the news appears to be bad, feasible options are available in many cases. Building materials can be made from recycled household and industrial wastes, slowing the speed with which we "run out" of both lumber and landfill sites. Even more dramatically, by changing the rules by which electrical utilities and their customers make supply-and-demand decisions, we could save enough electricity to eliminate any need for new coal-burning power plants. This latter assertion perhaps needs a brief elaboration.

Electrical utilities traditionally worried almost exclusively about supply, while demand management was primarily the customer's concern. The more the utility supplied, the more money they made. Utilities also rarely considered for long how durable or expandable their supply sources were; it was assumed that other supply sources could always be found, if necessary. Demand management frequently fell between the cracks as neither builders nor building managers were concerned about electricity bills because they did not pay them—tenants did. Builders avoided the higher capital costs of more efficient lighting and other devices. Many commercial tenants were unconcerned about electrical efficiency because they paid a share of electricity costs related to the square footage they occupied rather than the amount of electricity they actually used. In the late 1980s utilities in several states were ordered by state regulatory agencies to treat efficiency improvement as investments made on behalf of their customers. The savings have been considerable: for the utilities, for their customers, for the economy as a whole, and for the sustainability of energy supplies.[30] Demand reduction has generally proved to be cheaper than new supply; there are, it would seem, some win-win possibilities.

Nonetheless, policy choices remain because some jobs are placed at risk (while others are created) and some firms may suffer significant economic losses (while others gain). Those who supply or build new power plants are hit very hard by these changes. So, too, are some employees of utilities. Achieving greater sustainability may well require significant transformations throughout industrial society, but these transformations can be eased by intelligent public policy and forward-looking private initiatives (see chap. 12 for some specific examples and possibilities).

A final example here provides a clearer appreciation of the importance of this issue and leads to a discussion of integrating environmental, economic, and equity values. Automobiles, their manufacture and repair, and related industries, generate at least 25 percent of the gross national product (GNP) of North America. Related industries include road building, tires, auto parts, and significant proportions of the steel industry, the cement industry, aggregates (sand and gravel) extraction, fast foods, motels, advertising, and so forth. Yet the automobile itself may well be unsustainable—at least in present numbers, traveling current average annual distances. Automobiles consume land, pollute the air, use up the least durable of fossil fuels, contribute to global warming, reduce the habitat of other species, and are a major source of acid precipitation. All three core environmental values are simultaneously offended. It has increasingly been argued that a sustainable future will see more compact cities that in turn are less dependent on automobile transportation, however fueled.[31] European cities are at present typically twice as compact as North American cities, and citizens of those cities typically use half the transportation fuel of their North American counterparts.[32] Yet Europeans are equally prosperous overall and the cities in question are arguably more pleasant (Paris, London, Amsterdam). In addition, several European cities have very recently carved out core areas from which automobiles are completely excluded. Such efforts are already coming to North America, and this trend will accelerate with the next round of fossil fuel price increases.

The principal point here is that environmental values, if taken seriously, could transform the future of industrial societies. The economic, social, and political implications of these changes are important and wide-ranging. Governments will require, then, ways to integrate these new values with the other important values that have always served as at least implicit guides to public policy. Here one might speak of three fundamental value sets: environment, economy, and equity. Below, I consider the relationships between two pairs of value sets: environment/economy and environment/equity. Many such considerations have been implicit within the preceding analysis as well. Economy and equity are so central to politics as a value-integrating process that they deserve additional attention here.

The Environment and the Economy

As Charles Lindblom has observed, contemporary political leaders are held to be responsible for the success or failure of the economy.[33] Accordingly, rising unemployment or falling profits often result in electoral difficulties for incumbents. Increasingly our political leadership is also seen to be responsible for environmental damage. To the extent that environmental protection and economic growth are in conflict, political leaders are held to an impossible mandate. Some would prefer to abandon one set of goals, usually environmental. Others place an emphasis on win-win scenarios, on the possibility of sustainable development. In other words, the perhaps impossible mandate is seen by some to be achievable—the simultaneous maximization of environmental values and economic values is taken to lie somewhere between assumption and hope. But, putting aside equity considerations for the moment, *can* environment and economy be simultaneously advanced?

On the positive side, some significant economic sectors are highly compatible with environmental protection.[34] Growth in public transport systems results in improved air quality and the more efficient use of land, materials, and energy. Demand-side management by electrical utilities has similarly positive environmental effects, and it can also be a considerable economic stimulus to manufacturers and installers of electrical equipment for heating, cooling, lighting, and electrical motors. Recycling-based manufacturing of paper, building materials, packaging, metal products, and plastic products also enhances environmental quality on a variety of fronts. So, too, of course, do the production, installation, and maintenance of pollution abatement equipment. Similarly, reduced dependence on agricultural chemicals can result in more economically viable farming operations, in part because consumers are willing to pay more for organic produce. To the extent that governmental policies allow and/or encourage economic transformations of this sort, economy and environment can improve simultaneously.

In addition, many sectors of a modern economy have only very small, or readily avoidable, effects on the environment. Significant growth in these sectors would have negligible environmental effects. Additional expenditures on education, social services, health care, or the arts and entertainment, for example, add little to the burden borne by the environment. This is an aspect of the debate on the appropriate level of social and other expenditures that too often has been left aside. But other economic sectors also have quite modest net impacts. These include some of the more dynamic sectors of the global economy. Computers, automation, and telecommunications have modest impacts per dollar of value added. In addition, they may make offsetting contributions. Communications can substitute for travel with very significant energy savings and a corresponding pollution reduction. Robots need little lighting or heat and do not add to highway congestion at rush hour. Equity effects aside for the moment, automation has enormous potential for reducing the total energy and materials devoted to manufacturing work spaces. Total energy and materials use, much more than GNP, determines the level of environmental impact.

Some economic sectors, however, would appear irretrievably in conflict with environmental values in the long term—especially ecological and sustainability values. No one would propose eliminating any economic sector by fiat. Yet it is hard to imagine how environmental values will not increasingly come into conflict with the growth goals of some sectors of the contemporary economy. Sectors where clashes are likely include the automobile industry (and thereby other attendant industries), the forest industry, the chemical industry, coal mining and use, the packaging industry, and the construction industry (as regards suburban sprawl). And one should not omit tobacco producers. Often, but not always, such clashes can be resolved relatively painlessly as when less toxic substitutes can be found or new products or processes developed. Even when resolutions are not painless, the burden can be spread and softened through imaginative public policy initiatives.

Comfortable, happy, healthy lives for ourselves and our families are, it would appear, in conflict with exactly those same goals. The automobile that keeps us out of the rain on our way to basketball practice pollutes the air we breathe. The materials used to produce the extra rooms in our home may require the diminution of habitat and perhaps outdoor recreational space. Our dry-cleaned clothes mandate the production and use of hazardous chemicals.[35] The suburban lifestyle we have collectively embraced since the 1940s and 1950s may be environmentally inappropriate for the population levels and energy reserves of the twenty-first century. The potential value conflicts are clearly very deep and must be resolved both at the many points where polity and economy intersect and in the inner recesses of present and future minds. When we cannot have both economy and environment, which is the more important to us? (And exactly when can we not have both?)

These tensions, both potential and immediate, could be resolved in a number of ways. Even being able to step back and ask questions is, of course, a luxury. In poor nations the choices are more stark: food or nature? economic collapse or forests for tomorrow? a manufacturing sector or clean air? Choice is the ultimate luxury, and North Americans still have choices—so long as we do not just assume that economic values must always prevail, or that politics is a waste of time.

Changes in governmental tax and subsidy regimes could spur rapid adaptations. Many now agree that the extraction of energy and raw materials should no longer be subsidized and some European nations are moving toward closer linkages between environmental objectives and taxation patterns.[36] Also, some environmentalists have urged specifically that automobile transportation no longer be subsidized.[37] In broad terms, taxation burdens might be shifted at least in part from work (income tax), property ownership, and gross sales to energy, materials use, land use, and waste disposal. Such structural changes would allow the marketplace to gradually handle the multitude of production and consumption decisions associated with improving sustainability.

Such measures, combined with protection of environmentally sensitive lands and regulations to protect human health, could help to effectively integrate environmental and economic values. Also, through green products, green investment options, environmental audits, and other techniques, the private sector and individual consumers can take significant initiatives irrespective of the level of government commitment at a particular time. Those firms and sectors that are best able to anticipate change can make fundamental breakthroughs in both profitability and improved environmental protection (again, see chap. 12). Gains may not be achieved by every industry challenged by environmental values, but losses can often be minimized through far-sighted and ethically enlightened initiatives. Market-based initiatives and sustainability-oriented public policies can offset in part the challenges to environmental values posed by the forces of economic globalization discussed below.

The Environment and Equity

The integration of environmental values and economic values has received more consideration since the late 1980s. A good deal of attention has been devoted as well to the great challenges associated with achieving improved North-South equity and environmental protection simultaneously.[38] But political leaders have given less consideration to the linkages between environmental values and improvements in equity within wealthy economies. Such linkages are nonetheless both real and complex. They are so significant that some argue that environmental values are not likely to be politically successful unless and until major environment-equity tensions are at least partly resolved. Important points of value intersection—sometimes conflictual, sometimes mutually supportive—exist as regards gender and environment, class and environment, race and environment, and regional equity and environment.

Gender provides an interesting starting point because a commonality of interests between environmentalists and feminists has been frequently asserted.[39] Many of the complexities of these debates need not be reiterated here, but three matters are fundamental. The first is human population, the second is the parallel between the domination of women and of nature, and the third is women's distinctive perspective on sustainability.

All three core values of environmentalism would be more easily achieved if the total human population were stabilized or in gradual decline toward an optimal level. This is particularly true for ecology and sustainability values, which in all likelihood are unobtainable unless human population growth is halted. Many of the major objectives of the women's movement are thus essential to environmentalists. Access to family planning services and freedom of choice regarding abortion are obviously important. But perhaps even more important is the fact that there is no stronger determinant of ultimate family size than equal opportunity for women. Environmentalists and the women's movement concur, then, in a fundamental way on issues significant to both.

Second, there are parallels between the domination of women and the domination of nature. These parallels are so strong that they reach into the very structure of our language as in the "rape" of the land, "virgin" forests, and "mother" Earth. Another dimension of the parallel character of male-female and human-nature domination is that in both cases subjectivity is denied. The domination arises out of a self-regarding lack of respect. The habits and attitudes born of one form of domination re-create themselves within the other.

Third, women's distinctive biological (and cultural) role in childbearing and early nurture may well have other environmental implications.

Whether or not this distinctiveness has been overstated in the past, bearing children may well incline women to a greater sensitivity to the needs of future generations.

Sustainability issues are seen by women in perhaps a different light than they are seen by men. So, too, may be the habitat needs of other species. Women have frequently assumed leadership roles within the environmental movement.[40] Overall, there is some potential for cooperation between those advancing gender equity and those seeking environmental protection, and there would appear to be few points of tension.

The linkages between environmental values and class equity values are quite different. Here, tensions have been widespread, particularly over perceived threats to employment opportunities. A sense of threat has been particularly striking in the forest industry, but it has also arisen for workers in the nuclear industry, for coal miners, for ranchers (as regards protection or reintroduction of predators), for highway construction and packaging workers, and for farmers (regarding pesticide use). It exists as well within a variety of polluting industries where the cost of cleanup may appear to threaten competitiveness. It could also exist in the auto industry in the future, though the United Auto Workers' union has had a very long history of positive involvement with conservation and environmental protection.[41]

These tensions are both real and politically significant, but they do not reveal the whole story. As noted above, environmental protection initiatives also generate significant employment opportunities.[42] Renewable energy supply sources are more employment intensive and less environmentally threatening than are energy supply megaprojects. Energy efficiency improvements create jobs in manufacturing, installation, and construction. Recycling is highly labor intensive. Bottle bills, pushed through in ten states by environmental organizations, are net generators of employment. Urban reconfiguration and public transport expenditures create employment, as do pollution abatement and environmental restoration. Overall, the jobs gained may well be more numerous than the jobs put at risk. This does not necessarily help those who lose their jobs, but it could if transitions were accomplished in a more orderly and gradual fashion. Nonetheless, some political tension on the class-environment front is unavoidable.

Environmentalists, including European green parties, have become more thoughtful on such broad questions. Some have suggested that, given advances in the automation of industrial production, the time has or will come when there should be a greater decoupling of employment and income. Wealthy societies could perhaps afford to replace present transfer payments (social security, unemployment insurance, welfare, food stamps) with a universal social income. Net income would remain the same for most people, but some of it would come from a nonemployer source. The income level for some unemployed persons might rise, but only modestly. The largest difference would be that all adults would receive the income and thus there would be no disincentive to working (as with welfare) and no disincentive to education (as with unemployment insurance). Another problem with the present situation is that almost any risk to employment is seen as unacceptable, regardless of the tragedy attendant on continued employment (as in the cutting of the last of the old-growth forests). In effect, the problem lies in the distribution of work and income and the absence of full employment.[43] This may be the single largest political problem involved with the integration of equity values and environmental values, and it thus deserves a great deal of attention in the future.

Also increasingly important are the linkages between racial equity and environmental protection. However, here—as with gender—the interests tend to be parallel, although, as with class, perceptions sometimes diverge. In the 1970s some African American leaders saw environmental protection as likely to divert public funds from social justice needs. Given government's limited domestic budget, this was, and remains, an appropriate concern. But as with the issue of employment (itself, of course, a central concern of all visible minorities), there is another side captured in the new movement for environmental justice. Minorities have historically borne the brunt of occupational hazards, pollution, and waste disposal, including hazardous waste disposal.[44] The realization of this fact has had political and policy effects in some regions and communities in the 1990s, especially in the South. Robert Bullard's book *Dumping in Dixie* carefully portrays the growing environmental awareness among African Americans in their opposition to the disproportionate siting of hazardous waste dumps, incinerators, municipal landfills, plants using heavy metals, and chemical factories in their neighborhoods.[45] More than this, major environmental organizations are paying increasing attention to the environmental issues that affect minorities disproportionately, such as lead poisoning, the hazards faced by farm workers, and the general level of toxic exposures in minority communities.[46] The growing importance of the environmental justice movement in the early 1990s has brought these two important social movements into new forms of cooperation and some prospects for greater mutual respect in the future.[47]

An interesting environmental dimension of both racial and class inequality becomes visible in a closer examination of some of the links between wilderness protection and urban form. Poverty and crime in urban cores (and the associated high public costs for policing, social welfare, and education) have been part of the impetus that drives many families to distant suburban residential locations. Low density suburban sprawl, in turn, reduces the viability of public transportation systems. New construction reduces near-urban habitat and open spaces, and places a double pressure on remaining wilderness locations: as a source for extraction of new building materials and as a refuge from urban pressures (in terms of both the threat of crime and stressful commuting). One can see that it might be easier to alleviate some social and environmental problems simultaneously, rather than to imagine that governments must choose between addressing social problems and environmental problems, or that wilderness protection and environmental justice are somehow in conflict.[48]

Regionally based environment-equity matters also have a potential for future value conflict. For example, the strong push for recycling may have a negative effect on already depressed resource-producing regions. This is particularly pronounced in isolated regions in Canada, where many communities depend on pulp and paper production to survive. New plants to produce paper products from recycled stock will likely locate in high population areas near to the source of supply. Closure of distant mills will hurt some already economically marginal regions. Conversely, older urban cores in the United States, particularly in the Northeast, are as regionally underadvantaged as any places in North America. They may benefit from recycling and, as well, from any turn toward more compact urban areas and the corresponding increase in urban core restoration and public transport expenditures.

All of these environment-equity dilemmas must now be resolved within the context of a globalized economy and political reality. Few policy debates or value conflicts can remain purely domestic issues. What was once national has become international as all nations now struggle to remain competitive in terms of taxation and public spending, wages, technological capability, and environmental standards. Some analysts argue that in an era of globalization and "free trade," equity (in terms of social programs and wealth distribution) and environmental standards are in a world-wide "race to the bottom."[49] In fact, in most wealthy nations in the early 1990s, the rich gained significant further ground on the poor.[50] In many wealthy nations spending on environmental protection has declined throughout the decade.[51] It is possible, however, that these trends can be reversed through cooperation and coordination of policy initiatives between governments.

On the whole, the prospects for integrating equity and environmental values would seem promising, though neither easy nor simple. What is clear is that adding environment to the traditional political agenda will forever change the face of politics. Multidimensionality is accentuated and accelerated. Not that politics was ever simple. But ideology can no longer be seen in simplistic left-right/liberal-conservative terms. Not only the end of the cold war assures this new reality. Widely held environmental values will enormously diversify each citizen's coherent intellectual options while increasing the variety of possible political coalitions and combinations.

The integration of economy, equity, and environment is and must be primarily a political process, one fraught with ethical dilemmas and disputes. Moreover, these matters cannot be resolved solely on the basis of either facts or expertise. Solutions require a thoughtful collective sense of what kind of society we want. In a democracy, fundamental values are matters each of us must establish for ourselves. Democratic institutions succeed or fail on the basis of their ability to integrate citizen values within effective collective decisions. But more than that, our society itself will not succeed in the long run unless we face up to the difficult issues and choices now before us. That in turn requires that most, if not all, citizens understand environmental, economic, and equity values. It also requires both a widespread tolerance for the values of others and an ongoing prospect for broad participation in the political process.

Notes

1. David Easton, *The Political System* (New York: Knopf, 1953).
2. Evidence of wide acceptance of environmental values by the 1980s is contained in *Wildlife and the Public Interest* (New York: Praeger, 1989) and in Riley E. Dunlap, "Polls, Pollution and Politics: Public Opinion on the Environment in the Reagan Era," *Environment* 29 (July–August 1987): 6–11, 32–37.
3. Samuel P. Hays, "From Conservation to Environment: Environmental Politics in the United States Since World War Two," *Environmental Review* 6 (Fall 1982): 20.
4. George Sessions, "The Deep Ecology Movement: A Review," *Environmental Review* 11 (Summer 1987): 107.
5. See Max Oelschlaeger, ed., *After Earth Day: Continuing the Conservation Effort* (Denton: University of North Texas Press, 1992), chaps. by Susan Bratton and Oelschlaeger.
6. Ronald Inglehart, *The Silent Revolution: Changing Values and Political Styles among Western Publics* (Princeton, N.J.: Princeton University Press, 1977).
7. Riley E. Dunlap and K. Van Liere, "The New Environmental Paradigm," *Journal of Environmental Education* 9, no. 4 (1978): 10–19; and Lester W. Milbrath, *Environmentalists: Vanguard for a New Society* (Albany: State University of New York Press, 1984).
8. The movement of environmental values into the mainstream of American political culture is established and assessed in Willett Kempton, James S. Boster, and Jennifer A. Hartley, *Environmental Values in American Culture* (Cambridge, Mass.: MIT Press, 1995). Confirmation and updates in a comparative context are available in Alan Frizzell and Jon H. Pammett, *Shades of Green: Environmental Attitudes in Canada and Around the World* (Ottawa: Carleton University Press, 1997).
9. Robert Paehlke, *Environmentalism and the Future of Progressive Politics* (New Haven, Conn.: Yale University Press, 1989), 144–145.
10. Max Oelschlaeger, *The Idea of Wilderness: From Prehistory to the Age of Ecology* (New Haven, Conn.: Yale University Press, 1991), 292. For other views on these concerns see William Cronon, ed., *Uncommon Ground: Toward Reinventing Nature* (New York: Norton, 1995).
11. Ibid.
12. See Warwick Fox, *Toward a Transpersonal Ecology* (Boston: Shambhala, 1990); see also Bill Devall and George Sessions, *Deep Ecology: Living as if Nature Mattered* (Salt Lake City: Peregrine Smith Books, 1985), and Arne Naess, *Ecology, Community, and Lifestyle: Outline of an Ecosophy* (Cambridge: Cambridge University Press, 1989).
13. See, for example, Tom Regan, *All That Dwell Therein: Animal Rights and Environmental Ethics* (Berkeley and Los Angeles: University of California Press, 1982), and the extensive work of Peter Singer.
14. Oelschlaeger, *Idea of Wilderness*, ix.
15. Charles A. Wise and Kirk Emerson, "Regulatory Takings: The Emerging Doctrine and Its Implications for Public Administration," *Administration and Society* 26 (1994): 305–336.
16. Richard Lester, *Meltdown on Main Street* (New York: Plume/Penguin, 1997), 78.
17. Aaron Wildavsky, *Searching for Safety* (New Brunswick, N.J.: Transaction, 1988).
18. Mark Sagoff, *The Economy of the Earth* (New York: Cambridge University Press, 1988), 195–196.
19. Quoted at page 681 in Bob Benenson, "House Easily Passes Bills to Limit Regulations," *Congressional Quarterly Weekly Report*, March 4, 1995, 679–682; see also Margaret Kriz, "Risky Business," *National Journal*, February 18, 1995, 417–421.
20. Lester Milbrath, *Envisioning a Sustainable Society* (Albany: State University of New York Press, 1989), 338.
21. Joel J. Kassiola, *The Death of Industrial Civilization* (Albany: State University of New York Press, 1990).
22. See World Commission on Environment and Development, *Our Common Future* (New York: Oxford University Press, 1987), and, more recently, Hal Kane, "Shifting to Sus-

tainable Industries," in *State of the World, 1996,* ed. Lester R. Brown et al. (New York: Norton, 1996), 152–167, and John Elkington, *Cannibals With Forks: The Triple Bottom Line of 21st Century Business* (Stony Creek, Conn.: New Society Publishers, 1998).

23. Kempton, Boster, and Hartley, *Environmental Values,* 255–270; see especially responses to questions 23, 37, 42, 92, and 103.

24. Patrick Mazza, "The Spotted Owl as Scapegoat," *Capitalism, Nature, Socialism* (June 1990): 100.

25. Laura Westra, *An Environmental Proposal for Ethics: The Principle of Integrity* (Lanham, Md.: Rowman and Littlefield, 1994), xvii. See also Holmes Rolston III, *Conserving Natural Value* (New York: Columbia University Press, 1994).

26. Michael L. Nieswiadomy, "Economics and Resource Conservation," in *After Earth Day,* ed. Oelschlaeger, 123–124.

27. George Sessions, "Radical Environmentalism in the 90s," in *After Earth Day,* ed. Oelschlaeger, 16–27.

28. The best current source on human population issues is Joel E. Cohen, *How Many People Can the Earth Support?* (New York: Norton, 1995).

29. Robert C. Paehlke, "Occupational and Environmental Health Linkages," in *Controlling Chemical Hazards,* ed. Raymond P. Cote and Peter G. Wells (London: Unwin Hyman, 1991), 175–197.

30. See, for example, David Moscovitz, Steven Nadel, and Howard Geller, *Increasing the Efficiency of Electricity Production and Use: Barriers and Strategies* (Washington, D.C.: American Council for an Energy-Efficient Economy, 1991).

31. See, for example, Marcia D. Lowe, "Rethinking Urban Transport," in *State of the World, 1991,* ed. Lester R. Brown (New York: Norton, 1991), 56–73.

32. Peter Newman and Jeffrey Kenworthy, *Cities and Automobile Dependence: An International Sourcebook* (Hants, England: Gower, 1989).

33. Charles E. Lindblom, *Politics and Markets* (New York: Basic Books, 1977).

34. For more information on simultaneous gains noted in this paragraph, see, for example, Moscovitz, Nadel, and Geller, *Increasing Efficiency; State of the World, 1991,* ed. Brown, and *State of the World, 1992,* ed. Lester R. Brown (New York: Norton, 1992).

35. Kirk R. Smith, "Air Pollution: Assessing Total Exposure in the United States," *Environment* 30 (October 1988): 10–15, 33–38.

36. Regarding subsidy removals, see Jim MacNeill, Pieter Winsemius, and Taizo Yakushiji, *Beyond Interdependence* (New York: Oxford University Press, 1991); regarding environmental taxation, see Timothy O'Riordan, ed., *Ecotaxation* (London: Earthscan, 1997) and Robert Gale and Stephan Barg, eds., *Green Budget Reform: An International Casebook of Leading Practices* (London: Earthscan, 1995).

37. Francesca Lyman, "Rethinking Our Transportation Future," *E Magazine* 1 (September-October 1990): 34–41.

38. See, for example, MacNeill, Winsemius, and Yakushiji, *Beyond Interdependence,* and Lorraine Elliot, *The Global Politics of the Environment* (New York: NYU Press, 1998).

39. Perhaps the best single introductory article is still Karen J. Warren, "Feminism and Ecology: Making Connections," *Environmental Ethics* 9 (1987): 3–20. See also Roger Keil et al., eds., *Political Ecology: Global and Local* (London: Routledge, 1998), 193–255; Rosi Braidotti, *Women, the Environment and Sustainable Development: Towards a Theoretical Synthesis* (London: Zed Books, 1994); and Elliot, *The Global Politics of the Environment,* 147–157.

40. Carolyn Merchant, "Earth Care: Women and the Environmental Movement," *Environment* 23 (June 1981): 6–13, 38–40.

41. Robert Paehlke, "Environnementalisme et syndicalisme au Canada anglais et aux Etats-Unis," *Sociologie et Sociétés* 13 (April 1981): 161–179.

42. See Paehlke, *Environmentalism and the Future of Progressive Politics;* Michael Renner, "Creating Sustainable Jobs in Industrial Economies," in *State of the World, 1992,* ed. Brown; and Robert Paehlke, "Work in a Sustainable Society," in *Political Ecology: Global and Local,* ed. Keil et al.

43. Regarding work distribution, see Stanley Aronowitz and William DiFazio, *The Jobless Future* (Minneapolis: University of Minnesota Press, 1994); and Bruce O'Hara, *Working Harder Isn't Working* (Vancouver: New Star Books, 1993).

44. James C. Robinson, *Toil and Toxics: Workplace Struggles and Political Strategies for Occupational Health* (Berkeley and Los Angeles: University of California Press, 1991).

45. Robert D. Bullard, *Dumping in Dixie: Race, Class, and Environmental Quality* (Boulder, Colo.: Westview, 1991); and Charles Lee, *Toxic Waste and Race in the United States* (New York: United Church of Christ Commission for Racial Justice, 1987).

46. See, for example, the extensive treatment of environmental justice issues in *Environmental Action* (January–February 1990): 19–30, and the extensive sources cited therein.

47. The evolving politics of race and environment is discussed in Robert Bullard, ed., *Unequal Protection: Environmental Justice and Communities of Color* (San Francisco: Sierra Club Books, 1994); Christopher H. Foreman, Jr., *The Promise and Peril of Environmental Justice* (Washington, D.C.: Brookings, 1998); and Robert Bullard and Glenn S. Johnson, eds., *Just Transportation: Dismantling Race and Class Barriers to Mobility* (Stony Creek, Conn.: New Society Publishers, 1997).

48. For a broad overview of the links between social equity and sustainability, see Michael Carley and Philippe Spapens, *Sharing the World* (London: Earthscan, 1998); for an extended discussion of wilderness protection and environmental justice, see Robert Paehlke, "Biodiversity: The Policy Challenge," in *The Living Environment*, ed. Stephen Bocking (Peterborough, Ontario: Broadview Press, forthcoming).

49. William Greider, *One World, Ready or Not* (New York: Simon and Schuster, 1997); Hans-Peter Martin and Harald Schumann, *Global Trap* (Montreal: Black Rose Books, 1997); and Joshua Karliner, *The Corporate Planet* (San Francisco: Sierra Club Books, 1997).

50. Regarding recent wealth distribution trends, see, for example, Jeffrey Madrick, *The End of Affluence* (New York: Random House, 1997), and Robert H. Frank and Philip J. Cook, *The Winner-Take-All Society* (New York: Penguin, 1995).

51. Regarding reductions in environmental budgets, see Norman J. Vig and Michael E. Kraft, *Environmental Policy in the 1990s*, 3d ed. (Washington, D.C.: CQ Press, 1997), chap. 6, and chap. 6 in this volume.

5

Presidential Leadership and the Environment: From Reagan to Clinton

Norman J. Vig

Today we have a clear responsibility to conquer one of the most important challenges of the twenty-first century—the challenge of climate change—with an environmentally sound and economically strong strategy.

—President Bill Clinton,
National Geographic Society, October 22, 1997

What the president is proposing [on climate change] *is unilateral economic disarmament by the United States.*

—Rep. Thomas J. Bliley Jr., R-Va.,
Chairman of the House Commerce Committee

These remarks of the president and the powerful Republican chairman of the House Commerce Committee in October 1997, less than six weeks before the Kyoto conference on climate change, capture much of the frustration of the Clinton presidency in pursuing its environmental policy goals.[1] Bill Clinton and Al Gore had come to power with an ambitious environmental agenda. But the conservative Republican majority that won control of Congress in 1994 had no interest in this agenda; indeed, its leaders were determined to roll back much of the environmental regulation of the previous two decades (see chaps. 1 and 6). Nor had the Clinton-Gore administration been able to mobilize support within its own party for many of its environmental initiatives: the Senate had voted 95–0 in July 1997 against any climate change agreement that might seriously weaken the U.S. economy or that did not impose restrictions on developing countries as well as on industrial nations. The result was an agreement at Kyoto that satisfied no one and has little chance of ratification by the Senate in its present form. Nevertheless, despite a hostile Congress, Clinton was able to utilize the Oval Office to pursue many of his other environmental goals. Although unable to enact much new legislation, he and Gore used their formidable executive powers to reform environmental administration and reshape the terms of policy debate for the future.

We have often had divided government in America, but rarely have partisan and ideological differences reached the level of bitterness they did during the Clinton presidency. Clinton's own conduct in office contributed to the hostility that ultimately led to his impeachment by the House of Representatives in December 1998 and acquittal by the Senate in February 1999. The causes and effects of these historic actions will be debated for years to come. But whatever the final verdict on Clinton's tenure, it is important to examine the powers of the presidency to effect environmental change in various ways.

Presidents have used their powers over the past century to rally public support for environmental protection. In the early 1900s Theodore Roosevelt proclaimed the conservation era and set aside vast areas of public land for national forests, parks, and wildlife refuges.[2] During the New Deal in the 1930s, Franklin D. Roosevelt put millions of unemployed people to work on conservation and reclamation projects.[3] More recently, Richard Nixon, Gerald Ford, and Jimmy Carter dealt with an array of new issues involving air, water, and soil pollution; energy development; and toxic chemical use. By the late 1980s a host of international environmental problems including acid rain, stratospheric ozone depletion, and global warming were coming to a head. Despite notable lapses—especially during the administration of Ronald Reagan—presidents have played an important role in advancing environmental protection.

This chapter examines the impact recent presidents have had on national environmental policies, with particular emphasis on the administrations of Reagan, Bush, and Clinton. First, we briefly consider the general powers and limitations of the presidency and their relationship to policymaking.

Presidential Powers and Constraints

From a policy cycle perspective, presidents obviously have great potential influence (see chap. 1). First, they have a major role in *agenda setting*. They can raise issues to the public's attention, define the terms of public debate, and rally public opinion and constituency support through speeches, press conferences, and other media events. Without presidential endorsement, major policy initiatives have rarely been successful. Second, they can take the lead in *policy formulation* by devoting presidential staff and other resources to particular issues, by mobilizing expertise inside and outside government, and by consulting widely with interest groups and members of Congress in designing and proposing legislation. They can also stop legislation through use of the veto power. Third, presidents use their powers as chief executive to shape *policy implementation*. They make appointments to federal agencies, propose annual operating budgets, issue executive orders, and oversee management and efficiency in the bureaucracy. Another important function is regulatory oversight; that is, the president influences regulatory policymaking by agencies such as the Environmental Protection Agency (EPA). Finally, presidents play an increasingly important role in *international leadership*, as many environmental issues have become international or global in scope.

At the same time, presidents cannot govern alone; they are only part of a government of "separated powers."[4] They must rely on Congress to enact legislation and provide the funding to carry out all activities of the federal government. When Congress and the presidency are controlled by different parties, the president may have little control over the policy agenda (see chap. 6). But even when the president's own party has a majority in one or both houses, majority coalitions on particular issues may be difficult if not impossible to build. Moreover, congressional committees have substantial powers of legislative initiative, administrative oversight, and investigation that can blunt executive initiatives and embarrass the president. Nearly all major rules and regulations are also challenged in the courts by affected parties, often tying up administrative actions in litigation that goes on for years (see chap. 7). Finally, the media scrutinize the president more closely than any other public official and can make or break a president's reputation. Well before Clinton's troubled presidency, some scholars had argued that the era of bold presidential leadership is over.[5]

Nevertheless, we can assume that much will depend on the particular circumstances in which a president comes to office and on the skill of each incumbent in exploiting opportunities. Scholars of the presidency have pointed to several major variables in analyzing presidential performance.

One is the nature of the president's agenda and personal leadership style. Some presidents are "active" in the sense that they vigorously utilize presidential powers to pursue policy change. Others are more "passive" or pursue only incremental change; they are sometimes called "guardians." Agendas may be "expansive" in the sense of advocating new governmental programs, "contractionary" in seeking to reverse existing policies or reduce the role of government, or "consolidative" if their goal is to preserve or refine past gains.[6] Thus Reagan entered office as an "active contractionary" president, Bush as a "passive consolidator," and Clinton as an "active expansive" leader.

Whatever the president's personal agenda, his role also depends on the nature of the Congress he inherits.[7] If a president faces a Congress that is either split (with one party controlling each house, as during 1981–1986) or in the hands of the opposition party (as during 1987–1992 and 1995–2000), he may be forced to limit his policy agenda and choose between a more confrontational or conciliatory style of leadership. President Bush opted for a conciliatory, bipartisan strategy during the 101st Congress (1989–1990), but retreated to a more negative, confrontational stance during the 102d (1991–1992) as the Democratic Congress became more assertive in pursuing its own legislative agenda. (Bush exercised the veto twenty-one times in 1992 alone.) President Clinton attempted to capitalize on his party's control of the 103d Congress by following a generally partisan but conciliatory legislative strategy, yet he had only limited success as his expansive programs united the Republican opposition and alienated many conservative Democrats. After the 1994 election produced a radically different Congress, Clinton had little choice but to adopt an essentially defensive, confrontational posture, which continued during his second term.

A third factor is how the president organizes his office and utilizes his executive powers. Some presidents manage the White House much more coherently and effectively than others. Some, like Dwight Eisenhower, Nixon, and Reagan, have preferred a centralized, hierarchical style of management that concentrates power in a chief of staff and other top assistants. Others, like Franklin Roosevelt, John Kennedy, and Clinton, opted for a more open and decentralized "spokes in a wheel" model that encourages competition for the ear of the president from many policy sources.[8] Organizational styles seem to reflect the president's personality and temperament more than any model's inherent advantage, but some staff arrangements are markedly more successful than others in developing effective political strategies and managing the policy agenda.

A final dimension of presidential leadership concerns public confidence: ultimately, presidential power rests on an incumbent's ability to persuade the public that he is on the right course. Some presidents are much better public communicators than others (for example, Reagan as compared with Carter or Bush). In part, this is a matter of rhetorical skill, but the substance of the message is also important.[9] Clinton was able to maintain high public opinion ratings even during his impeachment trial because of his positive achievements and exceptional ability to articulate policy goals.

With these criteria in mind, we can turn to the records of the last three presidents in defining and shaping environmental policies. It should be emphasized that aside from public land use issues, environmental problems did not become a major federal responsibility until 1970. Riding the wave of the new environmental movement that peaked that year, President Nixon declared an "environmental decade," supported passage of the National Environmental Policy Act and Clean Air Act, and established the Environmental Protection Agency by executive order. Although Nixon later retreated from leadership on environmental issues, subsequent presidents largely cooperated with Congress in enacting a remarkable array of bipartisan environmental legislation in the 1970s (see app. 1).[10]

The Reagan Revolution: Challenge to Environmentalism

The "environmental decade" came to an abrupt halt with Reagan's landslide victory in 1980. Although the environment was not a major issue in the election, Reagan was the first president to come to office with an avowedly antienvironmental agenda. Reflecting the Sagebrush Rebellion—an attempt by several western states to claim ownership of federal lands—as well as long years of public relations work for corporate and conservative causes, Reagan viewed environmental conservation as fundamentally at odds with economic growth and prosperity. He saw environmental regulation as a barrier to "supply side" economics and sought to reverse or weaken many of the policies of the previous decade.[11] Although only partially successful, Reagan's contractionary agenda laid the groundwork for a renewed attack on environmental policy a decade later.

After a period of economic decline and weak leadership, Reagan's victory provided a strong mandate for policy change. With a new Republican majority in the Senate, he was able to gain congressional support for the Economic Recovery Act of 1981, which embodied much of his program. The law reduced income taxes by nearly 25 percent and deeply cut spending for environmental and social programs. Despite this initial victory, however, Reagan faced a Congress that was divided on most issues and did not support his broader environmental agenda. On the contrary, the bipartisan majority that had enacted most of the environmental legislation of the 1970s remained largely intact.

Faced with this situation, Reagan turned to what has been termed an "administrative presidency."[12] Essentially, this involved an attempt to change federal policies by maximizing control of *policy implementation within the executive branch*. That is, rather than trying to rewrite legislation, Reagan attempted to alter its content and effect through control of the bureaucracy.

The administrative strategy initially had four major components: careful screening of all appointees to environmental and other agencies to ensure compliance with Reagan's ideological agenda; tight policy coordination through cabinet councils and White House staff; deep cuts in the budgets of environmental agencies and programs; and an enhanced form of regulatory oversight to eliminate or revise regulations considered burdensome by industry.

Reagan's appointment of officials who were overtly hostile to the mission of their agencies aroused strong opposition from the environmental community. In particular, his selection of Anne M. Gorsuch (later Burford) to head the Environmental Protection Agency and James G. Watt as secretary of interior provoked controversy from the beginning because both were attorneys who had spent long years litigating against environmental regulation. Both made it clear that they intended to rewrite the rules and procedures of their agencies to accommodate industries such as mining, logging, and oil and gas.

In the White House, Reagan lost no time in changing the policy machinery to accomplish the same goal. He attempted to abolish the Council on Environmental Quality (CEQ), and when that effort failed because it would require congressional legislation, he drastically cut its staff and ignored its members' advice. In its place he appointed Vice President George Bush to head a new Task Force on Regulatory Relief to review and propose revisions or rescissions of regulations in response to complaints from business. All regulations were analyzed by a staff agency, the Office of Information and Regulatory Affairs (OIRA) in the Office of Management and Budget. To ensure broader policy coordination, Reagan appointed the Cabinet Council on Natural Resources and the Environment under Watt to oversee the EPA and other agencies. This hierarchical organization was designed to exert maximum policy control from above.

Finally, Reagan's budget cuts had major effects on the capacity of environmental agencies to implement their growing policy mandates. The EPA lost approximately one-third of its operating budget and one-fifth of its personnel in the early 1980s. The CEQ lost most of its staff and barely continued to function. In the Interior Department and elsewhere, funds were shifted from environmental to development programs.[13]

Perhaps the most controversial aspect of Reagan's pincer movement on environmental policy was his use of enhanced regulatory oversight through OIRA. This shadowy body, which originated in the Carter administration to deal with paperwork reduction, operated behind closed doors without the normal rules of administrative procedure and public accountability. Executive Order 12291 of February 1981 required all agencies to submit "regulatory impact statements" to OIRA. These statements were to include cost-benefit analyses justifying regulatory activity. Control was further extended by Executive Order 12498 of 1985, which required agencies to submit regulatory calendars a year in advance to allow more time to scrutinize pending regulations. Using this authority, OIRA held up, reviewed, and revised hundreds of EPA and other regulations to reduce their effect on industry. Although regulatory oversight is an accepted and necessary function of the modern presidency, the Reagan White House's effort to shape and control all regulatory activity in the interests of political clients raised serious questions of improper administrative procedure and violation of statutory intent.[14]

Not surprisingly, Congress responded by investigating OIRA procedures and other activities of Reagan appointees, especially Burford and Watt. Burford came under heavy attack for confidential dealings with business and political interests that allegedly led to "sweetheart deals" on such matters as Superfund cleanups. After refusing to disclose documents, she was found in contempt of Congress and forced to resign (along with twenty other high EPA officials), in March 1983. Watt was pilloried in Congress for his efforts to open virtually all public lands (including wilderness areas) and offshore coastal areas to mining and oil and gas development. In response, Democrats in the House attached riders to appropriations bills blocking many of his actions. Watt resigned later in 1983 over some ill-advised remarks he made about the ethnic composition of a commission appointed to investigate his coal-leasing policies. By that time he had alienated almost everyone in Congress.[15]

Because of these embarrassments and widespread public and congressional opposition to weakening environmental protection, Reagan's deregulatory campaign was largely spent by the end of his first term. Recognizing that his policies had backfired, the president took few new initiatives during his second term. His appointees to the EPA and Interior after 1983 were able to diffuse some of the political conflict generated by Watt and Burford. EPA administrators (William Ruckelshaus and Lee Thomas) were able to restore some funding and credibility to their agency, though the agency was permanently weakened by the drastic budget and personnel cuts of the early 1980s that made it difficult to cope with new legislative mandates (see chap. 8).

In other respects the 1980s were years of lost opportunity. The initiatives of the Ford and Carter administrations to promote fuel conservation and renewable energy development were largely abandoned, leading to renewed growth in energy consumption and oil imports after 1986. Opposition from the Reagan administration—as well as from certain key Democratic leaders in Congress, such as Sen. Robert Byrd of West Virginia and Rep. John Dingell of Michigan—blocked revision of the Clean Air Act to deal with acid rain, urban smog, and toxic pollutants throughout the decade. A new range of international environmental issues received only limited attention through 1988. The one exception was the leadership exerted by the United States in negotiating the Montreal protocol (1987) to limit production of chlorofluorocarbons (CFCs) and other ozone-depleting gases. On other international issues the administration reversed or weakened previous policy commitments. For example, it opposed the Law of the Sea Treaty and cut off funding for UN programs to promote family planning and population control.

Reagan clearly lost the battle of public opinion on the environment. His policies had the unintended effect of revitalizing environmental organizations. Membership in such groups increased by leaps and bounds, and polls indicated a steady growth in the public's concern for the environment that peaked in the late 1980s (see chap. 3). It is not surprising that Bush decided to distance himself from Reagan's environmental record in the 1988 election.

The Bush Transition

George Bush's presidency returned to a more moderate tradition of Republican leadership, particularly in the first two years. While promising to "stay the course" on Reagan's economic policies, Bush also pledged a "kinder and gentler" America. Although his domestic policy agenda was the most limited of any recent president, it included action on the environment. Indeed, during the campaign Bush declared himself a "conservationist" in the tradition of Teddy Roosevelt and promised to be an "environmental president." Like President Nixon twenty years earlier, he rode a wave of environmental concern during the first half of his term that culminated in passage of a new Clean Air Act. But, also like Nixon, he retreated to a harsher stance on the environment later in his term in the face of economic recession and business pressures. Indeed, by 1992 he sounded much like Reagan.

In a remarkable speech at Detroit's Metropark, near Lake Erie, on August 31, 1988, Bush laid out an ambitious environmental agenda calling for a new Clean Air Act and other reforms. Among other things, Bush committed himself to a program of "no net loss" of wetlands and called for strict enforcement of toxic waste laws. In reference to global warming, Bush stated, "Those who think we are powerless to do anything about the 'greenhouse effect' are forgetting about the 'White House effect.'" "In my first year in office," he said, "I will convene a global conference on the environment at the White House. . . . And we will act."[16]

If Bush surprised almost everyone by seizing the initiative on what most assumed was a strong issue for the Democrats, he impressed environmentalists even more by soliciting their advice and by appointing a number of environmental leaders to his administration.[17] William Reilly, the highly respected president of the World Wildlife Fund and the Conservation Foundation, became EPA administrator; and Michael Deland, formerly New England director of the EPA, became chairman of the Council on Environmental Quality. Bush promised to restore the CEQ to an influential role and made it clear that he intended to work closely with the Democratic Congress to pass a new Clean Air Act early in his administration.

Yet Bush's nominees to head the public land and natural resource agencies were not much different from those of the Reagan administration. In particular, his choice of Manuel Lujan Jr., a ten-term retired congressman (R-N.M.), to serve as secretary of the interior indicated that no major departures would be made in western land policies. The president's top White House advisers were also much more conservative on environmental matters than were Reilly and Deland.

Bush saw himself more as a consolidator and guardian of Republican gains than as a policy innovator. Indeed, the precautionary principle of "do no harm" appeared to guide his approach to leadership.[18] He did not attempt to restore the "administrative presidency." Lacking any clear agenda, he saw little need to exert tight control over the bureaucracy. He also had more respect for professional expertise than did Reagan and preferred a more pragmatic, collegial style of decision making. Although Bush appointed a strong chief of staff, John Sununu, he preferred to have several top aides work out policy compromises as a "team." On environmental matters, this approach gave enormous influence to several White House officials: Sununu, OMB director Richard Darman, science adviser D. Allan Bromley, and chairman of the Council of Economic Advisers Michael Boskin. This quadrumvirate, all former university professors, was to exert an increasingly conservative influence on policy.

Bush pursued a bipartisan legislative strategy in building a coalition to amend the Clean Air Act. Indeed, he had few other options, as the Democrats had large majorities in both houses of Congress. His party held only 175 seats in the House, the fewest of any twentieth-century president starting his term. At the same time, traditional Republican constituencies in business and industry were certain to oppose major environmental initiatives. Like President Nixon in 1970, he would have to take the lead to overcome this resistance and seek a bipartisan majority for new legislation.

Bush accomplished this in passage of the Clean Air Act of 1990, arguably the single most important legislative achievement of his presidency. His draft bill, sent to Congress on July 21, 1989, had three major goals: to control acid rain by reducing sulfur dioxide (SO_2) emissions from coal-burning power plants by nearly half by 2000; to reduce air pollution in eighty urban areas that still had not met 1977 air quality standards; and to lower emissions of 200 airborne toxic chemicals by 75 to 90 percent by 2000. To achieve the acid precipitation goals—to which the White House devoted most of its attention—Bush proposed an innovative approach advocated by environmental economists that relies on marketable pollution allowances rather than "command and control" regulation to achieve emission reductions more efficiently (see chap. 9).

Bush's staff negotiated with Senate majority leader George Mitchell, D-Maine, and others behind closed doors for ten weeks in early 1990 to reach a bipartisan Senate compromise on the basic outlines of the bill. Many of the technical details were subsequently filled in by the House Energy and Commerce Committee and by a joint conference committee. But without White House leadership, it is unlikely that the ten-year stalemate on clean air legislation would have been broken. As Richard Cohen concluded, "Ultimately the Clean Air Act showed that presidents matter. Once Bush was elected and decided to keep his vague clean-air campaign promises, the many constraints of divided government disappeared."[19]

The president drew a line against any further commitments in another highly contentious area: what to do about global climate change, especially pressures for the United States to agree to an international convention to stabilize CO_2 emissions. Although Bush had promised to confront "the greenhouse effect" with "the White House effect," it soon became apparent that strong forces within the administration (as well as from energy industries) opposed any policy that would limit fossil fuel production and consumption.

Climate change policy was formally put under control of the Domestic Policy Council, chaired by science adviser Allan Bromley. Sununu, Darman, and Boskin were skeptical of climate change theories and were concerned with the economic costs of limiting fossil fuel consumption, an area in which little information was available.[20] Other advice, including that from William Reilly, got a hostile reception in the White House.

President Bush, who showed little personal interest in the subject, thus adopted a policy stance on climate change similar to Reagan's policy on acid rain: more research was needed. In the meantime, the administration would follow a "no regrets" approach: actions would be taken against the possibility of global warming only if they could be fully justified on other grounds. For example, production of CFCs, which were considered a potent greenhouse gas as well as an ozone-depleting chemical, could be phased out because of their potential impact on the ozone layer. Thus, while the president substantially increased funding for global climate research and development (to a combined total of more than $1 billion annually) and supported accelerated curtailment of CFCs, he continued to resist all pressures to limit CO_2 emissions.

During the last eighteen months of the Bush administration, Vice President Dan Quayle entered the spotlight as head of the Council on Competitiveness, an obscure White House body that Bush had appointed in 1989. The "Quayle Council"—which included the secretaries of treasury and commerce, White House counsel C. Boyden Gray, and Sununu, Darman, and Boskin—assumed a role similar to that of Bush's own Task Force on Regulatory Relief in the early Reagan administration. (Its powers were later justified on the same legal basis, namely Reagan's Executive Order 12291 of 1981.) Its function was to invite and respond to industry complaints of excessive regulation, to analyze the costs and benefits of regulation, and to question any new regulations that were considered unnecessarily burdensome. It operated in secrecy, frequently pressuring the EPA and other agencies to ease regulations. During 1991 the council began to intervene in regulatory processes to rewrite environmental rules and regulations. And although the White House blocked some of the council's proposed orders during the campaign because they were considered too controversial, Bush and Quayle continued to push for reduced regulation.[21]

But it was probably Bush's stance toward the UN Conference on Environment and Development, held in June 1992, that most defined his environmental image. The president threatened to boycott the historic summit until he had ensured that the climate change convention to be signed would contain no binding targets for CO_2 reduction. He further alienated much of the world as well as the American environmental community by refusing to sign the biodiversity treaty at the conference, despite efforts by his delegation chief, William Reilly, to seek a last-minute compromise. To add insult to injury, Reilly's cable to the White House was leaked to the press, apparently by a Quayle Council staff member.[22] Thus, despite Bush's other accomplishments in foreign policy, the United States was isolated and embarrassed in international environmental diplomacy (see chap. 13).

In summary, what began as a productive environmental administration deteriorated into defensive disarray in its final year. Many environmentalists who had supported Bush were dismayed by the tenor of his reelection campaign, which became increasingly negative, angry, and harsh. In retrospect, Bush's retreat was an indication of more profound changes to come in American politics.

The Clinton Presidency: Embattled Environmentalism

Environmental issues were clearly overshadowed by the economy and other controversies during the 1992 election. According to one exit poll, only 6 percent of voters considered the environment one of the most important issues, ranking it ninth in importance. However, "green" voters reported that they voted for Clinton over Bush by more than a 5–1 margin.[23] Clinton and Gore also received endorsements from the Sierra Club, the League of Conservation Voters, and other environmental organizations.

Not surprisingly, the Clinton ticket won the support of most environmentalists. In early 1992 vice presidential candidate Al Gore, regarded as the Senate's leading environmentalist, had published a best-selling book, *Earth in the Balance.* Gore's environmental credentials were an important factor in his nomination because Clinton's environmental record as governor of Arkansas was mediocre at best. Under attack from both the White House and Democratic rival Jerry Brown, Clinton acknowledged his shortcomings in an Earth Day speech in April 1992, but he promised strong environmental action as president. The Democratic platform also took a strong environmental stance.[24]

Clinton's campaign promises included many environmental pledges: to raise the corporate average fuel economy (CAFE) standard for automobiles; encourage mass transit programs; increase the use of natural gas and oppose increased reliance on nuclear power; support renewable energy research and development; create a new solid waste reduction program and provide other incentives for recycling; pass a new Clean Water Act with standards for non-point sources; reform the Superfund program; tighten enforcement of toxic waste laws; protect ancient forests; make "no net loss" of wetlands a reality; preserve the Arctic National Wildlife Refuge as a wilderness area; emphasize pollution prevention and use of market forces to reward conservation and penalize polluters; limit U.S. CO_2 emissions to 1990 levels by 2000; negotiate more debt-for-nature swaps to preserve precious lands such as tropical rain forests; and restore funding to UN population programs.[25]

Beyond this impressive list of commitments, Clinton and Gore departed from traditional rhetoric about the relationship between environmental protection and economic growth. They argued that the jobs-versus-environment debate presented a "false choice" because environmental cleanup creates jobs and the future competitiveness of the U.S. economy will depend on developing environmentally clean, energy-efficient technologies. They proposed a variety of investment incentives and infrastructure projects to promote such "green" technologies. All of these promises created high expectations among environmentalists.

The Green Administration

President Clinton's early actions indicated that he intended to deliver on his environmental agenda. His appointments to key environmental positions were largely applauded by the environmental community, though there was some grumbling that more members of its ranks were not placed in higher positions.[26] Perhaps most important to them was the fact that Gore was given the lead responsibility for formulating and coordinating environmental policy. His influence was quickly seen in the reorganization of the White House and in Clinton's budget proposals, which contained elements of the new thinking on sustainable development that he and Gore had espoused during the campaign.

One of the administration's first acts was to abolish the Quayle Council on Competitiveness. Plans were announced to replace the Council on Environmental Quality with a new Office of Environmental Policy (OEP). The new office was to coordinate departmental policies on environmental issues and to ensure integration of environmental considerations into the work of other policy bodies such as the Domestic Policy Council, the National Security Council, and the new National Economic Council. The OEP director, Kathleen McGinty, and EPA administrator Carol Browner were both former Senate environmental aides of Gore.[27] Browner was given cabinet status pending enactment of legislation to transform the EPA into a cabinet department, and McGinty coordinated domestic environmental policy in the White House. There was also a considerable strengthening of the president's staff for international environmental affairs. Former senator Timothy Wirth was appointed the first under secretary of state for global affairs in the State Department, and Eileen Claussen, formerly head of atmospheric programs at EPA, became special assistant to the president for global environmental affairs at the National Security Council. A new President's Council on Sustainable Development was also appointed in June 1993.

Other appointments to the cabinet and executive office staffs were largely proenvironment, though they tended to be competent pragmatists rather than radicals. The most notable environmental leader was Bruce Babbitt, a former Arizona governor and president of the League of Conservation Voters, who was appointed secretary of the interior. In contrast to his predecessors in the Reagan and Bush administrations, Babbitt came to office with a strong reform agenda for western public land management.[28] Several environmental activists from such organizations as the Wilderness Society and the Audubon Society were also appointed to influential policy positions in his department.

Clinton's managerial style, like that of Franklin Roosevelt, favored freewheeling competition of ideas from many advisers to allow him to deliberate on policy options before making decisions. This "multiple advocacy" model differs sharply from the more hierarchical organization of the White House under strong chiefs of staff in the Reagan and Bush administrations.[29] Clinton appointed his boyhood friend and fellow Arkansan, Thomas F. "Mack" McLarty III, as his first chief of staff. McLarty, who had no experience in Washington politics, was not regarded as a success and was replaced by former representative Leon Panetta, in June 1994. He and subsequent chiefs struggled to overcome the disorder of the Clinton White House with limited success.[30]

The Frustrated Presidency

Although Clinton entered office with an expansive agenda and great talent and enthusiasm for policymaking, his administration quickly got bogged down in peripheral controversies that undermined confidence in his presidency. Disputes over gays in the military, Supreme Court nominees, the White House travel office, and the suicide of White House counsel Vincent Foster all derailed the administration during its first six months. Despite considerable success in enacting an economic program and other legislation during his first year in office, congressional blockage of health care reform and "gridlock" on most other initiatives during 1994 proved disastrous for the president. The Republican sweep in the midterm congressional elections appeared to be a repudiation of the Clinton administration as much as of Congress. Overall, Clinton's first two years turned out to be enormously frustrating.[31]

Two events early in the term gave the administration an appearance of environmental policy failure. Babbitt promptly launched a campaign to "revolutionize" western land use policies, including a proposal in Clinton's first budget to raise grazing fees on public lands closer to private market levels (something natural resource economists had advocated for many years). The predictable result was a furious outcry from cattle ranchers and their members of Congress. After meeting with several western Democratic senators, Clinton backed down and removed the proposal from the bill. Babbitt was left to fight a humiliating losing battle on the issue without presidential support.[32] Much the same thing happened on the "Btu tax." This was a proposal to levy a broad-based tax on the energy content of fuels as a means of promoting energy conservation and raising revenue. Originally included in the president's budget package at Gore's request, it was eventually dropped in favor of a much smaller gasoline tax (4.3 cents per gallon) in the face of fierce opposition from members of both parties in Congress.[33]

Clinton's failure to gain support even from his own party on these early initiatives undermined the confidence of environmentalists in the president. This loss of confidence was intensified by his active support for legislation to enact the North American Free Trade Agreement (NAFTA) and new General Agreement on Tariffs and Trade (GATT). During the election campaign he had promised not to support NAFTA unless protections for labor and the environment were added. Environmental groups were deeply divided over the treaty. Most of the larger Washington-based organizations supported the negotiation of a side agreement on environmental protection, and other groups, such as the Sierra Club and most grassroots organizations, adamantly opposed the treaty. Clinton alienated many environmentalists as well as a majority of congressional Democrats by allying with Republicans to pass NAFTA in 1993 and GATT in 1994.[34]

Clinton failed to satisfy environmentalists on other international issues as well. Although he signed the biodiversity treaty rejected by President Bush and announced his intentions to achieve the target proposed at the Rio summit for stabilizing carbon dioxide emissions by 2000, the administration failed to implement either policy. The biodiversity treaty was not brought up for ratification by the Senate, and the administration's climate change action plan announced in October 1993 called only for weak voluntary measures. These were soon admitted to be inadequate.[35]

The administration's overall legislative record during the 103d Congress (1993–1994) was mixed (see chap. 6). One of the administration's conspicuous failures was its inability to enact a bill elevating the EPA to cabinet rank. In this case the White House submitted legislation to establish a new

Department of Environmental Protection and worked with the relevant committees to move it along. The Senate passed an amended version of the legislation in May 1993, but it stalled in the House as additional amendments were added.[36] The White House eventually concluded that it was better to abandon the bill than to accept a version that would have crippled the EPA's regulatory authority. (Many of the amendments would reappear in more extreme form in the regulatory reform proposals of the new GOP majority in 1995.)

Despite these setbacks, the Clinton administration must be given credit for raising environmental considerations to a higher level of attention in the White House. The Office of Environmental Policy was in contact with the vice president's office, cabinet secretaries, and other White House staffs on a daily basis. At the end of 1994, it was decided to fold the OEP into the Council for Environmental Quality, which would have been abolished by the EPA cabinet bill but continued to exist. This arrangement was justified on grounds that the CEQ was being elevated to perform the policy functions of the OEP, so there was no longer need for a separate policy office.[37]

The White House also developed a more balanced approach to regulatory oversight in the OMB's Office of Information and Regulatory Affairs. Besides abolishing the Quayle Council, Clinton replaced Reagan's executive orders 12291 and 12498 with a new executive order (12866) on regulatory planning and review on September 30, 1993. The order set out the administration's regulatory philosophy as well as new procedures for reviewing individual regulations. In its statement of philosophy, the order declared:

> In deciding whether and how to regulate, agencies should assess all costs and benefits of available regulatory alternatives, including the alternative of not regulating. Costs and benefits shall be understood to include both quantifiable measures (to the fullest extent that these can be usefully estimated) and qualitative measures of costs and benefits that are difficult to quantify, but nevertheless essential to consider. Further, in choosing among alternative regulatory approaches, agencies should select those approaches that maximize net benefits (including potential economic, environmental, public health and safety, and other advantages; distributive impacts; and equity), unless a statute requires another regulatory approach.[38]

This guidance definitely suggests that agencies need to balance a variety of goals and values in justifying regulations but avoids any narrow economic definition of costs and benefits. Nevertheless, the Clinton OIRA has required the EPA and other agencies to seek greater cost-effectiveness.

The Congressional Challenge

The 1994 elections gave Republicans control of both houses of Congress and thirty-one governorships. Claiming a mandate for the "Contract with America" that some 300 GOP candidates for the House had pledged to support, the new House Speaker, Newt Gingrich, R-Ga., vowed "to begin decisively changing the shape of the government."[39] With the help of industry lobbyists, the new congressional leaders unleashed a massive effort to rewrite the environmental legislation of the past quarter-century (see chap. 6).[40]

Clinton could do little to stem the tide during the first "hundred days" of the Republican Congress, and the administration remained virtually silent on environmental issues. However, by the time the House of Representatives had passed a drastic revision of the Clean Water Act on May 16, opinion polls suggested that Republican environmental policies might be deeply unpopular with the public (see chap. 3). It was also evident that this and other legislation lacked both sufficient support to pass in the Senate and the two-thirds majority in the House necessary to override a presidential veto. The president and his new pollster, Dick Morris, saw an opportunity to regain public support by taking a tough stance against the "extremism" of the Republican environmental agenda.

Clinton's newly aggressive stance was signaled on May 30 in a fiery speech in Rock Creek Park in Washington, D.C.—a place "where Theodore Roosevelt loved to walk"—in which he vowed to veto the "Dirty Water Act" and castigated the Republicans for abandoning long-standing traditions of bipartisan support for the environment.[41] The threat of vetoes was frequently wielded throughout the summer, although Clinton enraged environmentalists by signing an appropriations rescission bill in late July that contained a provision allowing almost unlimited "salvage logging" without regard for environmental restrictions.[42] To mend fences, the president made highly publicized speeches in August at Baltimore Harbor and in Yellowstone National Park.[43]

The president and other members of his administration—especially interior secretary Babbitt, who campaigned throughout the country against the Republican proposals—appeared to have been successful by early fall in rallying public opinion against any significant weakening of environmental protection.[44] Indeed, a public backlash contributed to a revolt within House Republican ranks against the "mispositioning" of the party on environmental issues (see chap. 6). After a number of defeats in both houses, the GOP leadership switched to a strategy of burying provisions in riders to appropriation bills and in the budget reconciliation bill. Although most of the riders were stripped from the reconciliation bill before it was vetoed by Clinton, several important provisions (notably one that would open the Arctic National Wildlife Refuge to oil development) were dropped only in the final fiscal 1996 budget. Although this budget contained severe cuts in EPA funding, most of these funds subsequently were restored by Congress (see chap. 1 and app. 3).

Clinton's stout defense of the legislative and budgetary status quo against Republican onslaughts regained for him most of the support of environmentalists during the 104th Congress. Moreover, he was able to cooperate with a chastised GOP leadership in passing two significant environmental bills at the end of the session: the Food Quality Protection Act of 1996, which revised and strengthened pesticide regulation and set new standards for protection of infants and children, and the Safe Drinking Water Act Amendments of 1996, which set additional standards for drinking water contamination and created a new system for informing the public on local water quality (see chap. 6 and app. 1).

Clinton's relatively easy reelection victory over former senator Bob Dole in November 1996 did not fundamentally alter his relationship to Congress. Environmental policy was not a major issue in the campaign, although Clinton and Gore frequently criticized Dole and the Republicans for their attempts to gut environmental laws. In the congressional elections the Republicans maintained control of the House and gained two seats in the Senate, leaving Clinton little chance to enact further environmental legislation in the 105th Congress (see chap. 6). Indeed, his success in winning votes that session was among the worst for any modern president.[45] However, Clinton prevented any damaging environmental legislation from passing, and his agreement with the Republicans in 1997 on a bill to balance the budget contributed to budget surpluses during the remainder of his second term and provided room for increased spending for environmental programs.

Despite the distractions of the Monica Lewinsky affair and subsequent impeachment proceedings, Clinton continued to propose new environmental initiatives in his second term. In his State of the Union address in January 1998 he proposed a new $2.3 billion Clean Water Action Plan and a $6.3 billion program of tax credits and research and development spending over five years to implement the Kyoto Protocol on climate change (see chap. 13).[46] Congress funded the first program but not the second. In January 1999 he announced a Better America Bonds program, which would provide $700 million in new tax credits that could leverage almost $10 billion worth of state and local bonds to promote "livable communities," including additional green space in suburban areas. He and Gore endorsed "smart growth" strategies for controlling development and reducing congestion around cities—perhaps the most visible environmental issue to surface in the 1998 congressional elections. It also appeared that this would be a major theme in Gore's campaign for the presidency in 2000.[47]

The Administrative Presidency in Reverse

Like Reagan, Clinton was forced by congressional opposition to rely primarily on the "administrative presidency" to pursue his environmental agenda. But, unlike Reagan, he used his powers of appointment, budgeting, reorganization, and regulatory oversight to reform and strengthen environmental protection. Indeed, Clinton's most important environmental legacy may be the governmental "reinvention" effort carried out under the direction of Vice President Gore. This program, begun in March 1993 as the National Performance Review, developed into a much broader reform initiative known as the National Partnership for Reinventing Government, which focused on thirty-two "high impact" agencies, including the Environmental Protection Agency. A "reinventing environmental regulation" program launched at EPA on March 16, 1995, has produced more than forty new programs.[48] Essentially these programs invite states, industries, individual companies, and communities to collaborate with EPA to develop new performance-based management systems in return for greater regulatory flexibility. Although it is too early to evaluate their success, it appears that they have begun to create a new, more cooperative relationship between government and business while improving environmental quality (see chapter 8).

In addition to carrying out the most far-reaching administrative reforms in the history of the agency, EPA administrator Carol M. Browner strengthened existing regulations and enforcement. For example, in November 1996 she proposed tighter ambient air quality standards for ozone and small particulate matter to protect children, the elderly, asthmatics, and other vulnerable population groups against lung disease.[49] Despite howls of protest from industry and from many governors and mayors, as well as opposition from some White House advisers and threats in Congress to block the new regulations, Browner stuck to her guns and issued the final regulations in the summer of 1997. The EPA also accelerated the cleanup of hazardous waste sites under the Superfund program—completing more cleanups in five and a half years than under the first twelve years of the program—and launched a new effort to restore inner-city "brownfields" for economic redevelopment in more than 150 communities. At the same time, the EPA nearly doubled the number of chemical emissions that must be reported under the "community right to know" provisions of the Superfund Act.[50] Finally, while encouraging industries to disclose more information about their operations, the EPA set a new record for enforcement actions in 1997, referring more than 700 criminal and civil cases to the Justice Department for prosecution and assessing more fines and penalties than in any previous year in its history.[51]

Clinton deserves credit for substantial budget increases for environmental programs. For example, he proposed a 12 percent increase in EPA's budget for fiscal 1998 (to $7.6 billion, $7.4 billion of which was approved) and a 6 percent increase for fiscal 1999 (to $7.8 billion, $7.56 billion of which was enacted). With a projected budget surplus of $76 billion for fiscal 2000, Clinton proposed to spend a record $33.9 billion for all environmental and natural resource programs, an increase of about 5 percent over 1999 and 25 percent over 1993.[52]

In addition to strengthening the EPA, the Clinton administration has actively sought to collaborate with states and businesses to protect natural resources such as the Florida Everglades and Yellowstone National Park. It has pushed for new timber management plans and imposed a moratorium on construction of logging roads in some national forests.[53] It has also promoted voluntary agreements among multiple parties to establish habitat conservation plans to protect endangered species and other wildlife throughout the country. For example, in March 1999 a historic agreement was reached with Pacific Lumber Company for purchase of 10,000 acres of ancient redwood groves in the Headwaters Forest of northern California and for protection of endangered species habitat on another 211,0000 acres of timber land owned by the company.[54] When necessary, Clinton has utilized executive powers to remove scenic areas from mining and other potential development, most notably in September 1996 in creating the Grand Staircase–Escalante National Monument, which protects 1.3 million acres of the red rock canyon area of Utah. In this case he based his action on a little-used statute, the Antiquities Act of 1906, much to the chagrin of some western members of Congress.[55]

However belatedly, Clinton has also attempted to reestablish U.S. leadership in international environmental issues. Although the administration was slow to develop effective policies to deal with global warming, and postponed taking a position on the upcoming Kyoto negotiations until October 1997, ultimately Clinton authorized Gore to break the deadlock at the negotiations with an offer to reduce U.S. greenhouse gas emissions to 7 percent below 1990 levels by 2008–2012 (see chapter 13).[56] And, despite the fact that the final agreement imposed no limitations on the developing nations—a condition Congress had insisted upon as a condition for ratification—the United States signed the Kyoto Protocol in November 1998 during the followup negotiations in Buenos Aires.[57] Whether the treaty will ever be ratified in its present form is doubtful, but Clinton's support for action on climate change nevertheless stands in sharp contrast to the positions of Reagan and Bush on this overriding issue (see chap. 13). In the meantime, the administration has endorsed bipartisan legislation that would grant credits to companies for voluntary reductions of greenhouse gas emissions that could be counted against any future obligations under the Kyoto agreement.

Finally, Clinton and Gore have begun to lay the foundations for more comprehensive "sustainable development" policies in the future. The President's Council on Sustainable Development, comprising twenty-nine leaders from business, government, and nonprofit organizations, and working through multiple task forces, has issued a series of reports setting out principles and strategies for all sectors of society.[58] These in turn have helped to stimulate a host of new sustainable development initiatives in states and local communities across the nation.[59] In a draft report of January 1999, the council also offered extensive recommendations on strategies to combat climate change and on policies to foster U.S. leadership in international sustainable development policy.

Conclusion

The record of the past three presidents demonstrates that the White House has had a vital but hardly singular or consistent role in shaping national environmental policies. Most of Reagan's antienvironmental initiatives were repudiated by Congress, but he indirectly influenced the environmental agenda by intervening in regulatory processes, cutting agency budgets and personnel, delaying new environmental commitments, and challenging the cost and effectiveness of programs established in the 1970s. Bush attempted to strike a balance between cooperating with Congress (on the Clean Air

Act) and holding the line on other new policies, and he restored some of the funding and integrity of regulatory processes lost in the 1980s. However, his administration remained deeply divided internally, and Bush adopted an increasingly conservative stance during the second half of his term. Clinton seemed to adopt a reverse strategy of postponing environmental commitments at the beginning of his term when his party controlled Congress, taking a firm proenvironmental stance only after the opposition gained ascendancy in 1994. But he also established an "administrative presidency" that, unlike Reagan's, ultimately laid the groundwork for more innovative approaches to environmental protection and sustainable development policies. Most important, perhaps, Clinton began to restore America's flagging leadership on international environmental issues.

Notes

1. Quotations of President Clinton and Rep. Bliley are from Margaret Kriz, "Global Cooling," *National Journal,* Nov. 15, 1997, 2290, and Allan Freedman, "Clinton's Global Warming Plans Take Heat from Congress, *Congressional Quarterly Weekly Report,* Oct. 25, 1997, 2598, respectively.
2. See, for example, Paul R. Cutright, *Theodore Roosevelt: The Making of a Conservationist* (Urbana: University of Illinois Press, 1985); Donald E. Worster, ed., *American Environmentalism: The Formative Period, 1860–1915* (New York: Wiley, 1973); and Samuel P. Hays, *Conservation and the Gospel of Efficiency* (Cambridge: Harvard University Press, 1959).
3. Edgar B. Nixon, ed., *Franklin D. Roosevelt and Conservation, 1911–1945,* 2 vols. (Washington, D.C.: GPO, 1957). On the Roosevelts' use of presidential powers, see also Robert A. Shanley, *Presidential Influence and Environmental Policy* (Westport, Conn.: Greenwood, 1992).
4. Charles O. Jones, *The Presidency in a Separated System* (Washington, D.C.: Brookings, 1994), and *Separate but Equal Branches: Congress and the Presidency* (Chatham, N.J.: Chatham House, 1995).
5. Hugh Heclo and Lester M. Salamon, *The Illusion of Presidential Government* (Boulder: Westview, 1981); David K. Nichols, *The Myth of the Modern Presidency* (University Park: Pennsylvania State University Press, 1994).
6. These terms are from Jones, *Presidency in a Separated System,* chap. 5. Jones also adds a "fiscal" agenda orientation to refer to policymaking specifically to deal with the budget deficit. There is a large literature on presidential "leadership styles," including James David Barber's *Presidential Character: Predicting Performance in the White House,* 4th ed. (Englewood Cliffs, N.J.: Prentice-Hall, 1992), which emphasizes psychological traits of presidents; Colin Campbell, *Managing the Presidency: Carter, Reagan, and the Search for Executive Harmony* (Pittsburgh: University of Pittsburgh Press, 1988); and Richard T. Johnson, "Presidential Style," in *Perspectives on the Presidency,* ed. Aaron Wildavsky (Boston: Little, Brown, 1975).
7. See esp. Jones, *Presidency in a Separated System,* chaps. 6–7.
8. A classic work on White House organization is Stephen Hess, *Organizing the Presidency,* 2d ed. (Washington, D.C.: Brookings, 1988). See also John P. Burke, *The Institutional Presidency* (Baltimore: Johns Hopkins University Press, 1992); and John Hart, *The Presidential Branch: From Washington to Clinton,* 2d ed. (Chatham, N.J.: Chatham House, 1995).
9. See Samuel Kernell, *Going Public: New Strategies for Presidential Leadership* (Washington, D.C.: CQ Press, 1986); and Jeffrey Tulis, *The Rhetorical Presidency* (Princeton: Princeton University Press, 1987).

10. See, for example, Charles O. Jones, *Clean Air* (Pittsburgh: University of Pittsburgh Press, 1975); John C. Whitaker, *Striking a Balance: Environment and Natural Resources Policy in the Nixon-Ford Years* (Washington, D.C.: American Enterprise Institute, 1976); Charles O. Jones, *The Trusteeship Presidency: Jimmy Carter and the United States Congress* (Baton Rouge: Louisiana State University Press, 1988); and Shanley, *Presidential Influence.*

11. On Reagan's background and economic policies, see Lou Cannon, *Reagan* (New York: Putnam, 1982), esp. chap. 21; and William A. Niskanen, *Reaganomics* (New York: Oxford University Press, 1988). For a more detailed analysis of Reagan's environmental record, see Michael E. Kraft and Norman J. Vig, "Environmental Policy in the Reagan Presidency," *Political Science Quarterly* 99 (fall 1984): 414–439; and Vig and Kraft, eds., *Environmental Policy in the 1980s: Reagan's New Agenda* (Washington, D.C.: CQ Press, 1984).

12. Richard P. Nathan, *The Administrative Presidency* (New York: Wiley, 1983). See Robert F. Durant, *The Administrative Presidency Revisited* (Albany: State University of New York Press, 1992), for a somewhat different interpretation.

13. On the impact of the Reagan budget cuts, see esp. Robert V. Bartlett, "The Budgetary Process and Environmental Policy," and J. Clarence Davies, "Environmental Institutions and the Reagan Administration," in *Environmental Policy in the 1980s*, ed. Vig and Kraft.

14. See Barry D. Freedman, *Regulation in the Reagan-Bush Era: The Eruption of Presidential Influence* (Pittsburgh: University of Pittsburgh Press, 1995); Richard A. Harris and Sidney M. Milkis, *The Politics of Regulatory Change: A Tale of Two Agencies* (New York: Oxford University Press, 1989), 100–113, 257–265; and V. Kerry Smith, *Environmental Policy under Reagan's Executive Order: The Role of Cost-Benefit Analysis* (Chapel Hill: University of North Carolina Press, 1984).

15. For a more detailed summary of Watt's policies, see Paul J. Culhane, "Sagebrush Rebels in Office: Jim Watt's Land and Water Policies," in *Environmental Policy in the 1980s*, ed. Vig and Kraft, 293–318; and C. Brant Short, *Ronald Reagan and the Public Lands: America's Conservation Debate* (College Station: Texas A&M University Press, 1989). See also J. Clarence Davies III, "Environmental Institutions and the Reagan Administration," in *Environmental Policy in the 1980s*, ed. Vig and Kraft, 154–157. Burford tells her side of the story in Anne M. Burford (with John Greenya), *Are You Tough Enough?* (New York: McGraw-Hill, 1986).

16. John Holusha, "Bush Pledges Aid for Environment," *New York Times,* September 1, 1988; Bill Peterson, "Bush Vows to Fight Pollution, Install 'Conservation Ethic,'" *Washington Post,* Sept. 1, 1988.

17. Philip Shabecoff, "Bush Lends an Ear to Environmentalists," *New York Times,* Dec. 1, 1988, 13.

18. On Bush's decision-making style, see Michael Duffy and Dan Goodgame, *Marching in Place* (New York: Simon and Schuster, 1992); Colin Campbell and Bert Rockman, eds., *The Bush Presidency: First Appraisals* (Chatham, N.J.: Chatham House, 1991); and Burt Solomon, "In Bush's Image," *National Journal,* July 7, 1990, 1642–1647.

19. Richard Cohen, *Washington at Work: Back Rooms and Clean Air* (New York: Macmillan, 1992), 175. See also Gary C. Bryner, *Blue Skies, Green Politics: The Clean Air Act of 1990* (Washington, D.C.: CQ Press, 1993).

20. D. Allan Bromley, *The President's Scientists: Reminiscences of a White House Science Adviser* (New Haven: Yale University Press, 1994), 149–155. On the role of Sununu and other advisers in the White House, see also Fred Barnes, "Raging Bulls," *New Republic,* March 19, 1990, 11–12; Dan Goodgame, "Big Bad John Sununu," *Time,* May 21, 1990, 21–25; and Leslie H. Gelb, "Sununu v. Scientists," *New York Times,* Feb. 19, 1991, 17.

21. The most detailed analysis of the Quayle Council is Charles Tiefer, *The Semi-Sovereign Presidency* (Boulder: Westview, 1994), chap. 4. See also Kirk Victor, "Quayle's Quiet Coup," *National Journal,* July 6, 1991, 1676–1680; Christine Triano and Nancy Watz-

man, "Quayle's Hush-Hush Council," *New York Times,* Nov. 20, 1991; Bob Woodward and David Broder, "Quayle's Quest: Curb Rules, Leave 'No Fingerprints,'" *Washington Post,* Jan. 9, 1992; Robert D. Hershey Jr., "White House Sees a Mission to Cut Business Regulation," *New York Times,* March 23, 1992; and Keith Schneider, "Environment Laws Are Eased by Bush as Election Nears," *New York Times,* May 20, 1992.

22. Keith Schneider, "White House Snubs U.S. Envoy's Plea to Sign Rio Treaty," *New York Times,* June 5, 1992; Schneider, "Bush Aide Assails U.S. Preparations for Earth Summit." The press reported that the memo was leaked by the staff of the Quayle Council; Tiefer, *Semi-Sovereign Presidency,* 85.

23. *Newsweek,* special election issue, November–December 1992, 10.

24. Keith Schneider, "Clinton Relies on Voluntary Guidelines to Protect Environment in Arkansas," *New York Times,* April 4, 1992; Schneider, "Pollution in Arkansas Area May Be Key Campaign Issue," *New York Times,* April 21, 1992; and Gwen Ifill, "Clinton Links Ecology Plans with Jobs," *New York Times,* April 23, 1992. The Democratic and Republican platforms are reprinted in *Congressional Quarterly Weekly Report,* July 18 and August 22, 1992.

25. Bill Clinton and Al Gore, *Putting People First* (New York: Times Books, 1992), 89–99.

26. Margaret Kriz, "Their Turn," *National Journal,* Feb. 13, 1993, 388–391.

27. Ann Devroy, "Clinton Announces Plan to Replace Environmental Council," *Washington Post,* Feb. 9, 1993; Keith Schneider, "The Nominee for E.P.A. Sees Industry's Side Too," *New York Times,* Dec. 17, 1992.

28. Timothy Egan, "Sweeping Reversal of U.S. Land Policy Sought by Clinton," *New York Times,* Feb. 24, 1993; and Margaret Kriz, "Quick Draw," *National Journal,* Nov. 13, 1993, 2711–2716.

29. Bert A. Rockman, "The Leadership Style of George Bush," in *Bush Presidency,* ed. Rockman and Campbell; Campbell and Rockman, eds., *The Clinton Presidency: First Appraisals* (Chatham, N.J.: Chatham House, 1995); and Fred I. Greenstein, "The Presidential Leadership Style of Bill Clinton: An Early Appraisal," *Political Science Quarterly* 108 (winter 1993–1994): 589–601.

30. Peter Kerr and Thomas C. Hayes, "Praise for an Arkansan, and Criticism of a Deal," *New York Times,* Dec. 21, 1992. McLarty was replaced as chief of staff on July 17, 1994, by OMB director Leon Panetta. He was in turn succeeded by Erskine B. Bowles in 1996 and John D. Podesta in October 1998. See Carl M. Cannon, "And Now, Podesta," *National Journal,* Oct. 24, 1998, 2511.

31. The best early analysis of the Clinton administration is Campbell and Rockman, eds., *Clinton Presidency.* See also Stanley A. Renshon, ed., *The Clinton Presidency: Campaigning, Governing, and the Psychology of Leadership* (Boulder: Westview, 1995); Bob Woodward, *The Agenda: Inside the Clinton White House* (New York: Simon and Schuster, 1994); and Elizabeth Drew, *On the Edge: the Clinton Presidency* (New York: Simon and Schuster, 1994).

32. Drew, *On the Edge,* 110; Margaret Kriz, "Turf Wars," *National Journal,* May 22, 1993, 1232–1235; Richard L. Berke, "Clinton Backs Off from Policy Shift on Federal Lands," *New York Times,* March 31, 1993; Keith Schneider, "Clinton the Conservationist Thinks Twice," *New York Times,* April 4, 1993; and James Conaway, "Babbitt in the Woods: The Clinton Environmental Revolution That Wasn't," *Harpers,* December 1993, 52–60.

33. Drew, *On the Edge,* 71–72, 166–173; Richard E. Cohen, *Changing Course in Washington: Clinton and the New Congress* (New York: Macmillan, 1994); and Barbara Sinclair, "Trying to Govern Positively in a Negative Era: Clinton and the 103d Congress," in *Clinton Presidency,* ed. Campbell and Rockman, 105–107. Gore pushed hard for the tax, which passed the House, but was outmaneuvered by Treasury secretary Lloyd Bentsen and members of the Senate Finance Committee; see Woodward, *Agenda,* 89–92, 218–222.

34. See John J. Audley, *Green Politics and Global Trade: NAFTA and the Future of Environmental Politics* (Washington, D.C.: Georgetown University Press, 1997).

35. Richard L. Berke, "Clinton Supports Two Major Steps for Environment," *New York Times*, April 22, 1993; and William K. Stevens, "With Energy Tug of War, U.S. Is Missing Its Goals," *New York Times*, Nov. 28, 1995. See also Robert L Paarlberg, "Lapsed Leadership: U.S. International Environmental Policy since Rio," in *The Global Environment: Institutions, Law, and Policy*, ed. Norman J. Vig and Regina S. Axelrod (Washington, D.C.: CQ Press, 1999), 236–255.

36. Laura Michaelis, "Bill Elevating EPA to Cabinet Worries Environmentalists," *Congressional Quarterly Weekly Report*, March 27, 1993, 746; Catalina Camia, "Senate OKs Elevation of EPA; Hurdles Await in the House," ibid., May 8, 1993, 1140–1142.

37. Interview with Kathleen McGinty, Washington, D.C., June 10, 1995.

38. Executive Order 12866—Regulatory Planning and Review, *Federal Register*, vol. 58, no. 190, Oct. 4, 1993.

39. "Taking Speaker's Mantle, Gingrich Vows 'Profound Transformation,'" *Congressional Quarterly Weekly Report*, Dec. 10, 1994, 3522.

40. For a summary of the Republican agenda and responses to it, see "GOP Sets the 104th Congress on New Regulatory Course," *Congressional Quarterly Weekly Report*, June 17, 1995, 1693–1701; "The GOP's War on Nature," *New York Times*, May 31, 1995, A14; and Margaret Kriz, "The Green Card," *National Journal*, Sept. 16, 1995, 2262–2267.

41. Ann Devroy, "Veto Vowed for Clean Water Rewrite," *Washington Post*, May 31, 1995; "Clinton Vows to Veto Clean Water Rewrite," Minneapolis *Star Tribune*, May 31, 1995. Vice President Gore had planned to give the speech, but on the advice of Morris, the president "took the speech for himself." *Greenwire*, June 5, 1995.

42. Clinton vetoed an earlier version of the rescission bill on June 7 and gained restoration of some environmental funding, but the revised legislation signed on July 27, 1995, rescinded $16.4 billion of previously approved spending, including $1.3 billion from the EPA's budget. A congressional rider to the bill, which environmentalists fiercely opposed, was later ruled by a federal judge to allow logging of large areas of old-growth forests in Oregon and Washington while suspending most environmental regulations through 1996. Clinton later claimed, to the incredulity of observers, that he did not fully understand this section of the bill when he signed it, despite the warnings of environmentalists. See Timothy Egan, "Recriminations as Northwest Loggers Return," *New York Times*, Dec. 5, 1995.

43. Todd S. Purdum, "Clinton and Old Faithful Let Off Steam," *New York Times*, Aug. 26, 1995.

44. "It's Not Just Owls Anymore," *Newsweek*, Sept. 4, 1995, 23. Babbitt made more than 100 speeches attacking the Republican agenda; see, for example, "Springtime for Polluters," *Washington Post*, Oct. 22, 1995, C2.

45. David Hosansky, "Clinton's Biggest Prize Was a Frustrated GOP," *CQ Weekly*, Jan. 9, 1999, 75–77.

46. Margaret Kriz, "Fish and Fowl," *National Journal*, Feb. 28, 1998, 450; Allan Freedman, "Clinton's Global Warming Plan Meets Wall of Opposition," *Congressional Quarterly Weekly Report*, Feb. 7, 1998, 320.

47. "President Clinton's Fiscal Year 2000 EPA Budget: Building Healthy Communities for the 21st Century," EPA press release, Feb. 1, 1999 (*http://epainotes1.rtpnc.epa.gov:7777/opa*); "Clinton-Gore Livability Agenda: Building Livable Communities for the 21st Century" (*http://www.whitehouse.gov/CEQ/011499.html*); "Remarks prepared for delivery by Vice President Al Gore, American Institute of Architects," Jan. 11, 1999 (*http://www.whitehouse.gov/CEQ/011499-b.html*).

48. John Kamensky, "National Partnership for Reinventing Government, A Brief History," January 1999 (*http://www.npr.gov/whoweare/history2.html*). On EPA, see Bill Clinton and Al Gore, "Reinventing Environmental Regulation," March 16, 1995, reprinted in Al Gore, *Common-Sense Government Works Better and Costs Less* (New York: Random House, 1995), app. D.

49. John E. Cushman Jr., "E.P.A. Puts Forth Proposal for Tightened Air Standards, *New York Times*, Nov. 28, 1996; Margaret Kriz, "Heavy Breathing," *National Journal*, Jan. 4,

1997, 8–12; Allan Freedman, "Chafee Claims the Middle on Clean Air Standards," *Congressional Quarterly Weekly Report*, Feb. 15, 1997, 422–423; Freedman, "Latest Fight on Clean Air Rules Centers on Scientific Data," *Congressional Quarterly Weekly Report*, March 1, 1997, 530–532; Freedman, "Hill Foes of New Clean Air Rules United Behind Moratorium Bill," *Congressional Quarterly Weekly Report*, July 19, 1997, 1689–1690. In February 1999 the EPA indicated that it would soon propose tighter standards for auto and truck tailpipe emissions and for the sulfur content of gasoline to meet the new smog and particulate requirements. "EPA to Propose Tougher Standards in Effort to Reduce Air Pollution," Minneapolis *Star Tribune*, Feb. 19, 1999.

50. Carol M. Browner, "Remarks prepared for delivery, Brookings Institution," EPA, Speeches by the Administrator, Oct. 13, 1998 (*http://epainotes1.rtpnc.epa.gov: 7777/opa*).

51. "PR EPA Sets Records for Enforcement While Expanding Program for Industry to Disclose and Correct Violations," EPA press release, Dec. 22, 1997 (*http://epainotes1. rtpnc.epa.gov:7777:opa*).

52. "PR FY 98 Budget for EPA," EPA press release, Feb. 7, 1997 (*http://epainotes1.rtpnc. epa.gov:7777/opa*); "PR President Clinton's FY 1999 Budget for EPA: Protecting Public Health and the Environment," EPA press release, Feb. 2, 1998 (ibid.); Office of Management and Budget, *Budget of the United States Government Fiscal Year 2000* (Washington, D.C.: U.S. Government Printing Office, 1999).

53. Margaret Kriz, "Fighting over Forests," *National Journal*, May 30, 1998, 1232–1236; John H. Cushman Jr., "Government Moves to Conserve Remote Areas of National Forest," *New York Times*, Feb. 12, 1999, 1, A19.

54. Evelyn Nieves, "Lumber Company Approves U.S. Deal to Save Redwoods," *New York Times,* March 3, 1999, A1.

55. Allan Freedman, "Land Set-Aside by Clinton Prompts Outrage in Utah," *Congressional Quarterly Weekly Report*, May 3, 1997, 1016; and Freedman, "House Votes to Restrict Power of President to Protect Land," *Congressional Quarterly Weekly Report*, Oct. 11, 1997, 2481.

56. Allan Freedman, "Forecast Is Dim in the Senate for Global Warming Treaty," *Congressional Quarterly Weekly Report*, Dec. 13, 1997, 3068–3069.

57. John H. Cushman Jr., "U.S. Signs a Pact to Reduce Gases Tied to Warming," *New York Times*, Nov. 13, 1998.

58. See President's Council on Sustainable Development, *Sustainable America: A New Consensus for Prosperity, Opportunity, and a Healthy Environment for the Future* (Washington, D.C.: PCSD, February 1996); *Building on Consensus: A Progress Report on Sustainable America* (Washington, D.C.: PCSD, January 1997); *The Road to Sustainable Development: A Snapshot of Activities in the United States of America* (Washington, D.C.: PCSD, March 1997). These and other reports of PCSD can be found on *http://www.whitehouse.gov/PCSD/Publications/index.html*.

59. See Daniel A. Mazmanian and Michael E. Kraft, eds., *Toward Sustainable Communities: Transition and Transformations in Environmental Policy* (Cambridge: MIT Press, forthcoming 1999).

6

Environmental Policy in Congress: From Consensus to Gridlock

Michael E. Kraft

The American people sent us a message in November, loud and clear: Tame this regulatory beast!

—Thomas J. Bliley, Jr., R-Va.
Chair, House Commerce Committee, 1995

The highest lawmaking body in the land is paralyzed by partisanship [and] clear thinking and cooperation have been pushed aside. . . . . Especially in the environmental area, the will of the people has been forgotten.

—John H. Adams,
President, Natural Resources Defense Council, 1999

The 1994 elections marked a turning point in congressional action on the environment. For nearly three decades the U.S. Congress enacted—and over time strengthened—an extraordinary range of environmental policies (see chap. 1 and app. 1). In doing so, members of Congress within both political parties recognized and responded to rising public concern about environmental degradation. For the same reasons, they stoutly defended those policies during the 1980s when they were assailed by Ronald Reagan's White House.[1] The 104th Congress, elected in November 1994, and the 105th Congress that followed, brought a strikingly different posture on the environment to Capitol Hill.

With the conservative "Contract with America" as the cornerstone of their legislative agenda in 1995 and 1996, the Republicans in Congress fought intensely to rein in what they believed to be regulatory bureaucracies run amok. Environmental agencies such as the Environmental Protection Agency were prime targets of their efforts to curtail bureaucratic power and reduce the costs of regulation.[2]

Republican leaders and newly elected conservatives pursued these goals with a revolutionary fervor in the 104th Congress. They followed a similar agenda, although less openly and passionately, in the 105th Congress and at the beginning of the 106th Congress which took office in January 1999. The

Clinton administration and most congressional Democrats were equally intent on blocking what they characterized as ill-advised attempts to roll back twenty-five years of progress in protecting public health and the environment.

The short-term effect in both the 104th and 105th Congresses was environmental policy gridlock. For the most part, consensus proved elusive, and neither radical changes nor moderate reforms could be approved. Thus, existing policies—with their many acknowledged flaws—continued in force. The longer-term impacts are less clear. They depend on how a multiplicity of policy and budgetary conflicts are resolved over the next several years. The stakes are high, and the battles between congressional adversaries are certain to shape U.S. environmental policy for years to come.

In this chapter I examine some of the most significant efforts at policy change of the 104th and 105th Congresses and compare them with the way Congress dealt with environmental issues previously. I give special attention to the distinctive roles that Congress plays in the policymaking process and to the phenomenon of environmental policy gridlock, which has been a powerful influence on environmental lawmaking in recent years. I also suggest criteria for judging Congress's performance and what might be done to improve congressional decisions on environmental policy.

Congress and Environmental Policy

Under the U.S. Constitution, Congress shares responsibility with the president for federal policymaking on the environment. Congress is given chief responsibility for enacting public policies and for appropriating the funds necessary to implement them, powers that translate into a continuing role of overseeing, and often criticizing, executive agency actions. Presidents have greater opportunities than does Congress to set the political agenda and to govern policy implementation in the agencies. Historically, however, Congress has been equally as influential as the White House in setting the overall direction of environmental policies. For most of the modern environmental era, Congress also has operated with broad bipartisan agreement on the issues.[3]

The way in which Congress exercises its formidable policymaking powers is shaped by several key factors. Among the most important of these is whether the president's party also dominates Congress—and by what margins. In the U.S. political system, divided government, which has been common in recent decades, makes coalition building and policy compromise essential if anything is to be accomplished. The extent to which Congress is willing to work cooperatively with the White House, however, depends on the ideological and political differences between them, and on judgments members make about the president's legitimacy, as measured, for example, by his public approval ratings and leadership abilities.[4] President Clinton's capacity to cooperate with the 106th Congress remained in some doubt following his impeachment by the House in 1998 and the Senate trial—despite pledges by both the president and congressional leaders to work together.

Congress's actions on the environment reflect not only its partisan and ideological makeup but also its dualistic nature as a political institution. In addition to serving as a national lawmaking body, Congress is an assembly of politicians who are elected to represent politically disparate districts and states. This means they often focus as much on local and regional impacts of environmental and resource policies as they do on the effects of these policies on the nation as a whole. Members also tend to adopt a relatively short-term view of environmental policy issues compared with the long-term perspective frequently advocated by environmental scientists and policy analysts in touting such new approaches as ecosystem management and sustainable development.

These institutional characteristics mean that action on environmental policies in Congress is rarely easy. Sometimes it is impossible, at least in the short term. In the face of inaction the public may see a body of politicians who appear to do little about environmental and other public problems. This perception reinforces the prevailing negative image of Congress and its members—maintained in part by television comedians, radio talk show hosts, and journalists ever on the alert for a good Congress-bashing joke or story. The result of all these factors has been a public belief that Congress is, as two political scientists put it, "slothful, slow, conflict-ridden, immobilized, and inactive."[5]

Most of these criticisms, especially those related to legislative gridlock, miss the mark and focus our attention on the wrong issues. The "do-nothing Congress," for example, is better described as a deeply divided Congress. The fundamental political reality is that all too often members can find no way to reconcile their diverse and conflicting interests to build consensus on policy actions.

There are, however, some striking exceptions to this common pattern of deadlock. In 1990, for instance, Congress approved a far-reaching extension of the Clean Air Act, the nation's most demanding environmental statute.[6] In 1996 it ended a long stalemate on pesticide policy through adoption of the Food Quality Protection Act, and in the same year it approved a major revision of the Safe Drinking Water Act. An intriguing question is how it is possible for Congress to achieve a remarkable consensus on some environmental policies while remaining mired in gridlock on others. A brief examination of the way Congress has dealt with environmental issues over the past three decades helps to explain this seeming anomaly. Such a review also provides a useful context in which to examine and assess the actions of the 104th and 105th Congresses, and the outlook for environmental policymaking for the early 21st century.

The Causes and Consequences of Environmental Gridlock

As suggested above, policy gridlock refers to an inability to resolve conflicts in a policymaking body such as Congress, which results in governmental inaction in the face of important public problems. There is no consensus on *what* to do and therefore no movement in any direction. Present policies, or slight revisions of them, continue until agreement is reached on the direction and magnitude of change. Not uncommonly, environmental and other programs officially expire, but they continue to be funded by Congress through a waiver of the rules governing the annual appropriations process. The failure to renew the programs, however, contributes to administrative drift, ineffective congressional oversight, and a propensity, as discussed below, for members to use the appropriation process to achieve what cannot be gained through statutory change.[7]

Why Does Policy Gridlock Occur?

Political pundits and public officials regularly bemoan policy gridlock in Congress. They are less likely to ask why it occurs in the first place or what might be done to overcome the prevailing tendency toward institutional stalemate. Regrettably, there are no simple answers to those questions.

One of the major reasons for environmental policy deadlock in Congress is the sharply divergent policy views of Democrats and Republicans in combination with the constitutionally mandated separation of powers. The president may propose policy actions and submit budget recommendations that Congress ignores, and Congress may enact legislation that the president vetoes. Both are more likely, of course, when Congress and the White House are controlled by different parties. The House and Senate might also disagree with one another as well, as they frequently do on environmental issues, and committee actions may fail to command a majority on the House or Senate floor. Building consensus within Congress is made difficult as well by the political independence of members, who vigorously pursue their narrow district, state, or regional interests regardless of the preferences of party leaders, including the president.[8]

Although divided authority and these institutional and political incentives contribute significantly to policy gridlock, they are by no means the only causes. At least five others can be suggested.

One of these is the complexity and intractability of environmental problems, compounded by scientific uncertainty over their scope, causes, and implications. The more complex the issue and the less the consensus among scientists on causes and solutions, the more likely gridlock is to occur. Where scientific consensus reigns, Congress is less likely to impede policy action.

Another cause of policy stalemate is lack of public consensus. The more the public agrees on basic policy directions, the easier it is for Congress to act. That relationship should be good news for environmental policy because polls have long indicated widespread public support for environmental protection (see chap. 3). Yet the public's understanding of environmental issues often is quite limited and its views inconsistent. In part, this is because environmental issues are rarely foremost in people's minds. Absent a clear and forceful public voice, members cannot easily respond to their constituents' concern for the environment.

A third explanation is found in the power of organized or special interests. Interest groups willingly enter the political vacuum created by an inattentive and disengaged public. Most groups also have markedly increased their presence in the nation's capital over the past twenty-five years in what observers have termed an "advocacy explosion"—a sharp rise in the number of groups, the scope of their activities, and the intensity of their efforts. Business groups have become especially well represented and generally have greater resources than environmental organizations to use in furthering their legislative agenda.[9] Yet the more interest groups disagree (and are well positioned to act on their beliefs), the greater the probability of gridlock. In recent years business and environmental groups have proven adept at blocking each other's initiatives in Congress, thus assuring political stalemate.

A fourth reason for environmental gridlock concerns the high cost of environmental protection, and the way that policymakers think about and compare the costs with the benefits of taking action. Adopting policies to deal with problems such as climate change or protection of biological diversity—policies with highly visible short-term costs and uncertain long-term benefits—is difficult without compelling scientific evidence of the risks to human or ecological health or to economic well-being. Such evidence is rarely available, as scientific findings are nearly always subject to dispute. Moreover, there is no easy way to put a dollar value on many of the benefits of environmental policies. Thus attention tends to focus on short-term costs to the nation or to specific states or regions, making agreement on policy change difficult.

A final explanation for gridlock is the absence of effective political leadership. Scholars have argued for years that presidential leadership was one of the most assured ways to overcome institutional fragmentation within American government.[10] Similarly, strong leadership within Congress at either the committee level or among party leaders may help to forge the majorities needed for enacting legislation, as was evident in the House in the 104th Congress under Speaker Newt Gingrich, R-Ga., and his principal deputy, Majority Leader Dick Armey, R-Texas. Without effective leadership in the White House or on Capitol Hill, however, building consensus among highly disparate interests can be enormously difficult.

In sum, there is no single reason for environmental gridlock, and thus no simple solution. Policy paralysis of this kind reflects the structure of the political system, the nature of environmental problems, the state of public opinion, the power of organized interests, the high cost of environmental protection, and the difficulties political leaders face in the prevailing political climate in trying to build majority coalitions. The partisan, polarized, and caustic debates that have substituted for policy deliberation in recent Congresses have compounded the challenges of environmental policymaking. So, too, have public cynicism toward politics and the lack of a broadly-based vision for our collective environmental future. Overcoming policy gridlock requires dealing with all of these factors.

Gridlock's Effects

Generally the term "gridlock" has a negative connotation in the press and among the American public. It is seen as something to be ended quickly or avoided in the first place. Yet gridlock may be considered a positive political outcome, depending on how we appraise the consequences. Environmentalists might argue, for example, that when government cannot act on a pressing problem that creates adverse impacts on human health or the environment, the effects are clearly negative. Under these circumstances environmental groups and their allies see gridlock as something to be avoided.

However, if disagreement and immobility allow the continuation of policies that would otherwise be weakened by a legislative body (for example, the Endangered Species Act), environmentalists may welcome the outcome; the policies they prefer are left in place. In contrast, business interests concerned about the costs and burdens of environmental policies would likely judge the impacts negatively. So, too, would policy analysts who are convinced that many contemporary environmental policies, such as those dealing with hazardous waste cleanup and water pollution control, are in need of substantial reform. They would see such political stalemate as a lost opportunity to improve the effectiveness and efficiency of those policies.[11]

The implications of these general patterns of environmental policymaking and gridlock can be seen by examining specific actions Congress took on environmental policy from the 1970s through the early 1990s. Chapter 1 provided an overview of policy evolution during this period. In the rest of the chapter I turn to congressional efforts to grapple with environmental challenges both before and after the watershed election of the 104th Congress in 1994.

From Consensus in the Environmental Decade to Deadlock in the 1990s

The 1970s offer examples of both successful and unsuccessful environmental policymaking. The record for this "environmental decade" is nevertheless remarkable, particularly in comparison with actions taken during most of the 1980s and 1990s. The National Environmental Policy Act, Clean Air Act, Clean Water Act, Endangered Species Act, and Resource Conservation and Recovery Act, among others, were all signed into law in the 1970s, largely between 1970 and 1976. Their enactment demonstrates that the U.S. political system is capable of developing major environmental policies in fairly short order under the right conditions. Consensus on environmental policy could prevail in the 1970s because the issues were new and politically popular, and attention focused on broadly-supported program goals such as cleaning up the nation's air and water.

Environmental Gridlock Emerges

The pattern of the 1970s did not last. Congress's enthusiasm for environmental policy gradually gave way to apprehension about its impacts on the economy, and policy stalemate became the norm in the early 1980s. The shift had more to do with politics and ideology than economics. Ronald Reagan's election as president in 1980 altered the political climate. For the first time since 1955, the Republicans also captured the Senate, giving conservatives in both parties the opportunity to bar environmental policy proposals and to roll back some policies already in existence. The economic recession of 1980–1982 and the high cost of energy also shaped Reagan's decision to subordinate the environment to economic recovery (see chap. 5).

These alterations in the political environment threw Congress into a defensive posture. It was forced to *react* to the Reagan administration's aggressive policy actions. Rather than proposing new programs or expanding old ones, Congress focused its resources on oversight and criticism of the administration's policies. Bipartisan agreement became more difficult. Thus for most of Reagan's first term, political conditions were ripe for protracted conflict between the president and Congress.

As environmental issues became more complex, less prominent in voters' minds, and more contentious, there were fewer incentives for policy leadership on Capitol Hill than there were during the 1970s. Members were increasingly cross-pressured by environmental and industry groups, partisanship on these issues increased, and Congress and President Reagan battled repeatedly over budget and program priorities.[12]

The cumulative effect of these developments in the early 1980s was that Congress was unable to agree on new environmental policy directions. Members kept programs alive through continuing appropriations and short-term extensions of the existing acts, but they could not formally reauthorize them. During the 97th Congress, for example, eight comprehensive environmental programs were due for reauthorization; only two were enacted.

Gridlock Eases: 1984 to 1990

The legislative logjam began breaking up in late 1983, as the American public and Congress repudiated President Reagan's antienvironmental agenda (see chap. 5). These developments altered what John Kingdon has called the "politics stream."[13] Environmental groups took advantage of the favorable political mood to push policy goals deferred during the first part of the Reagan administration. The new pattern was evident by 1984 when, after several years of deliberation, Congress approved major amendments to the 1976 Resource Conservation and Recovery Act that strengthened the program and set tight new deadlines for Environmental Protection Agency (EPA) rulemaking on control of hazardous chemical wastes.

Although the Republicans still controlled the Senate, the 99th Congress (1985–86) compiled a record dramatically at odds with the deferral politics of the 97th and 98th Congresses. In 1986 the Safe Drinking Water Act was strengthened and expanded, and Congress approved the Superfund Amendments and Reauthorization Act, adding a separate Title III, the Emergency Planning and Community Right-to-Know Act (EPCRA). EPCRA was an entirely new program mandating nationwide reporting for toxic and hazardous chemicals produced, used, or stored in communities, as well as state and local emergency planning for accidental releases. By 1987 Congress reauthorized the Clean Water Act over a presidential veto.

The Democrats regained control of the Senate following the 1986 election, and the newly elected members of both the House and Senate were a more environmentally oriented group. Yet despite what was a highly productive period, several major environmental policy initiatives failed not only in the 99th Congress but in the 100th Congress (1987–88) as well. These measures included renewal of the Clean Air Act and the Federal Insecticide, Fungicide, and Rodenticide Act (FIFRA)—the nation's key pesticide control act—as well as new legislation to control acid rain.

The disappointment in this limited progress was captured in one analyst's assessment: "Congress stayed largely stalemated on a range of old environmental and energy problems in 1988, even while a generation of new ones clamored for attention."[14] Much the same could be said for the 101st and 102d Congresses (1989–92) during the Bush administration.

Yet Congress and President George Bush were able to agree on enactment of the monumental Clean Air Act Amendments of 1990 and of the Energy Policy Act of 1992. The latter was an important if modest advancement in promoting energy conservation and a restructuring of the electric utility industry to promote greater competition and efficiency.

Success on the Clean Air Act was particularly important because for thirteen years it symbolized Congress's inability to reauthorize controversial environmental programs. Congress was able to approve the 1990 amendments to the act for several reasons: improved scientific research, reports of worsening ozone in urban areas—which helped to reduce opposition by key interest groups such as the Chemical Manufacturers Association—and a realization by members that the American public would tolerate no further delays in dealing with air quality problems. President Bush also vowed to "break the gridlock" and support renewal of the act, and Sen. George Mitchell, D-Maine, newly elected as Senate majority leader, was equally determined to enact a clean air bill.[15]

The 103d Congress: Gridlock Returns

Unfortunately, enactment of the 1990 Clean Air Act was no signal that a new era of cooperative and bipartisan policymaking on the environment was about to begin. Nor was the election of Bill Clinton and Al Gore in 1992, even though the election returned control of both houses of Congress to the Democrats. Most of the major environmental laws were once again up for renewal. Yet despite an emerging consensus on reauthorization of the

Clean Water Act, Safe Drinking Water Act, Superfund, and FIFRA, among others, in the end the 103d Congress remained far too divided to act on these measures.

Coalitions of environmental groups and business interests clashed regularly on all of these initiatives, and congressional leaders and the Clinton White House were unsuccessful in resolving the conflicts. The administration came close with the much-criticized Superfund program. It brought all parties together through its National Commission on the Superfund (also known as the Keystone Commission), and by the end of 1994 there appeared to be agreement on needed reforms. Much the same was true for the Safe Drinking Water Act—a broad array of interest groups came close to reaching consensus on the act's renewal. But agreement proved impossible in both instances.

The search for consensus on environmental policy became more difficult as the 1994 election neared. Republicans increasingly believed they would do well in November, and partisan politics helped to scuttle whatever hopes remained for action in 1994. Like the environmentalists, the Republicans, their conservative Democratic allies in these battles, and business leaders thought they could strike a more favorable compromise in the next Congress. In the end, the only major environmental policy on which lawmakers could agree was the California Desert Protection Act, establishing new wilderness areas in that state. All the other proposals for reforming federal environmental laws were deferred to the 104th Congress beginning in 1995.

The 104th Congress:
Revolutionary Ambition Meets Political Reality

Few analysts had predicted the astonishing outcomes of the 1994 midterm elections, even after one of the most expensive, negative, and anti-Washington campaigns in modern times. Republicans captured both houses of Congress, picking up an additional fifty-two seats in the House and eight in the Senate. They also did well in other elections across the country, contributing to their belief that voters had endorsed the Contract with America, which symbolized the new Republican agenda.[16]

The contract had promised a rolling back of government regulations and a shrinking of the federal government's role. There was no specific mention of environmental policy, however, and the document's language was carefully constructed for broad appeal to a disgruntled electorate. For its policy recommendations, the contract drew heavily from the work of conservative and probusiness think tanks such as the Heritage Foundation, Cato Institute, and Competitive Enterprise Institute. For years they had waged a multifaceted campaign to discredit environmentalist thinking and policies and to shift public opinion on these issues. Those efforts merged with a carefully developed GOP plan to gain control of Congress to further a conservative political agenda.[17]

There is little persuasive evidence, however, that the Republican victory in November conveyed a public mandate to act on the contract's provisions related to environmental programs. Surveys indicated that voters were largely unaware of the contract and its provisions even as late as April 1995, and studies of voting behavior in the November election found no substantial basis for a voter mandate on the issues.[18] As the evidence presented in chapter 3 shows, voters continue to prefer a strong governmental role in environmental protection. Thus at best, one could read into the election results a *general* preference for less government and less regulation.

Whatever might be said about the meaning of the 1994 election, the political result was clear enough. It put Republicans in charge of the House for the first time in four decades and set the stage for an extraordinary period of legislative action on environmental policy characterized by exceptionally bitter relations between the two parties. Republican members were so accustomed to serving in a minority party capacity that initially they adopted an aggressive "take-no-prisoners" strategy that rejected political compromise with their ideological foes. Led by a determined Speaker, Newt Gingrich, and with many new members arriving on Capitol Hill without prior legislative experience, Republicans would struggle during the 104th Congress to learn the skills required for building broad support and governing Congress.[19] Deep conflicts within the party between conservatives and moderates, on other issues as well as environmental protection, exacerbated that challenge.[20]

The resulting environmental policy gridlock should have come as no surprise. With several notable exceptions, consensus on the issues simply could not be built, and the revolution failed for the most part. The lesson seemed to be that a direct attack on popular environmental programs could not work because it would provoke a backlash from environmentalists and the Clinton White House. Those who supported a new agenda turned to a strategy of emphasizing evolutionary or incremental environmental policy change through a more subtle and less visible exercise of Congress's appropriations and oversight powers. Here they were more successful.[21]

From Contract to Policy Action in the 104th and 105th Congresses

The varied efforts to change environmental policy during the 104th and 105th Congresses fall largely into three categories: initiatives to "reform" regulatory processes that are integral to policy implementation, efforts to use the appropriations process to curtail programs faulted by members, and attempts to reauthorize and modify the existing programs.[22] A brief review of actions within each permits some assessment of their success in light of the expectations that apply to any policymaking on the environment, and suggests ways of establishing new policy directions for the 21st century.[23]

Regulatory Reform

Regulatory reform has been a central theme in U.S. environmental policy since the late 1970s, and it was of special interest during Ronald Reagan's presidency (see chaps. 1 and 5). There is no real dispute among students of environmental policy on the need to reform agency rulemaking that has been widely faulted for being too inflexible, intrusive, cumbersome, and adversarial, and sometimes based on insufficient consideration of science and economics. Much disagreement exists, however, over precisely what elements of the regulatory process need to be reformed and the most legitimate way to institute such changes to be sure that they work as intended.

The Republican majority favored separate, "omnibus" regulatory reform legislation that would affect all environmental policies by imposing broad and stringent mandates on bureaucratic agencies, especially for the conduct and use of cost-benefit analysis and risk assessment. They also wanted to open agency technical studies and rulemaking to additional legal challenges to help protect the business community against what they viewed as unjustifiable regulatory action. Opponents argued that such impositions and opportunities for lawsuits would wreak havoc within agencies such as the EPA that already faced imposing procedural hurdles in developing regulations and frequent legal disputes over them. They preferred more limited changes that would be considered as each statute came up for renewal. They also sought to give agency professionals more discretion in considering how to weigh pertinent evidence and set program priorities.

The most notable attempt at regulatory reform occurred in the House early in 1995, with similar legislation considered in each subsequent year. Members were eager, in the words of the Contract with America, to "free Americans from bureaucratic red tape," which they saw in environmental, health, and safety regulations, and to spur economic growth. They also objected philosophically to a strong government role in regulation.

In pursuit of such goals, the contract's authors wanted to require "every new regulation to stand a new test: Does it provide benefits worth the costs?" Those ideas found expression in the Job Creation and Wage Enhancement Act of 1995, which mandated extensive cost-benefit analyses and risk assessments as part of the regulatory processes used by agencies such as the EPA to implement environmental policies. The act also would likely have thrown many contested decisions into the already crowded federal courts.

The final legislative package, HR 9, also included a "takings" provision that required compensation to landowners when regulations under certain laws reduced property values by 20 percent or more. In a telling comment about legislative politics in 1995, debate on the bill's provisions appeared to be anchored far more in colorful anecdotes of alleged regulatory abuses and pleas for relief for the business community than in scientific or economic facts.[24]

This act and its counterpart in the Senate, strongly supported by Bob Dole, R-Kan., then the Senate majority leader, reflected intense lobbying by business groups that sought to reduce the cost of complying with environmental, health, and safety regulation.[25] The business community's concerns were genuine, yet their political tactics were controversial and unlikely to succeed. Short-term economic relief might be gained, as it was in the Reagan administration, but at the expense of the more important goal of long-term reform of environmental statutes.

Despite serious misgivings about the bill by economists, scientists, policy analysts, and administration officials who favored *some* economic analysis of environmental proposals, the House overwhelmingly approved HR 9 by a vote of 277 to 141 in March 1995.[26] But parallel measures in the Senate fared poorly. Senator Dole tried three times to bring a companion bill to the Senate floor, but he failed to gain sufficient votes to end a filibuster by opponents who thought the legislation would jeopardize public health, safety, and the environment. In July 1995 Dole pulled the key bill from the Senate floor, signaling the GOP's retreat on sweeping regulatory reform legislation.

GOP leaders were successful, however, in gaining approval of several less ambitious reform measures. One of those was the Unfunded Mandates Reform Act of 1995, which Congress approved and the president signed in early 1995. The act erected new procedural barriers to keep Congress from approving statutes likely to impose unfunded federal mandates (requirements for action) of $50 million a year or more on state and local governments.

On other regulatory reform issues, Republicans remained too divided to act. The business community also was split, although at least some leaders signaled a strategic shift that recognized popular support for environmental protection. Those who worked closely with the President's Council on Sustainable Development announced that modest reforms of existing statutes might be better after all than the drastic changes they sought in 1995.[27]

In the 105th Congress in 1997, Senators Fred Thompson, R-Tenn., and Carl Levin, D-Mich., teamed up to draft a comprehensive regulatory reform measure (S. 981) that was less radical than the one rejected in 1996, but with similar goals of mandating cost-benefit analysis and risk assessment and expanding judicial review of agency actions. These efforts drew support from both parties and a broad coalition of business groups. But they were opposed by labor unions, environmentalists, consumer groups, and the Clinton administration, who argued that they would undermine critical environmental, health, and safety protections. Conservative Republicans, led by Senate majority leader Trent Lott, R-Miss., objected that the measure did no go *far enough* in placing limits on regulatory agencies; they still favored the approach that was rejected in 1995. These disagreements prevented adoption of any regulatory reform package in the 105th Congress. The Thompson-Levin bill was reported out of committee but never reached the Senate floor.[28] Several minor and more targeted regulatory reform initiatives also were introduced in the 105th Congress, but they failed to gain sufficient support to move forward.

Appropriation Politics: Riders and Budget Cuts

Perhaps the most striking element of the Republican strategy in the 104th and 105th Congresses was its use of the budget process to institute changes in policy as an alternative to enactment of new statutes. The Reagan administration used a similar approach in the 1980s with considerable short-term success (see chaps. 1 and 5). One of the most avid revolutionaries in the GOP freshman class, Rep. David McIntosh, R-Ind., explained the approach's logic: "The laws would remain on the books, but there would be no money to carry them out. It's a signal to the agencies to stop wasting time on these regulations."[29]

Appropriation Riders. The specific action to which McIntosh referred was the use of "riders"—legislative stipulations attached to appropriation bills—to achieve policy goals such as restricting, remaking, or even eliminating federal programs. In the 104th Congress, more than fifty antienvironmental riders were included in seven different budget bills, largely with the purpose of slowing or halting enforcement of laws by the EPA, the Interior Department, and other agencies until Congress could revise them. In one of the most controversial cases, seventeen riders were appended to the EPA appropriations bill in 1995 in an attempt to prohibit the agency from enforcing certain drinking-water and water quality standards and to keep it from regulating commercial development in wetlands and toxic air emissions from oil and gas refineries, among many other provisions. The EPA was told flatly that it could not spend any money on these activities.[30]

Such a legislative strategy is attractive to its proponents because appropriation bills, unlike authorizing legislation, typically move quickly and Congress must enact them each year. Many Republicans and business lobbyists also argue that use of riders is one of the few ways they have to rope in a bureaucracy that they believe needs additional constraints. This is because they are unable to address their concerns through changing the authorizing statutes themselves, a far more controversial and uncertain path to follow.[31]

Yet relying on riders is widely considered to be an inappropriate "backdoor" way to institute policy changes. The process provides little opportunity to debate the issues openly, and there are no public hearings or public votes on the policy questions involved. In one case, two sentences in an obscure passage buried within an $80 billion appropriation bill in 1995 would have barred the EPA from overseeing protection of wetlands.[32] By 1998 Kathleen McGinty, chair of the White House Council on Environmental Quality, complained about widespread use of the same tactics: "We have to literally comb through thousands of pages of legislative language and unearth these things." Other administration officials spoke of having to keep an eye out for "guerrilla activity" embedded in legislation, particularly budget bills.[33]

In 1995 the Natural Resources Defense Council (NRDC) had successfully characterized this appropriation rider strategy as a "stealth attack" on environmental statutes mounted at the behest of corporate polluters. Their charge was later repeated by both EPA administrator Carol Browner and President Clinton. Environmental groups worked steadily throughout 1995 to "shine a spotlight on the attacks" and gain media coverage that would enhance visibility of these kinds of activities on the Hill and mobilize an environmentally sympathetic but unaware public.[34] The environmentalists' campaign against what they termed Congress's "war on the environment" worked. Members were, as Rep. Sherwood Boehlert, R-N.Y., a moderate Republican, put it, "catching hell back home" over their environmental votes, and they learned that direct and open assaults on popular environmental laws would fail.[35]

The NRDC and other environmental groups used much the same political strategy during the 105th Congress to highlight the damage they believed would be inflicted by appropriation riders, which had become even more attractive to those seeking to weaken environmental policies than they were in the 104th Congress. Once again, the Clinton White House echoed the NRDC's critique in referring to the riders as a "sneak attack" by special interests seeking to bury their measures in budget bills "where they hope no one will find them."[36] Environmentalists managed to block or modify many of the riders but not all of them. According to an NRDC analysis, the 105th Congress enacted seven times as many environmental measures through riders on budget bills as it did through the conventional process of approving free-standing legislation that had gone through committee consideration, floor debate, and separate votes.[37]

The appeal of the budget rider strategy is easy to understand. There is little media attention, and the public tends not to get too worked up over such apparently "small" issues. Some of the riders do gain significant visibility, however, and the political calculus changes. For example, the fiscal year 1999 spending bill for the EPA prohibited the agency from using funds to prepare for implementation of the Kyoto Protocol on climate change protection (which Congress has strongly opposed), or even to educate the public about global warming. The latter part was later reversed by an amendment approved on the House floor after the Clinton White House characterized the legislation as a "gag order on federal agencies."[38]

Cutting Environmental Budgets. Despite the setback on appropriation riders, GOP leaders tried in 1995 and 1996 to capitalize on the momentum of their electoral success by representing the steep reductions they proposed for environmental spending as part of their larger—and broadly supported—effort to balance the federal budget. Their opponents argued that the depth of the cuts and the way they were targeted on enforcement actions suggested a quite different purpose. Indeed, House Budget Committee chair John Kasich, R-Ohio, a leading player in the new budget politics, acknowledged as much: "We're going to fund programs that we think are important and not fund the programs that we think are not important."[39]

Initial actions on the budget in the House in 1995 were surprising in light of public support for environmental policy. For fiscal year 1996 House members voted to cut the president's recommended EPA budget by 34 percent overall, proportionately the largest reduction for any major federal agency. The appropriations subcommittee that recommended the cuts explained why it favored deregulating the environment in this way: "The agency was headed in the wrong direction, for the wrong reasons, and in a manner that can impose unnecessary costs on American industry."[40]

The Senate was less drastic than the House but still harsh on the EPA. A House-Senate conference committee moved closer to the Senate's position. It reduced the EPA's overall budget by 22 percent, safe drinking-water grants to states and localities by 45 percent, and EPA's enforcement programs by 24 percent. As he had threatened, President Clinton vetoed the bill in mid-December 1995, saying the cuts were unacceptably large. Proposed reductions in other environmental agency budgets were generally smaller but nonetheless significant.

Irreconcilable differences between budgets that the president and the GOP Congress were willing to accept led to a period of prolonged stalemate in late 1995 and early 1996 and to two partial government shutdowns as money to operate agency programs ran out. The Republicans received the brunt of the public's wrath for the budget wars, which voters saw as yet another illustration of irresponsible gridlock in government.

By early 1996 Congress began to backtrack on its fiscal demands, and by late April 1996 it agreed to reinstate many of its earlier cuts in the EPA's budget as part of a broader compromise with the White House on the fiscal year 1996 budget. Although conflict continued in the 105th Congress over budget riders, spending levels were no longer targeted as they were in the previous Congress. There were some notable exceptions, such as the elimination of U.S. funding for the United Nations Population Fund in the fiscal year 1999 budget, which reflected a continuing conflict between the parties on population policy. Yet in 1998 the Clinton administration managed to gain full funding for its $1.7 billion Clean Water Action Plan (a five-year initiative to deal with polluted runoff from cities and farms), a 23 percent boost for programs to protect rare and endangered species, and a big jump in spending on global climate change research.[41]

Reauthorizing Environmental Statutes

For most of the 104th Congress members were absorbed in regulatory reform and budgetary battles and made little progress on the legislative front. Severe disagreements over the direction of environmental policy contributed to the lack of action. Partisan divisions were especially strong. The League of Conservation Voters (LCV) reported that for 1995, for example, votes on the environment showed the greatest disparity ever between the two parties. House Republicans averaged 15 percent on the league scorecard (supporting the LCV position on the selected votes 15 percent of the time) while Democrats averaged 76 percent. The ratios were similar in the Senate—11 percent and 89 percent, respectively, for Republicans and Democrats. For the 105th Congress, the partisan differences remained much the same.[42]

Partly because of such disagreement between the two parties, Congress was unable to act on renewal of the Clean Water Act, Endangered Species Act, Superfund, or Resource Conservation and Recovery Act. Where the House was prepared to move ahead, the Senate often blocked legislation that weakened environmental protection. For example, in May 1995 the House passed a revision of the Clean Water Act that the press and environmentalists promptly labeled the "dirty water act" for provisions that significantly weakened protection of wetlands and eased or revoked some of the law's requirements. The Senate's Environment Committee, chaired by John Chafee, R-R.I., chose not to move on similar proposals in the Senate.

The same outcome characterized action on most of the major environmental laws. In October 1995 the House Resources Committee approved a rewrite of the Endangered Species Act (ESA) backed by Rep. Don Young, R-Alaska, the committee's chair, and Rep. Richard W. Pombo, R-Calif. The Young-Pombo bill required greater consideration of property owners and economic impacts. Opponents argued that the bill would gut the ESA to appease small landowners and corporate developers, and they vowed to fight it.[43] As a result of these conflicts, neither house approved a final bill in the 104th Congress. Deadlock continued in the 105th Congress even though broad bipartisan agreement was reached on an ESA bill in the Senate, sponsored by Senators Dirk Kempthorne, R-Idaho, and Chafee; that bill also was endorsed by the Clinton White House.[44]

In both the 104th and 105th Congresses, members were unable to build consensus for revising the Superfund hazardous waste cleanup program despite long-standing concerns about its cost and effectiveness. The Senate Environment and Public Works Committee completed work on a bill in March 1998, but the committee split along party lines and the measure went no further. Two different bills were considered in the House, but neither made it out of committee. Environmentalists, most Democrats, and the Clinton White House objected that the measures would let polluters off the hook and weaken cleanup standards.[45]

Despite these failures to renew major environmental policies, there were some success stories in both the 104th and 105th Congresses. The 104th Congress approved a renewal of the Farm Bill, which contains significant land conservation provisions. Congress also enacted major amendments to marine fisheries conservation programs under the Magnuson Act. But the most important cases of legislative success involved control of pesticides and other agricultural chemicals, drinking water, and transportation. Especially for the first two of these actions, years of legislative gridlock were overcome as Republicans and Democrats uncharacteristically reached agreement on new policy directions.

The Food Quality Protection Act of 1996 was a major revision of the nation's pesticide law, which for decades had been a poster child for policy gridlock as environmentalists battled with the agricultural chemical and food industries. The new act required the EPA to use a new, uniform "reasonable risk" approach to regulating pesticides used on food, fiber, and other crops, and it required that special attention be given to the diverse ways in which both children and adults are exposed to such chemicals. EPA was to take special precautions to protect children against such risks. Remarkably, the act sped through Congress in record time without a single dissenting vote and was universally hailed as a key achievement of the 104th Congress. Such an unusual consensus emerged, however, only after court rulings that would have seriously and adversely affected the food industry by strictly interpreting the 1958 "Delaney Clause," which prohibited even minute traces of cancer-causing chemicals in processed food. Hence the industry was desperate to get the new law (which repealed the clause) enacted and was willing to compromise with public health and environmental groups. In addition, after the bruising battles of 1995, GOP lawmakers were eager to adopt an election-year environmental measure.[46]

The 1996 rewrite and reauthorization of the Safe Drinking Water Act (SDWA) sought to address many long-standing problems with the nation's drinking water program. It dealt more realistically with regulating contaminants based on their risk to public health and authorized over $7 billion through 2003 for state-administered loan and grant funds to help localities with compliance costs. It also created a new "right-to-know" provision that requires large water systems to provide their customers with annual reports on the safety of local water supplies. President Clinton signed the act into law in August 1996. Bipartisan cooperation on the SDWA amendments was unusual, and yet clearly illustrated that members of Congress could work together on resolving disputes over environmental policy. It was easier to do so when the legislation aided financially-pressed state and local governments and, like the pesticide bill, allowed Republicans to score some election-year points with environmentalists.[47]

Finally, after prolonged debate over renewal of the nation's major highway act, in mid summer 1998 the House and Senate overwhelmingly approved the Transportation Equity Act for the 21st Century. It was a sweeping six-year $218 billion measure that provided a 40 percent increase in spending to improve the nation's aging highways and included $5.4 billion for mass transit systems. The act also authorized new programs to reduce environmental impacts of transportation systems.[48]

Assessing Environmental Politics in the 104th and 105th Congresses

Policymaking on almost any major issue in the late 1990s has been difficult for many of the same reasons that environmental policies have faced gridlock in Congress: divided government, partisan rivalries, and insufficient public consensus. Nevertheless, it is important to ask how well environmental policymaking helps to pave the way for much-needed new policies. From that perspective, we should ask how well policymakers have assessed the problems the nation faces, evaluated current programs to see what works and what does not, and designed new policies that would do better over the next several decades, especially in light of strong public support for the goals of environmental protection.

By these standards, no recent Congress would get a high score. The 104th and 105th Congresses would have to be given a lower rating than most despite their considerable achievements in enacting new legislation on conservation of agricultural land, control of pesticides, safe drinking water, and transportation. The reason is that so many other important environmental problems, from energy use and climate change to global population growth, failed to get the attention they needed and so little progress was made in reconciling divergent interests and designing new policies.

Many students of Congress would add that the 104th Congress fell well short of common expectations for deliberation and debate among adversaries that is so vital to sound policymaking. The new Republican leadership was eager, of course, to move quickly on adoption of its conservative agenda and to capitalize on the political momentum created by the 1994 election. Even had more time been made available for public debate of policy proposals, however, many newer members likely would have rejected a strategy of consensus building and compromise as abandonment of their convictions.

Ultimately, such unwillingness to compromise led to widespread complaints about a new level of poisonous rhetoric and partisan rancor that came to dominate political dialogue on Capitol Hill. There is no question that the image of Republicans on the environment suffered as a result. Public opposition to Congress and its leadership grew throughout 1995, for example, and the Republican majority found itself censured by a revitalized and politically powerful environmental community and pilloried in the nation's press.[49]

The critics succeeded in shifting the terms of environmental policy debate. By 1996 senior Republicans began to signal a partial retreat from the revolution, worried that the party's antienvironmental image could cause it grievous harm in the fall elections.[50] They were right to worry about the electoral consequences. Environmental groups poured an unprecedented amount of money into both the 1996 and 1998 congressional elections, and they enjoyed considerable success in both.[51] In 1998, for example, the League of Conservation Voters reportedly spent some $2.3 million to help defeat nine of their "Dirty Dozen" candidates; 90 percent of the ninety-four candidates they endorsed won their races (see chap. 3).[52]

Despite the political price paid, the 104th Congress did achieve at least some of its goals—in addition to the enactment of legislation described above. It managed to reduce budgets for environmental agencies and programs, and it forced officials to reconsider their regulatory processes and priorities. It succeeded in gaining President Clinton's support for balancing the federal budget within seven years, with long-term implications for environmental policy. It also pushed the Clinton White House to escalate its own efforts at reinventing environmental regulation, which it reported prominently in March 1995 and emphasized strongly in subsequent years (see chap. 8). The result was that by 1996 the EPA, Interior Department, and other federal agencies had become more sensitive to the impacts of regulation. They quietly rolled back some regulations and softened enforcement of others. The EPA especially began to give much greater emphasis to cooperation with industry and use of incentive-based approaches to environmental protection.[53]

Intraparty squabbles among Republicans and battles between Congress and the Clinton White House made the 105th Congress less notable and less successful in enacting legislation than the 104th. Opportunities to resolve conflicts over environmental policies diminished as attention focused once again on policymaking through budget bills. Moreover, Newt Gingrich found himself increasingly unable to satisfy Republican conservatives or to rally his deeply divided party around a unified agenda; he also continued to suffer from persistent unpopularity with the public. An insurgent effort in July 1997 to remove him as Speaker failed. But three days after an unexpected five-seat Republican loss in the November 1998 elections (which many Republicans attributed to the Speaker's electoral miscalculations), Gingrich announced that he would leave the House in January 1999. In a stunning development closely linked to the House impeachment proceedings, Gingrich's designated successor, Rep. Robert Livingston, R-La., in turn resigned for personal reasons, and the Speakership went to a little-known member, J. Dennis Hastert, R-Ill.

In the 106th Congress, which convened in January 1999, Hastert quickly promised greater cooperation with Democrats, saying "The American people want Congress to work." He had little choice in adopting such a strategy. The Republicans had only a ten-vote margin over the Democrats, the smallest majority in nearly half a century, and thus could succeed only with Democratic support. Reeling from the public relations disaster over their attempt to remove President Clinton from office and plagued by continuing conflicts within the party between moderates and conservatives, the Republicans also were desperate to define a clear agenda around which to rebuild public support. Yet by almost any reckoning, the outlook for environmental policy in the 106th Congress remained highly uncertain, especially for major new initiatives. Members were more likely to act on popular but limited measures such as suburban growth management and protection of open land from development than to initiate far-reaching reforms.[54]

Conclusions

From many perspectives, environmental policies are at a critical crossroads. They have achieved much, but future gains cannot be assured by relying on conventional regulatory approaches governed by existing statutes. A search for new policy strategies has been underway for well over a decade as critical appraisals of existing programs have made their deficiencies clear. Innovative policy designs and experiments in collaborative decisionmaking, particularly at state and local levels, suggest the promise of new directions.[55] Such policy change can succeed at the federal level, however, only with the active assistance of Congress.

The political struggles on Capitol Hill summarized in this chapter reveal sharply contrasting visions for environmental policy. There may be consensus on broad principles of reform, but few signs point to an early resolution of conflict over the all-important details. To be sure, the revolutionary rhetoric of the 104th Congress had dissipated by 1999, and Congress was able to renew several major programs in an uncommon display of bipartisan cooperation. Nonetheless, for most other environmental programs policy gridlock continued to frustrate all participants, and partisan differences prevented emerging issues such as climate change from being seriously addressed.

The constitutional divisions between the House and the Senate guarantee that newly emergent political forces such as those represented in the House in the 104th and 105th Congresses will have no easy time pushing their legislative agendas. Even if they succeed, they may face a White House, as they did in the Clinton presidency, determined to slow or halt their advance. The 2000 elections may alter the equation by changing party control of Congress or the White House. Yet effective policymaking will always require cooperation between the two branches and leadership within both to advance sensible policies and secure public approval for them.

Whatever the short-term outcomes, setting new policy directions ultimately requires a greater level of public involvement in environmental politics. This is because such decisions must necessarily address fundamental questions about the role of government, the policies that are most appropriate, the setting of priorities for environmental protection, and the willingness of the American people to bear the costs.

Political institutions in a democracy, especially a representative legislature like Congress, are guided by public preferences. Yet the public's political influence will depend on its willingness to become more knowledgeable about environmental problems and to participate in the search for effective solutions, from local communities to the national level. Fortunately, detailed information about Congress and pending legislation is widely available on the Internet from interest groups as well as scientific and governmental Web sites.[56] Many of these sites provide direct links to facilitate communication with members of Congress, thus potentially enhancing the public's capacity to keep informed and influence the outcome of legislative decisionmaking.

Notes

The epigraph quotes Thomas Bliley, as reported in Bob Benenson, "GOP Sets the 104th Congress on New Regulatory Course," *Congressional Quarterly Weekly Report,* June 17, 1995, 1693. John Adams's statement is taken from his "Message from the President: A Congress Paralyzed," *The Amicus Journal* 21 (spring 1999): 2.

1. See chap. 1; and Michael E. Kraft, "Congress and Environmental Policy," in *Environmental Politics and Policy: Theories and Evidence,* 2d ed., ed. James P. Lester (Durham, N.C.: Duke University Press, 1995).
2. Ed Gillespie and Bob Schellhas, eds., *Contract with America: The Bold Plan by Rep. Newt Gingrich, Rep. Dick Armey, and the House Republicans to Change the Nation* (New York: Times Books/Random House, 1994); and Bob Benenson, "GOP Sets the 104th Congress on New Regulatory Course," *Congressional Quarterly Weekly Report,* June 17, 1995, 1693–1705.
3. Kraft, "Congress and Environmental Policy."
4. Charles O. Jones, *Separate but Equal Branches: Congress and the Presidency* (Chatham, N.J.: Chatham House, 1995); and James A. Thurber, ed., *Rivals for Power: Presidential-Congressional Relations* (Washington, D.C.: CQ Press, 1996).
5. Samuel C. Patterson and Gregory A. Caldeira, "Standing Up for Congress: Variations in Public Esteem since the 1960s," *Legislative Studies Quarterly* 15 (1990): 36. See also

John R. Hibbing and Elizabeth Theiss-Morse, *Congress as Public Enemy: Public Attitudes toward American Political Institutions* (New York: Cambridge University Press, 1995); and Hibbing and Theiss-Morse, "What the Public Dislikes About Congress," in *Congress Reconsidered*, 6th ed., ed. Lawrence C. Dodd and Bruce I. Oppenheimer (Washington, D.C.: CQ Press, 1997).

6. Richard E. Cohen, *Washington at Work: Back Rooms and Clean Air*, 2d ed. (New York: Macmillan, 1995); and Gary C. Bryner, *Blue Skies, Green Politics: The Clean Air Act of 1990*, 2d ed. (Washington, D.C.: CQ Press, 1996).

7. For a general discussion of the effects of programs that continue without formal reauthorization, see David Baumann, "Government on Autopilot," *National Journal*, March 13, 1999, 688–692.

8. Gary C. Jacobson, *The Politics of Congressional Elections*, 4th ed. (New York: Addison Wesley Longman, 1997).

9. Jeffrey M. Berry, *The Interest Group Society*, 3d ed. (New York: Addison Wesley Longman, 1997), chap. 2; Kay Lehman Schlozman and John T. Tierney, *Organized Interests and American Democracy* (New York: Harper and Row, 1986), 58–87; and Scott R. Furlong, "Interest Group Influence on Rulemaking," *Administration and Society* 29 (July 1997): 325–347.

10. David R. Mayhew, *Divided We Govern* (New Haven, Conn.: Yale University Press, 1991); Barbara Sinclair, *Unorthodox Lawmaking: New Legislative Processes in the U.S. Congress* (Washington, D.C.: CQ Press, 1997); and Jones, *Separate but Equal Branches*.

11. See National Academy of Public Administration, *Setting Priorities, Getting Results: A New Direction for EPA* (Washington, D.C.: NAPA, 1995); J. Clarence Davies and Jan Mazurek, *Pollution Control in the United States: Evaluating the System* (Washington, D.C.: Resources for the Future, 1998); and Daniel A. Mazmanian and Michael E. Kraft, eds., *Toward Sustainable Communities: Transition and Transformations in Environmental Policy* (Cambridge, Mass.: MIT Press, forthcoming, 1999).

12. Mary Etta Cook and Roger H. Davidson, "Deferral Politics: Congressional Decision Making on Environmental Issues in the 1980s," in *Public Policy and the Natural Environment*, ed. Helen M. Ingram and R. Kenneth Godwin (Greenwich, Conn.: JAI, 1985).

13. John W. Kingdon, *Agendas, Alternatives, and Public Policies*, 2d ed. (New York: HarperCollins, 1995).

14. Joseph A. Davis, "Environment/Energy," *1988 Congressional Quarterly Almanac* (Washington, D.C.: Congressional Quarterly Inc., 1989), 137.

15. For a fuller discussion of the gridlock over clean air and energy legislation, see Michael E. Kraft, "Environmental Gridlock: Searching for Consensus in Congress," in *Environmental Policy in the 1990s*, 2d ed., ed. Norman J. Vig and Michael E. Kraft (Washington, D.C.: CQ Press, 1994). See also Bryner, *Blue Skies, Green Politics*, and Cohen, *Washington at Work*.

16. Rhodes Cook, "Rare Combination of Forces May Make History of '94," *Congressional Quarterly Weekly Report*, April 15, 1995, 1076–1081; Gillespie and Schellhas, eds., *Contract with America*.

17. Katharine Q. Seelye, "Files Show How Gingrich Laid a Grand G.O.P. Plan," *New York Times*, December 3, 1995, 1, 16. See also John B. Bader, "The Contract with America: Origins and Assessments," in *Congress Reconsidered*, ed. Dodd and Oppenheimer.

18. Everett Carll Ladd, "The 1994 Congressional Elections: The Postindustrial Realignment Continues," *Political Science Quarterly* 110 (spring 1995): 1–23; and Alfred J. Tuchfarber et al., "The Republican Tidal Wave of 1994: Testing Hypotheses about Realignment, Restructuring, and Rebellion," *PS: Political Science and Politics* 28 (December 1995): 689–696.

19. Richard E. Fenno, Jr., *Learning to Govern: An Institutional View of the 104th Congress* (Washington, D.C.: Brookings Institution, 1997). See also Herbert F. Weisberg and Samuel C. Patterson, eds., *Great Theatre: The American Congress in the 1990s* (New York: Cambridge University Press, 1998); and Nicol C. Rae, *Conservative Reformers:*

The Republican Freshmen and the Lessons of the 104th Congress (New York: M. E. Sharpe, 1998).

20. Republican moderates on the environment, such as Rep. Sherwood Boehlert, R-N.Y., and Sen. John Chafee, R-R.I., had only modest success in pulling their party back from its more extreme positions on the environment. See John H. Cushman, Jr., "G.O.P. Backing Off from Tough Stand over Environment," *New York Times*, January 26, 1996, 1, A8; and Margaret Kriz, "The Green Card," *National Journal*, September 19, 1995, 2262–2267.

21. Allan Freedman, "GOP's Secret Weapon Against Regulations: Finesse," *CQ Weekly*, September 5, 1998, 1, 2314–2320; and Charles Pope, "Environmental Bills Hitch a Ride Through the Legislative Gantlet," *CQ Weekly*, April 4, 1998, 872–875.

22. For further details, see Benenson, "GOP Sets 104th Congress on New Regulatory Course"; and reports by the Natural Resources Defense Council: "Breach of Faith: How the Contract's Fine Print Undermines America's Environmental Success," February 1995; "The Year of Living Dangerously: Congress and the Environment in 1995," December 1995; and "Damage Report: Environment and the 105th Congress" *(www.nrdc.org/nrdcpro/damage/)*, November 4, 1998.

23. The general need for new directions in U.S. environmental policy is discussed in a number of chapters in this volume, especially chapters 1, 8, 9, 12, and 17. See also Mazmanian and Kraft, *Toward Sustainable Communities*; and Ken Sexton, Alfred A. Marcus, K. William Easter, and Timothy D. Burkhardt, eds., *Better Environmental Decisions: Strategies for Governments, Businesses, and Communities* (Washington, D.C.: Island Press, 1999).

24. John H. Cushman, Jr., "House Passes Bill That Would Limit Many Regulations," *New York Times*, March 4, 1995, 1, 8; Tom Kenworthy, "Letting the Truth Fall Where It May," *Washington Post National Weekly Edition*, March 27–April 2, 1995, 31; and Margaret Kriz, "Risky Business," *National Journal*, February 18, 1995.

25. David S. Cloud, "Industry, Politics Intertwined in Dole's Regulatory Bill," *Congressional Quarterly Weekly Report*, May 6, 1995, 1219–1224. The industry lobbying groups included two broad coalitions, Project Relief and the Alliance for Reasonable Regulation, in addition to the National Association of Manufacturers, trade associations representing diverse industries, and dozens of leading corporations with strong financial stakes in the outcome.

26. Bob Benenson, "House Easily Passes Bills to Limit Regulations," *Congressional Quarterly Weekly Report*, March 4, 1995, 679–682.

27. John H. Cushman, Jr., "House G.O.P. Chiefs Back Off on Stiff Antiregulatory Plan," *New York Times*, March 6, 1996, C20; Cushman, "Businesses Scaling Back Plans to Defang Federal Regulations," *New York Times*, February 3, 1996, 1, 7; and Cushman, "Adversaries Back Pollution Rules Now on the Books," *New York Times*, February 12, 1996, C1–11.

28. NRDC, "Damage Report"; Allan Freedman, "Rival Bills Cloud the Scene for Regulatory Overhaul," *Congressional Quarterly Weekly Report*, March 18, 1998, 658–659; and Freedman, "GOP Likely to Sidestep Overhaul, Fearing Environmental Showdown," *CQ Weekly*, April 4, 1998, 876–878.

29. McIntosh is quoted in Bob Herbert, "Health and Safety Wars," *New York Times*, July 10, 1995, A11.

30. John H. Cushman, Jr., "G.O.P.'s Plan for Environment Is Facing a Big Test in Congress," *New York Times*, July 17, 1995, 1, A9.

31. Pope, "Environmental Bills Hitch a Ride."

32. John H. Cushman, Jr., "Clause Would End an Agency's Veto on Wetland Plans," *New York Times*, December 12, 1995, 1, 15.

33. McGinty is quoted in Margaret Kriz, "Rough Riders," *National Journal*, September 5, 1998, 2022–2025. See also Pope, "Environmental Bills Hitch a Ride," 872.

34. See Natural Resources Defense Council, "Stealth Attack: Gutting Environmental Protection through the Budget Process," July 1995; and Gary Lee, "The Green Coun-

terattack," *Washington Post National Weekly Edition,* August 28–September 3, 1995, 15–16. For a broader review of environmental lobbying strategies, see Michael Kraft and Diana L. Wuertz, "Environmental Advocacy in the Corridors of Government," in *The Symbolic Earth: Discourse and Our Creation of the Environment,* ed. James G. Cantrill and Christine Oravec (Lexington: University Press of Kentucky, 1996).

35. John H. Cushman, Jr., "House Rejects Plan to Limit E.P.A.'s Power," *New York Times,* November 3, 1995, 1, A8; and Boehlert interview with *Greenwire,* October 30, 1995.

36. "Statement by Vice President Gore on Republican Anti-Environmental Riders" (Washington, D.C.: Office of the Vice President, September 29, 1998).

37. NRDC, "Damage Report: Environment and the 105th Congress," 1. For a more objective review of the rider strategy, see Kriz, "Rough Riders."

38. See Lori Nitschke, "Battles over Kyoto Treaty May Delay House Action on VA-HUD Spending Bill," *CQ Weekly,* June 27, 1998, 1767.

39. Quoted in Helen Dewar, "House Republicans Have a New Plan," *Washington Post National Weekly Edition,* January 22–28, 1996, 31.

40. Cushman, "G.O.P.'s Plan for Environment."

41. Carroll J. Doherty and the staff of *CQ Weekly,* "Congress Compiles a Modest Record in a Session Sidetracked by Scandal: Appropriations," *CQ Weekly,* November 14, 1998, 3086–3087 and 3090–3091.

42. League of Conservation Voters, "National Environmental Scorecard, 104th Congress, First Session" (Washington, D.C.: League of Conservation Voters, 1996); and "1998 National Environmental Scorecard" (Washington, D.C.: League of Conservation Voters, October 1998).

43. Bob Benenson, "House Panel Votes to Restrict Endangered Species Act," *Congressional Quarterly Weekly Report,* October 14, 1995, 3136–3137; and Margaret Kriz, "Caught in the Act," *National Journal,* December 16, 1995, 3090–3094.

44. John H. Cushman, Jr., "Linking Endangered Species Act to Spending," *New York Times,* October 10, 1998, A8; and Charles Pope, "In Senate, Hope Springs Again for Endangered Species Law," *Congressional Quarterly Weekly Report,* February 21, 1998, 437.

45. Charles Pope, "Politics Poisons the Debate over Superfund Rewrite," *Congressional Quarterly Weekly Report,* February 28, 1998, 486.

46. David Hosansky, "Rewrite of Laws on Pesticides on Way to President's Desk," *Congressional Quarterly Weekly Report,* July 27, 1996, 2101–2103; and Hosansky, "Provisions: Pesticide, Food Safety Law," *Congressional Quarterly Weekly Report,* September 7, 1996, 2546–2550.

47. David Hosansky, "Drinking Water Bill Clears; Clinton Expected to Sign," *Congressional Quarterly Weekly Report,* August 3, 1996, 2179–2180; and Allan Freedman, "Provisions: Safe Drinking Water Act Amendments," *Congressional Quarterly Weekly Report,* September 14, 1996, 2622–2627.

48. Alan K. Ota, "What the Highway Bill Does," *CQ Weekly,* July 11, 1998, 1892–1898.

49. See Margaret Kriz, "Not-So-Silent Spring," *National Journal,* March 9, 1996, 522–526.

50. See Allan Freedman, "Republicans Strive to Gain Environmental Advantage," *Congressional Quarterly Weekly Report,* May 18, 1996, 1384–1386.

51. Margaret Kriz, "The GOP Looks a Little Green," *National Journal,* November 16, 1996, 2516; and Kriz, "The Big Green Election Machine," *National Journal,* October 24, 1998, 2512–2513.

52. Deb Callahan, "Building Political Momentum for the Environment," *LCV Insider,* December 1998.

53. John H. Cushman, Jr., "Proposed Changes Simplify Rules on Pollution Control," *New York Times,* March 17, 1995, A8; and U.S. EPA, "EPA Strategic Plan" (Washington, D.C.: Office of the Chief Financial Officer, EPA, September 1997).

54. Staffs of *CongressDaily, Greenwire,* and *National Journal,* "Legislative Focus: Energy & Environment," supplement to *National Journal,* March 24, 1999. See also John H. Cushman, Jr., "Politicians of All Persuasions Rally Round Rival Bills to Protect Lands,"

New York Times, March 11, 1999, A10; and Charles Pope, "Suburban Sprawl and Government Turf," *CQ Weekly,* March 13, 1999, 586–590.

55. Sexton et al., *Better Environmental Decisions*; Mazmanian and Kraft, *Toward Sustainable Communities*; and Michael E. Kraft and Denise Scheberle, "Environmental Federalism at Decade's End," *Publius: The Journal of Federalism* 28: 1 (winter 1998): 131–146.

56. Nearly all activist groups, environmentalist and business organizations alike, have Web sites that track current legislation and facilitate e-mail communication with legislators. For example, see the Natural Resources Defense Council's site for coverage of environmental policy news and legislative issues *(www.nrdc.org/)* or the League of Conservation Voters' site for legislators' voting records on environmental issues *(www.lcv.org).* An overview of legislative issues also can be found at the Ecological Society of America's site *(http://esa.sdsc.edu/).* Policy studies from many different perspectives can be found at *www.policy.com/,* with some links to pending legislation in Congress and others that facilitate communication with members.

The EPA's home page *(www.epa.gov/epahome/)* has links to current laws and regulations and pending legislation, and to the Library of Congress's Thomas search engines for locating key congressional documents. Thomas can be accessed directly at *http://thomas.loc.gov/,* and it is the most comprehensive public site for legislative searches. Congressional Research Service reports are available at the Web site for the Committee for the National Institute for the Environment *(www.cnie.org).* General Accounting Office evaluations of environmental programs can be found at *www.gao.gov/.*

7

Environmental Policy in the Courts
Lettie McSpadden

The Role of the Courts in Environmental Policy

In 1803 the U.S. Supreme Court established the power of courts to oversee the constitutionality of actions by other branches of government when it declared that it is "the duty of the judicial department to say what the law is."[1] Even before Chief Justice John Marshall made this famous pronouncement, state and federal courts were helping to formulate and implement public policy through their powers to interpret and enforce laws, and they continue to do so to this day. Judicial decisions about public policies as diverse as abortion rights and desegregating public schools have been celebrated or deplored by commentators for the last three decades. Less well publicized, but just as important, has been their participation over the same period in shaping environmental policies from water pollution control to the preservation of endangered species. Were it not for court injunctions, even fewer ancient trees would be surviving in the United States. Were it not for enforcement actions brought by citizen activists, our waterways would be more choked by industrial wastes than they are.

Critics of judicial activism bemoan these developments; yet they are as much a part of the public policy process as congressional debates and executive management of the budget. Nevertheless, some analysts argue that judges are singularly unsuited to make policy decisions in technical areas such as pollution control because they must respond to individual demands for justice.[2] Other scholars caution against the dominance of technical experts and urge the continued use of lay judges to counterbalance inequities that arise when an unrestrained technocracy controls policy.[3] There is a tension between Americans' desire on the one hand for substantively "correct" decisions reached by experts and, on the other, for democratic decisions made through public participation and facilitated by the courts' insistence on due process. Like other government institutions, courts are caught between these two equally important values in the American polity, and they continue to struggle to reconcile them.

The Common Law: Compensation After Injury

Judicial involvement in environmental policy has evolved over three decades. Before environmental legislation exploded in the 1970s, common law concepts such as trespass, personal injury, and liability for damages provided the only legal recourse when people or organizations imposed the costs of their economic activities on others. Parties injured by polluted air, water, toxic wastes, or other hazards may still ask the courts for compensation for harm they suffer as a result of a degraded environment. In such cases, however, the burden of proof customarily falls on the plaintiff, who must show that each injury is the fault of a particular polluter. So many variables may have contributed to the victims' problems that most judges or juries find it difficult to assign fault to only one.

Relatively few victims successfully prove the culpability of the manufacturer of a product or the operator of a plant that dumps toxic materials into the air, water, or soil. And they are often dissatisfied by the outcome. The greatest drawback to the judicial remedy of damages is that nothing is done to modify the injurious behavior. It is often cheaper for businesses to pay damages and continue the harmful action. Theoretically, the fear of having to pay damages for injuries done to customers, workers, and innocent bystanders will affect the behavior of firms that manufacture products and dispose of wastes without concern for the consequences. The uncertainty of being sued, however, and the difficulty of establishing proof often diminish the impact of this fear.[4]

The equity suit is an alternative common law remedy to damage judgments. It gives courts the power to issue an injunction forcing the party causing the harm to cease doing so. Judges are loath, however, to order organizations performing essential services for a community, such as operating a hazardous waste landfill, to halt operations. The damage done to third parties is balanced against the economic good that the polluter provides; it is extremely difficult to shut down a business that is providing hundreds of jobs. Just as courts are reluctant to compensate for injuries, so too do they find it difficult to balance interests and restore equity.

Public Law: The Goal of Prevention

Because common laws of nuisance, trespass, and injury have remedied few environmental problems, proponents of resource conservation and pollution control have turned to public law. Rather than depending on the fear of a potential lawsuit after harm has been done, statutory law attempts to prevent the harm from occurring. By proscribing certain actions (for example, dumping crude oil into waterways) and prescribing others (for example, treating sewage before release into waterways), lawmakers hope to prevent many injuries to public health and the natural environment. Shifting legal recourse from private lawsuits against polluters to government enforcement of public law may redress the imbalance between the two parties in traditional common law cases. Prevention, rather than remediation, is the goal of public law.[5]

The number of statutory environmental laws intended to regulate behavior grew in the 1970s and increased the courts' workload, as some of the burden of resolving uncertainty was passed to the courts. The proliferation of new statutory laws not only creates the need for an administrative state to enforce them but also increases the need for courts to interpret them. Regulatory law forces courts to make prospective decisions about the potential for harm rather than retrospective judgments about the causes of demonstrated injuries. It casts judges in entirely new roles as quasi legislators and quasi administrators.[6]

Court Oversight of Administrative Discretion

In their traditional role as neutral arbiter of individual disputes, judges have finished their work once a verdict has been rendered. As makers of public policy, judges must now oversee how well the responsible agency carries out the court's orders. In many cases a judge will order an agency to comply with the letter of the law passed by Congress by writing regulations by a certain date, issuing a permit, or even rethinking the grounds for its previous decision. Sometimes a judge must exercise managerial control over the same case for years.

For the period preceding the court's verdict as well, the judge's role has greatly expanded. Judges today often act as intermediaries, bringing opposing parties into their chambers to work out a compromise before the case reaches trial. In so doing, judges' discretion and influence over policy are broadened greatly. Many cases are settled by the parties and their attorneys, often with judicial encouragement. Indeed, some adversaries in environmental disputes are now able to negotiate their differences without resort to the court system at all through a process called environmental dispute resolution (EDR). This method was pioneered by the Conservation Foundation in the 1980s, and its former president, William Reilly, urged business and environmental groups to use EDR after he was appointed administrator of the Environmental Protection Agency (EPA) by the Bush administration.[7]

Judges have disagreed among themselves about their role in overseeing administrative agency decisions. Judge Harold Leventhal, who in the 1970s sat on the U.S. Court of Appeals for the District of Columbia Circuit, argued that it is the courts' responsibility to guarantee that agencies take a "hard look" at all factors when making their decisions.[8] Judge Leventhal also argued that judges need access to court-appointed scientific experts to help them understand the conflicting testimony of adversarial expert witnesses.

One of Judge Leventhal's colleagues on the D.C. Circuit in the 1970s, Judge David Bazelon, was skeptical of the suggestion that experts be assigned to the courts. Instead, Bazelon proposed that all opinions about an issue be incorporated into the agency's decision-making process. Although he did not dispute the complexity of the technical problems facing the courts, Bazelon believed that science and technology are not the exclusive domain of scientists and engineers. Many cases before the courts, he argued, involve major value choices. Although cloaked in technical questions, such cases should nevertheless be open to public scrutiny and participation. Rather than curing the problem with separate, expert advisers for judges, he preferred that all contending groups be able to have their own experts heard before administrative agencies and in court as well.[9]

Interest Groups and the Federal Courts

Judge Bazelon's affinity for a pluralist competition of ideas in the judicial process has been adopted by many interest groups concerned with environmental policy. The same groups that try to influence Congress to pass and modify environmental laws are usually active in tracking the way agencies carry out these laws. Not surprisingly, environmental groups that urged Congress to pass legislation also come before the courts to have the law enforced. Business groups and others who were disappointed in the outcomes in either the legislative or executive branch also have another chance to influence policy in court. Given the ambiguity of many of the policies made by both legislative and administrative actors, the shift to the courts for further debate is the obvious next step.

Most environmental litigation is initiated by one of three actors. The best known are groups like the National Audubon Society and Sierra Club, which worked to get environmental protection and natural resource legislation passed and reformed in the 1970s. Subsequently, these groups and newer organizations such as the Natural Resources Defense Council (NRDC) and the Environmental Defense Fund (EDF) sued government agencies to carry out their congressional mandates. During the early 1970s they went to the federal courts to get the new laws enforced, where they often succeeded in having their strict interpretations of the laws accepted.

Initially caught off guard by environmental litigation, economic interests are now responding with increasing confidence and stridency. With their superior legal and economic resources, major corporations and trade associations have asked the courts to reinterpret environmental laws in a more probusiness light. It is common, for example, for both business and environmental groups to simultaneously sue the EPA over the same regulation. One litigant claims the regulation is too strict; the other, that it is too lenient. Often businesses and private property owners outstrip environmental groups in the extreme nature of their demands, arguing that the laws themselves should be declared unconstitutional and unenforceable.

Government is the third major actor in environmental law, and it participates on both sides of the issues. When challenged by environmental groups, it often represents an economic or development interest normally associated with major corporations. When challenged by industry, it must defend the law and the environmental point of view. In addition, government agencies have a sizable agenda of their own. After all, their official role is to enforce statutory laws, ensure the conditions of permits, and halt violations of regulations by businesses and private property owners.

Originally, government cases were restricted to asking the courts for civil fines. However, in 1981 the EPA established an Office of Criminal Enforcement and began referring cases to the Department of Justice for prosecution. This development met with mixed reviews. Proponents argued that the possibility of incarcerating corporate officials would increase their willingness to comply with environmental laws. Critics complained about the possibility of civil rights violations and claimed that accommodations could be reached without resort to such extreme measures.

Environmental cases were originally classified into three modal types at the trial level—environmental groups vs. government, business vs. government, and government vs. business. At the appellate level any loser may choose to appeal, which creates a fourth type in which government appeals an environmental victory at the trial level. These became common in the 1980s when the Reagan Justice Department grew defensive about lax environmental regulation. There is also a fifth type of case between different agencies and levels of government. In such cases one government body accuses the other of polluting the environment. Reacting against the emphasis in the Reagan and Bush administrations on deregulation, state authorities have increasingly assumed a regulatory stance against such federal agencies as the Department of Defense for not cleaning up polluted bases in their states.

Litigants and Their Changes in Strategy

The traditional approach of environmental groups was to sue government for regulating too loosely. But in the 1980s these groups began confronting business corporations directly in court in addition to suing the government. Congress facilitated this type of suit by writing into several of the environmental laws provisions for private attorneys general (citizen suits) to enforce them. This power enables a private citizen or group to take legal action against a polluter when a government agency does not.

Disappointed by the EPA's unwillingness to undertake enforcement actions in the 1980s, environmental groups sued to force individual industries and plants to conform to the limits written into water pollution discharge permits. In this way environmental groups have been able to pursue their disagreements directly with their chief rival, business interests, when the responsible agencies are unwilling to play their proenvironmental role. This trend has continued throughout the 1990s as groups such as the NRDC, EDF, and Sierra Club combed reports filed with EPA to locate self-reported violations of Clean Water Act permits and sued for fines the administrators had not demanded.

Calling these cases instances of "judicial activism," conservative critics argue that the litigants do not deserve standing before the courts. Implementation of the laws should be left, they contend, to technical experts in the administrative agencies; environmental groups should not be allowed to involve the courts. This argument has received a sympathetic hearing in some courts, especially the U.S. Supreme Court, and is used not only by business defendants but also by government defendants against environmental initiatives.

During the Reagan and Bush administrations, Congress was so convinced of the need for these citizen suits that it continued to add authority for private attorneys general to pollution control laws. In 1990, for example, it amended the Clean Air Act to require permits for plant emissions similar to those issued to industries that discharge wastes into waterways. The reporting system required by permits creates a clear paper trail for private groups to use in court.[10] One ambitious goal in the Republican Party's 1994 "Contract with America" was to change pollution control laws by eliminating private attorney general suits. However, this effort proved unsuccessful.

In addition to objecting to environmental groups' standing in court, business groups have found a new theme around which to focus their arguments against government regulation. Developers and other landowners argue that almost any government regulation, federal or state, constitutes an unconstitutional violation of their property rights if it diminishes the value of their land. These litigants use the Fifth Amendment language ("nor shall private property be taken for public use without just compensation") to attack such federal laws as wilderness preservation and endangered species protection. They also cite the Fourteenth Amendment's due process clause to challenge state police powers such as zoning laws. Moreover, in cases where the property owner wins the right to develop, he or she may also claim compensation from the government for losses suffered in the interim.[11] These arguments have frequently been upheld by the U.S. Court of Claims, which hears suits against the U.S. government for monetary damages, and in many cases by the U.S. Supreme Court (see discussion below in "Patterns in Court Outcomes"). During the 1990s twenty-six state legislatures passed laws establishing a right of property owners to be compensated if regulations reduce their property values. This development sent a chill through federal and state policymakers, who may relax their regulations rather than face large damage judgments.[12]

Developers and other business interests have also developed the strategic lawsuit against public participation (SLAPP suit) to use against public interest groups, such as consumer protection advocates and environmentalists. These suits attempt to prevent environmentalists from testifying in public hearings, lobbying zoning boards, and advertising against development projects by arguing that the public interest group has defamed or libeled the developer in opposing the projects. The majority of SLAPP suits are thrown out of court on the ground that they interfere with citizens' right to petition their government for redress of grievance.[13] Because they are filed in various state trial courts, however, they may go unresolved for years, running up legal expenses for the defendants. The threat of SLAPP suits may deter public interest groups from becoming involved in issues in their communities.

The Types of Issues in Federal Courts

Most federal cases about the environment fall into three categories: (1) National Environmental Policy Act (NEPA) cases, in which public interest groups challenge government projects because of their adverse environmental effects; (2) public health threats, from air and water pollution as well as from toxic materials such as pesticides and hazardous wastes; and (3) natural resource management issues, including disputes over energy development, the use of public lands, and wildlife and wilderness protection.

The Rise and Fall of NEPA

During the "environmental decade" of the 1970s, many cases concerned NEPA, which requires the federal government to write an environmental impact statement (EIS) before undertaking a government-funded or -regulated project, such as highway or dam construction, or permitting the operation of a nuclear reactor. Federal courts initially responded by treating such questions substantively, insisting that agencies should prove that they had indeed taken Judge Leventhal's "hard look" at all aspects of such projects.[14] District and circuit court judges also fashioned stringent procedural requirements for federal agencies to ensure that all interested parties had an opportunity to enter the process, in accordance with Judge Bazelon's desire for complete procedural protection.

By the end of the 1970s, however, the U.S. Supreme Court had narrowed the scope of NEPA by overturning many of these cases. In *Vermont Yankee* v. *NRDC* (1978), the Court reversed two District of Columbia Circuit Court decisions remanding Nuclear Regulatory Commission (NRC) decisions for inadequate treatment of environmental issues.[15] Writing for a unanimous Supreme Court, Justice William H. Rehnquist chastised the D.C. Circuit for interfering with NRC discretion and substituting its own policy preferences for that of an expert commission. After having their decisions overturned by the Supreme Court repeatedly in the 1970s, the federal courts came to treat writing EISs as a paper exercise. They generally ruled in favor of government projects as long as the EIS requirement had been observed. As a consequence, the number of NEPA cases declined dramatically in the 1980s as environmental groups turned their resources to pollution control and natural resource management issues.

Public Health Threats

Although air pollution cases constitute a modest percentage of environmental cases, water pollution cases are abundant chiefly because permits are required for every point source, which opens the door to enforcement actions. During the 1980s government enforcement actions dropped off dramatically, but environmental groups replaced government implementation with their own private attorneys general cases. If the EPA or a state agency begins a public enforcement action, or if industry reduces its pollution in response to the citizen action, the courts often dismiss environmental groups' cases. Nevertheless, they have achieved their desired end—reduced pollution. When pollution continues and enforcement at either the state or federal level is not forthcoming, the courts are willing to give private attorneys general standing and are likely to decide these cases for the environmental groups, even awarding them attorney's fees afterward. With the renewed attack on environmental groups' standing in courts, however, this type of victory may become less common.

New and amended laws treating solid and hazardous waste disposal and cleanup created additional litigation as government, industry, and environmental groups competed to have courts accept their interpretation of the legislation. The 1980 Comprehensive Environmental Response, Compensation, and Liability Act (CERCLA, or Superfund) provides for recovery of costs from owners and former users of abandoned waste sites, but Congress failed to define liability or explain how to divide it among multiple responsible parties, creating an increased workload for many federal courts.

Trial courts have interpreted the Superfund law to imply strict liability, which relieves government of the need to prove intent or negligence when demonstrating blame. They have also been willing to assess liability quite broadly on former and present owners, operators, haulers, and users of sites, sometimes holding a few parties responsible for the entire cost when others went bankrupt or could not be located.[16] Amending Superfund to eliminate strict, retroactive, and joint liability was one of the most important items on the 104th and 105th Congresses' agenda, but gridlock prevailed and the law went unchanged (see chap. 6). Meanwhile, government and industrial litigants continue to search for additional responsible parties, and courts continue to struggle to assess liability and divide the expenses.

Often EPA or a state agency will initiate a case against one or more large polluters of a leaking toxic waste site, and the corporations named will immediately counter by conducting their own delay-inducing investigation to locate evidence of other dumpers who contributed waste. In many cases these additional parties are municipal administrators of dump sites or contributors of trivial amounts of wastes. At the end of the 1990s many environmental cases were squabbles among multiple contributors and their insurance agencies over which responsible party will pay for how much of the cleanup. Protracted conflicts of this kind enabled opponents of the Superfund law to claim that at some sites more money is spent on legal disputes than on actual cleanup operations.

Natural Resources Cases

Energy issues were rarely contested in the courts until the energy crisis in the mid 1970s. Related to energy issues are cases that concern publicly owned land and other natural resources located primarily in the western United States. Although the number of such cases declined somewhat in the early 1980s, energy–public land issues now constitute an important subject for environmental cases. The March 1989 Exxon *Valdez* disaster, which spilled 11 million gallons of oil into Prince William Sound, Alaska, generated one misdemeanor conviction of the tanker's captain in state court. It sparked numerous additional civil actions. The federal government settled its water pollution suit against Exxon for $1 billion. In September 1994, a federal jury awarded fishers, native Alaskans, and other residents of the area nearly $300 million in compensatory damages for loss of income and $5 billion in punitive damages designed to force Exxon into greater vigilance to prevent future spills. This award was appealed and, at the tenth anniversary of the accident, was still not resolved. Exxon argued that its expenditure of $2.3 billion in cleanup operations in 1989 should have ended the matter and denied that any effects from the spill lingered in the sound. Local residents, however, remained bitter about what they perceived as continued harm to the ecosystem and their livelihood.[17]

In the early 1990s a dispute in the Pacific Northwest over proposals to harvest the last large remaining stands of old-growth timber not protected by wilderness or park status joined conservationists and the timber industry in controversy. Conservationists argued that further loss of virgin forests would reduce biodiversity and set a negative example for developing nations that are rapidly depleting their own forests. The timber industry responded by saying that preserving old growth would throw loggers and mill workers out of work at a time of economic depression in the Northwest. Environmentalists countered that the industry's automation and its trade in raw logs to Japan eliminated more jobs than conservation ever could.

In court the controversy centered around the Endangered Species Act (ESA), which the Fish and Wildlife Service (FWS) interpreted to prohibit anyone from destroying the habitat of endangered or threatened plants and animals. Although the northern spotted owl, which lives in the Northwest forests, had been in decline for years, the FWS would not label the species threatened—much less endangered—until a federal judge in Washington State, responding to a suit from the Sierra Club, ordered it to reconsider.[18] Once the FWS had labeled the owl threatened, its interpretation of the ESA's language forced judges to issue injunctions that halted logging in several national forests because of the threat to habitat. At the urging of Washington and Oregon representatives and senators, Congress took the unusual step of stripping the federal courts of jurisdiction over these cases in 1989 and again in 1990. Environmentalists challenged the constitutionality of these acts, but the U.S. Supreme Court upheld the Congress.[19]

After Congress failed to pass similar laws in 1991, trial judges renewed their injunctions against logging areas where the spotted owl lives. The Bush administration argued the law should be amended to accommodate logging, but environmentally oriented members of Congress countered with new bills that would afford protection for old-growth forests for the sake of biodiversity itself rather than relying on finding endangered species that depend on them for habitat. Neither side won the congressional debate before the Clinton administration took office. In 1993 a Clinton-arranged "timber summit" in Oregon defused the situation with a compromise that allowed some logging and also provided federal funds to retrain out-of-work loggers.

Patterns in Court Outcomes

There are noticeable trends in the way federal courts interpret environmental laws. Since the 1970s judges in certain regions of the country have tended to reflect the worldviews of the other residents in those areas. Federal courts in the Northeast and Midwest and on the West Coast have tended to favor environmental litigants, whereas judges in the Southeast, Southwest, and Rocky Mountain states have tended to favor development and economic growth.[20] Democratic judges have tended to favor environmental arguments more than Republican judges in all the regions. This became especially apparent during the 1980s when the Reagan and Bush administrations carefully screened candidates for the federal bench for their ideological purity, including opposition to governmental regulation. In the early 1990s, when Reagan-Bush appointees dominated the federal circuits, fewer environmental victories were recorded in federal courts.[21]

The Lower Federal Courts

Because courts tend to favor official government actors in all areas of litigation, government agencies win more often than either their business or environmental opponents. In fact, the Supreme Court established a precedent in 1991 that federal courts should defer whenever possible to the expert judgments of administrative agencies.[22] Although environmentalists tended to win more victories in the 1970s than business litigants, in the 1990s the balance shifted. The EPA increased its success rate over environmental groups and lost several significant legal battles to business litigants. In October 1991 the Fifth Circuit Court of Appeals in New Orleans overruled the EPA on banning asbestos, a regulation the agency had spent ten years perfecting. The court ruled that the agency had not considered the costs to industry for finding substitutes and that insufficient benefits were to be gained.[23] An extreme example of judicial intervention into administrative decisionmaking, this case contradicts the assertion often made by Presidents Ronald Reagan and George Bush that they chose federal judges who would uphold agency decisions and refrain from inserting their own values into their opinions. In December 1991 a panel of D.C. Circuit judges—consisting of two Reagan appointees and Clarence Thomas, who was subsequently appointed to the Supreme Court by President Bush—threw out the EPA's twelve-year-old definition of hazardous wastes, which included certain wastes from the petroleum industry.[24]

Divided decisions made by the D.C. Circuit Court of Appeals illustrate how volatile the political balance can be in one circuit. In 1993 the logging industry attacked the Fish and Wildlife Service's reading of the Endangered Species Act in the D.C. Circuit, traditionally a favored forum for environmental litigants. In July 1993 Chief Judge Abner Mikva, a Carter holdover, ruled against the loggers, agreeing with the FWS that the word "harm" in the

ESA meant that private property owners could not destroy the habitat of endangered species. Judge David Sentelle, a Reagan appointee, vigorously dissented, arguing the only meaning of "harm" means killing the species directly.[25] In March 1994 the third member of the panel, another Reagan appointee, changed his mind on rehearing the case and decided that the FWS had misinterpreted the ESA. This decision flew in the face of the Supreme Court's admonition to lower courts to defer to government agencies when interpreting statute law, and the High Court overturned it in 1995 when it ruled 6–3 that the FWS can interpret the ESA to include habitat destruction in the definition of harm.[26] The D.C. Circuit's decision signaled a new willingness on the part of Reagan and Bush appointees to view agency decisions more critically after the Democratic Party gained control of the executive branch.

In August 1994 the entire D.C. Circuit court voted on whether to hear the case again in order to settle the disagreement within the three-judge panel. The only judges who voted to rehear were Mikva, another Carter holdover, one Reagan appointee, and the newest judge, who was appointed by President Bill Clinton.[27] All six judges voting not to rehear were either Reagan or Bush appointees. After this vote, Judge Mikva left the bench, and President Clinton named his replacement. With three Clinton appointees, two Carter holdovers, and six Reagan-Bush appointees, the D.C. Circuit will be a polarized circuit for some time to come.

The U.S. Court of Claims

One forum in which the new property rights movement has received a warm reception is the U.S. Court of Claims, where landowners take their allegations that the government must compensate them for any diminution in the value of their property because of regulations. Two cases about filling wetlands exemplify the court's generosity toward business. In one case the Corps of Engineers, the agency that regulates wetlands, refused to permit a New Jersey developer to build a subdivision on 12.5 acres of wetlands. Although the Corps had authority to deny the permit, the Court of Claims found that the owner had lost all economic use of the wetlands and was entitled to $2.6 million in compensation.[28] The judge accepted the developer's argument that the "best use" for the land was residential development despite the clear objective of preserving wetlands found in the Clean Water Act. In a second case, the Corps refused a permit to quarry limestone in an area where the aquifer was rapidly becoming polluted by such strip-mining operations. The judge awarded the company $1 million for the loss of all use of its property despite evidence that the land could be sold for about $4,000 an acre.[29]

In both cases the judges rejected the government's argument that the parcels of land were small parts of larger holdings from which their owners had already reaped huge profits. The proposed housing development in New Jersey was part of 250 acres, bought for $300,000, most of which had already been developed. The Florida quarry was 98 acres out of 1,560 acres of wetland, most of which had already been mined. The land in both cases had escalated in value, and the court ruled the owners were entitled to the present-day fair market value of the land because they had expected to gain from their initial investment.[30] In both cases the judges also found that the burden on the private property owners outweighed any public benefit from preserving wetlands or preventing groundwater contamination.

In addition to private land use cases, the Court of Claims has been receptive to numerous complaints from timber, mining, and ranching interests, as well as from inholders of private lands inside public parks, that the government's efforts to control uses and to preserve the ecology of public lands interfere with their property rights. These decisions are supported by the property rights philosophy increasingly being espoused by conservative judges and law professors. They have also been supported by recent decisions in the Supreme Court, which has looked favorably on private landowners' claims against state land use regulations.

The Supreme Court and Environmental Issues

Under the leadership of Chief Justice Warren Burger, the Supreme Court in the 1970s and the first half of the 1980s was less receptive to environmental claims than were the lower federal courts, overturning almost all proenvironmental cases brought before it. After William Rehnquist became chief justice in 1986, the High Court became even more business oriented as most of the remaining liberal justices were replaced by Reagan and Bush appointees; most environmental litigants stopped taking appeals there. After Reagan appointees in the lower federal courts began upholding property rights arguments, businesses increased their inputs and government agencies such as the Fish and Wildlife Service felt they had no alternative but to appeal to the High Court when federal and state regulations were attacked.

At the beginning of the 1980s the original Burger court was severely divided, with some holdover liberal justices vigorously opposed to their colleagues' desire to reduce government regulation. At that time, the Court came to opposite conclusions in two similar industry challenges to regulations set by the Occupational Safety and Health Administration (OSHA) to protect workers' health.

The first came from the U.S. Court of Appeals for the Fifth Circuit in New Orleans, known for its probusiness point of view. That court agreed with the American Petroleum Institute that estimated risks to workers from exposure to benzene were not worth the costs to industry to avoid them. In 1980 the Supreme Court upheld this ruling in a 5–4 decision. But in the same year the D.C. Circuit upheld a cotton-dust standard set by OSHA, and the Supreme Court upheld the agency's decision on the grounds that the same law as in the benzene case did not mandate cost-benefit justification.[31] In this case, three of the majority justices in the benzene standard case became dissenters. One changed his position and voted in favor of the cotton-dust standard because the agency had shown that 25 percent of all workers in the industry suffered from a disease caused by inhaling cotton fibers. Five of the justices who made the two OSHA decisions have been replaced, among them the most health-conscious of the original Burger Court: Justices William Brennan and Thurgood Marshall.

Justice Antonin Scalia, who leads the conservative wing of the Court, has responded favorably to business's attacks on the constitutionality of government regulation of property on the grounds that overregulation amounts to taking property without due process. In one case, Justice Scalia, writing for the Court majority, agreed with landowners that the California Coastal Zone Commission attempted to take their property without due process when it tried to force them to provide public access to the ocean in exchange for a permit to rebuild their beachfront house.[32] In another case, Chief Justice William Rehnquist addressed an additional question that the Court had avoided until then. Instead of restricting the remedy for any regulatory taking of property to striking down the unconstitutional regulation, he stated that landowners are entitled to be compensated by the state for any loss of value from the property that occurred between the time the regulation was put in place and its invalidation.[33]

In 1992 *Lucas* v. *South Carolina Coastal Council* was decided in favor of a South Carolina landowner who had invested in property before the state passed a law prohibiting developers from building on erodible beach land. Although the Court did not determine whether Lucas had lost all economic use of the land itself, it sent the case back to state court to decide this fact. Justice Scalia's decision said the state's only rationale for justifying its regulation would be through the common law of nuisance, which normally requires proof that harm would be done to adjacent property.[34] This ruling effectively interprets the taking doctrine to mean the state's regulatory powers are restricted to those it would have under the nuisance doctrine in common law. Taken to an extreme, this interpretation could reduce the police powers of the states to prevent property owners from imposing externalities on the larger society only when the state can prove individual harm to specific individuals. The *Lucas* decision eventually forced the state to buy his property at such an inflated figure that it subsequently had to sell the property for development.

Following the logic of these property rights cases, in 1994 the Supreme Court ruled that the town of Tigard, Oregon, could not force a commercial property owner to dedicate 10 percent of her land to runoff drainage and a bicycle and walking path in exchange for doubling the size of the store and paving the parking lot.[35] Chief Justice Rehnquist, in writing the majority decision, made it clear that in all land use regulations the government agency must demonstrate to the courts' satisfaction that the public benefits the agency seeks are roughly equivalent to the loss in property value the owner suffers from the regulation.

Together these two cases have caused some analysts to speculate that the Court is moving gradually toward a return to the New Deal Court's interpretation of the Fourteenth Amendment's due process clause as protecting private property from most regulation by all levels of government. Most constitutional law students in the late twentieth century assumed that the substantive interpretation of "due process" had been reserved to civil liberties cases. At the beginning of the twenty-first century, however, a rise in popularity of the "law and economics" school of law betokens the preeminence of economic rights over personal liberties by a majority on the Court.

Standing to Sue

For environmental litigants another development is equally ominous. This stems from several recent Supreme Court decisions that threaten to remove environmentalists' access to all federal courts. In 1972 a far different Supreme Court from the current Rehnquist Court signaled its willingness to look sympathetically on nontraditional litigants who hoped to raise ecological and even esthetic issues in court. Earlier courts had created a barrier for noneconomic grievances through the concept of "standing to sue," which holds that only persons or groups with a particular injury can present their arguments in court. Although the Court did not give the Sierra Club standing in this landmark case, it laid out how this status could be achieved by claiming specific injury to individual club members on the grounds that they used the area in question.[36]

Other environmental groups were quick to take the Court up on this suggestion, and lower federal courts followed precedent by opening their doors to these kinds of suits. This movement quickly reached its peak, however, when a group of law students got into court by alleging they hiked in scenery that might be injured if railroad rates on recycled materials were higher than those on virgin materials.[37] The Burger Court throughout the remainder of the 1970s refused to open the door further to the federal courts. Since then the Rehnquist Court has been gradually narrowing the opening that many on the Court, including Justice Scalia, believe was wrongly left ajar.[38]

This trend was demonstrated in 1990 when the Court refused to allow the National Wildlife Federation to protest a Bureau of Land Management decision to open up some public land to development. Justice Scalia wrote the majority decision that denied standing on the ground that the federation had not demonstrated that it suffered from any specific injury aside from asserting that its members use the public land under consideration for recreation.[39] This case was followed by another in 1992 against the Defenders of Wildlife, who wanted the courts to force the Department of the Interior to challenge overseas projects funded by the State Department that endangered the survival of rare species. Justice Scalia opined again that because the Defenders had suffered no particularized injury (despite language in the Endangered Species Act that permits citizen suits), they had no right to sue.[40]

In 1998 Justice Scalia got another opportunity to reject an environmental group's standing. The case involved the Emergency Planning and Community Right to Know Act of 1986, which allowed citizens to sue when industry failed to file timely hazardous chemical storage and emission reports. The Seventh Circuit found the environmentalists' claim to a hearing to be legitimate despite the fact that the offending company had complied after the suit was filed. The Supreme Court overturned the lower court's decision, ruling that the Citizens for a Better Environment had no standing to sue because if the industrial plant paid a penalty for violating the law, this would in no way remedy the organization's injury which existed, if at all, only in the past.[41] Only Justices Ruth Bader Ginsburg, David Souter, and John Paul Stevens dissented, but Justices Anthony Kennedy, Sandra Day O'Connor, and Stephen Breyer wrote a separate concurrence to indicate they would not have restricted standing to the degree that Justices Scalia, Rehnquist, and Thomas did.

In the same term Justice Breyer wrote for a unanimous Court that the Sierra Club could not sue the Forest Service to challenge the environmental impact of a plan to log in Ohio's Wayne National Forest because the issue was not ripe. The Forest Service had not yet identified specific areas to be logged, although they had specified the total acreage, board feet, and method of logging (clear cutting).[42] The case is particularly important because, while it involved environmental groups challenging the U.S. government, it was appealed to the Supreme Court by a trade association representing the logging industry, which had intervened. The case demonstrates the eagerness of business groups to take disputes all the way to the Supreme Court even if the federal executive branch does not choose to appeal.

These precedents go beyond those that simply find against the merits of environmental arguments. They imply that the groups with the most effective arguments are not eligible to make them in any federal court. Many critics of the courts agree with Justice Scalia that judges, because of their focus on individual rights, are unsuited to make decisions that can influence broad social policy. They believe technical decisions are better left to administrators with appropriate expertise who can determine priorities for agencies pressed to respond to multiple legislated requirements.[43]

Opponents of this restrictive view of the courts' role argue that executive agencies are no more democratically elected than judges and that Congress would not have provided the mechanism of citizen suits if it trusted administrators to render unerringly correct decisions. Judges admittedly do not have the agencies' concerns for efficient use of resources foremost in mind. But other values, such as individual justice, should outweigh these considerations. Experts do disagree about many technical issues regarding pollution and resource management. Eliminating standing for one group of experts will mean that much information, and even some issues, such as the spotted owl's status as a threatened species, may be precluded from discussion at any level in the federal court system.

Another development that bodes ill for environmental groups is tort litigation reform promised by the Republican majority in Congress. One change passed by the House, but not by the Senate, is that losers of lawsuits will be forced to pay the court costs of the winners. This innovation would assist groups hit with SLAPP suits, but it would also hurt groups attempting to enforce environmental statutes. If they were to lose, they could be liable for the legal costs of their governmental or business opponents. Until now environmental groups have benefited by having cost-recovery written into some of the statute laws, such as the Clean Air and Water Acts, to favor private attorneys general. If all losers were made liable for their opponents' costs, the extravagant hourly billing rates of corporate attorneys would dampen environmental groups' enthusiasm for litigation.

Some Projections

The presidential election in November 1992 created an opportunity to begin the slow evolution of the Supreme Court to a more moderate position on the environment. President Clinton's first appointment in 1993 was Ruth Bader Ginsburg, a moderate judge from the D.C. Circuit who had been appointed by President Jimmy Carter. She replaced Byron White, the only remaining Democrat on the Court, who resigned soon after Clinton came into office. Although White had been appointed by President John F. Kennedy, he was quite probusiness in his rulings; Justice Ginsburg is therefore likely to push the Court in a less prodevelopment direction.

In 1994 Clinton got a second opportunity to appoint a justice when the liberal Justice Harry Blackmun resigned. Although a Republican appointed by Nixon, he had a more proenvironment record than White. His replacement was Stephen Breyer, an appellate judge from the First Circuit Court of Appeals known for his expertise in regulatory affairs and administrative law and therefore likely to take an active role in environmental cases. Justice Breyer is especially knowledgeable about comparative risk assessment and cost-benefit analysis and is eager to increase the rationality of agency decisions.[44] He is less likely to accept without economic justification public health arguments, as Justice Blackmun did. Taken together, the two Clinton appointments may stop the Court's drift to the right but leave its rulings on the environment in approximately the same position they have been since President Bush replaced Justice Thurgood Marshall with Justice Clarence Thomas in 1992.

It takes a long time to change the ideology of the Supreme Court, as its members have life tenure. President Clinton's opportunities are limited to voluntary resignations and deaths of sitting justices. Except for the two most recent appointees, all remaining justices are Republicans. These High Court incumbents will strive to hold on to their positions, as customary, until a Republican president can appoint their successors. John Paul Stevens, an independent-thinking appointee of President Gerald R. Ford and the oldest justice, is the most likely candidate to follow the example of Justice Blackmun, but it seems unlikely. Also he is a moderate regarding the environment, and as a lame duck, President Clinton will be hard-pressed to get a more liberal appointee through a Republican-dominated Senate.

The same logic applies to the lower federal courts, where more than half the judges have been appointed by either President Reagan or President Bush. After Orrin Hatch, R-Utah, became chair of the Senate Judiciary Committee, confirmation of federal judges at all levels slowed to a crawl. During most of 1998, while Capitol Hill and the White House were preoccupied with the Independent Counsel Kenneth Starr's investigations of President Clinton, Senator Hatch scheduled few hearings for confirmation, and the vacancies on the federal bench swelled to over two hundred positions.

It seems probable that most federal courts will begin the twenty-first century by carefully scrutinizing any regulation of economic behavior whether at the local, state, or federal level. This is likely to take three forms: an increased use of cost-benefit analysis and other economic tools such as effluent charges, continued favorable reception to arguments about taking property without due process, and reduced standing for public interest organizations.

Congress is likely to reinforce the judiciary's preference for increased use of cost-benefit and risk-benefit standards in specific pollution control laws, such as the Clean Air or Clean Water Acts. In addition, the Clinton administration is inclined to increase the use of economic calculations in setting environmental standards. If such laws as the Endangered Species Act are amended to provide for compensation for the owners of private property for regulatory "takings," there will be no disagreement between federal law and the Rehnquist Court's interpretation of the Constitution. Instead, conflict will be more likely between the states' attempts to control land uses and the latest interpretation of the due process clause.

One principle of the 1994 "Contract with America" was to increase state authority at the expense of federal control. Nevertheless the Republican majority in the House of Representatives labored to pass a bill to require all levels of government to compensate landowners if regulation diminishes their property value. The Senate did not follow suit, but if it had the Republicans would have been in the ironic position of having the central government coerce all states to comply while continuing to claim a preference for local government decisionmaking.

Because it is easier to show a specific monetary loss than any other kind, the Supreme Court's standing-to-sue rulings favor economic interests over ecological ones. Industry by definition has a material interest in its cases, and this may mean that only one side of some controversial cases will be fully aired in court. Although the Clinton administration could choose not to make standing arguments against allowing environmental interest groups into court, business litigants would still be able to initiate such claims. The Republican Congress could decrease or eliminate the citizen suit provisions in some laws, reducing the zone of interest the legislation is designed to protect. Even if environmental groups are unlikely to win the cases they bring, a reduction in their ability to sue is even more important because it prevents them from even making their arguments.

In addition to the three patterns in Supreme Court decisions, there is a more general societal trend toward negotiated rulemaking and alternative forms of dispute resolution. Many environmental disputes are now settled out of court, with or without judicial supervision. This trend is likely to continue given the high costs of litigation and the increased reluctance of industry and environmental groups to prolong cleanup controversies. Another factor pushing alternative methods of dispute settlements is the fact that multinational corporations have been developing voluntary standards of operation in order to reduce the possibility of multiple and conflicting regulations. The European Union has been particularly active in this area, and European nation states have long preferred to cooperate with industry rather than confront it in court.

A final complication is the internationalization of many environmental issues. As policies like reducing global warming by international agreements, such as that made in 1997 in Kyoto, Japan, are adopted by international treaties and protocols, the role of U.S. courts in interpreting environmental standards could diminish. Given the lack of effective enforcement powers in international bodies, however, U.S. courts could face an increasing volume of cases brought by foreign parties challenging U.S. policies that affect their territory. How U.S. courts will respond to such new challenges remains to be seen.

Notes

1. *Marbury* v. *Madison*, 5 U.S. (1 Cranch) 137; 2 L.Ed. 60 (1803).
2. Donald L. Horowitz, *The Courts and Social Policy* (Washington, D.C.: Brookings, 1977); and R. Shep Melnick, *Regulation and the Courts* (Washington, D.C.: Brookings, 1983).
3. Lawrence Tribe, "Policy Science: Analysis or Ideology?" *Philosophy and Public Affairs* 2 (1972): 56; and Joel Yellin, "High Technology and the Courts: Nuclear Power and the Need for Institutional Reform," *Harvard Law Review* 94 (1981): 489.
4. Lettie M. Wenner, *One Environment under Law* (Pacific Palisades, Calif.: Goodyear, 1976), 7–9. In 1997 a best selling nonfiction book, *A Civil Action*, publicized the plight of the community of Woburn, Massachusetts. Its author, John Haar, described the tortuous path taken by one attorney in attempting to obtain damages for families with multiple injuries. Later made into a movie starring John Travolta, this book did much to demonstrate the plight of groups trying to prove damage from several sources.
5. James Willard Hurst traced the law's development from common law in the nineteenth century through the development of public laws to regulate individual behavior for the common good. See Hurst, *Law and Social Order in the United States* (Ithaca, N.Y.: Cornell University Press, 1977). Also see Norman Vig and Patrick Bruer, "The Courts and Risk Assessment," *Policy Studies Review* 1 (May 1982): 716–727.
6. Among those who applaud this development are Hurst, *Law and Social Order;* and Abram Chayes, "The Role of Judges in Public Law Litigation," *Harvard Law Review* 89 (1976): 1281–1316. Among those who criticize it are Nathan Glazer, "Toward an Imperial Judiciary?" *Public Interest* 41 (1975): 104–123; and Horowitz, *Courts and Social Policy.*

7. Douglas J. Amy, "Environmental Dispute Resolution: The Promise and the Pitfalls," in *Environmental Policy in the 1990s: Toward a New Agenda,* ed. Norman J. Vig and Michael E. Kraft (Washington, D.C.: CQ Press, 1990).

8. Harold Leventhal, "Environmental Decisionmaking and the Role of the Courts," *University of Pennsylvania Law Review* 122 (1974): 509–555.

9. David L. Bazelon, "Coping with Technology through the Legal Process," *Cornell Law Review* 62 (1977): 817–832. Consistent with these expectations, during the 1990s the Supreme Court attempted to set guidelines for the use of science in judicial proceedings. See Jeffrey Mervis, "Supreme Court to Judges: Start Thinking Like Scientists," *Science,* July 2, 1993, 22. In addition, legal scholars increasingly have asked how the courts can reconcile legal and scientific reasoning in dispute resolution, and have examined the implications for public policies dealing with environmental quality, health, and safety. See Kenneth R. Foster and Peter W. Huber, *Judging Science: Scientific Knowledge and the Federal Courts* (Cambridge, Mass.: MIT Press, 1997); and Sheila Jasanoff, *Science at the Bar: Law, Science, and Technology in America* (Cambridge, Mass.: Harvard University Press, 1997).

10. Pub.L. 101-549, Title V, Section 501, 104 Stat. 2635 28.

11. Richard A. Epstein, *Takings, Private Property, and the Power of Eminent Domain* (Cambridge, Mass.: Harvard University Press, 1985).

12. Mark W. Cordes, "Leapfrogging the Constitution: The Rise of State Takings Legislation," *Ecology Law Quarterly* 24 (1997): 187–242.

13. Penelope Canan, "The SLAPP from a Sociological Perspective," *Pace Environmental Law Review* 7 (1989): 23–32; and George W. Pring, "SLAPPs: Strategic Lawsuits against Public Participation," *Pace Environmental Law Review* 7 (1989): 3–21.

14. The high point of the Supreme Court's acceptance of this doctrine came in *Citizens to Preserve Overton Park* v. *Volpe,* 401 U.S. 402 (1971). The Supreme Court in this decision agreed with the lower federal court that the Department of Transportation had exercised too much discretion in deciding to take a public park in order to build a highway under the Federal Aid Highway Act of 1968.

15. James F. Raymond, "A *Vermont Yankee* in King Burger's Court: Constraints on Judicial Review under NEPA," *Boston College Environmental Affairs Law Review* 7 (1979): 629–664; Richard Stewart, *"Vermont Yankee* and the Evolution of Administrative Procedure," *Harvard Law Review* 91 (1978): 1805–1845; and Katherine B. Edwards, "NRC Regulations," *Texas Law Review* 58 (1980): 355–391.

16. *U.S.* v. *Monsanto Company,* 858 F.2d 160 (4th Circuit, 1988); *U.S.* v. *Maryland Bank & Trust Company,* 632 F. Supp. 573 (D. Md. 1986).

17. *New York Times,* March 7, 1999, 1.

18. *Northern Spotted Owl* v. *Hodel,* 716 F. Supp. 479 (1988).

19. *Robertson* v. *Seattle Audubon,* 112 S. Ct. 1407 SC (1992).

20. Lettie M. Wenner, "Contextual Influences on Judicial Decision Making," *Western Political Quarterly* 41 (March 1988): 115–134.

21. "Courthouse No Longer Environmentalists' Citadel," *New York Times,* March 23, 1992, 1.

22. *Chevron U.S.A., Inc.* v. *Natural Resources Defense Council,* 467 U.S. 837, 104 S.Ct. 2778 (1984).

23. *Corrosion Proof Fittings* v. *EPA,* 33 ERC 1961 (1991).

24. *Shell Oil* v. *EPA,* 34 ERC 1049 (1991).

25. *Sweet Home Chapter of Communities for a Great Oregon* v. *Interior Department,* 1 F.3d 1 (1993).

26. *Bruce Babbitt* v. *Sweet Home Chapter of Communities for a Great Oregon,* 515 U.S. 687 (1995).

27. *Sweet Home Chapter of Communities for a Great Oregon* v. *Interior Department,* 39 ERC 1278 (1994).

28. *Loveladies Harbor* v. *United States,* 21 Cl. Ct. 153 (1990).

29. *Florida Rock Industries* v. *United States,* 21 Cl. Ct. 161 (1990).

30. Lee R. Epstein, "Takings and Wetlands in the Claims Court: *Florida Rock* and *Love-ladies Harbor,*" *Environmental Law Reporter* 10 (1990): 10517–10521. Thomas Hanley, "A Developer's Dream: The U.S. Claims Court's New Analysis of Section 404 Takings Challenges," *Environmental Affairs* 19 (1991): 317–353.
31. *Industrial Union Department AFL-CIO* v. *American Petroleum Institute,* 100 S.Ct. 244 (1980); *Textile Manufacturers Institute Inc.* v. *Donovan,* 425 U.S. 490 (1981). See William H. Rodgers Jr., "Judicial Review of Risk Assessments: The Role of Decision Theory in Unscrambling the Benzene Decision," *Environmental Law* 11 (1981): 301–320.
32. *Nollan* v. *California Coastal Zone Commission,* 107 S.Ct. 3141 (1987).
33. *First English Evangelical Lutheran Church* v. *Los Angeles,* 107 S. Ct. 2378 (1987).
34. *Lucas* v. *South Carolina Coastal Council,* 112 S. Ct. 2886 (1992).
35. *Dolan* v. *City of Tigard,* 114 S. Ct. 2309 (1994).
36. *Sierra Club* v. *Morton,* 405 U.S. 727 (1972).
37. *U.S.* v. *Students Challenging Regulatory Agency Procedures,* 412 U.S. 669 (1973).
38. Antonin Scalia, "The Doctrine of Standing as an Essential Element of the Separation of Powers," *Suffolk University Law Review* 17 (1983): 881–899.
39. *Lujan* v. *National Wildlife Federation,* 110 S. Ct. 3177 (1990).
40. *Lujan* v. *Defenders of Wildlife,* 112 S. Ct. 2130 (1992).
41. *Steel Company* v. *Citizens for a Better Environment,* No. 96-643 (1997).
42. *Ohio Forestry Association* v. *Sierra Club,* No. 97-16 (1998).
43. In *Sierra Club* v. *Gorsuch,* 18 ERC 1549 (1982), a federal district court in California forced the EPA to set radioactive nuclides standards, which may have taken attention away from other types of priorities the EPA had under the Clean Air Act. See Melnick, *Regulation and the Courts.*
44. Stephen Breyer, *Breaking the Vicious Circle* (Cambridge, Mass.: Harvard University Press, 1993).

8

Escaping the "Battered Agency Syndrome": EPA's Gamble with Regulatory Reinvention

Walter A. Rosenbaum

[EPA] is now staggering under the assault of its enemies—while still gravely wounded from the gifts of its "friends."

—William Ruckelshaus, former EPA administrator

In mid July 1997, the U.S. Environmental Protection Agency (EPA) officially occupied its new headquarters in the massive Ronald Reagan Building and International Trade Center. For the EPA it was a rags-to-riches triumph, an overdue liberation from cramped, aging, and improvised quarters in unfashionable Southwest Washington to new facilities not just luxurious but palatial. The $818 million Reagan Building—the "crown jewel of Pennsylvania Ave"—covers eleven acres adjacent to the Mall in the federal government's heartland, bedazzling the eye and begging superlatives. Second only to the Pentagon in size, the building's thirteen levels surround an acre of atrium crowned by an impressive carved glass dome. There, ensconced amidst a two-story exhibit hall, 620-seat auditorium, conference center, reception hall, day care center, 980-seat food court, four restaurants, and thirteen floors of other federal agencies, the EPA's suddenly expansive offices hardly crowded an interior with more floor space than the Empire State Building.[1] The event, coinciding with the agency's twenty-fifth anniversary, marked the beginning of perhaps the most important, and most risky, period in the EPA's turbulent history.

Celebration Laced with Apprehension

Most satisfying to EPA was the symbolism of its new headquarters. The setting was deliciously ironic—a sort of revenge for the many EPA employees who recalled the Reagan administration's implacable hostility to the agency and the president's unremitting efforts to undermine its authority.[2] More important, the occasion was testimony to the EPA's having survived that bitter season—and many succeeding controversies—and come out the other side, ready to prosper.

The new headquarters clearly confirmed the agency's importance, for the EPA, charged with enormous and still growing responsibilities, badly needed the working room as well as the glossy public image it conveyed. The

EPA had become the federal government's largest and costliest regulatory agency, with 18,000 employees and a budget in fiscal year 1998 of $7.3 billion.[3] By the mid 1990s, it was responsible for administering part or all of twelve major federal environmental laws (see table 8-1). The enormous breadth of EPA's regulatory mission meant that its authority affected virtually every aspect of the U.S. environment, all major sectors of the American economy, and almost all Americans in some manner. And this responsibility continues to grow. Between 1995 and 1998, Congress added to the agency's tasks the implementation of amendments to the Safe Drinking Water Act, pesticide regulation, new provisions for management of smog in U.S. border areas, additional requirements for reporting the economic impact of federal environmental legislation, and much more.[4] Enlarged authority and improved facilities, however, were not the most important transformations at EPA in the late 1990s.

In one crucial respect, all this celebration implied a counterfeit success, for EPA was still under enormous pressure to accomplish major reforms across vital areas of its organization and activities. In differing ways, most of these reforms reflect the agency's efforts to resolve problems that Congress

Table 8-1 Major Environmental Laws Administered by the EPA

A dozen major statutes form the legal basis for the programs of the EPA:

The **Pollution Prevention Act** seeks to prevent pollution through reduced generation of pollutants at their point of origin.

The **Clean Air Act** requires the EPA to set mobile-source limits, ambient air quality standards, hazardous air pollutant emission standards, standards for new pollution sources, and significant deterioration requirements, and to focus on areas that do not attain standards.

The **Clean Water Act** establishes the sewage treatment construction grants program and a regulatory and enforcement program for discharges of wastes into U.S. waters. Focusing on the regulation of the intentional disposal of materials into ocean waters and authorizing related research is the **Ocean Dumping Act.**

The **Safe Drinking Water Act** establishes primary drinking water standards, regulates underground injection disposal practices, and establishes a groundwater control program.

The **Solid Waste Disposal Act** and the **Resource Conservation and Recovery Act** authorize regulation of solid and hazardous waste, while the **Comprehensive Environmental Response, Compensation, and Liability Act**, known as CERCLA or Superfund, establishes a fee-maintained fund to clean up abandoned hazardous waste sites.

The **Emergency Planning and Community Right-to-Know Act** requires reporting of toxic releases and encourages response for chemical releases.

The **Toxic Substances Control Act** regulates the testing of chemicals and their use, and the **Federal Insecticide, Fungicide, and Rodenticide Act** governs pesticide products and their use.

The **National Environmental Policy Act** requires, in part, the EPA to review environmental impact statements.

Source: Adapted from National Academy of Public Administration, *Setting Priorities, Getting Results* (Washington, D.C.: NAPA, 1995), 182.

has so far failed to address through new legislation or amendments to EPA's many existing statutory programs. Many of these compelling problems are discussed elsewhere in this volume, including dealing with environmental justice (see chap. 11), promoting the "greening" of industry by encouraging voluntary industry programs for environmental protection (see chap. 12), and creating more effective market incentives in pollution regulation (see chap. 9).

This chapter concerns another agenda of EPA reforms: the agency's high-profile "reinvention" initiatives launched in the 1990s to address a number of serious organizational and programmatic flaws rooted in the agency's congressional design. The reinvention campaign is perhaps the most critical, riskiest reform program in EPA history. It is a massive effort at institutional transformation prompted by a realization that fundamental changes in organization and administrative style were mandatory for the agency's future effectiveness, and perhaps for its survival. Reaching for imagery that would communicate sweeping reform and implacable optimism, the EPA advertises these reforms as nothing less than "Reinventing Environ. ental Regulation." Despite the upbeat rhetoric, the agency's leadership knows that success at this work (hereafter called "reinventing regulation") will be problematic, for the reforms are targeted at deeply entrenched problems stubbornly resisting many previous reform assaults. Moreover, the EPA in many instances is not itself the primary source of these problems.

In this chapter, a brief description of the chronic problems compelling the reinvention effort leads to a description of the initiatives themselves, the obstacles confronting them, their progress, and the outlook for reform in the next several years. However, to understand why these pressures on the EPA are so formidable, it is helpful to retrace briefly the turbulent historic course culminating in the EPA's present predicament.

The Path to Reinventing Regulation

As noted in chapter 1, the EPA is the most important institutional expression of the "environmental era" that began in the 1960s with emergence of environmentalism as an organized political force and vaulted to national importance with the first Earth Day in April 1970. Created by presidential order in 1970, EPA quickly inherited a rapid succession of unprecedented, highly complex new environmental laws written by Congress between 1970 and 1980 in response to a new public environmental consciousness.[5] These numerous laws, such as the Clean Air Act, the Clean Water Act, and the Toxic Substances Control Act, became the statutory foundation of federal environmental regulation, enlarged by continual congressional amendments and additions throughout the 1980s and 1990s.

The Stormy Epicenter of Environmental Regulation

Since the first Earth Day, the EPA has been the nation's principal environmental regulator and thus the political epicenter of controversy over federal environmental regulations. The EPA is compelled by its authority and design to work satisfactorily—if it can—with a large, varied, and politically aggressive constituency. Environmentalists regard themselves as the EPA's primary constituency. It has been, more than any other federal or state agency, the regulatory institution that environmentalists hold accountable for the success or failure of federal environmental law. However, the EPA has assumed equal importance for the thousands of industrial and commercial interests affected by the regulations it enforces, and they too consider themselves a major agency constituency. Since the states are responsible for enforcing most federal environmental laws with EPA oversight (see chap. 2), they are yet another significant constituency. Furthermore, Congress exercises budgetary control over the EPA in addition to writing and overseeing the implementation of environmental laws entrusted to the agency. And other federal agencies, such as the Department of the Interior, share with EPA the responsibility for environmental management in different ways. Finally, a multitude of other interests—including the scientific community, economists, legal professionals, and engineers—are often deeply concerned with EPA's work.

Considering its multiple constituencies and broadly construed mission, EPA was predestined to controversy. By the mid 1980s, the EPA had become, as its first administrator, William Ruckelshaus, complained, a victim of the "battered agency syndrome."[6] This, too, was inevitable, for it is the EPA's misfortune to have an absolutely essential but politically distasteful mission, making criticism from all environmental quarters as routine as paper clips in the agency's worklife. The EPA's vital job is also scientifically complex, administratively difficult, and economically expensive, and is carried out amid chronic disagreement over what its regulatory goals ought to be and without prior experience for guidance. Moreover, its congressionally mandated mission thrusts its authority unwelcomed upon virtually every important political and economic sector. When President George Bush complained that the EPA always came to the president with bad news, he was merely repeating the received White House wisdom. Thus, the EPA early became a prime candidate to blame for real or alleged environmental misregulation but not to praise for substantial environmental accomplishments.

A Turbulent History

The EPA's political passage from 1970 to the 1990s leads through an ebb and flow of unceasing controversy shaping the agency's institutional culture and exacerbating administrative problems that seemed to elude repeated reform efforts. Throughout most of the 1970s the EPA and Congress were largely occupied with creating the legal, political, and institutional foundations of the nation's environmental politics. Like the environmental movement, the EPA generally prospered in a benign political climate assured by sympathetic congressional majorities and a succession of White House occupants tolerant, if not always sympathetic, to its objectives. This was a period of expanding annual budgets and a rapidly enlarging agenda of new legislation to implement. While the agency was already struggling with administrative problems that would deepen with time, their character and severity were still emergent.

The advent of the Reagan administration changed all of this. The president and his appointed leaders at the EPA, particularly its newly designated administrator, Anne Gorsuch Burford, believed that they were elected to bring "regulatory relief" to the U.S. economy, and environmental regulations topped their hit list of laws to be "reformed." Environmentalists, regarding the Reagan administration as the most environmentally hostile in a half-century, believed the president's persistent criticism of the EPA was the cutting edge of an assault on the institutional foundations of federal environmental protection erected during the 1970s. During most of Reagan's two terms, EPA budgets increasingly lagged behind the levels needed for the agency to implement a host of new environmental laws passed in the 1980s. Controversies between Reagan Republicans and the EPA were continually in the news. Attacks on the competence of EPA's staff issuing from the White House, and even from the EPA's own administrator, depressed agency morale, as did the continual controversies between EPA's leaders and the Democratic congressional majority opposing Reagan's regulatory reform. The Reagan years severely tested the new environmental movement, but the foundations held.[7] Still, little was done to advance the implementation of existing policy, to enhance EPA's organizational resources, or address EPA's emerging regulatory problems.

President Bush awakened expectations of major reform from the environmental movement after the drift and indecision of the Reagan years. Bush brought to the White House a much more sympathetic and active environmentalism and sponsored new, if episodic, environmental policy initiatives and administrative reforms. EPA's budget and morale improved significantly under a new, popular, and politically skilled administrator, William K. Reilly. Discussion of more constructive EPA reform became common. However, the Bush administration was never more than mildly environmentalist. The modest enlargement of EPA's budget and staff during Bush's administration, however welcome after the lean Reagan years, still left the agency severely understaffed and underfunded for managing its still-growing administrative tasks.

Bill Clinton's election in 1992 seemed a portent of much better times for the EPA and environmentalism, particularly since Vice President Al Gore, an outspoken environmentalist, was now a strong White House presence and his former staff director and protégé, Carol Browner, was appointed EPA's new administrator. Clinton's early performance failed to meet the expectations inspired among environmentalists by his campaign rhetoric, although his environmental record improved somewhat after his 1996 reelection. At the EPA, however, Browner and her leadership team, convinced that the agency's mounting problems were nearing critical proportions, were deeply committed to sweeping reforms in organization and activities. If suc-

cessful, the reforms would constitute the most important institutional reno-
vation in EPA's brief history and a major legacy of the Clinton years.

Reinvention Arrives

In 1995 EPA's leadership officially announced it was "reinventing
EPA"—in effect, changing the fundamental legal and political character of
its regulatory programs. It looked more like gambling than reform to many
observers. "EPA has survived daunting challenges in its short history," com-
mented one informed analyst, "but demands that it reinvent the methods it
uses to control pollution may turn out to raise the highest stakes."[8]

The initiatives collectively called "Reinventing EPA" were but a part of
the Clinton administration's highly touted campaign to "Reinvent Government." EPA was expected to be reinvention's regulatory showcase. A national
news conference by Vice President Gore and EPA administrator Browner in
March 1995 had announced "an ambitious agenda to reinvent environmental
protection."[9] Earlier, Gore had promised no merely modest results:

> Drawing on the lessons of the past 25 years, the Clinton/Gore Adminis-
> tration is committed to reinventing our environmental protection system.
> This is a positive effort to build upon the strengths of the current system,
> while overcoming its limitation. We will reform the system, not undermine
> it. We will bring people together in support of reform, rather than further
> polarizing a debate that has been polarized for too long already.[10]

Gore and Browner's comments previewed all subsequent EPA reinvention rhetoric, invoking images of unprecedented and sweeping change, of
new ideas and inspirations, of profound institutional transformations essential in the twenty-first century. Twenty-five high-priority projects, cutting
across many different existing EPA programs and offices, were announced—
fourteen more appeared later—all to "promote innovation and flexibility,
increase community participation and partnerships, improve compliance
with environmental laws, and cut red tape and paperwork."[11]

The reinvention initiative is the most highly publicized, coherent, comprehensive, and institutionally focused reform program in EPA history. The
EPA and the White House are gambling substantial political capital and
administrative resources on its success. The high stakes for the agency are
apparent in the scale of resources and visibility the EPA is giving to the project. In early 1997, the agency created a new Office of Reinvention, appointed
a new associate administrator to direct a large staff, and provided a separate
budget for the work. Reinvention has become a leadership mantra. Reinvention initiatives are continually advertised and promoted to all of EPA's important constituencies and stakeholders through such strategies as a new monthly
magazine, *New Directions*, reinvention newsletters and press releases, and a
Web site dedicated entirely to news about the ongoing programs.[12]

For all its potential benefits, reinvention is freighted with enormous
political risk. It is the agency's best effort to respond to the broadly shared
conviction among both supporters and critics that fundamental changes are

essential to EPA's programs and organization—a conviction that slowly gathered strength over the three decade's of EPA regulatory and political experience. In particular, the EPA's leadership hopes that the new initiatives will deflect the relentless legislative attacks on the agency instigated by congressional Republicans since they captured control of both chambers in 1994.[13] It may also be the last opportunity for the EPA to come to terms with deeply embedded problems without a politically wrenching and demoralizing overhaul of EPA's fundamental structure and staff.

Why Reinvention?

Several specific problems, increasingly troublesome throughout EPA's history, provoke most of the reform pressure now coming from so many different agency constituencies.

Regulatory Accomplishments? Yes, But . . .

Controversy has often eclipsed the agency's important regulatory accomplishments. EPA's many achievements in several of its most vital regulatory domains—air quality, pesticide control, and hazardous waste—include the following:

- Reducing the number of metropolitan areas failing to meet national air quality standards by more than half: from 199 cities to fewer than 70.
- Reducing the total emissions of six common air pollutants by an average of 32 percent from 1970 to 1996 despite a doubling of the nation's economy and substantial growth in both its population and vehicle miles traveled.
- Banning or eliminating the use of over 230 pesticides and 20,000 pesticide products, including DDT.
- Accelerating the cleanup of the thirteen hundred worst abandoned toxic waste sites on the Superfund program's National Priority List; completing cleanup at over five hundred of these sites by early 1998.[14]

Despite these and many other important achievements (see chap. 1), the EPA has experienced great difficulty in implementing most of the major programs for which it is responsible. It has frequently missed mandated program deadlines, failed to achieve regulatory goals, moved at a glacial pace in implementing vital program elements, and struggled to find the appropriate scientific resources for its tasks.[15] Equally important, in politics appearances matter as much as reality, and EPA has been widely perceived as a failed regulator, especially in Congress. These difficulties, however, often arose not primarily from administrative incompetence but from the following problematic elements in the legislative design of the many statutes defining the agency's mission:

1. *Too much reliance on a "command-and-control" strategy for pollution control.* This policy strategy required regulatory officials to declare

acceptable pollution standards, specify the appropriate control technology for every regulated pollution source, issue each source a permit specifying the acceptable limit of its pollution emissions, and enforce the standards through inspections and, if necessary, legal action, including fines. Rather than encourage the prevention of pollutants, "command-and-control" emphasized "end-of-the-pipe" technology controls. An increasingly common criticism of this approach is that it is economically inefficient.[16] It assumes "that pollution control requirements must be imposed on all sources across the board, without regard to either the costs of compliance or the benefits of emission reduction," argues Rena Steinzor. "Because such standards rely on arbitrary judgments that industry should use whatever technologies deliver the best control, sources of pollution are forced to install equipment even if its costs could be achieved by less expensive, more flexible methods."[17] The best alternatives, in the opinion of many economists and other critics, rely heavily on marketplace incentives to control pollutants (see chap. 9).

2. *Excessive and unrealistic regulatory deadlines, too many detailed and inflexible administrative rules, and ambitious but virtually unattainable program objectives.* "Politicians, eager to appear environmentally conscious, pass statute after statute establishing unrealistic and unaffordable goals," laments one careful analyst. "Then they delegate enforcement to the EPA and its state and local counterparts without giving the agency enough money to implement the mandates. Bureaucrats without independent political power are forced to reconcile impossible goals with reality, irrevocably damaging their credibility in the process."[18] Much of this congressional "micromanagement" is inspired by suspicion of the EPA and its leadership. The EPA is also chronically overwhelmed by regulatory tasks because it had been avalanched with a multitude of new environmental laws within a relatively few years, but left virtually powerless to set priorities or allocate resources appropriately between its multiplying new responsibilities. The cost of this misdirected legislative oversight is paid in protracted, extremely expensive lawsuits, and in administrative complexity. As an example, litigation and administration accounted for 20 to 33 percent of the average cost for a Superfund site cleanup in the mid 1990s.[19] These costs, and the inevitable failed deadlines, continually exacerbate the widely deplored institutional antagonism between the EPA and its congressional overseers.

3. *Too little use of cross-media strategies for pollution control.* Virtually all federal environmental laws focus on controlling pollution by its different media—air, water, or solid waste, for instance. A pollutant might be regulated one way if it appears in water, another way if it is airborne, yet a different way if it appears in the soil. This approach frequently appears only to remove a pollutant from one medium and put it into another. Often a more effective and economically efficient

approach appears to be "cross-media" regulation in which a pollutant is regulated by one authority and one strategy through all the different media in which it may be found.[20] The EPA, however, has been designed so that the major regulatory offices are organized by air, water, toxics and hazardous waste, and other media, and virtually all budgets, programs, and staffs are focused on pollution control through these offices (see figure 8-1).

4. *The absence of a comprehensive regulatory law.* The most pernicious and fundamental flaw in EPA's mission appears to be a lack of clear priorities and chronic inconsistency between its foundational programs. An influential review of EPA's performance in the mid 1990s got the emphasis right:

> The large number of detailed pollution control laws makes rational priority setting difficult. . . . The overlap and numerous inconsistencies among these laws are additional impediments to efficient and effective implementation. . . . The major problems with environmental legislation are their rigidity and lack of coherence. *The laws are complex, unrelated to each other, and lacking any unified vision of environmental problems or EPA's mission* (emphasis added).[21]

Reform pressures were intensified by numerous high-visibility, national evaluations—most from expert panels, all involving former EPA officials, including several past EPA administrators. They had comprehensively examined the EPA since 1990 and declared, often harshly, a compelling need to reorganize and redirect the agency.[22] The severity of this criticism is exemplified by the verdict of William Ruckelshaus, a consistently outspoken friend and defender of the agency's mission: "A quarter century after the birth of the Environmental Protection Agency, the system it administers is broken— severely broken, beyond hope of easy repair," he warned. "The country needs to form a new consensus about what it wants in environmental protection, and how much it is willing to give up to have it."[23] The root of this perceived problem was summarized by a report for the Mellon Foundation:

> Despite [EPA's] accomplishments, we conclude that the pollution control system has deep and fundamental flaws. There is a massive dearth of scientific knowledge and data. The system's priorities are wrong, it is ineffective in dealing with many current problems, and it is inefficient and excessively intrusive. . . . The future system should be results-oriented, integrated, efficient, participatory, and information rich.[24]

Congressional Dissatisfaction

Additional reform pressure on the EPA emanates from Congress, where the Republican majority has been joined by many Democrats in sponsoring a tide of legislative proposals intended to recast the agency's organization and authority. In many respects, this situation seems perverse, for Congress has often contributed directly and indirectly to EPA's difficulties by the manner in which it has written the nation's environmental legislation, its often highly

Figure 8-1 Organizational Chart of the EPA

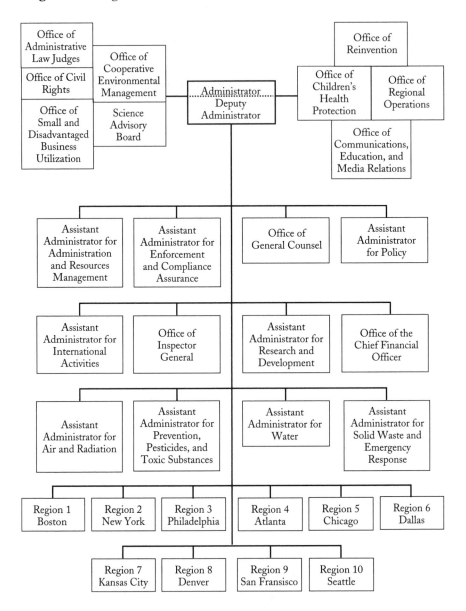

Sources: EPA, Office of Administration and Resources Management; National Academy of Public Administration, *Setting Priorities, Getting Results* (Washington, D.C.: NAPA, 1995), 17; and EPA web page at *www.epa.gov/epahome/organization* (January 21, 1999).

disruptive political forays into EPA's activities, and its efforts to microman-age EPA operations.

During the 104th Congress (1995–96) especially, the Republican lead-ership attempted to pass a multitude of proposals intended to reduce the costs of environmental regulation, to speed and to simply the regulatory process, to give the states more influence in administering federal environmental pro-grams, to reduce the number and complexity of regulations, and to achieve many changes in the EPA that Republicans considered essential (see chap. 6). Few of these proposals were passed, largely because of opposition by congres-sional Democrats and the White House. Both believed the way the proposals were written was actually intended to dangerously weaken the EPA and undermine its important environmental programs.[25] Still, leaders in both con-gressional parties, as well as many influential environmental interest groups, recognized that major reforms were required, even while they often disagreed vigorously about the details. The legislative mood was obviously reformist. EPA leaders expected that major congressional reform legislation would eventually emerge before the decade's end.

Rising Costs

Another impetus toward reform is the growing consensus among critics and proponents of past environmental regulation that regulatory costs are rising too precipitously and somehow must be controlled. Arguments about the true cost of environmental programs are endless, and actual costs are dif-ficult to fix precisely. Yet rising costs are a reality and, equally important, they are widely believed to be a problem. The regulated U.S. economic sectors currently spend altogether a relatively modest 2.8 percent of all capital out-lays for pollution abatement, but the compliance costs for individual indus-tries and factories has often risen steeply over the last decade. The costs of administering many environmental programs also has been climbing relent-lessly throughout the 1990s. The Superfund program to clean up abandoned toxic waste sites, for example, will greatly exceed the $15.2 billion Congress authorized for it in 1980 and the $26.4 billion the EPA later estimated would be necessary. Completed site cleanups, averaging about $2.1 million each in the early 1990s, were predicted to exceed $26 million by the decade's end.[26] The federal Waste Treatment Grant Program, created by Congress in 1972 to assist local governments in constructing waste treatment facilities to meet new federal water quality standards, was originally authorized at $18 billion, but had cost nearly $70 billion by 1998; another $140 billion may be needed to meet program goals.[27]

The Restive States

Finally, reform pressure has also been growing among those states that bear most of the responsibility for implementing and enforcing environmen-tal programs administered by the EPA (see chap. 2). The states have acquired considerable experience and growing competence in environmental regulation, often by creating highly imaginative, successful approaches themselves. As their capabilities grow, the states have been increasingly dissatisfied with the constraints imposed on them by the EPA, whose approach to regulatory federalism, in their view, allowed them too little freedom to interpret and apply federal laws to their enormously varied constituencies. As Michael Kraft and Denise Scheberle note, centralizing the responsibility for standard-setting and overall management of state programs with EPA reflected the congressional belief during the 1970s, when most of the laws were written, that the states were less willing and able than Washington to enforce environmental regulations. As new federal environmental laws have imposed ever-increasing responsibilities and mounting implementation costs on the states during the 1990s, friction with Washington has increased. "The sheer number of new environmental laws, coupled with the enormity of the tasks required of the EPA and the states," write Kraft and Scheberle, "have put a considerable strain on intergovernmental relations. Among the most salient issues that have arisen in this decade have been the adequacy of federal financial assistance, the extent of federal 'micromanagement' of state programs, and the degree to which states are given flexibility to set policy priorities reflecting problems of local importance."[28]

The Centerpiece Reforms So Far

More than forty high-priority EPA reinvention projects have been undertaken at different times since 1995. Almost all were intended to attack several of EPA's most troublesome problems simultaneously. EPA's own evaluations have been resolutely upbeat since the campaign's inception in 1995. In mid 1998, for example, EPA's third-year report was eulogistic. "EPA has achieved real progress in reinventing the nation's environmental regulatory system," proclaimed a press release. "[T]he improvements in environmental regulation . . . make government work better and more cost-effective for all citizens, communities and businesses."[29] The executive summary of the third-year report spoke similarly: "For 3 years, EPA Administrator Carol Browner has led EPA in pursuing an unprecedented agenda for consistently delivering cleaner, cheaper, smarter results from environmental and public health protection programs."[30]

Privately, EPA officials acknowledge that it will take considerably more time to determine accurately the success of most initiatives. In fact, the agency is still trying to define evaluation standards for many of these initiatives, and, consequently, current appraisals are impressionistic and fragmentary. If one accepts EPA's definitions of success uncritically, the news seems good indeed. The facade of official optimism, however, cloaks a more complex reality where formidable political and administrative obstacles often frustrate program goals and success is a sometime thing, frequently difficult to measure. It was quickly apparent, moreover, that several of the initiatives, packaged in the most politically attractive language, had become centerpiece programs because of their great scope, their potential broad-range impact, and the considerable administrative resources and political capital the EPA has invested in them. The outcome of these signature initiatives, consequently, merits particular attention.

The Common Sense Initiative

The Common Sense Initiative (CSI), explained EPA's new associate administrator for reinvention to a congressional oversight committee, "is one of the most ambitious efforts undertaken by the Agency . . . as a fundamentally different system of environmental protection." Its promotion has been freighted with ambitious promises and high expectations about its impact on EPA's most troublesome problems. "In contrast to the traditional system which controls pollution to air, water, and land separately," explained the associate administrator, "CSI works with selected industries using a consensus approach to engage multiple stakeholders in looking, on a cross-media basis, at all aspects of an industry's performance. The goal is to develop more flexible, cost-effective, and environmentally-protective solutions tailored to industries' needs. Moreover, by involving all stakeholders up-front, CSI helps avoid challenges in court, ultimately paving the way for faster, more cost-effective results."[31]

The CSI is targeted at six major economic sectors rather than at individual companies: auto manufacturing, computers and electronics, iron and steel, metal finishing, petroleum refining, and printing. The initiative will encourage innovative, experimental approaches that depart from traditional regulatory styles to regulate each sector. The EPA believes that a crucial component in the CSI's success will be committees created from key stakeholders–business, labor, environmental groups, and state officials—who will try to reach a consensus on the appropriate administrative and regulatory approaches for each sector, thus avoiding costly delays and litigation.

In EPA's opinion, CSI has been an early success. By the end of 1998 the EPA reported that it has more than forty projects under way involving the development of industry-by-industry environmental control standards. One example has been the adoption of an unprecedented set of performance goals for the entire metal finishing industry. The EPA believes that these goals could affect as many as eleven thousand firms nationwide and cut the industry's toxic emissions by 75 percent.[32]

The recommendations that have thus far evolved from the CSI, however, are far fewer, and have taken far longer to materialize, than the EPA had expected. According to a U.S. Government Accounting Office (GAO) review of the CSI in 1997, most of the recommendations so far do not make the kind of changes that the EPA had anticipated.[33] The CSI process, much to the annoyance of many stakeholders, has also been time-consuming. "Although stakeholders have begun to work collaboratively," explains the GAO, "progress toward the Initiative's goal has been limited by . . . the length of time needed to collect and analyze data; the difficulties stakeholders have had in reaching consensus on the approaches needed to address large, complex issues or policies; and variations in stakeholders' commitments of time and understanding of the technical aspects of environmental issues."[34] Additionally, the EPA has so far measured program accomplishments largely by the number of committees, meetings, and stakeholder interests involved rather than by the results of the process.

Project XL

Project XL (shorthand for "eXcellence and Leadership") is intended to facilitate cooperation between the EPA and individual companies in developing alternative management strategies to improve environmental performance beyond what would be achieved under the traditional regulatory system. "If you have a proposal that promises better environmental results than what would be achieved under the traditional regulatory system," explains EPA's reinvention office, "and if you commit to engaging all stakeholders in developing alternative approaches and appropriate safeguards, then EPA will give you the operational flexibility to put those good ideas to the test."[35]

The EPA considers this initiative especially important because it extensively involves the states and local governments in deciding how to regulate specific facilities and because it can become "a laboratory for testing innovative environmental management strategies for the future." The most important component of Project XL so far has been the "facilities XL" that focuses on large manufacturing companies. It assumes that "companies should be allowed to develop their own site-specific plans for achieving environmental benefits in exchange for exemptions from existing and future command and control requirements." In return, the company is pledged to achieve "superior" environmental controls.[36]

By the end of 1998, Project XL had undertaken fifty pilot projects. The first Project XL operational project, the Intel Corporation's new facility near Phoenix, Arizona, has become an EPA showpiece. The EPA allowed the corporation unprecedented flexibility in setting its pollution control targets and securing the necessary permits. In return, Intel has pledged to achieve a higher standard of pollution control than the law requires. The EPA has also begun testing new strategies negotiated with the Jack M. Berry Corporation, a Florida citrus juice processor, and the lumber industry's giant Weyerhaeuser Corporation. As of 1998, twenty-two additional projects were far advanced or in actual operation.[37] It is too early to determine the effect of Project XL on any of the facilities where it is currently being implemented. But the disappointing response of most constituencies so far is a source of private leadership misgivings.

The EPA had expected several hundred proposals when Project XL began in 1995, but fewer than one hundred had appeared by late 1998.[38] Most of the non-agency constituencies for Project XL have expressed dissatisfaction with the early process. Environmental and other public interest groups frequently suspect that the EPA is negotiating "sweetheart" agreements with facilities in the program. Many also believe that nonindustrial groups are disadvantaged in the process because they do not have the legal and technical resources available to regulated business and because the process demands enormous time. The Intel Final Project Agreement, for example, required one hundred meetings, each four to six hours, through ten months.[39] Many states believe the EPA still retains to itself too much authority in the process of negotiating Project XL agreements. And a great many major manufacturers are reluctant to begin negotiations over possible Project XL facilities because they believe the long-term savings they may achieve through the agreements are less important to their firms than the short-term additional costs involved in negotiating a Project XL agreement in comparison to accepting a traditional regulatory scheme. In an effort to address some of these concerns, the EPA has made a number of "midcourse" corrections, with as yet unclear results.

NEPPS

The National Environmental Performance Partnership System, or NEPPS, is designed to appeal strongly to the states by addressing many problems they now consider the most important in current regulatory federalism. The foundation undergirding NEPPS is an agreement between EPA's administrator and leaders of the Environmental Council of the States, signed in 1996, that provides a framework through which EPA and the states will jointly set priorities and ensure appropriate action. The EPA and the states will negotiate agreements based on a comprehensive assessment of state environmental problems. The agreements are intended to identify many areas where the EPA can reduce its oversight of delegated or authorized state programs when a state has a strong record of environmental performance. The EPA strongly believes the NEPPS will "provide a more effective, collaborative framework for managing state and federal environmental programs and resources" by giving the states much more freedom in developing and implementing federally required environmental regulations without EPA intrusions.[40] Beginning with six states in 1996, agreements had been signed with thirty-three states by the end of 1998. However, as many as forty-three states have participated in at least some element of the initiative.

The program is too recent to provide evidence of its impact—the EPA and the states reached an agreement on criteria for evaluation only in 1997. However, by late 1998 the EPA described "a growing acceptance of NEPPS by the states as a substantive, carefully thought-out program that can improve environmental program efficiency and effectiveness. . . . [A]ll states, whether participating or not, will benefit from streamlined joint-planning and priority-setting processes that have evolved as a result of state/EPA collaboration."[41] As evidence, the EPA cited Florida's experience. There, state and EPA officials "reviewed every reportable document" in several federal environmental programs and were able to reduce Florida reporting requirements in one major program by 75 percent. Although other independent reviews of the NEPPS program have spoken encouragingly about its potential, the EPA is still hard pressed to produce measurable results so early in the program's history.

Performance Partnership Grants

In another initiative directed to state and local governmental complaints, the Performance Partnership Grants (PPGs) will permit states and tribes to combine the funding from two or more among a dozen existing federal categorical grants (those dealing with specific programs) into a new kind of consolidated grant. In this way, the EPA hopes that the combined single grant will enable the states to integrate approaches to pollution control across different pollution control programs and separate media such as air and water.

By the end of 1998, forty-three states had negotiated an agreement with the EPA. One of the PPGs' most attractive features, from the states' perspective, is that it enables them to combine several different kinds of environmental grant into a single award, and to spend it with greater flexibility than had previously been possible. While the PPG initiative has not received the high-profile attention the EPA has lavished on some other aspects of regulatory reinvention, the PPGs appear likely to become a quietly successful effort based on its enthusiastic early endorsement by most states.

Cutting Red Tape and Paperwork

One of EPA's more dismal statistics is the 81 million hours it estimates must be spent annually on paperwork for its programs.[42] The work and cost required to comply with federal environmental regulations—most prescribed by the EPA—annoy everyone involved. A war on paperwork gratifies multitudes and offends no one, so EPA's early decision to bundle several paperwork reduction proposals into a "Cutting Red Tape and Regulatory Burden" initiative aimed for immediate appeal to all of the agency's constituencies. The first EPA campaign is a "line-by-line" review of new and proposed regulations to identify where excessive paperwork could be eliminated. Another reform encourages simpler, quicker ways of reporting essential environmental information to local, state, and federal agencies while another intends to make compliance with environmental laws easier for small business by providing more assistance in understanding and following environmental regulations.[43] The EPA is giving this endeavor a very high profile, diligently producing, even at an early stage, an impressively detailed volume of statistics about program success.

If EPA's public assertions are accurate, bastions of paperwork have been relentlessly falling before the reinvention onslaught. In a 1998 annual report, the EPA estimated that it had "slashed more than 1,300 pages of requirements" from its programs, thereby reducing the regulatory burden by 20 million hours. The reduction, it asserted, was the equivalent of returning more than a half million work weeks, valued at about $600 million, "back to our society for more productive use." [44] The EPA has publicized many additional illustrations of work reduction and paperwork simplification, including the following:

- Negotiating with state and local governments, and other stakeholders in the Clean Water Act, to reduce the number of new permits required for waste water dischargers under amendments to the Clean Water Act. The EPA believes that, when approved, a new agreement signed in 1997 will eliminate at least seventy thousand industrial permits, numerous municipal permits, and save approximately $511 million in administrative costs.
- Reducing the emergency plans to be prepared by industrial facilities for combating a chemical spill at each facility from nine plans to one. This will, states the EPA, "minimize confusion and response time in an emergency situation."
- Reviewing for the first time federal regulations written in 1980 concerning the disposal of PCBs at industrial sites. By simplifying the rules and the required administrative work, the EPA asserts that the affected industries will save a half billion dollars in compliance costs in the next twenty years. [45]

Time and money have undoubtedly been saved, but EPA's scorekeeping is suspect. After reviewing early EPA paperwork reduction estimates, the GAO decided they were overstated. The agency, noted GAO, claimed a reduction of 1.2 million hours by eliminating a long form previously required by companies reporting for the Toxics Release Inventory. But the EPA had not, said GAO, offset this reduction by an additional 800,000 hours required by the same companies to fill out a new form in lieu of the original one. Citing other examples, GAO concluded that "some of the larger reductions claimed by EPA are overstated because of the way EPA calculated them." [46] The EPA has reportedly reviewed its arithmetic, but the disputed figures still appear in current EPA reports about the initiative. Is this honest reporting or creative bookkeeping? Statistics of this sort are elusive at best, and the EPA is probably innocent of deliberate deception. It is fair to conclude that EPA's paperwork savings are probably less than it claims and more than its critics believe.

The Underside of Reinvention

Reinventing environmental regulation is reform barely begun. But developing and launching these ambitious programs has exposed an organizational underside of reinvention: formidable impediments embedded within EPA's own organization, its staff, and its constituencies. These are less publicized but still disruptive problems with which the EPA must deal if the gamble on reinvention is to yield the political and regulatory results the agency urgently needs.

The Struggle Within the EPA

Early experience with reinvention has revealed an EPA struggling with itself, and with its inherited organizational design, to make reform work. Reform has evoked conflicts within the EPA's organizational culture, and replicated them across many different initiatives, that must be satisfactorily resolved for the initiatives to be successful. These conflicts arise from EPA's organizational pluralism: a workforce embracing many different and often contentious professional viewpoints and organizational interests that collide over the fate of specific initiatives. "Because the agency is responsible for many different aspects of policymaking ranging from toxicity standard-setting to law enforcement, it employs a wide range of professionals including lawyers, economists, and engineers," explains a well-informed agency analysis. "The modes of thought characteristic of these professions . . . often breed misunderstanding and conflict"—and one should also add EPA's scientists and political appointees to the mix. Two organizational cleavages, in particular, are likely to powerfully shape the future direction of reinvention.[47]

The Media Offices and Integrated Regulation. EPA's major "media" offices—those regulating air, water, and hazardous waste, especially—have been the organizational and regulatory centers of power within the EPA by its organizational design. They have been, from the beginning, ambivalent about the effectiveness of the numerous reinvention initiatives that in some way encourage "integrated" approaches to regulation—that is, approaches that cut across and combine techniques from different media offices. This attitude, buttressed by strong, sincere professional convictions, frequently translates into apathy, if not opposition, to reinvention efforts. One task confronting EPA's leadership is to convince the staff of the media offices to "buy into regulatory reinvention."[48]

Bringing the media offices "under the tent" of reform will not be easy. These offices are delegated the major authority, separate budgets, and most of the administrative personnel for implementing major pollution control laws. This reflects the traditional style of environmental regulation in the United States: pollution control professionals are trained, and their technology developed, to deal with pollution medium by medium, an approach powerfully reinforced by the professional schools, associations, and political groups representing each medium specialty. EPA's administrators have very limited power and influence over the media offices. "The EPA administrator has more authority over the constituent parts than many federal agency heads," concluded one expert agency study, "but the authority is limited by the fragmented statutes, and, in some administrations, by the reluctance of the administrator to do battle with the media-oriented offices."[49] Several years into the reform effort, the GAO concluded that EPA's rank-and-file were still to be converted, having "grown accustomed to prescriptive, medium-by-medium regulation during the agency's 27-year history."[50]

Rallying Support from Regional Offices and the States. EPA's reinvention campaign, originating during Carol Browner's term as EPA administrator, has been strongly identified with Browner and her agency leadership team. Browner has enjoyed the longest tenure of any EPA administrator and consistently strong White House support through Vice President Al Gore. She has been in many respects a strong and effective agency leader and spokesperson, particularly in successfully defending the EPA and its core programs from the aggressive attacks of the Republican majority in the 104th Congress. Nonetheless, her relationship with EPA's permanent staff and existing offices has been highly variable, partially because Browner came to her job outspokenly critical of EPA's internal management and organizational effectiveness.[51] Her subsequent performance as administrator has inspired support and respect from EPA personnel on many occasions. Yet many EPA staff, especially among the ten regional offices, remain uncertain about the durability of EPA's leadership commitment to the initiatives, particularly after Browner's term ends in the year 2000. Many EPA managers, especially in the regional offices, and state officials find the outpouring of initiatives confusing and disruptive to their existing tasks. GAO discovered several common complaints:

> Officials . . . cited the large number of initiatives as a problem and indicated that setting priorities among the initiatives would make the most efficient use of the Agency's resources. Under the current situation . . . the regional offices are expected to carry out reinvention activities with few resources beyond those the regions receive to carry out traditional program responsibilities.[52]

Additionally, initiatives so expansive in their organizational impact have incited the predictable turf fights between different EPA offices and interests who perceive a threat to their institutional fortunes, or an opportunity to promote them, in specific proposals. Overcoming these and other obstacles to reform deeply rooted in EPA organizational history cannot be easy or quick.

Increasing Stakeholder Support

The EPA has a large, diverse constituency of "outside" interests deeply concerned with its work: state and local officials, environmental organizations, pollution control professionals, scientists, regulated commercial and industrial facilities and their trade organizations, academics, and others. The agency is investing enormous time and resources in promoting the involvement of these stakeholders in the reinvention process, and it considers broad stakeholder participation and endorsement for the initiatives a major test of their success. Stakeholder response so far has been highly variable, although the EPA considers it encouraging.

Stakeholders generally commend the EPA for undertaking these initiatives and largely support the broad objectives but, as with legislation, the devil is in the details. Three problems in particular are frequently mentioned by stakeholders in assessing the way the initiative process is implemented. First, the EPA is often faulted for trying to achieve 100 percent agreement among all the stakeholders involved with initiatives, such as the CSI, that promote negotiation about changes in regulatory rules and procedures. Many stakeholders believe this goal is unachievable. Many believe the search for absolute consensus prolongs and complicates negotiations, making final agreements difficult.[53] Second, stakeholders have often found the goals of specific initiatives mystifying and, consequently, difficult to define or measure. What criterion, for instance, should be used to judge stakeholder involvement a "success"? How much agreement among stakeholders on specific changes in regulatory practices should be expected? One of the continuing challenges for the EPA emerging from this early experience is to create evaluation criteria for its initiatives that will satisfy stakeholders. Finally, many environmental organizations believe, or strongly suspect, that changes in regulatory procedures that appear to benefit industry, or other regulated interests, constitute an EPA "sellout" to big business or its allies. A few environmental leaders and organizations, convinced the reinvention process itself is unnecessary, steadfastly resist most EPA initiatives.

These problems are probably inevitable for a reform agenda so ambitious and novel. Many difficulties, such as the tensions between environmental interests and regulated industries, are a manifestation of political cleavages embedded in the whole fabric of environmental policymaking. Others, such as confusion over measures of program progress, result from the newness of the initiatives and may be ameliorated with time. Still others, like the conflicts within the EPA among its program offices, may be unsolvable with EPA's existing organizational structure. Ultimately, however, the most important issue of all in reinvention's future is whether the problems to which it is addressed require a solution that lies not with the EPA but with Congress.

What About Congress?

Many informed observers, otherwise disunited about the efficacy of specific EPA initiatives, believe the ills that the reinvention initiatives address require a cure only the Congress can provide: a major rewriting of the numerous but disorganized and inconsistent environmental laws the EPA now administers into a coherent, consistent array of complimentary regulatory programs. Many legislators agree. This would be no easy accomplishment, however, especially in light of the congressional mood in the late 1990s.

Virtually every major study of EPA's organization and performance in the 1990s has prescribed some sort of congressional comprehensive statute to clarify EPA's mission. Former EPA administrator William Ruckelshaus perhaps best summarized the issue with characteristic cogency:

> The nation needs a new, single, unified environmental statute supervised by a single authorizing committee and a single appropriations committee in each House of Congress. Not the 12 laws and 70 committees we now have.[54]

The National Academy of Public Administration's extensive 1995 report on EPA's activities made its first recommendation in a similar vein:

"Congress and EPA should develop an integrating statute to . . . clarify EPA's mission and encourage the agency to use performance-based tools and integrated approaches to address the nation's outstanding environmental problems."[55] Other expert studies have recommended that Congress provide the EPA with a charter, or an "organic act," that defines its mission explicitly, defines the priorities between different pollution control activities, identifies the major regulatory approaches it should emphasize, and otherwise clarifies what the EPA is expected to do, in what order, and to what ends. Such an enactment would not eliminate a need for specific regulatory laws such as the Clean Air Act or Clean Water Act, but it would greatly facilitate EPA's work and the administrator's responsibilities within the EPA. In any case, while the many expert panels evaluating the EPA in the 1990s disagree over details, they all advocate legislative action that provides a strategic plan and vision that the agency presently cannot derive from the hodgepodge of statutes currently entrusted to its implementation.

The irony in these recommendations is that most of the EPA's fundamental problems, such as inflexibility in writing regulatory rules, inconsistency between different pollution control laws, and failure to achieve mandated program deadlines, originate on Capitol Hill. EPA's many complex environmental statutes, with their heavy dependence on command-and-control pollution management, end-of-the-pipe controls and micromanagement of the agency, betray a legislative style not easily changed. The EPA will need to deftly educate Congress about the need for legislative reform without antagonizing it. Especially after the aggressive effort by the Republican majority in the 104th Congress to enfeeble many EPA programs through draconian "reform" legislation, EPA and its friends may fear that any current congressional reform will become a cure worse than the disease, and so is best discouraged. Neither congressional party, moreover, relishes the political bloodletting sure to arise among all the stakeholders in existing environmental legislation when their different political agendas collide over which priorities Congress should assign to the EPA. In short, looking to Congress for a charter, however desirable it may be, could be a very risky strategy for the EPA to initiate or Congress to encourage.

Conclusion

EPA's new Washington headquarters building boasts 13,000 doors, 21,000 light fixtures, and 94 stairways, but not a single crystal ball. The EPA, as its leaders clearly recognize, is gambling enormous political and organizational stakes on the success of its current reform initiatives. It is in many respects a risky wager, made urgent by the agency's imperative need for major reform but inherently problematic in its outcome.

Issues vital for the nation's environmental future are involved. How effectively will EPA's reforms attack the agency's now widely recognized problems? How well does reinventing environmental protection serve EPA's best interests? How well does it advance EPA's vital regulatory mission? Reinventing environmental regulation is too new to permit firm judgments about its lasting impact on the agency or on the many constituencies with stakes in the many specific initiatives involved. At best, the current results are mixed and inconclusive. Looming always in the political background are portents both ominous and beneficent for the EPA, depending on whether the initiatives achieve their stated objectives. Equally important is whether they acquire the political luster that subdues much of the current criticism of EPA's performance within Congress and among EPA's many constituencies, friendly or hostile. The EPA has never confronted reforms more consequential for its future. The agency has reached a stage in its history when demands for radical recasting of its organization and mission have gathered a strength and breadth of political appeal that signals the potential for a profound change in EPA's fundamental character, perhaps its permutation into some very different entity, should reinvention prove to be largely illusory.

It seems apparent, in any event, that the future impact of the reinvention program will be based on several factors. It will depend on how well the EPA's leadership can rally EPA's own stakeholders and constituents behind reform, how effectively leadership can win over EPA's media offices to the initiatives, and how well the leadership can convince the majority of EPA's professional staff that reinvention is no charade and leadership commitment is durable. The most decisive institution in shaping reinvention's future may ultimately be Congress. It is also the most currently enigmatic element in EPA's future. Congress may, against conventional political opinion, accept the political risks and challenges involved in creating a needed legislative charter for EPA, thereby perhaps accelerating the changes envisioned by the reinvention initiatives. It may also resurrect the belligerent antiregulatory mood of the 104th Congress, and in the name of "reform" launch another assault on EPA's existing authority. It may do nothing. Whatever it does, there will be an impact on EPA and its reformist leadership. For the EPA, in any case, reinvention will be a high-stakes game for many years more.

Notes

1. "A Big One for the Gipper," *Seattle Times*, July 22, 1997; and Ann Hartzell and Michael Pope, "The Ronald Reagan Building and International Trade Center," *Archeological Investigations at the Federal Triangle* at *http://www.gsa.gov/regions/r11/projects/rrarch.htm* (October 3, 1998).
2. A summary of the Reagan administration's relationship to EPA is found in Richard A. Harris and Sidney M. Milkis, *The Politics of Regulatory Change: A Tale of Two Agencies* (New York: Oxford University Press, 1989); Thomas F. Walton and James Langenfeld, "Regulatory Reform Under Reagan—The Right Way and the Wrong Way," in *Regulation and the Reagan Era*, ed. Roger E. Meiners and Bruce Yandle (New York: Holmes and Meier, 1989), 41–71; and Marc K. Landy, Marc J. Roberts, and Stephen R. Thomas, *The Environmental Protection Agency: Asking the Wrong Questions from Nixon to Clinton* (New York: Oxford University Press, 1994), chap. 8.
3. The $7.3 billion figure refers to budget authority as reflected in President Clinton's fiscal 1999 budget submission to Congress in early 1998. See appendix 3 in this volume.
4. Martin R. Lee, *Environmental Protection Legislation in the 105th Congress*, Issue Brief No. 97020 (Washington, D.C.: Congressional Research Service, November 9, 1998). See also appendix 1 in this volume.

5. For histories of the EPA, see Alfred A. Marcus, *Promise and Performance: Choosing and Implementing Environmental Policy* (Westport, Conn.: Greenwood, 1980); John C. Whitaker, *Striking a Balance: Environmental and Natural Resources in the Nixon-Ford Years* (Washington, D.C.: American Enterprise Institute, 1976); and Landy, Roberts, and Thomas, *The Environmental Protection Agency.*

6. William D. Ruckelshaus, "Stopping the Pendulum," *The Environmental Forum* 12, no. 6 (November 1995): 25; see also Richard J. Lazrus, "The Tragedy of Distrust in the Implementation of Federal Environmental Law," *Law and Contemporary Problems* 311, no. (1991).

7. On this period of EPA history, see Samuel P. Hayes, *Beauty, Truth and Permanence: Environmental Politics in the United States, 1955–1985* (Cambridge: Cambridge University Press, 1987), chaps. 14–16; Susan Tolchin and Martin Tolchin, *The Rush to Deregulate* (Boston: Houghton Mifflin, 1983); and Norman J. Vig and Michael E. Kraft, eds., *Environmental Policy in the 1980s: Reagan's New Agenda* (Washington, D.C.: CQ Press, 1984).

8. Rena I. Steinzor, "Reinventing Environmental Regulation: The Dangerous Journey from Command to Self-Control," *Harvard Environmental Law Review* 22, no. 1 (1998): 150; see also Margaret Kriz, "A Kinder (More Realistic) EPA—In a Shift, the Agency's Trying to Squeeze More Environmental Protection out of Laws Already on the Books," *National Journal*, March 28, 1998; and Scott R. Furlong, "Reinventing Regulatory Development at the Environmental Protection Agency," *Policy Studies Journal* 23, no. 3 (July 1995): 466–482.

9. U.S. Environmental Protection Agency (EPA), Office of Reinvention, "Reinventing Environmental Protection: EPA's Approach to the Reinvention Strategy" (Washington, D.C.: EPA, Office of Reinvention, 1995).

10. Vice President Al Gore, "Reinventing Environmental Regulation: Clinton Administration Regulatory Reform Initiatives" (Washington, D.C.: EPA, Office of Reinvention, August 22, 1996).

11. Ibid.

12. The Web site can be found at *http://www.epa.gov/reinvent.*

13. For a review of the Republican reform agenda, see Walter A. Rosenbaum, "The EPA at Risk: Conflicts over Institutional Reform," in *Environmental Policy in the 1990s*, 3d ed., ed. Norman J. Vig and Michael E. Kraft (Washington, D.C.: CQ Press, 1997), 143–167.

14. EPA, "Twenty-Five Years of Environmental Progress," at *http://www.epa.gov/25year/intro.html* (December 20, 1998). See also chapter 1 in this volume for a review of comparable achievements in environmental protection efforts.

15. For a summary of EPA's compliance problems, see Walter A. Rosenbaum, *Environmental Politics and Policy*, 4th ed. (Washington, D.C.: CQ Press, 1998), chaps. 1, 6, and 7.

16. For a thorough review of the problems involved with the command-and-control approach and the alternatives, see the National Academy of Public Administration (NAPA), *The Environment Goes to Market* (Washington, D.C.: NAPA, 1994), chap. 1; Gary Bryner, "Market Incentives in Air Pollution Control," in *Flashpoints in Environmental Policymaking: Controversies in Achieving Sustainability*, ed. Sheldon Kamieniecki, George Gonzalez, and Robert O. Vos (Albany: State University of New York Press, 1997), 85–109; and Steinzor, "Reinventing Environmental Regulation," 110–125.

17. Steinzor, ibid., 115.

18. Ibid., 119.

19. U.S. General Accounting Office (GAO), "Superfund: Cleanups Nearing Completion Indicate Future Challenges," GAO/RCED 93-188 (Washington, D.C.: GAO, September 1993). See also Marc Landy and Mary Hague, "The Coalition for Waste: Private Interests and Superfund," in *Environmental Politics: Public Costs, Private Rewards*, ed. Michael S. Greve and Fred L. Smith (New York: Praeger, 1992).

20. On integrated pollution regulation, see Conservation Foundation, *America's Waste: Managing for Risk Reduction* (Washington, D.C.: Conservation Foundation, 1987).

21. Clarence Davies and Jan Mazurek, *Regulating Pollution: Does The U.S. System Work?* (Washington, D.C.: Resources for the Future, 1997), 7.

22. These studies include the following: Landy, Roberts, and Thomas, *The Environmental Protection Agency*; Davies and Mazurek, *Regulating Pollution*; NAPA, *The Environment Goes to Market*; NAPA, *Resolving the Paradox of Environmental Protection* (Washington, D.C.: NAPA, 1998); and National Commission on the Environment, *Choosing a Sustainable Future* (Washington, D.C.: Island Press, 1993).

23. Ruckelshaus, "Stopping the Pendulum," 25–26.

24. Davies and Mazurek, *Regulating Pollution*, 48.

25. The various reform proposals and their intent are discussed in Gary Bryner, "Congressional Decisions About Regulatory Reform: The 104th and 105th Congresses," in *Better Environmental Decisions: Strategies for Governments, Businesses, and Communities*, ed. Ken Sexton, Alfred A. Marcus, K. William Easter, and Timothy D. Burkhardt (Washington, D.C.: Island Press, 1999), 91–112.

26. GAO, "Duration of the Superfund Process," GAO/RCED 97-20 (Washington, D.C.: GAO, 1997), 15.

27. See Claudia Copeland, "Clean Water Act Reauthorization in the 105th Congress," Report No. 97001 (Washington, D.C.: Congressional Research Service, October 29, 1998); and "Water Quality: Implementing the Clean Water Act," Report No. 89102 (Washington, D.C.: Congressional Research Service, December 4, 1998).

28. Michael E. Kraft and Denise Scheberle, "Environmental Federalism at Decade's End: New Approaches and Strategies," *Publius* 28, no. 1 (Winter 1998): 131–146

29. EPA, "EPA Reports Real Progress in Reinvention of Nation's Environmental Regulatory System," press release, March 3, 1998, at *http://epainotes1.rtpnc.epa.gov:7777/opa* (December 12, 1998).

30. EPA, Office of Reinvention, *Reinvention 1997 Annual Report: Executive Summary* (Washington, D.C.: EPA, 1998), 1.

31. J. Richard Fox, *Testimony Before House Commerce Committee, Investigations and Oversight Subcommittee, Hearing on Reinvention at EPA*, November 4, 1997, at *http://www. epa.gov/reinvent/notebook/1104test.htm* (December 13, 1998).

32. EPA, "EPA Reports Real Progress in Reinvention of Nation's Environmental Regulatory System."

33. GAO, "EPA's Common Sense Initiative," GAO/RCED 97-164 (Washington, D.C.: GAO, May 1997), 5.

34. Ibid.

35. Fox, *Testimony*.

36. Steinzor, "Reinventing Environmental Regulation," 122.

37. EPA, Office of Reinvention, *Managing for Better Environmental Results: A Two Year Anniversary Report on Reinventing Environmental Protection: Executive Summary* (Washington, D.C.: EPA, 1998), 2.

38. Steinzor, "Reinventing Environmental Regulation," 128.

39. Ibid., 142.

40. EPA, Office of Reinvention, *A Stronger Partnership With State Agencies* (Washington, D.C.: EPA, 1998), available at *http://www.epa.gov/reinvent* (January 2, 1999).

41. Ibid.

42. GAO, "Assessing EPA's Progress in Paperwork Reduction," GAO/T-RCED-96-107 (Washington, D.C.: GAO, March 1996), 1.

43. EPA, Office of Reinvention, *Cutting Red Tape and Regulatory Burden* (Washington, D.C.: EPA, 1998).

44. EPA, "EPA Reports Real Progress."

45. EPA, Office of Reinvention, *Cutting Red Tape*.

46. GAO, "Assessing EPA's Progress," 2–3.

47. Landy, Roberts, and Thomas, *The Environmental Protection Agency*, 11.

48. On the problems associated with promoting integrated regulatory strategies at the EPA, see GAO, "An Integrated Approach Could Reduce Pollution and Increase Regulatory Efficiency," GAO/RCED 96-41 (Washington, D.C.: GAO, January 1996); GAO, "Reinventing Environmental Regulation," 6–11; GAO, "EPA's Common Sense Initiatives," 5–7; GAO, "EPA's Progress in Reinventing Regulation," GAO/T-RCED 98-33 (Washington, D.C.: GAO, July 1998), 9–11; Davies and Mazurek, *Regulating Pollution*, 8–13; and NAPA, *Resolving the Paradox*, chap. 2.

49. Davies and Mazurek, *Regulating Pollution*, 8.

50. GAO, "Reinventing Environmental Regulation," 6.

51. Landy, Roberts, and Thomas, *The Environmental Protection Agency*, 306–309.

52. GAO, "Reinventing Environmental Regulation," 8.

53. Ibid., 9.

54. Ruckelshaus, "Stopping the Pendulum," 28–29.

55. NAPA, *Setting Priorities, Getting Results*, chap. 2.

9

Economics, Incentives, and Environmental Regulation

A. Myrick Freeman III

It is helpful to think of the environment as a resource system that contributes to human welfare in a variety of ways. The source of the basic means of life support—clean air and clean water—the environment provides the means for growing food. It is the source of minerals and other raw materials that go into the production of the goods and services that support modern society's standard of living. The environment can be used for a variety of recreational activities such as hiking, fishing, and observing wildlife. It is also the source of amenities and esthetic pleasure, providing scenic beauty and inspiring our awe at the wonder of nature. Finally, the environment is the place where we deposit the wastes from the economic activities of production and consumption. It is this latter use and the conversion of natural environments to more intensively managed agricultural ecosystems and to residential and commercial development that give rise to today's environmental problems.

The environment is a scarce resource. This means that it cannot provide all the desired quantities of all its services at the same time. Greater use of one type of environmental service usually means that less of some other type of service is available. Thus, the use of the environment involves trade-offs. Increasing the life-sustaining or amenity-yielding services it provides may require reducing the use of the environment's waste-receiving capacities or cutting back on development, and vice versa.

Economics is about how to manage the activities of people and the ways we use the environment to meet our material needs and wants in the face of scarcity. Environmental protection and the control of pollution are costly activities. We wish to protect the environment and reduce pollution presumably because the value we place on the environment's life-sustaining and -enhancing services is greater than the value we place on what we must give up to achieve environmental improvement.

Devoting more of our scarce resources of labor, capital, and so forth to controlling pollution necessarily means that fewer of these resources are available to do other things that we value. Similarly, the protection of a particular environmental resource to preserve amenities or wildlife habitat typically requires reductions in other uses of that resource, such as mining of minerals and production of forest products. The costs of environmental protection are the values of these alternative uses that are forgone and the labor, capital, materials, and energy that are used up in controlling the flow of wastes to the environment. Because pollution control and environmental protection are costly, it is in our best interest to be economical in our decisions about environmental protection and improvement.

There are two senses in which this is true. First, we need to be economical about our objectives for environmental protection. If we are to make the most of our endowment of scarce resources, we should compare what we receive from devoting resources to pollution control and environmental protection with what we give up by taking resources from other uses. We should undertake more pollution control activities only if the results are worth more to us than the values we forgo by diverting resources from other uses such as producing food, shelter, and comfort. This is basically what benefit-cost analysis is about.

Second, whatever pollution control targets are chosen, the means of achieving them should minimize the costs of meeting these targets. It is wasteful to use more resources than is absolutely necessary to achieve pollution control objectives. Yet many environmental protection and pollution control policies are wasteful in just this sense. One of the major contributions of economic analysis to environmental policy is that it can reveal when and how these policies can be made more cost-effective.

In the next section of this chapter, I will describe how benefit-cost analysis can be used to decide how far to go in the direction of environmental protection. I also discuss recent applications of benefit-cost analysis to environmental policy decisions and contributions that this economic approach to environmental policymaking might make in the future.

In the third section I will briefly describe the basic approach to achieving pollution control objectives that is embodied in the major federal statutes—the Clean Air Act of 1970 and the Federal Water Pollution Control Act of 1972. The fourth section is devoted to the concept of cost-effectiveness.

In the final three sections I describe and evaluate a variety of economics-based incentive devices (such as pollution taxes, deposit-refund systems, and tradable pollution discharge permits) that encourage pollution-control activities by firms and individuals and reduce the overall costs of achieving environmental protection targets. I also discuss the possibility of increasing the use of economic incentives in environmental policy early in the twenty-first century.

Benefit-Cost Analysis and Environmental Policy

The basic premise underlying benefit-cost analysis is that the purpose of economic activity is to increase the well-being of the individuals who make up the society and that each individual is the best judge of how well off he or she is in a given situation. If we are to make the most of our scarce resources, we should compare what we receive in the form of increased well-being from pollution control and environmental protection activities with what we give up by taking resources from other uses. We should measure the values of what we gain (the benefits) and what we lose (the costs) in terms of the preferences of those who experience these gains and losses. We should undertake environmental protection and pollution control only if the results are worth more, in terms of individuals' values, than what is given up by diverting resources from other uses. This is the underlying principle of the economic approach to environmental policy. Benefit-cost analysis is a set of analytical tools designed to measure the net contribution of any public policy to the economic well-being of the members of society.

Although in some respects benefit-cost analysis is nothing more than organized common sense, the term is usually used to describe a more narrowly defined, technical economic calculation that attempts to reduce all benefits and costs to a common monetary measure (that is, dollars). It seeks to determine if the aggregate of the gains that accrue to those made better off is greater than the aggregate of losses to those made worse off by the policy choice. The gains and losses are both measured in dollars and are defined as the sums of each individual's willingness to pay to receive the gain or to prevent the policy-imposed losses. If the gains exceed the losses, the policy should be accepted according to the logic of benefit-cost analysis.

Policies where the aggregate gains outweigh the aggregate costs can be justified on ethical grounds because the gainers could fully compensate the losers with monetary payments and still themselves be better off with the policy. Thus, if the compensation were actually made, there would be no losers, only gainers.[1]

Setting Environmental Standards

Selection of environmental quality standards illustrates some of the issues involved in using benefit-cost analysis for environmental policymaking. An environmental quality standard is a legally established minimum level of cleanliness or maximum level of pollution in some part of the environment. Once established, a standard can form the basis for enforcement actions against a polluter whose discharges cause the standard to be violated. Benefit-cost analysis can provide a basis for determining what the standard should be. In general, economic principles require that each good be provided at the level for which the marginal willingness to pay for it (the maximum amount that an individual would be willing to give up to get one more unit of the good) is just equal to the cost of providing one more unit of the good (its marginal cost).

Consider an environment that is badly polluted by industrial activity. Suppose that successive one-step improvements are made in some measure of environmental quality. For the first step, individuals' marginal willingnesses to pay for a small improvement are likely to be high. The cost of the first step is likely to be low. The difference between them is the net benefit of the first step. Further increases in cleanliness bring further net benefits as long as the aggregate marginal willingness to pay is greater than the marginal cost. But as the environment gets cleaner, the willingness to pay for additional units of cleanliness typically decreases, at least beyond some point, while the additional cost of further cleanliness rises. At that point where the marginal willingness to pay equals the marginal cost, the net benefit of further cleanliness is zero, and the total benefits of environmental improvement are at a maximum. This is the point at which the environmental quality standard should be set, if economic reasoning is followed.

The logic of benefit-cost analysis does not require that those who benefit pay for those benefits or that those who ultimately bear the cost of meeting a standard be compensated for those costs. Whether compensation should be paid is considered to be a question of equity or distributive fairness. Benefit-cost analysis is concerned exclusively with economic efficiency as represented by the aggregate of benefits and costs. If standards are set to maximize the net benefits, then the gainers could fully compensate the losers and still come out ahead. But when beneficiaries do not compensate losers, there is political asymmetry. Those who benefit call for ever-stricter standards and more cleanup because they obtain the benefits and bear none of the costs, while those who must bear the costs of controlling pollution call for less strict standards.

An environmental quality standard set according to the benefit-cost rule will almost never call for complete elimination of pollution. Contrast this economic approach to setting standards with what the Clean Air Act says about establishing air quality standards for conventional air pollutants such as fine particles and ozone. Section 109 requires that these standards be set so as to "protect human health" with "an adequate margin of safety." If even the smallest amount of pollution increases the risk of disease or death at least for some sensitive individuals (as may be the case for ozone and fine particles), a literal reading of the Clean Air Act would require the complete cleanup of these pollutants. But this may result in marginal costs that are substantially greater than society's willingness to pay for additional cleanup.

The Uses of Benefit-Cost Analysis

Benefit-cost analysis can be used to evaluate proposed regulations and new environmental policies in the manner just described. Establishing environmental regulations on the basis of benefits and costs is presently authorized by the Toxic Substances Control Act; the Federal Insecticide, Fungicide, and Rodenticide Act; and the recently amended Safe Drinking Water Act. Its use in setting standards is effectively precluded, however, under provisions of the Clean Air Act of 1970 and the 1972 Federal Water Pollution Control Act.[2] Since the mid 1970s, the U.S. Environmental Protection Agency (EPA) has been conducting benefit-cost analyses of major regulations even though in many cases they could not base decisions on the results. These analyses are major components of the regulatory impact assessments required under a series of Executive Orders issued by Presidents Jimmy Carter, Ronald Reagan, and Bill Clinton.

In at least one important case, the EPA's careful analysis of the benefits and costs of a regulation led to the adoption of stricter environmental protection. In 1985, the EPA reduced the maximum allowable lead in gasoline from 1.1 grams per gallon to 0.1 grams per gallon. Reducing the lead in gasoline means less lead in the environment. This, in turn, means a reduced incidence of adverse health and cognitive effects in children, a lower incidence of high blood pressure and cardiovascular disease in adults, and lower automotive maintenance expenditures. Not all these benefits can be easily measured in monetary terms. But counting only measurable benefits resulted in a benefit-cost ratio in excess of 10:1, thus justifying the regulation on economic grounds.[3]

More recently, the regulatory impact analyses for the proposed revisions to the air quality standards for fine particles and ozone air pollution helped to illuminate the issues involved. For fine particles, the estimated benefits of the new standard substantially exceeded the costs, partly because of the high value placed on reducing the premature mortality associated with this pollutant and partly because major sources (fossil fuel power stations) could be controlled at reasonable additional costs. In contrast, the costs of meeting the new ozone standard are expected to substantially exceed the benefits.[4] Because of the requirements of the Clean Air Act mentioned above, both standards were adopted in 1997. But the controversy about the costs and benefits of the ozone standard may prompt a reconsideration of the legal basis for setting air quality standards.

Another possible use of benefit-cost analysis is to evaluate existing policies by estimating the benefits actually realized and comparing them with the costs of the policies. Where retrospective analysis shows that costs have exceeded benefits, it may be possible to find ways to reduce the costs through adopting more cost-effective policies. But excessive costs may also indicate that the targets or environmental standards need to be reconsidered. As mandated by Congress in 1990, the EPA has recently conducted a retrospective benefit-cost assessment of the Clean Air Act of 1970. The analysis reveals benefits that exceed costs by as much as perhaps a factor of 40. Almost all of the benefits come from the control of particles and airborne lead.[5]

Benefit-Cost Analysis: An Assessment

A major question is whether the state of the art of measurement is sufficiently well developed to provide reliable estimates of benefits and costs. It must be acknowledged that the physical and biological mechanisms by which environmental changes affect human beings are often not well understood. And the economic values people place on environmental changes can seldom be measured with precision. As a consequence, the results of a benefit-cost analysis are usually (or at least should be) expressed as most likely values with ranges of uncertainty. For example, the conclusion might be:

> The most likely value for benefits is $50 million with a range of uncertainty of plus or minus 50 percent; the most likely value for costs is $30 million with a range of uncertainty of plus or minus 25 percent.

Even when ranges of uncertainty overlap, as in this example, information of this sort should be useful for decisionmakers who are concerned with how proposed policies would affect people's welfare.

A second question concerns the political context in which analyses of benefits and costs are carried out and used. The typical textbook discussions of the use of benefit-cost analysis implicitly assume a disinterested decisionmaker who has access to all the relevant information on the positive and negative effects of a policy and who makes choices based on this information so as to maximize social welfare. The real world, however, seldom corresponds to the textbook model. First, as noted above, decisionmakers seldom have perfect information on benefits and costs. But more important, environmental policy decisions are usually made in a highly politicized setting in which the potential gainers and losers attempt to influence the decision.

Some contend that the benefits of environmental regulation are difficult to quantify and value compared to the costs. They point out that in such a setting the businesses that would bear the costs will be better organized to represent their views. If this is correct, then relying on benefit-cost analysis as the basis for setting environmental standards would appear to justify less environmental protection and pollution control than is really desirable. There are three responses to this argument.

First, this is not so much an argument for rejecting the benefit-cost criterion for decisionmaking as it is for electing and appointing decisionmakers who are more capable and for trying to achieve greater objectivity and balance of conflicting views. Second, the argument is based on, at best, an oversimplified view of the process. To be sure, proindustry groups will present information that minimizes estimates of benefits and maximizes estimates of costs. However, policy analysts within government seldom accept industry estimates at face value and, for major regulations, usually prepare their own estimates of benefits and costs or have them prepared by consultants. At the EPA, most benefit-cost analyses are subject to a rigorous peer review by panels of outside experts established under the guidance of the agency's Science Advisory Board. And there is room in the process for the presentation of alternative estimates and points of view.

Finally, as a factual matter, it is not true that benefit-cost analysis is always biased against environmental protection. For many years decisions on funding for federal water resource development projects were nominally based on benefit-cost analyses. But these analyses used techniques that systematically overstated the benefits of development; understated the economic costs; and ignored the environmental costs of building dams, diverting water for irrigation, and so forth. As a consequence, a number of economically wasteful and environmentally damaging projects were undertaken. Indeed, serious consideration was once given to building a dam in the Grand Canyon.[6] Competent and objective benefit-cost analyses clearly demonstrated that many of these projects were uneconomical even without taking into account their environmental costs. And more recently, a comparison of the benefits to recreational fishing expected to come from removal of an existing dam with the costs of removal, including the forgone hydroelectric power generation, was used by the Federal Energy Regulatory Commission to help justify its order to remove the Edwards Dam on the Kennebec River in Maine.[7]

The Future of Benefit-Cost Analysis

The United States has made substantial progress in controlling some forms of pollution over the past twenty years. Examples include emissions of soot and dust from coal-burning power plants and municipal trash incinerators and the discharge of sewage and other organic wastes into rivers. In part, this is because these problems were highly visible and the costs of cleaning them up were relatively low. But the pollution problems of the present and future are likely to be much more costly to deal with. Thus, it will be important to try to estimate what the benefits of cleanup will be.

For some kinds of problems, analysis of the benefits and costs is made very difficult by the scientific uncertainties concerning the physical and ecological consequences of certain policies. The most important example is the question of preventing or controlling global climate change due to emissions of carbon dioxide (CO_2) and other greenhouse gases. Nevertheless, some effort to describe and quantify benefits and costs may provide useful information to decisionmakers. For example, William Cline has attempted to estimate the benefits of controlling emissions of CO_2 and to compare them with estimates of the costs of controlling emissions provided by other authors. Although he finds the benefit-cost ratio to be somewhat less than 1, his estimates contain great uncertainties. He concludes that if society is prudent and wishes to avoid unnecessary risks, "it appears sensible on economic grounds to undertake aggressive abatement to sharply curtail the greenhouse effect."[8]

The twin questions of whether to conduct benefit-cost analyses of environmental policies and how the results should be used by decisionmakers were brought to center stage in the 104th and 105th Congresses. These Congresses considered several bills that would have substantially changed the way that environmental policies are evaluated in this country. These bills would have required that all new major regulations be subjected to a benefit-cost analysis and that only those regulations that passed a benefit-cost test could be approved. Some bills would also have allowed firms to request that existing regulations be reviewed and revoked unless their benefits exceeded costs.

Although most economists laud the principles expressed in these proposals, many have serious reservations about some of their specific features. Some of the proposals spell out in some detail the methods to be used in conducting the analyses; but the methods are not always state of the art. Some proposals would offer affected parties the opportunity to seek judicial review of the analyses. But judicial review is a costly and time-consuming process. Judges without training in economics would be obliged to make decisions about economic theory and method that are outside their areas of expertise. These requirements could bottle up proposed beneficial regulations in court for long periods of time. As of late 1998 none of these bills seemed likely to pass both houses of Congress. However, the issue of the role of benefit-cost analysis in environmental regulation is likely to be with us for some time.

Direct Regulation in Federal Environmental Policy

The major provisions of the federal laws controlling air and water pollution embody what is often termed a direct regulation (or command and control) approach to achieve the established pollution control targets. This direct regulation approach involves placing limits on the allowable discharges of polluting substances from each source, coupled with an administrative and legal system to monitor compliance with these limits and to impose sanctions or penalties for violations.

In this approach the pollution control authority must carry out a series of four steps:

1. Determine the rules and regulations for each source that will achieve the given pollution control targets. These regulations might include the installation of certain types of pollution control equipment; restrictions on activities; or control of inputs, such as limiting the sulfur content in fuels. The regulations typically establish maximum allowable discharges of polluting substances from each source.
2. Establish penalties or sanctions for noncompliance.
3. Monitor sources so that incidents of noncompliance can be detected. Alternatively, the authorities might establish a system of self-reporting with periodic checks and audits of performance.
4. Punish violations. If violations of the regulations are detected, the authorities must use the administrative and legal mechanisms spelled out in the relevant laws to impose penalties or to require changes in the behavior of the sources.[9]

Economists have criticized the direct regulation approach on two grounds. First, the regulations require a pattern of pollution control activities that tends to be excessively costly—in other words, not cost-effective. Second, the incentive structure created for firms and individuals is inappropriate. Because compliance is so costly, there is no positive incentive to control pollution, although there is the negative incentive to avoid penalties. Not only is there no incentive to do better than the regulations require, but also the incentives to comply with the regulations themselves may be too weak to overcome the disincentive of bearing the costs of compliance.

Efficiency and Cost-Effectiveness

Even if one objects, for either philosophical or pragmatic reasons, to basing environmental policy on benefit-cost analysis, it still makes good sense to favor cost-effective environmental policies. Cost-effectiveness means the stated environmental quality standards are achieved at the lowest possible total cost. The importance of achieving cost-effective pollution control policies should be self-evident: cost savings free resources that can be used to produce other goods and services of value to people.

When several sources of pollution exist in the same area, a pollution control policy must include some mechanism for dividing the responsibility for cleanup among the several sources. The direct regulation form of policy typically does this by requiring all sources to clean up by the same percentage. But such a policy will rarely be cost-effective. A pollution control policy is cost-effective only if it allocates the responsibility for cleanup among sources so that the incremental or marginal cost of achieving a one-unit improvement in environmental quality at any location is the same for all sources of pollution. Differences in the marginal costs of improving environmental quality can arise from differences in the marginal cost of treatment or waste reduction across sources; also, discharges from sources at different locations can have different effects on environmental quality.

Suppose that targets for air pollution control have been established by setting an ambient air quality standard for sulfur dioxide. To illustrate the importance of differences in marginal costs of control, suppose that two adjacent factories are both emitting sulfur dioxide. A one-ton decrease in emissions gives the same incremental benefit to air quality whether it is achieved by factory A or factory B. Now suppose that to achieve the ambient air quality standard, emissions must be reduced by fifty tons per day. One way to achieve the target is to require each factory to clean up twenty-five tons per day. But suppose that with this allocation of cleanup responsibility, factory A's marginal cost of cleanup is $10 per ton per day, while at factory B the marginal cost is only $5 per ton per day. Allowing factory A to reduce its cleanup by one ton per day saves it $10. If factory B is required to clean up an extra ton, total cleanup is the same and the air quality standard is met. And the total cost of pollution control is reduced by $5 per day. Additional savings are possible by continuing to shift cleanup responsibility to B (raising B's marginal cost) and away from A (reducing A's marginal cost). This should continue until B's rising marginal cost of control is made equal to A's now lower marginal cost. Emissions of a pollutant may have different impacts on air quality depending on the location of the source. This must also be taken into account in finding the least-cost or cost-minimizing pattern of emissions reductions.[10]

Nothing in the logic or the procedures for setting pollution control requirements for sources ensures that the conditions for cost minimization will be satisfied. In setting discharge limits, federal and state agencies usually do not take into account the marginal cost of control, at least in part because of the difficulties they would have in getting the data. Thus, discharge limits are not likely to result in equal marginal costs of reducing discharges across different sources of the same pollutant. One analysis of the marginal cost of removing oxygen-demanding organic material under existing federal water pollution standards found a thirtyfold range of marginal costs within the six industries examined.[11]

Another way to look at the question of cost-effectiveness is to ask how to get the greatest environmental improvement for a given total budget or total expenditure on pollution control. The answer is to spend that money on those pollution control activities with the highest level of pollution control benefit per dollar spent (the biggest "bang for the buck"). For example, if society decides for whatever reason to spend $1 million to control organic forms of water pollution, it should require that the money be spent on industries with the highest pollutant removal per dollar, which is to say, the lowest cost per pound of removal. The study cited in the preceding paragraph shows that spending an extra dollar for controlling organic pollution in a low-cost industry will buy thirty times more pollution removal than spending the same dollar in an industry with high marginal costs.

A number of environmental protection and public health policies are cost-ineffective because of large differences across activities in the marginal costs of control, or in the benefit per dollars spent. For example, a study of the costs of regulating toxic chemicals in the environment and the workplace found that the costs of each life year saved varied widely, both across chemicals and for different regulations on the same chemical. The costs of meeting an exposure standard for benzene varied from $76,000 per life year saved in rubber and tire factories to $3 million per life year saved in coke and coal chemical factories. And the costs of controlling arsenic emissions varied from $74,000 per life year saved at copper smelters to $51 million at glass manufacturing plants.[12] These examples clearly show that it would be possible both to lower the compliance cost burden for industry and to increase the number of life years saved by somewhat reducing the requirements imposed on the highest-cost factories and placing stricter requirements on those sources with the lowest cost of compliance.

Probably the greatest opportunities for more cost-effective pollution control are in the realm of the conventional pollutants of air and water. The problem of cost-effectiveness has stimulated many empirical studies comparing the costs of direct regulation policies (under provisions of the Clean Air Act and Federal Water Pollution Control Act) with cost-effective alternatives based on equalizing the marginal costs of meeting environmental quality standards across all sources of pollution. In his review of these studies, T. H. Tietenberg found that least-cost pollution control planning could generate cost savings of 30 to 40 percent, and in some cases more than 90 percent.[13] This means that in some instances pollution control costs are ten times higher than they need to be.

How can cost savings of this magnitude be realized? Can pollution control policies be made more cost-effective without causing further environmental degradation? The answer lies in changing the incentives that face polluters.

Incentives vs. Direct Regulation

In an unregulated market economy pollution arises because of the way individuals and firms respond to market forces and incentives. Firms find that safe and nonpolluting methods of disposing of wastes are usually more costly than dumping them into the environment, even though such disposal harms others. Because polluters are generally not required to compensate those who are harmed, they have no incentive to alter their waste disposal practices.

Incentives Under Direct Regulation

In deciding how to respond to a system of regulations and enforcement, polluters will compare the costs of compliance with the likely costs and penalties associated with noncompliance. The costs of compliance may be substantial, but the costs of noncompliance are likely to be uncertain. Incidents of noncompliance might not be detected. Minor violations, even if detected, might be ignored by the authorities. Rather than commit itself to the uncertain legal processes involved in imposing significant fees and penalties, the overburdened enforcement arm of the pollution control agency might negotiate an agreement with the polluter to obtain compliance at some future date. And even if cases are brought to court, the court might be more lenient than the pollution control agency would wish. All of these problems of monitoring and enforcement of regulations add up to a weak incentive for polluters to comply with the regulations.

One of the consequences of these weak incentives has been high rates of violations of existing standards. In one early study, the U.S. General Accounting Office (GAO) compared the actual discharges of a sample of water polluters with the permissible discharges under the terms of their discharge permits. They found that 82 percent of the sources studied had at least one month of noncompliance during the study period. Twenty-four percent of the sample was in "significant noncompliance," with at least four consecutive months during which discharges exceeded permitted levels by at least 50 percent.[14] More recently, the GAO found that in 1994 about one in six of the major industrial and municipal sources that were inspected were in significant violation of their discharge permits.[15] Finally, in 1998 the EPA's own inspector general reported finding serious enforcement problems for both air and water pollution control at the state level, where most of the responsibility for enforcement resides.[16]

Improving the Incentives

Economists have long argued for an alternative approach to pollution control policy; it is based on the creation of strong positive incentives for firms to control pollution. One form that the incentive could take is a charge, or tax, on each unit of pollution discharged. The tax would be equal to the monetary value of the damage that pollution caused to others. Each discharger wishing to minimize its total cost (cleanup cost plus tax bill) would compare the tax cost of discharging a unit of pollution with the cost of controlling or preventing the discharge. As long as the cost of control was lower than the tax or charge, the firm would want to prevent the discharge. In fact, it would reduce pollution to the point where its marginal cost of control was just equal to the tax and, indirectly, equal to the marginal damage caused by the pollution. The properly set tax would cause the firm to undertake on its own accord the optimum amount of pollution control.

The pollution tax (or charge) strategy has long appealed to economists because it provides a sure and graduated incentive to firms by making pollution itself a cost of production. And it provides an incentive for innovation and technological change in pollution control. Also, because the polluters are not likely to reduce their discharges to zero, the government would collect revenues that could be used to finance government programs, reduce the deficit, or make possible cuts in taxes.

A system of marketable or tradable discharge permits (TDPs) has essentially the same incentive effects as a tax on pollution. The government would issue a limited number of pollution permits, or "tickets." Each ticket would entitle its owner to discharge one unit of pollution during a specific time period. The government could either distribute the tickets free of charge to polluters on some basis or auction them off to the highest bidders. Dischargers could also buy and sell permits among themselves. The cost of purchasing a ticket or of forgoing the revenue from selling the ticket to someone else has the same incentive effects as a tax on pollution of the same amount.

Polluters can respond to the higher cost of pollution imposed by a tax or TDP system in a variety of ways. They could install some form of conventional treatment system if the cost of treatment were less than the tax or permit price. But more important technical options also exist. Polluters can consider changing to processes that are inherently less polluting. They can recover and recycle materials that otherwise would remain in the waste stream. They can change to inputs that produce less pollution. For example, a paper mill's response to a tax on dioxin in its effluent might be to stop using chlorine as a bleaching agent. Finally, because the firm would have to pay for whatever pollution it did not bring under control, this cost would result in higher prices for its products and fewer units of its products being purchased by consumers. The effects of higher prices and lower quantities demanded would be to reduce the production level of the firm and, other things being equal, to further reduce the amount of pollution being generated.

A system of pollution taxes or TDPs can make a major contribution to achieving cost-effectiveness. If several sources are discharging into the environment, they will be induced to minimize the total cost of achieving any given reduction in pollution. This is because each discharger will control discharges up to the point where its marginal or incremental cost of control is equated to the tax or permit price. If all dischargers face the same tax or price, their marginal costs of pollution control will be equal. This is the condition for cost-effectiveness. Low-cost sources will control relatively more, thus leading to a cost-effective allocation of cleanup responsibilities. There is no reallocation of responsibilities for reducing discharges that will achieve the same total reduction at a lower total cost.

One difficulty with implementing a pollution-charge system is knowing what the charge should be. In some cases enough is already known about the costs of control for average polluters so that the appropriate charge could be calculated. The charge can be adjusted, too, if experience reveals that it was initially set too high or too low.

One advantage of the TDP system is that the pollution control agency does not have to determine the level of the tax. Once the agency determines the number of permits, the market determines the permit price. Another advantage of a system of TDPs in comparison with effluent charges is that it represents a less radical departure from the existing system. Because all sources are presently required to obtain permits specifying the maximum allowable discharges, it would be relatively easy to rewrite them in a divisible format and to allow sources to buy or sell them. A source with low marginal costs of control should be willing to clean up more and to sell the unused permits as long as the price of a permit were greater than the marginal cost of control. A source with high pollution control costs would find it cheaper to buy permits than to clean up itself.

Recent Developments

A marketable permit program is a key component of the federal program to reduce acid deposition resulting from emissions of sulfur dioxide. The Clean Air Act Amendments of 1990 called for a reduction of sulfur dioxide emissions of 10 million tons per year (to about 50 percent of 1980 levels) by the year 2000. Starting in 1995, major sources of these emissions (primarily coal-burning electric power plants) are receiving permits for emissions (called allowances) equal to a percentage of their historic emissions levels. The numbers of permits will be reduced to the target level in 2000. The cost savings relative to direct regulation are expected to be several billion dollars per year.[17]

The Air Quality Management District in Los Angeles has set up a TDP system for nitrogen oxides emissions as part of its plan to reduce ozone air pollution (smog). The first set of permits was issued to existing sources of emissions in 1994. Each year for the next ten years, the number of permits will be reduced by between 5 percent and 8 percent. Each source has the choice of reducing emissions in step with the reduced number of permits it receives, reducing emissions by more than the required amount and selling the extra permits, or keeping emissions constant and purchasing additional permits, depending on whether the marginal costs of reducing emissions are less than or greater than the market price of a permit.

Many state and local governments have also been experimenting with various forms of pollution fees in other contexts. Examples include tying the annual fee paid for licenses to operate industrial facilities to the expected quantities of emissions of air and water pollutants, charging households and others "by the bag" for trash collection and disposal, and taxing purchases of automobile tires and motor oil and using the revenues for safe disposal of these products.

More Modest Reforms

The EPA has found several ways to use economic incentives in a more limited way to introduce greater flexibility into the existing legal framework and to foster cost-effectiveness in meeting existing targets. Two of the most interesting of these are the creation of "bubbles" and pollution control "offsets."

Major industrial facilities often have several separate activities or processes, each of which is subject to a different pollution limit or standard. Many of these activities discharge the same substances, yet the incremental costs of pollution control may vary a great deal across activities. Regulators apply pollution control requirements to the aggregate of emissions leaving the plant rather than to each individual stack or source. The bubble concept allows plant managers, with EPA or state approval, to adjust the levels of control at different activities if they can lower total control costs. But the total amount of a pollutant discharged from the plant must not exceed the aggregate of the emissions limitations for individual processes. Aggregate savings have probably amounted to several billion dollars. Because EPA regulations sometimes require a net reduction in emissions from the "bubble," the net effect on air quality has probably been positive.[18]

The offset policy was created in the mid 1970s to resolve a potential conflict between meeting federal air quality standards and allowing economic growth and development. The Clean Air Act of 1970 prohibited the licensing of new air pollution sources if they would interfere with the attainment of federal air quality standards. Taken literally, this would prohibit any new industrial facilities with air pollution emissions in those parts of the country not in compliance with existing air quality standards. In response to this dilemma, the EPA issued a set of rules that allowed new sources to be licensed in nonattainment areas provided they could show that there would be an offsetting reduction in emissions from existing sources of pollution in the area above and beyond what had already been required, either by installing additional controls on these sources or by shutting them down.

For firms desiring to expand or to enter a region, the offset rules provide an incentive to reduce emissions from existing sources in the region. Firms are free to seek offsets from other firms as well. The policy also encourages technological innovation to find means of creating offsets and probably encourages older, dirty facilities to shut down sooner than they otherwise would in order to sell offsets.

Economic Incentives and Environmental Policy in the Early Twenty-First Century

Interest in the use of economic incentives appears to be growing in Congress as well as at EPA. Evidence of this can be found in two reports released in 1989 and 1991 under the banner of Project 88. The first report stated that "conventional regulatory policies need to be supplemented by market-based strategies which can foster major improvements in environmental quality by enlisting the innovative capacity of our economy in the development of efficient and equitable solutions."[19] The report urged much greater use of incentive-based systems such as TDPs and pollution taxes. It also suggested how these systems can be applied to many different environmental problems. The second report, *Project 88—Round II,* provided more detailed proposals for using incentive-based policies to deal with global climate change, energy conservation, solid and hazardous waste management, the supposed scarcity of water in the arid West, and the management of our timber and other resources of the National Forest system.[20]

Drawing on these two reports and other sources, I will briefly discuss several possible applications of economic incentive strategies. They include using taxes or tradable permits to reduce carbon dioxide emissions and excessive applications of pesticides, using deposit-refund systems to prevent improper disposal of hazardous wastes, and "getting the prices right" to prevent excessive use of scarce resources.

CO_2 Emissions

If present trends in emissions and atmospheric concentrations of CO_2 continue, average temperatures worldwide could increase by 1.8 to 6.3 degrees Fahrenheit by the year 2100.[21] If this global warming is to be avoided, or at least retarded, global emissions of CO_2 must be held steady if not substantially reduced. This issue was addressed by 160 nations meeting in Kyoto, Japan, in December 1997. The result was the Kyoto Protocol, which commits the industrialized nations of the world to reducing emissions of CO_2 by an average of about 5 percent below 1990 levels by sometime between 2008 and 2012. The United States is committed to a 7 percent reduction. However, the commitments are not binding until the Protocol is ratified by the signatories, and ratification by the U.S. Senate is very unlikely in the near future.

There are two major policy questions facing the signatories of the Protocol. The first question is what policy instrument should each nation choose to meet its own commitment? One possibility is to implement an economic incentive system such as a tax or TDP program. The case for preferring an incentive-based system over direct regulation is strong. In terms of incentives, enforcement, cost-effectiveness, and administrative ease, both the tax and TDP system come out ahead of direct regulation. One important consideration in choosing between a tax and TDP system is the different ways in which the consequences of uncertainty are felt. With a tax, there is uncertainty about the magnitude of the reduction in emissions that will be achieved for any given tax rate. With a TDP system, there is no uncertainty because the reduction in emissions is determined by the number of permits the government chooses to issue. But there is uncertainty about the price of permits and the costs that will be incurred in achieving the required reduction in emissions. Thus, given a specific commitment to stabilize greenhouse gas emissions, the certainty about the size of the emissions reductions makes a TDP system more attractive than a tax on CO_2 emissions.

If no such commitment had been made, however, there would be a stronger case for taxing CO_2 emissions. This is because very little is known about the economic costs of controlling these emissions, leaving a TDP system at a disadvantage. A compromise position would be to start off with a relatively modest tax on CO_2 emissions. The response to the tax would then provide information on the relationship between the marginal cost of controlling emissions and the size of the emissions reduction. Various tax rate proposals have been made, with most falling in the range of $10 to $100 per ton of carbon content of the fuel. To put these numbers in perspective, a tax of $75 per ton of carbon is equivalent to an increase in the gasoline tax of about fifty cents per gallon.

The second major question facing all nations collectively is what role, if any, should trading of emissions rights between countries play? Many economists argue that the total costs of controlling emissions of CO_2 could be substantially reduced if nations were allowed to trade CO_2 emissions permits with other nations. The Kyoto Protocol allows for the development of a trading system for emissions rights among industrialized nations. However, most industrialized nations, with the exception of the United States, are opposed to this. Another option is to allow the industrialized nations, or firms in those nations, to pay developing nations to reduce their emissions and then take credit for these reductions in meeting their own commitments under the Protocol. Most observers believe that there are many more options for low cost emissions reductions in developing countries through improvements in energy efficiency and reductions in conventional pollutants. In fact, the Clinton administration is basing its estimates of relatively low economic costs of meeting the U.S. commitment for emissions reductions on the development of some kind of trading framework.[22]

Pesticide Use

Heavy use of chemical pesticides in agriculture has resulted in two kinds of environmental problems. First, pesticide residues can adhere to soil particles that erode from the land, causing ecological problems in downstream lakes and rivers. Second, these residues can leach directly into aquifers and contaminate water supplies to households.

The EPA currently has the power to ban specific pesticides entirely or to ban or otherwise regulate applications on particular crops. The degree of erosion and the potential for pesticide residues to leach into groundwater vary widely across different regions of the country. Also the value of pesticide use varies widely by crop and region. Thus, any system of direct regulation is likely to be very cost-ineffective in protecting surface and groundwater quality. The first Project 88 report suggests placing a tax on the use of certain pesticides both to discourage their use and to encourage the development and utilization of environmentally sound agricultural practices. In the absence of specific knowledge about the costs to farmers of reducing their applications of pesticides, it is difficult to know at what level to set a tax for each pesticide in question.

A better alternative might be a regionally based system of marketable pesticide application permits (PAPs). Local officials could estimate the maximum allowable applications of each pesticide in the region that are consistent with protecting surface and groundwater quality. Farmers could then bid for PAPs in an auction. Some farmers would find that the auction price was greater than the value to them of using the pesticide, so they would seek out other ways to deal with pest problems. Assuming adequate monitoring and enforcement, the maximum safe levels of pesticide application would not be exceeded.

Hazardous Waste Disposal

Federal policy on hazardous wastes focuses on regulating disposal practices. The effectiveness of this policy is highly dependent on the government's ability to monitor and enforce these disposal regulations and to detect and penalize illegal practices. Both industry and government have recognized that the problem of safe disposal can be made more manageable by reducing the quantities of hazardous wastes being generated. The high cost of complying with disposal regulations is itself an incentive for industry to engage in source reduction, but it is also an incentive to violate the regulations on safe disposal, the so-called midnight-dumping problem.

For some types of wastes, a deposit-refund system could provide better incentives to reduce hazardous wastes at their source as well as to dispose of them safely. The system would resemble the deposits on returnable soda and beer cans and bottles established in some states. For example, the manufacturer of a solvent that would become a hazardous waste after it is used could be required to pay the EPA a deposit of so many dollars per gallon of solvent produced. The amount of the deposit would have to be at least as high as the cost of recycling the solvent or disposing of it safely. Because paying the deposit becomes, in effect, part of the cost of producing the solvent, the manufacturer would have to raise its price. This would discourage the use of the solvent and encourage source reduction. The deposit would be refunded to whoever returned one gallon of the solvent to a certified safe disposal facility or recycler. Thus, the user of the solvent would find it more profitable to return the solvent than to dispose of it illegally. In this way private incentives and the search for profit are harnessed to the task of environmental protection.[23] A deposit-refund system has potential applications for a wide variety of products where improper disposal is environmentally damaging but difficult to prevent. Examples include motor oil, car tires, and mercury and lead-acid batteries.

Getting the Prices Right

A surprising number of environmental problems are caused, at least in part, by inappropriate prices for some of the goods and services that people buy and by barriers to the effective functioning of markets. A basic economic principle is that if the price of a good is increased, the quantity purchased decreases, while the quantity that producers are willing to sell increases. Many environmental problems are linked to government policies that keep the prices of some things artificially low. For example, the federal government sells water to farmers in the West at prices that are far below the government's cost of supplying the water. And most states in the arid West either prohibit or place substantial restrictions on the ability of private owners of water rights to sell their water to others who might be able to make better use of it. As a consequence, vast quantities of water are wasted in inefficient irrigation practices while some urban areas face water shortages. This increases the political pressure to build more dams and to divert larger quantities of water from rivers already under ecological stress from inadequate water flows.[24]

The U.S. Forest Service often sells rights to harvest its timber at prices that do not cover the government's own cost of supervising the harvest and constructing access roads. Not only do taxpayers bear the direct financial cost, but there is an indirect cost in that too much forest land is subject to cutting with the attendant loss of wildlife habitat and recreation opportunities.[25]

Free access to public facilities is a special case of a low price. In many urban areas, access to the public highway system is free. Even where tolls are charged, these do not always cover the cost of constructing and maintaining the highways. More important, the tolls do not reflect the costs that each driver imposes on others when he or she enters an already congested highway, slows traffic even further, and increases the emissions of air pollution. If each driver were charged a toll that reflected his or her marginal contribution to congestion, this would reduce the incentives drivers have to use the highway during peak traffic hours. Average speeds would be higher with more efficient use of fuel and less air pollution. This would diminish the pressure to build more roads with their impacts on land use, and so forth.[26]

In some cases, prices are too high. In the past the government has supported the prices of some agricultural products at artificially high levels. This gave farmers incentives to plant more of these crops on less productive lands and to apply excessive quantities of pesticides and fertilizers. The result was excess soil erosion and pollution of streams and rivers in rural areas as runoff carried sediments, pesticides, and nutrients into adjacent waters. At present these subsidies are being phased out. We can only hope that future Congresses will resist the temptation to curry political support in agricultural states by raising farm prices artificially again.

Conclusion

Economic analysis is likely to be increasingly useful in grappling with the environmental problems of the twenty-first century for at least four reasons. First, as policymakers address the more complex and deeply rooted national and global environmental problems, they are finding that solutions are more and more costly. Thus, it is increasingly important for the public to get its "money's worth" from these policies. This means looking at benefits and comparing them with costs. Therefore, some form of benefit-cost analysis, such as that required by President Clinton's Executive Order 12866, will play a larger role in policy debates and decisions in the future.

Second, the slow progress over the past thirty years in dealing with conventional air and water pollution problems shows the need to use private initiative more effectively through altering the incentive structure. This means placing greater reliance on pollution charges, tradable discharge permits, and deposit-refund systems. I have suggested three possible applications of incentive-based mechanisms to emerging problems, but the list of potential applications is much longer, as is made clear in the Project 88 reports. The institution of tradable permit programs at the federal level and in Southern California demonstrate the political feasibility of this type of instrument. However, the current political climate appears to be quite hostile to any form of tax increase, even taxes on "bads" such as pollution.

Third, the high aggregate cost of controlling various pollutants and environmental threats makes it imperative to design policies that are cost-effective. Incentive-based mechanisms can play a very important role in achieving pollution control targets at something approaching the minimum possible social cost.

Finally, economic analysis can help us to identify those cases where government policies result in prices that send the wrong signals to consumers and producers and fail to provide the right incentives to make wise use of scarce resources and the environment.

Notes

1. For more discussion of the principles of benefit-cost analysis and applications in the realm of environmental policy, see one of the recent textbooks on environmental economics. Examples include Tom Tietenberg, *Environmental and Natural Resource Economics*, 4th ed. (New York: HarperCollins, 1996); Barry C. Field, *Environmental Economics: An Introduction*, 2d ed. (New York: McGraw-Hill, 1997); and James R. Kahn, *An Economic Approach to the Environment and Natural Resources*, 2d ed. (New York: Dryden Press, 1998).
2. Paul R. Portney, ed., *Public Policies for Environmental Protection* (Washington, D.C.: Resources for the Future, 1990), esp. 21.
3. For a discussion of the role of benefit-cost analysis in the regulation of lead in gasoline, see George M. Gray, Laury Saligman, and John D. Graham, "The Demise of Lead in Gasoline," in *The Greening of Industry: A Risk Management Approach*, ed. John D. Graham and Jennifer Kassalow Hartwell (Cambridge, Mass.: Harvard University Press, 1997).
4. See John W. Anderson, "Revising the Air Quality Standards," at *www.rff.org/issue_briefs/PDF_files/ozprimer.htm#ozprimer* (February 15, 1999).
5. U.S. Environmental Protection Agency (EPA), *The Benefits and Costs of the Clean Air Act: 1970 to 1990* (Washington, D.C.: EPA, 1997).
6. For a description of how bad economic analysis is used to justify proposals of this sort, see Alan Carlin, "The Grand Canyon Controversy: Or, How Reclamation Justifies the Unjustifiable," in *Pollution, Resources, and the Environment*, ed. Alain C. Enthoven and A. Myrick Freeman III (New York: Norton, 1973).

7. *New York Times,* November 26, 1997.
8. William R. Cline, *The Economics of Global Warming* (Washington, D.C.: Institute for International Economics, 1992), 9. For other perspectives on the economics of global warming, see William D. Nordhaus, "To Slow or Not to Slow," *Economic Journal* 101 (1991): 920–938, and Thomas C. Schelling, "Some Economics of Global Warming," *American Economic Review* 82, no. 1 (1992): 1–15.
9. For more detailed discussions of the major provisions of federal air and water pollution law, see Paul R. Portney, "Air Pollution Policy," and A. Myrick Freeman III, "Water Pollution Policy," in *Public Policies for Environmental Protection,* ed. Portney.
10. For more detail on this, see any of the texts cited in note 1.
11. Wesley A. Magat, Alan J. Krupnick, and Winston Harrington, *Rules in the Making: A Statistical Analysis of Regulatory Agency Behavior* (Washington, D.C.: Resources for the Future, 1986), table 6-1.
12. Tammy O. Tengs et al., "Five-Hundred Life-Saving Interventions and Their Cost-Effectiveness," *Risk Analysis* 15 (1995): 369–390.
13. T. H. Tietenberg, *Emissions Trading: An Exercise in Reforming Pollution Policy* (Washington, D.C.: Resources for the Future, 1985), 38–47.
14. U.S. General Accounting Office (GAO), *Waste Water Dischargers Are Not Complying with EPA Pollution Control Permits* (Washington, D.C.: GAO, 1983).
15. GAO, *Water Pollution: Many Violations Have Not Received Appropriate Enforcement Attention* (Washington, D.C.: GAO, 1996).
16. See John H. Cushman, Jr., "EPA and States Found to Be Lax on Pollution Control," *New York Times,* June 7, 1998, 1.
17. For a review of the allowance trading program and what has been happening in this market, see Renee Rico, "The U.S. Allowance Trading System for Sulfur Dioxide: An Update on Market Experience," *Environmental and Resource Economics* 5 (1995): 115–129, and Dallas Burtraw, "Trading Emissions to Clean the Air: Exchanges Few But Savings Many," *Resources,* no. 122 (Winter 1996): 3–6.
18. The "bubble concept" was so called because it treats a collection of smokestacks or sources within a large factory as if it were encased in a bubble.
19. *Project 88, Harnessing Market Forces to Protect Our Environment: Initiatives for the New President,* a public policy study sponsored by Sen. Tim Wirth (D-Colo.) and Sen. John Heinz (R-Pa.) (Washington, D.C.: Project 88, December 1988). See also Bruce A. Ackerman and Richard B. Stewart, "Reforming Environmental Law: The Democratic Case for Market Incentives," *Columbia Journal of Environmental Law* 13 (1988): 171–199; and Richard B. Stewart, "Controlling Environmental Risks through Economic Incentives," *Columbia Journal of Environmental Law* 13 (1988): 153–169.
20. *Project 88—Round II, Incentives for Action: Designing Market-Based Environmental Strategies,* a public policy study sponsored by Sen. Tim Wirth (D-Colo.) and Sen. John Heinz (R-Pa.) (Washington, D.C.: Project 88, May 1991).
21. J. T. Houghton et al., eds., *Climate Change 1995: The Science of Climate Change* (New York: Cambridge University Press, 1996), 6.
22. U. S. Council of Economic Advisors, *The Kyoto Protocol and the President's Policies to Address Climate Change: Administration Economic Analysis* (Washington, D.C.: Government Printing Office, July 1998).
23. See *Project 88,* chap. 7; Clifford S. Russell, "Economic Incentives in the Management of Hazardous Waste," *Columbia Journal of Environmental Law* 13 (1988): 1101–1119; and Molly K. Macauley, Michael D. Bowes, and Karen L. Palmer, *Using Economic Incentives to Regulate Toxic Substances* (Washington, D.C.: Resources for the Future, 1992).
24. *Project 88—Round II,* chap. 4.
25. Ibid.
26. Kenneth A. Small, Clifford Winston, and Carol A. Evans, *Road Work: A New Highway Pricing and Investment Strategy* (Washington, D.C.: Brookings, 1989); and James J. MacKenzie, Roger C. Dower, and Donald D. T. Chen, *The Going Rate: What It Really Costs to Drive* (Washington, D.C.: World Resources Institute, 1992).

10

Risk-Based Decisionmaking

Richard N. L. Andrews

Environmental regulation as it enters the twenty-first century is pervaded by the language of risk, and environmental policy analysis by the concepts and methods of quantitative risk assessment (QRA). In 1984 the administrator of the U.S. Environmental Protection Agency (EPA), William Ruckelshaus, officially endorsed "risk assessment and risk management" as the primary framework for EPA decisionmaking.[1] In 1987 a major agency report stated flatly that "the fundamental mission of the Environmental Protection Agency is to reduce risks"; another influential report, issued in 1990, recommended that the EPA "target its environmental protection efforts on the basis of opportunities for the greatest risk reduction."[2] By the end of the 1980s risk-based decisionmaking had become the dominant language for discussing environmental policy in the EPA, and in some other agencies as well.[3]

The adoption of this risk-based framework has important implications for the future of U.S. environmental policy. Originally developed as a technical procedure for evaluating the health risks of toxic chemicals, the risk-based approach has since been promoted as a broader comparative basis for setting priorities across the whole range of EPA's environmental policy mandates—and by other federal agencies, state and local governments, and other countries as well. Risk assessment is now the focus of intensive political debate over trade-offs between environmental concerns and regulatory burdens more generally, and recent legislative proposals to mandate risk-based decisionmaking by statute could either reform or undermine many of the environmental protection statutes put in place during the "environmental era" that began in 1970.

Risk assessment remains controversial, both among scientists and policymakers and in general political debate; even many of its advocates are uneasy that it is often oversold or abused. Risk-based decisionmaking may also be too narrow and too negative to deal adequately with many of the most important policy issues of the present and future. To appraise its significance, one must first understand how it has come to be so widely used, what it is, why it is controversial, and how it is now being applied.

The Regulatory Legacy

U.S. environmental policy before 1970 included more than seven decades' experience in managing the environment as a natural resource base—

lands and forests, minerals, water, fish and wildlife—but pollution control had been left almost exclusively to state and local governments. Beginning in 1970, however, U.S. policy shifted dramatically from managing the environment to regulating it, and from state and local to national primacy. The EPA was created by reorganizing most of the few existing regulatory programs into one agency. Within a decade Congress enacted more than a dozen major new regulatory statutes for federal pollution control, each requiring many individual standards and permits for particular technologies, practices, and substances (see chap. 8).

Risk-Based Regulation

Initially these laws emphasized the use of known technologies to reduce the most obvious problems: urban sewage, automotive air pollution, and the major industrial pollutants of air and water. The Clean Air Act of 1970, for instance, directed the EPA to set national minimum ambient air quality standards for six major pollutants, based on health criteria, and set deliberately "technology-forcing" statutory timetables for reducing emissions from motor vehicles. The Federal Water Pollution Control Act Amendments of 1972 required federal permits for all new water pollution sources, again using technology-based standards—that is, "best practicable" and "best available" technologies—to force improved control of wastewater discharges from each industrial process.

As these measures took effect, however, environmental politics became increasingly intertwined with public fears that pesticides and other manufactured chemicals might be significant causes of cancer.[4] The environmental control agenda was broadened and redirected, therefore, to address the far larger domain of chemical hazards as a whole: toxic air and water pollutants, pesticides, drinking-water contaminants, hazardous wastes, and toxic substances in commerce generally. This domain included thousands of compounds, far too many to address explicitly in statutes. At the time, many of these compounds had not even been well studied, and many of them were not just wastes but had important economic uses.[5]

These substance-by-substance decisions raised serious new problems for environmental protection policy. Asbestos, for instance, clearly caused cancer in shipyard workers who were continuously exposed to it at high concentrations as they installed it in ships during World War II. But did this mean that asbestos in floor and ceiling tiles was a serious threat to children? Serious enough to require that every school and day care center spend large sums to remove it rather than to improve their educational programs? Similar questions about risk and cost could be raised about many other chemicals the EPA might regulate: industrial chemicals such as polychlorinated biphenyls (PCBs), pesticides such as DDT (dichlorodiphenyltrichloroethane), trace contaminants such as radon in drinking water, and consumer products such as lead in gasoline, pentachlorophenol (PCP, a wood preservative in outdoor paint), and others. Which of these thousands of chemicals should the EPA regulate, and how should it decide? Should it regulate them to eliminate all risk (if that were even possible)? Or to reduce the risk to some minimum level (one in a million, for instance)? Or to some level comparable to other risks people routinely accept voluntarily (driving a car or crossing the street, for instance)? Or to a level justified by economic estimates of the costs and benefits of control? Finally, how much proof of these risks should the agency have to have before regulating?

To control toxic chemicals, Congress enacted "risk based" and "risk balancing" statutes, which required the EPA to assess the risks of each substance it proposed to regulate, and then either to protect the public with "adequate margins of safety" against "unreasonable risks," or to make choices that would balance those risks against economic benefits. In turn, the EPA had to develop methods for *setting risk priorities* among many possible candidates for regulation; for *justifying particular regulatory decisions*, balancing risks against benefits; and for *approving site decisions*, based on an "acceptable risk" for certifying a cleaned-up hazardous waste site or permitting construction of a new facility.[6] A Supreme Court decision in 1980 reinforced these requirements by holding in effect that many proposed environmental health standards for chemicals could be invalidated if the agency did not justify them by quantitative risk assessments.[7]

Risk Assessment and Risk Management

Quantitative risk assessment has been defined as "the process of obtaining quantitative measures of risk levels, where risk refers to the possibility of uncertain, adverse consequences."[8] To the EPA, "risk" normally means "the probability of injury, disease, or death under specific circumstances," and risk assessment means "the characterization of the potential adverse health effects of human exposure to environmental hazards."[9] Note that these definitions combine two separate concepts: hazard (adverse consequence, usually assumed to be a health hazard) and probability (quantitative measures of likelihood or uncertainty). This mixing of two concepts is one cause of the confusion and controversy that surrounds risk assessment.

One fundamental doctrine of this approach was that risk "assessment" should be clearly distinguished from risk "management." Risk assessment, in this view, was a purely scientific activity based on expert analysis of facts. Risk management was the subsequent decision process in which the scientific conclusions were considered along with other elements (such as statutory requirements, costs, public values, and politics).

A National Research Council report endorsed this view in 1983, and it was adopted as the EPA's policy by administrator William Ruckelshaus. It remains a basic tenet in the literature on risk assessment, though Ruckelshaus himself later acknowledged the difficulty of maintaining such a clear distinction in practice.[10]

Risk Assessment

Quantitative health risk assessment was rapidly elaborated into a detailed analytical procedure that included four elements:

- *hazard identification,* in which the analyst gathers information on whether a substance may be a health hazard;
- *dose-response assessment,* in which the analyst attempts to describe quantitatively the relationship between the amount of exposure to the substance and the degree of toxic effect;
- *exposure assessment,* in which the analyst estimates how many people may actually be exposed to the substance and under what conditions (how much of it, how often, for how long, from what sources); and
- *risk characterization,* in which the analyst combines information from the previous steps into an assessment of overall health risk: for example, an added risk that one person in a thousand (or a hundred, or a million) will develop cancer after exposure at the expected levels over a lifetime.

Suppose, for instance, that the EPA decides to assess the health risks of an organic solvent used to degrease metal parts: a liquid, moderately volatile, that is somewhat soluble in water and degrades slowly in it.[11] The hazard identification step uncovers several experimental animal studies between 1940 and 1960, all showing lethal toxicity to the liver at high doses but no toxic effects below an identifiable "threshold" dose; cancer was not studied. One more recent study, however, appears to show that lifetime exposure to much lower doses causes significant increases in liver cancers in both mice and rats. The only human data are on exposed workers, too few to draw statistically valid conclusions (two cases of cancer diagnosed in fewer than two hundred workers, when one case might have been expected). From these data the EPA decides that the solvent is a "possible" (as opposed to "probable" or "definite") human carcinogen.

In dose-response assessment, the analyst then uses a mathematical model to predict a plausible "upper-bound" estimate of human cancer risk by extrapolating from the animal studies: from high to low doses, and from laboratory species (such as rats and mice) to humans. Applying these models to the measured animal data, the EPA estimates a "unit cancer risk" (the risk for an average lifetime exposure to 1 milligram per kilogram [mg/kg] of body weight per day) of about two in one hundred for lung cancer from inhalation, based on studies of male rats, and about five in one hundred for liver cancer from ingestion, based on studies of male mice.

In exposure assessment, the analyst then uses monitoring data and dispersion models to calculate that approximately 80 neighbors may be exposed to about eight ten-thousandths mg/kg of body weight per day, and 150 workers to about one thousandth mg/kg per day; and through gradual groundwater contamination, about 50,000 people may be exposed to one to two thousandths mg/kg per day in their drinking water after about twenty years.

Finally, the risk characterization combines these calculations into numerical upper-bound estimates of excess lifetime human cancer risk. In this hypothetical case, the result might be eight in one hundred thousand of the general population, one in one thousand nearby residents, and three in a thousand workers. Note from the previous paragraph that the actual numbers of neighbors and workers are far smaller, but risk assessments are normally expressed in numbers per thousand for consistency's sake. These estimates are then to be used by the EPA's "risk managers"—that is, the officials responsible for its regulatory decisions—to decide what risks are the highest priority for regulation and what regulatory action (if any) is justified.

Risk Management

In the context of the EPA's statutory authorities, risk "management" primarily means choosing and justifying regulatory decisions. The EPA administers a complex patchwork of separate statutes, each of which addresses a particular set of problems, establishes its own range of authorized management actions (usually regulations), and specifies its own criteria for making decisions. Some of the laws direct that health risks be minimized regardless of costs; others that the risks be balanced against costs; and still others that the best available technology be used to minimize risks, allowing some judgment about what technologies are economically "available," or that new technologies be developed to meet a standard.[12]

In practice, the EPA and other regulatory agencies appear to apply their own rules of thumb, based on risk and cost, to manage health risks. In one study that examined 132 federal regulatory decisions on environmental carcinogens from 1976 through 1985, two clear patterns emerged. Every chemical with an individual cancer risk greater than four chances in one thousand was regulated and, with only one exception, no action was taken to regulate any chemical with an individual risk less than one chance in one million. In the risk range between these two levels, cost-effectiveness was the primary criterion. That is to say, risks were regulated if the cost per life saved was less than $2 million, but not if the cost was higher.[13]

Science and Values

Quantitative risk assessment is now used to varying degrees by all the federal environmental and health regulatory agencies. It has also been institutionalized in a professional society (the Society for Risk Analysis), several journals, and a large professional community of practitioners in government agencies, chemical and other industries, consulting firms, universities and research institutes, and advocacy organizations.

Despite its widespread use, however, serious dispute remains as to how much of risk assessment is really scientific and how much is merely a recasting of value judgments into scientific jargon. The language of risk assessment is less accessible to the general public; does it nonetheless provide a more scientifically objective basis for public policy decisions?

Risk Assessment Policy

Risk assessment in practice is permeated by judgments that cannot be reduced to science. One such judgment governs the selection of substances for risk assessment in the first place. In practice, these judgments are based not only on preliminary evidence of risk but also on publicity, lawsuits, and other political pressures. Another judgment concerns what effects, or "end points," are considered: most assessments focus on cancer, with less attention and usually far less data for other health hazards, species, ecosystems, and environmental consequences.

In conducting each risk assessment, the analysts' own value judgments come into play whenever they must make assumptions or draw inferences in the absence of objective facts. Such judgments are identified collectively as "risk assessment policy." Hazard identification, for example, relies on evidence from epidemiological studies of human effects, from animal bioassays, from short-term laboratory tests (*in vitro*), or simply from comparison of the compound's molecular structure with other known hazards. In practice, these data are usually few and fragmentary, often collected for different purposes, and of varied quality; the analyst must make numerous judgments about their applicability.

For both dose-response and exposure assessment, analysts must routinely use mathematical models to generate risk estimates. Even the best dose-response models, however, are based on simplified biology and fragmentary data. Scientists must interpolate the dose-response relationship between a small number of observations, extrapolate it to lower doses (often far beyond the observed range), and adjust for the many possible differences between species and conditions of exposure.

Similarly, in exposure assessment, analysts must make many assumptions about variability in natural dispersion patterns and population movements, about other sources of exposure, and about the susceptibility of those exposed (for instance, healthy adults compared with children or chemically sensitive persons).

Finally, the analyst must synthesize a characterization of overall risk out of the diverse, uncertain, and sometimes conflicting estimates derived from the previous three steps. Such choices include weighing the quality, persuasiveness, and applicability of differing bodies of evidence; deciding how to estimate and adjust for statistical uncertainties; and even choosing which estimates to present ("best estimate" or "upper bound," for instance, or a range defined by degree of probability).

Given these many unavoidable judgments, the conclusions of health risk assessments are inevitably shaped more by their assumptions than by "facts." The EPA and other agencies therefore developed guidance documents called "inference guidelines," which specify what assumptions and rules of thumb are to be used in calculating risks. Such guidelines cannot be scientifically definitive because the underlying science contains fundamental uncertainties. They are, rather, policy directives, based on a mixture of scientific consensus and political choices about the appropriate level of prudence. These guidelines often have important substantive differences, specifying different assumptions and procedures to be used in producing and presenting risk assessments.[14]

A Conservative Bias?

A major reason for differences among the guidelines is an intense and continuing debate, both scientific and political, over whether the regulatory agencies' risk estimates are systematically biased in favor of excessive caution. If each assumption includes some extra "safety factor" favoring health protection, for instance, and especially if those factors are then multiplied (as they often must be), the overall safety factor might be far greater than any of them individually, and sometimes far costlier to achieve. Critics of the regulatory agencies argue that these practices render the agency's risk assessments excessively cautious, and that they should be revised to reflect only "best estimates" of risk rather than large margins of safety.[15] Other risk experts argue, however, that many of these assumptions might not be excessively cautious at all. Both human susceptibility and exposure levels can be underestimated as well as overestimated, as can the toxicity of a substance itself and its interaction with other risk factors.

A distinguished risk research group in 1988 identified plausible biological reasons showing that existing risk assessment methods—despite all their "safety factors"—might in fact underestimate some risks of low-level exposure. Given scientific uncertainty, moreover, "best estimate" methods could not themselves avoid value judgments, errors, and biases: they might simply substitute different ones, favoring less prudence toward health protection.[16] Many risk experts therefore argued against using any single "point estimate" of risk as a basis for decisions, and for substituting a range defined by degrees of probability or uncertainty.[17]

Multiple Risks and Risk Management

Value judgments pervade risk assessment even in its simplest forms, such as the risk of a single result (cancer) from a single substance. Most of the "risk management" decisions that the EPA and other agencies must actually make, however, involve far more complex choices among combinations of substances causing several or many kinds of risks to multiple populations.

Imagine, for instance, a relatively common decision issue: the EPA must establish requirements for air and water emissions and hazardous waste storage permits at a new facility for chemical reprocessing and incineration. Many risks must be considered in setting such standards: cancer, respiratory illness, fish mortality, stream eutrophication, crop damage, diminished visibility, and economic hardship to the surrounding community, to list just a few. There may be many beneficial effects as well: reduced damage to health and ecosystems because of improved waste disposal practices, economic benefits to the surrounding community, and others.

In principle, risk assessment can estimate the probability of each of these effects individually. It does not specify, however, which should be considered, nor make them commensurable, nor provide weights specifying their relative importance. In practice, risk assessment has dealt with these issues by simplifying them, focusing on just a few human health effects. This simplification may, however, obscure the many considerations that must be balanced in more complex decisions.

Risk Assessment and Environmental Decisions

By the end of the 1980s risk assessment had become established as the EPA's primary language of analysis and management. The agency's statutes did not contain this consistency of discourse, but most EPA administrative decisions were now couched in terms of how much risk they would reduce: allocating budget priorities among programs, justifying individual regulatory proposals, even framing the EPA's proposed research program for the 1990s. Why?

A Management Tool

From the perspective of senior EPA administrators, such as Ruckelshaus and his successors, formal risk assessment offered an essential management tool. Every head of the EPA faced two nearly intractable problems. One was setting priorities and justifying regulatory decisions for literally thousands of individual chemicals that were candidates for regulation under its several hazardous-substance statutes: hazardous air pollutants, toxic water pollutants, pesticides, drinking-water contaminants, hazardous wastes, and toxic substances generally. Every one of these decisions was likely to be challenged in court, either by industry for regulating too tightly or by environmental groups for failing to protect public health. The second problem was setting priorities across the EPA's many separate programs. The EPA has never had a single overall statutory mission or operating framework: it was created by a presidential reorganization plan, not an act of Congress. Each program was created under a different statute, overseen by different congressional subcommittees, and advocated (and opposed) by powerful constituencies in the glare of the mass media—leaving little discretionary authority for the administrator to set priorities among them.

Risk assessment provided a common denominator—human health risk—by which the administrator could rationalize and defend the administrative decisions he or she ultimately had to make, both among individual chemicals and across the agency's many mandates. Lacking any unified framework or criteria in statutes, the administrator used risk assessment in effect to *create* a more consistent approach, justified by common-sense arguments of reasonableness, consistency, and scientific objectivity. Assistant administrator Milton Russell argued in a 1987 article, for instance, that risk balancing was the only alternative to a much cruder and more fragmented approach, in which priorities were set mainly by historical accident and political influence, and uncoordinated actions might create new risks as great as those they were correcting (for instance, simply moving pollutants from water to land or land to air).[18]

In addition, risk assessment reaffirmed the principle that environmental and health consequences, rather than just the economic costs of compliance, should be the primary criterion for evaluating and justifying the EPA's decisions. During the early 1980s the Reagan administration had greatly expanded the authority of the Office of Management and Budget (OMB) to impose cost-benefit requirements—"regulatory impact assessments"—on environmental regulatory proposals. Risk assessment made risk rather than dollars the focus for justification, permitting the EPA to wrap its decisions in the legitimacy and apparent objectivity of science and in the language of health effects rather than merely economic benefits. Whatever its imperfections, risk assessment redefined the issues in scientific terms, in which the EPA administrator's decisions and staff expertise were normally accorded greater deference than in the broader domains of economics and politics.[19]

Risk Perception and Communication

Although risk assessment strengthened the EPA's hand in dealing with the OMB, it exacerbated conflict between the agency and the general public. First, most controversies over environmental hazards turned on the question of how much evidence was needed before regulating. Public advocacy groups tended to take the position, "If in doubt, regulate to protect health," whereas businesses would reply: "If in doubt, don't regulate until you have proof." Many critics of the EPA used risk assessment to argue *against* aggressive regulation on the grounds that the agency did not have sufficient proof of hazards to justify regulating them.[20] From the perspective of the public, quantitative risk assessment thus tipped such controversies in favor of business, implicitly accepting the view that proof rather than prudence was required to justify regulations and thus imposing costly and time-consuming burdens—analysis, review, and sometimes new research—before any regulatory action.

Second, the professionalization of risk assessment created a new commonality of perspective among risk "experts," who shared a technical view of risks and often disdained the broader concerns of the general public as ignorant, irrational, or self-interested. Many expert risk analysts seemed to believe that their relatively narrow and specialized methods were not just one source of relevant information, but the *only* proper basis for environmental decisions; and these attitudes heightened public distrust of risk analysis.[21] Why were technical estimates of hypothetical cancer risks any more "real," or any more exclusively the proper basis for policy decisions, than public concerns about unanticipated leaks, spills, or plant malfunctions, about risks to their economic well-being, or about harm to their community because of industrial waste disposal? Indeed, what if the estimates made by today's risk analysts turned out to be wrong? Risk analysts reacted by advocating better "risk communication," but many such efforts were essentially one-way attempts—often unsuccessful—to convince the public that the technical understanding of risks was the correct one.[22]

Risk assessment thus remained a controversial procedure, even as it increasingly became the dominant language for justifying regulatory decisions. Beyond a few well-studied substances and health effects, data remained scarce and expensive, basic mechanisms and magnitudes of toxicity remained uncertain, exposure patterns remained vulnerable to many confounding factors, and other important decision considerations could not easily be captured in the language of "risk." Like cost-benefit analysis, therefore, risk assessment became an important tool, but not the ultimate rule, for making environmental decisions.[23]

Comparative Risk Analysis

Quantitative health risk assessment was developed to estimate health risks associated with specific chemicals and exposures, and thus to permit comparisons among the magnitudes of health hazards they posed. It was not originally designed for setting priorities among diverse *kinds* of environmental problems, such as between a chemical threatening health and a development project threatening a wetland. Beginning in the mid 1980s, however, EPA administrators undertook a more ambitious initiative: to use the language of risk as an agencywide framework for setting priorities among all its programs and mandates.

Unfinished Business and Reducing Risk

A pioneering study by the EPA in 1987, entitled *Unfinished Business,* compared the "relative risks" of some thirty-one environmental problems spanning the full range of the agency's responsibilities in relation to four different kinds of risk: cancer, noncancer health risks, ecological effects, and other effects on human welfare. Significantly, this study was *not* a formal quantitative risk assessment, because both data and methodology were lacking for most noncancer risks. Rather, it was based on the consensus of perceptions of relative risk offered by some seventy-five EPA senior managers and on comparisons of those perceptions with opinion-poll data on perceptions held by the general public. These perceived risks were then compared with the amount of effort the agency was devoting to each problem.

The *Unfinished Business* study found that the information available to assess risks for virtually any of these problems was surprisingly poor, and that the agency's actual risk management priorities were more consistent with public opinion than with the problems EPA managers thought most serious. For example, the agency was devoting far more resources to the problem of chemical waste disposal than to indoor air pollution and radon, which appeared to have much greater health risks. The study also found that in most of its programs, the EPA had been far more concerned with public health than with protecting the natural environment itself. Finally, it found that even for public health, localized hazards caused much higher risks to individuals than overall risk estimates revealed.[24]

This study was a remarkably candid step by the EPA to compare its diverse responsibilities and to lay the groundwork for setting priorities among them. In effect, it used the scientifically based language of relative risk to try to build consensus about priorities. By doing so, however, the agency implicitly redefined risk to include not only quantifiable health hazards but also all environmental concerns—making risk assessment a more general language of political debate about environmental priorities. It also implied that such priorities were reducible to a precise technical procedure for risk estimation rather than to a broader process of political choice.

A follow-up study by EPA's Science Advisory Board (SAB) in 1990, entitled *Reducing Risk,* encouraged the EPA to go further with this approach and made substantive recommendations for addressing several high-priority environmental threats. It recommended increased emphasis, for instance, on reducing human destruction of natural habitats and species and on slowing stratospheric ozone depletion and global climate change—and correspondingly less emphasis on more localized concerns such as oil spills and groundwater contamination. Finally, it urged that the EPA use a wider and more flexible range of "market-oriented incentives" to promote cost-effective reduction of environmental risks—pollution charges, tradable emissions permits, emission disclosure requirements, and liability principles, for instance— in place of the more rigid "command-and-control" regulatory requirements that had been its primary policy "tools" so far.[25]

In effect, the *Reducing Risk* report proposed a major reorientation of EPA priorities and tools. More fundamentally, it argued that the agency should *set* priorities and *choose* among policy tools for implementing them rather than mechanically carrying out all the statutory mandates Congress had assigned to it. EPA administrator William Reilly publicly endorsed the report and its recommendations, and made its implementation a personal priority: EPA offices and regions were to use comparative risk studies to justify their annual budget requests, and enforcement priorities were to be based on relative-risk estimates as well.[26]

Despite such strong advocacy from the Science Advisory Board and the administrator, however, the EPA's actual priorities continued to be dominated by its statutes and annual appropriations, which were unusually detailed, prescriptive, and fragmented among separate statutory programs. This rigidity had existed since the EPA's creation and was reinforced by a parallel fragmentation of oversight among separate congressional oversight subcommittees. It was exacerbated in the 1980s by many new restrictions and requirements, which were added to the laws by Congress in response to the Reagan administration's attempts to radically weaken the agency by unilateral administrative actions. These new requirements included rigid statutory deadlines, enforced by "hammer clauses"—serious consequences that would go into effect automatically if the agency missed its deadlines—plus new provisions for citizen suits, court orders, and consent decrees.[27]

The result was that without statutory changes, the EPA administrator had little or no real authority to carry out the SAB's recommendations either to shift priorities or to use more effective policy "tools" to achieve environmental protection.

Technical Comparisons or Public Consensus?

A key unresolved issue for comparative risk assessment was whether it really was a technical procedure to be carried out by experts (as quantitative health risk assessments were claimed to be), or a broader process of assigning value judgments, which should involve public input rather than merely the subjective consensus of technical or administrative elites. Comparative risk assessment modeled on the technocratic procedures of QRA implied that risks of different sorts could be reduced to simple measures, and that these measures could be compared. Such comparisons, however, required judgments going well beyond science, even for different health risks (cancer versus acute poisoning or developmental disabilities, for instance), let alone for risks to other species and whole ecosystems.[28] Skeptics also criticized narrowly technical comparative risk assessments for forcing false choices by comparing environmental risks too narrowly with one another, a procedure which implicitly biased the comparison by leaving out broader and perhaps more effective policy strategies for reducing risk.[29]

Pollution Prevention and Life-Cycle Risks

In 1989, in the midst of its shift toward risk-based priorities, the EPA adopted a new policy statement emphasizing pollution prevention over treatment and safe disposal, establishing the Office of Pollution Prevention to guide its implementation.[30] This policy reflected a growing belief that traditional waste management methods—dilution of wastes in the environment, isolation of materials in shallow landfills, and "end of pipe" waste treatment technologies—were both more costly and less effective than changing the materials and production processes that generated the wastes in the first place. Congress endorsed the new emphasis in the Pollution Prevention Act of 1990 but did not require pollution prevention initiatives. Nor did it supersede the EPA's existing regulatory statutes, many of which—by mandating specific control approaches and investments—remained serious obstacles to prevention incentives.[31]

Pollution prevention provided a valuable step forward in the debate about risks, demonstrating in case after case that preventing environmental risks often costs far less—and provides greater benefits—than building capital-intensive treatment facilities or cleaning up contaminated sites. Two important issues remained, however. One was to assure that pollution prevention initiatives really did reduce pollution and its related risks and did not just introduce different risks that were unregulated. This required a new form of comparative risk study called "life-cycle analysis." Life-cycle analysis would compare products with their substitutes throughout their whole life-cycles—from resource extraction through production, consumption, reuse, and recycling to ultimate disposal. Such analysis provided valuable new insights into opportunities for pollution prevention and risk reduction, but like other forms of risk assessment, it depended on many assumptions and judgments.

The second important issue was to focus pollution prevention efforts on the most serious risks, rather than just on reducing waste quantities. Up until the 1990s, most pollution prevention initiatives were voluntary. They were used in situations where reducing risks served both the polluters' economic self-interest and broader social goals: reducing energy and raw materials costs, cutting waste disposal and insurance expenses, and bringing down the sheer cost of regulation, for instance, or of improving companies' public image. But what about reducing risks when it costs the polluter more to do so? In principle, polluters should pay for the full environmental risks of their decisions. But many of these risks were difficult or impossible to calculate, and no institutional mechanism usually existed to impose and collect such payments.

The Political Debate over Debate Environmental Risks

From the 1970s to the 1990s, beginning with the pesticide and toxic chemicals statutes, the EPA itself took the lead in promoting risk-based decisionmaking and developing risk assessment procedures to accomplish it. Both the procedures and the resulting decisions remained controversial, however, and by the 1990s the issue of environmental risk became a focal point for a far broader national political battle: about trade-offs between environmental protection and public health on the one hand, and the burdens and costs of regulation on the other.

Questioning Environmental Health Risks

Throughout the 1980s, even as the EPA was committing itself to risk-based decisionmaking, skeptics questioned whether many environmental risks had in fact proved significant. Some of these voices could be viewed as merely self-serving industrial interests or antiregulatory publicists.[32] Others, however, included some respected academic scientists and commentators. British epidemiologists Richard Doll and Richard Peto argued that no clear epidemiological evidence demonstrated increases in most cancers from general public exposure to industrial chemicals. Biochemist Bruce Ames, inventor of the Ames toxicity test, argued that people routinely ingest natural carcinogens far more potent than most exposures to manmade chemicals, without evident ill effects. Philip Abelson, editor of *Science,* repeatedly questioned the assumptions and extrapolations used in the EPA's risk assessments, arguing that they raised needless public fears and wasted money on costly and unnecessary protective measures.[33]

By the 1990s influential critiques had been published that challenged the risks of a number of costly environmental regulations, such as those pertaining to asbestos. Prominent academics and journalists joined the chorus of skeptics. Even some federal officials—including one who played a major role in the decision to evacuate the town of Times Beach, Missouri, following an incident of dioxin contamination—wondered in retrospect if their judgments had been correct.[34] Defenders of the EPA's regulations countered with new evidence suggesting additional risks that had not yet been carefully studied, such as hormonal hazards posed by dioxin to wildlife (and potentially to humans) owing to the toxin's estrogen-mimicking properties. A major review by the National Academy of Sciences also reaffirmed the EPA's risk assessment methods and assumptions.[35] Despite these counterarguments, skeptics gained increasing influence in challenging the EPA's use of scientific risk claims to justify its regulatory decisions.

Regulatory Burdens and Risk Priorities

During the same period, though little noticed by the media and the general public at the time, environmental regulatory mandates were also imposing changing and cumulatively increasing burdens on those who were regulated. The environmental statutes of the 1980s were not only more prescriptive and inflexible than previous ones, but they also imposed far greater burdens on far more targets. Thousands of "small quantity generators" such as dry cleaners must now report their hazardous wastes, and pay high costs for disposal. Thousands of gas stations must dig out and replace their underground storage tanks and pay huge sums for cleanup if they had leaked. Many small manufacturers faced the prospect of MACT standards ("maximum achievable control technology") to reduce toxic air emissions under the 1990 Clean Air Act amendments. The banking and insurance industries, meanwhile, found themselves unexpectedly sharing huge financial liabilities for Superfund sites with their clients.

For local governments, the burden was also becoming far greater. The Clean Water Act required cleanup of municipal wastewater discharges, yet federal wastewater-treatment construction grants were being phased out and replaced by repayable loans. The EPA's landfill standards increased the cost of traditional municipal solid waste management methods by as much as ten times, while its new drinking-water standards required more expensive monitoring and purification efforts. Local governments, too, were required to replace their underground fuel tanks, and many school systems were compelled to remove asbestos from ceilings, floors, and insulation. The 1990 Clean Air Act amendments added costly automatic penalties on cities that failed to achieve new compliance timetables; Superfund liability imposed costs to clean up contaminated municipal landfills, and cities became owners by default of many abandoned industrial sites. Yet local governments had no new revenues to pay for these tasks, and the laws provided no mechanism for setting priorities among them.

In short, while the environmental regulations of the 1970s primarily affected large corporations, those of the 1980s placed much greater burdens on smaller businesses and local governments, whose resources were far more limited and which did not fit the populist image of corporate villain. Local governments themselves, early and important political allies of the EPA, became adversaries. Faced with burgeoning federal mandates, no discretion to set priorities, and disappearing federal subsidies, many cities by the 1990s had joined small businesses and other antiregulatory forces to demand an end to "unfunded federal mandates." The alienation of such an important constituency, particularly at a time when federal budget politics offered no realistic chance of increased funding, posed a serious threat to the EPA.

In fairness to the EPA, the real blame for these regulatory burdens lay not so much with the agency as with the rigid and prescriptive statutes enacted by Congress in the wake of President Reagan's unilateral deregulation initiative. These new laws mandated a vast expansion of federal regulations without funding their implementation and gave the EPA itself no discretion to set priorities or to use more economical tools for their implementation. The result was to fuel a radical backlash against federal environmental regulations that materialized in the 1994 elections and the 104th Congress.

Congress Discovers Risk Analysis

In the early 1990s risk assessment suddenly emerged as a focal point for congressional debate over federal environmental regulation, though the debate was fraught with misunderstandings and hidden agendas. As one knowledgeable observer noted, "no other issue is marked more by confusion and misinformation than the current debate over risk assessment."[36] Some members, such as Sen. Patrick Moynihan, D-N.Y., proposed bills to make risk assessment a more explicit and visible basis for setting EPA priorities, essentially supporting the agency's own comparative risk initiatives. Others proposed legislation to prescribe changes in risk assessment methodology by statute, such as requiring the EPA to use "best estimates" of risk rather than "upper bounds." Still others sought to make risk assessment a procedural weapon to block environmental regulation, by proposals that would add industry representatives to scientific "peer reviews" and open EPA risk assessments to additional litigation and judicial review.

These proposals were all presented as seemingly reasonable demands for analysis of the risks and costs of regulatory proposals and could easily be confused with one another. Most were unacceptable to EPA supporters, however, out of concern that they would grind the regulatory process to a halt in paperwork and litigation. A coalition of congressional conservatives discovered that they could thus block environmental legislation by attaching risk-assessment requirements to proposed bills. A 1993 bill to upgrade the EPA to the status of a cabinet department was derailed by such an amendment, and similar threats ultimately blocked nearly all environmental legislation in the 103d Congress. For regulatory opponents, supported by a Republican-dominated 104th Congress elected in 1994 and led by Newt Gingrich, statutory risk assessment requirements became one of three tactical devices—along with "unfunded mandates" and "takings" bills—for blocking new environmental laws.[37]

Throughout the rest of the 1990s most federal environmental legislative proposals, including most proposals for risk-assessment requirements, remained stalemated by ideological conflicts between these opponents of federal environmental regulation programs and the programs' defenders. The 1994 congressional elections dethroned many of the architects and protectors of the EPA's statutes, and installed in their stead far more radical opponents of the agency as chairs and members of key committees. The EPA's programs retained broad public support, but politically they were under siege. In effect, the EPA was now reprising its political battles of the early Reagan years, only this time its opponents were in the Congress and its defenders in the White House.

Lost in this ideological conflict were most serious proposals to reform the regulatory programs in ways that would benefit both their economic and environmental effectiveness. A strong and coherent set of reform recommendations was proposed in a 1995 report of the National Academy of Public Administration (NAPA), for instance, which had been commissioned by the congressional appropriations committees. The NAPA report recommended that Congress give the EPA both a coherent statutory mission and the flexibility to carry it out; that the agency continue to set and enforce national standards but allow state and local governments far greater freedom as to how to achieve them ("accountable devolution"); that Congress pass legislation allowing flexibility and market-based incentives to encourage firms to perform better than required ("beyond compliance"); that the EPA improve its own management systems and expand its use of risk analysis and cost-benefit analysis to set priorities and justify decisions; and that the EPA's fragmented environmental statutes and programs be integrated into a single coherent framework.[38]

Leading congressional risk assessment bills, however, appeared more likely to cause ineffectual stalemate than productive reform. These bills would not increase the EPA's authority to set priorities among its mandates, nor its authority to allow more efficient and effective approaches to fulfill them. They would simply require far more paperwork for each regulation, with less funding to produce it and additional opportunities for litigation, thus increasing rather than reducing bureaucratic red tape and hamstringing rather than reforming the regulatory process.

The main exceptions to this stalemate were two statutes passed in the midst of the 1996 election campaign, the Food Quality Protection Act and amendments to the Safe Drinking Water Act, both of which were driven by bipartisan perceptions of strong public demand for environmental protection and represented genuine and constructive reforms.

The Food Quality Protection Act replaced the 1958 Delaney clause, which flatly prohibited the addition of any potential human carcinogen to food products, with new criteria based on risks, particularly to children. This achieved a long-standing goal of regulatory skeptics, many of whom believed that such an absolute ban was both unwarranted and impractical, but it also achieved major reforms desired by environmentalists, by requiring documentation of all risks of pesticide residues rather than just cancer risks, and particularly risks to children rather than just to the general adult population. In addition, it required food stores to post information on agrichemical residues on their products—a "right to know" provision for their customers, which environmental advocates hoped would substitute consumer pressures for the difficulties of achieving effective government regulation. The amended Safe Drinking Water Act directed EPA to focus on the most hazardous drinking-water contaminants, thus requiring more risk-based priorities and easing the burdens on both EPA and local water utilities, but it also required the water utilities to disclose contaminant levels to their customers—another "right to know" policy. Unfortunately, both of these statutes represented only election-driven exceptions to the more general antienvironmental congressional politics of the 1990s.

Toward the Twenty-First Century

As the twenty-first century dawns, risk-based decisionmaking has become a powerful idea in U.S. environmental policy, yet it remains fraught with political agendas and assumptions rather than fulfilling the purely "scientific" role its early proponents claimed for it. Broader questions also remain as to whether the risk-based approach is the most appropriate way to address the far wider range of environmental issues the EPA now faces, let alone the larger global environmental issues that are arguably most important for the future.

EPA's administrative leaders since William Ruckelshaus have fostered the development of systematic procedures for risk-based decisionmaking, initiated comparative risk processes for setting priorities, and advocated market-oriented policy incentives to reduce these risks. Yet the EPA's statutes remain a fragmented patchwork of disparate mandates, most of them dictating specific command-and-control regulatory programs with rigid timetables and little discretion either for establishing priorities or devising solutions; some promote risk reduction more by their regulatory burdens than by purposeful incentives. Some pollutants that appear to pose only remote risks continue to be regulated, while many other important environmental risks remain ineffectively managed: nonpoint sources of water pollution; losses of natural habitat; global climate change; and archaic subsidies that promote excessive mining, logging, grazing, water use, energy use, auto emissions, and so forth.

In 1997 a Presidential/Congressional Commission on Risk Assessment and Risk Management issued a major report on risk-based decisionmaking, which echoed many previous reform recommendations and added worthwhile proposals of its own.[39] Created by the Clean Air Act amendments of 1990, the commission urged that risk management be redefined away from the fragmented and increasingly cumbersome procedures for analyzing individual substances toward a more comprehensive and systematic framework for examining the multiple contaminants and sources of exposure, and the multiple value perspectives, that are characteristic of most real risk-management decisions. It proposed a new, six-stage framework for risk management that would focus at each stage on the basic goal of reducing or preventing risk to human health and ecosystems, not just characterizing the technical details of particular substances, and would engage all stakeholders' concerns throughout the process. It also urged that this framework be used to address not just individual chemicals, but the full ranges of risks in air and watersheds, work sites, and indoor and outdoor environments. If adopted, such a framework would re-invigorate and significantly broaden the standardized substance-by-substance procedure for risk assessment and risk management that has dominated EPA's decisionmaking since the 1980s. However, it remains to be seen whether these recommendations will be adopted.

National Environmental Goals

Even if the ongoing debate over risk assessment and risk management were to produce meaningful reforms within the EPA, however, risk-based decisionmaking might not produce better decisions for many environmental problems unless it were combined with broader measures to address the fundamental causes of these problems. Better risk-based decisions about regulating individual pesticide compounds, for instance, will probably never be as effective in reducing pesticide hazards as incentives for agricultural businesses to reduce overuse of pesticides in general—yet reducing overall pesticide use may require changes in agricultural policy incentives rather than just in EPA regulations. Similarly, better risk-based decisions about regulating motor vehicle emissions might begin to target enforcement on the worst-polluting vehicles, but without changing more fundamental policies promoting increased auto use, mobile source pollution will continue to increase despite less pollution per car. The EPA's regulatory mandates alone may never effectively reach these causes, even with better risk-based decisionmaking. Similar problems remain unsolved in many sectors, and others will undoubtedly emerge.[40]

Reducing many important environmental risks will thus require changes not just in the EPA's policies, but across all of the agencies whose policies create important incentives, such as the Departments of Agriculture, Energy, Transportation, and others. Some other countries are well ahead of the United States in this effort. The Dutch National Environmental Policy Plan, for instance, sets specific targets and timetables for pollution reduction by each ministry and each sector of its economy, updating these each year in its environmental program document. So far the United States has no institutional mechanism for orchestrating such governmentwide risk-reduction initiatives. In 1993 the EPA initiated a "National Environmental Goals Project," which might provide a basis for such a strategy. But to succeed, this project will require far broader commitment from the president, Congress, and the federal agencies—not to mention the industries and other constituencies that would have to be involved.[41]

From Risk Reduction to Sustainable Development

Beyond the domestic politics of the risk debate lies the larger question of whether risk-based decisionmaking is an adequate approach to the most important environmental issues. Risk assessment in concept seems as self-evidently appropriate to its advocates as common sense: how could reasonable people possibly object to basing environmental decisions on better science, setting priorities based on evidence, or using the most cost-effective actions to reduce the most serious risks? In practice, however, the costs and complexity of such assessments may sometimes outweigh their value: prudence in action is ultimately more important than proof in analysis. The causes are often reasonably clear, the magnitudes and probabilities are imperfectly understood but serious enough to command attention, and the goal need not always be a finely tuned regulation but changes in the directions of gross trends.

Even more important, the environmental risks that are arguably most serious for the future include international and global issues for which a domestic regulatory approach is inadequate. Examples include transboundary pollution, maintenance of ocean fisheries, stratospheric ozone depletion, global climate change, the environmental impacts of international trade arrangements, and unsustainable pressures of population and economic development on natural processes worldwide. Are these problems amenable to quantitative risk assessment? In principle, perhaps. But in practice these decisions are about far more complex choices than "risk" alone. They are about risks, but they are also about other environmental values—sustainability of natural resources and ecosystems, and esthetics and the appreciation of nature, for instance—and about legitimate nonenvironmental values as well, such as self-determination, fairness, basic human needs, economic welfare, and other considerations just as central to the environmental decisions being made. Calling all these considerations "risks" may simply obscure rather than clarify the issues at stake.

Ultimately, environmental management cannot be *only* a matter of "reducing risks." To sustain human civilizations, we must sustain the environmental conditions and ecosystems that make them possible. As René Dubos has so articulately noted, we humans and our environment constantly shape each other, in beneficial and beautiful ways as well as in damaging and ugly ones.[42] To sustain environmental quality therefore requires positive action and creative vision, not merely control of risks. Where in the language of risk would one find the creative vision of environmental design, or the "City Beautiful"? Or even the stewardship concept of environmental conservation?

On a more concrete level, where would one place the idea of rehabilitating degraded ecosystems? The vocabulary of risk-based decisionmaking is a valuable step forward from the patchwork of disparate and sometimes conflicting laws that still defines much of U.S. environmental regulation. But it is ultimately too narrowly focused on justifying the regulation of adverse outcomes to provide an adequate framework for the more complex and creative tasks of environmental management.

These questions require a broader understanding of the interactions between human societies and their environments and a more systematic and positive vision of their future than is provided by the concept of risk. One framework for such a vision was proposed in 1987 by the United Nations' World Commission on Environment and Development in the concept of "sustainable development": meeting the needs of the present in ways that do not compromise the ability of future generations to meet their own needs. This idea was further developed by the U.N. Conference on Environment and Development (the Earth summit) in Brazil in 1992; but as yet it remains more an idealized concept than a specific program. Perhaps the highest-priority task for environmental policy in the twenty-first century is to spell out its details and work toward its implementation.[43]

Notes

1. William D. Ruckelshaus, "Science, Risk, and Public Policy," *Science* 221 (1983): 1027–1028.
2. U.S. Environmental Protection Agency (EPA), *Risk Assessment and Risk Management: Framework for Decisionmaking* (Washington, D.C.: EPA, 1984); EPA, *Unfinished Business: A Comparative Assessment of Environmental Problems* (Washington, D.C.: EPA, 1987), 1; and EPA, *Reducing Risk: Setting Priorities and Strategies for Environmental Protection* (Washington, D.C.: EPA, 1990), 16.
3. Curtis C. Travis, Samantha A. Richter, Edmund A. C. Crouch, Richard Wilson, and Ernest D. Klema, "Cancer Risk Management: A Review of 132 Federal Regulatory Decisions," *Environmental Science and Technology* 21 (1987): 415–420.
4. Mark E. Rushefsky, *Making Cancer Policy* (Albany: State University of New York Press, 1986), 74–80.
5. Ibid., 59–84.
6. Milton Russell and Michael Gruber, "Risk Assessment in Environmental Policy-Making," *Science* 236 (1987): 286–290.
7. Executive Order No. 12291, February 17, 1981; and *Industrial Union Department, AFL-CIO v. American Petroleum Institute*, 448 U.S. 607 (1980). As a legal matter, the extent to which quantitative risk assessment (QRA) is required must be decided on a statute-by-statute basis. Although this decision actually involved a proposed standard by the Occupational Safety and Health Administration for occupational exposure to benzene, it influenced all the regulatory agencies to put increased emphasis on QRA.
8. Vincent Covello and Joshua Menkes, *Risk Assessment and Risk Assessment Methods: The State of the Art* (Washington, D.C.: Division of Policy Research and Analysis, National Science Foundation, 1985), xxiii.
9. ENVIRON Corp., *Elements of Toxicology and Chemical Risk Assessment*, rev. ed. (Washington, D.C.: ENVIRON, July 1988), 9; and National Research Council, *Risk Assessment in the Federal Government: Managing the Process* (Washington, D.C.: National Academy Press, 1983), 18.

10. National Research Council, *Risk Assessment in the Federal Government*; William D. Ruckelshaus, "Science, Risk, and Public Policy"; and Ruckelshaus, "Risk in a Free Society," *Risk Analysis* 4 (1984): 157–162.
11. Example adapted from the EPA, "Workshop on Risk and Decision Making" (materials prepared for the EPA by Temple, Barker, and Sloane Inc. and ENVIRON Corp., 1986).
12. For a list see Rushefsky, *Making Cancer Policy*, 68–70.
13. Travis et al., "Cancer Risk Management."
14. EPA, "Health Risk and Economic Impact Assessments of Suspected Carcinogens: Interim Procedures and Guidelines," *Federal Register* 41, May 25, 1976, 21402–21405; *Federal Register* 51, September 24, 1986, 33992–34054; *Federal Register* 53, June 30, 1988, 24836–24869; and Rushefsky, *Making Cancer Policy*, chaps. 3–6.
15. See, for example, Philip H. Abelson, "Risk Assessments of Low-Level Exposures," *Science* 265 (1994): 1507.
16. See, for instance, Adam M. Finkel, "Has Risk Assessment Become Too 'Conservative'?" *Resources* (Summer 1989): 11–13; and John C. Bailar III, Edmund A. C. Crouch, Rashid Shaikh, and Donna Speigelman, "One-Hit Models of Carcinogenesis: Conservative or Not?" *Risk Analysis* 8 (1988): 485–497. See also Adam M. Finkel and Dominic Golding, eds., *Worst Things First? The Debate over Risk-Based National Environmental Priorities* (Baltimore: The Johns Hopkins University Press, 1995).
17. National Academy of Public Administration (NAPA), *Setting Priorities, Getting Results: A New Direction for EPA* (Washington, D.C.: NAPA, 1995), 41–43.
18. Russell and Gruber, "Risk Assessment," 286–290.
19. Terry F. Yosie, "Science and Sociology: The Transition to a Post-Conservative Risk Assessment Era" (Plenary address to the annual meeting of the Society for Risk Analysis, Houston, Texas, November 2, 1987). Dr. Yosie was then director of the EPA's Science Advisory Board.
20. Rushefsky, *Making Cancer Policy*, 92–94; see also, for example, American Industrial Health Council (AIHC), *AIHC Recommended Alternatives to OSHA's Generic Carcinogen Proposal* (Scarsdale, N.Y.: AIHC, 1978).
21. Sheldon Krimsky and Alonzo Plough, *Environmental Hazards: Communicating Risks as a Social Process* (Dover, Mass.: Auburn House, 1989).
22. Ibid.; see also K. S. Shrader-Frechette, *Risk and Rationality: Philosophical Foundations for Populist Reforms* (Berkeley and Los Angeles: University of California Press, 1991).
23. The "tool versus rule" issue has also been discussed in relation to cost-benefit analysis of regulatory proposals: see Richard N. L. Andrews, "Cost-Benefit Analysis as Regulatory Reform," in *Cost-Benefit Analysis and Environmental Regulations: Politics, Ethics, and Methods*, ed. Daniel Swartzman, Richard A. Liroff, and Kevin G. Croke (Washington, D.C.: Conservation Foundation, 1982).
24. EPA, *Unfinished Business.*
25. EPA, *Reducing Risk.*
26. William Reilly, "Aiming Before We Shoot: The Quiet Revolution in Environmental Policy," *Northern Kentucky Law Review* 18 (1991): 159–174.
27. Norman Vig and Michael Kraft, eds., *Environmental Policy in the 1980s: Reagan's New Agenda* (Washington, D.C.: CQ Press, 1984).
28. Donald T. Hornstein, "Reclaiming Environmental Law: A Normative Critique of Comparative Risk Analysis," *Columbia Law Review* 92 (1992): 562–633.
29. Donald T. Hornstein, "Lessons from Federal Pesticide Regulation on the Paradigms and Politics of Environmental Law Reform," *Yale Journal on Regulation* 10 (1993): 369–446. Some advocates of comparative risk assessment also urged broader risk comparisons, arguing that some nonenvironmental regulations reduced health risks far more cheaply and effectively than many of the EPA's environmental regulations. See, for example, Stephen Breyer, *Breaking the Vicious Circle* (Cambridge, Mass.: Harvard University Press, 1993); but also Adam Finkel, "A Second Opinion on an Environmental Misdiagnosis: The Risky Prescriptions of *Breaking the Vicious Circle*," *NYU Environmental Law Journal* 3 (1994): 295–381.

30. EPA, "Pollution Prevention Policy Statement," *Federal Register* 54, January 26, 1989, 3845–3847.
31. Robert Gottlieb, ed., *Reducing Toxics: A New Approach to Policy and Industrial Decision-Making* (Washington, D.C.: Island Press, 1995), 73–83.
32. The American Industrial Health Council, for instance, was formed in the 1980s to develop industrywide positions on environmental health risks and risk assessment methods. See, for example, "Special Edition: Need for Re-Examination of Risk," *AIHC Science Commentary* 5, no. 1 (1994): 1–26. Popular-literature critiques included Edith Efron, *The Apocalyptics: Cancer and the Big Lie* (New York: Simon and Schuster, 1984); and Elizabeth Whelan, *Toxic Terror* (Ottawa, Ill.: Jameson Books, 1985).
33. Richard Doll and Richard Peto, "The Causes of Cancer: Quantitative Estimates of Avoidable Risks of Cancer in the United States Today," *Journal of the National Cancer Institute* 66 (1981): 1191–1285; Bruce Ames, Renae Magaw, and Lois Swirsky Gold, "Ranking Possible Carcinogenic Hazards," *Science* 236 (1987): 271–280; and Philip H. Abelson, "Risk Assessments of Low-Level Exposures," *Science* 265 (1994): 1507.
34. See, for example, Brooke T. Mossman et al., "Asbestos: Scientific Developments and Implications for Public Policy," *Science* 247 (1990): 294; John D. Graham, L. Green, and Marc Roberts, *In Search of Safety: Chemicals and Cancer Risk* (Cambridge, Mass.: Harvard University Press, 1988); Breyer, *Breaking the Vicious Circle;* and Aaron Wildavsky, *But Is It True? A Citizen's Guide to Environmental Health and Safety Issues* (Cambridge, Mass.: Harvard University Press, 1995). In the media, a major change was the replacement of the lead environmental reporters for the *New York Times* and some other influential papers with more skeptical successors: see, for example, Keith Schneider, "What Price Cleanup?" *New York Times,* March 21–26, 1993.
35. Theodora Colborn, Frederick von Saal, and Ana M. Soto, "Developmental Effects of Endocrine-Disrupting Chemicals in Wildlife and Humans," *Environmental Health Perspectives* 101, no. 5 (1993): 378–384; National Academy of Sciences-National Research Council, *Science and Judgment in Risk Assessment* (Washington, D.C.: National Academy Press, 1994). See also Finkel, "Second Opinion."
36. Terry [J. Clarence] Davies, "Congress Discovers Risk Analysis," *Resources* (Winter 1995): 7.
37. Ibid., 5–8.
38. NAPA, *Setting Priorities.*
39. Presidential/Congressional Commission on Risk Assessment and Risk Management, *Risk Assessment and Risk Management in Regulatory Decision-Making*, Final Report, vol. 2, 1997 (*http://www.riskworld.com*).
40. Hornstein, "Lessons from Federal Pesticide Regulation," 369–446; James J. MacKenzie, Roger C. Dower, and Donald D. T. Chen, *The Going Rate: What It Really Costs to Drive* (Washington, D.C.: World Resources Institute, 1992); and Robert Repetto, *Jobs, Competitiveness, and Environmental Regulation: What Are the Real Issues?* (Washington, D.C.: World Resources Institute, 1995).
41. Ministry of Housing, Physical Planning, and Environment, *Highlights of the Dutch National Environmental Policy Plan* (The Hague: Ministry of Housing, Physical Planning, and Environment, 1990); EPA, *The New Generation of Environmental Protection* (Washington, D.C.: EPA, 1994).
42. René Dubos, *The Wooing of Earth* (New York: Scribner's, 1980).
43. World Commission on Environment and Development, *Our Common Future* (New York: Oxford University Press, 1987); and Ismail Serageldin and Andrew Steer, eds., *Making Development Sustainable: From Concepts to Action* (Washington, D.C.: World Bank, 1994). See also chapters 13 and 15 in this volume.

11

Environmental Justice:
Normative Concerns and Empirical Evidence

Evan J. Ringquist

The context of environmental policy at the cusp of the twenty-first century is vastly different from that of twenty, or even ten, years ago. Environmentalists are skeptical about many of the new elements of this context,
viewing risk assessment, relieving states from federal mandates, protecting
"property rights," and some economic approaches to environmental protection as tactics to roll back environmental regulations (see chaps. 2, 9, and 10).
One new element of the environmental policy context, however, has the
potential to expand efforts in environmental protection: concerns over the
unequal distribution of environmental risk, or "environmental justice."

As early as 1971 federal regulators recognized that exposure to environmental pollutants was not distributed equally: minority communities experienced disproportionately high levels of environmental risk.[1] These inequities
were largely ignored until the late 1980s, when a number of studies concluded that minority neighborhoods generally suffered from worse air quality, worse water quality, more landfills, more sources of toxic pollution, more
hazardous waste sites, and weaker enforcement of environmental regulations
than did wealthier neighborhoods with smaller minority populations. This
evidence has led many activists to charge that environmental protection
activities are affected by "environmental racism." Concerns over racial and
class biases in environmental protection have mobilized hundreds of small,
grassroots groups into what is generally referred to as the "environmental justice movement." The environmental justice movement has the potential to
broaden the base of support for the traditional environmental movement,
and it may reinvigorate and refocus the forces of progressive politics behind
environmental concerns.[2] In short, it has the potential to change the face of
environmental politics and policy.

My discussion of the role played by environmental justice concerns in
the policy context is divided into six sections. First, I examine instances of
"environmental racism." This is followed by a discussion of the development
and demands of the environmental justice movement. I then examine the
empirical evidence that supports, and sometimes contradicts, the claims of
environmental justice advocates. Although the evidence presented in this
chapter focuses on toxic chemicals and waste disposal facilities, similar evidence is available regarding the distribution of risk from air and water pollution. Next, I consider five potential causes of environmental inequity. I
then look at actions that local, state, and federal officials have taken to rem-

edy environmental inequities. Finally, I evaluate the prospects for continued progress in addressing perceived racial and class biases in environmental protection.

Environmental Injustice: You'll Know It When You See It

South Chicago, Illinois

One six-by-six-mile area on the South Side of Chicago contains fifty active or closed commercial hazardous waste landfills, one hundred factories (including seven chemical factories), and more than one hundred abandoned toxic waste sites. Near the middle of this toxic wasteland sits the residential development of Altgeld Gardens, a neighborhood of roughly ten thousand residents. In addition to being surrounded by the greatest concentration of hazardous waste sites in the country, Altgeld Gardens itself was built atop the old Pullman Railroad Car company landfill—for decades, an industrial and municipal dumping site.[3] As one might imagine, Altgeld Gardens is not a pleasant place to live. Residents have had a difficult time getting state and federal environmental officials to address the contamination problems in their neighborhood. State officials became more receptive to the residents' complaints, however, when, during an inspection of one particularly noxious toxic waste lagoon, the boat carrying the state environmental inspectors began to disintegrate beneath them.[4] The federal Environmental Protection Agency (EPA), however, has been unwilling to place any of the abandoned hazardous waste sites on the Superfund National Priorities List. Residents do not believe that the many hazardous waste sites in their neighborhood or government officials' reluctance to clean up these facilities are random occurrences. Altgeld Garden's population is 70 percent African American, 11 percent Latino, and suffers a poverty rate nearly double the state's average. Residents believe they are the victims of environmental racism.

Kettleman City, California

In the late 1980s Chemical Waste Management Incorporated (CWM Inc.), one of the nation's largest hazardous waste disposal firms, proposed construction of a large commercial hazardous waste incinerator in Kettleman City, California. The governing board of Kings County approved the facility, and several of the necessary permits were in the process of being issued when the residents of Kettleman City filed a lawsuit to stop construction of the facility. One of the major motivations behind this lawsuit was the belief on the part of the residents that they were the victims of environmental racism. The population of Kettleman City is 95 percent Latino, and a full 40 percent of the residents speak only Spanish. In spite of this, neither the county nor CWM Inc. provided announcements of public meetings, technical reports, or any other official documents in Spanish. Moreover, the county refused to provide residents with a Spanish-language interpreter at the one public meeting held before the county board approved the incinerator. In 1992 a California Superior Court judge ruled that the county government had to translate these environmental review documents into Spanish to ensure meaningful involvement by the residents of Kettleman City. This court case also brought to light the fact that, before approving the incinerator, the Kings County board did not adequately evaluate the effects the facility would have on air quality, local agriculture, or the health of area residents.[5]

St. Regis Reservation, New York

For hundreds of years the Mohawk tribe hunted, fished, and farmed the land that is now the St. Regis reservation. The Mohawks are not the only people, however, who have made productive economic use of the land near the reservation. On the banks of the St. Lawrence River, which is the centerpiece of the St. Regis reservation, sits an abandoned General Motors factory that is now a toxic waste site. Nearby are similar industrial facilities owned by ALCOA, Reynolds Aluminum, and several Canadian companies. Over the past thirty years, pollution from these facilities has destroyed the Mohawk way of life. The St. Lawrence has become so contaminated that tribal members cannot eat fish from the river. The herds of cattle that once roamed the reservation are gone, victims of fluoride poisoning from the nearby GM site. Mohawk families are even advised not to eat the vegetables they grow in their own gardens, for fear of toxic contamination.[6] In short, pollution from the nearby industrial facilities has undermined the entire economic infrastructure of the reservation. With poverty and unemployment at high levels, and with no other viable options for reviving their economy, tribal leaders are being wooed by numerous developers seeking to place everything from solid waste landfills to hazardous waste incinerators on the St. Regis reservation.

This scenario is frequently repeated across the country. Often isolated, reservations have high levels of unemployment and few sources of economic development. This makes them attractive targets for companies seeking to build noxious facilities. A few observers go so far as to claim that the federal Bureau of Indian Affairs is promoting these waste facilities as an economic development strategy for reservations. Because Native American tribes retain some sovereign rights, environmental regulations on reservations are often less strict than those of the states surrounding the reservation, and enforcement of these regulations is often weak (for example, in 1990 only 30 of 280 reservations had offices of environmental protection). For all these reasons, reservations are increasingly viewed as potential dumping grounds, and many Native American leaders claim that reservation residents are being victimized by environmental racism.[7]

The Environmental Justice Movement

Although cases like those described above have been relatively common over the past several decades, the initial prospects for a coalition between the environmental movement and advocates for civil rights and social justice looked bleak. Conventional wisdom held that poor and minority individuals were generally unconcerned with pollution and did not share the values of environmentalists. Equally important, critics of environmentalism claimed that the movement was full of upper-middle-class elites who did not care about the urban environmental problems faced by members of disadvantaged groups. There is some evidence to support these contentions. Early in their history, environmental groups sought to keep the environmental movement separate and distinct from general social justice concerns because they feared that an alliance might dilute their effectiveness and detract from their ability to attract members. In addition, mainstream environmental groups often emphasize wilderness preservation and the protection of endangered species over reducing pollution in inner cities, and the membership lists and leadership positions of these groups are hardly crowded with racial minorities.[8]

On the other hand, the potential for an alliance between environmentalists and social justice advocates has always been present. Public opinion polls have repeatedly shown that the poor and members of minority groups are no less concerned about environmental protection than is the general population, and the Congressional Black Caucus routinely has the best environmental voting record of any group in Congress.[9] Moreover, a few national environmental groups have a strong history of minority group involvement and of attending to social justice (Greenpeace, the National Toxics Campaign, and the Earth Island Institute). Partially in response to criticism from environmental justice advocates, partially in recognition that social justice and the environment are intimately linked, and partially because poor and minority citizens provide an opportunity to increase their membership base, the other mainstream environmental groups have more recently become involved in the environmental justice movement. In 1989 the ten largest environmental groups embarked on a minority outreach campaign to increase minority membership and the number of minorities in leadership positions. Some of these groups, particularly Greenpeace and the National Wildlife Federation, now actively seek out partnerships with local grassroots groups to combat environmental injustice. Local environmental and social justice groups have also forged alliances on their own. Beginning with small grassroots groups protesting the location of hazardous waste facilities, the alliances grew stronger as these groups developed a permanent presence in local politics. Today the common interests of environmentalists and social justice advocates are advanced through a multifaceted nationwide network of organizations generally referred to as the environmental justice movement.

The Origins of the Environmental Justice Movement

Nearly all observers agree that the environmental justice movement began in 1982 outside a small town in North Carolina. A hazardous waste management firm, in conjunction with the EPA and the state of North Carolina, proposed construction of a large hazardous waste landfill in Warren County. The residents of Warren County initially received little information about the proposed landfill. When they were finally alerted to the nature of the facility, large demonstrations ensued, during which more than five thousand arrests were made. The local residents were not the only ones protesting the landfill. Representatives from the United Church of Christ, the Southern Christian Leadership Conference, and the Congressional Black Caucus also took part in the demonstrations. Because Warren County was the poorest county in the state, with a population that was 65 percent African American (more than three times the state average), many of the protesters believed this landfill was as much a violation of the residents' civil rights as it was a threat to public health and environmental quality. By linking environmental and civil rights concerns, opponents of the Warren County landfill served as the prototype for the modern environmental justice movement.[10]

Grassroots Opposition to Environmental Injustice

After the Warren County episode, local civil rights and social justice groups across the country began to protest the location of polluting facilities. Soon, these temporary groups that had mobilized around a single facility began to maintain a permanent presence in local politics in order to advance the cause of environmental justice. For example, Concerned Citizens of South Central Los Angeles (CCOSCLA) organized in 1985 to fight a proposed solid waste incinerator. Although the group succeeded in defeating the incinerator proposal, the members of CCOSCLA have since learned that existing facilities in their neighborhood release more toxic chemicals than are released in the entire San Francisco Bay area, making theirs the most toxic neighborhood in America. CCOSCLA remains a force in Los Angeles politics and now focuses not only on preventing the siting of new polluting facilities but also on reducing pollution from existing ones. Finally, CCOSCLA forges alliances with national environmental groups, such as Greenpeace, when seeking to stop the construction of polluting facilities, and works with other grassroots groups to oppose polluting facilities in neighboring communities.[11]

From Local Grassroots Groups to an Environmental Justice Movement

As the number of local grassroots environmental justice groups grew, and their activities expanded, local activists inevitably came into contact with each other. Through these contacts, environmental justice advocates across the country realized that they shared similar values, faced similar adversaries, employed similar tactics, and faced similar obstacles in pressing for environmental justice. Local groups had initially surmounted these obstacles with the help of national environmental organizations. Although these national organizations still respond each year to several thousand requests for assistance from grassroots environmental groups, local environmental justice groups have banded together into large, regional assistance networks.[12]

The Southwest Network for Environmental and Economic Justice (SNEEJ) is one of the largest and best known of these regional environmental justice networks. It provides local groups with technical assistance and advice on effective organizational management, organizing protests, effective lobbying techniques, and technical analysis. In this capacity, SNEEJ has helped local groups oppose numerous facilities across the Southwest and has even worked with local groups in Mexico to protest hazardous waste incinerators and the waste disposal practices of numerous *maquiladoras* (factories owned by U.S. companies but located just south of the U.S.-Mexican border). SNEEJ itself is guided by a twenty-three-member governing council comprised entirely of activists from minority groups.[13]

The success of SNEEJ inspired the creation of other large regional environmental justice organizations. In 1990 representatives from several of these groups organized the nation's first conference on race and the incidence of environmental hazards. The final report from this conference was forwarded to the EPA, and several of the coalition's suggestions served as the basis for the agency's efforts to improve environmental equity. In 1991 environmental justice groups from around the country participated in the first People of Color Leadership Summit on the Environment, held in Washington, D.C. The summit drew more than six hundred participants from all fifty states and several foreign countries, and also attracted the participation of the leaders of most of the nation's mainstream environmental groups.

The major product of the summit was a statement of the "principles of environmental justice." These principles serve as criteria for developing and evaluating policies aimed at attaining social and environmental justice. Movement activists view these twin goals as inseparable. Substandard housing, health care, and employment opportunities contribute as much or more to the low quality of life in poor and minority communities as does environmental pollution. Thus, the movement aims to remedy social inequities as it pursues environmental equity. To accomplish these goals, the statement calls for full representation of minority groups and the poor in the policy-making process through membership in traditional environmental groups and through government provision of the legal and technical advice required for effective participation; for increased emphasis on pollution prevention; and for resident participation in corporate decisions affecting the well-being of their communities.[14]

Environmental Injustice: A Look at the Evidence

The most serious concern of environmental justice advocates is that inequities in exposure to environmental risks will result in higher rates of disease and death among minorities and the poor. It is extraordinarily difficult to test this concern directly. First, many diseases caused by environmental pollution have other causes as well. Thus, even if we find that poor and minority populations suffer higher levels of these ailments, we can't be sure that these diseases are caused by exposure to pollution. Second, the United States is the only advanced industrial nation that does not gather disease data by income and education, and environmental health data are not routinely collected by race and income.[15]

As a substitute for these data, we can evaluate the evidence that we do have regarding the complex chain of causal relationships that lead to adverse environmental health effects among poor and minority populations. First, I will examine the charge that polluting facilities are located closer to these communities. Second, I will assess the evidence that racial minorities and the poor are exposed to higher levels of pollution. Third, I will look at the evidence on the link between pollution and disease and injury. Finally, I will briefly discuss the rates of disease and injury among the poor and minorities. If proximity to facilities leads to higher levels of pollutant exposure, if exposure leads to disease, and if poor and minority populations experience disproportionately high levels of proximity, exposure, and disease, then we might logically conclude that at least some of this disease is caused by their greater exposure to environmental risk.

The Location of Polluting Facilities

Solid Waste Landfills and Incinerators. The earliest research into environmental racism in facility siting examined the location of solid waste landfills and incinerators. There is no national database on the location of these facilities, so these studies had to examine siting patterns in particular communities. One study found that all the landfills constructed in King and Queen County, Virginia, between 1969 and 1990 were located in communities where a majority of the residents were African American. In another study, sociologist Robert Bullard found that five of six municipal landfills, three of four private landfills, and six of eight municipal incinerators were located in Houston neighborhoods where African Americans made up more than 50 percent of the population. Overall, 82 percent of Houston's waste facilities were located in majority black neighborhoods, though only 28 percent of Houston's population was African American. Bullard claims that the results from the Houston and Virginia studies are not uncommon and that minority communities across the country receive more than their fair share of landfills and incinerators.[16] A more systematic study by the General Accounting Office (GAO), however, reached a different conclusion. After examining the characteristics of populations surrounding nearly three hundred nonhazardous waste facilities, the GAO found no evidence that poor or minority residents were overrepresented near these landfills compared with the county as a whole.[17]

Hazardous Waste Treatment, Storage, and Disposal Facilities. Most research examining the location of polluting facilities has focused on commercial hazardous waste treatment, storage, and disposal facilities (TSDFs), and the degree to which these facilities are located disproportionately in poor and/or minority communities is the subject of some debate. In 1983 the GAO examined the location of the four commercial hazardous waste landfills in EPA's Region IV (the Southeast). The average minority population of this region was 20 percent, but these hazardous waste landfills were located in four communities where racial minorities made up 38 percent, 52 percent, 66 percent, and 90 percent, respectively, of the local population. Moreover, poverty rates in these communities were significantly higher than for the region as a whole. The GAO concluded that there was enough evidence to be concerned about inequities in the siting of these facilities. Other local community studies have produced similar results. In Baton Rouge, Louisiana, the ten neighborhoods with the highest percentage of white residents contain five TSDFs and 1 percent of the local TSDF capacity, while the ten neighborhoods with the highest percentages of African American residents contain fifteen facilities with 99 percent of the local TSDF capacity.[18] Finally, researchers at the University of Michigan examined the demographics of neighborhoods with hazardous waste TSDFs in Detroit. They discovered that of the people who lived within one mile of these facilities, 48 percent were minorities and 29 percent had incomes below the poverty line. Of the people living more than 1.5 miles from any TSDF, 18 percent were minorities and only 10 percent were poor.[19]

The first nationwide study of the location of TSDFs was undertaken in 1987 by the United Church of Christ's Commission for Racial Justice (CRJ). The CRJ gathered data on the location of every commercial hazardous waste TSDF in the country and then examined the racial and socioeconomic composition of the ZIP codes within which these facilities were located. The CRJ's statistical analysis demonstrated that as the percentage of poor and minority residents of a neighborhood increased, so did the likelihood that the neighborhood had a TSDF. This relationship between race and facility location held even when controlling for region, urbanization, and land value. An update to the CRJ report found these same relationships holding in the 1990s.[20] At least one group of researchers, however, disputes the conclusion that hazardous waste facilities are located in poor and minority communities. Douglas Anderton and his colleagues at the University of Massachusetts believe that the positive association between race and facility location is an artifact of data aggregation. Indeed, when these scholars compared the demographics of census tracts (areas smaller than ZIP codes) that had commercial TSDFs with nearby census tracts with no facilities, they found no relationship between race, poverty, and the location of TSDFs.[21] Vicki Been, however, demonstrates that the results reached by Anderton and his colleagues are themselves artifacts of a peculiar and questionable research design. While finding that the relationship between race, class, and facility location is more pronounced at the ZIP code level, Been also finds that census tracts with commercial TSDFs have significantly higher percentages of Hispanic and African American residents.[22]

One potential limitation of each of these studies is that they only examine the location of commercial TSDFs (that is, facilities that accept hazardous wastes generated elsewhere and make a profit by disposing of these wastes). Fewer than 1 in 10 hazardous waste facilities are commercial facilities, however, and commercial facilities handle less than 5 percent of all hazardous wastes generated in the United States. In an examination of all TSDFs nationwide, I found that race is an important predictor of facility location, but that poverty is not, when controlling for other factors.[23] This relationship is illustrated in table 11-1.

Exposure to Environmental Pollutants

Simply because a person lives close to a polluting facility does not mean he or she is exposed to higher levels of pollution. If regulated facilities are operating properly, if the pollution control equipment on these facilities is working correctly, and if environmental regulations are diligently enforced, the level of exposure near these facilities should be minimal. We must look at the pollution data themselves to determine if pollutant exposure is distributed inequitably.

Toxics Release Inventory Pollutants. The 1986 Superfund Amendment and Reauthorization Act requires thousands of factories across the country to report their releases of more than two hundred toxic chemicals. Together, this information makes up the Toxics Release Inventory (TRI). The first TRI in 1987 showed that industry released a total of 5.2 billion pounds of toxic pollutants into the environment. By 1992 this figure had dropped 40 percent to 3.16 billion pounds.[24] These data are relatively new, so few researchers have examined the distribution of these pollutants. We do know, however, that in Los Angeles and Florida those facilities that emit TRI pollutants are concentrated in poor and minority areas; we also know that releases of these pollutants in South Carolina are concentrated in poor areas with racially mixed populations.[25]

In order to examine the distribution of these toxic pollutants more closely, I have aggregated all the TRI data from 1987 to 1991 by ZIP code and merged them with information on the race and class composition of all residential ZIP codes in the country (see table 11-2). The table shows that as the percentage of all minorities in a neighborhood increases, so too does the level of toxic pollution. On the other hand, TRI releases appear to be unrelated to poverty or to the percentage of Latino residents in a neighborhood. In a much more complicated analysis published elsewhere, I demonstrate that ZIP codes with large minority populations are much more likely

Table 11-1 Minorities and the Poor in ZIP Codes with Hazardous Waste TSDFs (in percentages)

No. of TSDFs	African American	Latino	Minority	Poor
None	6.66	4.17	10.93	15.64
1 or more	11.59	6.93	18.77	14.76
At least 5	14.59	9.09	23.72	16.34

Source: Compiled from EPA RCRIS database and U.S. Bureau of the Census 1990 STF 3B.

to contain a single or multiple TRI facilities and to exhibit higher levels of TRI pollutant emissions.[26]

Other Harmful Pollutants. Certain subpopulations of the United States are exposed to exceptionally high levels of certain pollutants. For example, agricultural workers, especially migrant farm laborers, are exposed to far more pesticides than are other citizens. Researchers estimate that more than three hundred thousand farm workers per year suffer pesticide-related illnesses, attributing from eight hundred to one thousand deaths per year to pesticide exposure. Roughly 90 percent of all migrant farm laborers are African American or Latino.[27] Similarly, African American residents in Detroit, and Native Americans across the country, are exposed to significantly higher levels of PCB (polychlorinated biphenyl) and mercury contamination because these subpopulations eat four to five times the amount of fish assumed by EPA models when setting "safe" levels of these pollutants. One study in Wisconsin concluded that the number-one environmental threat faced by Native Americans was the contamination of their food supply, particularly fish, by toxic pollutants.[28] Finally, a handful of studies have shown that air pollution is particularly severe in areas with large concentrations of poor and minority residents.[29]

Overall Evaluations of Inequities in Exposure to Environmental Risk. Four studies have surveyed the research on inequitable exposure to environmental risk. In their examination of fifteen studies evaluating the distribution of twenty-one separate environmental hazards, Paul Mohai and Bunyan Bryant found that 94 percent of the relevant studies demonstrated racial inequities in the distribution of environmental risk, and 80 percent of the relevant studies pointed up inequalities based on wealth.[30] A 1993 report commissioned by the National Wildlife Federation surveyed sixty-four relevant empirical studies; sixty-three of them found significant environmental disparities by income or race.[31] In 1995 a group of researchers from Colorado State University scrutinized thirty studies on the distribution of forty-six different environmental risks and found race or class disparities in more than 80 percent of the cases.[32] Finally, in a dissenting report the GAO examined ten previous studies and concluded that in aggregate they showed an inde-

Table 11-2 Toxic Pollutant Emissions in Poor and Minority ZIP Code Areas (in lbs.)

Percentage of the Population	African American	Latino	Minority	Poor
< 5	10,799	14,163	10,133	18,014
5 to 25	25,467	17,017	20,151	12,629
> 25	27,695	11,789	24,315	17,003

Source: Compiled from EPA TRI 1987–1991 and U.S. Bureau of the Census 1990 STF 3B.

terminate relationship between race, class, and the risks posed by hazardous facilities.[33] On balance, the available empirical evidence suggests a strong positive association between race, poverty, and environmental risk that works to the detriment of these traditionally disadvantaged groups.

Health Effects of Environmental Pollutants

Evidence that environmental pollution causes adverse health effects in humans comes from two sources: experimental research and epidemiological research. Experimental research, with random assignment of subjects and laboratory controls, provides the best evidence. But the ethical problems of asking human subjects to breathe polluted air or drink water laced with toxic chemicals prevent experimentation. Most of our evidence regarding the health effects of pollutant exposure therefore comes from epidemiological studies, or studies that examine populations of persons accidentally exposed to varying levels of pollution. Epidemiological evidence has its problems as well: the symptoms epidemiologists study are caused by multiple diseases; the diseases studied have multiple causes; and the subjects of these studies are often exposed to multiple pollutants and other risk factors. In short, epidemiological studies can never conclusively prove that exposure to a particular pollutant caused a particular subject to contract a disease or to die. By ruling out alternative explanations for disease and by producing consistent results across a number of studies, however, epidemiology can provide us with solid evidence of the health effects of pollution.

Toxic Chemicals. Industrial and hazardous waste facilities produce hundreds of toxic pollutants, occurring in literally thousands of possible combinations. It is difficult to find instances where a particular population was exposed to one particular substance. We do, however, have reasonably good evidence regarding the toxicity of certain hazardous chemicals. For example, contamination of the water supply of Woburn, Massachusetts, with chlorinated organics resulted in significantly higher levels of childhood leukemia, birth defects, and perinatal deaths in the population exposed to this water. In addition, after reviewing dozens of studies, Rae Zimmerman found that exposure to TCDD dioxin increases by 300 percent to 700 percent the risk of developing soft-tissue sarcomas, while exposure to formaldehyde significantly increases the risk of nasopharyngeal cancer.[34]

Most of the epidemiological research with respect to toxic substances, however, examines the effects of exposure to whole classes of hazardous chemicals. One nationwide study examined all municipalities whose groundwater supplies had been contaminated by toxic chemicals. These researchers found strong relationships between contamination and all forms of cancer. Additional research has found that residents downwind from hazardous waste incinerators are 20 to 90 percent more likely to have emphysema, asthma, pneumonia, or allergies. Exposure to these incinerators is also associated with numerous neurological disorders.[35] In one of the most comprehensive studies to date, Sandra Geschwind and her colleagues found that proximity to hazardous waste sites increased the probability of birth defects by 12 to 32 percent and that this risk increased even more if the hazardous wastes had leaked into the surrounding community. Dozens of other studies find that persons living near hazardous waste sites have significantly higher levels of respiratory illnesses, stress, psychological ailments, and immune system disorders than do people who do not live near these facilities.[36]

Inequitable Health Consequences? The evidence is nearly overwhelming that poor citizens and members of minority groups live closer to polluting facilities and are exposed to higher levels of pollution. The evidence also shows that exposure to these pollutants leads to more adverse health effects. We also know that minorities and the poor suffer more illnesses and have shorter life expectancies. Nevertheless, while all of this research provides a mountain of circumstantial evidence, the data limitations described in the introduction to this section prevent us from stating absolutely that environmental pollution disproportionately harms the health of minorities and the poor. Indeed, after surveying much of the same evidence presented here, the EPA concluded that "although there are clear differences between ethnic groups for disease and death rates, there are virtually no data to document the environmental contribution to these differences."[37] The National Environmental Health Association concurred with EPA, though it did issue a call for detailed, high quality studies to investigate connections between environmental risk and public health in low income and minority communities.[38]

The one exception to this conclusion is lead poisoning. All Americans have benefited from a remarkable reduction in exposure to lead due to the phaseout of leaded gasoline. A great deal of lead remains in certain localized environments, however. The Centers for Disease Control and Prevention (CDCP) in Atlanta recommends hospitalization when blood lead levels rise to 25 micrograms per deciliter ($\mu g/dl$). As part of the second National Health and Nutrition Examination Survey, the CDCP examined blood lead levels in children younger than six years. This study found average blood lead levels of 20 $\mu g/dl$ for poor children, 21 $\mu g/dl$ for African American children, and 23 $\mu g/dl$ for poor African American children living in urban areas—a level nearly as high as the suggested hospitalization guideline. Eighteen percent of these poor, inner city black children had blood lead levels above 180 $\mu g/dl$. A 1988 study by the Agency for Toxic Substances and Disease Registry reached similar conclusions: 60 percent of poor, inner-city black children had elevated levels of lead in their blood, largely due to the presence of lead-based paint in the household.[39]

Causes of Environmental Inequity

The evidence is clear that minorities and the poor face disproportionately high levels of environmental risk, even if the health consequences of this exposure remain unclear. Simply describing this situation, however, is not enough. Social scientists, policymakers, and the citizens who live in these polluted communities are all interested in causation: how and why did this situation arise? Five explanations are generally given for the distribution of polluting facilities, and thus for the distribution of environmental risk: scientific rationality, market rationality, neighborhood transition, political power, and explicit discrimination. The appropriate role for government in assuring environmental equity depends on which causes of environmental injustice are most important.

Scientific Rationality

Engineers, EPA officials, and others are extremely skeptical of the claims of environmental justice advocates. According to these experts, the siting of polluting facilities, especially landfills and hazardous waste TSDFs, is driven by technical criteria. When looking to site a hazardous waste landfill, for example, companies will regard the area's demographics as irrelevant. What matters, they would argue, are the geological characteristics of the site (for example, does the site sit on top of an important drinking-water aquifer?). If the scientific rationality explanation is correct, then these facilities should be randomly distributed in all types of communities. The reality that polluting facilities are concentrated in poor and minority areas strongly suggests that technical criteria alone do not explain the distribution of these facilities.

Market Rationality

According to proponents of the market rationality explanation, economic factors drive decisions regarding the location of hazardous waste facilities. For companies, the most important economic factors in deciding where to site facilities are cheap land, available labor, access to transportation infrastructure (highways, railroads, ports, and so forth), and access to raw materials. Ignoring these factors to target poor and minority communities for polluting facilities would be economically irrational. Although certain economic forces may lead a company to locate a facility in a poor community, economics rather than discrimination drive this decision. The evidence supports the notion that economic considerations are important in siting polluting facilities. The CRJ study discussed earlier found that commercial hazardous waste facilities were located in areas with low property values, while the sociologists at the University of Massachusetts concluded that these same facilities were located in areas with large numbers of skilled manufacturing employees. My own research demonstrates that hazardous waste TSDFs are more likely to be located where land is cheap and where raw materials (in this instance, hazardous wastes) are abundant. Much of this same research, however, concludes that the racial and class characteristics of the surrounding area are important even after controlling for these economic factors. In other words, it is unlikely that economic rationality alone explains the distribution of these facilities.[40]

Neighborhood Transition

Any attempt to evaluate the degree of discrimination in siting polluting facilities faces one very large problem: which came first, the facility, or the people in the surrounding neighborhood? Although these facilities may presently be located in poor and minority areas, an argument could be made that when they were first built, the surrounding area was neither minority nor poor. The "neighborhood transition" explanation paints the following scenario. Many polluting facilities originally located in urban, working-class areas for many of the reasons cited by the market rationality explanation. Over time, those residents with the resources to move away did so. Because these facilities had reduced the value of the surrounding property, the departing residents were replaced by people who were poor and/or members of minority groups. Thus, although the present-day risks from these facilities may be distributed inequitably, the process of siting these facilities was not discriminatory.

The neighborhood transition explanation is plausible. Each year between 17 and 20 percent of all households in the United States move, so neighborhoods are constantly changing. Moreover, research by Kerry Smith and others shows that hazardous waste sites and other polluting facilities do drive down the value of surrounding property, and wealthier, better educated residents will pay more to move away from polluting facilities.[41] In short, as the middle class moves away from these facilities, the vacated housing is likely to attract the poor.

Considered carefully, the neighborhood transition thesis poses two propositions. First, neighborhoods receiving hazardous waste facilities were no different from those that did not receive them at the time the facilities first opened. Second, the proportion of poor and/or minority residents has increased more rapidly in neighborhoods that host hazardous waste facilities than in those that do not. Social scientists have only recently been able to test these propositions. With respect to the first proposition, the group at the University of Massachusetts found that commercial hazardous waste facilities built during the 1970s and 1980s were not placed in neighborhoods with larger than average concentrations of poor and minority residents.[42] Vicki Been found the same to be true for landfills in Houston, Texas. In other analyses, however, Been found that hazardous waste facilities in EPA Region IV were all originally located in areas with disproportionately large poor and minority populations.[43] Moreover, Been found once again that the null results of researchers at the University of Massachusetts were a function of a peculiar research design. Her own research found that commercial hazardous waste facilities built in the 1970s were more likely to be located in African American and Latino areas, while those built in the 1980s were more likely to be located in Latino areas. Been found the strongest relationship between race and facility location for firms that opened for business prior to 1970.[44] There is more consensus with respect to the second proposition. No study has found that building hazardous waste facilities causes "white flight" or unusual increases in the concentrations of poor and minority residents in the surrounding area.[45]

Political Power

Although the right to vote is distributed equally, political power is not. Political power is a function of wealth, education, group organizational skills, frequent participation in the political process, and so forth. Certain citizens, particularly members of minority groups and the poor, have fewer of these resources. Since the rational political actor will attempt to site polluting facilities where they will face the least amount of political resistance, political rationality, rather than outright discrimination, may best explain the location of polluting facilities.

A report commissioned by the state of California explicitly recommends that the state target areas that "lack social power" when trying to site incinerators. Moreover, when investigating which hazardous waste facilities seek to expand their capacity, James Hamilton of Duke University found that neither race nor class matters much. Instead, facilities are least likely to expand when they are located in neighborhoods where the residents are politically active. Finally, my own research shows that one of the best predictors of whether a permit to operate a hazardous waste TSDF will be approved or denied is not the demographic characteristics of the surrounding neighborhood, but the percentage of neighborhood residents who own their own homes.[46] To sum up, nearly all of the available evidence suggests that when it comes to siting hazardous waste facilities, neighborhood political power matters.

Intentional Discrimination

Many observers, including prominent members of the environmental justice movement like Robert Bullard, claim that minority (and poor) neighborhoods are explicitly targeted to receive polluting facilities, thus proposing that the process of facility siting is driven by environmental racism. Hazardous waste industry officials completely reject this claim. Still, it is difficult to overlook the fact that CWM Inc. has chosen to site all four of its commercial hazardous waste incinerators in communities where African Americans and Latinos constitute the overwhelming majority of the population.

Governmental decisions, as well as private decisions, may generate environmental inequities. EPA officials reject the contention that government environmental policy decisions intentionally discriminate against poor and minority communities, yet a 1974 EPA report identifying the most suitable locations for a large hazardous waste landfill selected ten counties where minorities made up 32 percent of the population (the national average is 20 percent).[47] Moreover, my own research indicates that EPA officials are significantly more likely to approve permits for hazardous waste facilities in neighborhoods with large numbers of minority residents.[48] On the other hand, we should not overstate government contributions to environmental inequities. A 1992 study by reporters at the *National Law Journal* found that average civil penalties for violating environmental laws were higher in white, wealthy neighborhoods than in poor and/or minority neighborhoods.[49] A close examination, however, shows that these conclusions do not hold up under statistical scrutiny. In fact, penalties for violating environmental laws are neither larger nor smaller in areas with large numbers of poor and minority residents.[50]

In many ways, the intentional discrimination theory is the most difficult to test. Although suggestive, the evidence presented above does not prove discriminatory intent. Moreover, as the other explanations for environmental inequities make plain, discriminatory intent is not necessary to produce discriminatory outcomes. Nevertheless, even though intentional discrimination may not be the most plausible explanation for environmental inequities, we would do well to remember that "harm perpetuated by benign inadvertence is as injurious as harm by purposeful intent."[51]

Remedying Environmental Injustice

In response to the evidence presented above and pressure from environmental justice advocates, private and governmental actors are undertaking a wide variety of activities to remedy environmental inequities.

Policy Changes at the National Level

Presidential Actions. President Bill Clinton has identified environmental justice as a top administrative priority. In February of 1994 the president issued Executive Order (EO) 12898, which requires that "each federal agency . . . make achieving environmental justice part of its mission by identifying and addressing, as appropriate, disproportionately high and adverse human health or environmental effects of its programs, policies, and activities on minority populations and low-income populations in the United States and its territories and possessions." In addition, EO 12898 created an interagency workgroup on environmental justice to coordinate the environmental justice plans of all affected federal agencies. Accompanying EO 12898, President Clinton released a Memorandum on Environmental Justice that requires all federal agencies to (a) ensure that all programs or activities receiving federal financial assistance that affect human health or the environment do not discriminate on the basis of race, color, or national origin; (b) analyze the environmental and health effects on poor and minority communities whenever an Environmental Impact Statement is required under the National Environmental Policy Act; and (c) ensure that poor and minority communities have adequate access to public information relating to human health, environmental planning, and environmental regulation. EO 12898 also requires the EPA to fully analyze the environmental effects on poor and minority communities precipitated by the actions of other federal agencies. In his second term, however, President Clinton has been noticeably silent on the issue of environmental justice, and there has been no executive leadership in this policy area.

Congressional Actions. In 1992 Congress enacted the Residential Lead-Based Paint Reduction Act. This legislation authorizes $375 million for inspection and lead abatement actions in low-income housing, requires the EPA to set up training and certification programs for lead abatement contractors, and provides grants to the states to develop their own lead abatement and training programs.[52] Additional environmental justice legislation introduced this same year, however, did not fare as well. John Lewis, D-Ga., and Al Gore, then a Democratic senator from Tennessee, introduced the Environmental Justice Act (EJA). The EJA required the EPA to identify the one hundred areas of the country most polluted by toxic chemicals and designate them as "environmental high-impact areas," or EHIAs. For each EHIA, the act required the EPA to impose a moratorium on siting new sources of toxic pollution if the agency found evidence of adverse health effects. Cardiss Collins, D-Ill., proposed the "Environmental Equal Rights Act," which prevented siting additional hazardous waste TSDFs in poor or minority communities already hosting these facilities. Finally, amendments to the Resource Conservation and Recovery Act proposed by Rep. Bill Clinger, R-Pa., and Sens. Mike Synar, D-Okla., and John Glenn, D-Ohio, required private developers and government officials to prepare "community information statements" that would identify the socioeconomic and demographic composition of the areas surrounding any proposed hazardous waste TSDF. None of this proposed legislation was enacted. The "heyday" for environmental justice in Congress came during the 1993–94 session, when six pieces of legislation were introduced. Once again, none passed. After the 1994 elections placed Republicans in charge of both houses of Congress, however, no environmental justice legislation was introduced for three years. And while two more environmental justice bills were introduced in 1998, it is extraordinarily unlikely that policy leadership in this area will come from Congress in the near future.

Administrative Actions. The EPA has undertaken a variety of efforts aimed at producing environmental justice. These actions can be grouped into three general categories: agency reorganization, environmental litigation, and research and education. The EPA first responded to the concerns of environmental justice advocates in 1990 by creating an internal environmental equity workgroup to examine evidence regarding the inequitable distribution of environmental risk. The results of the workgroup's research convinced EPA to create a new Office of Environmental Equity (now the Office of Environmental Justice). In addition, the EPA now has an Office of Civil Rights and participates in the National Environmental Justice Advisory Council that helps local communities pursue remedies for instances of environmental discrimination. Finally, each EPA regional office has appointed an Environmental Justice Coordinator to oversee efforts at improving environmental equity.

One way to reduce inequitable exposures to environmental risk is to sue the actors responsible for producing that risk. In 1993 EPA's Office of Civil

Rights began an investigation into the process by which permits were granted to operate polluting facilities in Louisiana's "cancer alley." This investigation bore fruit in 1994, when the EPA sued Borden Chemicals and Plastics for illegally storing and disposing of large quantities of hazardous chemicals that eventually contaminated the groundwater in nearby poor and minority communities. The Borden case is the first in which the EPA has raised the issue of environmental racism.[53]

In several areas, the EPA is going beyond the requirements of EO 12898, embarking on additional research and education activities with respect to environmental justice. For example, in 1990 the EPA began the first survey of pollution on Native American reservations. In 1991 EPA headquarters required all regional offices to complete research on elements of environmental justice that were particularly relevant in their region.[54] Finally, in 1992 the EPA created the Minority Academic Institutions Task Force to enhance the interaction between the agency and historically minority academic institutions. Responding to the recommendations of this task force, the EPA created the Cooperative Progression Program, with which the EPA recruits promising minority students to pursue careers in the environmental field and eventually work at the agency. In addition, the EPA has either started or expanded research programs at several historically minority academic institutions, and these faculty are encouraged to work at the agency through the EPA's faculty fellows program.[55]

Policy Changes at the State Level

Many state governments have struck out on their own to address the issues raised by environmental justice advocates. At least four states (California, Florida, Texas, and Wisconsin) have created environmental justice study commissions. The California legislature twice passed legislation requiring applicants for toxic facility permits to present data on the demographic and socioeconomic makeup of the area surrounding the proposed facility. However, Gov. Pete Wilson vetoed both bills because they placed an unreasonable burden on business. The Texas Department of Health now requires these data from developers of hazardous waste disposal sites. The state of Arkansas bans waste facilities from being sited within twelve miles of each other, and Alabama now prohibits siting more than one commercial hazardous waste TSDF in a single county.[56] Of the forty-four states responding to a national survey, twenty-seven have taken some action to study potential problems of environmental inequity, while only three had changed state statute to remedy environmental injustices.[57]

Policy Changes at the Local Level

Most environmental justice advocates are skeptical of the effectiveness of the traditional tools of public policy—legislation and litigation—especially at the national level. Because of this, the environmental justice movement generally targets its political action and pressure at the local level.[58] The contemporary model for local efforts to ensure environmental justice is New York City's "fair share" policy. In 1989 New York adopted a new city charter with two unique provisions ensuring that each borough and neighborhood bears its fair share of locally undesirable land use burdens (for example, prisons, waste facilities, and homeless shelters). The city has developed explicit criteria for determining each borough's "fair share." Each year the mayor produces a list of undesirable facilities that must be built, expanded, or closed. The list specifies the exact location of these facilities in accordance with the "fair share" criteria and also take into account the extent to which the character of the neighborhood will be changed by the concentration of these facilities. Borough presidents and community residents then have at least two years to comment on these plans.[59]

Obstacles to Remedying Environmental Injustice

The environmental justice movement has been quite successful at getting its concerns onto the environmental policy agenda. The movement has also instigated a large amount of research assessing the presence and causes of inequities in the distribution of environmental risk, and in some instances has prompted policy solutions that seek to remedy these inequities. However, continued progress will require significant changes in the national political climate, the science underlying claims of environmental inequity, and the environmental justice movement itself.

This assessment is shared by Christopher Foreman, author of one of the best evaluations of the environmental justice movement to date.[60] Foreman identifies five difficulties faced by activists seeking to pursue social justice through environmental policy. First, Foreman points out that the evidence supporting inequities in the distribution of environmental risks is inconclusive. Second, he argues that the current national political climate is generally unreceptive to new initiatives in the area of environmental protection—especially those dealing with the redistribution of environmental risk or compensatory actions—and that the leading role of state and local governments in environmental protection leaves the movement's focus on the federal level misplaced. Third, Foreman notes that environmental justice activists are motivated by more than a concern over environmental quality; they are driven as well by aspirations for political empowerment, social justice, improved public health, and other goals that are difficult to address through environmental means. Fourth, aggressive pursuit of environmental justice concerns by EPA may exacerbate well-known problems with its traditional environmental regulations (for example, difficulty in setting priorities and inefficient use of resources with respect to risk). Finally, Foreman fears that efforts to remedy perceived environmental inequities may divert attention away from more serious threats to the health and well-being of minority communities (for example, lifestyle choices) and thus be counterproductive.

The strength of some of these conclusions is open to debate. For example, the evidence for significant inequities in the distribution of environmental risk is much stronger than he claims. Moreover, criticizing environmental justice efforts for diverting attention and resources away from other factors contributing to the low quality of life in poor and minority neighborhoods is kind of like criticizing crime policy for diverting attention and resources away from education. We know that the latter may have a larger effect on addressing certain social ills than the former, but public policy decisions that take these cross-issue substitution effects into account are extraordinarily rare. Foreman has nevertheless identified the most important factors limiting the political effectiveness of the environmental justice movement today. Specifically, his last three points are emblematic of what Foreman characterizes as a "chronic inability to define and pursue a coherent policy agenda." In calling for social empowerment, pollution prevention, direct access to environmental decisionmaking, attention to community preferences in environmental priorities, and the redistribution of economic power, the environmental justice movement is "almost boundary-less, covering all races and classes, and all manners of perceived environmental slights."[61]

A National Normative Consensus Regarding Environmental Justice

What should government do about observed environmental inequities? According to Foreman, the environmental justice community's response to this question is "everything," which in a world of limited political and economic resources is the same thing as "nothing." The difficulties faced in answering this question, however, go beyond those identified by Foreman. To answer this question, we must forge a national consensus first on what constitutes "discrimination" in environmental protection and second on what we mean by "equity."

Defining Discrimination. Does every decision-making process that produces discriminatory outcomes deserve the government's attention, or are such decisions only legally actionable when there is actual discriminatory intent? This is a difficult question, and even our laws apply different definitions of discrimination. For example, violating the Fourth Amendment's equal protection clause requires discriminatory intent, while violating Title VI of the 1964 Civil Rights Act requires only that an action produce a discriminatory outcome. If we adopt the "discriminatory intent" definition when examining the five causes of environmental inequity presented earlier in this chapter, only the fifth cause is clearly an example of discrimination. If we adopt the "discriminatory outcome" definition, however, then any of the causes of environmental inequities presented above require governmental remedy.

Defining Equity in the Distribution of Polluting Facilities. We routinely use the term "equity" as if there were one, universally accepted definition. There are, however, many different definitions. For example, an economist might characterize as equitable a system that requires those who benefit from the production of pollution to also pay its costs. Since wealthy individuals consume more and thus produce more pollution, equity requires that these individuals either live with higher numbers of polluting facilities, or pay others to accept them. A geographic conception of equity, on the other hand, might require that all states, cities, or communities have equal numbers of polluting facilities. Still other conceptions might require that polluting facilities be divided proportionately among income classes, racial groups, or even individuals.

One problem with each of these definitions of equity is that a distribution that is equitable at one level often produces inequities at another level. For example, even if polluting facilities were distributed equally between rich and poor, and white and minority neighborhoods, not every neighborhood would receive a facility. Moreover, each of these facilities would not be equally "risky." Thus, some poor/rich/African American/Latino/Caucasian residents will be exposed to higher levels of environmental risk than others. In short, an equitable distribution of facilities according to group status will produce an inequitable distribution of environmental risk among individuals. Finally, some experts argue that when it comes to disposing of hazardous and radioactive wastes, we should either lock them away from the environment for hundreds of years (for example, in sealed landfills) or ship them to other countries for disposal. But, eventually, all landfills leak, which only transfers the environmental risk across generations, while shipping the wastes to other nations for disposal simply produces environmental inequities on an international scale.

What Definitions of Discrimination and Equity Mean for Public Policy. Defining discrimination and equity is of more than academic interest. How we define these two terms determines the dividing line between acceptable and unacceptable governmental responses to the concerns of environmental justice advocates. If "discrimination" includes only those actions with clear discriminatory intent, and "equity" is defined as communities paying the full costs of the pollution they produce, then government efforts to ensure environmental equity are relatively simple: narrowly enforce antidiscrimination laws, prevent the illegal disposal of wastes, and have rich communities pay poor communities for accepting polluting facilities. In short, government would do few things differently. On the other hand, if we define "discrimination" as any action that produces a discriminatory outcome and "equity" in very broad terms (for example, equalizing exposure to all environmental risks for all individuals and generations), ensuring environmental equity would require the government to intervene in developers' decisions to build houses and factories, to redistribute income and political power, and to guarantee equal access to medical care, the political process, and so forth. Regardless of the specific definitions one selects, the point is that until we have clearly defined criteria for what constitutes "discrimination" and "equity," it is impossible to develop practical policies to address the problem of environmental inequity.[62]

Conclusion

We can draw several conclusions from the material presented in this chapter. First, there is solid evidence that minority groups and the poor suffer higher levels of exposure to environmental risk, though the evidence on just what causes this inequitable distribution of risk is less certain. Moreover, there is a strong likelihood that members of these same groups suffer higher levels of environmentally generated disease and death as a result of this elevated risk. Second, national, state, and local governments (and mainstream environmental groups) have all responded to the concerns of environmental justice advocates. Few of these policy responses, however, have produced long-lasting changes in the process of allocating environmental risk. Third, the resources and strategies necessary for mobilizing a constituency and moving an issue on to the public agenda are very different than those necessary for articulating a coherent policy agenda and for forging consensus regarding policy change. While the environmental justice movement has experienced significant success at the former, it is clear that the latter hampers realization of the movements' full potential. Fourth, it is evident that we will have no standards with which to judge either the adequacy or the effectiveness of governmental efforts to ensure environmental equity until we can arrive at some common social understanding of what "discrimination" and "equity" mean in the context of environmental protection. Finally, for the foreseeable future, environmental justice concerns will continue to occupy a place next to risk assessment, federal mandates to the states, property rights, and economic incentives as the major forces reshaping the context of environmental policymaking into the twenty-first century.

Notes

1. U.S. Council on Environmental Quality, *Environmental Quality* 1971 (Washington, D.C.: GPO, 1971).
2. See Robert Bullard, ed., *Confronting Environmental Racism: Views from the Grassroots* (Boston: South End Press, 1993); and Robert Paehlke, *Environmentalism and the Future of Progressive Politics* (New Haven, Conn.: Yale University Press, 1989).
3. Robert Bullard, "Introduction," in *Unequal Protection: Environmental Justice and Communities of Color*, ed. Robert Bullard (San Francisco: Sierra Club, 1994); and Marianne Lavelle and Marcia Coyle, "Unequal Protection: The Racial Divide in Environmental Law," *National Law Journal*, September 21, 1992.
4. Michael Ervin, "The Toxic Doughnut," *Progressive* 56, no. 1 (1992): 15.
5. Jane Kay, "The Kettleman City Story," *EPA Journal* 18, no. 1 (1992): 47–48.
6. Robert Tomsho, "Indian Tribes Contend with Some of Worst of America's Pollution," *The Wall Street Journal*, November 29, 1990, A1.
7. Ibid., and Jane Kay, "California's Endangered Communities of Color," in *Unequal Protection*, ed. Bullard. For a different view, see Kevin Gover and Jana Walker, "Escaping Environmental Paternalism: One Tribe's Approach to Developing a Commercial Waste Disposal Project in Indian Country," *University of Colorado Law Review* 63 (1992): 933.
8. Philip Shabecoff, "Environmental Groups Told They Are Racist in Hiring," *New York Times*, February 1, 1990, sec. A.
9. Everett Ladd, "Clearing the Air: Public Opinion and Policy on the Environment," *Public Opinion* 5 (1982): 16–20; Paul Mohai, "Black Environmentalism," *Social Science Quarterly* 71 (1990): 744–765; and Henry Vance Davis, "The Environmental Voting Record of the Congressional Black Caucus," in *Race and the Incidence of Environmental Hazards*, ed. Bunyan Bryant and Paul Mohai (Boulder, Colo.: Westview, 1992).

10. Robert Bullard, "Environmental Justice for All," and Ken Geiser and Gerry Waneck, "PCBs and Warren County," in *Unequal Protection*, ed. Bullard.

11. Cynthia Hamilton, "Concerned Citizens of South Central Los Angeles," and Kay, "California's Endangered Communities of Color," in *Unequal Protection*, ed. Bullard.

12. Andrew Szasz, *Ecopopulism: Toxic Waste and the Movement for Environmental Justice* (Minneapolis: University of Minnesota Press, 1994).

13. L. Pulido, "Restructuring and the Expansion and Contraction of Environmental Rights in the United States," *Environment and Planning* 26 (1994): 915–936; and Richard Moore and Louis Head, "Building a Network That Works: SWOP," in *Unequal Protection*, ed. Bullard.

14. Szasz, *Ecopopulism*; Benjamin Chavis, "Foreword," Karl Grossman, "The People of Color Environmental Summit," and Regina Austin and Michael Schill, "Black, Brown, Red, and Poisoned," in *Unequal Protection*, ed. Bullard.

15. U.S. Environmental Protection Agency (EPA), *Environmental Equity: Reducing Risk for All Communities*, Vol. 1 (Washington, D.C.: EPA, 1992).

16. Robert Bullard, *Dumping in Dixie: Race, Class, and Environmental Quality* (Boulder, Colo.: Westview, 1990). See also Bullard, ed., *Confronting Environmental Racism*.

17. U.S. General Accounting Office (GAO), *Hazardous and Nonhazardous Waste: Demographics of People Living Near Waste Facilities* (Washington, D.C.: GPO, 1995).

18. GAO, *Siting of Hazardous Waste Landfills and Their Correlation with Racial and Economic Status of Surrounding Communities* (Washington, D.C.: GPO, 1983). See also Bullard, ed., *Confronting Environmental Racism*.

19. Paul Mohai and Bunyan Bryant, "Environmental Racism: Reviewing the Evidence," in *Race and the Incidence of Environmental Hazards*, ed. Bryant and Mohai.

20. Commission for Racial Justice, *Toxic Wastes and Race in the United States* (New York: United Church of Christ and Public Data Access, Inc., 1987); and Benjamin Goldman and Laura Fitton, *Toxic Wastes and Race Revisited* (Washington, D.C.: Center for Policy Alternatives, 1994).

21. Douglas Anderton, Andy Anderson, John Michael Oates, and Michael Fraser, "Environmental Equity: The Demographics of Dumping," *Demography* 31 (1994): 229–248.

22. Vicki Been, "Analyzing Evidence of Environmental Justice," *Journal of Land Use and Environmental Law* 11 (1995): 1–36.

23. Evan Ringquist, "Race, Class, and the Politics of Environmental Risk," Unpublished manuscript, 1998.

24. EPA, *1992 Toxics Release Inventory National Report* (Washington, D.C.: Office of Solid Waste and Emergency Response, 1994).

25. Lauretta Burke, "Race and Environmental Equity: A Geographic Analysis in Los Angeles," *Geo Info Systems* (October 1994): 44–50; Susan Cutter, "The Burdens of Toxic Risks: Are They Fair?" *Business and Economic Review* 40 (1994): 101–113; and Philip Pollock III and M. Elliot Vittas, "Who Bears the Burdens of Environmental Pollution? Race, Ethnicity, and Environmental Equity in Florida," *Social Science Quarterly* 76 (1995): 294–310.

26. Evan Ringquist, "Equity and the Distribution of Environmental Risk," *Social Science Quarterly* 78 (1997): 811–29.

27. EPA, *Environmental Equity*, Vol. 1; and Ivette Perfecto and Baldemar Velasquez, "Farm Workers: Among the Least Protected," *EPA Journal* 18, no. 1 (1992): 13–14.

28. EPA, *Environmental Equity*, Vol. 2; and Patrick West, "Health Concerns for Fish-Eating Tribes," *EPA Journal* 18, no. 1 (1992): 15–16. See also "Invitation to Poison? Detroit Minorities and Toxic Fish Consumption from the Detroit River," in *Race and the Incidence of Environmental Hazards*, ed. Bryant and Mohai.

29. Peter Asch and Joseph Seneca, "Some Evidence on the Distribution of Air Quality," *Land Economics* 54 (1978): 278–297; and Julian McCaull, "Discriminatory Air Pollution: If Poor, Don't Breathe," *Environment* 18 (1976): 26–31.

30. Mohai and Bryant, "Environmental Racism," in *Race and the Incidence of Environmental Hazards*, ed. Bryant and Mohai.

31. Benjamin Goldman, *Not Just Prosperity: Achieving Sustainability with Environmental Justice* (Washington, D.C.: National Wildlife Federation, 1993).

32. David Allen, James Lester, and Kelly Hill, "Prejudice, Profits, and Power: Assessing the Eco-Racism Thesis at the County Level" (Paper presented at the annual meeting of the Western Political Science Association, Portland, Oregon, 1995).

33. GAO, *Hazardous and Nonhazardous Waste.*

34. S. W. Lagatos, B. J. Wessen, and M. Zelen, "An Analysis of Contaminated Well Water and Health Effects in Woburn, Massachusetts," *Journal of the American Statistical Association* 81 (1986): 583–596; and Rae Zimmerman, "When Studies Collide: Meta-Analysis and Rules of Evidence for Environmental Health Policy—Applications to Benzene, Dioxins, and Formaldehyde," *Policy Studies Journal* 23 (1995): 123–240.

35. J. Griffith et al., "Cancer Mortality in United States Counties with Hazardous Waste Sites and Groundwater Pollution," *Archives of Environmental Health* 44 (1989): 69–74; and "Hazardous Incinerators," *Science News* 143 (1993): 334.

36. Sandra Geschwind, "Risk of Congenital Malformations Associated with Proximity to Hazardous Waste Sites," *American Journal of Epidemiology* 135 (1993): 1197–1207; D. B. Baker et al., "A Health Study of Two Communities Near the Stringfellow Waste Disposal Site," *Archives of Environmental Health* 43 (1988): 325–334; D. Ozonoff et al., "Health Problems Reported by Residents of a Neighborhood Contaminated by a Hazardous Waste Facility," *American Journal of Industrial Medicine* 11 (1987): 581–597; Dennis Peck, ed., *Psychosocial Effects of Hazardous Toxic Waste Disposal on Communities* (Springfield, Ill.: Charles C. Thomas, 1989); and National Research Council, *Environmental Epidemiology: Public Health and Hazardous Wastes* (Washington, D.C.: National Academy Press, 1991).

37. EPA, *Environmental Equity*, Vol. 1, 3.

38. National Environmental Health Association, "NEHA's Position on Environmental Justice," at *http://www.fcla.ufl.edu/cgi-bin/cgiwrap/~louisr/cgi2iac/FS?18832405* (November 16, 1998).

39. Joel Schwartz and Ronnie Levin, "Lead: An Example of the Job Ahead," *EPA Journal* 18, no. 1 (1992): 42–44; and Michael E. Kraft and Denise Scheberle, "Environmental Justice and the Allocation of Risk: The Case of Lead and Public Health," *Policy Studies Journal* 23 (1995): 113–122.

40. Commission for Racial Justice, *Toxic Wastes and Race*; Anderton et al., "Environmental Equity"; and Ringquist, "Race, Class, and the Politics of Environmental Risk."

41. V. Kerry Smith, "The Value of Avoiding a LULU: Hazardous Waste Disposal Sites," *Review of Economics and Statistics* 68 (1986): 293; Robert Anderson and Thomas Crocker, "Air Pollution and Property Values: A Reply," *Review of Economics and Statistics* 68 (1972): 293; Gregory Michaels and V. Kerry Smith, "Market Segmentation and Valuing Amenities with Hedonic Models: The Case of Hazardous Waste Sites," *Journal of Urban Economics* 28 (1990): 233; and Janet Kolhase, "The Impact of Toxic Waste Sites on Housing Values," *Journal of Urban Economics* 30 (1991): 1–21.

42. John Oakes, Douglas Anderton, and Andy Anderson, "A Longitudinal Analysis of Environmental Equity in Communities With Hazardous Waste Facilities," *Social Science Research* 25 (1996): 125–148.

43. Vicki Been, "Locally Undesirable Land Uses in Minority Neighborhoods: Disproportionate Siting or Market Dynamics?" *Yale Law Journal* 103 (1994): 1383–1422.

44. Vicki Been, with Francis Gupta, "Coming to the Nuisance or Going to the Barrios? A Longitudinal Analysis of Environmental Justice Claims," *Ecology Law Quarterly* 24 (1997): 1–56.

45. Been, "Coming to the Nuisance or Going to the Barrios?; and Oakes et al., "A Longitudinal Analysis of Environmental Equity Claims."

46. Cerrell and Associates Inc., *Political Difficulties Facing Waste-to-Energy Conversion Plant Siting: Report for the California Waste Management Board* (Los Angeles: Cerrell and Associates, 1984); James Hamilton, "Politics and Social Costs: Estimating the Impact of Collective Action on Hazardous Waste Facilities," *Rand Journal of Eco-*

nomics 24 (1993): 101–125; Hamilton, "Testing for Environmental Racism: Prejudice, Profits, Political Power?" *Journal of Policy Analysis and Management* 95 (1995): 107–132; and Ringquist, "Race, Class, and the Politics of Environmental Risk."

47. EPA, *Report to Congress: Disposal of Hazardous Waste* (Washington, D.C.: EPA, 1974).
48. Ringquist, "Race, Class, and the Politics of Environmental Risk."
49. Lavelle and Coyle, "Unequal Protection."
50. Evan Ringquist, "A Question of Justice: Equity in Environmental Litigation, 1974–91," *Journal of Politics* 60 (1998): 1148–1165.
51. Deeohn Ferris, "A Challenge to EPA," *EPA Journal* 18, no. 1 (1992): 28–29.
52. Kraft and Scheberle, "Environmental Justice."
53. "Clinton Actions on Race and the Environment," *National Law Journal*, December 6, 1993, 1; and "Agency Watch," *National Law Journal*, December 5, 1994, A16.
54. EPA, *Environmental Justice Initiatives: 1993* (Washington, D.C.: EPA, 1994).
55. Clarice Gaylord and Robert Knox, "Helping Minorities Help the Environment," *EPA Journal* 18, no.1 (1992): 88–90.
56. Kelly Michelle Colquette and Elizabeth Henry Robertson, "Environmental Racism: The Causes, Consequences, and Commendations," *Tulane Environmental Law Journal* 5 (1991): 153–208; Vicki Been, "What's Fairness Got to Do with It? Environmental Justice and the Siting of Locally Undesirable Land Uses," *Cornell Law Review* 78 (1993): 1001–1085; Deeohn Ferris, "A Call for Justice and Equal Environmental Protection," in *Unequal Protection*, ed. Bullard; and Hamilton, "Testing for Environmental Racism."
57. Evan Ringquist and David Clark, "Issue Definition and the Politics of State Environmental Justice Policy Adoption," *International Journal of Public Administration* (forthcoming).
58. Bullard, ed., *Confronting Environmental Racism*; Kay, "California's Endangered Communities of Color," in *Unequal Protection*, ed. Bullard; and Luke Cole, "Empowerment as the Key to Environmental Protection: The Need for Environmental Poverty Law," *Ecology Law Quarterly* 19 (1993): 619–683.
59. Been, "What's Fairness Got to Do with It?"
60. Christopher Foreman, *The Promise and Peril of Environmental Justice* (Washington, D.C.: Brookings, 1998).
61. Ibid. 12.
62. Been, "What's Fairness Got to Do With It?"

12

Understanding the Transition to a Sustainable Economy

Daniel Press and Daniel A. Mazmanian

*Having spent the last 25 years focused on cheaters and laggards, we
are ill prepared to understand the motivations and the methods of
industry leaders. But policymakers who are willing to leave some
cherished beliefs behind and journey into the strategic core of innovative corporations will discover the most radical restructuring of
production since Henry Ford—one with far-reaching implications
for the environment.*

—David Rejeski (Director of Technology Programs at
EPA's Office of Economy and Environment)

It is becoming increasingly evident, as we approach the twenty-first century, that the unparalleled success of the industrial revolution and the market economy was achieved by depleting much of the regenerative capacity of
nature's economy. With a world population that has doubled to 6 billion
people in only fifty years and expected to peak at 8 to 10 billion in the twenty-
first century, it is no wonder that tension continues to mount over the future
of civilization. Viewed on a global scale, four essential strategies would stabilize and significantly reduce the environmental burdens caused by the current rates of population growth, consumption, and industrial development:
(1) decreasing the size of the human population; (2) reducing the level of
material consumption (particularly among the most affluent of today's societies); (3) altering fundamentally our use of the planet's nonrenewable and
renewable resources through the development of new technologies; and (4)
devising public policies that will foster environmentally responsible business
practices. The focus of this chapter is on these latter two strategies. We explore the extent and pace of business and industry efforts to develop the appropriate technologies and key features of the market economy that bring
the design, production, and use of natural and human-made resources into
alignment with nature's economy.

As a starting point, we assume that everyone would prefer to live and
work in a cleaner, more sustainable economy, and it is thus in the collective
(public) interest of business and industry to expedite the needed alterations.
We also recognize that the institutions of the market economy—with their
practice of exploiting nature's economy while shielding consumers from the

environmental costs of their consumption and affluent life—too often deter or prevent business and policymakers from undertaking transformational steps. While some business and industries will by their nature be change-agents and entrepreneurs in the transformation process, others will resist change in view of their presently limited capacity to adapt and their position within the market economy. A successful transformation to economic sustainability, therefore, is inextricably linked to finding ways within today's market economy to encourage change and, to a substantial though presently unspecified degree, finding the best array of transformative public policies that will permanently alter business and industry behavior.

This chapter surveys the first generation of market-based or nonregulatory initiatives designed to move U.S. business and industry toward a sustainable economy, pointing to both the successes and impediments of these efforts. The greening of industry has only emerged as a serious topic of discussion and analysis among business leaders and policymakers over the past ten years. In this initial stage, there continues to be confusion over exactly what it is about business and industry that needs to be changed—is it waste generation, air and water pollution, or energy consumption? Production methods? Product design? The end products themselves? Researchers have focused on these questions, and fields of study have emerged around each.

From Command-and-Control to Greening: A Cup Half-Full or Half-Empty?

Often vilified for their roles in causing pollution, for close to thirty years business and industry have been the target of sustained, vigorous command-and-control regulation in the campaign for pollution reduction. This massive regulatory effort—the U.S. Environmental Protection Agency (EPA) has the largest total budget of any federal regulatory agency at $7.3 billion for fiscal year 1998—has substantially reduced the release of certain pollutants into the environment.[1] Indeed, in the first quarter-century of the environmental movement, stringent government rules and regulations have strongly correlated with pollution reductions in the United States, which is reflected in the literature on the greening of industry and noted at numerous points throughout this book (see esp. chaps. 1 and 9).[2]

Abatement expenditures in the public and private sectors have definitely risen, both in terms of total dollars and as a percentage of the gross national product, and with them the costs borne by industry. In 1973 U.S. industries spent about $4.8 billion on pollution abatement, almost equally split between capital and operating costs. U.S. industries spent a total of about $28.6 billion on pollution abatement in 1994—$7.9 billion on capital costs and $20.7 billion on operating costs.[3] Almost half of this total, $12.8 billion, was spent by chemical and petroleum companies.

The results of these effects are captured in aggregate terms in emissions and resource consumption patterns. Nationwide air emissions trends from all manufacturing sources show that most air emissions reached a peak in the early to mid 1970s, declined, then plateaued from the mid 1980s on. Manufacturing firms have slowly reduced their annual energy consumption, going from 23.97 quads (quadrillion British thermal units, or Btus) in 1970 to 21.66 quads in 1994.[4] This decline occurred while manufacturing output increased nearly 10 percent from 1989 to 1994.[5] Manufacturing industries decreased their energy intensity by 26.7 percent (usually measured in Btus per dollar value of shipments and receipts) between 1980 and 1988, but then experienced a 4.1 percent increase from 1988 to 1991.[6]

Over the past decade, policymakers have begun to shift their sights from pollution reduction to pollution prevention per se, and to do so by devising "incentive-based" and voluntaristic policy approaches (see chap. 9). The leading edge today is in the drive toward a sustainable economy, where firms are encouraged to move away from products and production processes that require high inputs of virgin raw materials and energy and that release high volumes of waste. Although far from universal, industrial greening is being pursued by many leading companies across the spectrum of U.S. manufacturing sectors through internal industry initiatives and partnerships that operate well ahead of the formal public policy process. Not all is going smoothly, however. Many firms resist both existing and new environmental policies, which they see as only adding to their responsibilities and stretching their capacities. In effect, two quite different trends in business and industry can be detected. One is characterized by shallow, often defensive short-term status-quo actions, while the other is a deeper, long-term movement toward sustainability evident in both public policy and industry behavior. In the extreme, fearing real or potential costs in the short term, industries will often seek to curtail and even roll back established environmental rules and regulations. At the same time, several corporate leaders and industry associations are beginning to recognize the long-term need not only to reduce pollution, but also to chart a new course toward a sustainable economy.

Defining a Sustainable Economy

The concept of a sustainable economy has several meanings but is essentially analogous to a healthy biological system in which little is wasted and human activity does not significantly undermine species diversity and resource availability. Although it is important to gauge progress toward this goal empirically, the process is necessarily a dynamic one, making industry attitudes and practices as important as the measurements of sustainability we choose.[7] For the transformation to endure, firms must change the ways they think about their products within the constraints of their local natural environment as well as the planet more broadly. Growing evidence suggests that some of the world's major corporations are moving in the right direction, although reducing waste and harmful emissions in the production process and developing redesigned or new, less harmful products are two very different tasks.[8] Douglas Lober proposes a twenty-four-point checklist of criteria for assessing whether a particular firm is greening (see box 12-1).[9]

Box 12-1   Criteria for Evaluating a Corporation's Greenness

1. Environmental Policy
2. Code of Environmental Ethics and Standards of Practice
3. Corporate Structure
4. Employee Involvement
5. Environmental Management Systems
6. Total Quality Management
7. Materials, Energy, Water Usage
8. Pollution Prevention, Waste Minimization, and Recycling Activity
9. Product and Process Stewardship
10. Environmental Accounting of Benefits/Costs
11. Environmental Auditing
12. Environmental Releases
13. Sustainable Relationship with Natural Ecosystems
14. Environmental Liabilities, Compliance, and Penalties
15. Environmental Accidents
16. Relationships with the Public/Media
17. Relationships with the Local Community
18. Relationships with Shareholders
19. Relationships with Suppliers
20. Relationships with Environmental Groups
21. Relationships with Political/Regulatory System
22. Participation in Cooperative Environmental Councils and Partnerships
23. Communication of Environmental Activity
24. Industrial Ecology

Source: Douglas J. Lober, "Evaluating the Environmental Performance of Corporations," *Journal of Managerial Issues* VIII, no. 2 (Summer 1996).

As Robert Paehlke asserts in chapter 4, environmental improvements need not always occur at the cost of economic growth and expansion. Evidence suggests that no necessary diminution of overall economic growth accompanies even the most stringent environmental regulation, though there are specific industrial winners and losers.[10] Research on the consequences of greening for economic growth has grown in breadth and clarity. First, it is widely accepted today that many pollution prevention and source reduction measures associated with the initial steps toward greening can and do eliminate waste and increase the efficiency of business firms. In a systematic empirical analysis of numerous companies, Stuart Hart and Gautam Ahuja found that the costs of implementing such measures are fully recovered within one to two years.[11] They point out, however, that the lowest hanging fruits are being picked fast. Further improvements are likely to face increasing costs and decreasing benefits.

Second, there is some evidence and a strong theoretical argument that stricter environmental requirements spur innovations by business, which are important sources of competitive advantage in today's business world.[12] Third, based on recent U.S. experience, it is reasonable to argue that future economic growth, especially in the developed countries, will be driven by quality-of-life considerations that produce stable populations and jobs in areas of high environmental quality. Fourth, researchers and practitioners point to the creation of jobs in pollution control technology as a source of economic welfare and employment even within the framework of the conventional market economy, which is a result of today's environmental regulation.[13]

An important caveat in interpreting these trends is that greening is not uniform across all business and industrial sectors. One indicator of the difference across sectors is the level of voluntary self-reporting on environmental and pollution characteristics, which ranged (as of 1996) from a high of 57 percent for utilities, 47 percent for forest and paper, and 43 percent for pharmaceuticals industries to 10 percent for motor vehicles parts and 5 percent for the food industry.[14]

When it comes to greening, researchers have found critical differences between leading-edge, large companies that have launched impressive greening initiatives and small- and medium-sized businesses that exhibit an absence of equally dramatic change.[15] The latter group appears to be systematically handicapped by lack of many of the requisite "environmental competencies" of the larger, more professionally managed and well-heeled companies.[16] In general, four major factors explain the widespread reluctance to embrace even the most rudimentary level of greening:

1. Despite financial benefits, many managers view P2—pollution prevention—as an extension of existing costly and burdensome regulatory programs.
2. Accounting systems are still inadequate to measure the costs and savings of pollution prevention.
3. P2 involves changing production processes, which introduces risks that some plant managers are reluctant to take.
4. Investments in waste reduction programs compete with other demands on capital that are thought by managers to be of more strategic importance. Top management of many companies, while supporting the concept of pollution prevention, is not involved closely enough in promoting its implementation.[17]

Changes will not come easily. To make a significant improvement in the situation, the key is not simply "incremental" or even "breakthrough" innovations, but "radical innovations" that "sweep away much of a firm's existing investment in technical skills and knowledge, designs, production techniques, plant, and equipment."[18]

Stuart Hart characterizes the necessary changes as moving through three stages: from pollution prevention to product stewardship to, inevitably and most importantly, clean technology. And, he concludes, in view of the fact that "technology is the business of business," it is not simply a matter of legal obligation but the moral responsibility of business to lead the way to a sustainable economy.[19]

It may be tempting to imagine that the green industrial evolution will take place naturally, that is, in response to the growing scarcity of natural resources and public awareness of the need for firms to change as they compete in the global economic marketplace. But the crucial driving forces of the market and natural economies rarely operate in concert. A key difference is that the two do not value nature's resources similarly nor do they work on the same timetable. Thus, when left solely to market considerations, substantial and irreparable harm to biodiversity and natural environments can occur before patterns of extraction, pollution, and depletion are significantly altered. The imperative today is to design the appropriate mix of public and private policies that promote and provide a comprehensive framework that strikes a balance between the two economies.[20]

Pollution Reduction Programs

In the late 1980s and early 1990s policymakers began to design policies that fostered the greening of industry by encouraging firms to look inward and develop pollution prevention strategies that were suited to their specific company and that were in keeping with conventional business practices. What resulted was better internal monitoring of material and energy flows, more efficient use of primary materials, and reuse of materials within the production process. Together, these improvements helped to minimize the generation of waste while increasing the bottom line. With the exception of the monitoring and management of toxic materials, which are closely regulated by the federal (and sometime state) government, pollution prevention programs are mostly incentive-based and voluntary. Business itself, it is thought, can best decide how to minimize pollution in production. At the same time, information-gathering and reporting requirements have been added to the 1970s generation command-and-control statutes already on the books that address air, water, and land pollution.

Required Information Disclosure: The Toxics Release Inventory

The trend toward this new generation of environmental programs began in 1986 with the Superfund Amendments and Reauthorization Act. Title III of the statute established the Toxics Release Inventory (TRI), the first major federal environmental program that moved away from the traditional command-and-control approach (characterized by heavy fines, specified emission levels, and mandatory pollution abatement technologies) toward a "softer, gentler" self-reporting and cooperative framework. While most of the new pollution prevention programs are voluntary, the TRI is not. Under the Emergency Planning and Community Right-to-Know Act, companies that fall within Standard Industrial Classification codes 20–39, have ten or more employees, and use significant amounts of any of more than six hundred listed chemicals must report their annual releases and transfers of these chemicals to the EPA, which then generates an annual report—the *TRI Public Data Release*—detailing the information.[21] The reporting requirements are extensive, including the maximum amount of chemicals onsite, the number of pounds released to different media (air, land, water), and information on whether discharges are treated, recovered for energy, or recycled.

Like the National Environmental Policy Act of 1970, the TRI requires companies to report their activities but does not mandate that they modify their behavior. To view such policies as "all study and no action," however, would be to miss their contribution to what David Morell calls "regulation by embarrassment."[22] Indeed, environmental groups like Citizens for a Better Environment, INFORM, and Greenpeace have seized on the data released by the EPA to publicize particularly heavy polluters.[23] Moreover, many state environmental agencies are basing their rulemaking on the TRI reports for industries in their states. Some industries have called for ending the TRI reporting process because of these new regulatory uses.

The Pollution Prevention Act of 1990

The nation's first federal law aimed at curbing pollution at the source by mostly voluntary means, the Pollution Prevention Act (PPA) expands the level and quality of information available to industry and regulators. The law directs the EPA to establish standard methods of measurement and audits for industrial pollution prevention goals. It created the Source Reduction Clearinghouse to help states disseminate information and to provide technical assistance to businesses. The statute also directs the EPA to form a pollution prevention advisory panel made up of industry, states, and public interest groups. In an effort to promote environmentally benign manufacturing processes and to "jump start" markets for greener products, the law requires the EPA to establish federal procurement guidelines for environmentally preferable products. The act also established a new pollution prevention awards program. Finally, the law adds requirements to TRI reports that include information on toxic chemical source reduction, recycling, and industry estimates of total production-related chemical wastes. Total production-related wastes refers to all TRI chemical wastes generated by a firm, whether they were subsequently released to the environment, treated onsite, shipped offsite, or recycled.

Measuring Industry Success Based on the TRI and the PPA

Making year-to-year comparisons in toxic releases is difficult, because the EPA has expanded the kinds of facilities required to report releases as well as added to the list of chemicals to report. But if we limit ourselves to the three hundred or so "core chemicals," we find that total releases decreased

45.6 percent from 1988 to 1996.[24] This news is certainly good; however, it is tempered by other information from the TRI.

First, not all sectors are responding equally well to the challenge of toxics reduction. Second, there has been relatively little source reduction accomplished overall. Between 1991 and 1996, quantities of core chemicals actually released into the environment dropped by 26.4 percent, but at the same time total production-related waste of core chemicals increased by 2 percent. Thus while industries required to report to the TRI have decreased their core chemical releases, they have not changed the amount of core chemicals they generate as waste, which must then be recycled, used as a source of energy, or disposed of. Most of the reductions in chemical releases that were reported to the TRI were the result of increases in recycling and energy recovery. These are laudable achievements, to be sure, but the only way to accomplish significant decreases in total production-related waste is through source reduction. The data available suggest that the transition from waste management to source reduction for core chemicals is simply not occurring. This lack of source reduction would perhaps be less discouraging if facilities were at least moving up the EPA's waste management hierarchy from treatment (the least desirable) to energy recovery to recycling to, finally, source reduction (the most desirable), but they are not.[25]

Voluntary Programs and Partnerships

One of the major thrusts today is to encourage collaborations between business, environmental groups, and government agencies in developing solutions to pollution problems. Indeed, the many voluntary programs that the EPA coordinates range across sector and issue areas, and are managed by the agency's Office of Reinvention and its Partnership Programs Coordinating Committee. Box 12-2 provides a catalogue of EPA's partnership programs organized by the specific pollution topics they address.

Three of these programs are noteworthy. These are the EPA's 33/50, Energy Star, and Project XL programs.

The 33/50 Program. The 33/50 program was the first of many new voluntary programs, and the favorable responses it received inside and outside of the EPA helped usher in the additional initiatives, most of which began between 1991 and 1995. In 1989, the EPA had sufficient TRI data to rank the largest polluters and the chemicals they release. Just nine chemical and petroleum manufacturers were responsible for vast releases of toxics. Rather than call for further regulation of these corporations, William Reilly, EPA administrator, convened meetings with their senior management, environmental organizations, and agency staff. He emerged with a pledge to lead the way in industry-wide voluntary reductions.

Thus, in 1991 the EPA launched the 33/50 program, named for its goal of reducing releases of seventeen high-priority chemicals by 33 percent by 1992 and 50 percent by 1995. The seventeen chemicals were selected from the TRI list based on "their relative toxicity, volumes of use, and the poten-

Box 12-2   Partners for the Environment: Toxics Reduction, Reporting, and Efficiency

General

Design for the Environment (DfE)—Include environmental considerations in product design.

Environmental Accounting—Increase business identification of environmental costs and encourage incorporation of these costs into decisionmaking.

Green Chemistry Program—Promote and recognize breakthroughs in chemistry that accomplish pollution prevention cost effectively.

33/50 Program—Reduce toxic releases of seventeen high-priority chemicals.

Common Sense Initiative (CSI)—Reinvent environmental regulation to achieve cleaner, cheaper, smarter results for six industry sectors: auto manufacturing, computers and electronics, iron and steel, metal finishing and plating, petroleum refining, and printing.

EPA Standards Network—Coordinate agency involvement in international standards development and provide public information.

Project XL—Develop alternative regulatory approaches to achieve greater environmental benefits.

Agriculture

AgSTAR—reduce methane emissions from manure management.

Ruminant Livestock Methane Program—Reduce methane emissions from ruminant livestock.

Pesticide Environmental Stewardship Program—Promote integrated pest management and reduce pesticide risk in agriculture and non-agriculture settings.

Global Climate Change

Climate Wi$e—Reduce industrial greenhouse gas emissions and energy costs through comprehensive pollution prevention and energy efficiency programs (an EPA/Department of Energy partnership).

Coalbed Methane Outreach Program—Increase methane recovery at coal mines

U.S. Initiative on Joint Implementation—Promote international projects that reduce greenhouse gases.

Indoor Environments Program—Reduce risks from indoor air pollution.

Voluntary Aluminum Industrial Partnership—Reduce perfluorocarbon gas emissions from aluminum smelting.

(continues on next page)

Box 12-2   *(Continued)*

Energy Efficiency and Conservation
Water Alliances for Voluntary Efficiency (WAVE)—Promote water efficiency in lodging industry.
Energy Star—Maximize energy efficiency and reduce atmospheric pollution.
Energy Star Buildings—Maximize energy efficiency in commercial and industrial buildings.
Energy Star Residential Programs—Promote energy efficiency through new home design and residential use of energy efficient products.
Energy Star Office Equipment—Increase manufacture of energy efficient products.
Energy Star Transformer Program—Increase use of high efficiency distribution transformers by utilities and manufacturers.
Green Lights—Increase use of energy efficient lighting technologies.
Landfill Methane Outreach Program—Develop landfill gas-to-energy projects.
Natural Gas Star—Reduce methane emissions from natural gas industry.
Transportation Partners—Reduce carbon dioxide emissions from transportation sector.

State and Local
State and Local Outreach Program—Reduce greenhouse gas emissions by empowering state and local decisionmakers.

Solid Waste
Waste Minimization National Plan—Reduce persistent, bioaccumulative and toxic chemicals in hazardous waste.
WasteWi$e—Reduce business solid waste through prevention, reuse and recycling.

Compliance
Environmental Leadership Program (ELP)—Recognize facilities defined as environmental leaders and promote environmental management systems.

Source: EPA, Partners for the Environment: A Catalogue of the Agency's Partnership Programs EPA 100-B-97-003 (Washington, D.C.: EPA, Spring 1998).

---

tial for pollution prevention opportunities." [26] Significant decreases in the release levels for these chemicals was not the program's only objective. The EPA also wanted to promote flexibility by challenging corporations to reduce toxic emissions by whatever means they felt most appropriate. Participants were encouraged to adopt source reduction rather than end-of-pipe control methods. More than 8,000 companies were identified as potential program participants and invited to enroll in the program. According to the *1995 TRI Public Data Release,* roughly 1,300 companies signed up more than 6,000 facilities for the 33/50 program.

EPA reported that the cumulative reduction achieved by participants during the program's first five years (1988–1993) totaled 46 percent.[27] The 1996 TRI report indicated a 60 percent overall reduction in the releases and transfers of the seventeen chemicals between 1988 and 1996.[28]

In some ways, the 33/50 program is a success story. Not only were the reduction goals achieved, but an EPA-sponsored study revealed that source reduction accounted for 58 percent of the decrease in releases and transfers for the 33/50 chemicals.[29] In 1997, the program was recognized by *Innovations in American Government Award Program* as one of the 25 best government innovations in the country, an award sponsored by the Ford Foundation and Harvard's John F. Kennedy School of Government. At the same time, caution is warranted. The General Accounting Office (GAO) has pointed out that "paper reductions" accounted for 400 million pounds—or 27 percent—of the reductions achieved between 1988 and 1991. In addition, many of the reductions in 33/50 program chemicals cannot be directly attributed to the program because 26 percent of the 1988–1991 reductions were reported by nonparticipants, and 40 percent of the reductions occurred before the program was established.[30]

Energy Star. The EPA launched the Energy Star program in June 1992. Energy Star certifies energy-efficient equipment, appliances, and many other products. The most successful part of the program has been with computers and computer equipment. In a few short years, the EPA has signed partnership agreements with 90 percent of all computer, printer, or monitor manufacturers to install power-down, or "sleep," features in their equipment. In the mid 1990s computers accounted for 5 percent of all commercial electricity consumption; by the year 2000, that figure could rise to 10 percent. In 1998, more than two thousand Energy Star-compliant products were widely available in the United States and in many other countries.[31] The EPA estimates that in 1997 energy and cost savings stemming from Energy Star compliance rose to 2 billion kilowatt hours and $740 million.[32] The corresponding emissions avoided amounted to 1.85 MMTCE (million metric tons of carbon equivalent).[33]

Another success of the Energy Star program has been the Green Lights initiative. Noting that lighting accounts for 20 to 25 percent of all electricity sold in the United States, and that 80 to 90 percent of total lighting electricity is consumed by industrial and commercial end users, the EPA in 1991 launched its Green Lights program, which was quickly incorporated into the Energy Star Program. Green Lights encourages large facilities to install high-efficiency lighting systems, particularly where these systems will pay for themselves within five years or less. The agency provides technical support (including lighting-upgrade manuals), a database of financial assistance programs and energy service companies, information on specific products, and public recognition for individual companies participating in the program.

In its first three years, nearly seventeen hundred organizations participated in the program. As of the summer of 1998, the Green Lights program had over twenty-five hundred members.[34] Typical savings in energy bills have been in the range of 20 to 40 percent per year, far above the minimum return of 15 percent suggested by the EPA. In 1994 alone, Green Lights participants reduced their electricity consumption by 1 billion kwh (kilowatt-hour), for a savings of approximately $92 million.[35]

Project XL. Project XL (e*X*cellence and *L*eadership), launched by the Clinton administration in 1995, represents a more recent policy initiative aimed at finding a positive response to the complaints from business and industry that the cumulative regulatory burdens of air, water, toxic, and other environmental laws are onerous and unnecessary. Project XL was designed to be collaborative, bringing together representatives from industry; federal, state, and local government; and environmental organizations. It was to be site-specific, with the focus on developing an environmental plan for a particular major industrial facility. It was to respond to the complaints about slow and multiple-layered permitting, which extended across media and governmental jurisdictions. It was to be more flexible with respect to how the firm would be required to reduce emissions in each of the different media and, in this way, presumably be more economic, while at the same time exceed the aggregate level of emission reduction that could be expected under conventional regulation.[36]

EPA estimated that five hundred firms would submit proposals for participation in the program, and it would select fifty for purposes of the pilot. Through 1997, however, only fifty-one proposals had been submitted.[37] Seven Project XL programs have been completed to date; a handful more are in the proposal and development stages.

It turned out that the agency's decision not to establish firm standards and requirements for participation discouraged more than inspired firms to take the program seriously. Even more troubling, thirty of the initially interested firms—some with exemplary environmental track records—withdrew after entering the program, many disappointed with EPA's unwillingness or inability to live by the program's promises of flexibility, collaboration, and fast-track multi-media permitting. In practice, the difficulties encountered in the Washington office of EPA in its efforts to support its field representatives, the realization by firms that there may not be greater gains over the conventional regulatory approach, and the uncertainties about the legally binding nature of specific facility-level arrangements raise serious questions about the program's long-range viability.

Ultimately, EPA's pollution prevention programs are still relatively new and must be evaluated cautiously. Benefits have been forthcoming. However, Walter Rosenbaum points out that these programs are also part fanfare and guesswork. For example, the problems with the self-reported industry data—on energy and material inputs and waste streams—make it very difficult to assess what is truly happening in a firm. Moreover, EPA evaluators have not performed life-cycle assessments to determine if greening is truly occurring, as opposed to displacing problems to other media.[38]

The Transition to Stewardship and New Technologies

There is ample evidence today that many industry executives and manufacturing associations are beginning to reach beyond specific government programs and pollution prevention to embrace the philosophy of greening as a matter of good business, customer relations, and corporate citizenship.[39] This is evidenced by the emergence of Canada's environmental roundtables; California's Business Environmental Assistance Center; the Business for Social Responsibility trade association (formed in 1992 with fifty-four members and now nearing seven hundred); firms adopting the CERES principles (formerly the Valdez principles); the Responsible Care Program developed by the Chemical Manufacturers Association (CMA) and now required of all its 175 members; the GEMI (Global Environmental Management Initiative) program, intended to ensure that U.S. corporations stay competitive while going green; and the code of conduct adopted by the International Chamber of Commerce.[40]

Even investment brokers have begun to respond to the greening movement with "socially responsible" environmental investment portfolios, though today they are only a small part of the investments market. By the mid 1990s there were about forty mutual funds managing $3 billion offered green investments.[41] In 1998, the *Greenmoney Journal* reported that socially-responsible investment (SRI) funds, which select companies through a wide range of social screens, had reached $1.18 trillion, or 10 percent of worldwide investments. Since 1990 the Domini 400 Social Index tracks four hundred companies that pass a number of social screens.[42] Managers of green mutual funds are constantly updating their "social ratings" of industries worthy of investment. Indeed, a number of studies now suggest a strong correlation between profitability and greening, although researchers are quick to point out that just how a company's profits are tied to its investments in pollution prevention or abatement is not clear.[43]

These commitments demonstrate that many of the leaders of industry do recognize the environmental imperative of greening. Yet if the need is so apparent, and the path fairly well laid out, the obvious question is why is the transformation not occurring more rapidly? More precisely, why is it not occurring fast enough to satisfy those in business, government, the environmental community, and the general public who champion it? Several answers have been suggested, from lack of awareness and technical know-how to organizational resistance, high production costs, and substantial marketplace constraints. All surely impede progress toward a sustainable economy.

Scholars in organizational behavior and economics are helping to fill in the gaps in our understanding of these barriers. They have examined business firms for internal motives and changes in organizational design and have profiled those at the leading edge of their industry in greening. Researchers have chronicled how these companies evolved from being heavy polluters to conscientious pollution abaters by significantly reducing emissions, better managing wastes, reformulating products and production processes in order to use fewer natural resources and energy, and making goods recyclable, more durable, and less toxic.[44]

Leading-edge firms share several characteristics, including visible involvement of corporate leadership in developing and promoting new management philosophies and infiltration of upper management by younger executives and women. To reinforce green strategies, firms have introduced corporate environmental pledges, internal training programs, environmental education programs, and use of "cradle-to-grave" systems of management control, such as full-cost accounting and total quality management (TQM).[45] Of the elements, the two most important appear to be commitment at the top of the corporate hierarchy and a management system designed to track the flow of raw materials, energy, labor, quality, and costs through the operations of the firm.[46] The most frequently identified external factor influencing a change in environmental management is the trauma (for example, legal liability, consumer backlash) directly experienced by a firm or its industry as a result of some environmental catastrophe.[47]

Economists look at greening from a more theoretical viewpoint, and in doing so provide a persuasive case for why the transition to greening is less successful than many had hoped. They frame the issues of pollution and greening as a subset of the classic externalities problem (see chap. 9). Firms have little or no incentive to absorb pollution abatement costs or to go green so long as society does not hold them accountable. From a competitive standpoint, it makes little sense for them to voluntarily take on the added expenses of pollution abatement or production line modification. The central message of the economic analysis is that greening will not come voluntarily. It will take hold if the problem of acting progressively when others do not—the classic problem of collective action—is solved for the firm.

Economists offer a host of policy prescriptions designed to internalize unwanted environmental externalities, most frequently by imposing emissions taxes or fees, or by instituting programs of emissions trading (see chap. 9). For these to be effective, their cost to the businesses involved needs to be substantial. Yet imposing such costs requires strong and effective environmental regulations, monitoring, and enforcement—that is, a dedicated, powerful government. This is the dilemma of the economists' prescriptions. Though their research may be analytically persuasive and their remedies internally consistent, they offer few avenues for overcoming the political hurdles and business costs of implementing their recommendations, making their adoption highly improbable and minimizing their effectiveness, especially on the global scale required.

The Sectoral Approach to Greening and
the Problem of Collective Action

Motivations for Greening

Greening can be accelerated by public policy aimed at reducing the costs and barriers associated with bringing like firms together to overcome common managerial, technological, and marketplace barriers to greening. Reducing costs and overcoming obstacles are efforts most likely to occur regionally, rather than nationally, and within industrial sectors. This suggests that a sectoral-based greening policy will be the most likely to succeed.[48] A "sector" is an industry network related by the production life-cycle, which consists of primary producers; a second tier of direct material/energy suppliers; and an outer group of equipment suppliers, associated producers, sales and distribution channels, and end users. Moving to a sector-based policy has the added advantage of permitting researchers to develop "benchmarks" against which to judge changes at levels more meaningful than single firms (where changes can be idiosyncratic) or "all manufacturing" (a level that averages out the achievements of progressive sectors with laggard ones).

Recognizing the importance of cross-sector and cross-media approaches to pollution prevention, the EPA proposed a new "cluster rule" for the pulp and paper industry in late 1994. The cluster rule combined regulations from the federal Clean Water and Clean Air Acts and set emissions standards for hazardous air pollutants. The idea was to avoid regulating one part of the pulp and paper sector only to have pollution increase elsewhere in the production cycle. Similarly, reductions in air emissions would not be gained at the expense of water quality. Perhaps the most visible result of the cluster rule has been the decrease in the use of elemental chlorine as a bleaching agent, which has been replaced by a number of totally chlorine-free processes as well as chlorine dioxide.

The important point is that an individual firm's decisions about greening need not be based solely on the conventional market calculations such as total costs and discounted future benefits of a given change or innovation. If the transaction costs of greening can be reduced for a firm through coventuring, cost sharing, and horizontal integration of technical expertise, it is much more likely to be in the firm's interest to "voluntarily" go green, not because of government policy but as a matter of good business practice.[49] Consequently, industries are forming sectorwide networks and collaborations to gain sectoral—as opposed to single-firm—advantage in the increasingly competitive global economy. Sectorwide cooperation allows firms to address technical problems arising not just with the primary producer of a product, but also with its raw material (or semimanufactured component) suppliers and consumers. As Jacqueline Cramer and Johan Schot point out: "Since most firms are not themselves involved in all phases of [the product life] cycle, cooperation among firms is necessary. The need for cooperation is not limited to the development of environmentally sound products. Innovation processes of any kind most often do not occur within companies, but between companies."[50]

Market advantage can be gained on the basis of flexibility, responsiveness, adaptation, and innovation, which in turn can be cultivated and reinforced through sectoral business networks. The chief chronicler of this development, Michael Porter, argues that the firms in sectoral arrangements are best positioned not only to succeed in business but also to go green and to do so the most quickly.[51] Others have also argued that competitive advantage will become more and more tied to innovations in environmental technologies and management.[52]

From a strategic perspective, sectorwide policy and collaboration appear to offer several advantages to both the participating firms and specific regions of the country:

- If an entire sector acts, each of its members is far less likely to suffer from fear that others won't change and that they will be left at a comparative disadvantage in the marketplace.
- Informal communications can complement the formal, and this is most likely to occur within a sector.
- Professional organizations already exist and can serve as "change entrepreneurs."
- Governments can and do target sectors, not entire economies; thus, the threat of government intervention is more realistic if focused on sectors.
- Self-policing (providing monitoring and assurance) is more likely within an existing sector (particularly if it is highly networked).
- It is in the sector's collective interest to foster a positive public image.

If public policy and industry efforts move to a sector-based strategy, we should have a way of measuring their progress at reducing environmental impacts and determining if Porter's predictions about environmental innovations are being borne out. The examples of emissions, resource extraction, and pollution control cost that follow thus focus on several industrial sectors.

The Chemical, Computer Electronics, and Paper Sectors: Brief Overviews

Not all industries are moving at the same pace, and the aggregate industrial indicators mask the significant efforts of individual sectors. Cases from three important manufacturing industries provide a picture of how sectoral efforts at greening are being pursued in practice.

Chemical Manufacturing. Chemical manufacturing facilities are among the largest net polluters in U.S. industry. They release more toxics, by far, than any other single manufacturing sector.[53] But the 1996 figures reported for core chemicals by this sector are also vastly smaller—by just over 50 percent—than in 1988. And although chemical companies increased their total emissions of most conventional air pollutants from approximately 8 percent to 15 percent (depending on the pollutant) between 1985 and 1993, they did so while increasing production by 15 to 20 percent.

Pollution prevention has been taken quite seriously in the chemical sector, not only because compliance, liability costs, and enforcement fines are so high, but also because chemical company practices undergo tremendous public scrutiny. In addition, most chemical manufacturing firms are large enough to devote considerable resources, in terms of both staff and money, to exploring and implementing environmental management innovations.

Battered by negative publicity, the Chemical Manufacturers Association (CMA) adopted the "Responsible Care" program in 1988. This sector-wide code of conduct is now required of all CMA members and has been adopted in some form by chemical manufacturers in thirty-seven countries.[54] It consists of ten guiding principles and six management practice codes. The guiding principles emphasize responding to community concerns; ensuring safety in all phases of production, transportation, use, and disposal; developing safe chemicals and supporting research on health, safety, and environmental effects of products, processes, and wastes; and helping to create "responsible" laws and regulations. The management codes are designed to improve each facility's emergency response capabilities; pollution prevention; and safety in production, sales, distribution, and final disposal. The CMA has been adopting quantitative benchmarks to measure its members' progress on each of these codes.[55]

The Responsible Care program is quite self-consciously sectoral. As Porter might predict, CMA members expect the program to succeed with collaborative efforts:

> The Responsible Care program has also spawned an extensive mutual assistance network within the chemical industry, a network that includes very senior management. Companies that are far along in their implementation of the codes are asked to help those companies having difficulty complying. Through its Partnership Program, CMA actively pushes the envelope of Responsible Care beyond the chemical industry. Partners are industries and associations that are not CMA members, but that make, use, formulate, distribute, transport, and/or treat or dispose of chemicals.[56]

It is too early to draw conclusions about the Responsible Care program. Critics point to a large gap between improvements to which CMA members have committed themselves and what companies have actually achieved. Part of the problem is that some of the management codes lack clear performance indicators and company statistics are not yet independently validated by any third-party observers.[57]

Industrial end users of chemicals are also pulling chemical manufacturers toward environmentally benign practices. Cramer and Schot report that corporate consumers are increasingly reluctant to take delivery of highly toxic chemicals or compounds "that receive a great deal of negative publicity," such as polyvinyl chloride, cadmium, or chlorofluorocarbons.[58] And to make good on some manufacturers' claims of recyclability, the automobile industry is pressuring chemical companies to use plastics that "have the same chemical structure, which makes it easier to recycle and reuse them."[59] Finally, most firms are seriously concerned about the cost and liability of hazardous waste disposal. As a result, they are requesting that chemicals be delivered in the exact amounts needed, preferably in returnable containers.

Computer Electronics. Computer manufacturers also have modified their environmental impacts substantially over the past decade. In 1988 manufacturers of computer equipment, circuit boards, and semiconductors reported total toxic releases to the environment of 18.3 million pounds. In 1992 this sector reported releases of 13.0 million pounds and in 1995 releases of 4.27 million pounds, decreases of 29 and 76 percent, respectively.[60] Once considered the cleanest of industries, computer manufacturers lost that reputation as the result of stunning groundwater contamination cases (mostly in California) in the 1980s. Circuit board and semiconductor companies were storing toxic solvents in underground storage tanks that leaked into groundwater supplies, eventually creating twenty-nine Superfund sites in Silicon Valley alone. The government and high-tech firms responded with groundwater remediation programs, but soon afterward the sector faced new evidence of environmental damage from its use of ozone-depleting chlorofluorocarbons (CFCs) and perfluorocarbons (PFCs) for circuit board cleaning.

Although semiconductor manufacturers continue to use 90 percent of the perfluoroethane sold in the United States, chemical and high-tech firms have been rapidly replacing CFCs, PFCs, and solvents with more benign cleaners in addition to developing emissions recovery systems for those applications that still rely on the ozone depleters.[61] Widespread participation in the EPA's Energy Star program has also helped to reduce this sector's environmental impacts.

Because of the rapid turnover in their products, computer electronics firms face some unusual problems and opportunities in the transition to greening. Frequent innovations make any given model of computer or printer obsolete after about eighteen months, at which time companies usually discontinue a particular model in favor of the next version. While rapid obsolescence can lead to more wastes, there is also tremendous potential to redesign products with environmental goals in mind. Moreover, most of a computer's costs—and its environmental impacts—are determined by its design, literally before engineers draw up the manufacturing blueprints. So product design changes can reduce those costs and environmental impacts before manufacturing begins.[62]

Because of these sector-specific characteristics, computer electronics firms have focused their environmental innovations on product design and recyclability. The Design for Environment initiative, coordinated by the American Electronics Association (AEA), is the most notable. Design for Environment focuses on sharing management and engineering practices concerning the design, production, distribution, and ultimate disposal of computers, printers, copiers, and telecommunications devices. The initiative also promotes mutual aid on regulatory compliance and provides concrete examples of production changes that other firms can implement on the shop floor.[63]

Similarly, industry leaders like Hewlett-Packard and Xerox are beginning to design their products for disassembly (making components easy to take apart), and for recycling (by choosing materials that, once disassembled, yield valuable materials). Some larger firms also take back or remanufacture products or parts of products, using extensive networks of third-party brokers, which provide the critical link in the recycling chain.[64]

Pulp and Paper. Some segments, though by no means all, of the pulp and paper sector are undergoing an aggressive transition to greening. On the whole, paper companies have been steadily reducing many of their emissions, as well as their energy intensity, on a per ton of product or dollar output basis.

The pulp and paper industry used 2,665 trillion Btus of energy for all purposes in 1994, which accounts for 12.3 percent of U.S. energy consumption from manufacturing in that same year and ranks the pulp and paper industry as the third largest energy consumer among manufacturing sectors.[65] That figure, however, represents a substantial drop in energy intensity from an industry average of 19.1 million Btus per ton of paper produced in 1972 to 11.7 million Btus per ton of paper produced in 1992.[66]

Between 1985 and 1994 the pulp and paper sector increased its conventional air emissions by approximately 3 to 9 percent, depending on the pollutant.[67] This rise occurred while the industry increased its total output of paper and paperboard from about 52 million tons in 1970 to just under 66 million tons in 1980 to 81 million tons in 1996.[68]

The paper sector is still a significant polluter in U.S. industry, but it has vastly reduced its emissions, energy demands, and resource usage on a per-unit-produced basis. Without command-and-control, and without pollution prevention and the rising costs of waste management, this sector would impose much greater burdens on the American landscape. There is undeniably tremendous room for improvement as this industry moves toward recycling much more wastepaper, phasing out chlorine and other toxic chemicals in its production process, and reaping further energy efficiency gains.

The paper industry's environmental innovations are being abetted by sectorwide partnerships, communications, and collaboration, many of these occurring with the help of engineering consultants and trade associations.[69] Such collaboration is on the rise, particularly among the greener recycling segment of the sector and among companies that are expanding or siting new facilities.

The professional organizations of the pulp and paper industry play a key role in the sector's collective action efforts. The Technical Association of the Pulp and Paper Industry is especially effective and attracts literally thousands of members to its major meetings. These meetings offer technical panels on wide-ranging topics, including those with implications for competitiveness as well as for reducing environmental impacts. The major lobbying organization for this sector, the American Forest and Paper Association, is also viewed as a particularly effective coordinating entity.

In sum, sector-based cooperation and networking have become more important than ever before, and key industry actors have responded by increasing the importance of collaborative mechanisms for innovation and learning. Leading-edge developments tend to involve greener firms, because these are the very ones that must innovate the most; they have fewer years of research and development behind them. But the whole sector is certainly not greening at the same pace. Many firms still rely on virgin wood fiber and harmful chemicals like chlorine to produce paper. They tend to be located near cheap and plentiful sources of timber and water and thereby hold on to their market shares with very competitive pricing. The future of greening in the paper sector may depend on replacement of these plants with deinking facilities located in the heart of the "urban forest," with its vast sources of multiple grades of recovered wastepaper.[70]

Backlash and Forward Movement

The greening of industry in the 1990s has been marked by differential progress: some firms in some sectors are consistently out in front, while others vigorously resist change. Progress toward greening has spread unevenly within and across industrial sectors. And libertarian ideology strongly motivates some corporate leaders to resist not only command-and-control regulation but the nontraditional pollution prevention programs as well.

Despite the good image nurtured by corporate public relations officers, many industry lobbyists today still work assiduously at blocking or rolling back environmental mandates. Indeed, the chemical industry's strong lobbying to weaken existing environmental protection legislation and to prevent new legislation undermines the credibility of its own Responsible Care program.[71] Industry political action committees are keeping up a steady stream of campaign contributions to antienvironmentalist legislators, just as they have done for years.[72] In the spring of 1995 congressional Republicans were sharply criticized for drafting environmental reform bills with the help of industry lobbyists. Many Democrats and environmentalists accused Republicans of inviting industry to rewrite the Clean Water Act and to vastly complicate the ability of federal agencies to regulate polluters.[73]

The implication is that greening will be more of a corporate aspiration than a reality as long as political and business leaders struggle with the kind of backlash against command-and-control environmentalism that characterized the mid 1990s. But a backlash against command-and-control is not the same as opposition to greening. The challenge for industry and public policy will be to move greening into the shallow political currents now occupied by conflicts over traditional regulatory approaches. The deep and shallow currents of public policy and corporate management need to merge long enough to forge both support for and sustained efforts on behalf of greening.

The Clinton administration moved greening onto the national policy agenda by forming the President's Council on Sustainable Development and by creating the Environmental Technology Initiative (ETI), which is designed to stimulate development and use of innovative environmental technologies through technology and process redesign partnerships. The ETI's goals of economic competitiveness are a central feature of this initiative—indeed, the administration frames the ETI as a way of maintaining competitiveness in a rapidly growing economic sector.

The experience of the last thirty years demonstrates that manufacturing industries are capable of making tremendous strides toward greening. Certainly, the potential for greening today is much higher than it was in 1970, thanks to innovations in product designs, production processes, and technologies. To realize that potential, public policies must focus not just on individual firms and their products but also on the market demands made by consumers and other producers. Nevertheless, the problem is larger than just one end of the economy. It lies at the intersection of production and consumption. But the consumption end has been conspicuously ignored by major federal actors—witness Congress's refusal to impose substantial increases in the fuel economy of today's automobiles—and industry. There is simply no visible governmental or corporate leadership devoted to reducing extreme consumption and the perceived need for high-volume, high-polluting, high-obsolescence products.

Notes

1. U.S. Environmental Protection Agency (EPA), *EPA FY 1999 President's Budget* (Washington, D.C.: EPA, Spring 1998).
2. Stephen Meyer, "Environmentalism and Economic Prosperity: Testing the Environmental Impact Hypothesis" (Cambridge, Mass.: MIT Project on Environmental Politics and Policy, 1992).
3. Department of Commerce, *Pollution Abatement Costs and Expenditures*, MA-200(80)-1 (Washington, D.C.: Department of Commerce, Bureau of the Census, 1980, 1985, 1993, 1994).
4. Department of Energy, *Annual Energy Review* (Washington, D.C.: Department of Energy, Energy Information Administration, 1980, 1985, 1991, 1997).
5. EPA, *1996 Toxics Release Inventory Public Data Release*, EPA 745-R-98-005 (Washington, D.C.: EPA, April 1998).
6. Department of Energy, *Annual Energy Review*, 1991, 1997.
7. Douglas J. Lober, "Evaluating the Environmental Performance of Corporations," *Journal of Managerial Issues* VIII, no. 2 (Summer 1996): 184–205.
8. Faye Rice, "Who Scores Best on the Environment?" *Fortune*, July 1993, 114–122; and Ted Saunders and Loretta McGovern, *The Bottom Line of Green Is Black: Strategies for Creating Profitable and Environmentally Sound Business* (San Francisco: HarperSanFrancisco, 1993). See also the World Resources Institute's online annotated guide to environmental management and sustainability case studies at *www.wri.org/wri/meb/guide/gde.html*.
9. Lober, "Evaluating the Environmental Performance of Corporations."
10. Robert C. Repetto, *Jobs, Competitiveness, and Environmental Regulation: What Are the Real Issues?* (Washington, D.C.: World Resources Institute, 1995).
11. Stuart Hart and Gautam Ahuja, "Does It Pay to Be Green? An Empirical Examination of the Relationship between Emission Reduction and Firm Performance," *Business Strategy and the Environment* 5 (1996): 30–37.
12. Michael E. Porter and Claas van der Linde, "Green and Competitive: Ending the Stalemate," *Harvard Business Review* 73, no. 5 (September–October 1995): 120–134.

13. Doris Fuchs and Dan Mazmanian, "The Greening of Industry: Needs of the Field." *Business Strategy and Environment* 7 (1998): 193–203.

14. Douglas J. Lober, David Bynum, Elizabeth Campbell, and Mary Jacques, "The 100+ Corporate Environmental Report Study" (Durham, N.C.: Duke University Center for Business and the Environment, January 1996).

15. Stuart L. Hart, "Beyond Greening: Strategies for a Sustainable World," *Harvard Business Review* 75, no. 1 (January–February 1997): 65–76.

16. Alfred Marcus and William McEvily, "Environmental Competence in Two Small Firms," in *Better Environmental Decisions*, ed. Ken Sexton, Alfred A. Marcus, K. William Easter, and Timothy D. Burkhardt (Washington, D.C.: Island Press, 1999).

17. National Pollution Prevention Center for Higher Education (NPPC), "Strategic Environmental Management: Pollution Prevention Educational Resources Compendium," at *www.umich.edu/~nppcpub/resources/compendia/SEM.html* (June 1998).

18. *Radical innovation* is a term employed by Mark Rossi in "Environmental Technology Innovation in the U.S. Pulp and Paper: The Role of Public Policy," unpublished monograph, February 19, 1998, which he draws from James Utterback, *Mastering the Dynamics of Innovation* (Cambridge, Mass.: Harvard Business School Press, 1994), 200.

19. Hart, "Beyond Greening: Strategies for a Sustainable World"

20. Michael E. Porter and Claas van der Linde, "Green and Competitive: Ending the Stalemate," 120–134.

21. The Standard Industrial Classification (SIC) system assigns a number to all major industrial categories. The U.S. Census Bureau has replaced SIC codes with the North American Industry Classification System (NAICS). Information about NAICS and SIC can be found at *http://www.census.gov/epcd/www/naics.html*.

22. David Morell, ERM-West, Inc., personal communication, June 1994.

23. As with most self-reported data, there are limitations inherent in the TRI and thus in any conclusions drawn with respect to greening. First, companies are seldom, if ever, audited by the EPA, so some reports may not be reliable. Second, companies unfamiliar with the reporting requirements may have made significant errors in the first few years reports were due; indeed, the first year's reports, 1987, are often left out of new TRI analyses. Third, the TRI does not cover a host of other environmental indicators, such as energy and water usage, solid waste (nonhazardous) generation, and most greenhouse gas emissions. Fourth, the EPA does not rank the relative hazards of all releases reported to the TRI; thus, it is difficult to compare the health or ecosystem effects of large or small chemical releases. Fifth, chemical and process substitutions are not accounted for in the TRI data; thus, if companies reduced their use of one chemical agent, the TRI does not permit one to see whether they substituted that chemical with one of similar or lesser toxicity. Finally, there is no way of identifying "paper reductions"—reductions achieved by changes in the way a company estimates releases, or by decreases in production levels, or by plant closures. Despite these limitations, the TRI is the best, most complete database of industry toxic releases available in the world.

24. EPA, *1996 Toxics Release Inventory Public Data Release*.

25. Ibid.

26. EPA, *1995 Toxics Release Inventory Public Data Release*, EPA 745-R-97-005 (Washington, D.C.: EPA, April 1997).

27. EPA, *1993 Toxics Release Inventory Public Data Release*, EPA 745-R-95-010 (Washington, D.C.: EPA, 1995).

28. EPA, *1996 Toxics Release Inventory Public Data Release*.

29. EPA, *1995 Toxics Release Inventory Public Data Release*.

30. U.S. General Accounting Office (GAO), *Toxic Substances: Status of EPA's Efforts to Reduce Toxic Releases* (Washington, D.C.: GAO, 1994).

31. INFORM Inc., *Toxics Watch 1995* (New York: INFORM, 1995).

32. Ibid.

33. Ibid.
34. Ibid.
35. EPA, *Green Lights—Fourth Annual Report*, EPA-430-R-95-004 (Washington, D.C.: EPA, Office of Air and Radiation, 1995).
36. Emily L. Dawson, "Looking at Voluntary Participation Programs: A Case Study of Project XL at the Weyerhaeuser Flint River Facility," Senior Honors Thesis, School of Natural Resources and Environment, University of Michigan, May 1998.
37. EPA, Project XL, at *www.epa.gov/ProjectXL/* (March 19, 1999).
38. Walter A. Rosenbaum. "Why Institutions Matter in Program Evaluation: The Case of EPA's Pollution Prevention Program," in *Environmental Program Evaluation: A Primer,* ed. Gerrit J. Knaap and Tschangho John Kim (Urbana: University of Illinois Press, 1998); and Douglas J. Lober, "Pollution Prevention as Corporate Entrepreneurship," *Journal of Organizational Change Management* 11, no. 1 (1998): 26–37.
39. Stephen Schmidheiny, *Changing Course: A Global Business Perspective on Development and the Environment* (Cambridge, Mass.: MIT Press, 1992); Anne T. Lawrence and David Morell, "Leading-Edge Environmental Management: Motivation, Opportunity, Resources, and Processes," in *Special Research Volume of Research in Corporate Social Performance and Policy: Sustaining the Natural Environment: Empirical Studies on the Interface between Nature and Organizations,* ed. Denis Collins and Mark Starik (Greenwich, Conn.: JAI, 1994); and Thomas Gladwin, "The Meaning of Greening: A Plea for Organizational Theory," in *Environmental Strategies for Industry: International Perspectives on Research Needs and Policy Implications*, ed. Kurt Fischer and Johan Schot (Washington, D.C.: Island Press, 1993).
40. Gladwin, "Meaning of Greening," 48. The Coalition for Environmentally Responsible Economies (CERES) maintains a website at *http://www.ceres.org/.* The website explains the CERES principles and lists participating organizations.
41. Ricardo Sandoval, "How Green Are the Green Funds?" *Amicus Journal* 17 (Spring 1995): 29–33. One widely respected eco-rating of Fortune 500 companies is provided by the Investor Responsibility Research Center in Washington, D.C. at *http://www. irrc.org/.*
42. *Greenmoney Journal* at *http://www.greenmoney.com/* (March 19, 1999).
43. David Austin, "The Green and the Gold: How a Firm's Clean Quotient Affects Its Value," *Resources* 132 (Summer 1998): 15–17.
44. Patricia S. Dillon and Kurt Fischer, *Environmental Management in Corporations: Methods and Motivations* (Medford, Mass.: Center for Environmental Management, Tufts University, 1992); and Mark Dorfman, Warren Muir, and Catherine Miller, *Environmental Dividends: Cutting More Chemical Wastes* (New York: INFORM, 1992).
45. John T. Willig, ed., *Environmental TQM*, 2d ed. (New York: McGraw-Hill Executive Enterprises Publications, 1994).
46. Bruce Smart, ed., *Beyond Compliance: A New Industry View of the Environment* (Washington, D.C.: World Resources Institute, 1992); and Schmidheiny, *Changing Course.*
47. See, for example, Joel Makower, *The E Factor: The Bottom-Line Approach to Environmentally Responsible Business* (New York: Tilden, 1993).
48. Michael E. Porter, *The Competitive Advantage of Nations* (New York: Free Press, 1990); AnnaLee Saxenian, *Regional Advantage: Culture and Competition in Silicon Valley and Route 128* (Cambridge, Mass.: Harvard University Press, 1994); and Kenichi Ohmae, *The End of the Nation-State* (New York: Free Press, 1995).
49. Transactions costs are those borne by the players when devoting time and energy to bargaining and negotiating over what should be done to provide a collective good, who should bear the risks involved in the venture, and which institutional mechanisms should be used. They are associated with nurturing the personal ties that engender trust and build reputations. These costs result from uncertainties over how other self-seeking, rational players will behave and the task of devising mechanisms of assurance once an agreement on the production of a good is attained. They are the costs of long-term monitoring and interaction among the players.

50. Jacqueline Cramer and Johan Schot, "Environmental Comakership among Firms as a Cornerstone in the Striving for Sustainable Development," in *Environmental Strategies for Industry,* ed. Fischer and Schot, 312.
51. Michael E. Porter, "America's Green Strategy," *Scientific American,* April 1991, 168.
52. Joseph M. Petulla, "Environmental Management in Industry," *Journal of Professional Issues in Engineering* 113, no. 2 (1987): 167–183; Johan W. Schot, "Credibility and Markets as Greening Forces for the Chemical Industry," *Business Strategy and the Environment* 1 (1992): 35–44; R. H. Bezdek, "Environment and Economy—What's the Bottom Line?" *Environment* 35 (September 1993): 7–11, 25–32; and Cramer and Schot, *Environmental Strategies for Industry.*
53. EPA, *1996 Toxics Release Inventory Public Data Release.*
54. Lois R. Ember, "Responsible Care: Chemical Makers Still Counting on It to Improve Image," *Chemical and Engineering News,* May 29, 1995.
55. Ibid., 12.
56. Ibid., 11.
57. Ibid., 13.
58. Cramer and Schot, *Environmental Strategies for Industry,* 319.
59. Ibid.
60. EPA, *1987–1992 Toxic Release Inventory,* EPA 749/C-94-001 (Washington, D.C.: EPA, Office of Pollution Prevention and Toxics, 1994), and EPA, *1996 Toxics Release Inventory Public Data Release.* Figures were compared for firms in SIC codes 3571–3579, 3672, and 3674.
61. Elisabeth Kirschner, "Praxair Aims to Cool Fluorocarbon Dilemma," *Chemical and Engineering News,* July 24, 1995, 28.
62. Bruce Paton, "Design for Environment: A Management Perspective," in *Industrial Ecology and Global Change,* ed. R. Socolow, C. Andrews, F. Berkhout, and V. Thomas (New York: Cambridge University Press, 1994).
63. Braden R. Allenby and Ann Fullerton, "Design for Environment: A New Strategy for Environmental Management," *Pollution Prevention Review* (Winter 1991–1992): 51–61.
64. Paton, "Design for Environment."
65. Department of Energy, *Annual Energy Review* (Washington, D.C.: Department of Energy, Energy Information Administration, 1997).
66. American Forest and Paper Association, "U.S. Pulp and Paper Industry Energy Efficiency: Calendar Year 1993," unpublished report, November 1994.
67. Sharon Nizich, EPA, personal communication, September 8, 1995.
68. *U.S. Industry and Trade Outlook* (New York: McGraw Hill, 1998); Department of Commerce, Bureau of Economic Analysis, *Survey of Current Business,* Vol. 77 (Washington, D.C.: Government Printing Office, 1997).
69. Daniel Press and Daniel A. Mazmanian, "The Greening of Industry as a Problem of Collective Action" (Paper delivered at the annual meeting of the American Political Science Association, New York, September 1–4, 1994).
70. Deborah Vaughn Nestor, "Issues in the Design of Recycling Policy: The Case of Old Newspapers," *Journal of Environmental Management* 40 (1994): 245–256. From 1994 to 1998, the United States deinked recycled market pulp capacity increased from 704,000 metric tons to 1.75 million metric tons (*U.S. Industry and Trade Outlook*).
71. Ember, "Responsible Care," 13.
72. Larry Makinson and Joshua Goldstein, *The Cash Constituents of Congress* (Washington, D.C.: Center for Responsive Politics, 1994).
73. David S. Cloud, "Industry, Politics Intertwined in Dole's Regulatory Bill," *Congressional Quarterly Weekly Report,* May 6, 1995; and Stephen Engelberg, "Wood Products Company Helps Write a Law to Derail an EPA Inquiry," *New York Times,* April 26, 1995.

13

Climate Policy on the Installment Plan
Lamont C. Hempel

Climate change may be the most significant and enduring environmental problem of the twenty-first century, especially if it exacerbates
the late twentieth century's most pervasive and persistent environmental
problem—loss of biodiversity. Human alterations of climate epitomize what
are sometimes called "third generation" environmental issues: global in scale,
long-term in scope, plagued by scientific uncertainty, and seemingly unmanageable within the constraints of existing policies, practices, and institutions.
Prior generations of issues featured local and regional concerns about air and
water quality, land use, and nonrenewable resource depletion. They centered
on health-based, point-source regulation of pollution, along with natural
resource management. Today, they must share their place in history with a
new generation of environmental concerns and a new direction in environmental policy, one that is principally shaped by the worldwide implications
of enhanced greenhouse warming.

This new direction calls for more "glocal" and "intermestic"—that is,
transboundary and multilevel—approaches to environmental problem solv-
ing, while at the same time requiring more flexible, contingent, and collaborative forms of policy design and implementation. The policy approaches
and jurisdictional responsibilities that functioned reasonably well to limit
resource use and pollution in the past—at least when faithfully executed
and enforced—are proving inadequate for the emerging task of managing
the Earth's climate system. Despite extensive experience with sophisticated
policy instruments for managing air, land, and water resources, advanced industrial nations appear woefully unprepared to undertake climate stabilization. Because they emit over half of all anthropogenic greenhouse gases, their
reputations for environmental leadership are under attack both at home and
by critics from developing countries. The United States, which emits nearly
a quarter of all anthropogenic greenhouse gases, is the most striking example
of this. While unquestionably a world leader in many aspects of environmental protection, the United States has at times been viewed as the world's
leading laggard when it comes to climate issues.

In this chapter I will examine the basis for this perception within the
larger context of the international climate change debate. The role of U.S.
science and politics is unquestionably central to this debate, though it is clear
that developments in other countries have also played an influential and
sometimes decisive role. The focus here is on policy evolution and on the
political and economic dilemmas that have arisen in the course of interna-

tional negotiations over climate policy.[1] I will then examine these dilemmas as they pertain to problems and opportunities emerging within the domestic arena of U.S. energy policy. Each dilemma finds expression in the continuing struggle to transform contestable science and newfangled technology into prudent policy and economically affordable action.

"Political" Science

The conversion of science into policy is seldom a smooth process, particularly if scientific consensus is tentative—and therefore fragile—and the economic implications of that fledgling consensus are inimical to the interests of powerful stakeholders. The climate change debate exemplifies this better perhaps than any other issue of our time. Uncertain, potentially catastrophic, complex beyond human comprehension, and susceptible to costly overreaction and underreaction by policymakers, climate issues offer a revealing glimpse of what happens when probabilistic science meets the crystallized objectives of interest group politics.

While science has been a powerful force in environmental policymaking for several decades, emerging climate concerns have elevated science higher than ever before. These growing concerns have also helped to redefine the practice of applied science and the public role of scientists. Climate research represents a major impetus for the "new directions in environmental policy" envisioned for the twenty-first century. Until recently, science-based environmental policymaking was largely a matter of quantifying and managing potential harm to the health of people and ecosystems. Increasingly, however, environmental scientists are confronted with the inherently unmanageable and chaotic behavior of climate systems. As a result, science may never be able to predict adequately the changes in climate caused by human activity.

This growing realization has not been lost on political leaders, some of whom still yearn for a society in which science provides almost indisputable authority for policy action, and many others who are relieved that science is unlikely to reign over politics in the future, hence preserving their political options for dealing with what could be enormously costly, high-stakes issues of climate change.

Risk Assessment

Because it goes to the heart of policy decisions about energy, transportation, natural resource management, and many other issues, the climate debate can be characterized as a high-stakes political contest between "risk takers" and "risk avoiders." Risk takers oppose action unless there is solid proof that the benefits of proactive policy outweigh the potential costs of adaptation to climate change. Risk avoiders adhere to the so-called "precautionary principle," which calls for proactive policy in the absence of scientific proof, especially when large-scale threats with potentially irreversible outcomes are involved (see chap. 10 for a discussion of risk-based decisionmaking).

To be sure, simple dichotomies of this type fail to capture the enormous range of opinion that characterizes the views of climate change held by most citizens, scientists, business leaders, and policymakers. Moreover, framing the issue in terms of risk behavior presumes that participants in the climate debate agree on the probability and severity of climate threats. They do not. Nor do they agree on what constitutes risky behavior. For example, opponents of climate protection initiatives claim to be responsibly risk averse, arguing that it is the environmentalists and other "Chicken Littles" who are the true risk takers, foolishly promoting costly prevention measures that will disrupt our way of life and our free-market economy without compelling evidence that such measures are necessary. Environmentalists counter that such rationales merely shift the risk exposure to future generations. Inaction, in their view, poses the highest risk of all for our descendants, along with millions of other species.

Many scientists believe that enhanced greenhouse warming may have severe effects on human settlement patterns, food and freshwater supplies, energy production, and the health and integrity of natural ecosystems. Potential impacts include loss of wetlands and other wildlife habitat, increased frequency and severity of storms and droughts, reduced forest productivity, changes in species composition, ocean flooding, increased salt-water intrusion in estuaries, and a myriad of other problems resulting from interactive shifts in temperature, precipitation, wind patterns, sea level, ocean currents, and cloud behavior.

But it is also possible that climate change will occur slowly enough to permit incremental adaptation without severely straining the capacities of natural systems or human ingenuity. In the opinion of some scientists, the central challenge of climate policy will be "adapting to the inevitable."[2] Some regions may benefit from changes in climate, while those that are less fortunate may have plenty of time to prepare for a less favorable climate. In the long run, advances in science and technology may prove adequate to the challenges of climate adaptation and environmental protection, without having to alter human lifestyles and economic priorities. The key question in the face of potentially large and irreversible climate risks is whether it is prudent to assume that such advances will occur in a timely fashion. Moreover, even if human beings possess sufficient technoscientific capacity to cope with climate change, many other living species remain vulnerable to changes in temperature and precipitation. Their migration and adaptation rates may not be fast enough to keep pace with human alterations of climate.

Regardless of how the problem is framed, the debate over climate policy involves two key questions that inevitably bring together science and politics. The first question addresses the need for action on potential climate threats; the second addresses our ability to influence outcomes through public policy, market forces, life-style changes, and new technologies.[3] The usual response to the "need for action" question begins with a scientific risk assessment and ends with a political judgment about what constitutes an *acceptable* risk. The response to the "ability to influence" question begins with an assessment of

institutional and financial capacity and culminates in a judgment about political and technical feasibility, administrative competence, and the efficacy
of markets to implement decisions and policies.

Policy responses to climate threats are inevitably a product of such
reasoning, whether consciously and systematically or by some haphazard
process of trial and error. They are constructed not only from tentative agreements about what the facts are, but from even more tentative agreements
about what the facts *mean*. Positions on climate policy reflect *political* needs
assessments that, in turn, influence the funding and interpretation of scientific needs assessments. They also reflect beliefs about the desirability of government, market, technological, and life-style solutions—that is, the ability
to influence outcomes—that draw heavily on the claims-making activities of
scientists and political leaders. Hence, to understand the policy debate in this
domain, one must first understand the claims-making activities of scientists
and how scientific disputes about climate change get reframed to serve political ends.

Evaluating claimsmaking, particularly with regard to the perceived
costs of inaction or overreaction, requires a clear sense of where scientific
consensus reigns and where it gives way to disputes over data, methods, interpretation of findings, and "contaminating" influences of politics and economics. To assist in this understanding, it is helpful to review some of the
basic consensus about what today's "facts" are, as well as disputes over what
those facts mean.

Claims of Scientists

Life as we know it depends on the greenhouse effect, whereby incoming
ultraviolet radiation from the sun is partially absorbed at the Earth's surface,
redistributed through the oceans and atmosphere, then radiated back to
space in infrared wavelengths. Due to infrared trapping by natural greenhouse gases—mostly water vapor, along with carbon dioxide (CO_2) from
cellular respiration—the Earth's surface temperature is about 33°C (59°F)
warmer than it would otherwise be. Prior to the industrial era, outgoing
terrestrial radiation was roughly in balance with incoming solar radiation,
thanks to relatively stable concentrations of these natural greenhouse gases.
In this century, however, human activities have measurably "enhanced"
the greenhouse effect by increasing the concentrations of key trace gases—
principally CO_2, chlorofluorocarbons (CFCs), methane (CH_4), nitrous oxides
(N_2O), and tropospheric ozone (O_3 in the form of urban smog).

Atmospheric concentrations of CO_2, the most important of these gases,
are projected during the next one hundred years to double from pre-industrial
levels of about 270 parts per million by volume (ppmv), due primarily to
fossil fuel combustion, deforestation, and other large-scale transformations
wrought by industrial and agricultural development.[4] Unfortunately, there is
no reason to assume that concentrations will stop increasing at that point.
Because CO_2 has a long atmospheric lifetime, perhaps hundreds of years, lag-

time effects must be carefully considered in the formulation of policy responses. For example, if the world attempted to stabilize atmospheric CO_2 concentrations at the 500 ppmv level by the end of the next century, global emissions would probably have to be reduced to their 1990 levels by the year 2050 and then further reduced sharply during the second half of the century.[5]

The consequences of increased greenhouse warming are much harder to predict than the warming itself. While virtually all scientists agree that the chemistry of our atmosphere is changing and that the average surface temperature of the Earth is rising, there is much less consensus about the rate and magnitude of any resulting climate disturbances that can be attributed to emissions from human activities. Scientists recognize that other factors—some natural, some anthropogenic—may play a significant role in the observed warming. The only consensus is that a combination of greenhouse gases, aerosols (for example, sulfates, fine particles of dust, volcanic emissions), deforestation, and changes in our sun (for example, sunspot activity) may be forcing perceptible changes in climate.

The overall global climate trend can be summarized as warmer and wetter, with rising sea levels, but regional variations and microclimatic conditions make prediction hazardous. Modeling the interaction of feedback mechanisms for climate systems is exceedingly complex. Further complicating efforts at prediction are recent marine geochemistry studies suggesting that incremental global warming may trigger abrupt cooling by shutting down major ocean currents. Of particular concern is the enormous current that carries heat to the North Atlantic. Researcher's studying this ocean "conveyor belt" and its interactions with other climate systems have warned that global warming may cause sudden shifts in ocean circulation, plunging much of Europe and Asia into a steep cooling trend.[6] Such a shift could occur within a single decade, producing catastrophic consequences for agriculture and jeopardizing the integrity of major ecosystems. Findings such at these illustrate why many scientists and sophisticated policymakers no longer use terms like "global warming" and "greenhouse warming" to frame the problem, choosing instead the more neutral term "climate change."

Issue Evolution

The evolution of climate issues and policies can be roughly divided into the following five developmental stages: Stage I. scientific assessment (1950s–1988); Stage II. agenda setting (1988–1992); Stage III. policy frameworks (1992–1997); Stage IV. national targets and timetables (1997–current); and Stage V. contingent implementation (twenty-first century). Obviously, these stages overlap. The temporal demarcations represent approximate shifts in emphasis and in the preoccupations of policymakers. They serve to distinguish the relative importance of different activities in shaping the development of climate policy issues.

Scientific assessment has occurred and will continue to occur throughout each stage. But this does not mean that the visibility and influence of science remains constant over time. The focus of policy debate has already shifted somewhat from scientific risk assessment to the economic implications of recently adopted targets and timetables for greenhouse gas reduction. In the future the focus will presumably shift more toward political matters of implementation. And, if implementation follows its usual pattern, the focus will continue shifting as setbacks in implementation or advances in science and technology result in the reformulation of policy responses.

Like Anthony Down's famous issue attention cycle,[7] the five eras suggested here can also be thought of as common stages in the development of most major environmental policies. The cycle is almost certain to repeat itself as new questions and issues arise in both the scientific and political realms. Hence, it is likely that over periods of months and years climate issues will move on and off the policy agenda as successive advances in science alarm or calm the attentive public, and as displacement by other emerging issues takes place. It is equally likely that changes in economics, politics, and technology will provide an impetus for new policy frameworks and revised targets and timetables. All of these changes will in turn affect the scale and speed of efforts at implementing climate protection measures, not to mention the content of what is being implemented.

Each of the five stages or evolutionary phases that have helped to frame the climate debate can be described historically in terms of key issues, actors, and focusing events, beginning with the scientific production of climate research findings.

Stage I. Scientific Assessment

Although calculations of the greenhouse effect of CO_2 were made by Svante Arrhenius in the 1890s, it was not until the 1950s that scientists began to test the theory of global warming, using the Mauna Loa Observatory in Hawaii to measure a possible atmospheric buildup of CO_2.[8] By the late 1960s warnings by scientists about human-induced climate change began to appear in the popular literature. Because most scientists expected that the oceans would absorb increases in carbon emissions, these warnings were widely dismissed as unduly alarmist. In fact, many scientists subscribed to the view that global cooling was the more likely future trend, not warming. Lacking the yet-to-be-discovered evidence linking incremental warming to abrupt cooling, scientists initially debated climate issues in the either/or terms of "greenhousers" versus "ice agers."[9]

The debate over future global temperature trends provided a healthy stimulus for further climate research but contributed little to what was by that time a rapidly emerging environmental movement. However, as evidence of rising CO_2 and possible warming effects accumulated in the 1970s, the climate debate became sharper and more closely tied to questions of energy and environmental policy. Prominent scientists began to call for serious and sustained attention to the climate implications of energy consumption. For example, Wallace Broeker, one of the world's leading scientists on greenhouse geochemistry, argued in 1977 that the warming effects of fossil fuel combustion "could become the single most important environmental issue of the next 30 years."[10] Twenty years later, he amplified his claim, warning that greenhouse effects on ocean currents could spur catastrophic cooling in Eurasia.[11]

Stage II. Agenda Setting

Prior to the summer of 1988, the debate over global warming was largely confined to a few thousand scientists. It was only in the midst of that summer's intense heat spells and droughts that widespread media attention was drawn to the issue and public interest was piqued. The political focusing event came in the form of much publicized testimony before the Senate Committee on Energy and Natural Resources by Dr. James Hansen, director of NASA's Institute for Space Studies. At the invitation of then Senator Tim Wirth, D-Colo., Hansen testified that the "signal" of climate change had been detected with a high level of confidence and, furthermore, that human activities were almost certainly the major cause.

Within a week following Hansen's testimony, an international group of scientists and policymakers meeting in Toronto called for a 20 percent reduction in global carbon emissions by the year 2005. Convinced that conclusive evidence of atmospheric destruction would arrive too late for preventive measures to be effective, they implored world leaders to act on the basis of incomplete information. Greenhouse skeptics in science and industry, fearing that a small group of overzealous scientists were prematurely setting the policy agenda, began a lobbying campaign of their own to emphasize the uncertainty in the research data and the extent of counterevidence.[12] They did not have to dig deeply to uncover disagreement.

The resulting battle of the experts led to the creation of the Intergovernmental Panel on Climate Change (IPCC), an international scientific review body that serves informally as a "science court" of last resort. This high-level group of climate scientists and related experts advises world leaders on the technical aspects of climate change, its impact on human and other life forms, and possible policy responses. The U.N. General Assembly's establishment of the IPCC in December 1989 brought together the activities of scientific assessment and agenda setting in a highly visible manner. Almost from its inception, the panel's assessment activities strongly influenced the scope and pace of policy debate on climate issues. In fact, virtually all national and international climate initiatives to date have been crafted in light of the science assessments performed by the IPCC. By enlisting hundreds of the world's leading climate scientists and thousands of noted technical advisors and reviewers, the IPCC has become the principal source of authoritative information about the science of climate change and its societal implications.

The IPCC's influence on agenda setting in national and multinational policy arenas was heavily supplemented by informal groups of scientists and environmental opinion leaders. Anticipating the release of the panel's first assessment in 1990, more than 700 scientists, including 49 Nobel laureates, petitioned President George Bush to take prompt action on global warming so that "future generations will not be put at risk."[13] An even stronger action statement, the 1993 "World Scientists' Warning to Humanity," was signed by more than 1,600 senior scientists, including many Nobel laureates. This was followed in 1997 by the "Scientists Call for Action at the Kyoto Climate Summit," a document that included signatures from 104 of the surviving 172 Nobel Prize winners in science.[14]

These efforts by scientists to mobilize political leaders and the general public did not go unchallenged by skeptical science and industry groups. The resulting controversy marked a critical transition in the role of many scientists from detached observer to passionate advocate. Scientists, more than any other group, shaped the policy debate before 1992, but once they succeeded in moving climate issues high on the institutional agendas of governments, the political and economic determinants of policy became dominant once again. For some policymakers, this meant that scientific advice could be safely judged on the basis of its political and economic acceptability, rather than on its technical merits.

Stage III. Policy Frameworks

The political mobilization and media coverage surrounding the weather disasters of the late 1980s, the IPCC assessments, and the orchestrated warnings by prominent scientists succeeded in placing climate issues at the center of international environmental policy discussions, but they did not produce a ready consensus about *which* climate protection measures to adopt and how fast to introduce them. For that purpose, a general guide for climate action—a framework convention—was needed, one that could secure general commitments from many different nations without threatening to jeopardize their economic development with specific mandates. Recognizing this need, the United Nations established the International Negotiating Committee in 1990 to draft a climate policy framework. The committee's work culminated in the Framework Convention on Climate Change, which was signed by more than 150 governments at the Earth Summit in 1992. Today, over 175 countries are parties to the convention.

Although international in scope, the framework convention bore the unmistakable imprint of U.S. negotiators, who succeeded in keeping emissions targets and timetables for greenhouse gas abatement out of the initial agreement. This was in keeping with the Bush administration's steadfast position that abatement measures were too costly and that existing scientific evidence did not justify economic sacrifices. Instead of mandates, the United States and other industrialized democracies publicly embraced the nonbinding goal of reducing their own carbon and other greenhouse gas emissions to 1990 levels by the year 2000. Few, however, adopted effective strategies or policies for accomplishing this goal. They agreed merely to prepare inventories of their emissions and to adopt unspecified national policies for future abatement and mitigation.

While hailed as a major first step, the climate treaty signed in Rio de Janeiro permitted a great deal of political posturing. Whether naively or strategically, it combined very demanding objectives and very weak instruments for achieving them. The principal objective of the convention was, as stated in Article 2,

> stabilization of greenhouse gas concentrations in the atmosphere at a level that would prevent dangerous anthropogenic interference with the climate system. Such a level should be achieved within a time frame sufficient to allow ecosystems to adapt naturally to climate change, to ensure that food production is not threatened and to enable economic development to proceed in a sustainable manner.

Given the enormous emissions reductions needed to stabilize greenhouse gas concentrations, the nonbinding measures agreed to in the convention were widely viewed as palliatives. All parties agreed to develop emissions inventories and action plans, cooperate in research, and share relevant information and technology. But from the very start a division between North and South threatened to impede more meaningful action. Developing countries, by downplaying their role in future emissions and pointing to the heavy responsibility of the United States and other industrialized countries for past emissions, argued successfully for a two-track approach that confined the need for action initially to the North.

Separating the duties of rich and poor countries under the framework convention was essential for achieving international consensus, but it threatened to further undermine U.S. support. Countries that were already developed or in transition—listed in the Convention as "Annex I" parties—were assigned most of the burden for climate protection. This seemed acceptable at the time because these countries were annually producing two-thirds of global emissions. Today, however, annual emissions from non-Annex I countries, which include most of the developing world, are expected to surpass Annex I countries by as early as 2015. In anticipation of increasing emissions from the South, opponents have complained that the Convention sacrifices equity and science for the sake of political expediency.

On closer inspection, the comparison of annual emissions rates is itself highly political. Annual accounting methods attribute greater responsibility to developing countries than is warranted, since their *cumulative* emissions remain small in comparison to those of their industrial counterparts, and it is the cumulative emissions that determine the atmospheric concentrations of CO_2 and other gases. Given the long residence time of some greenhouse gases in the atmosphere, it may take until the end of the twenty-first century before developing countries surpass the industrialized world in cumulative emissions. Eventually, however, this unwitting emissions "race" is one the developing countries are likely to win. No matter how one calculates future greenhouse gas emissions, the expected CO_2 contributions of non-Annex I countries, es-

Table 13-1   Key Events in Climate Policy Evolution

1979:	World Meteorological Organization and U.N. Environment Program establish World Climate Program and sponsor first World Climate Conference.
1988:	Summer weather disasters are linked by mass media to global warming; N.A.S.A. scientist James Hansen testifies about climate threats before U.S. Senate (July); United Nations establishes International Panel on Climate Change (IPCC).
1989:	Leaders participating in the G-7 Summit endorse proposal for an international climate protection treaty.
1990:	IPCC First Assessment released, projecting mean global temperature increases of 3.5–8°C by the year 2050; Second World Climate Conference convened; U.N. establishes International Negotiating Committee to draft Framework Convention on Climate Change.
1992:	Framework Convention on Climate Change signed by over 150 nations meeting at the Earth Summit in Rio de Janeiro.
1993:	Clinton proposes energy consumption tax—the "BTU tax"—which is opposed by a majority in Congress; Clinton observes Earth Day with pledge to stabilize U.S. greenhouse gas emissions at 1990 levels by the year 2010 (April); U.S. announces Climate Change Action Program based on voluntary actions (October).
1995:	First Conference of the Parties (COP-1) is held in Berlin (March–April), resulting in the Berlin mandate, which exempts developing countries from any limits on emissions adopted in the near future.
1996:	Parties attending COP-2 in Geneva (May) endorse second IPCC Assessment, which includes projections of mean global temperature increases of 1.8–6.3°C by 2100 and a statement that "discernible human influence" on climate systems was now evident. The U.S., in a reversal of position, endorses idea of binding emissions reduction targets.
1997:	Clinton addresses special session of the U.N., calling for "realistic and binding limits" on emissions, but offering no specific targets for the U.S (June). Senate resolution passed 95–0 instructing the Clinton administration to refrain from signing any forthcoming climate protocol that does not include measures to be undertaken by developing countries (July). Clinton announces that the U.S. will commit to reducing emissions to 1990 levels by 2012, and then pursue further reductions (October). COP 3 is held in Kyoto, Japan (December), leading to agreements in concept on a protocol for binding emissions targets and timetables.
1998:	The Kyoto Protocol is signed by the U.S. at COP-4 in Buenos Aires, Argentina (November). Argentina and Kazakhstan break ranks with other developing countries by pledging reductions in their own emissions.

pecially China, loom increasingly large on the horizon. Hence the complaints of U.S. critics, while premature, may ultimately prove to be justified.

The cautious response of U.S. policymakers to the framework convention was strongly encouraged by business and industry stakeholders, who organized major lobbying programs to ensure that political leaders understood the potential costs of overreaction. Although their most extensive lobbying campaigns were reserved for later negotiations on emissions targets and timetables, these interest groups were effective from the start in framing climate issues as trade-offs between economic vitality and environmental risk. Opponents of aggressive climate protection policies, led by the fossil fuels industry's Global Climate Coalition and by business-funded public relations consortia, such as the Global Climate Information Project, pressed for inexpensive and, at most, incremental responses to the problem of greenhouse gas emissions.

Environmental lobbyists, led by Greenpeace, sought to counter industry opponents and policy incrementalists with sometimes confrontational tactics and media campaigns designed to alarm the public about the potentially catastrophic consequences of climate change. The resulting polarization—visible in the way issues were framed, political support distributed, and arguments constructed—continued long after the U.S. elections of 1992, severely limiting efforts by the Clinton administration to achieve a domestic consensus on climate policy. As a consequence, the administration's Climate Change Action Plan, which was called for by the framework convention and released in October 1993, relied almost exclusively on voluntary actions and very gradual shifts in energy consumption and investment. These measures quickly proved inadequate for achieving the national goal of reducing projected greenhouse gas emissions by roughly 100 million tons by the year 2000.

Stage IV. National Targets and Timetables

Following the agreement on a framework convention, a series of international meetings to refine and extend climate protection policy were held in Berlin, Geneva, Kyoto, and Buenos Aires. Known officially as conferences of parties (COPs), these meetings were prescribed in the framework convention for the purpose of providing a deliberative process out of which might emerge realistic targets and timetables for emissions reduction beyond the year 2000.

The environmental enthusiasm that set in motion the Earth summit and its centerpiece, the climate convention, had waned considerably by the time the first meeting of the parties (COP-1) took place in Berlin in early 1995. Despite this atmosphere, some delegates forcefully raised the issue of reduction targets and deadlines as a test of national commitments to climate protection. Although the United States continued its opposition to international mandates in favor of voluntary national measures, most of the parties agreed to a multiyear process from which specific mandates would be developed. It was also agreed that developing countries would be exempt from any new commitments for the time being. Somewhat presumptively, perhaps, this agreement became known as the Berlin Mandate. By calling for a set of "quantified limitation and reduction objectives within specified time frames," the mandate laid the groundwork for the Kyoto Protocol, which was negotiated almost three years later. By excluding developing countries from any new and additional commitments, it also created one of the most contentious issues for opponents of climate action to exploit during subsequent negotiations.

By the time the Second Conference of the Parties (COP-2) met in Geneva in July 1996, it was clear that at least fifteen developed nations, collectively responsible for over half of the world's greenhouse gas emissions, were not on course to reduce their emissions to 1990 levels by the year 2000. Members of the U.S. delegation used the Geneva meeting to promote reliance on international emissions trading as a basis for U.S. acceptance of binding limitations and time frames. The abrupt shift in the U.S. position was announced by Tim Wirth, then Undersecretary of State for Global Affairs and head of the U.S. delegation at COP-2. Wirth essentially repudiated the U.S. emphasis on voluntary action in favor of a "realistic, verifiable and binding medium-term emissions target."[15]

In response to these initiatives by the Clinton administration, critics at home stepped up their opposition to proposed mandates and performance standards.[16] By early 1997, a strategy had emerged whereby opponents publicly challenged the differential treatment of North and South called for by the Berlin Mandate. In essence, they appealed to the ordinary American's sense of fairness by insisting that the United States should not make any sacrifices for global climate protection that other countries were not willing to make. In July, the Senate voted 95–0 in favor of the Byrd-Hagel Resolution instructing the president to refrain from signing any prospective climate protocols that did not include developing countries in the prescribed actions. Although merely advisory, the unanimous support for the resolution signaled a major escalation in the climate treaty controversy.

Under mounting pressure from every direction, Clinton attempted in October 1997 to stake out a pre-conference position on acceptable emissions limits and time frames, announcing that the United States would reduce its emissions to 1990 levels by the year 2012 and pursue further, unspecified reductions after that time. Critics seized the opportunity to warn the attentive public that the White House was preparing to commit Americans to undertake sacrifices that would not be asked of many countries with which the United States competed in global and regional markets. As efforts to weaken U.S. commitments gained bipartisan support from some powerful members of Congress, further strains began to appear between U.S. negotiators and their European and Japanese counterparts. Only four weeks before the widely anticipated December meeting in Kyoto, U.S. negotiators began backtracking on the Berlin Mandate, arguing that developing countries should not be exempted from actions required of the Annex 1 parties.

It was against this backdrop that delegates arrived in Kyoto in December 1997 for COP-3, many expressing strong doubts about the prospects for a meaningful outcome. After eleven days of grueling negotiations, the nearly exhausted delegates came to agreement in an all-night session on the final day of the meeting. As part of the agreement, they established country-by-country emission targets using 1990 emissions levels as the baseline. The proposed Kyoto Protocol was to become legally binding ninety days after being ratified by 55 percent of the parties to the 1992 Climate Treaty. The protocol called for thirty-nine industrialized nations (Annex B parties) to achieve emissions reductions averaging about 5 percent below 1990 levels by 2012. The United States agreed to a 7 percent cut, though it should be noted that this translates into a 30–35 percent reduction from projected "business-as-usual" levels for 2012.[17] Members of the EU pledged to cut emissions collectively by 8 percent (though cuts by individual members would vary), while Japan committed to a 6-percent reduction.

The protocol was comprehensive in that it applied to all major greenhouse gases not already controlled under the Montreal Protocol for Ozone Protection. It also established a number of mechanisms to promote flexibility in national policy responses. Most important were provisions for emissions trading among Annex B parties (Article 17), joint implementation (Article 6)—a project-based crediting system for offsetting carbon emissions within developed countries—and a major new program called the Clean Development Mechanism (Article 12), which encourages developed countries to provide financial and technical assistance programs to developing countries for the purpose of achieving certified emissions reductions.

In other respects, the agreement left many issues unresolved, including one of great importance to U.S. negotiators: the form and extent of emissions trading to be permitted among developed countries. Also unclear was the degree to which compliance with the protocol could be made verifiable and enforceable. As in so many other policy domains, flexibility in climate policy came at the cost of increased complexity.

In November 1998, over 160 countries meeting at COP-4 in Buenos Aires attempted to deal with the problems of retaining flexibility in policy responses while promoting fairness in the allocation of responsibilities. Serving to remind his fellow delegates of the North-South divisions that remained, a representative from China declared that the only legitimate policy responses under the convention would be those that targeted the "luxury" emissions of the North without impinging on the "survival" emissions of the South. Fortunately, the divisions between North and South were not strong enough to prevent needed refinement and elaboration of the Kyoto Protocol.

Like the meetings in Kyoto, many of the achievements took place during an all-night session on the final day of the conference. Among the most important accomplishments were commitments to develop within two years monitoring and enforcement mechanisms for greenhouse gas abatement. Progress on emissions trading rules, the Clean Development Mechanism, and related technology and finance mechanisms was also achieved. The most important political accomplishment was the announcement by host President Carlos Menem that Argentina would break ranks with other developing countries and voluntarily reduce its emissions in line with the Kyoto Protocol—a pledge shared by the representatives of Kazakhstan and given serious consideration by several other developing countries attending the conference. Encouraged by symbolic support from developing countries and from a growing circle of U.S. business leaders, the Clinton White House marked the occasion by becoming the sixtieth signatory to the Kyoto Protocol. Rebuke by U.S. senators was immediate and strong, suggesting a difficult road ahead for ratification.[18]

Stage V. Contingent Implementation

In many respects, the era of implementation has not yet begun. International debate remains focused on interpretation and adjustment of the Kyoto Protocol. Parties to the convention are still weighing the economic implications of the protocol for their own trade and development agendas. As with many other treaties, national implementation efforts are likely to be contingent on the efforts made by other parties to the agreement, as well as on advances in science and technology, economic development, and perceived fairness. In short, implementation progress is likely to be contingent on multiple factors, most of which are beyond the control of national policymakers.

Although the precise course to be followed remains unknowable, the broad outlines of a probable U.S. implementation strategy are already discernible: make the cheapest cuts first, tie performance levels to the progress of other parties, and promote "no regrets" measures to limit and reduce emissions. Such measures (for example, energy efficiency improvements) serve collaterally to improve domestic economies, even if climate threats turn out to be false alarms. This strategy, which is popular in many countries, represents a compromise between bold international mandates, based on precise abatement targets and timetables, and voluntary, incremental domestic adjustments, based on the need for economic flexibility in policy responses.

The lack of correspondence between the relatively ambitious emissions targets developed by international negotiators and the rather anemic reduction measures promoted by domestic implementers is not surprising. As with so many other breakthroughs in international environmental protection, negotiators have tended to evaluate the success of the climate convention and protocol in terms of multilateral cooperation. Unfortunately, the ability of government parties to secure cooperation among themselves is probably greater than the ability of most governments to secure cooperation from their own citizens, in the form of reduced energy consumption, stronger protection of forests, and so forth. Within the United States, gaining the cooperation of other elements of the government may prove to be even more difficult than gaining general public support. Leaders of Congress declared the Kyoto Protocol "dead on arrival" (for ratification) unless China, India, and other major developing countries were prepared to join the Annex I parties in abatement efforts. Clearly, it was not agreement among countries that mattered so much as agreement among domestic publics over the quantity, direction, and timing of abatement measures. The ability of national governments to secure the cooperation of their own citizens probably remains the most difficult task in climate protection today.

The contest between international and domestic politics is not the only tension that lies in the way of effective implementation of climate policy. Throughout the 1990s, the climate policy debate has been embedded in a much older and more familiar debate about theoretically elegant policies versus workable programs. Solutions on paper have too often failed in practice, especially when the roles of policy designers and implementers have been functionally and temporally separated.

In the case of greenhouse gas abatement, the practicality debate has revolved around the use of market-based policy instruments—principally emissions trading—to meet agreed-on targets and timetables. The idea of trading is to allow those for whom emissions reduction is expensive to buy abatement services or emissions allowances from those for whom it is relatively cheap. Advocates of trading seek to harness the power of markets to ensure that climate protection measures are accomplished at the least cost and with incentives that encourage participants to achieve more than the minimum reductions required.

The United States has steadfastly maintained that the best way to inject flexibility and efficiency into climate policy responses is to rely on trading schemes. In fact, 75 percent of the costs of planned reductions in U.S. emissions are premised on trading approaches.[19] Critics contend that market solutions have been oversold; that they appear much more promising in academic circles than in real policy environments. Even some leading academic economists have questioned the feasibility of international trading to achieve binding targets and timetables. They point to the difficulty of finding allocation rules for emissions credits that would be acceptable to all the major emitters of greenhouse gases.[20] Noting the powerful tendency for parties to international treaties to behave as "free riders," some critics argue that the only workable climate policy is to tax fossil energy consumption or emissions.[21]

Opponents argue that emissions taxes are politically unwise and that their supporters are "out of touch with reality."[22] The feasibility of emissions trading, they argue, has already been demonstrated with the U.S. experiment in sulfur trading begun in 1990.[23] The only remaining obstacles to an effective trading system for greenhouse gases, in their estimation, arise from standard disputes over the allocation of credits, monitoring and enforcement measures, and questions about banking of credits. This last item has become particularly troublesome in the case of Russia, which seeks to bank all carbon emissions reductions that have resulted from its continuing economic crisis as "paper tons" that can be credited toward meeting future targets. In essence, Russia wants to treat a severe economic problem as a greenhouse gas solution, a view that critics regard as trading in "hot air."

Implementation of climate stabilization programs and policies, whether of the market-based, technology-based, or command-and-control (regulatory) variety, will require extensive cooperation between China, North America, the EU, and the newly industrializing countries of Asia and Latin America. Eventually, development and population pressures in developing countries will necessitate truly global levels of cooperation.[24] Because of large differences in the capacities and capabilities of these nations to curb their emissions, joint action will almost surely be guided by the principle of "common but differentiated responsibilities," whereby the richest nations are expected to undertake the most costly climate stabilization programs. If climate change turns out to be a catastrophic problem, urgent measures to stabilize both human population and per capita consumption of carbon-based energy and forest products may be needed. Implementation in this case would be further impeded by the fact that the political and economic consequences would vary tremendously throughout the world.

A related problem is that the physical impacts of climate change are likely to be felt very unevenly across countries and regions. Although this is partly attributable to the natural variation of climate systems, many of the most important climate effects may be the result of co-existent impacts of poverty, population growth and density, inadequate institutional capacity, and ecological vulnerability. Regions with large, impoverished, high-density populations, lacking efficient infrastructures and flexible social and political systems, are particularly susceptible to rapid changes in climate. For example, it is possible that small changes in climate could have large human impacts in some African regions, while comparatively large climate changes in North America or Western Europe might have relatively modest human impacts.

For all of these reasons, the course of future implementation of climate policy is likely to vary significantly from region to region, country to country, and even community to community. From the perspective of U.S. policy-makers, implementation success will depend heavily on development of in-centive structures that promote voluntary changes in consumption behavior. By far the most important of these center on energy consumption.

The Role of U.S. Energy Policy in Climate Protection

Mapping the constraints on climate policy formation and implementa-tion leads inexorably to matters of energy policy. Fossil energy combustion alone accounts for nearly 90 percent of U.S. greenhouse gas emissions, most of it in the form of CO_2. While other emissions sources—such as landfills, CFC-based refrigerants, and nitrogen fertilizers—emit greenhouse gases that are much more potent than CO_2, molecule for molecule, their aggregate and cumulative contribution to potential global warming remains far below that of carbon-based fuels. Further complicating the picture is the fact that coal, oil, and gas vary significantly in their carbon emissions per unit of energy pro-duced, with coal being the highest and natural gas the lowest. Hence, the most critical factors in controlling greenhouse gas emissions may be the choice of fuel type and the efficiency with which it is used. Given the enor-mous quantities of coal, oil, and natural gas used in global trade and devel-opment, it is not surprising that efforts to reduce carbon emissions through energy conservation and alternative energy technologies have become the centerpiece of climate stabilization strategies.

Under a business-as-usual scenario, U.S. carbon emissions are expected to increase by 32 percent from 1995 to 2015, due in large measure to an-ticipated retirement of nuclear power plants, which, in view of today's in-vestment risks, would presumably be replaced by fossil fuel-fired plants.[25] Meanwhile, low oil prices and growth in sales of fuel-inefficient vehicles, particularly sport utility vehicles, are expected to result in increased carbon emissions from the transportation sector. Given that U.S. oil imports have increased by about 40 percent since the 1973 OPEC oil embargo, and are forecast to supply over 60 percent of U.S. oil consumption by 2015, there is no escaping the conclusion that trade, climate policy, energy security, and American consumption behavior are becoming tightly interlinked.[26]

Efforts to reduce carbon emissions produced by rising U.S. energy consumption have involved three basic measures: (1) use of energy-saving devices and promotion of energy efficiency improvement; (2) desubsidization of fossil energy extraction and use; and (3) development of alternative energy technologies, such as hydrogen vehicles, wind turbines, photovoltaics, fuel cells, and gas turbines. The success of each of these measures depends to a large extent on the interaction of market and political forces in setting energy prices. While this is obvious in the case of desubsidization strategies, getting energy prices "right" (that is, internalizing externalities) is also fundamental for making alternative energy sources and efficiency improvements more attractive.

Energy conservation is by many accounts the key to emissions avoidance and reduction. While most experts agree that major efficiency improvements are both possible and desirable, there are sharp differences of opinion over which improvements are cost-effective, in which combinations, and under what circumstances. Even if climate concerns were to evaporate, many energy conservationists claim that investments in energy efficiency will produce large net savings by avoiding the costs of constructing new power plants and reducing energy consumption of households, manufacturers, and the transportation sector.[27] Those who are skeptical about energy conservation benefits argue that massive investments in energy efficiency, especially if induced by carbon taxes or draconian efficiency standards, will mean a lower standard of living for most of the world.[28] Many object to the notion that fossil energy prices should be increased now, as a matter of prudence, in order to internalize *potential* social costs of carbon that cannot be authoritatively estimated.

Still others argue that energy prices are already grossly distorted. Opponents of subsidies claim that efforts to perpetuate them, ostensibly to maintain economic stability, are more often than not the self-serving strategies of special interests who directly benefit from these redistributive policies. Direct government subsidies for fossil energy sources and technologies worldwide are estimated at $200 billion annually. U.S. government support, both direct and indirect, for fossil energy sources and technologies—particularly gasoline-powered vehicles—is well over $100 billion annually.[29] Reducing these subsidies inevitably pits environmental and energy conservation enthusiasts against powerful stakeholders in the energy, manufacturing, and transportation sectors. Not surprisingly, desubsidization has shown less progress than the other two major approaches to energy reform.

The hoped for "silver bullet" of climate protection is often said to lie in the third approach—alternative energy technology. Although oversold in some instances, technological solutions show genuine promise for reducing carbon emissions sharply by the middle of the twenty-first century, if not before.[30]Among the exciting innovations are hybrid electric vehicles made of super lightweight materials, solar-powered hydrogen production systems, and wind turbines, which presently lead the alternative energy competition with a growth rate in generating capacity of 25 percent per year. Advanced nuclear generators, while controversial, may also play an important role in future climate protection, although remaining problems with waste management, safety, and security are likely to perpetuate perceived risks within the U.S. investment community.

While most of these technologies provide carbon-free energy services, low carbon technologies, such as gas-fired absorption heat pumps and advanced repowering systems for fossil fuel-fired plants, are likely to contribute more to emissions reduction goals in the short-term than are technologies based on renewable energy. Even so-called "clean coal" programs are showing progress in reducing carbon emissions or capturing them before they can get into the atmosphere. Most promising of all in the near term are advanced technologies for energy conservation, such as super-efficient windows, lights, appliances, and electric motors, all of which provide alternatives that increase end-use efficiency and thereby reduce emissions, regardless of the carbon content of the energy input. The major impediments to widespread use of these technologies appear to be consumer ignorance about, or indifference to, life-cycle cost benefits and the associated tendency of consumers to apply very high discount rates to energy efficiency investments (that is, expecting a payback of between three and thirty-six months for any new energy-saving device).[31]

If the most promising alternative energy sources and efficiency improvements were combined and swiftly introduced, it might be possible to keep atmospheric CO_2 concentrations below about 500 ppmv—a level many scientists believe would produce only modest shifts in climate, thereby allowing humans and most other species to adapt without significant stress. Few energy analysts, however, believe that action of this magnitude is achievable without the use of steep carbon taxes and other drastic measures to wean consumers away from heavy reliance on fossil fuels. And even fewer believe that the United States is politically ready to accept the taxes or regulations such a transformation apparently requires.

Recent political history appears to support this view. A case in point is President Clinton's unsuccessful attempt in 1993 to establish a broad-based tax on the heat content of fuels—the so-called "Btu tax"—which would have added about $3.47 to the price of a barrel of oil (nearly 60 cents per million Btus, or 8.3 cents per gallon of gasoline). Coal, natural gas, and nuclear energy would have been taxed at about 26 cents per million Btus. Although energy conservation and carbon emission reductions were cited as benefits of the Btu tax, most of the public debate centered on the tax implications for deficit reduction and economic competitiveness. Critics argued that the tax would unfairly hamper U.S. firms competing in the global market. Congress, bowing to pressure from the fossil fuel lobby and energy-intensive industries, not only discarded the broad-based tax proposal in favor of a much narrower gasoline tax but also reduced the tax rate by about 50 percent (to 4.3 cents per gallon).

Framing the energy tax proposal as a large, new, and additional burden on the economy—an economy designed to run on cheap energy—ensured congressional opponents a victory in terms of public opinion. Carbon taxes and similar alternatives to the Btu tax have not fared any better in U.S. politics, although some have succeeded in Europe. Polling results show that climate issues have low salience for most Americans, and few are willing to support significant taxes on carbon fuels or emissions.[32]

Interestingly, when energy tax proposals are presented to the public in the form of revenue-neutral tax shifts, public opinion is far more positive. A poll conducted in the summer of 1998 revealed that over 70 percent of respondents favored a proposed tax shift from income and payroll to fossil fuel consumption.[33]

On a global level, tax shifting could have profound effects on greenhouse gas emissions of all kinds. When combined with government desubsidization strategies, carbon taxes could transform global and regional markets for fossil fuels, depending of course on how gradually they were phased in. A recent tax-shift strategy developed at the Worldwatch Institute would arguably lead to massive emissions savings within a few decades. The global strategy calls for sharp reductions in government subsidies for environmentally destructive activities—estimated at $650 billion per year—plus a gradual shift of an additional $1 trillion per year in taxes on income, savings, and investment to consumption taxes that "make prices tell the ecological truth" and, in the process, provide a net tax cut of approximately $500 for each American.[34] While such a massive tax shift and desubsidization effort appears politically inconceivable today, the long-term outlook for such measures may improve with developments in climate science, international trade, and public awareness of climate threats. In any event, the *political* climate for tax shifts may depend on whether those who pay the taxes personally experience shifts in the *physical* climate that adversely affect their surrounding temperature, precipitation, and sea level—and by extension their food, water, and material production systems.

Conclusion

In this chapter, we have examined the issue evolution of climate concerns in the arenas of both science and public policy, emphasizing long-term environmental and political considerations over those of a short-term economic nature.

From the standpoint of science it is clear that *certainty* is not only a luxury we cannot afford in the short run, but quite possibly an unattainable goal in the long run, due to the chaotic properties of climate systems. The current scientific ability to separate out observed trends from the enormous range of natural variability and "background noise" is quite limited. So much depends on confidence in scientific models by which to steer, since the expected climate benefits of planned emissions reductions will be virtually undetectable for many decades.

From the standpoint of policy, we have learned that the political rewards and penalties for climate action vary greatly. If climate threats are real, leaders who resist taking action today will probably be safely out of office by the time unambiguous climate impacts are felt by the general public. By the same token, leaders who push for precautionary abatement measures may incur high political costs, while finding no tangible climate benefits in the short term to serve as justification.

But what does this mean in terms of policy directions for the twenty-first century? We can only speculate, of course, but based on the preceding analysis, future progress in climate protection policy will depend to a great extent on how governments respond to the following three dilemmas:

1. The dilemma of temporally separated costs and benefits creates perverse incentives to defer needed policy responses. Inaction may turn out to be the most costly policy option of all, but because the costs are predominantly borne by future generations, the political system remains biased in favor of inaction. To overcome this bias, more attention will have to be given by educators, policymakers, and business leaders to the concepts of sustainability and intergenerational equity.

2. The tension between the goals of comprehensive policy and adaptive management continues to confound climate protection efforts. In the future, policy will have to be more adaptive and flexible, with abatement targets that can shift rapidly in step with scientific knowledge and economic opportunities, much like the "flip-flop" pattern of past climate change itself. While emissions trading and other market approaches look promising, it should be remembered that the virtues of markets are often oversold.

3. Good policy design will reflect the creative tensions between international and domestic politics, as well as the synergistic tensions between theory and practice in the choice of policy instruments and implementation plans. Eventually, policymakers may have to move beyond the conventional two-level test of international and domestic political acceptability toward a more "glocal" perspective on climate issues.[35] In the meantime, however, increasing efforts to distinguish "survival" emissions from "luxury" emissions will ensure that tensions within and between nations remain high.

Because of what scientists call "atmospheric commitment," there is little margin for error in today's policy responses to climate threats. Today's emissions are producing effects on climate that may not show up for fifty years or more. It remains to be seen whether the modest abatement targets and timetables already agreed to by the White House will be ratified and enforced in time to prevent massive new commitments. But even if they are—and such action is probably contingent on getting China, India, Brazil and other developing countries to participate in meaningful emissions reductions—the likelihood remains that major new and additional measures for prevention, abatement, and adaptation will be needed early in the twenty-first century.

Reducing atmospheric commitment will require *environmental* commitment on the part of policymakers. At the intersection of such scientific and political commitments will emerge the next installment in what is likely to be a long line of policy responses to climate change.

Notes

1. For a detailed analysis of climate negotiations, see the *Earth Negotiations Bulletin*, published by the International Institute for Sustainable Development, and available at *http://www.iisd.ca/climate*. See also Resources for the Future's climate policy Web site at *http://www.weathervane.rff.org*.
2. Martin Parry, Nigel Arnell, Mike Hulme, Robert Nicholls, and Matthew Livermore, "Adapting to the Inevitable," *Nature*, October 22, 1998, 741.
3. A systematic treatment of these questions is provided by Susan Walter and Pat Choate, *Thinking Strategically: A Primer for Public Leaders* (Washington, D.C.: Council of State Planning Agencies, 1984).
4. Since pre-industrial times (circa 1750), atmospheric concentrations of CO_2, CH_4, and N_2O have increased by approximately 30 percent, 145 percent, and 15 percent, respectively. The Intergovernmental Panel on Climate Change projects increases in concentrations of CO_2, the most important of the long-lived trace gases, from today's level of about 360 ppmv to 500 ppmv by the end of the twenty-first century, nearly double their pre-industrial level.
5. Intergovernmental Panel on Climate Change, *Climate Change 1995: The Science of Climate Change*, ed. J. T. Houghton et al. (New York: Cambridge University Press, 1996).
6. Richard Kerr, "Warming's Unpleasant Surprise: Shivering in the Greenhouse?" *Science*, July 10, 1998, 156–158.
7. Anthony Downs, "Up and Down with Ecology: The Issue Attention Cycle," *The Public Interest* (Summer 1972): 38–50.
8. Svante Arrhenius, "On the Influence of Carbonic Acid in the Air upon the Temperature of the Ground," *The London, Edinburgh, and Dublin Philosophical Magazine and Journal of Science* 41 (April 1896): 237–276.
9. William H. Calvin, "The Great Climate Flip-flop," *Atlantic Monthly*, January 1998, 47–64.
10. Quoted in "Is Energy Use Overheating World?" *U.S. News and World Report*, July 25, 1977.
11. Kerr, "Warming's Unpleasant Surprise," 156.
12. Among the most influential of these critics were members of the Marshall Institute, a small group of scientists whose opinions were repeatedly used by President George Bush's chief of staff, John Sununu, to oppose climate protection initiatives.
13. *Science News*, February 10, 1990, 95.
14. Signatures for the "Scientist's Warning" and "Scientists Call for Action" were collected by the Union of Concerned Scientists beginning in 1992. For a summary of the Union's efforts in this regard, see Warren Leon, "A Strong Statement," *Nucleus* 19, no. 4 (Winter 1997–1998): 1–3.
15. Address to the Second Conference of the Parties, Framework Convention on Climate Change, Geneva, Switzerland, July 17, 1996.
16. The largest of these efforts was a $13 million ad campaign opposing climate treaties launched by the Global Climate Coalition in September 1997.
17. Because of changes in accounting methods for carbon sequestration and changes in the baseline years—from 1990 to 1995—for three synthetic greenhouse gases, the overall 7-percent cut agreed to by U.S. negotiators at Kyoto represented no more than a 3-percent real reduction from President Clinton's pre-Kyoto proposal.
18. For example, U.S. senator Chuck Hagel, co-author of the 1997 resolution opposing unilateral climate action by the United States and its allies, declared tersely: "In

signing the Kyoto Protocol, the President blatantly contradicts the will of the U.S. Senate." (Press release, November 14, 1998).

19. President's Council of Economic Advisors, *The Kyoto Protocol and the President's Policies to Address Climate Change* (Report to Congress, July 31, 1998).

20. See, for example, Richard Cooper, "Toward a Real Global Warming Treaty," *Foreign Affairs* 77, no. 2 (March–April 1997): 66–79.

21. The free rider problem posits that "the wide distribution of expected but distant benefits in response to collective action provides an incentive for every country to encourage all to act but then to shirk itself." Ibid., 69.

22. Stuart Eizenstat, "Stick with Kyoto" (Response to Richard Cooper), *Foreign Affairs* 77, no. 3 (May–June 1997): 119.

23. The permits traded for sulfur dioxide emissions are expected to reduce emissions in the year 2000 by 50 percent from 1980 levels while providing savings of at least $2 billion to participating utilities when compared with conventional regulatory approaches.

24. See, for example, Frederick Myerson, "Population, Carbon Emissions, and Global Warming: The Forgotten Relationship at Kyoto," *Population and Development Review* 24, no. 1 (March 1998): 115–130.

25. Conference Proceedings (Overview), "Energy Technology Availability to Mitigate Future Greenhouse Gas Emissions," Paris, France, June 16, 1997, 37.

26. James J. Mackenzie, *Climate Protection and the National Interest: The Links Among Climate Change, Air Pollution, and Energy Security* (Washington, D.C.: World Resources Institute 1997), 22.

27. See, for example, Howard Geller, Jeffrey Harris, Mark Levine, and Arthur Rosenfeld, "The Role of Federal Research and Development in Advancing Energy Efficiency: A $50 Billion Contribution to the U.S. Economy," *Annual Review of Energy* (1987).

28. See, for example, Ronald Cooper, "Energy Conservation and Renewable Energy Supplies: A Survey," *Journal of Energy and Development* 21, no. 2 (1997): 259–281. Cooper complains that "many energy conservation enthusiasts have forgotten that the improvement in living standards among industrial nations has come about through technological development, exploitations of natural resources, and large increases in energy consumption, particularly electricity" (p. 269).

29. Christopher Flavin and Seth Dunn, "Rising Sun, Gathering Winds: Policies to Stabilize the Climate and Strengthen Economies," *Worldwatch Paper* 138 (November 1997).

30. Despite such advances, both U.S. and U.N. energy models indicate that large regions of the world are likely to remain dependent on fossil fuels for many decades to come—perhaps until late in the twenty-first century—even if major breakthroughs in alternatives can be commercialized rapidly in industrial countries.

31. Cooper, "Energy Conservation and Renewable Energy Supplies," 263.

32. Robert O'Connor and Richard Bord, "Implications of Public Opinion for Environmental Policy: Risk Perceptions, Policy Preferences, and Management Options for Climate Change" (Paper presented at the annual meeting of the American Political Science Association, Boston, September 3–6, 1998).

33. International Communications Research, poll conducted for Friends of the Earth, June 1998.

34. David Roodman, *The Natural Wealth of Nations* (Washington, D.C.: Worldwatch Institute, 1998).

35. For a discussion of the two-level approach, see Robert D. Putnam, "Diplomacy and Domestic Politics: The Logic of Two-level Games," *International Organization* 42, no. 3 (Summer 1988): 427–460. For a discussion of "glocal" perspectives, see Lamont C. Hempel, *Environmental Governance: The Global Challenge* (Washington, D.C.: Island Press, 1996).

14

Natural Resource Policies in the Twenty-First Century

William R. Lowry

In 1997, the city of San Diego announced the launching of its model Nature Habitat Plan, an innovative attempt to protect habitat while still allowing economic growth in the San Diego area. Secretary of the Interior Bruce Babbitt lauded the plan as the "latest and best example of a new era in American conservation."[1] What is the "new era" to which Secretary Babbitt refers, and what does it mean for natural resource policies? In this chapter I will define the "new era in American conservation" as a third stage in the evolution of natural resource policies. The first stage, running from colonial times to the end of the nineteenth century, involved little government control and a view of resources as perpetually abundant. In the second, ongoing stage, natural resource policies are developed within the public sector, allowing government a prominent policy-making role. In the United States, this role is carried out mainly by public agencies that are created by Congress. The decisions produced by these political institutions have always inspired controversy, but in recent years natural resource policies have become even more contentious. Many of the controversies discussed by Norman Vig and Michael Kraft in chapters 5 and 6 are connected to natural resource policies. Richard Tobin's chapter on population growth (see chap. 15) suggests that global conditions contribute to increased tensions affecting natural resource policies. Indeed, disagreements are inevitable. People hold vastly different views on the appropriate handling of natural resources. Preservationists want to see lands and waters set aside to be kept in relatively natural condition. Growth advocates see resources as opportunities for use and development. Between these two poles lies a wide range of perspectives on the most desirable fate of resources. As a result, natural resource policymaking is both important and controversial.

Dissatisfaction with conventional public sector mechanisms for resolution of disputes over land, water, and species has stimulated a variety of proposals that may well constitute a third stage in the evolution of natural resource policies. In fact, several projects described in detail later in this chapter, including San Diego's Nature Habitat Plan, offer evidence that a third stage is already under way. These new programs generally involve coordination between economic and environmental goals, innovative techniques for area management, scientific input into planning, and cooperation between people who have traditionally disagreed over the handling of natural resources.

The key ingredient to successful policies in this new era is the ability to synthesize different, and traditionally competing, preferences and perspectives.

In the first section of this chapter I will review conventional approaches to natural resource policies and some of the controversies that have motivated reform ideas. In the second section I will assess some recent proposals and evaluate how they might lead to policies that will better meet natural resource needs in the twenty-first century.

Traditional Approaches to Natural Resource Policies

During the twentieth century, public sector agencies assumed or were assigned responsibility for management of natural resources in the United States. This arrangement resulted from the perception that the absence of governing institutions led to neglect and excessive exploitation of lands and waters. The management framework that evolved is one of segmentation and differentiation: different types of natural resources are managed by separate agencies.

The Growth of Public Sector Management

Public sector management of natural resources developed in response to perceived abuses of lands, waters, and species. These perceptions are largely a product of twentieth-century life, although earlier warnings were voiced by such writers as Ralph Waldo Emerson and Henry David Thoreau. These early warnings, faced with a lack of understanding about environmental destruction, a public sense of perpetual abundance, and the omnipresent opportunity to move further west, received little attention during the first stage of natural resource policies. Starting in the late nineteenth century, however, more critical views gained prominence. The frontier had closed and there was increasing evidence that the lack of public land management was resulting in excessive and irreparable exploitation of resources: forests were disappearing; rangeland was losing productive capability; entire species were being destroyed.

In response, the federal government assumed a greater role in management of resources. That role grew during the second stage of resource policies until the 1980s, when serious questions were raised about their efficacy and efficiency. By then, the federal government owned nearly one third of the total U.S. land area and its policies affected natural resources even on lands that were not publicly owned. The institutional framework for federal management was organized around different types of resources whereby a designated agency managed specific categories.

Public sector management of natural resources produced varying degrees of success. In many cases practices that caused damage to land and water were halted. In other instances, however, the delegation of responsibility to a public agency led to detrimental policy-making arrangements: subgovernments—so-called iron triangles composed of local economic interests, congressional representatives, and public sector employees—emerged, each element assisting the others in abusing the resource under agency management. The most prominent resource agencies are discussed below. Statistics for these agencies are summarized in table 14-1.

Waterways. Largely because they provided such an important means of transportation, the earliest federal policies regarding management of natural resources concerned rivers and harbors. The federal government explicitly assumed responsibility for these resources in 1802 with the creation of the U.S. Army Corps of Engineers, which was charged with making and keeping inland waterways navigable. As its name suggests, the Corps early on displayed a fondness for "engineering" waterways, a fondness that translated into a policy emphasis on use of structural modifications such as dams, dredging, and levees that could divert and seemingly control wetlands and waterways. When Congress established the Bureau of Reclamation (BuRec) to pursue water projects in the arid West a century later, it too adopted a structural approach.

This structural approach to waterways was instituted within a subgovernment of water users. Members of Congress, by supplying the fiscal resources, could claim credit for dams and other water projects. Public agencies overseeing these projects were rewarded with larger budgets. And local economic interests gained federal dollars and the jobs and revenue that come with new programs. Both BuRec and the Corps thrived in this supportive environment and developed an ability to expand in response to shifting demands. Their statutory responsibilities grew to include flood control, hydroelectric power generation, and, eventually, environmental protection. The Corps in particular benefited, enabling it to command significant political resources (see table 14-1).[2]

Table 14-1   Statistics on Natural Resource Agencies (1995)

Agency	Acres (millions)	Staffing (in FTEs)[a]	Visits (millions)	Budget (millions)
Bureau of Land Management	267.1	11,046	58	$ 1,240
Bureau of Reclamation	8.6	6,954	87	859
Army Corps of Engineers[b]	12.4	27,661	386	3,339
Forest Service	191.6	40,712	830	3,362
Fish and Wildlife Service[c]	91.8	2,215	27	168
National Park Service	76.6	19,876	270	1,474
Total	648.1	108,464	1,658	$10,442

Source: U.S. General Accounting Office (GAO), *Land Management Agencies: Major Activities at Selected Units Are Not Common Across Agencies* GAO/RCED-97-141 (Washington, D.C.: GAO, June 1997), 20.

[a] A full-time equivalent (FTE) equals the number of hours worked divided by the number of compensable hours in a fiscal year.

[b] Figures are for civil works programs only.

[c] Figures refer to the National Wildlife Refuge System only. The full Fish and Wildlife Service employment totals about 6,700 (see app. 4).

Forests. National policies regarding forest resources in the United States have long centered on the goal of multiple use. These policies first appeared at the end of the nineteenth century amid growing recognition of the damages resulting from unsustainable logging. Created in 1905, the U.S. Forest Service quickly adopted the philosophy that forests should provide the greatest good for the greatest number of people. All potential uses of national forests, ranging from timber harvesting to watershed protection to grazing to recreation, were to be balanced. The Multiple Use–Sustained Yield Act of 1960 served to sanction this already ingrained agency ethos.

In practice, however, the multiple use policy often translated into "tree farming" of vast areas of national forests. Timber was the one forest output that could be easily measured and used to quantify incentives for local forest managers. The amount of boardfeet of timber produced from the national forests increased each year until the 1970s. While that total has dropped some since then, the devastating result of Forest Service-sanctioned tree farming is apparent in that today less than 15 percent of the original, old-growth forests remain.[3]

Parklands. The national park system contains what are often called the "purest" or most precious of America's natural resources. Beginning with the establishment of Yellowstone in 1872, Congress and the president have since set aside more than 365 parks, monuments, battlefields, and other areas containing almost 80 million acres of land (see table 14-1). The National Park Service (NPS) was created in 1916 to manage this system for the enjoyment of current visitors but also to preserve these sites in "unimpaired" condition for future generations.

Since 1916, the NPS has faced the difficult task of balancing these often conflicting policy goals of use and preservation. The agency has been criticized, with some justification, for everything from "locking up" precious lands to catering too much to concessionaires and developers. In fact, the NPS is one of the most micromanaged agencies in the federal government. The specific policies pursued and the lands assigned to be protected are as likely to be determined by congressional overseers as by agency personnel.[4]

Rangelands. Public rangelands are supervised by the federal government's largest landlord, the Bureau of Land Management (BLM). The BLM evolved in 1946 out of an executive branch reorganization of largely ineffectual public land agencies. Its creation stemmed in large part from the demands of cattle ranchers and their congressional representatives who recognized that without greater institutional control public grazing lands were doomed to "dust bowl" futures from overuse and severe erosion.

Because the new agency did not receive authorizing legislation from Congress until 1976, it developed its own policy emphasis, one consistent with the needs of its closest constituents—ranchers and miners. This service focus has been sustained through a classic subgovernment involving agency personnel, grazing and mining interests, and cooperative western state representatives and senators.[5]

Species and Wildlife Refuges. Policies toward species and wildlife refuges are largely the jurisdiction of the U.S. Fish and Wildlife Service (FWS). Like the BLM, the FWS was created by an executive reorganization of weak existing agencies. Ultimately, it gained responsibility for over 90 million acres of wetlands, hatcheries, and wildlife refuges.

A relatively vague policy mission of protecting the nation's fish and wildlife resources was made much more prominent with passage of the Endangered Species Act (ESA) in 1973. Congress mandated that the FWS list and provide for the protection of threatened and endangered species. Specific sections of the act called for designation of "critical habitat" areas for species recovery and for all federal actions to be cleared through the FWS when those actions might affect endangered species.[6] As discussed later, the ESA has been one of the most controversial of resource policies.

Other Land and Water Designations. The lands described above constitute the majority of federal land designations in the United States, but they do not exhaust the targets of natural resource policies in this country. The 1964 Wilderness Act called for the designation of undeveloped lands as wilderness areas to be kept in their natural state. Such lands can be found in national parks, forests, and refuges and are managed by the federal agency responsible for the relevant geographic location.[7] Public agencies are also responsible for maintaining the pristine nature of the wild and scenic rivers that traverse their jurisdictions. In 1968 Congress passed the Wild and Scenic Rivers Act, which designated twelve rivers as federally protected waterways. Since then, over two hundred rivers in the United States covering roughly 10,000 miles have become part of this system.[8] Finally, state and local governments have developed their own policies concerning natural resource protection. For example, every state has its own system of parks and reserves.[9]

Minerals and Energy Sources. Mineral and energy sources existing on public lands or in public waters are also controlled by federal natural resource policies. The United States is responsible for nearly one fourth of the world's energy consumption. The vast majority of its energy supplies comes from fossil fuel sources such as coal, oil, and natural gas. While imports play a significant role in supplying these energy needs, domestic production of energy is significant and involves public areas. Over the years, federal policies targeted at mineral and energy source protection have included regulation of the price of natural gas and other commodities, subsidization of oil exploration and nuclear development, and restriction of access to certain public areas. However, the United States has never had a comprehensive energy policy and today continues its precarious reliance on fossil fuels. Policies concerning hard-rock minerals remain similarly outdated, the primary statutory authority controlling their disposition being the 1872 Mining Law, described in detail below.[10]

Summary. Natural resource policies have evolved as a series of separate and fairly ambiguous mandates. These mandates include the structural emphases of the Corps of Engineers and BuRec; the multiple-use agenda of the Forest Service; the conflictory dual mandate of the NPS; the service mission of the BLM; and an unfocused, outdated approach to energy use. The failure of Congress to specify any overarching vision of natural resource policies is consistent with its tendency to delegate difficult tasks rather than make explicit decisions. The resulting segmentation and lack of prioritization has led to chronic disagreement and numerous controversies.

Public Sector Management Controversies

Over the past two centuries, public sector approaches to natural resource management have evolved in response to perceptions of abuse and neglect in the absence of adequate government supervision of resources. Recently, controversies over public sector management have fostered arguments in favor of new approaches. These controversies center on criticisms of natural resource policies as conflictual, inefficacious, and inefficient.

Lack of Consensus. Consensus over the ultimate disposition of natural resources has never existed. In recent decades, however, the intensity of disputes between different advocacy groups has escalated dramatically.

The growth of the environmental movement since the late 1960s has spawned a variety of groups focused on natural resource issues (see chap. 3). Some of these groups, such as the Sierra Club, have been around for over a century, but have only recently become consciously political. Others, such as Friends of the Earth and Earth First!, formed precisely to pursue a less compromising, more confrontational approach to resource preservation than their more traditional counterparts. While finding consensus within the environmental community has never been easy, in recent years the splits between these groups have been explicit and intense. An accompanying increase in confrontational tactics has occurred at the state level as well.[11]

Opponents of environmental groups have also become much more visible and outspoken. The Sagebrush Rebels of the 1970s, a group focused on diminution of federal authority, gave way to the Wise Use and County Supremacy movements in the 1980s and 1990s. Under an umbrella goal of "find[ing] ways to use the earth wisely," the Wise Use movement specifically proposes more development of public lands and increased construction of visitor accommodations in places such as national parks.[12] Wise Users argue that the Earth is more resilient than environmentalists think and that resources are limited only when people fail to find new sources or approaches. Wise Use leaders explicitly encourage oil development in the Arctic National Wildlife Refuge and timber production in the Tongass National Forest.[13] Both places are wilderness areas in Alaska, highly regarded by environmentalists who adamantly oppose Wise Use proposals. Consistent with some Wise Use demands, the County Supremacy movement calls for a drastic reduction in the role of the federal government in management of natural resources. Proponents maintain that management is more appropriately carried out at the local level.[14]

The heightened intensity of debate between interest groups over natural resource policies has often been matched by confrontations between the two major political parties. For example, Congress passed the monumental Alaska Lands Act of 1980 only after much heated debate and several years of filibusters. Differences between the parties intensified during the 1980s as the Reagan administration pursued a deregulatory agenda that included selling off large parcels of public lands and opening up other areas for oil, gas, and mineral development. Ronald Reagan's first secretary of the interior, James Watt, was a lightning rod for controversy. His explicit goals for development of public lands and his penchant for controversial statements led to petition drives by environmental groups and environmentally minded Democrats demanding his removal. Ultimately, calls for his resignation sounded within the ranks of the Republican Party as well. Even after Watt left office in 1983, unresolved issues such as the debate over the Arctic National Wildlife Refuge continued to fester through the 1990s.[15]

When the Republicans gained the majority position in Congress in 1995 and began considering major changes in environmental laws, party differences were again magnified.[16] An early indication of the Republican agenda occurred when the new majority party changed the name of one major House committee from "Natural Resources" to just "Resources." Party differences became increasingly apparent in specific debates, most notably the one over reauthorization of the Endangered Species Act. A Republican task force headed by representatives Don Young of Alaska and Rich Pombo of California initiated a series of hearings designed to highlight the impositions on property owners caused by protection of species. Democratic supporters of the ESA protested. Subsequently, even moderate Republicans called for more even-handed hearings and greater input from scientists as well as propertied interests. Eventually, Speaker of the House Newt Gingrich of Georgia encouraged his party to find less confrontational resolutions to ESA issues.[17]

Many of these debates are now being fought in the courts. Property rights advocates have gained considerable attention in recent years as a result of "takings" litigation. These cases (see chap. 7) involve claims that government actions may affect the use of private property to the point of unlawful violation of the Fifth Amendment. The key constitutional clause is the prohibition against "private property taken for public use without just compensation." Since the 1992 case of *Lucas v. South Carolina Coastal Commission*, federal courts have often restricted perceived government interventions in development of private property. In many ways, these cases and the land rights groups pursuing them have shifted the debate from controversy over use of public lands to reconsideration of just how "public" these lands really are.[18]

Lack of Efficacy. The second stage of natural resource policies produced many positive results such as the recovery of some endangered species and an enviable system of national parks. For all the positives, however, the lack of successes in many other issue areas has received considerable attention in recent years.

Some of these critiques are directed at areas of apparent success. The warnings regarding inefficacious protection of endangered species have become ominous and prominent. Good news concerning revitalization of specific species such as the bald eagle and California condor is tempered by the fact that hundreds of species await listing or specific plans for recovery. Prominent scientists warn that "humanity has initiated the sixth great extinction spasm, rushing to eternity a large fraction of our fellow species in a single generation" and point out the lack of systematic progress in protection.[19] Even the most revered of natural resources, the national parks, have been the subject of much concern lately. Parks are often characterized as overcrowded and excessively commercial. While not necessarily blaming the NPS, observers and agency personnel themselves have questioned the effectiveness of current practices in pursuing preservation goals. In an internal review commemorating the agency's seventy-fifth anniversary, the NPS concluded that "there is a wide and discouraging gap between the Service's potential and its current state, and the Service has arrived at a crossroads in its history."[20]

Other complaints focus on how resources are used. Major floods in the Midwest and elsewhere during the 1990s elicited compelling questions regarding the structural policy approach of the Corps of Engineers and the Bureau of Reclamation. According to critics, the subgovernment that traditionally dominates water policy decisions produced modifications to riverways resulting in a loss of floodplains that contributed to flooding during periods of high precipitation and ensuing severe property damage.[21] These criticisms renewed debates over the historical tendency of the Corps and BuRec to support structural modifications to riverways and their ability to justify such changes using questionable cost-benefit analyses. Even relatively favorable assessments of Corps behavior have identified instances of inflated benefits and unrealistic interest rates producing positive calculations encouraging project initiation when in fact more objective analyses would have scrapped those proposals.[22]

Often using the same theoretical construct of subgovernments, analyses of Forest Service behavior have been critical as well. Critics suggest that catering to timber interests with the use of clearcuts and other land abuses have left the national forests on the verge of losing their regenerative abilities.[23]

Lack of efficiency. Natural resource policies are also criticized for inefficiency. For example, not only do the structural policies of the Corps contribute to flooding, but they cost significant amounts of taxpayer money both in capital contributions up front and in disaster relief afterwards. Many of these arguments assess blame to bureaucrats who, at least theoretically, have few incentives to pursue efficient behavior.[24]

Critics are particularly vocal in the cases of the Forest Service and the Bureau of Land Management. The Forest Service annually brings in less revenue than it spends. This deficit is largely the result of subsidies to loggers who pay below-market rates for timber; recreationists, who often pay no fees to use forest lands, also contribute. The price to American taxpayers is millions of dollars each year.[25] The BLM has been chastised for years for its subsidization of grazing and mining. The BLM traditionally spends two to three times as much on administering an acre of rangeland than it receives in grazing fees.[26]

The easiest target for inefficiency criticism involves mining fees and royalties paid on use of public lands. These prices are still determined by the 1872 Mining Law and are therefore incredibly low or even nonexistent. Basically, mining companies can patent claims to public land at 1872 prices (generally $5 per acre) and then, if they spend a minimum of $100 per year on improvements, can treat the land like private property. Unlike the 8- to 12-percent royalty payments from mining of coal, oil, or natural gas, mining of hard-rock minerals involves no payment of royalties at all. By simply imposing an 8-percent royalty on hard-rock minerals millions of dollars of revenue could be generated every year. Instead, mining companies enjoy the ultimate sweet deal. In 1995, for example, ASARCO Inc. patented 347 acres of national forest containing an estimated $2.9 billion worth of minerals for just $1,735.[27] Attempts to change such gross underpricing of public lands have consistently been unsuccessful in the face of stiff opposition from western lawmakers sympathetic to mining interests. As recently as 1998, Clinton administration attempts at reform led by Secretary Babbitt were stopped by the mining lobby and their congressional allies.[28]

The lack of emphasis on efficiency is noticeable in other natural resource policies as well. Until recent years, entrance and user fees in national parks and other areas have been quite low compared to what visitors might pay for other recreational venues. Further, until 1996 revenue collected from these fees did not stay in the parks; instead, it went into the general treasury to be spent on everything from welfare to defense.[29] Park employees had little incentive to ensure adequate fee collection or support higher fees. Contracts for concessionaires operating on public lands have also been notoriously unprofitable. In 1989, for example, national park concessions generated only a 2.2-percent return to the government.[30]

Summary. Criticisms regarding inefficacious and inefficient use of natural resources are summarized in table 14-2. These problems have fueled demands for change in natural resource policies. When criticisms reinforce one another, they are particularly powerful arguments for reform. In numerous instances, for example hard-rock mining and clear-cutting, conventional policies have been both economically inefficient and environmentally destructive. This creates the potential for development of powerful coalitions between fiscal conservatives and environmentalists.[31]

Awareness of egregious abuses of economic and environmental principles are already causing breaks in strong traditional usage patterns. For example, the Florida Everglades ecosystem suffered for decades as its wetlands were removed to create sugar farms and its waterways were inundated with polluted farm runoff. Intensive agricultural activity was facilitated by federal policies that kept sugar prices high by restricting foreign imports.[32] These policies made little environmental or economic sense. Since the mid 1990s, however, new plans have been drawn to take thousands of acres of sugar farms out of production and restore some of the water quality to the ecosystem.

Table 14-2   Criticisms of Existing Resource Policies

Resource	Efficacy	Efficiency
Waterways	Destroyed floodplains; destroyed wetlands	Dollar losses from flooding; unjustified capital expenses
Forests	Excessive clear-cutting; damaged habitat/topsoil	Subsidized logging; subsidized recreation
Parklands	Inadequate protection; excessive commercialization	Subsidized concessions; subsidized recreation
Species	Inadequate protection; insufficient habitat	High expenditures on some species; impacts on business/jobs
Minerals	Use of fragile areas; failure to reclamate	Subsidized development; artificially low fees

Another example of change involves the behavior of the Forest Service. In some areas the agency is now more likely to emphasize environmental concerns than in previous periods of intense tree farming.[33] However, recent actions involving salvage logging raise doubts about dramatic change. Salvage logging occurs when certain trees in forests are deemed unhealthy. The presence of such trees provides justification for wholesale clearing in the affected sections, prompting the cutting of both diseased and healthy trees. In 1995, an attachment to an appropriations bill allowed the Forest Service to bypass other environmental laws in declaring areas suitable for salvage logging. After President Bill Clinton reluctantly signed the appropriations bill, this salvage logging rider facilitated a surge in cutting in many national forests.

Recent Proposals for Institutional Changes

With the twenty-first century comes increasing pressure for changes in natural resource policies. Certainly, suggestions for different approaches have existed for quite some time, and various proposals have been debated since lands were first declared public spaces. However, demands for systematic reconsideration of these policies have become increasingly prominent since the early 1980s.[34] Change now seems inevitable. Indeed, many new approaches are already being tried on a fairly large scale. In the next sections we will look at these various proposals for institutional change according to their major (not sole) emphasis: privatization, devolution, prioritization, or syntheses.

Privatization

Much of the support for major overhaul of natural resource policies derives from demands to privatize the public sector. Privatization proposals are motivated by the recognition that scarce natural resource commodities can theoretically be used in ways that maximize the value of net output. Advocates criticize public bureaucracies as centralized and inefficient and claim that without direct incentives, agency employees will not manage natural resources to achieve the greatest benefits for society. Privatizing resource policies, particularly through establishment of private property rights, will enable the use of market-determined prices to provide measures of true social preference. As one proponent writes, "the essential notion is to grant private property rights to own and control the land itself, fee simple, and thus internalize the significant external benefits and costs that under government ownership are a commons, resulting in inefficient production, investment, and distribution decisions."[35]

Privatization proposals received considerable attention in the 1980s. A supportive President Reagan used Executive Order 12348 to establish a Property Review Board to oversee the selling off of numerous federal properties under his administration's Federal Real Property Initiative. The Board's stated target was to raise $17 billion over five years, but many privatization advocates encouraged much more extensive action. Some called for divesting major portions of public lands to the marketplace. One study critical of the BLM asserted the "need for secure property rights to the western range."[36] Today, privatization proposals are still offered as solutions to many resource issues. Recently, scholars at the Political Economy Research Center (PERC) in Montana made forceful arguments in favor of privatizing instream water flows.[37]

Privatization proposals are compelling for several reasons, not the least of which are persuasive analyses of past public sector failures. But they are not immune to criticism. For one, most such proposals are based on assumptions of an idealized market economy in which perfect knowledge and proper incentives always exist. Such conditions are, as one critic notes, "elegant, alluring, and hopeless."[38] Second, while markets are well suited to reveal individual preferences, they are less adept at assessing collective values for qualities such as clean air and water. Law professor Joseph Sax notes, "there are collective values both important and distinctive to the political community."[39] Third, the emphasis on efficiency may neglect crucial questions of equity, questions that may only be resolved through distinctions between different types of land and resources.[40] Fourth, critics argue that people benefit just by knowing that certain resources, such as preserved lands, are there for perpetuity. Privatization advocates counter that if there is a demand, then private ownership will retain wilderness conditions.[41] However, the long-term effects of privatization are anything but certain. Economists recognize that markets do not easily assess demand from future generations. As Nobel Laureate Robert Solow says, "the future is not adequately represented in the market, at least not the far future."[42]

Privatization proposals are most compelling when applied to commodity extraction policies such as those guiding timber harvesting. Scholars at the pro-market PERC concur, admitting: "The case for private management is strongest on lands that are valued primarily for commodity production, since the ease of establishing property rights prevents external effects."[43] These proposals also offer valuable lessons for the appropriate pricing of resource uses ranging from production to recreation. They are less successful at valuing wilderness and land preservation efforts.

Devolution

Devolution proposals call for decentralization of natural resource policies to the state, local, or county levels. Inspired by severe distrust of the federal government (see chap. 2), advocates of these proposals argue that state and local governments are much more attuned to the needs of their constituents and much more capable of addressing specific circumstances affecting natural resources within their jurisdiction. Proponents argue that such transfers of power would facilitate wiser decisionmaking and be more consistent with the spirit of localized democratic processes.[44]

Support for such proposals remains inconsistent. The Sagebrush Rebellion received considerable attention in some state legislatures in the late 1970s. The Nevada legislature, for example, passed legislation in 1979 claiming jurisdiction over the 48 million acres of BLM land that constitutes nearly 80 percent of its territory. Other western states (Arizona, New Mexico, Utah, and Wyoming) followed suit, but similar measures failed elsewhere (notably, in California, Colorado, and Montana).[45] Sporadic support since then, even in western states where so much federal land is located, has slowed the momentum of devolution proposals. In fact, analysts have found no correlation between the percentage of federal land in a state and the degree of state support for devolution. Rather, individual legislators are more likely to support devolution if they are Republicans and represent a less densely populated area.[46] While the Wise Use and County Supremacy movements have assumed a leadership role in pushing these ideas, they continue to find little support either through popular referenda or judicial rulings.[47]

If devolution were in fact adopted, how would it affect natural resource policies? Scholars have offered predictions that cover a wide range of possible outcomes, from intensive development as state legislatures cater to and compete for business and industry to increased environmental regulation as local citizens worry more about their own spaces.[48] From my own research on state approaches to pollution control and park management, I would expect three outcomes. First, empowered states would display considerable variance in emphases. Second, many policies would be altered significantly. One need look no further than comparisons of national and state parks to see how different incentives at the state level, in particular a greater emphasis on self-sufficiency, have led to more development and greater commercialization of parks at subnational levels. Third, conflict over resource usage would not be reduced; it would simply resume at more local levels of government.[49]

While current rhetoric in American politics continues to call for a transfer of regulatory power to state governments, wholesale devolution remains unlikely. Support for such a shift is inconsistent even in areas where it might be most expected. Overall, opposition to devolution has been and remains strong.[50]

Prioritization

Prioritization, while retaining a significant role for the federal government in natural resource policymaking, would require a shift in regulatory emphasis toward redefining goals. Led largely by biologists and ecologists, advocates urge high priority for the principles of biodiversity and ecosystem management. Biodiversity refers to all components of life in a given region, their distribution, and interrelationships. Ecosystem management proposes to protect biodiversity through dynamic use of scientific techniques, such as Geographic Information Systems, over long periods of time. Its goal is to conserve native species and ecological types in areas large enough to sustain diversity, evolutionary processes, and genetic potential.[51]

While the roots of scientific management of ecosystems are deep, dating formally to President Theodore Roosevelt and forester Gifford Pinchot, official adoption of these goals by federal institutions has proceeded slowly. Proponents of prioritization have been critical of existing efforts to protect natural resources as mere landscape maintenance that does not really address ecological issues, as patchwork protection that does not conserve enough area to facilitate migratory patterns of species, or as simply a collection of fragmented efforts that do not afford holistic protection of areas or species. As one author concluded in 1994, "because various land management agencies have different missions and mandates, each agency views ecosystem management differently."[52] Thus, even high profile areas such as the Greater Yellowstone Ecosystem are affected by an uncoordinated set of federal and state agencies as well as by private landowners.

Recent developments suggest an increasing acceptance of the ideas of biodiversity and ecosystem management among federal agencies. The Gap Analysis Project was initiated by the Fish and Wildlife Service in the late 1980s to assess "gaps" in habitat protection necessary to species preservation. In 1991 the Keystone National Policy Dialogue on Biological Diversity brought together various interests in an attempt to forge common goals. Members of some agencies have also expressed at least rhetorical support for biodiversity goals, although real acceptance of ecosystem goals among personnel remains uncertain.[53]

Projects emphasizing these goals have been attempted in various settings. The NPS has had a plan on its books since the early 1970s for systematic representation of diverse ecosystems, although it has received neither the funds nor the commitment from political leaders to see it implemented.[54] The National Forest Management Act of 1976 called for comprehensive ecological planning and maintenance of biological diversity. This legislation has contributed some legitimacy to various attempts to make forest management practices more ecologically oriented. The Forest Service has attempted to establish Research Natural Areas to protect all types of reserves, but so far most are too small to sustain many vegetation types. [55] The U.S. Environmental Protection Agency (EPA) has recently attempted to protect aquatic habitats using a watershed approach. In doing so, agency officials are recognizing that "environmental protection should be place-based, rather than environmental media- or national program-based." [56] Finally, in a review of over one hundred ecosystem management projects in the United States, one group of analysts admits that, while obstacles have proven challenging and implementation remains preliminary, they are generally "hopeful" about future progress. [57]

Two major initiatives at prioritization have received official endorsement from the Clinton administration. Difficulties in their implementation illustrate the complexities of pursuing such wide institutional changes. Secretary of the Interior Bruce Babbitt established a National Biological Service to survey and identify the biological resources of the United States. The goal was identification of critical ecosystems and habitats so that protection of biodiversity could occur on a more comprehensive scale. However, the program has received little financial support from Congress. A second effort has been more visible. Stimulated by controversial court cases involving protection of the northern spotted owl in the Pacific Northwest, the administration encouraged development of a wide-ranging project to protect old-growth forest ecosystems. Planning involved as many as four different federal agencies and hundreds of scientists. Their ecosystem management plan for the Northwestern forests has been called a "blueprint" for ecosystem management. The plan includes a system of forest and aquatic reserves, strong emphasis on scientific input, and dynamism through the inclusion of adaptive areas for experimentation. However, others remain less confident of success, warning that planning, like talk, is cheap. [58]

Efforts to prioritize biodiversity and ecosystem management within natural resource policies have made some progress. However, controversy remains and full implementation is stalled. Overall commitment from most political leaders has been inconsistent at best. Further, the term *ecosystem* is used so frequently that it often defies precise definition. As a result, managers may still be pursuing goals that are not ecologically or economically sound. Many "federal land managers have hitched their wagon to ecosystem management" without knowing quite where that wagon will take them. [59]

Achieving Sustainability: Syntheses

Perhaps the most promising reform proposals for natural resource policies are those that combine different institutional forms to provide innovation and synergy. These approaches are being attempted in the international as well as the domestic arena. [60] Such efforts may bring together public and private sectors and involve different levels of government. To oversimplify somewhat, many of the proposals described here focus on the same end, but differ in their approach.

The desirable end state under which these proposals unite is the pursuit of sustainable development. The term dates at least to the 1987 Brundtland Commission, which called for development that meets the needs of present generations without compromising those of future generations. This concept has received significant international attention as well as domestic support.[61] For example, in 1996 the President's Council on Sustainable Development assessed U.S. natural resources by concluding: "America's continued prosperity directly depends on its ability to protect this natural heritage and to learn to use it in ways that do not diminish it."[62]

The concept of sustainable development emphasizes broad goals but specific targets. The broad goal is to maximize both environmental and economic benefits in resource policy. Specific targets include participatory planning, greater incorporation of scientific data, facilitation of both commodity usage and resource protection, realistic pricing of various forms of use, and concern for long-term as well as short-term outcomes.

Not surprisingly, such a blanket concept is susceptible to tugging at all sides. Like ecosystem management, sustainability is a term that defies easy and consistent definition. Many will ask sustainable for whom, or sustainable for how long? Three somewhat different approaches to achieving sustainable development are discussed below.

New Resource Economics. One broad category of efforts to synthesize reform proposals in pursuit of sustainable development is often referred to as New Resource Economics (NRE). NRE was motivated by perceived failures to efficiently sustain natural resources in previous eras of laissez-faire allocation, scientific management, or public sector control. According to NRE advocates, the market alone could not protect against failures such as externalities. Scientific management was a myth undermined by the inability of scientists to connect to the real world. The public sector has been dominated by interest group capture of agencies and logrolling in political oversight bodies. Overall, central planning lacks objective information, individual accountability, or emphasis on efficiency.[63]

The NRE school takes aspects of neoclassical economics, property rights theory, public choice theory, and Austrian economics to focus on the incentives facing decisionmakers who use natural resources. The goal of NRE is to "structure institutions that stimulate self-interested bureaucrats to act as if they were acting for the public good."[64] A simple example is making individual national forest managers accountable for expenses and revenues in their jurisdictions. Specific proposals include privatizing where possible through establishment of property rights, using the government to regulate externalities, incorporating scientific data to specify regulations, charging realistic fees on commodity extraction and recreational use of public lands, and locating public authority at the lowest level of government that still allows control of externalities.[65]

The response to NRE has been mixed. Some scholars are quite laudatory, asserting that in NRE "sound economics and sound ecology finally merge."[66] Others are more cautious, arguing that economic instruments are better thought of as tools than as a solution in themselves. Such tools can be quite useful, but "only after the most difficult environmental decisions have already been made."[67] These critics maintain that while NRE adds to the public debate some needed emphasis on efficiency, it will not replace the public sector in formulating policy.

In fact, as one would expect from such a new and major reform initiative, a unanimous verdict on the success of empirical application is still out. According to one analysis, the incorporation of NRE has already produced modifications in the practices of some logging companies. In Idaho, for example, Louisiana-Pacific Corporation replaced clear-cutting with NRE-based mixed-stand management to achieve greater sustainability on 45,000 acres of land. Potlatch Corporation is also developing cooperative programs with the Forest Service on over 600,000 acres.[68] NRE principles are also evident in the projects of such groups as the Nature Conservancy, which purchases ecologically important land in order to preserve it.[69] NRE-based international projects include debt-for-nature swaps whereby a financially poor developing nation agrees to protect certain areas within its borders in return for relaxation of debt pressures.

Collaborative Planning. Another approach to achieving sustainability engages the private sector in participatory planning. This approach is inspired by a sense that the present institutional arrangements are insufficient: federal agencies are hampered by lack of resources and no single agency has clear funding responsibility. Together, these deficiencies make for inefficient, often ineffective programs.[70]

What distinguishes this approach is the emphasis on focusing diverse viewpoints into a collaborative, ad hoc, voluntary process directed at specific areas of land. One recent example is the creation of the Tallgrass Prairie National Preserve in Kansas. After decades of debate over preservation of what little remained of tallgrass prairie ecosystems, proponents of the site achieved authorization in 1996. This unique arrangement within the NPS will see just 180 acres managed by the National Park Trust itself; the other 10,714 acres of the site will be overseen by an advisory commission made up of representatives of the Trust, historic societies, and local landowners. Another example of collaborative planning, this one outside the United States, involved efforts to revise management of Canada's Banff National Park. A plan developed by outside experts utilized all relevant viewpoints in a thorough and lengthy planning process. While the park areas at Banff will continue to be managed by the Canadian parks agency, the town of Banff will function as an incorporated unit. Activities affecting both will be directed by a plan that coordinates public, private, federal, and provincial priorities.[71]

The collaborative planning process is frequently stimulated in the United States by a need to acquire federal permits to develop land or water resources. Developers need the permits. Environmental groups want to retain protection of the lands. Public agencies can neither reconcile diverse views nor fund protective compromises simply on developers' fees. Thus, planners engage all viewpoints (private developers, environmentalists, local authorities), often using mediators or dispute resolution techniques, in an attempt to achieve a legally enforceable agreement. One of the most prominent of these efforts involved planning for the Chesapeake Bay. The eventual agreement between diverse parties, several states, and the EPA was sufficiently comprehensive to facilitate state legislative protection of wetlands and other sensitive areas.[72]

Collaborative planning has been most evident in the use of Habitat Conservation Plans (HCPs). HCPs are motivated by provisions in the Endangered Species Act allowing developers to seek "incidental taking" permits if their proposed actions might affect, harm, or harass an endangered species. To receive the permit, a plan must be offered that specifies steps taken to minimize impact on threatened species, why alternatives to the taking were not pursued, how funding will be supplied for the plan, and other issues. The planning process usually involves a steering committee made up of representatives from all relevant interests, a technical committee of experts (often biologists), and the use of outside consultants to prepare the plan. Since the first HCP was prepared in 1982 for the development of offices and houses on land near San Bruno, California, that was home to rare butterflies, several hundred others have been completed or are in progress. Timothy Beatley has reviewed dozens of these HCPs and calls them a "badly needed pressure-release valve" for otherwise potentially intense confrontations.[73]

Similar endorsements have been made for collaborative planning in general, but not without reservations. These efforts can replace conflict and find compromises, but they are also resource-intensive, lengthy, and provide no guarantee of long-term benefits. Still, as one study of these programs concludes, "for all its faults, collaborative planning is worth the effort if it succeeds in reconciling otherwise intractable environmental and development issues."[74]

The most telling analysis for collaborative planning will likely result from the San Diego project mentioned at the beginning of this chapter. The project centers around a fifty-year plan to reconcile natural preservation and development interests in the areas surrounding this fast-growing city. The plan calls for economic interests to give up the rights to develop thousands of acres of remaining natural habitat in return for freedom from any future obligations to protect imperiled species on already developed lands. In other words, existing property owners are guaranteed a "no surprises" policy in the future. If completed, the nine-hundred-square-mile region would include 172,000 acres of protected habitat. Proponents, including Secretary Babbitt and the Republican mayor of San Diego, promise that this arrangement will assist an entire ecosystem, one that is home to nearly two hundred imperiled species, without impairing economic growth. The plan required six years of collaborative negotiations between developers, preservationists, scientists, and politicians at both the state and federal levels.[75] While it still has its critics, many aspects of the plan, including the "no surprises" policy, are being touted for other habitat protection efforts and for revisions to the federal ESA.

Grassroots Restoration. Finally, thousands of people in the United States and elsewhere are involved in a variety of efforts to restore and sustain specific ecosystems. These efforts are neither guided by a particular school of experts nor motivated by a federal permitting procedure. They are, however, decentralized, focused on biodiversity, and receptive to economic motivations. Their common goal is to restore ecosystems as much as possible to their pre-industrial states. A variety of grassroots organizations have attempted to establish protected ecosystems in their own regions. Many of these efforts have found assistance through a nonprofit organization called the Wildlands Project, which connects biologists with activists in order to provide technical advice and coordination.[76]

Grassroots restoration efforts vary dramatically in scale. One local program, an attempt to restore the tallgrass savanna ecosystem along the Chicago River, is small in scope but has received considerable national attention. In this case, a group of determined residents have turned a devastated area into a vibrant, sustainable ecosystem.[77] On quite a different scale, and in a different country, is the program to restore the tropical dry forest ecosystem of the Guanacaste region of Costa Rica. Led by biologist Dan Janzen and other scientists, this project involves government agencies and the local citizenry in a comprehensive attempt to gather a large area of private lands, national parks, and other land designations into one coordinated ecosystem. The Guanacaste project is the prototype for the Costa Rican national park system and, some would say, a model for future preservation efforts around the world.[78]

Grassroots efforts face obvious difficulties and raise serious questions. For example, will enough funding be available to make up for the loss of economies of scale that is inevitable in pursuing decentralized projects? Will the loss of central coordination result in a lack of consistency across different areas that precludes desirable large-scale changes? Answers to these and other questions concerning grassroots activities are not readily apparent. What is apparent, however, is the success of grassroots efforts such as those described here in establishing ecosystem sustainability.

Summary

Table 14-3 sketches, albeit in simplified form, many of the reform proposals discussed in this section. This table is by no means exhaustive; it merely summarizes the most prominent of the numerous innovative ap-

Table 14-3   Natural Resource Policy Reform Proposals

Proposal	Role of Public Sector	Role of Private Sector	Primary Emphasis
Privatization	Reduce	Fundamental	Efficiency
Devolution	Decentralize	Increase	Efficiency
Prioritization	Focus	Maintain	Efficacy
Syntheses	Complement	Incorporate	Both

proaches currently being pursued in the third stage in the evolution of natural resource policies.

Conclusion

Will the "new era in American conservation" witness dramatic change in the handling of natural resource policies? Has this third stage of policy formation brought with it significant alterations to the traditional management of the Earth's resources? Some scholars have concluded that "unlikely partnerships may be the hallmark of the West in the closing years of the twentieth century."[79] In this chapter we have seen that in fact unusual partnerships mated to innovative approaches may indeed hold the greatest promise toward achieving sustainable use of natural resources in the United States and elsewhere. Just as significant problems with an earlier lack of institutional protection of natural resources led to a dramatic increase in federal government management, perceived weaknesses in today's public sector framework are motivating ongoing reform. Many current policies are criticized as conflictual, ineffective, and inefficient. Advocates of privatization, devolution, and prioritization encourage redress of these problems. The most promising of the new proposals are those that combine elements of several different perspectives in an innovative synthesis of ideas aimed at promoting environmental and economic benefits.

Though the focus of this chapter has been on the United States, the same dynamic questioning of traditional governance structures is occurring in other nations as well. The decentralization in Costa Rica and the collaborative planning at Banff are just two examples.[80] The future promises even greater challenges the world over as pressure to develop existing natural areas mounts and already endangered species are increasingly imperiled. In these new approaches, with their emphases on public participation and collaboration between groups with diverse points of view, many perceive our best prospects for achieving both short-term and long-term goals for effective natural resource management.

Notes

1. Quoted in B. Drummond Ayres, Jr., "San Diego Council Approves 'Model' Nature Habitat Plan," *New York Times*, March 20, 1997, A16.
2. For more on the Corps, see Jeanne Nienaber Clarke and Daniel C. McCool, *Staking Out the Terrain*, 2d ed. (Albany: State University Press of New York, 1996), 17–49, 129–156; John A. Ferejohn, *Pork Barrel Politics* (Palo Alto, Calif.: Stanford University Press, 1951); and Daniel A. Mazmanian and Jeanne Nienaber, *Can Organizations Change?* (Washington, D.C.: Brookings, 1979).
3. Clark and McCool, *Staking Out the Terrain*, 49–66; Roger Dower, Daryl Ditz, Paul Faeth, Nels Johnson, Keith Kozloff, and James J. MacKenzie, *Frontiers of Sustainability* (Washington, D.C.: Island Press, 1997), 191–280; George Hoberg, "From Localism to Legalism," in *Western Public Lands and Environmental Politics*, ed. Charles Davis (Boulder, Colo.: Westview, 1997), 47–73; and Herbert Kaufman, *The Forest Ranger* (Baltimore: Johns Hopkins University Press, 1960).

4. Ronald A. Foresta, *America's National Parks and their Keepers* (Washington, D.C.: Resources for the Future, 1984); John Freemuth, *Islands Under Siege* (Lawrence: University Press of Kansas, 1991); Michael Frome, *Regreening the National Parks* (Tucson: University of Arizona Press, 1992); and William Lowry, *The Capacity for Wonder* (Washington, D.C.: Brookings, 1994).

5. Clarke and McCool, *Staking Out the Terrain*, 157–175; Charles Davis, "Politics and Public Rangeland Policy," in *Western Public Lands and Environmental Politics*, ed. Davis, 74–94; Robert F. Durant, *The Administrative Presidency Revisited* (Albany: State University of New York Press, 1992); and Philip O. Foss, *Politics and Grass* (Seattle: University of Washington Press, 1960).

6. Clarke and McCool, *Staking Out the Terrain*, 107–125; and Winston Harrington and Anthony C. Fisher, "Endangered Species," in *Natural Resource Policy*, ed. Paul R. Portney (Washington, D.C.: Resources for the Future, 1982), 117–148.

7. Craig W. Allin, "Wilderness Policy," in *Western Public Lands and Environmental Politics*, ed. Davis, 172–189; and Walter A. Rosenbaum, *Environmental Politics and Policy*, 3d ed. (Washington, D.C.: CQ Press, 1995), 297–328.

8. Tim Palmer, *Endangered Rivers and the Conservation Movement* (Berkeley: University of California Press, 1986).

9. Phyllis Myers and Sharon N. Green, *State Parks in a New Era* (Washington, D.C.: Conservation Foundation, 1989).

10. David H. Davis, *Energy Politics*, 4th ed. (New York: St. Martin's Press, 1993); Christopher M. Klyza, "Reform at a Geological Pace," in *Western Public Lands and Environmental Politics*, ed. Davis, 95–121.

11. Sandra K. Davis, "Fighting over Public Lands," in *Western Public Lands and Environmental Politics*, ed. Davis, 11–31; and Debra Salazar, "Political Resources and Activities of Environmental Interest Groups in Washington State," in *Public Lands Management in the West*, ed. Brent S. Steel (Westport, Conn.: Praeger, 1997), 65–81.

12. Alan Gottlieb, *The Wise Use Agenda* (Bellevue, Wash.: Free Enterprise Press, 1989), xvii.

13. Ibid., 5–6.

14. Ron Arnold, "Overcoming Ideology," and John Freemuth, "Wise Use Movement and the National Parks," in *A Wolf in the Garden*, ed. Philip D. Brick and R. McGregor Cawley (Lanham, Md.: Rowman and Littlefield, 1996), 15–26, 207–213; William L. Graf, *Wilderness Preservation and the Sagebrush Rebels* (Savage, Md.: Rowman and Littlefield, 1990); and S.L. Witt and L.R. Alm, "County Government and the Public Lands," in *Public Lands Management in the West*, ed. Steel, 95–110.

15. Paul J. Culhane, "Sagebrush Rebels in Office," in *Environmental Policy in the 1980s*, ed. Norman J. Vig and Michael E. Kraft (Washington, D.C.: CQ Press, 1984), 293–317.

16. Norman J. Vig, "Presidential Leadership and the Environment," and Michael E. Kraft, "Environmental Policy in Congress," in *Environmental Policy in the 1990s*, 3d ed., ed. Norman J. Vig and Michael E. Kraft (Washington, D.C.: CQ Press, 1997), 95–118, 119–142.

17. Margaret Kriz, "Aiming for the Green," *National Journal*, October 4, 1997, 1958–1960.

18. Philip D. Brick and R. McGregor Cawley, "Knowing the Wolf, Tending the Garden," Glenn P. Sugameli, "Environmentalism: The Real Movement to Protect Property Rights," in *A Wolf in the Garden*, ed. Brick and Cawley, 1–12, 59–72.

19. Edward O. Wilson, *The Diversity of Life* (New York: Norton, 1992), 32; see also Rosenbaum, *Environmental Politics and Policy*, 333–340.

20. U.S. National Park Service (NPS), *National Parks for the 21st Century* (Washington, D.C.: NPS, 1992), 12; see also Lowry, *The Capacity for Wonder*.

21. Karl Hess, Jr., "John Wesley Powell and the Unmaking of the West," in *The Next West*, ed. John A. Baden and Donald Snow (Washington, D.C.: Island Press, 1997), 151–180; and Todd Shallat, *Structures in the Stream* (Austin: University of Texas Press, 1994).

22. Mazmanian and Nienaber, *Can Organizations Change?*, 22–23.

23. Rocky Barker, "New Forestry in the Next West," in *The Next West*, ed. Baden and Snow, 29; Nels Johnson and Daryl Ditz, "Challenges to Sustainability in the U.S. Forest Sector," in *Frontiers of Sustainability*, ed. Dower, 191–280.

24. Terry L. Anderson and Pamela Snyder, *Water Markets* (Washington, D.C.: Cato Institute, 1997).
25. Robert H. Nelson, "The Future of Federal Forest Management," in *Federal Lands Policy*, ed. Philip O. Foss (New York: Greenwood, 1987), 159–176; and Randal O'Toole, *Reforming the Forest Service* (Washington, D.C.: Island Press, 1988).
26. John Baden and Dean Lueck, "Bringing Private Management to the Public Lands," in *Controversies in Environmental Policy*, ed. Sheldon Kamieniecki, Robert O'Brien, and Michael Clarke (Albany: State University of New York Press, 1986), 54; John G. Francis, "Public Lands Institutions and Their Discontents," in *Federal Lands Policy*, ed. Foss, 61–76; and Gary D. Libecap, *Locking Up the Range* (Cambridge, Mass.: Ballinger, 1981).
27. "Merry Christmas, Mining Companies," editorial, *St. Louis Post-Dispatch*, December 11, 1995, 6B.
28. Charles Davis, "Gold or Green? Efforts to Reform the Mining Law of 1872," *Natural Resources and Environmental Administration* 19, no. 2 (February 1998): 2–4.
29. The NPS began a pilot program in 1997 of retaining most entrance fee revenue at nearly one hundred units in the system. For more on the traditional approach, see William R. Lowry, "Land of the Fee," *Political Research Quarterly* 46 (1997): 823–845.
30. U.S. General Accounting Office (GAO), "Recreation Concessionaires Operating on Federal Lands," GAO/RCED-91-16 (Washington, D.C.: GAO, 1991).
31. Nelson, "The Future of Federal Forest Management," 161; Donald Snow, "Introduction," in *The Next West*, ed. Baden and Snow, 1–9.
32. Bill Gifford, "The Government's Too-Sweet Deal," *Washington Post*, January 9, 1994, C3.
33. Charles Davis, "Conclusion," in *Western Public Lands and Environmental Politics*, ed. Davis, 193–202; and Hoberg, "From Localism to Legalism," 47–73.
34. See, for example, Marion Clawson, "Major Alternatives for Future Management of the Federal Lands," in *Rethinking the Federal Lands*, ed. Sterling Brubaker (Washington, D.C.: Resources for the Future, 1984), 195–234.
35. B. Delworth Gardner, "The Case for Divestiture," in *Rethinking the Federal Lands*, ed. Brubaker, 169; see also Terry L. Anderson and Peter J. Hill, "Introduction," in *The Political Economy of the American West*, ed. Terry L. Anderson and Peter J. Hill (Lanham, Md.: Rowman and Littlefield, 1994), x; and Nelson, "The Future of Federal Forest Management," 170–171.
36. Libecap, *Locking up the Range*, 101.
37. Anderson and Snyder, *Water Markets*, 111–132.
38. R.W. Behan, "The Polemics and Politics of Federal Land Management," in *Federal Lands Policy*, ed. Foss, 180.
39. Joseph Sax, "The Claim for Retention of the Public Lands," in *Rethinking the Federal Lands*, ed. Brubaker, 139.
40. Christopher K. Leman, "How the Privatization Revolution Failed," in *Western Public Lands*, ed. John G. Francis and Richard Ganzel (Towota, N.J.: Rowman and Allanheld, 1984), 115.
41. Gardner, "The Case for Divestiture," 174.
42. Robert M. Solow, "Sustainability," in *Economics of the Environment*, 3d ed., ed. Robert Dorfman and Nancy S. Dorfman (New York: Norton, 1993), 182.
43. Baden and Lueck, "Bringing Private Management," 60.
44. John G. Francis and Richard Ganzel, "Introduction," in *Western Public Lands*, ed. Francis and Ganzel, 1–22; and Hess, "John Wesley Powell," 177.
45. R. McGreggor Cawley, *Federal Lands, Western Anger* (Lawrence: University Press of Kansas, 1993), 2.
46. John G. Francis, "Environmental Values, Intergovernmental Politics, and the Sagebrush Rebellion," in *Western Public Lands*, ed. Francis and Ganzel, 29–46.
47. Christopher A. Simon, "The County Supremacy Movement and Public Lands in Oregon," in *Public Lands Management in the West*, ed. Steel, 111–127; Witt and Alm, "County Government and the Public Lands."

48. Francis and Ganzel, "Introduction"; Howard E. McCurdy, "Environmental Protection and the New Federalism," in *Controversies in Environmental Policy*, ed. Kamieniecki, O'Brien, and Clarke, 85–107.
49. William R. Lowry, *The Dimensions of Federalism* (Durham, N.C.: Duke University Press, 1992); Lowry, "State Parks Found to Be Source of Innovation," *Public Administration Times* 19, no. 10 (1996): 1, 12–13; see also Francis, "Public Lands Institutions," 74.
50. Clawson, "Major Alternatives for Future Management," 210.
51. Jerry F. Franklin, "Ecosystem Management: An Overview," in *Ecosystem Management*, ed. Mark S. Boyce and Alan Haney (New Haven, Conn.: Yale University Press, 1997), 21–53; Reed F. Noss and Allen Y. Cooperrider, *Saving Nature's Legacy* (Washington, D.C.: Island Press, 1994); and Steven L. Yaffee, Ali F. Phillips, Irene C. Frentz, Paul W. Hardy, Sussanne M. Maleki, and Barbara E. Thorpe, *Ecosystem Management in the United States* (Washington, D.C.: Island Press, 1996).
52. Alan Haney and Mark S. Boyce, "Introduction," in *Ecosystem Management*, ed. Boyce and Haney, 9. See also Reed F. Noss and J. Michael Scott, "Ecosystem Protection and Restoration," in ibid., 239–264.
53. Noss and Cooperrider, *Saving Nature's Legacy*, 87, 329; Jack Ward Thomas, "Foreword," in *Ecosystem Management*, ed. Boyce and Haney, x–xi; Yaffee et al., *Ecosystem Management in the United States*, 33–34; Hanna J. Cortner and Margaret A. Moote, *The Politics of Ecosystem Management* (Washington, D.C.: Island Press, 1999); and Todd Wilkinson, *Science Under Siege* (Boulder, Colo.: Johnson Books, 1998).
54. William R. Lowry, *Preserving Public Lands for the Future* (Washington, D.C.; Georgetown University Press, 1998).
55. John Kotar, "Silviculture and Ecosystem Management," in *Ecosystem Management*, ed. Boyce and Haney), 265–275; Noss and Scott, "Ecosystem Protection," 250.
56. Douglas J. Norton and David G. Davis, "Policies for Protecting Aquatic Diversity," in *Ecosystem Management*, ed. Boyce and Haney, 279.
57. Yaffee et al., *Ecosystem Management in the United States*, 39.
58. Franklin, "Ecosystem Management," 47–48; see also the April 1994 issue of *Journal of Forestry*.
59. Brick and Cawley, "Knowing the Wolf," 5.
60. For a discussion of international regimes as lightly administered sets of rules to address environmental problems, see Oran Young, "Global Governance," in *Global Governance*, ed. Oran Young (Cambridge, Mass.: MIT Press, 1997), 273–299.
61. Herman E. Daly, *Beyond Growth* (Boston: Beacon Press, 1996); Dower et al., *Frontiers of Sustainability*, 3; and National Commission on the Environment, *Choosing a Sustainable Future* (Washington, D.C.: Island Press, 1993).
62. Daniel Sitarz, ed., *Sustainable America* (Carbondale, Ill.: EarthPress, 1998), 116.
63. John Baden and Andrew Dana, "Toward an Ideological Synthesis in Public Land Policy," in *Federal Lands Policy*, ed. Foss, 1–20; and Mark Sagoff, "Saving the Marketplace from the Market," in *The Next West*, ed. Baden and Snow, 131–149.
64. Baden and Dana, "Toward an Ideological Synthesis," 14; and Baden and Lueck, "Bringing Private Management," 39–45.
65. Baden and Dana, "Toward an Ideological Synthesis," 15; and Sagoff, "Saving the Marketplace," 139–144.
66. Donald Snow, "Introduction," in *The Next West*, ed. Baden and Snow, 2.
67. Thomas M. Power, "Ideology, Wishful Thinking, and Pragmatic Reform," in *The Next West*, ed. Baden and Snow, 253.
68. Rocky Barker, "New Forestry in the Next West," in *The Next West*, ed. Baden and Snow, 25–44.
69. W. William Weeks, *Beyond the Ark* (Washington, D.C.: Island Press, 1997).
70. David A. Salvesen and Douglas R. Porter, "Introduction," in *Collaborative Planning for Wetlands and Wildlife*, ed. Douglas Porter and David A. Salvesen (Washington, D.C.: Island Press, 1995), 1–6.

71. Lowry, *Preserving Public Lands for the Future*, chap. 5.
72. Erik Myers, Robert Fischman, and Anne Marsh, "Maryland Chesapeake Bay Critical Areas Program," in *Collaborative Planning for Wetlands and Wildlife*, ed. Porter and Salvesen, 181–201.
73. Timothy Beatley, "Preserving Biodiversity through the Use of Habitat Conservation Plans," in *Collaborative Planning for Wetlands and Wildlife*, ed. Porter and Salvesen, 57, 35–74; and Scott Sonner, "Clinton Administration Has 'Junked the Law,' Critics Charge," *St. Louis Post-Dispatch*, May 9, 1997, 3A.
74. Douglas R. Porter and David A. Salvesen, "Conclusion," in *Collaborative Planning for Wetlands and Wildlife*, ed. Porter and Salvesen, 275; Beatley, "Preserving Biodiversity," 57–68; and Salvesen and Porter, "Introduction," 4–5.
75. Ayres, "San Diego Council Approves 'Model' Nature Habitat Plan"; and William K. Stevens, "Disputed Conservation Plan Could be Model for Nation," *New York Times*, February 16, 1997, I18.
76. Noss and Scott, "Ecosystem Protection," 254.
77. William K. Stevens, *Miracle Under the Oaks* (New York: Pocket Books, 1995).
78. Lowry, *Preserving Public Lands for the Future*, chap. 6.
79. John A. Baden and Donald Snow, "Preface," in *The Next West*, ed. Baden and Snow, ix.
80. See also Noss and Cooperrider, *Saving Nature's Legacy*, 333–334; and Young, "Global Governance."

15

Environment, Population, and the Developing World
Richard J. Tobin

Environmental problems occasionally make life in the United States unpleasant and inconvenient, but most Americans tolerate this unpleasantness in exchange for the benefits and comforts associated with a developed, industrial economy. Most Europeans, Japanese, and Australians share similar lifestyles, so it is not unexpected that they too typically take modern amenities for granted.

When lifestyles are viewed from a broader perspective, however, much changes. Consider, for example, what life is like in much of the world. The U.S. gross national product (GNP) per capita was almost $28,740, more than $550 per week in 1997, but millions of people live in countries where weekly incomes are less than 5 percent of this amount, even when adjusted for differences in prices and purchasing power. In Mozambique, the world's most impoverished country, real per capita incomes are about three hundred times smaller than those in the United States. Throughout sub-Saharan Africa about half the population survives on less than a dollar a day.[1]

Low incomes are not the only problem facing many of the world's inhabitants. In some developing countries, women, often illiterate with no formal education, will marry as young as age thirteen or fourteen. Indeed, in several African countries 40 percent of all females are married before their twentieth birthday. During their childbearing years, women in many developing countries will deliver as many as six or seven babies, most without the benefit of trained medical personnel. This absence is not without consequences. The chance of a woman dying due to complications associated with pregnancy, childbirth, or an unsafe abortion is hundreds of times higher in many poor countries than it is in Europe or the United States.[2]

Many of the world's children are also at risk. Only six out of one thousand American children die before the age of five; in some Asian and African countries as many as 25 to 30 percent do. *Every day* thousands of children under five die in developing countries from diseases that rarely kill Americans. Most of the deaths are caused by tetanus, measles, malaria, diarrhea, whooping cough, or acute respiratory infections, most of which are easily and cheaply prevented or cured.[3]

Of the children from these poor countries that do survive their earliest years, millions will suffer brain damage because their pregnant mothers had no iodine in their diets; others will lose their sight and die because they lack vitamin A. Many will face a life of poverty, never to taste clean water, enter a classroom, visit a doctor, have access to even the cheapest vitamins or medicines, or eat nutritious food regularly. To the extent that shelter is available, it is rudimentary, rarely with electricity or proper sanitary facilities. When a poor child in Jakarta wants to bathe, as an example, he might lower himself into the open sewer that flows through his family's squatter settlement. Because their surroundings have been abused or poorly managed, millions of those in the developing world will also become victims of floods, famine, desertification, water-borne diseases, infestation of pests and rodents, and exceedingly noxious levels of air pollution. Nearly all sewage in developing countries is discharged into lakes and rivers without any treatment, and pesticides and human wastes often contaminate well water.

As these children grow older, many will find that their governments do not have or cannot provide the resources to ensure them a reasonable standard of living. Yet all around them are countries with living standards well beyond their comprehension. The average American uses about thirty-four times more electricity and consumes about 50 percent more calories per day—far in excess of minimum daily requirements—than does the typical Indian. The Indian might wonder why Americans consume a disproportionate share of the world's resources when she has a malnourished child she cannot afford to clothe or educate.

In short, life in much of Asia, Africa, and Latin America provides a different array of problems than those encountered in developed nations, which are responding to the benefits and consequences of development. The residents of poor countries, in contrast, must cope with widespread poverty and a lack of economic development. Yet both developed and developing nations often undergo environmental degradation. Those without property, for example, may be tempted to denude tropical forests for land to farm. Alternatively, pressures for development often force people to overexploit their base of environmental resources.

These issues lead to the key question addressed in this chapter: can the poorest countries, with the overwhelming majority of the world's population, improve their lot through sustainable development? According to the World Commission on Environment and Development, sustainable development meets the essential needs of the present generation for food, clothing, shelter, jobs, and health without "compromising the ability of future generations to meet their own needs." To achieve this goal, the commission emphasized the need to stimulate higher levels of economic development without inflicting irreparable damage on the environment.[4]

Whose responsibility is it to achieve sustainable development? One view is that richer nations have a moral obligation to assist less fortunate ones. If the former do not meet this obligation, not only will hundreds of millions of people in developing countries suffer but the consequences will also be felt in the developed countries as well. Others argue that poorer nations must accept responsibility for their own fate; outside efforts to help them only worsen the problem and lead to an unhealthy dependence. As an illustration, biologist Garrett Hardin insists that it is wrong to provide food to famine-stricken nations because they have exceeded their environment's carrying capacity. In Hardin's words, "if you give food and save lives and thus increase the number of people, you increase suffering and ultimately increase the loss of life."[5]

The richer nations, whichever position they take, cannot avoid affecting what happens in the developing world. It is thus useful to consider how U.S. actions influence the quest for sustainable development. At least two related factors affect this quest. The first is a country's population; the second is a country's capacity to support its population.

Population Growth: Cure or Culprit?

Population growth is one of the more controversial elements in the journey toward sustainable development. Depending on one's perspective, the world is either vastly overpopulated or capable of supporting as many as thirty times its current population (about six billion in mid 1999 and increasing at an annual rate of about 1.4 percent).[6] Many of the developing nations are growing faster than the industrial nations (see table 15-1), and

Table 15-1   Estimated Populations and Projected Growth Rates

Region or Country	Estimated Population (millions)			Annual Net Percentage Increase	Number of Years to Double Population Size
	1998	2010	2025		
World total	5,926	6,903	8,082	1.4	49
More developed countries	1,178	1,217	1,240	0.1	548
United States	270	298	335	0.6	116
Japan	126	128	121	0.2	330
Canada	31	35	40	0.5	136
Less developed regions	4,748	5,687	6,842	1.7	40
China	1,243	1,394	1,561	1.0	69
India	989	1,197	1,441	1.9	37
Sub-Saharan Africa	624	805	1,076	2.6	27
Brazil	162	184	208	1.4	48
Bangladesh	123	148	166	1.8	38
Nigeria	122	150	203	3.0	23
Mexico	98	118	140	2.2	32
Uganda	21	26	34	2.7	26
Yemen	16	24	39	3.3	21

Source: Population Reference Bureau, *1998 World Population Data Sheet* (Washington, D.C.: Population Reference Bureau, 1998).

more than 80 percent of the world's population lives outside the developed regions. If current growth rates continue, the proportion of those in developing countries will increase even more. Between 1998 and 2050 nearly all of the world's population increase will occur in the latter regions, exactly where the people and the environment can least afford such a surge.

Africa is particularly prone to high rates of population growth. Populations in Angola, the Democratic Republic of the Congo, Mozambique, Niger, Tanzania, Togo, and Uganda were growing by at least 3 percent per year in the late 1990s. This may not seem to be much until we realize that such rates will double the countries' populations in about twenty-three years. Of the fourteen countries with crude birth rates of at least forty-five per thousand in 1997, all but two are in Africa. Fertility rates measure the number of children an average woman has during her lifetime. Eighteen of the twenty-two countries with fertility rates at six or above are in Africa. By comparison, the birth rate in the United States was fourteen per thousand in 1997, and its fertility rate was two.

High rates of population growth are not necessarily undesirable, and criticisms of high rates often bring rebuke. In the 1970s, for example, when the United States and other industrial nations urged developing countries to stem their growth, many responded with hostility. To pleas that it initiate family planning programs, China complained that they represented capitalist efforts to subjugate the world's poorer nations. China viewed a rapidly growing population as highly desirable because it contributed to increases in domestic production and "accelerated social and economic development."[7]

By the late 1970s and early 1980s, however, many developing countries no longer viewed high population growth as desirable. They found themselves with many young, dependent children, increasing rates of unemployment, a cancerous and unchecked growth of urban areas, and a general inability to provide for the social and economic demands of ever-larger populations. Many developing countries also realized that if their living standards are to improve, their economic growth must exceed their rate of population increase.

Although many countries altered their attitudes about population growth, they soon realized the immensity of the task. The prevailing theory of demographic transition suggests that societies go through three stages. In the first stage, in premodern societies, birth and death rates are high, so populations remain stable or increase at low rates. In the second stage, death rates decline and populations grow more rapidly because of vaccines, better health care, and more nutritious foods. As countries begin to reap the benefits of economic development, they enter the third stage. Infant mortality declines, but so does the desire or need to have large families. Population growth slows considerably.

This model explains events in the United States and many European countries. As standards of living increased, birth rates declined. The model's weakness is that it assumes economic growth; in the absence of such growth, many nations are caught in a "demographic trap."[8] They get stuck in the second stage. This is the predicament of many developing countries today. In some of these countries the situation is even worse. Their populations are growing faster than their economies, and living standards are declining. These declines create a cruel paradox. Larger populations produce increased demands for health and educational services; stagnant economies make it difficult to respond.

The opportunity to lower death rates can also make it difficult to slow population growth. In nearly twenty Asian and African countries the average life expectancy at birth is less than fifty years (compared with 76.5 in the United States and eighty in Japan, as of 1997). If these Asians and Africans had access to the medicines, vitamins, and nutritious foods readily available in the developed nations, then death rates would drop substantially. Life expectancies could be extended by twenty years or more.

There is good reason to expect death rates to decline. Over the past twenty-five years the United Nations and other development agencies have attempted to reduce infant mortality by immunizing children against potentially fatal illnesses and by providing inexpensive cures for diarrhea and other illnesses. These programs have met with enormous success, and more is anticipated. One of the goals of the World Health Organization is to reduce mortality among children under age five by as much as 20 percent by 2000 and to prevent most deaths due to tetanus and measles. These two diseases now kill more than 1.7 million children per year.[9] Reduced mortality rates among children should also reduce fertility rates, but the change will be gradual, and millions of children will be born in the meantime. Most of the first-time mothers of the next twenty years have already been born.

Given these problems, the success that Côte d'Ivoire, Cuba, Kenya, South Korea, Thailand, and Zimbabwe have had in lowering their population growth rates is remarkable. Thailand cut its growth rate by half in fifteen years by using both humor and showmanship. A private association distributes condoms at movie theaters and traffic jams, sponsors condom-blowing contests, and organizes a special cops-and-rubbers program each New Year's Eve. The association also offers free vasectomies on the king's birthday; for those who cannot wait, the normal charge is $20.[10]

Perhaps the best known but most controversial population programs are in India and China. India's family planning program started in the early 1950s as a low-key educational effort that achieved only modest success. The program changed from an initiative of volunteerism to one of compulsion in the mid 1970s. The minimum age for marriage was increased, and India's states were encouraged to select their own methods to reduce growth.

Several states chose coercion. Parents with two or more children were expected to have themselves sterilized. To ensure compliance, states threatened to withhold salaries or to dismiss government workers from their jobs. Public officials were likewise threatened with sanctions if they did not provide enough candidates for sterilization. One result was a massive program of forced sterilization that caused considerable political turmoil.[11] Although the program was eventually relaxed, India was able to cut its fertility rate by almost 35 percent between 1980 and 1997. This is remarkable progress, but cultural resistance may stifle further gains. India currently adds about sixteen million inhabitants each year, more than any other country. If such growth continues, India could become the world's most populous country within the next half-century.

Whether India becomes the world's most populous nation depends on what happens in China. Sharply reversing its earlier position in the late 1970s, the Chinese government conceded that too-rapid population growth was leading to shortages of jobs, housing, and consumer goods, further frustrating efforts to modernize its economy.[12] To reduce the country's population growth rate, the government now discourages early marriages. It also adopted a one-child-per-family policy in 1979, and the policy is applied in most urban areas. The government gives one-child families monthly subsidies, educational benefits for their child, preference for housing and health care, and higher pensions at retirement. Families that had previously agreed to have only one child but then had another are deprived of these benefits and penalized financially.

The most controversial elements of the program involve the government's monitoring of women's menstrual cycles; instances of forced abortions and sterilizations, some occurring in the last trimester; and even female infanticide in rural areas. Chinese officials admit that abortions have been forced on some unwilling women. These officials quickly add, however, that such practices represent aberrations, not accepted guidelines, and that they violate the government's policies.

China's initial efforts lowered annual rates of population growth considerably. Total fertility rates declined from 5.8 in 1970 to 1.8 in 1998. Perhaps because of this success, the program began to encounter extensive resistance and, in some areas, outright disregard. Consequently, the government relaxed its restrictions and exempted certain families, particularly in rural areas, from the one-child policy. Rather than mandating limits on the number of children a couple can have, the government of China has gradually adopted approaches to population control that encourage women to have fewer children. These policy changes led to a 20 percent increase in the birth rate between 1985 and 1987, and China soon announced that it had abandoned its goal of a population of 1.2 billion by 2000, which the country exceeded in 1997.[13] Abandoning this goal does not mean that China has forsaken its population objectives. Renewed concern about population growth in the late 1980s caused the Chinese government to reassess the effectiveness of its programs and to renew its efforts to limit births. If these programs fail and birth rates increase, China's population could approach two billion by the middle of the twenty-first century.

The U.S. government's position toward China's population policies has been inconsistent. For many years the U.S. government viewed rapidly growing populations as a threat to economic development. The United States backed its rhetoric with money; it was the single largest donor to international population programs. The official U.S. position changed dramatically during the Reagan administration in the 1980s. Due to its opposition to abortion, the administration said the United States would no longer contribute to the U.N. Population Fund because it subsidized some of China's population programs. None of the fund's resources are used to provide abortions, but the U.S. ban on contributions nonetheless continued during the Bush administration.

Within a day of taking office, President Bill Clinton announced his intention to alter these policies, to provide financial support to the fund, and to finance international population programs that rely on abortions. The 1994 U.N. International Conference on Population and Development in Cairo provided an opportunity for the Clinton administration to advocate its preferences before an international audience. A draft Program of Action acknowledged an interdependence among population, economics, environmental quality, and human rights. The program also advocated increased reliance on family planning, which became a hotly contested issue at the conference. Delegates from the United States promoted the universal availability of reproductive health services. Without urging abortion, these delegates argued that women should have access to safe abortion services.

Not all discussion focused on abortion, and a majority of the countries represented in Cairo were able to agree on many common ideas. Perhaps the most important of these gave "prominence to reproductive health and the empowerment of women while downplaying the demographic rationale for population policy."[14] In adopting this perspective, the meeting reflected a major victory for the United States, which was widely perceived as one of the conference's most effective participants.

In tandem with this achievement, the Clinton administration dramatically increased financial support for family planning in developing countries even in the face of cuts in the overall U.S. budget for foreign assistance. With the Republicans gaining control of the Congress in 1995, however, much of this momentum was soon reversed. In the federal budget for fiscal year 1996, for example, Congress cut U.S. foreign assistance for population and family planning programs in developing countries by 35 percent. As a result of the cuts, the head of the U.N. Population Fund estimated that 17 to 18 million unwanted pregnancies would occur. Disagreements between the Congress and the Clinton administration about funding for international family planning programs continued throughout the 1990s. President Clinton vetoed a bill in 1998 that would have paid nearly one billion dollars in back dues to the United Nations because the bill contained a provision that would have prohibited federal support for organizations that seek to alter policies on abortion in developing countries.

Concerns about abortion are not the only reason that many people have qualms about efforts to affect population increases. Their view is that large populations are a problem only when they are not used productively to enhance development. The solution to the lack of such development is not government intervention, they argue, but rather individual initiatives and the spread of capitalist, free-market economies. Advocates of this position also believe that larger populations can be advantageous because they enhance

political power, contribute to economic development, encourage technological innovation, and stimulate agricultural production.[15] Other critics of population control programs also ask if it is appropriate for developed countries
to impose their preferences on others. As one scholar has asked: "Isn't it time
wealthy white people stopped telling Third World peasants who aspire to a
better life how many children and what kind of economy to have?"[16]

Another issue that has been much debated involves the increased access
to abortions, and who chooses to have them. For example, the consequences
of efforts to limit population growth are not always gender neutral. In parts
of Asia male children are highly prized as sources of future financial security,
whereas females are viewed as liabilities. In years past the sex of newborns
was known only at birth, and in most countries newborn males slightly out-
number newborn females. With the advent of amniocentesis and ultrasound,
however, the sex of a fetus is easily ascertained months before a child is due.
This knowledge is often the basis of a decision to abort female fetuses.

In sum, the appropriateness of different population sizes is debatable.
There is no clear answer to whether growth by itself is good or bad. The important issue is a country's carrying capacity. Can it ensure its population a
reasonable standard of living?

Providing Food and Fuel for Growing Populations

Sustainable development requires that environmental resources not be
overtaxed so that they are available for future generations. As Lester Brown
points out, however, when populations exceed sustainable yields of their forests,
aquifers, and croplands, "they begin directly or indirectly to consume the resource base itself," gradually destroying it.[17] The eventual result is an irreversible collapse of biological and environmental support systems. Is there any
evidence that these systems are now being strained or will be in the near future?

The first place to look is in the area of food production. Nations can
grow their own food, import it, or, as most nations do, rely on both options.
The Earth is richly endowed with agricultural potential and production.
Millions of acres of arable land remain to be cultivated, and farmers now
produce enough food to satisfy the daily caloric and protein needs of a world
population exceeding twelve billion, far more than are already alive.[18] These
data suggest the ready availability of food as well as a potential for even
higher levels of production. This good news must be balanced with the sobering realization that nearly a billion people in the developing world today
barely have enough food to survive.

As with economic development, the amount of food available in a country must increase at least as fast as the rate of population growth; otherwise,
per capita consumption will decline. If existing levels of caloric intake are
already inadequate, then food production (and imports) must increase faster
than population growth in order to meet minimum caloric needs. Assisted
by the expanded use of irrigation, pesticides, and fertilizers, many developing
countries, particularly in Asia, dramatically increased their food production

over the past two or three decades. Asia's three largest countries—China, India, and Indonesia—are no longer heavily dependent on imports.

Despite these and a few other notable successes, much of the developing world is in the midst of an agricultural crisis. Nearly thirty African countries produced less food per capita in 1996 than they had in 1980. Not surprisingly, daily caloric consumption decreased in these countries. In many developing countries the average daily caloric consumption, already below subsistence levels in the early 1980s, declined still further by the late 1990s as agricultural productivity per capita plunged in many places (see table 15-2). These nations consequently face severe problems with food security. In several African countries it is not unusual for farming families to exhaust their supplies of food several months before the next harvest.

Some people consume more and others less than the average daily caloric intake in each country. The result is that in many countries that exceed average caloric requirements, a large number of people are on the brink of

Table 15-2   Changes in Agricultural Production and Daily Caloric Intake

Country	Index of Food Production Per Capita (1989–1991 = 100) Year 1997	Daily Caloric Supply Per Capita Years			Aggregate Household Food Security Index[a] Years	
		1969–1971	1989–1991	1993–1995	1990–1992	2010
Cuba	61.7	2,660	3,080	2,350	—	—
Zambia	79.6	2,180	2,070	1,950	72.0	72.0
Madagascar	85.8	2,410	2,130	2,010	80.3	83.2
Kenya	86.5	2,150	1,930	1,960	69.6	72.8
Sierra Leone	87.4	2,200	2,020	1,990	66.3	70.8
Malawi	91.0	2,280	1,980	2,000	69.6	74.4
Bangladesh	99.9	2,120	2,060	2,040	76.6	79.7
Canada	105.8	2,890	3,010	3,080	—	—
India	107.3	2,080	2,350	2,390	83.0	86.8
United States	109.6	3,170	3,450	3,610	—	—
China	152.1	2,320	2,650	2,710	87.9	93.4

Sources: U.N. Food and Agriculture Organization (FAO), *FAO Yearbook: Production 1997* (Rome: FAO, 1998), 43–44; FAO, *Food and Agricultural Sector Profiles: Country Tables 1997* (Rome: FAO, 1998); FAO, Committee on World Food Security, Twentieth Session, *Assessment of the Current World Food Security Situation and Medium Term Review* (Rome: FAO, February 1995), 12–13.

[a] The Aggregate Household Food Security Index (AHFSI) "calculates the food-gap between the undernourished and average national requirements, the instability of the annual food supply and the proportion of undernourished in the total population." See FAO News Release PR 94/6, "32 African Nations Face Food Security Problems" (March 27, 1994). Scores range from 0 (total famine) to 100 (complete, risk-free food security). Scores above 85 indicate high food security; scores from 76 to 85 indicate medium food security; scores between 65 and 75 represent low food security; scores below 65 indicate a critical food security situation. The FAO computes the AHFSI only for low-income, food-deficit countries.

starvation. In India, Indonesia, Nepal, Nigeria, Pakistan, Sri Lanka, and Vietnam, the average resident consumes more than the required number of calories each day, but more than a third of the children under five in these countries are malnourished.[19]

Low levels of production can be attributed to inefficient farming practices: lack of irrigation, fertilizers, appropriate strategies for managing pests, and in some instances corruption or incompetence. The Democratic Republic of the Congo (formerly Zaire) exemplifies several of these problems. According to the Food and Agriculture Organization (FAO), the Congo is "land abundant." With few agricultural inputs (that is, with traditional farming practices), the country was capable of producing almost twelve times as much food as it needed in 1975, according to FAO calculations. With a higher level of inputs, the country could feed all Africans several times over. Despite its potential, the Congo's increase in food production per capita between 1980 and 1996 significantly lagged behind its population growth, and more than one-third of its children are malnourished.

If current agricultural practices are continued, more than half of the 117 developing countries studied by the FAO will not be able to provide minimum levels of nutrition by the turn of the century. If, however, their agricultural practices are improved significantly to include complete mechanization and other high-technology approaches, then 98 of the countries could feed themselves by 2000.[20]

It is possible to increase agricultural outputs, as the FAO found, but its calculations did not incorporate practical limitations. No consideration was given to whether money would be available to purchase the higher level of inputs.[21] The calculations also assumed that all land that could be cultivated would be cultivated; no cropland would be lost to degradation or soil erosion; no livestock would be allowed to graze on land that had the potential to grow food; and no nonfood crops, such as tea, coffee, or cotton, would be grown! The study also assumed that only minimum nutrition levels would be satisfied and that production could be distributed appropriately. In short, the current-practice scenario is likely to offer a better indication of the state of agricultural production over the near term.

This scenario is discouraging. In many countries there is not enough arable land to support existing populations, and some developing countries have already reached or exceeded the sustainable limits of production. Up to 80 percent of the land in sub-Saharan Africa is threatened by degradation, and millions of acres of forested areas are destroyed on the continent each year.[22] Kenya had the agricultural potential to support less than 30 percent of its population in 1975. With its anticipated growth, Kenya will be able to provide for an even smaller share of its population, at least with continued low levels of agricultural inputs. Many Asian countries face similar predicaments. Their populations are already overexploiting the environment's carrying capacity. These people are thus using their land beyond its capacity to sustain agricultural production. One estimate suggests that farmers in India, Pakistan, Bangladesh, and West Africa are already farming virtually all the land suitable for agriculture. Unless changes are made soon, production will eventually decline. Millions of acres of barren land will be added to the millions that are already beyond redemption.

Increased use of fertilizers can boost agricultural production, but increases in production rarely match (and often lag) increases in the use of fertilizer. Pakistan's use of fertilizer increased by more than 90 percent between the late 1970s and the early 1990s, but per capita agricultural production declined by about 1 percent per year in the 1990s.

It is important to appreciate as well that the nature of diets changes as nations urbanize. Irrespective of differences in prices and incomes, according to the International Food Policy Research Institute, "urban dwellers consume more wheat and less rice and demand more meat, milk products, and fish than their rural counterparts."[23] This preference leads to increased requirements for grain to feed animals, the need for more space for forage, greater demands for water, and increased pollution from animal waste. China provides one of the best examples of this phenomenon. Its consumption of red meat is increasing at about 10 percent per year, and the number of cattle in China increased by almost 50 percent between 1989–1991 and 1997. China's per capita production of livestock doubled during this period. Changes in the composition of diets can be anticipated in many other countries. In fact, in virtually every low-income country, urbanization is increasing faster than overall population growth (in many instances, three to four times faster).

Increased demand for meat has several environmental consequences. On the one hand, more grain must be produced to feed the livestock and poultry. In a typical year, as much as 35 to 40 percent of the world's grain production is used for animal feed, but the conversion from feed to meat is not a neat one. As many as ten pounds of grain are required to produce one pound of beef. On the other hand, ruminant livestock need grazing land, which is already in short supply in many areas. Throughout the world about twice as much land is devoted to animal grazing as is that designated for crop production. If a land's carrying capacity is breached due to excessive exploitation, then the alternative is to use feedlot production, which, in turn, requires even higher levels of grain and concentrates waste products in smaller areas.

Food imports offer a possible solution to deficiencies in domestic production, but here, too, many developing countries encounter problems. In order to finance imports, countries need foreign exchange, usually acquired through their own exports or from loans. Few developing countries have industrial products or professional services to export, so they must rely on minerals, natural resources (such as timber or petroleum), or cash crops (such as tea, sugar, coffee, cocoa, and rubber). Advances in biotechnology can also affect the developing countries' ability to find export markets for their crops. Scientists can produce artificial vanilla in laboratories. If they can do so on a large scale, Madagascar will lose opportunities to export one of its largest sources of foreign exchange. Similarly, genetically produced sweeteners could eliminate the export of sugarcane from several developing countries.

Economic recessions and declining demand in the developed world cause prices for many of these commodities to fluctuate widely. At the end of 1998, the price of a "basket" of twenty-two international commodities was at a twenty-six-year low. To cope with declining prices for export crops, farmers are forced to intensify production, which implies increased reliance on fertilizers and pesticides, or to expand the area under cultivation in order to increase production. Unfortunately, these seemingly rational reactions are likely to depress prices even further as supply outpaces demand. As the area used for export crops expands, less attention is given to production for domestic consumption.

There are opportunities to increase exports, but economic policies in the developed world can discourage expanded activity in the developing countries. Farmers in developed countries—especially Japan, Europe, and the United States—received more than $335 *billion* in annual subsidies from their governments in the 1990s, often resulting in overproduction and surpluses. These surpluses discourage imports from developing countries, reduce prices further, and remove incentives to expand production. Subsidies and protectionist trade policies in the developed nations also prevent access to many markets. The United Nations estimated in 1992 that subsidies and trade barriers cost developing countries about $500 billion a year in lost income,[24] about ten times as much as they received in foreign assistance. There is obvious irony in these figures. Without access to export markets, developing countries are denied their best opportunity for economic development, which, historically, has provided the best cure for rapid population growth and poverty.

Developing countries could once depend on loans from private banks or foreign governments to help finance imports. Now, however, many developing countries are burdened with massive debts, which exceeded $2.1 trillion in 1996—more than three times larger than in 1980. This debt often cannot be repaid because of faltering economies, as governments in Indonesia, Korea, Russia, and Thailand learned in 1997 and 1998. Failures to make interest payments are common, and banks are increasingly hesitant to lend more money.

Developing countries that attempt to repay their debts find that interest payments alone take a large share of their earnings from exports. In the late 1970s about $40 billion in net aid per year was transferred to the developing countries. The flow of resources was reversed in the 1980s. Poor countries' payments of principal and interest were higher than the value of new loans and foreign aid received from rich countries.[25]

A common measure of a nation's indebtedness is its debt service, which represents the total payments for interest and principal as a percentage of the country's exports of goods and services. These exports produce the foreign currencies that allow countries to repay their debts and to import foreign products, including food, medicines, and machinery. When debt service increases, nations find that more of their export earnings are required to repay loans, and less money is available for national development. Many developing nations have encountered this problem over the past twenty-five years. Between 1970 and 1996, for example, dozens of developing countries experienced a tripling of their debt service. Many developing countries have asked that their repayments be rescheduled or their debts forgiven. Many banks have been forced to accept the former; most have rejected the latter. In sum, at a time when many countries are not growing enough food, they also find that they cannot afford to import the shortfall, particularly when droughts and poor harvests in exporting countries cause prices to rise.

Shortages in developing countries are not limited to food. Rather than rely on electricity or natural gas, as is common in developed countries, more than three billion people in these countries depend on wood or other traditional fuels for heating and cooking. For approximately two-thirds of these people, according to the FAO, fuelwood is the main or sole source of all domestic energy. In much of the world, however, fuelwood is in short supply, and efforts to acquire it are time-consuming and environmentally destructive. A typical household in some parts of East Africa spends as many as three hundred days per year searching for and collecting wood. Despite such efforts, the FAO believes that about one hundred million people, half in Africa, are unable to meet their daily minimum needs for fuelwood. Another one billion, mostly in Asia, are able to satisfy their needs, but only through unsustainable exploitation of existing resources.

The Destruction of Tropical Forests

Shortages of fuelwood point to a much larger and potentially catastrophic problem—the destruction of tropical forests. The rain forests of Africa, South America, and Southeast Asia are treasure chests of incomparable biological diversity. These forests provide irreplaceable habitats for as much as 80 percent of the world's species of plants and animals, most of which remain to be discovered and described scientifically. Among the species already investigated, many contribute to human well-being. More than one-quarter of the prescription drugs used in the United States have their origins in tropical plants. Viable forests also stabilize soils, reduce the impact and incidence of floods, and regulate local climates, watersheds, and river systems.[26] In addition, increasing concern about the effect of excessive levels of carbon dioxide in the atmosphere (the greenhouse effect) underscores the global importance of tropical forests. Through photosynthesis, trees and other plants remove carbon dioxide from the atmosphere and convert it into oxygen. The functions that tropical forests perform are so ecologically priceless that some people argue that these forests should be protected as inviolable sanctuaries. However desirable such protection might be, what often occurs is exactly the opposite. Tropical rain forests, contend Paul and Anne Ehrlich, "are the major ecosystems now under the most determined assault by humanity."[27]

At the beginning of this century, tropical forests covered approximately 10 percent of the Earth's surface, or about 5.8 million square miles. The deforestation of recent decades has diminished this area by about one-third. If current rates of deforestation continue unabated, only a few areas of forest will remain untouched. Humans will have destroyed a natural palliative for the greenhouse effect and condemned half of all species to extinction.

Causes and Solutions

Solutions to the problem of tropical deforestation depend on the root cause. One view blames poverty and the pressures associated with growing populations and shifting cultivators.

Landless peasants, so the argument goes, invade tropical forests and denude them for fuelwood, grazing, or to grow crops with which to survive. Frequent clearing of new areas is necessary because tropical soils are often thin, relatively infertile, and lack sufficient nutrients. Such areas are ill-suited for sustained agricultural production.

In spite of this knowledge, some governments have actively encouraged resettlement schemes that require extensive deforestation. In Brazil, which has about 30 percent of the world's tropical forests, the government opened the Amazon region in the name of land reform. After the government built several highways into the interior and offered free land to attract settlers, the population of some Amazonian states soared by as much as a hundredfold between the mid 1960s and the late 1980s. Thousands of square miles of forest were cleared each year to accommodate the new arrivals and to provide them with permanent settlements.

Indonesia's transmigration program moves people from the densely populated islands of Java and Bali to sparsely populated, but heavily forested, outer islands. Other forested land is being cleared to increase the acreage allotted to cocoa, rubber, palm oil, and other cash crops intended for export.

Another explanation for deforestation places primary blame on commercial logging intended to satisfy demands for tropical hardwoods in developed countries. Whether strapped for foreign exchange, required to repay loans from foreign banks, or subjected to domestic pressure to develop their economies, governments in the developing world frequently regard the resources of tropical forests as sources of ready income. Exports of wood now produce billions of dollars in annual revenues for developing countries, and some countries impose few limits in their rush to the bank. Southeast Asia contains about 25 percent of all tropical forests, but the region produces more than three-quarters of the value of all exports of tropical hardwoods.

If tropical forests were managed in an environmentally sustainable manner, the flow of income and benefits to local populations could continue indefinitely. Unfortunately, few tropical forests are so managed, and many countries are now becoming victims of past greed and too-rapid exploitation. About three dozen countries were exporters of tropical hardwoods in the late 1980s, but fewer than ten of these countries will have enough wood to export at the end of the 1990s.

Recognizing the causes and consequences of deforestation is not enough to bring about a solution. Commercial logging is profitable, and few governments in developing countries are equipped to manage their forests properly. These governments often let logging companies harvest trees in designated areas under certain conditions. All too frequently, however, the conditions are inadequate or not well enforced because there are too few forest guards. Paltry wages for guards also create opportunities for corruption.

Although penalties can be imposed on those who violate the conditions, violators are rarely apprehended. When they are, the fine is often less than the profits that accrue from the violation. Some countries require companies with concessions to post bonds, which are returned once the companies complete mandatory reforestation projects. Here again, however, the amounts involved are often so low that many companies forfeit their bonds rather than reforest. Moreover, concessions are typically granted for brief periods that discourage reforestation.

An Alternative View of the Problem

As the pace of tropical deforestation has quickened, so have international pressures on developing countries to halt or mitigate it. In response, leaders of developing countries quickly emphasize how ironic it is that developed countries, whose increasing consumption creates the demand for tropical woods, are simultaneously calling for a reduction of logging and shifting cultivation in developing countries.

In addition, the developing countries correctly note Europe's destruction of its forests during the industrial revolution and the widespread cutting in the United States in the nineteenth century. Why then should developing countries be held to a different standard than the developed ones? Just as Europeans and Americans decided how and when to extract their resources, developing countries insist that they too should be allowed to determine their own patterns of consumption. One observer, examining the situation in Indonesia, cast the problem in economic terms. He wondered how bureaucracies in poor countries can overcome domestic pressures for economic development. He raised this question after hearing the views of an Indonesian involved with logging. As the Indonesian businessman declared, "We are a profit-oriented company, and if that means destroying the environment within the legal limit, then we will do it."[28]

Such views are not universally shared, and change is in evidence in many developing countries. Thailand imposed a nationwide ban on logging in 1989, despite projections that the ban would cause thousands of people to lose their jobs. Ghana, Côte d'Ivoire, and the Philippines similarly announced restrictions on logging in the late 1980s. These are well-intentioned efforts, but in each instance the restrictions were imposed well after they could do much good. Moreover, such restrictions can be counterproductive. Without an assured stream of revenue from timber sales, incentives for sustainable management decline.[29]

International collaboration between wood-producing and wood-consuming nations offers one hope in the battle against deforestation. To date, however, such collaboration has only a modest record. The International Tropical Timber Organization (ITTO), formed in 1985, was on the brink of collapse just a few years later.[30] Several importing nations had refused to pay their full dues, Japanese importers boycotted ITTO's meetings, and the organization could claim few accomplishments other than its tenuous survival. The ITTO issued best-practice guidelines for the management of tropical forests in 1990; it has asked all countries to adhere to these guidelines by 2000 and to ensure that all exports of tropical timbers after that date are from sustainably managed forests. This is a highly ambitious and probably unrealistic goal.

More recently, despite repeated efforts, the Intergovernmental Panel on Forests, which included more than seventy countries, was unable to reach agreement about how to preserve the world's forest resources. The European Union and several timber-exporting countries favored an international convention that would require nations to meet certain standards for logging and preservation. Other exporting nations asserted that it is inappropriate for other countries to determine how and when domestic natural resources, including forests, are exploited. The United States opposed a convention in the belief that it would impose unacceptable economic costs on the American timber industry.

Will tropical forests survive? Solutions abound. What is lacking, however, is a consensus about which of these solutions will best meet the essential needs of the poor, the reasonable objectives of timber-exporting and timber-importing nations, and the inflexible imperatives of ecological stability.

Fortunately, there is a growing realization that much can be done to stem the loss of tropical forests. For example, nearly ninety countries had developed tropical forest "action plans" by 1994. These plans describe the status of tropical forests in each country as well as strategies to preserve them for future generations. Unfortunately, implementation of these plans does not always parallel the good intentions associated with them. Likewise, rather than seeing forests solely as a source of wood or additional agricultural land, many countries are now examining the export potential of forest products other than wood. The expectation is that the sale of these products—such as cork, rattan, oils, resins, and medicinal plants—will provide economic incentives to maintain rather than destroy forests.

Other proposed options to maintain tropical forests include programs to certify that timber exports are from forests that are managed sustainably. Importers and potential consumers would presumably avoid timber products without such certification. For such programs to be successful, however, exporters would have to accept the certification process and there would have to be widespread agreement about what sustainable management means. That agreement is still absent. In addition, no country would want to subject itself to the process only to be told that its timber exports do not meet the requirements for certification.

Another approach would impose taxes on timber exports (or imports). The highest taxes would be imposed on logging that causes the greatest ecological costs; timber from sustainable operations would face the lowest taxes.[31] Yet another option would increase reliance on community-based management of forest resources. Rather than allowing logging companies with no long-term interest in a forest to harvest trees, community-based management would place responsibility for decisions about logging (and other uses) with the people who live in or adjacent to forests. These people have the strongest incentives to manage forest resources wisely, particularly if they reap the long-term benefits of their management strategies.

Debt-for-nature swaps provide still another means to protect fragile environments. These swaps allow countries to reduce their foreign debts, which are usually denominated in dollars, in exchange for agreements to increase expenditures of local currencies on environmental activities. Sustained concern about tropical forests suggests that many other imaginative ways to protect these forests will soon emerge. Having noted these causes for optimism, it is important to emphasize that much remains to be done if tropical forests are to be preserved.

Conflicting Signals from the Industrial Nations

Improvements in the policies of many developing countries are surely necessary if sustainable development is to be achieved. As already noted, however, industrial countries sometimes cause or contribute to environmental problems there.

Patterns of consumption provide an example. Although the United States and other industrial nations can boast about their own low rates of population growth, developing nations reply that patterns of consumption, not population increases, are the real culprits. This view suggests that negative impacts on the environment are a function of population growth plus consumption and technology.

Applying this formula places major responsibility for environmental problems on rich nations, despite their relatively small numbers of global inhabitants. The inhabitants of these nations consume far more of the Earth's resources than their numbers justify. Consider that the richest one-fifth of the world's nations control about 85 percent of the world's income and consume about 45 percent of all meat and fish, nearly 60 percent of its energy, and three-quarters of its paper, chemicals, iron, and steel. These nations similarly generate more than 90 percent of all hazardous and industrial wastes. The United States leads the world in per capita production of trash and has one of the lowest rates of recycling among industrialized countries. Consider as well that these relatively few rich nations are likewise responsible for releasing more than two-thirds of all greenhouse gases and more than 90 percent of all ozone-depleting chlorofluorocarbons into the atmosphere.[32]

In contrast, consumption patterns among the 20 percent of the world's population living in the lowest income countries account for less than 1.5 percent of the world's private consumption and only about 5 percent of the world's consumption of meat and fish. According to the U.N. Development

Programme, consumption declined in seventy countries between the early 1970s and the mid 1990s.[33]

Comparing such a decline with the situation in the United States is instructive. Americans represent less than 5 percent of the Earth's inhabitants, yet they consume almost 30 percent of the world's commercial energy. Much of this energy is used to fuel Americans' love for the automobile, one of the most environmentally harmful technologies known to humans. While Americans increased their numbers by about 20 percent in the 1970s and 1980s, the total number of automobiles in use in the United States grew by more than 50 percent. One-fifth of American households now have three or more cars (as compared to one family in twenty-five in 1969), and the average horsepower of the typical American vehicle increased by nearly 60 percent between the early 1980s and the late 1990s.[34] American drivers also encounter some of the world's lowest prices for gasoline and have one of the highest rates of per capita consumption of gasoline in the world.

Adjusted for inflation, the cost of gasoline in the United States was lower in the late 1990s than at any time in the previous thirty years and less than half of what it had been in the early 1980s. In fact, despite having to import about half of its petroleum, the price for a gallon of gasoline consumed in the United States is often lower than the price of an equivalent amount of bottled water, *even when tap water is used to fill these bottles.* As might be expected, low prices for petroleum encourage consumption rather than conservation, and rates of growth in consumption of gasoline exceed U.S. rates of population growth.

Although the United States made sizable gains in fuel efficiency in the 1970s and 1980s, many of these gains are being eroded in the late 1990s as Americans drive faster and farther, and as they increasingly rely on vans and sport utility vehicles rather than cars.[35] The typical American still uses about two and one-half times more gasoline per year than does the typical German. Americans' profligacy with fossil fuels provides part of the explanation for U.S. production of almost one-fifth of the emissions that contribute to global warming.

Americans' patterns of food consumption are also of interest. As noted in table 15-2, an average American consumes over 3,600 calories per day, one of the highest levels in the world. About 20 percent of these calories come from sugars. The United States (and New Zealand) lead the world in annual per capita consumption of meat. Few nations waste as much food as does the United States. The U.S. Department of Agriculture estimates that Americans waste about ninety-six billion pounds of edible food each year—about one-quarter of all the food available to them and about a pound a day for each American.[36]

As environmental scholar Paul Harrison has noted, because of such inequalities in consumption, continued population growth in rich countries is a greater threat to the global environment than it is in the developing world. He adds that if relative consumption and levels of waste output remain unchanged, the 57 million extra inhabitants likely to be born in rich countries in the 1990s will pollute the globe more than the extra 900 million born else-where. Other experts suggest that if Americans want to maintain their present standard of living and levels of energy consumption, then the ideal population for the United States is between 40 million and 100 million, far less than the current population of 270 million.[37]

Causes for Optimism?

Although there is cause for concern about the prospects for sustainable development among developing countries, the situation is neither entirely bleak nor beyond hope. Millions of people throughout the world have been the beneficiaries of considerable social and economic development over the past two decades. The number of chronically malnourished people in devel-oping countries declined by more than 150 million between 1970 and 1990, and the number of families in developing countries with access to sanitary facilities and clean water surged in the 1980s and 1990s. Smallpox, a killer of millions of people every year in the 1950s, has been eradicated. Between 1970 and 1998, infant mortality rates declined in nearly all developing coun-tries—in many by significant amounts. These and other dramatic improve-ments prompted the World Bank to conclude that "health conditions around the world have improved more in the past forty years than in all previous human history."[38]

The international community is also demonstrating a new recognition of the Earth's ecological interconnectedness. At the request of the U.N. General Assembly, the World Commission on Environment and Develop-ment was established in 1983 and charged with formulating long-term envi-ronmental strategies for achieving sustainable development. In its report, *Our Common Future*, the commission forcefully emphasized that although environmental degradation is an issue of survival for developing nations, fail-ure to address the degradation satisfactorily will guarantee unparalleled and undesirable global consequences from which no nation will escape.[39] The re-port's release in 1987 prompted increased international attention to environ-mental issues.

This attention manifested itself most noticeably in the U.N. Conference on Environment and Development in Río de Janeiro in 1992, which, in turn, led to the creation of the U.N. Commission on Sustainable Development (CSD). The commission, which meets annually, reviews nations' efforts to implement international environmental agreements and their progress in achieving sustainable development.[40]

Delegates at the Río conference also approved Agenda 21, a plan for enhancing global environmental quality. The price tag for the recommended actions is huge—an estimated $600 billion per year for seven years, of which developed nations would be expected to provide at least $125 billion per year, or about twice as much as they now devote to all foreign assistance each year. Rich nations could afford to provide this amount if they donated as little as 0.70 percent (*not* 7 percent, but seven-tenths of 1 percent) of their total eco-nomic output to the developing world each year. Only Norway, Sweden,

Denmark, and the Netherlands exceeded this target in the 1990s. The Japanese pledged to move toward the recommended target, but U.S. foreign assistance as a percentage of its gross domestic product (GDP) declined steadily between the 1960s and 1997. At 0.08 percent of GDP in 1997, U.S. foreign assistance was well below the target level and the lowest among twenty-two advanced industrial countries, leading one observer to label the United States as the "global Scrooge." According to the U.N. Development Programme, official development aid from all donor nations in 1997 was the lowest it had been since record keeping began.

The prospects for increasing U.S. assistance to address environmental problems in developing countries are not good. Most Americans believe that Asians and Africans should solve their own environmental problems. According to one opinion survey, most Americans also believe that the U.S. government provides far more assistance than it actually does to poor countries. The survey found that the average respondent thinks that about 18 percent of the U.S. federal budget is devoted to foreign assistance, but that 8 percent would be an appropriate amount. The actual amount is less than 1 percent.[41]

In contrast to Americans' seeming reluctance to share their wealth, other nations have demonstrated an increased willingness to address globally shared environmental problems. The international community now operates a Global Environment Facility (GEF), a multibillion-dollar effort to finance environmental projects in developing countries. The World Bank, the U.N. Development Programme, and the U.N. Environment Programme implement the GEF and distribute funds to address four priority areas: global warming, loss of biological diversity, pollution of international waters, and depletion of the ozone layer.

In addition, more than 170 countries have ratified the Convention on Biological Diversity. Participating nations meet each year to discuss accomplishments and next steps. Many of these nations approved a Convention to Combat Desertification in late 1996. The following December representatives from more than 100 countries met in Kyoto, Japan, to discuss implementation of the U.N. Framework Convention on Climate Change, which more than 175 countries have ratified. In an historic agreement, industrialized nations agreed to reduce emissions that contribute to global warming by an average of about 5 percent below 1990 levels in the period from 2008 to 2012. The United States, because it is one of the largest producers of these emissions, agreed to reduce them by 7 percent (see chap. 13).

Meeting this goal will create considerable challenges for U.S. policymakers. U.S. emissions of greenhouse gases are already well over the target for 2008–2012. If current trends in consumption of fossil fuels continue, emissions of greenhouse gases will be more than 40 percent higher than the target allows. Convincing politicians to impose restraints on U.S. energy consumption will be difficult. Although many developing nations applauded pledges to reduce greenhouse gases in the industrialized world, most of these nations refused to make any commitments to reduce their own emissions until they saw results from Europe and the United States. The developing nations argue that self-imposed limits on emissions would stifle their economic growth and put them at a competitive disadvantage if the developed nations do not meet the goals they set for themselves.

The United States did not sign the Convention on Climate Change until November 1998, but this still leaves the need for Senate ratification, which is highly unlikely in the near future due to intense opposition. In an effort to allay this opposition, the Clinton administration negotiated an agreement at the Kyoto meetings that allows industrialized countries, including the United States, to pay developing nations to reduce their emissions so that the rich nations do not have to do so. Paying others to reduce their emissions would ensure that development in rich nations would not be slowed, or so it is argued. The payment plan is controversial because it allows rich nations to avoid imposing potentially large constraints on their citizens' consumption of energy. Despite the opposition to the payment plan, it is not without some merit. The burning of fossil fuels is highly inefficient in most developing countries, and few of their motor vehicles, which are major sources of pollution, have emission-control devices. The payment plan has the potential to promote the transfer of technology to developing nations, to improve the health of millions of people, and to reduce energy consumption as efficiency improves.

Many developing nations recognize their obligations to protect their environments as well as the global commons. At the same time, however, these nations argue that success requires technical and financial assistance from their wealthy colleagues. However desirable the protection of tropical forests and biological diversity and the prevention of global warming and a depleted ozone layer, the poor nations cannot afford to address these problems in the absence of cooperation from richer nations. The prospects for achieving such cooperation are uncertain. Developing nations like China and India want to provide refrigerators to as many of their inhabitants as possible. These hundreds of millions of refrigerators will require extraordinary amounts of chlorofluorocarbons (CFCs) unless companies in developed nations are willing to share the scientific secrets associated with substitutes for the CFCs. These companies are reluctant to do so, arguing that they are in business to make money, not to give away valuable trade secrets.

This reluctance has important consequences. China's economic growth over the past decade boosted its share of the world's CFC emissions from 3 percent in 1986 to nearly 20 percent in 1995. From 1990 to 1997 alone, Chinese emissions of carbon into the atmosphere increased by more than 35 percent. Over the same period sales of new cars in China increased by an average of 33 percent per year.[42] China's emissions of gases that contribute to global warming can also be expected to increase rapidly as it industrializes. China has vast reserves of coal, which are burned to produce electricity, albeit without the pollution control devices typically installed on power plants elsewhere. Unfortunately, the Chinese are among the least efficient users of energy in the world. They require more energy to produce a given level of economic output than all but a few other countries.

The economic, population, and environmental problems of the developing world dwarf those of the industrial nations and are not amenable to immediate resolution, but immediate action is imperative. Millions of people are steadily destroying their biological and environmental support systems at unprecedented rates in order to meet their daily needs for food, fuel, and fiber. Driven by poverty and the need to survive, they have become ravenous souls on a planet approaching the limits of its tolerance and resilience. Whether this situation will change depends on the ability of residents in the developing countries not only to reap the benefits of sustained economic development but also to meet the demands of current populations while using their natural resources in a way that accommodates the needs of future generations. Unless the developing nations are able to do so soon, their future will determine ours as well. It is both naive and unreasonable to assume that the consequences of population growth, environmental degradation, and abysmal poverty in developing countries will remain within their political boundaries.[43]

Notes

1. World Bank, *World Development Report 1998–1999* (New York: Oxford University Press, 1999), 190–191. Due to differences in the costs of goods and services from one country to another, gross national product per capita does not provide comparable measures of economic well-being. To address this problem, economists have developed a measure that reflects purchasing-power parity (PPP). Such a measure attempts to equalize the prices of identical goods and services across all countries, with the United States as the base economy. For a humorous but helpful explanation and application of the PPP concept, see "Big MacCurrencies," *Economist*, April 11, 1998, 58, which compares the price of a McDonald's Big Mac hamburger in more than thirty countries.

2. Population Action International (PAI), *Reproductive Risk: A Worldwide Assessment of Women's Sexual and Maternal Health* (Washington, D.C.: PAI, 1995).

3. U.N. Children's Fund (UNICEF), *State of the World's Children 1989* (New York: Oxford University Press, 1989), 37. UNICEF's annual report on this subject, and a companion report, *The Progress of Nations*, are excellent sources of information about the status of children in developing countries. These reports can be accessed at *http://www.unicef.org/*. Other good sources of information about the environment and development include the U.N. Development Programme's annual report on human development (available at *http://www.undp.org/hdro/*), the U.N. Environment Programme's *Global State of the Environment Report* (available at *http//www.unep.org/unep/eia.geo1/ch/toc.htm*), the Food and Agriculture Organization's *State of the World Forests* (available at *http://www.fao.org/WAICENT/faoinfo/forestry/SOFOPDF/SOFO97.pdf*), and the World Bank's *World Development Report*, which Oxford University Press publishes. The *Economist*, another excellent source, published a "A Survey of Development and the Environment" in its issue of March 21, 1998.

4. World Commission on Environment and Development, *Our Common Future* (London: Oxford University Press, 1987), 8, 43.

5. John N. Wilford, "A Tough-Minded Ecologist Comes to Defense of Malthus," *New York Times*, June 30, 1987, C3.

6. United Nations, Population Division, Department of Social and Economic Affairs, "Revision of the World Population Estimates and Projections," (New York: United Nations, 1998; available at *http://www.popin.org/pop1998/*). Colin Clark, *Population Growth and Land Use*, 2d ed. (London: Macmillan, 1977), 153 ("the world's potential agricultural and forest land could supply the needs of 157 billion people"); Paul Ehrlich and Anne Ehrlich, *Extinction* (New York: Random House, 1981), 243 (start-

348   Richard J. Tobin

ing a gradual decline of the human population is "obviously essential"). For an excellent discussion of the world's carrying capacity, see Vaclav Smil, "How Many People Can the Earth Feed?" *Population and Development Review* 2 (June 1994): 255–292.

7. Richard Bernstein, "World's Surging Birthrate Tops the Mexico City Agenda," *New York Times*, July 29, 1984, sec. 4, 3; "Speech by the Head of the Delegation of the People's Republic of China at the World Population Conference," Bucharest, August, 1974," in *Population and Development Review* 2 (June 1994): 452.

8. Lester R. Brown, "Analyzing the Demographic Trap," in *State of the World, 1987*, ed. Lester R. Brown (New York: Norton, 1987), 20.

9. World Health Organization (WHO), *Executive Summary of the World Health Report 1995: Bridging the Gaps* (Geneva: WHO, 1995), 13.

10. "The Good News: Thailand Controls a Baby Boom," *Time*, Asian international ed., January 2, 1989, 37; and G. Tyler Miller, "Cops and Rubbers Day in Thailand," in *Living in the Environment*, 8th ed. (Belmont, Calif.: Wadsworth Publishing Co., 1994).

11. K. Srinivasan, "Population Policy and Programme," in U.N. Economic and Social Commission for Asia and the Pacific, *Population of India* (New York: United Nations, 1982), 161. For a discussion of India's family planning programs, see Sharon L. Camp and Shanti R. Conly, *India's Family Planning Challenge: From Rhetoric to Action* (Washington, D.C.: Population Crisis Committee, 1992).

12. U.N. Department of International Economic and Social Affairs, *World Population Policies*, vol. 1 (New York: United Nations, 1987), 127–129.

13. Marshall Green, "Is China Easing Up on Birth Control?" *New York Times*, April 23, 1986, A25; "The Mewling That They'll Miss," *Economist*, August 13, 1988, 27. For an analysis of the application of China's population policies, see Susan Greenhalgh, Zhu Chuzhu, and Li Nan, "Restraining Population Growth in Three Chinese Villages, 1988–1993," *Population and Development Review* 20 (June 1994): 365–395. See also Elisabeth Rosenthal, "For One-Child Policy, China Rethinks Iron Hand," *New York Times*, November 1, 1998, A1.

14. C. Alison McIntosh and Jason L. Finkle, "The Cairo Conference on Population and Development: A New Paradigm?" *Population and Development Review* 21 (June 1995): 223.

15. As an example of this perspective, see Julian Simon, *The Ultimate Resource* (Princeton, N.J.: Princeton University Press, 1981). See also Ester Boserup, *The Conditions of Agricultural Growth* (London: Allen and Unwin, 1965).

16. Sheldon L. Richman, letter to the editor, *New York Times*, June 30, 1992, A22.

17. Brown, *State of the World*, 21.

18. Per Pinstrup-Anderson, the director-general of the International Food Policy Research Institute (IFPRI), believes the world can easily feed twelve billion people one hundred years from now. See "Will the World Starve?" *Economist*, June 10, 1995, 39.

19. U.N. Development Programme, *Human Development Report 1998* (Oxford: Oxford University Press, 1998), 160–161; and World Bank, *World Development Report 1998–1999*, 192–193.

20. FAO, *Potential Population-Supporting Capacities of Lands in the Developing World* (Rome: FAO, 1982).

21. Brown, *State of the World*, 24. The criticisms of the study are from Brown's analysis of the FAO report.

22. Ousmane Badiane and Christopher L. Delgado, eds., *A 2020 Vision for Food, Agriculture, and the Environment in Sub-Saharan Africa* (Washington, D.C.: IFPRI, 1995), 7.

23. Jikun Huang, Scott Rozelle, and Mark Rosegrant, *China's Food Economy to the Twenty-First Century: Supply, Demand, and Trade* (Washington, D.C.: IFPRI, 1997), 5.

24. André de Moor and Peter Calamai, *Subsidizing Unsustainable Development: Undermining the Earth with Public Funds* (San José, Costa Rica: Institute for Research on Public Expenditures and the Earth Council, 1997); and U.N. Development Programme, *Human Development Report 1992* (New York: Oxford University Press, 1992), 67.

25. Organization for Economic Co-operation and Development (OECD), Development Assistance Committee, *Development Cooperation 1994* (Paris: OECD, 1994), 58–59, 62–63.

26. National Academy of Sciences (NAS), *Population Growth and Economic Development: Policy Questions* (Washington, D.C.: NAS, 1986), 31; FAO, Committee on Food Development in the Tropics, *Tropical Forest Action Plan* (Rome: FAO, 1985), 2, 47.

27. Ehrlich and Ehrlich, *Extinction*, 160.

28. Michael Vatikiotis, "Tug-of-War over Trees," *Far Eastern Economic Review*, January 12, 1989, 41.

29. FAO, *World Agriculture: Towards 2010* (New York: Wiley, 1994), 223.

30. Margaret Scott, "Unequal to the Task," *Far Eastern Economic Review*, January 12, 1989, 38; Marcus Colchester, "The International Tropical Timber Organization: Kill or Cure for the Rainforest?" *Ecologist* (September–October 1990).

31. Edward B. Barbier, Joanne C. Burgess, Joshua Bishop, and Bruce Aylward, *The Economics of the Tropical Timber Trade* (London: Earthscan, 1994); Alan Thein Durning, "Redesigning the Forest Economy," in *State of the World 1994*, ed. Lester R. Brown (New York: Norton, 1994), 31.

32. U.N. Development Programme, *Human Development Report 1998*, 2; and "Trash as Treasure," *Washington Post*, October 17, 1998, A14.

33. U.N. Development Programme, *Human Development Report 1998*, 7.

34. Allen R. Myerson, "U.S. Splurging on Energy After Falling Off Its Diet," *New York Times*, October 22, 1998, A1.

35. Agis Salpukas, "What Next, Tail Fins? Fast Speeds and Big Cars Send Gas Consumption Up," *New York Times*, February 15, 1996, D1.

36. Linda Scott Kantor, Kathryn Lipton, Alden Manchester, and Victor Oliveira, "Estimating and Addressing America's Food Losses," *Food Review*, vol. 20 (January–April 1997). The article can be accessed at *http://151.121.66.126:80/Whatsnew/Feature/ARCHIVES/JULAUG97/final.PDF*.

37. Paul Harrison, *The Third Revolution: Environment, Population and a Sustainable World* (New York: I. B. Taurus, 1992), 256–257; David Pimintel and Marcia Pimentel, "Land, Energy and Water: The Constraints Governing Ideal U.S. Population Size," *NPG Forum*, January 1990, 5.

38. World Bank, *World Development Report 1993* (New York: Oxford University Press, 1993), 21. Data on birth rates are from the World Bank, *World Development Report 1998–1999*, and U.N. Development Programme, *Human Development Report 1998*, 156.

39. World Commission on Environment and Development, *Our Common Future*.

40. *Linkages—A Multimedia Resource for Environment and Development Policy Makers (http://www.iisd.ca/linkages/welcome.html)* provides a handy way to remain informed about the formulation and implementation of international environmental agreements. *Linkages* provides scores of text pages on ongoing negotiation processes as well as an archive for past negotiations, including the U.N. Conference on Population and Development.

41. Marcy E. Mullins, "How Three Nations View the Future," *USA Today*, June 1, 1992, 8A; Rae Tyson, "Poll: Environment Tops Agenda," *USA Today*, June 1, 1992, 1A. Both articles report the results of public opinion surveys conducted in May 1992 by the Gordon S. Black Corp.

42. Tom Boden, Antoinette Brenkert, Bob Andres, and Cathy Johnston, "Revised National CO_2 Emissions from Fossil-Fuel Burning, Cement Manufacturing, and Gas Flaring: 1751–1995," Carbon Dioxide Information Analysis Center, Oak Ridge National Laboratory, January 1998 (available at *http://cdiac.esd.ornl.gov/ftp/ndp030/nation95.env*). This report provides estimates of total carbon emissions and per capita carbon emissions for most countries. The annual average growth rate for car sales in China is from "Emerging-Market Indicators: Cars," *Economist*, June 13, 1998, 102. China led the world in annual average growth rates of car sales between 1990 and 1997 and is expected to do so between 1997 and 2005.

43. Lester R. Brown and Christopher Flavin, "A New Economy for a New Century," in *State of the World 1999*, ed. Lester R. Brown (New York: Norton, 1999), 3–21.

16

International Trade and Environmental Regulation

David Vogel

This chapter explores the increasingly important and often contentious relationship between international trade and environmental regulation. It begins by explaining why these two policy areas have recently become more closely linked, and then reviews environmentalists' criticisms of trade liberalization. The next two sections explore the environmental dimensions of the World Trade Organization (WTO), formerly the General Agreement on Tariffs and Trade (GATT), and the North American Free Trade Agreement (NAFTA), including the unsuccessful effort to extend the latter to Chile. The concluding section of the chapter assesses the likely impact of trade liberalization on environmental standards.

The Growth of Policy Linkages

The growth of policy linkages between the formerly distinct policy areas of trade and environmental regulation is related to the convergence of two critical postwar trends: an increase in both the volume of world trade and the amount and scope of environmental regulation.[1]

Thanks to the GATT and the WTO at the global level, and to other treaties and agreements at a regional level, such as those associated with the European Union (EU), tariff levels have declined steadily throughout the postwar period. As a consequence, trade negotiations have begun to pay greater attention to nontariff barriers (NTBs)—government policies that discriminate against imports through means other than tariffs. Examples of NTBs include quotas, procurement policies favoring domestic producers, and subsidies. Another important category of NTBs consists of government regulations and, more specific to the topic of this chapter, environmental standards. Many of these regulations, often inadvertently, but sometimes intentionally, restrict trade by imposing greater burdens on foreign producers than on domestic ones.

Accordingly, reducing the role of government regulations as obstacles to trade has become an important priority of both regional and international trade negotiations and agreements. In the second half of the 1980s, for example, the EU's precursor, the European Community (EC), chose to harmonize many environmental and consumer regulations to prevent them from being used to restrict trade among member states. EC law also required its member states to admit any product approved for use in another member state. Likewise, a major result of the Uruguay Round GATT negotiations, which created the World Trade Organization (WTO), was to strengthen the Standards Code, originally established in 1979 to prevent national standards from serving as "technical barriers to trade." NAFTA also includes a number of provisions that seek to restrict its members (Canada, Mexico, and the United States) from using NTBs to undermine regional economic integration.

Economic integration has thus subjected an increasing number of public policies that were formally the exclusive purview of national governments to both regional and international scrutiny. Trade liberalization has made the politics of environmental protection more global: it means that governments, in formulating their environmental policies, must now take into account their impact not only on national producers but on their foreign competitors as well. At the same time—as the trade disputes discussed below will illustrate—trade agreements have also provided foreign producers with a legal vehicle for challenging the domestic regulations of their trading partners, if those regulations appear to unfairly discriminate against their exports. Consequently, agreements to expand trade have frequently challenged national regulatory sovereignty.

The second trend fostering increased policy linkages between trade and regulation has been the steady expansion of environmental regulation. The past three decades have witnessed a significant increase in the number of government regulations that directly affect traded goods. These include automobile emission standards; rules governing the content and disposal of packaging; chemical safety regulations; regulations for the processing, composition, and labeling of food; and rules to protect wildlife and natural resources. The steady growth of protective regulation has forced exporters to cope with an increasingly diverse and complex array of national standards, many of which have made trade more difficult. Because nations generally want to maintain their own standards in spite of—or sometimes because of—the burdens they impose on imports, the continual growth of national environmental regulations represents a growing source of trade conflict.

The scope of environmental policy also grew steadily during the second half of the 1980s. Many environmental issues have taken on a global dimension that requires the coordination of national regulatory policies. These include saving endangered species located in foreign lands or international waters, protecting the ozone layer, safeguarding the shipment and disposal of hazardous wastes, and preserving tropical forests in developing countries. This coordination often involves trade restrictions, however, either as a means to prevent "free riding" or because the harm itself is trade related. Many developing countries have strongly criticized the use of trade restrictions by developed countries as a form of "eco-imperlialism."

As a result of the expansion of both trade and regulation, the debate between supporters of environmental regulation and advocates of free trade has become both more visible and more contentious. Free trade advocates want to limit the use of regulations as barriers to trade, while environmentalists and consumer advocates want to prevent trade agreements from serving as barriers to regulation. The trade community worries about an upsurge of "eco-protectionism"—the justification of trade barriers on environmental grounds. For their part, consumer and environmental organizations fear that trade liberalization will serve to weaken both their own country's regulatory standards as well as those of its trading partners.

Environmentalists and Free Trade

Many environmental groups have become increasingly critical of treaties and trade agreements that promote liberalization. As one activist put it, "When they call me protectionist, I respond, 'Well, if protecting the earth, if protecting the air, if protecting the water, and indeed human life is protectionist, then I have to admit I am protectionist'." [2] Although their views are by no means uniform, those within the environmental community do share a number of criticisms of free trade.

A primary concern of environmentalists is that growing international competition will weaken national regulatory standards. As tariffs and other trade barriers between developed and developing nations fall, producers in the developed nations are increasingly forced to compete with goods produced in nations with laxer standards. Environmentalists fear that producers in industrial nations will demand the relaxation of their country's regulatory standards in order to remain competitive; alternatively, they may relocate their production to "pollution havens," thus giving developing nations a still greater incentive to keep their standards lax or even to lower them further. Hence, trade liberalization is likely to result in a regulatory "race to the bottom" as nations compete with one another by weakening their environmental standards.

Environmentalists also worry that trade liberalization is directly harming environmental quality. Trade liberalization increases the level of global economic activity; indeed, that is among its major purposes. But the Earth's ability to sustain current levels of economic growth is limited. By increasing the rate at which the Earth's scarce natural resources such as forests, fossil fuels, and fisheries are consumed, free trade is said to undermine sustainable development. Liberal trade policies may also indirectly contribute to the greenhouse effect by stimulating an increase in the use of fossil fuels, thus endangering the welfare of the entire planet. Finally, environmentalists worry that accelerating the rate at which goods and raw materials are transported around the world increases not only energy use but also the likelihood of accidents, such as oil or chemical spills in international waters.

The GATT

The Tuna/Dolphin Case

Environmentalists have been particularly critical of international trade rules that limit a signatory nation's ability to use trade measures to influence the environmental policies of its trading partners. This was a central issue in the tuna/dolphin case, the most visible and controversial trade-dispute panel decision in the GATT's nearly fifty-year history. Indeed, environmental opposition to the Uruguay Round GATT agreement was mobilized largely in reaction to the 1991 decision that declared sections of the Marine Mammal Protection Act to be in violation of U.S. obligations under the GATT.

In the eastern tropical Pacific, where approximately one-quarter of tuna are harvested, dolphins commonly swim above schools of tuna. As a result, the large purse-seine nets used to catch tuna also kill large numbers of dolphins. By the late 1960s dolphin fatalities had reached roughly five hundred thousand per year. In order to protect dolphins, the United States imposed limits on the number of dolphins that could be killed annually by U.S. commercial tuna-fishing vessels.

By the late 1980s, thanks to the tightening of U.S. regulatory standards, along with various improvements in fishing technology, incidental dolphin mortality by U.S.-registered vessels had declined by more than 90 percent. Foreign fishing fleets, however, continued to kill dolphins at a higher rate than did their American counterparts. A major portion of these tuna were then exported to the U.S. market, which accounts for approximately half of global tuna consumption. Following a 1990 federal court decision, the United States prohibited imports of tuna from Mexico, Venezuela, and the Pacific islands of Vanuatu. This embargo affected approximately $30 million worth of tuna imports annually.

Mexico challenged the U.S. embargo on the grounds that GATT rules prohibit a nation from using trade policies to affect regulatory policies outside its legal jurisdiction. The GATT disputes panel ruled in favor of Mexico. According to the panel, GATT rules permit signatory nations to issue regulations to protect their own citizens or land. Thus, a nation can impose whatever restrictions it wishes on products consumed within its borders—provided they do not discriminate between foreign and domestic products—as well as on the production of goods or natural resources within its borders. The panel ruled, however, that a nation cannot regulate how foreign nationals produce goods or raw materials outside its legal jurisdiction. Accordingly, the United States cannot dictate to Mexico how it can harvest tuna: it cannot make access to its domestic market contingent on Mexico's adopting dolphin protection practices similar to its own.

This decision outraged American environmentalists. As an article in the magazine of the Sierra Club put it, "Meeting in a closed room in Geneva . . . three unelected trade experts . . . conspired to kill Flipper."[3] An environmental activist predicted: "In the 1990s, free trade and efforts to protect the environment are on a collision course."[4] Lori Wallach, a spokesperson for Congress Watch, a public interest lobbying group founded by Ralph Nader, proclaimed: "This case is the smoking gun. We have seen GATT actually declaring that a U.S. environmental law must go. These [trade] agreements must be modified to allow for legitimate consumer and environmental protections."[5] Many American environmental and consumer groups subsequently announced their opposition to the new "Uruguay Round" GATT agreement that was then being negotiated on the grounds that it threatened the ability of the United States to establish and enforce its own regulatory standards.

Environmentalists specifically argued that the GATT dispute panel ruling rested on an artificial and outdated distinction between domestic and extrajurisdictional environmental regulations. They claimed that because all mankind shares a common biosphere, the U.S. environment *is* adversely affected by the killing of dolphins by Mexican fishing fleets, even if this takes place in international waters. As two environmental lawyers argued, "The panel's domestic limitation is nonsensical because it fails to take into account the fact that domestic environmental harms are now, increasingly, being traced to actions occurring beyond a nation's borders. Limiting the reach of a nation's environmental laws to domestic activities substantially undercuts its ability to protect itself from adverse extraterritorial activities."[6] Moreover, "the GATT's focus on 'products' makes it virtually incapable of capturing the environmental costs of externalities related to methods of production."[7]

The CAFE Dispute

After the Uruguay Round negotiations were concluded, but before the Uruguay Round agreement was voted on by Congress, a GATT dispute panel issued a decision in a second trade dispute involving a challenge to an American environmental regulation. The European Union had requested the convening of a dispute panel to determine the GATT consistency of three American automobile regulations and taxes, namely corporate average fuel economy standards (CAFE), the so-called gas-guzzler tax, and a tax on luxury cars. The former two were environmental/conservation measures, while the third was revenue related. The EU claimed that all three measures were discriminatory since their burdens fell disproportionately on European car exports to the United States. While vehicles manufactured in Europe accounted for only 4 percent of American car sales in 1991, they contributed 88 percent of the revenues collected by these measures.

Of the three regulations and taxes addressed in the EU's complaint, CAFE was the most politically important. Originally established in 1975 in the midst of the energy crisis, and subsequently tightened in 1980, CAFE standards are designed to promote fuel efficiency. They are based on the miles per gallon achieved by the sale-weighted average of all vehicles sold by each manufacturer. If a manufacturer's vehicles fall below this standard, they are subject to a substantial financial penalty. Although the penalty applies equally to all car makers doing business in the United States, it has been paid exclusively by European firms. American and Japanese firms have been able to avoid CAFE penalties by averaging their smaller, more fuel-efficient vehicles with their larger, less fuel-efficient ones. However, the European car manufacturers do not have this option since they only export inefficient, luxury vehicles to the United States; they have no smaller cars to bring up the average fuel-efficiency of their fleet.

The *Financial Times* predicted that "should the United States lose this case, it would face as much outcry as the so-called 'tuna-dolphin decision.'"[8] However, in October 1994, the GATT disputes panel ruled in favor of the United States. It concluded that product regulations were GATT-consistent as long as they did not explicitly discriminate on the basis of country of origin and were necessary to protect public health or the environment. This GATT panel decision helped diffuse environmental opposition to the Uruguay Round agreement, which was approved by Congress two months later.

The Uruguay Round Agreement

The Uruguay Round agreement, which concluded in 1994 and was ratified by the U.S. Congress the following year, addressed few of the specific criticisms of environmentalists. But largely as a response to the criticisms of the GATT made by environmentalists, it did explicitly acknowledge one formerly tacit principle. The preamble to the Standards Agreement, now incorporated into the provisions of the newly established WTO, marks the first mention of the word "environment" in the GATT itself. It states that each country "may maintain standards and technical regulations for the protection of human, animal, and plant life and health and of the *environment*" [emphasis added].[9] It also notes that a country should not be prevented from setting technical standards (which include environmental regulations) "at the levels it considers appropriate," a phrase meant to discourage nations from harmonizing standards in a downward direction.[10] In addition, the Agreement on Subsidies and Countervailing Measures permits governments to subsidize up to 20 percent of one-time capital investments to meet new environmental requirements, provided that its subsidies are directly linked and proportional to environmental improvements. This provision makes the granting of environmental subsidies somewhat easier.

At the same time, in an effort to reduce the use of national consumer and environmental regulations as nontariff barriers, the Uruguay Round agreement also requires that national standards or "technical barriers to trade" "not be more trade-restrictive than necessary to fulfill a legitimate objective, taking into account the risks nonfulfillment would create."[11] An earlier draft would have imposed a stricter test of technical barriers to trade by requiring that standards be the "least trade-restrictive available." But this was modified at the insistence of the United States, once again reflecting the influence of the American environmental movement on trade policy.[12]

The WTO

Reformulated Gasoline

The fact that the first trade dispute adjudicated by the WTO involved the alleged use of an environmental regulation as a nontariff trade barrier suggests the continued importance of trade and environmental linkages. On

October 17, 1996, a dispute panel ruled that American compliance standards for reformulated gasoline violated American obligations under the WTO.[13] The standard in dispute, issued by the Environmental Protection Agency under the 1990 Clean Air Act Amendments, required the sale of clean-burning gasoline in the nation's smoggiest cities beginning on January 1, 1995. To provide refiners with sufficient time to adjust their production, the EPA issued a five-year interim standard rather than a fixed one. Each year between 1995 and 1997, refiners were required to reduce the amount of olefins, a chemical that contributes to ground-level ozone concentration, by a certain percentage, with 1990 as the base year.

However, because the EPA believed that foreign data for 1990 was unreliable, this rule applied to only American refiners. Foreign producers of gasoline were required to use the 1990 American average as their baseline. This meant that the standards applied to imported gasoline would in some cases be stricter and in other cases more lax than those for domestic producers. Venezuela, one of the primary suppliers of gasoline to the United States, filed a formal complaint with the GATT. It argued that the American rule violated the trade agreement's national treatment clause, which requires that all "like" products be held to similar standards, regardless of their country of origin. The EPA responded by proposing a corrective rule that allowed foreign refiners to establish their own baseline if they could supply adequate documentation. Venezuela's national oil company was able to do so, and Venezuela withdrew its complaint.

This compromise upset both American environmentalists, who regarded it as weakening an American regulatory standard in order to appease a foreign producer, and the American domestic refinery industry, which, having been forced by the 1990 Clean Air Act to invest billions of dollars in new technologies for refining gasoline, wanted to maintain a federal rule which protected them from less expensive imported gasoline. A coalition of American oil companies and environmentalists persuaded Congress to require the EPA to reinstate its original rule. Venezuela responded by resubmitting its complaint, first to the GATT and then to the newly established WTO. It was joined by Brazil, another gasoline exporter to the United States.

The WTO ruled in favor of Venezuela on the grounds that the United States had treated gasoline produced by foreign refiners differently than that made by domestic ones and that it had not demonstrated that this difference was necessary to protect American air quality. The United States appealed the decision to a WTO internal review board, which in April 1996 affirmed the panel's ruling. Two months later the Clinton administration announced that it would propose changes in the application of clean air rules to bring the United States into compliance with its obligations under the WTO. In August 1997 the EPA rules were formally revised.

Although roundly criticized by environmentalists, the decision in the Venezuelan gasoline case generated relatively little political fallout compared with that incited by the tuna/dolphin case. Not only was it difficult for the public to become outraged over different methods for calculating the baseline standard for a relatively obscure pollutant, but even some environmentalists were prepared to admit that the American rule was motivated more by protectionism than by environmental protection. As a report issued by the International Institute for Sustainable Development noted:

> The facts of the case speak against the United States: by all accounts, the measures Brazil and Venezuela complained against are discriminatory and statements by U.S. officials exist indicating that they were aware of this. This was also the case in which the trade barriers erected by the United States provided little environmental benefit, except perhaps to ease the political difficulties in applying the law.[14]

The Shrimp/Turtle Dispute

No sooner had the reformulated gasoline dispute been resolved than another environmentally related trade dispute emerged. In 1989 the U.S. Congress passed legislation requiring that American-registered shrimp boats be fitted with a device to protect turtles from becoming entrapped in their nets. In 1995 this regulation was applied to foreign fishing vessels. As a result, shrimps and shrimp products caught by foreign nationals whose countries did not require turtle protection devices could no longer be imported into the United States. India, Malaysia, Pakistan, and Thailand requested the formation of a WTO dispute panel in October 1996. The four countries, whose complaint was supported by a number of other Pacific Rim nations including Australia, argued that WTO rules prohibit a nation from imposing its domestic environmental laws outside its borders. The United States countered that international trade rules permit nations to take measures that are necessary "to protect natural resources" and that most of the turtle species being killed by shrimpers were endangered.

Although Thailand did enact legislation mandating turtle exclusion devices (TEDs) on the shrimp-crawl nets used by its fisherman, and was therefore exempt from the American ban, it supported the complaint as a "matter of principle."[15] For its part, the U.S. shrimp industry was divided. While firms that did business with shrimp importers criticized the law as discriminatory, American shrimpers endorsed the ban on the grounds that it created a level playing field. In May 1998 a WTO disputes panel ruled against the United States, basing its decision on principles similar to those that the GATT had applied in the tuna/dolphin decision. Although the political heat generated by this decision was less intense than that produced by the tuna/dolphin ruling—in part because no trade agreement was being negotiated or considered by the U.S. Congress at the time—it served to reinforce environmentalists' criticism of the WTO.

American environmentalists claimed that the TEDs could save 97 percent of the 150,000 sea turtles killed in shrimp nets each year, and Dan Seligman of the Sierra Club predicted that "environmentalists will oppose further trade negotiations until the Clinton administration gets serious about fixing these badly broken trade rules."[16] For its part, in July 1998, the Clinton administration announced that it would appeal the disputes panel decision.

Three months later, the WTO's appellate body issued its ruling. Although it decided against the United States, it did so in terms that represented a significant departure from the tuna/dolphin ruling. It stated that trade restrictions based on production methods could be used to protect the environment and to guard natural resources outside a nation's borders. However, it found the U.S. embargo inconsistent with WTO rules because the United States had insisted that its trading partners adopt regulations essentially identical to its own. The appellate body also faulted the United States for not having done enough to pursue bilateral or multilateral approaches before applying its own unilateral sanctions.[17]

Tuna/Dolphin: The Resolution

In May 1992 the United States, Mexico, and eight other tuna-catching nations signed the first major international accord to protect dolphins. This agreement was endorsed by the Earth Island Institute and other American environmental organizations. In October Congress approved the International Dolphin Conservation Act, which authorized the United States to pursue an international agreement to establish a global moratorium on the use of purse-seine nets that encircle dolphins, and provided for an embargo of up to 40 percent of a nation's fish exports to enforce compliance. David Phillips, executive director of the Save the Dolphins Project at the Earth Island Institute, described the legislation as "a breakthrough proposal for dolphins."[18]

Nevertheless, the U.S. tuna embargo remained in effect because a 1993 amendment to the Marine Mammal Protection Act (MMPA) had reduced the U.S. quota of dolphin kills to eight hundred in 1993 and to zero after February 28, 1994. Thus, even though the fifty Mexican boats fishing in the eastern tropical Pacific (ETP) were killing, on average, less than one dolphin for every shoal of tuna they netted, they were still in violation of the MMPA's 1.25 kill ratio since so few dolphins were still being killed by the handful of American flagged vessels tuna fishing in the ETP. Although American officials admitted that "there is no longer a viable environmental argument" for continuing to enforce the embargo, environmentalists and their allies in Congress appeared "determined to enforce the law to the letter."[19]

Finally, after three years of intensive negotiations, a compromise was reached between the United States and the Latin American nations whose vessels fished in the ETP. In exchange for allowing their tuna to be sold in the United States, Mexico and ten other countries pledged to cap their annual dolphin kill at five thousand animals per year. This compromise bitterly divided the environmental community. A number of important environmental organizations including Greenpeace and the World Wildlife Fund supported the compromise on the grounds that opening U.S. markets was the best way to encourage more countries to fish in a dolphin-friendly manner.

However, it was strongly opposed by eighty-five environmental and animal rights groups, who viewed the compromise as a trade treaty masquerading as environmental policy. After intensive lobbying by both the Mexican government and the Clinton administration, legislation was enacted in the summer of 1997 that finally ended the seven-year tuna embargo.

The WTO Committee on Trade and the Environment

At the GATT's April 1994 ministerial meeting during which the Uruguay Round agreement was formally ratified, a resolution was approved committing the soon-to-be-established WTO to undertake a systematic review of "trade policies and those trade-related aspects of environmental policies which may result in significant trade effects for its members."[20] In January 1995 the WTO General Council officially established a Committee on Trade and the Environment (CTE). This committee, which is open to all WTO members, has met six to seven times each year. It has debated a number of issues, including WTO rules governing the export of domestically prohibited goods and the growing use of eco-labeling by developed countries. The latter issue has proven especially contentious. Those nations, primarily in northern Europe, that have made widespread use of eco-labels, which certify that a product is environment-friendly, have defended them as a valuable source of information to consumers. Many of their trading partners, however, have expressed concern that the criteria used to award labels are biased in favor of domestically produced goods. A similar controversy has arisen over the compatibility of national packaging requirements with fair trade rules.

The most important issue addressed by the CTE concerns the relationship between multinational environmental agreements (MEAs) and WTO rules. A number of international environmental agreements contain provisions obligating their signatories to restrict the importation of goods that are either proscribed as environmentally harmful or are produced in harmful ways. For example, the Convention on International Trade in Endangered Species of Wild Fauna and Flora (CITES) restricts or prohibits trade in endangered species, while the Montreal Protocol restricts trade in ozone-depleting chemicals as well as in products made using proscribed chemicals. If a nation is a signatory to both an MEA and the WTO, the two obligations compliment one another. But a potential problem can arise if a nation is a member of the WTO but not a signatory to an MEA, since, under current WTO rules, the exports of one WTO member to another cannot be restricted.

The European Union (EU), which maintains that "trade measures can be necessary to achieve the environmental objectives of these [environmental] agreements," has urged the CTE to support a change in the WTO agreement that would exempt trade restrictions sanctioned by MEAs from WTO challenges.[21] Such a change would affect approximately 180 agreements. However, the EU's proposal has been strongly opposed by developing nations, which fear that it could be used to coerce them into adopting the environmental policies and priorities of their "greener" trading partners. But unless WTO rules are changed, they may well conflict with the provisions of a future treaty on global climate change. For example, such a treaty might well include an agreement to tax products based on the amount of carbon emitted by their production. Yet WTO rules currently prohibit a nation from taxing an imported product on the basis of how it was produced outside its legal jurisdiction. Thus, a signatory to a global climate change treaty could apply the tax only to goods within its borders, leaving domestic producers disadvantaged.

The CTE had hoped to resolve at least some of the issues on its agenda before the WTO ministerial meeting in Singapore in June 1996, but it was unable to do so. This impasse was due in part to the strong opposition of developing countries to any change in WTO rules that would weaken the WTO's current strictures against trade restrictions on environmental grounds. In fact, several developing countries indicated that they would like the CTE to be abolished and its work turned over to the WTO's Standing Committee on Trade and Development. They argued that the latter body would be more sympathetic to the economic development interests of the WTO's poorer members.

But an equally important reason for the impasse was the lack of leadership by the United States. Although it was the main supporter of the creation of the CTE, the Clinton administration showed little interest in proposing "greener" trade rules. As one official in Geneva observed, "The U.S. is proposing nothing and systematically trashing everyone's else's proposals. It is a major obstacle to getting anything done." [22] As a result, the only decision relevant to trade and the environment made by the WTO conference in Singapore was to make the CTE a permanent body of the WTO. This outcome was frustrating to environmentalists who, following the conclusion of the Uruguay Round, had looked forward to changes in WTO rules that would make the trade agreement more environmentally friendly. As the CTE remains stalemated, a number of environmentalists have decided that the environmental community should abandon any hope of "greening" the WTO.

The North American Free Trade Agreement (NAFTA)

Terms of NAFTA

NAFTA, the free trade agreement negotiated among the United States, Mexico, and Canada, has raised a number of environmental issues. [23] The agreement's most innovative feature is its supplemental agreement on the environment, though this is not part of NAFTA itself. It was negotiated by the Clinton administration with considerable input from American environmental organizations. The supplemental agreement established a Commission for Environmental Cooperation (CEC), headed by a secretariat and council composed of senior environmental officials from each country and advised by representatives of environmental organizations. Addressing some of the criticisms of GATT dispute resolution procedures made by environmental groups following the tuna/dolphin decision, it extends to citizens the right to make submissions to the commission on any environmental issue, requires the secretariat to report its responses to these submissions, and, under certain circumstances, permits its reports to be made public. In fact, these provisions provide more opportunities for nonbusiness participation than does current U.S. law, which permits only aggrieved producers to file complaints with or to sue the International Trade Commission, the body responsible for enforcing U.S. trade laws.

In addition, the CEC was given the authority to consider the environmental implications of production methods or, in its words, the "environmental implications of products throughout their life-cycles." This ruling departed from the position of the GATT tuna/dolphin dispute panel, which had ruled that no nation may regulate how other nations produce goods or raw materials outside its borders.[24] Although the side agreement does not require any of the three signatories to enact new environmental laws, it does authorize the use of fines as well as trade sanctions for the nonenforcement of new or existing ones, though only fines may be applied against Canada. Although the CEC is empowered to address any environmental or natural resource issue, the range of issues subject to dispute settlement panels is limited to the enforcement of those environmental laws related to trade or competition among the parties.

NAFTA seeks to prevent its signatory nations from using environmental regulations to gain a comparative advantage by making them either too strict or too lax. The agreement both prohibits any country from lowering its environmental standards to attract investment and permits its signatories to impose stringent environmental standards on new investments, provided they apply equally to foreign and domestic investors. It also requires all three countries to cooperate on improving the level of environmental protection and encourages, but does not require, the raising of regulatory standards.

As the direct response to the concerns of environmentalists over the implications of the GATT decision in the tuna/dolphin case, the agreement specifically states that the provisions of several international environmental agreements—including the Montreal Protocol, the Basel Convention on hazardous wastes, and CITES—take precedence over NAFTA. In some cases it also allows each nation to continue to enforce "generally agreed upon international environmental or conservation rules or standards," provided they are "the least trade-restrictive necessary for securing the protection required."[25] At the same time, "while NAFTA in no way attempts to reduce national standards to a lowest common denominator . . . it does seek to limit the ability of signatories to use such regulations as surreptitious protectionist devices."[26] A Committee on Standards-Related Measures will attempt to develop common criteria for determining the environmental hazards of products as well as methodologies for risk assessment.

The debate over NAFTA sharply divided the environmental community, as it did the business community. A number of nongovernmental organizations (NGOs), including Friends of the Earth, Public Citizen, and the Sierra Club, strongly opposed NAFTA. They viewed the agreement as both too weak and too powerful: they feared the environmental side agreement would be ineffective in making Mexico enforce its environmental laws and highly effective in making the United States lower its regulatory standards. But equally significant, six major national environmental organizations, including the Natural Resources Defense Council, the Audubon Society, the Environmental Defense Fund, and the World Wildlife Fund, endorsed the agreement. They concluded that the provisions of the supplementary environmental agreement, on which they had insisted and which they helped the Clinton administration to negotiate, offered adequate regulatory safeguards. They were disappointed, however, that the supplementary agreement did not include any procedure for raising environmental standards or their enforcement to the highest common denominator.[27]

The Impact of NAFTA

As of September 1998 the CEC, which established its office in Montreal, had received four petitions from environmental organizations. Two of the complaints, which were brought by American NGOs alleging the failure of the United States to enforce its own environmental laws, were rejected on the grounds that the actions about which they complained were actually changes in national legislation rather than the lack of enforcement of existing laws.

A third petition requested the CEC secretariat to prepare a factual record explaining the death of forty thousand migratory birds in the Silva Reservoir, located two hundred miles northwest of Mexico City. It did not allege an enforcement failure by Mexico but simply requested information. The petition was accepted, and the Mexican government cooperated with an extensive investigation by a trinational scientific panel. The panel concluded that the deaths were caused by botulism, probably attributable to untreated urban and industrial sewage emptying into the reservoir. The CEC proposed that a sewage treatment facility be constructed with some of the costs shared by the three NAFTA signatories.

In August 1996 the CEC agreed to prepare a factual record based on a petition by Mexican environmental NGOs. The petition alleged that the Mexican government had failed to follow its own environmental laws when it authorized the construction of a five-hundred-meter pier and cruise ship terminal that threatened an important coral reef at Cozumel. This marked the first time that the CEC secretariat had acted on a complaint under Article 14 of the environmental side accord, which permits any person or organization to file a petition alleging the lack of enforcement of environmental laws by any of the three NAFTA countries.

The Mexican government reluctantly agreed to the preparation of a report by the CEC but sharply dissented from the report's finding that it had violated its own environmental laws by permitting construction of the pier and terminal. It claimed that approval for the project predated NAFTA and that therefore the CEC lacked jurisdiction. Construction of the pier and terminal, which Mexico claimed was needed to handle increased tourism that was a major source of revenue in this very impoverished region, has continued to go ahead but on a smaller scale. Under the provisions of the side agreement, either the United States or Canada could petition for the imposition of trade sanctions or fines against Mexico, but to date neither has done so.

The CEC does have some accomplishments. For example, it has established a North American environmental research program, begun development on a North American Pollutant Release Inventory to monitor air quality, and has initiated a plan to protect various threatened and endangered species. Most important, the three NAFTA signatories have agreed to phase out or reduce the use of a number of dangerous chemicals and pesticides, including DDT. "Taken together, these actions suggest that the CEC may be developing into an institution that could have significant effect on some environmental issues in North America."[28]

However, NAFTA has had only a modest impact on the most pressing environmental issue associated with Mexican-American relations—namely, the reduction of transboundary pollution. Although sixteen transborder projects have been certified with a combined cost of $230 million and construction has begun on six, none has been completed. The impact of NAFTA on domestic Mexican environmental policies and practices has been more encouraging. A number of Mexican environmental standards have been tightened and their enforcement strengthened. More than four hundred firms have signed environmental compliance action plans, and there has been a 72 percent reduction in serious environmental violations in the industrial region bordering the United States since NAFTA was signed. But Mexico's overall efforts to grapple with its environmental problems have been undermined by the severe economic difficulties it has experienced since the agreement came into effect.

Expanding NAFTA

The most important environmental impact of NAFTA has been a political one: it has made it more difficult to secure the U.S. Congress's approval of future trade agreements. An important case in point is the politics surrounding the possible extension of NAFTA to include Chile. From the onset of negotiations between the United States and Chile, it was clear that the latter's environmental record would be an important issue. As the *Financial Times* noted in May 1994, "The environment is likely to prove the biggest sticking point. Chile's mining, fishing forestry and fruit industries—backbone of the export sector—have been criticized on environmental grounds."[29] For its part, Chile began to make a number of efforts to improve its environmental performance. It also indicated its willingness to include environmental provisions in a trade agreement with the United States, provided that American demands did not damage the competitiveness of its economy. In

December 1995 Chile and Canada announced their intention to negotiate an agreement on environmental cooperation as part of a free trade agreement between the two countries. Based on the North American Agreement on Environmental Cooperation, this agreement reflected the strong and growing public interest in Chile in environmental issues and was intended to facilitate the eventual inclusion of Chile into NAFTA. Chile subsequently entered into free trade agreements with both Canada and Mexico.

But in the United States the place of trade-environment linkages in any future trade agreement has proved to be a contentious issue. On balance, since the approval of both NAFTA and the Uruguay Round agreement, those in the American environmental community have become even more skeptical of the role of trade agreements in improving or even protecting environmental quality. They have been disappointed with the lack of progress in changing WTO rules to make them more compatible with stricter national and global regulatory standards and with the WTO disputes panel decision in the shrimp/turtle case. They have also been disappointed with the environmental impact of NAFTA. As a specialist on trade policy for the Sierra Club put it, "The side agreements really haven't delivered on commitments made by the Clinton Administration in 1993." [30] According to Richard Gephardt, D-Mo., the Democratic House leader, NAFTA has proven a failure: along the Mexican border "each day the environment dies another death." [31] Even those environmental organizations that supported the passage of NAFTA now insist that the environment become a priority "on the par with other negotiating objectives" in trade talks rather than be included in a side agreement as it was under NAFTA. [32] Not surprisingly, those environmental groups that opposed NAFTA remained equally opposed to a free trade agreement with Chile and other Latin American nations.

The Failure of Fast Track

The extent to which the issue of trade/environmental linkages had become highly polarized was revealed in the debate in the U.S. Congress over renewal of the president's "fast-track" authority in fall 1997. Under this authority, trade agreements negotiated by the president could be submitted to Congress for expedited approval. Congress would then have ninety days to vote either yes or no on proposed agreements, which could not be amended. Republicans strongly opposed including either labor or environmental standards in the provisions of any new trade agreement. Their position was endorsed by a group of more than fifty American international economists who claimed that American insistence on uniform standards in the face of large international differences in regulatory requirements would hurt poor countries and "slow down or even possibly halt the opening up of world markets through trade-liberalizing negotiations." [33] Unions and environmental groups were equally insistent that fast track reauthorization mandate negotiations on environmental and labor standards.

The Clinton administration, under increasing pressure from business to secure reauthorization of fast track—not only to extend NAFTA to Chile and other Latin American nations but also to write new WTO rules for services, such as transportation and communication, and the protection of intellectual property rights—decided to back the Republican position.[34] Abandoning an earlier promise to make America's trading partners adopt labor and environmental standards as part of any future trade agreement, the administration announced that it would not seek to include such standards as part of an agreement's core provisions. However, in an effort to appease congressional Democrats, the administration did promise both to negotiate separate environmental and labor side agreements when appropriate and to work through international organizations to strengthen labor and environmental standards on a global basis.

Nonetheless, the administration was unable to secure congressional approval of fast-track reauthorization, though this had more to do with the strong and effective opposition of organized labor than with the influence of the American environmental community. Still, the fact that labor unions relied so heavily on environmental organizations' arguments about the threat posed by free trade to American regulatory standards reveals the extent to which trade/environmental linkages have become a permanent part of the political agenda of trade policy in the United States. Until Congress agrees to reauthorize fast track, no new trade agreement can be entered into by the United States.

The Environmental Impact of Trade Liberalization

What is likely to be the overall impact of more liberal trade policies on environmental protection? To a significant extent, any assessment of the environmental impact of trade liberalization depends in large measure on one's analysis of the relationship between environmental quality and economic development. If the two are viewed as incompatible, then clearly trade liberalization will, by definition, have adverse environmental consequences, especially for developing countries. Alternatively, if economic development is understood as making possible an improvement in environmental quality, then trade liberalization can have a positive environmental impact.

For relatively poor countries, increased economic growth and economic interdependence generally does result in a deterioration of domestic environmental quality: pollution levels increase and natural resources are depleted at an accelerating rate. But environmental quality tends to improve as per capita income increases because nations are in a better position to devote resources to conservation and pollution control. Thus, in the long run, economic development may actually contribute to the strengthening of environmental standards.

Nor is it the case that trade liberalization necessarily results in more environmentally irresponsible economic practices. On the contrary, the experiences of Latin America and the formerly communist nations of eastern and central Europe indicate that the polluting and energy-inefficient firms are also likely to be economically inefficient. By exposing these firms to global competition, trade liberalization improves local environmental conditions.[35] In agriculture the lowering of barriers to trade tends to transfer production from developed to developing nations. Because farming in developing countries tends to be less capital intensive, overall environmental quality improves. Simultaneously, land is freed up in the developed nations for conservation and other purposes.[36]

As the recent changes in Mexico's domestic environmental policies suggest, increased economic interdependence has not resulted in a regulatory "race to the bottom." With the exception of a handful of industries, the costs of compliance with environmental standards are modest. Accordingly, firms seem to have little incentive to migrate to "pollution havens" to lower their production costs, even with the removal of barriers to trade. Contrary to the fears of both environmentalists and unions, American firms have not relocated to Mexico in order to take advantage of its less-well-enforced environmental standards. Nor is there any evidence that nations have lowered their environmental standards in order to retain or attract investment.[37]

Indeed, in many cases, stricter domestic regulatory standards represent a source of competitive *advantage* because it is often easier for domestic firms to comply with them. For example, recycling requirements almost invariably work to the advantage of those firms that produce close to their customers, thus providing domestic firms with an important incentive for supporting the requirements. Moreover, the lure of access to green export markets has played a critical role in encouraging firms to support stricter domestic product standards. For example, in the early 1970s Japan modeled its automobile emission standards on those of the United States—its major export market— while an important factor underlying the support of German auto firms for stricter European Community emissions standards during the 1980s was the fact that the vehicles they were producing for sale in California were already meeting the world's stricter emission standards. Likewise, according to a recent study conducted by the U.S. General Accounting Office, countries that export significant quantities of agricultural products to the United States frequently take U.S. standards into account in establishing their domestic pesticide regulations.[38] Moreover, as Michael Porter has argued, stricter regulatory standards can also encourage domestic firms to develop improved pollution control technologies, which they can then export as the regulatory standards of their trading partners become stronger.[39] Thus, in a number of cases, increased economic interdependence has led to the strengthening rather than the weakening of environmental standards—a "race to the top" that has been characterized as "the California effect."[40]

It is also important to note that many of the environmental abuses attributable to trade liberalization have more to do with domestic politics than international economics. Trade liberalization does not dictate the rate at which a nation allows its natural resources to be exploited or the value it accords to hardwood forests, jungles, or endangered wildlife. These determinations are made by national governments. Developed nations have made enormous progress in protecting their domestic environments; there is nothing in the terms of international trade agreements that prevents developing nations from doing likewise. Moreover, if the developed nations are dissatisfied with the environmental practices of developing nations, they have no shortage of vehicles with which to improve them. Trade restrictions are rarely the most effective or efficient mechanisms.

The tension between trade liberalization and environmental regulation should not be exaggerated. Only three American environmental regulations have been held to be inconsistent with the GATT/WTO agreements, and none has been weakened by NAFTA. Both the WTO and NAFTA explicitly protect the right of nations to establish whatever regulatory standard they deem appropriate, provided they can be scientifically justified and are as "least trade-restrictive" as possible. Even more important, these agreements have not prevented a steady increase in the number and scope of regional and international environmental agreements.

Tensions between both national and international environmental policies and trade liberalization will continue to persist. Yet, on balance, the postwar period has witnessed both a strengthening of environmental standards and an increase in trade liberalization. There is no reason to expect that this trend will change significantly in the future. However, there is every reason to expect that the relationship between trade advocates and environmentalists will remain contentious.

Notes

1. See David Vogel, *Trading Up: Consumer and Environmental Regulation in a Global Economy* (Cambridge, Mass.: Harvard University Press, 1995).
2. Quoted in Stewart Hudson, "Coming to Terms with Trade," *Environmental Action* (summer 1992): 33.
3. Paul Rauber, "Trading Away the Environment," *Sierra* (January–February 1992).
4. James Brooke, "America—Environmental Dictator?" *New York Times*, May 3, 1992, 7.
5. Stuart Auerbach, "Endangering Laws Protecting the Endangered," *Washington Post National Weekly Edition*, October 7–13, 1991, 22.
6. Robert Housman and Durwood Zaelke, "The Collusion of the Environment and Trade: The GATT Tuna-Dolphin Decision," *Environmental Law Reporter* (April 1992): 10271.
7. Matthew Hurlock, "The GATT, U.S. Law, and the Environment: A Proposal to Amend the GATT in Light of the Tuna-Dolphin Decision," *Columbia Law Review* 92 (1992): 2100.
8. Quoted in "U.S. Auto Fuel-Efficiency Taxes to be Examined by GATT Panel," *Trade and the Environment: News and Views from the GATT,* June 3, 1993, 4.
9. Richard Steinberg, "The Uruguay Round: A Legal Analysis of the Final Act," *International Quarterly* 6, no. 2 (April 1994): 35.
10. Ibid.
11. Daniel Esty, *Greening the GATT* (Washington, D.C.: Institute for International Economics, 1994), 170.
12. Ibid., 50.

13. For a more detailed discussion of this trade controversy and the background to it, see David Vogel, "Trouble for Us and Trouble for Them: Social Regulations as Trade Barriers," in *Comparative Disadvantages? Social Regulations and the Global Economy*, ed. Pietro Niovola (Washington D.C.: Brookings Institution, 1997), 119–124.

14. *The World Trade Organization and Sustainable Development: An Independent Assessment* (Winnipeg, Manitoba: International Institute for Sustainable Development, 1996), 41.

15. Chana Schoenberger, "Shrimp Dispute Tests U.S. Use of Trade to Protect Environment," *Wall Street Journal*, July 18, 1997, A 14.

16. Nancy Dunne, "Anger over WTO Turtle Ruling," *Financial Times*, March 5, 1998, 3.

17. Nancy Perkins, "The World Trade Organization Holds That Trade Barriers May, If Properly Designed and Applied, Be Used to Protect the Global Environment," *Legal Times*, February 8, 1999.

18. "Congress Considers New Bill to Save Dolphins," *Dolphin Alert* (Fall, 1992): 2.

19. "Must Try Harder," *Economist*, August 21, 1993, 22.

20. "Decisions Adopted by Ministers in Marrakesh," *Focus: The GATT Newsletter* (May 1994): 9.

21. Quoted in William Lasch, III, "Green Showdown at the WTO," *Contemporary Issues Series* 85, Center for the Study of American Business (March 1997): 12.

22. Frances Williams, "U.S. Holding Up Green Trade," *Financial Times*, July 26, 1996, 3.

23. For a detailed discussion of the politics surrounding the approval of NAFTA by the United States, see John Audley, *Green Politics and Global Trade: NAFTA and the Future of Environmental Politics* (Washington, D.C.: Georgetown University Press, 1997).

24. Quoted in James Sheehan, "NAFTA—Free Trade in Name Only," *The Wall Street Journal*, September 9, 1993, A21.

25. Michelle Swenarchuk, "NAFTA and the Environment," *Canadian Forum* 71 (January–February 1993): 13.

26. Roberto Salinas-Leon, "Green Herrings," *Regulation* (Winter 1993): 31.

27. For criticisms of the environmental provisions of both NAFTA and the side agreement, see Gary Hufbauer and Jeffrey Scott, *NAFTA: An Assessment*, rev. ed. (Washington, D.C.: Institute for International Economics, 1993), 92–97.

28. Richard Steinberg, "Trade-Environment Negotiations in the EU, NAFTA, and WTO: Regional Trajectories of Rule Development," *American Journal of International Law* 91 (1997): 250–251.

29. David Pilling, "NAFTA Accord Back on Chile's Agenda," *Financial Times*, May 27, 1994, 7.

30. Anthony DePalma, "NAFTA Environmental Lags May Delay Free Trade Expansion," *New York Times*, May 21, 1997, A4.

31. David Sanger, "Republicans Say the Trade Bill Is in Big Trouble," *New York Times*, October 1, 1997, A14.

32. Nancy Dunne, "Chile's NAFTA Hopes Fade as Trade Pacts Lose U.S. Favor," *Financial Times*, October 2, 1997, 6.

33. Nancy Dunne, "Clinton Boost on Fast-Track," *Financial Times*, October 2, 1997, 11.

34. Amy Borrus, "Business Is in a Hurry For Fast-Track," *Business Week*, September 15, 1997, 38–39. For alternative views of the impact of the global economy on environmental quality in Latin America, see *Difficult Liaison: Trade and the Environment in Latin America*, ed. Heraldo Munõz and Robin Rosenberg (New Brunswick, N.J.: Transaction Publishers, 1993).

35. See for example, Nancy Birdsall and David Wheeler, "Trade Policy and Industrial Pollution in Latin America: Where Are the Pollution Havens?" in *International Trade and the Environment*, ed. Patrick Low (Washington, D.C.: World Bank, 1992), 159–168. For a more critical view of the impact of economic globalization on ecological policy, see *Ecological Policy and Politics in Developing Countries*, ed. Uday Desai (Albany: State University of New York Press, 1998).

36. For a comprehensive analysis of the impact of trade liberalization on both economic efficiency and environmental quality, see *The Greening of World Trade Issues*, ed. Kym Anderson and Richard Blackhurst (Ann Arbor: University of Michigan Press, 1992).

37. There is an extensive literature on the relationships among economic regulation and trade patterns, international competitiveness, and corporate location decisions. See, for example, Richard Stewart, "Environmental Regulation and International Competitiveness," *Yale Law Journal* 102, no. 8 (June 1993): 2077–2079; and Judith Dean, "Trade and the Environment: A Survey of the Literature," in *International Trade and the Environment,* ed. Patrick Low, 16–20.
38. Quoted in Charles Pearson, "Trade and Environment: The United States Experience" (New York: U.N. Conference on Trade and Development, January 1994), 52.
39. See Michael Porter, *The Competitive Advantage of Nations* (New York: Free Press, 1990), 685–688; and also Curtis Moore and Alan Miller, *Green Gold* (Boston: Beacon Press, 1994).
40. See Vogel, *Trading Up,* chap. 8.

17

Toward Sustainable Development

Norman J. Vig and Michael E. Kraft

Our vision is of a life-sustaining Earth. We are committed to the achievement of a dignified, peaceful, and equitable existence. A sustainable United States will have a growing economy that provides equitable opportunities for satisfying livelihoods and a safe, healthy, high quality of life for current and future generations. Our nation will protect its environment, its natural resource base, and the functions and viability of natural systems on which all life depends.

—President's Council on Sustainable Development
February 1996

The pace of change in our world is speeding up, accelerating to the point where it threatens to overwhelm the management capacity of political leaders. This acceleration of history comes not only from advancing technology, but also from unprecedented world population growth, even faster economic growth, and the increasingly frequent collisions between expanding human demands and the limits of the earth's natural systems.

—Lester R. Brown
1996

As the twenty-first century dawns, environmental quality has come to occupy a central place in the public policy of the United States and other advanced industrial countries. There is an emerging consensus that all nations must move rapidly toward new forms of "sustainable development" if future generations are to survive and prosper. Indeed, it is no longer possible to think about economic growth and development without considering the ecological impacts of virtually all human activities. Yet, as Lester Brown suggests above, it is by no means certain that the human race will succeed in managing the planetary balance.

The concept of sustainable development was first defined and popularized by the World Commission on Environment and Development in its 1987 report, *Our Common Future*,[1] and was further elaborated at the 1992 U.N. Conference on Environment and Development. It has also been adopted as the framework for all environmental policy in the European Union.[2] In the

United States the National Commission on the Environment, a prestigious group of private individuals including four former heads of the Environmental Protection Agency (EPA), similarly called for rethinking environmental policies in terms of this concept:

> U.S. leadership should be based on the concept of *sustainable development.* By the close of the twentieth century, economic development and environmental protection must come together in a new synthesis: broad-based economic progress accomplished in a manner that protects and restores the quality of the natural environment, improves the quality of life for individuals, and broadens the prospects for future generations. This merging of economic and environmental goals in the concept of sustainable development can and should constitute a central guiding principle for national environmental and economic policymaking.[3]

The President's Commission on Environmental Quality, a committee of corporate, foundation, and environmental group executives set up by President George Bush, issued a report in early 1993 that called for establishing a national council on sustainable development. President Bill Clinton took up the challenge by appointing a new President's Council on Sustainable Development. The council, consisting of some twenty-five leaders from industry, government, and the environmental community, was charged with formulating sustainable development strategies for the United States. The council's first report, issued in February 1996, called for a new generation of flexible, consensual environmental policies that would maximize economic welfare while achieving more effective and efficient environmental protection. It concluded that "in order to meet the needs of the present while ensuring that future generations have the same opportunities, the United States must change by moving from conflict to collaboration and adopting stewardship and individual responsibility as tenets by which to live."[4]

To recognize environmental sustainability as a guiding principle will not, however, solve the problem of making difficult policy choices that involve other important social values. Although many of these choices may no longer be regarded as zero-sum trade-offs, they will often require financial sacrifices and changes in social behavior. This means that environmental policies will continue to generate strong political resistance from established economic and bureaucratic interests. Political opposition is also likely to persist among antienvironmental and property rights organizations (see chaps. 3, 7, and 14). And as environmental protection deepens, success in policy implementation will increasingly depend on public understanding and acceptance of the need for social and behavioral change—because policymakers otherwise would be reluctant to act.

The current impasse over environmental regulation in the U.S. Congress illustrates the difficulties ahead. The Republican majority elected in 1994 has demonstrated little awareness or acceptance of the concept of sustainable development (see chap. 6). Nor does there appear to be much support in either party for action on such critical international issues as global climate change or protection of biological diversity.[5] Environmentalists, for their part, have largely adopted a defensive strategy of blocking most congressional initiatives in the hope of preserving the statutory foundations of environmental policies built up over the past three decades.

The overwhelming evidence presented in this book and other recent studies suggests, however, that neither the current policy structure nor a major regulatory rollback and retreat from global environmental responsibilities will provide satisfactory solutions in the future. Environmental policy success will require, as the National Commission on the Environment, the President's Council on Sustainable Development, and the National Academy of Public Administration all suggest, more innovative strategies and tools than have characterized past regulation.[6] Many chapters in this book have emphasized the need for new policy approaches, including greater use of economic incentives, comparative risk assessment, voluntary partnerships, and community involvement.

The remainder of this chapter discusses the need for better integration of environmental values into national policymaking and identifies seven of the most pressing environmental issues on the national agenda. It also outlines seven innovative approaches to environmental management and concludes with some general reflections on the need to rethink political strategies and the long-term choices that must be made if we are to maintain the health of the planet.

Integrating Environmental Policies

Perhaps the greatest obstacle to more rational and effective environmental policymaking at present is the absence of any mechanism for coordinating and integrating policy actions on the basis of an overall strategy or set of priorities. As Rosenbaum argues in chapter 8, the EPA lacks both a statutory charter defining its priorities and authority over most matters involving natural resources and land use. Even within its own areas of competence, it is driven by separate legal mandates that make it difficult to set priorities based on comparative risk assessment or some other common standard. Other agencies, such as the Council on Environmental Quality (CEQ), have lacked the legal and political stature to coordinate the policies of cabinet departments and other executive agencies, while efforts to control agency policies through budgetary and regulatory oversight or special bodies such as the Bush administration's Council on Competitiveness have focused too narrowly on reducing administrative and regulatory costs.

To remedy these shortcomings, President Clinton created a new White House Office of Environmental Policy (OEP) and appointed a special assistant on international environmental affairs attached to the National Security Council (see chap. 5). He also proposed legislation to establish a cabinet-level Department of Environmental Protection. None of these innovations succeeded, however, and in 1994 the OEP was merged into the CEQ. Institutionalized policy coordination thus remains weak and at the mercy of the incumbent president.

To achieve sustainable development in the future we will need to move beyond policy coordination to *policy integration*—that is, to making environmental protection an essential part of the mission of *all* federal agencies. Departments such as Interior, Energy, Agriculture, Commerce, Transportation, and Housing and Urban Development implement most of the national policies that affect environmental quality. Scientific agencies like the White House Office of Science and Technology Policy, the National Oceanic and Atmospheric Administration, and the National Aeronautics and Space Administration support critical research that must be incorporated more fully into the policymaking process. There must also be much greater integration of international and domestic environmental policy, since most serious threats to the environment are now regional or global in scope. Agencies such as the State Department, Defense Department, and Office of Trade Representative must assume greater responsibilities for the international environment.

Policy integration on this scale will require both more comprehensive environmental legislation and transformation of the institutional cultures within many agencies. Such major changes are not likely in the near future. The remainder of this chapter focuses on some of the most important substantive issues and alternative strategies for improving policy effectiveness.

Critical Policy Issues

As noted throughout this book, many important environmental policy issues remain unresolved despite the progress we have made in the past three decades. Here we briefly note some of the most important problems likely to confront the nation in the future. It should be emphasized that this list is not exhaustive and that Congress and the public are likely to attach different orders of priority to the issues than that suggested here.

Energy Consumption and Climate Change

Fossil fuel burning is the source of many of our environmental problems, but its greatest potential impact is on global climate change (see chap. 13). Although many uncertainties remain, evidence continues to mount that carbon dioxide and other greenhouse gases generated by human activity are altering the temperature and climate patterns of the Earth. The warmest surface temperatures ever recorded occurred in 1998, following previous records in 1990, 1995, and 1997.[7] Possible effects of global warming include rising sea levels; an increased volume and intensity of hurricanes and other storms; shifts in rainfall patterns and, consequently, in patterns of droughts and flooding; massive loss of species and habitats; and the spread of pests and infectious diseases to new geographical areas.

President Clinton reversed the position of the Bush administration by endorsing the goals of the 1992 Framework Convention on Climate Change (FCCC) and signing the 1997 Kyoto Protocol (chaps. 5 and 13). The latter agreement requires the United States to reduce greenhouse gas emissions by

7 percent below 1990 levels over the period 2008–2012—that is, by nearly one-third of what U.S. emissions would be at that time without any policy changes. Attaining this goal is likely to require substantial reductions in U.S. fossil fuel consumption, even though the Kyoto treaty allows the nation to meet some of its obligations through credits gained by emissions trading (a practice by which the United States buys from other nations the right to emit carbon dioxide) and investment in clean energy technologies in other countries.[8] In January 1998 Clinton proposed a $6.3 billion program for tax incentives and research to promote the development of more fuel-efficient cars and other energy-saving technologies, but Congress has refused to fund it.[9] Moreover, it is very unlikely that the Senate will ratify the Kyoto treaty in its present form, raising doubts about this nation's commitment to the FCCC. Future presidents will have to give much higher priority to building a national consensus on this issue if any significant progress is to be made.

Biodiversity and Endangered Species

Loss of biodiversity ranks with climate change as the greatest long-term threat to the global environment. Scientists believe that a mass extinction of plants and animals is underway and predict that as many as 20 percent of all species could disappear within thirty years. According to one study published in 1998, at least one in eight plant species in the world—and nearly one in three in the United States—is already threatened by extinction.[10] Natural systems that support the greatest diversity of species—such as rainforests, wetlands, and coastal estuaries—are threatened by human development throughout the world.

Biodiversity was therefore a central focus of the 1992 Río conference and resulted in a Convention on Biological Diversity (CBD) that was signed by all major nations except the United States (see chap. 5). To his credit, President Clinton promptly signed the CBD after taking office in 1993, but the Senate has not ratified the treaty and the United States remains outside the convention. Moreover, in 1999 the U.S. and several other nations blocked implementation of provisions regarding export of genetically altered crops on grounds that the treaty would unduly restrict international trade.[11]

Within the United States, the Clinton administration has sought to increase protection of endangered species and to preserve critical habitats. The secretary of interior, Bruce Babbitt, established a National Biological Service to survey the remaining biological resources of the United States. His department has pursued a wide range of new strategies to identify and protect important natural areas before individual species are threatened, including support for habitat conservation plans (see chap. 14). Clinton and Vice President Al Gore have actively sought compromises over such controversial issues as protection of the spotted owl in old-growth forests of the Pacific Northwest, restoration of the Florida Everglades, and preservation of ancient stands of redwood trees in northern California.

Despite some successes in these areas, the future of the Endangered Species Act (ESA) remains in doubt. Congress has been gridlocked over reauthorization of the law throughout the 1990s (see chap. 6). However, bipartisan consensus may be emerging on amendments that would codify some of the practices of the Clinton administration, such as negotiation of "no surprises" voluntary agreements with landowners who agree to protect critical habitats for extended periods (for example, fifty years) in return for immunity from new restrictions under the ESA. More positive incentives may be needed to encourage cooperation among the wide range of public and private stakeholders whose help is needed to deal with such massive problems as restoration of threatened salmon species in the Pacific Northwest.[12]

Clean Water and Wetlands

The Clean Water Act (CWA), last amended in 1987, is also up for reauthorization. One of the most important unresolved issues is how to control "nonpoint" water pollution from farm fields, construction sites, mines, forestry sites, and cities, which together account for as much as two-thirds of all surface water pollution. Solutions may require tighter regulation of pesticide and fertilizer use as well as new land use controls to protect watersheds. Under the 1987 CWA revisions, states are required to develop plans for control of nonpoint sources of water pollution, but they are not mandatory and Congress has provided little funding for this purpose. President Clinton proposed in his 1998 State of the Union address a new Clean Water Action Plan which provides $1.7 billion of additional funding over five years to help state and local governments deal with this problem, and Congress approved the funding late in the year.[13]

Another critical issue is protection of wetlands. President Clinton promised a "no net loss policy" for wetlands during his 1992 election campaign and has threatened to veto any legislation weakening section 404 of the Clean Water Act which is intended to protect wetlands. However, his administration has bowed to pressure from state and local governments as well as from a wide array of property rights groups and development interests by easing enforcement of some wetlands restrictions, especially for small property owners. EPA administrator Carol Browner has tried to reduce confrontation by working out voluntary agreements among land developers, farmers, and environmentalists to preserve or restore certain wetlands in exchange for releasing others. But it remains to be seen how effective these restoration projects are and whether pressure will mount to pay compensation to landowners affected by regulatory "takings" (see chap. 7).

Hazardous and Nuclear Waste

The storage, treatment, and disposal of hazardous and toxic wastes present another series of intractable problems in our industrial society. Despite growing efforts by manufacturers to reduce the use of hazardous and toxic materials (see chap. 12), the volume of dangerous waste continues to grow. Many solid and hazardous waste facilities have been closed, while others, such as incinerators, are meeting increasing public opposition. Nuclear power plants built in the 1960s and 1970s are also running out of space for storing spent fuel long before a permanent repository for civilian high-level radioactive wastes is available. The safety of the permanent disposal facility under consideration at Yucca Mountain, Nevada, remains highly controversial, while efforts to find interim solutions have bogged down in Congress.[14] The cleanup of contaminated nuclear weapons production facilities and the storage and disposal of radioactive military wastes also present enormous ongoing challenges to the Department of Energy; it is estimated that it will cost several hundred billion dollars to clean up these facilities in the new century.[15]

Congress failed to reauthorize the Comprehensive Environmental Response, Compensation and Liability ("Superfund") Act in the 1990s despite bipartisan consensus that the law badly needs revision (see chap. 6). The Superfund program is considered excessively costly owing to the extensive litigation involved in determining responsibility for cleanups, wasteful spending on elaborate remediation plans, and long delays in implementation (although completion of cleanups has been considerably accelerated during the Clinton administration). However, despite repeated attempts to reach compromise the parties have remained deadlocked over such issues as elimination of retroactive liability (responsibility for contamination prior to passage of the law in 1980), allocation of costs for cleanups among responsible parties, and the role of state and local governments in designing and monitoring Superfund projects.[16] Congress has also allowed the taxes supporting Superfund to expire, requiring new sources of funding if the nearly fourteen hundred sites currently on the National Priority List for cleanup are to be addressed in the new century.

Suburban Sprawl and Sustainable Communities

Environmentalists and policymakers increasingly have argued that sustainable development can best be pursued at the local and regional levels—in a manner consistent with the well-established axiom, "think globally, act locally." The movement toward sustainable communities, or what the EPA calls "community-based environmental protection," has spread across the nation in the last few years and has fostered hundreds of local efforts to address interrelated environmental, economic, and social issues through community dialogue and "visioning" exercises. At the local level citizens are coming together to identify the major problems affecting a community, such as degradation of local surface water or loss of natural habitats, and are developing appropriate solutions. They are especially likely to do so through voluntary partnerships involving government, business, and citizen groups. The EPA has encouraged such innovative actions (and has supported them through grants to states and communities) as part of its broader effort to redefine its mission and to prepare for "a new era of environmental protection" that is more integrative and collaborative than prior actions have been.[17]

It is too early to tell how successful such intriguing community sustainability efforts will prove to be, yet there is little question of their appeal. This is especially so in areas affected by rapid growth and suburban sprawl, and thus by problems such as highway congestion, air pollution, and loss of open space. In the November 1998 elections voters across the nation endorsed growth management policies proposed in some 250 state and local ballot initiatives, many of them promoted by environmental groups. These actions were designed to limit regional growth or otherwise preserve open space. Some 72 percent of the measures were approved, and they authorized about $7.5 billion in additional conservation programs at the state and local level.

Only two months later, in early 1999, the Clinton administration proposed spending nearly $1 billion in its fiscal 2000 budget to initiate a "livability agenda" that would "provide communities with new tools and resources to preserve green space, ease traffic congestion, and pursue regional 'smart growth' strategies." A complementary Lands Legacy proposal encouraged federal partnerships with states and local communities to preserve open spaces. The political popularity of such ideas was evident as politicians from both parties were quick to endorse a variety of legislative measures dealing with suburban sprawl, including some that advocated spending substantially more money than now available to buy endangered farmland and conserve other lands for ecological purposes or to improve quality of life.[18] The extent to which such growth management initiatives can build a foundation for true community sustainability and more effective and efficient environmental policies remains to be seen.

Environmental Justice

Another side of community development policy must focus on the distributive effects of activities that negatively affect people and the environment. There is substantial evidence that low-income and minority groups are disproportionately exposed to environmental hazards such as lead poisoning, industrial air pollution, and toxic waste sites (see chap. 11). African Americans, Hispanics, Asians, and Native Americans have formed hundreds of new grassroots organizations to fight pollution in their communities, and mainstream environmental groups have become more sensitive to such inequities.

Beginning in the Bush administration and accelerating under Clinton, the EPA and other federal agencies have begun to document unequal patterns of pollution exposure and investigate their causes. In February 1994 President Clinton issued Executive Order 12898, which called for all federal agencies to develop strategies for achieving environmental justice. But little further progress appears to have been made toward reducing these inequities in the 1990s, and some have questioned both the evidence of racial discrimination and the priorities of the environmental justice movement.[19] Nevertheless, more attention must be given to environmental inequities and ways to reduce them in the future if environmental policy is to maintain its political and ethical foundations (see chap. 4).

International Issues

In addition to the global problems of climate change and biodiversity discussed earlier, a host of other critical environmental issues will require much greater international cooperation in the new century. They include population growth, transboundary pollution, preservation of ocean fisheries, international hazardous waste shipment, export and use of agricultural pesticides and chemicals, and many issues relating to nuclear fuel reprocessing, destruction of nuclear weapons, and weapons proliferation. Some of these issues are beginning to be perceived as critical foreign policy and national security concerns. For example, environmental degradation is increasingly a source of local and regional conflict that produces large numbers of "environmental refugees." As a result, "eco-terrorism" could become an important weapon in the future.[20]

One of the most contentious issues for international environmental policy is support for U.N. and other multilateral family planning and population programs. The Reagan and Bush administrations cut off aid for such programs because of concern that funds could be used to promote abortions. President Clinton restored funding for population programs and increased financial support for other international bodies such as the Global Environment Facility, a fund operated by the World Bank to support environmental projects in developing countries. However, the Republican Congress has severely cut funding for these and other foreign assistance programs, and the United States remains deeply in arrears to the U.N.[21] There appears to be little support in Congress for any programs that address the problems of developing nations discussed by Richard Tobin in chapter 15. Indeed, the current majority appears hostile to all international environmental treaties and commitments, raising profound doubts about the ability of the United States to lead in the future.

Another increasingly important issue concerns the relationship between international trade and environmental protection (see chap. 16). Until recently environmental problems were considered outside the scope of trade negotiations. But passage of the North American Free Trade Agreement (NAFTA) in 1993 and completion of the Uruguay Round of the General Agreement on Tariffs and Trade (GATT) in 1994 raised serious concerns about the potential impacts of free trade on national environmental restrictions. President Clinton refused to sign NAFTA until a side agreement on environmental and labor safeguards was added, but the GATT treaty left such issues to be resolved by the new World Trade Organization (WTO).[22] However, environmental protection has taken a back seat to expansion of trade under both treaties. Little headway has been made in cleaning up pollution along the U.S.-Mexico border, and several WTO panels have made decisions striking down environmental protection actions as unfair restraints on trade. Partly for this reason, environmentalists, among others, strongly (and successfully) opposed the further extension of "fast track" negotiating authority to the Clinton administration in 1997. (This authority would have permitted the president to submit trade agreements to Congress for expedited approval.) But the relationship between trade liberalization and sustainable development is likely to remain a highly contentious issue in the twenty-first century.[23]

New Strategies and Methods

The 1990s saw major new efforts to "reinvent government" to make it more efficient and effective. The EPA has been a leader in this campaign (see chap. 8). Yet in most areas it is still charged with writing detailed regulations requiring individual polluters to install specific technologies to mitigate emissions or discharges at "the end of the pipe." Such "command and control" regulation of major pollution sources has had considerable success in improving environmental quality (see chap. 1) and will continue to be needed to protect public health and environmental resources from many immediate threats. But a broad consensus has developed among economists, business leaders, government officials, and environmental professionals that more efficient and cost-effective methods are necessary if we are to address the expanding environmental agenda of the next century. The following section lists seven areas in which new policy approaches are receiving wide attention.

Pollution Prevention

Perhaps no idea has received more widespread general support than the wisdom of preventing pollution before it occurs rather than trying to clean it up later. Prevention or "source reduction" is often far less expensive for companies and eliminates potential liability. Moreover, it spares people from harmful exposure to wastes. It is the only way to halt deterioration of the environment in the long run.[24] Yet only a tiny fraction of the EPA's resources is devoted to *prevention*, while the remainder is directed to end-of-the-pipe cleanups. The reason is that most of the environmental statutes (see app. 1) require after-the-fact controls. They are based on the assumption that environmental problems can be managed without significant changes in existing production technologies and consumption patterns. This assumption can no longer be sustained in the face of continuing environmental degradation.

The Bush administration deserves credit for passage of the Pollution Prevention Act of 1990, which established prevention as an EPA priority for the first time and authorized cooperative programs with industry to install energy-efficient lighting and to encourage source reduction of toxic wastes. Hundreds of companies voluntarily participate in these programs mainly because pollution prevention reduces costs. Companies are also becoming more sensitive to their environmental image. These voluntary programs have been expanded and extended to new sectors by the Clinton administration, and some industries are now pursuing sustainable development practices that augur well for the future (see chap. 12). Pollution prevention will have to be integrated more explicitly into all of our regulatory statutes in the future. In the meantime, all of the other strategies discussed below can also contribute to prevention.

Risk Assessment

Virtually all environmental regulation is now based on some form of scientific risk assessment (see chap. 10). Moreover, "regulatory reform" legislation introduced in the 104th and 105th Congresses would have required extensive additional risk analysis to justify any new regulation (see chap. 6). Although some of these bills were clearly designed to paralyze the regulatory process, there is a strong logical case for using risk assessment as one of several important tools for deciding what and how much to regulate.[25] Comparative risk assessment can be especially useful in setting priorities for action by the EPA and other agencies in order to concentrate resources on the most pressing problems. The case for such an approach has been made by the EPA since 1987, and it became a major policy objective under William Reilly in the early 1990s (see chaps. 8 and 10). EPA still lacks statutory authority, however, to allocate its budget on the basis of comparative assessment of risk.[26]

More effective use of risk assessment will depend on improving methodologies for measuring risk in the future. As Richard Andrews notes in chapter 10, present methods are subject to significant limitations, which have led to uncertainty about the actual risks posed and thus about the need for corrective action. The uncertainty fuels controversy over the use of these methods to set public policy, for example, over the health effects of extremely small particulates in the air or allowable concentrations of chemicals in drinking water.

Another major challenge is the need to reconcile public and expert perceptions of risks. The two are often sharply at odds. In some cases the public is more concerned about environmental and health risks (for example, from hazardous wastes and oil spills) than are the experts. In other cases (such as indoor air pollution, drinking-water quality, and loss of biological diversity), the experts are more worried than is the public. Without greater public involvement in risk assessment processes it is unlikely that they will become more legitimate and effective tools for policymaking.[27] Rather than mandating specific risk assessment methodologies or requiring unrealistic levels of scientific certainty before any regulation can be undertaken, Congress should give EPA greater flexibility to experiment with a variety of risk analysis techniques, including more participatory processes that can help to build consensus between experts and citizens.

Environmental Taxes, Incentives, and Markets

Economists have long espoused the concept of internalizing environmental costs by taxation or other means of pricing "externalities." As A. Myrick Freeman points out in chapter 9, use of such devices as environmental taxes or fees and tradable pollution allowances can often achieve environmental goals more efficiently than command-and-control regulation. In an era of scarce public resources, it makes sense to maximize environmental quality benefits from pollution control expenditures. The idea of using market incentives to encourage behaviors that prevent pollution and conserve resources now has broad support among environmentalists as well as in the business community.[28] Indeed, many believe that if environmental damage were fully accounted for (through "full cost pricing") the level of environmental protection would be much higher than it is at present.

Energy taxes have been among the most widely discussed market-oriented approaches, and the Btu tax proposed in 1993 by President Clinton was designed to motivate changes in both consumer preferences and industrial production. In the absence of higher fuel prices, energy will continue to be wasted as indicated by growing sales of vans, light trucks, and sport utility vehicles which get considerably lower gas mileage than do cars. Taxes or fees could be designed to discourage use of such gas guzzlers, to reduce use of toxic chemicals and virgin materials, and to discourage generation of solid and hazardous waste. Conversely, tax credits could be offered for a wide range of "green" business practices, and rebates could be given for the purchase of environmentally benign products. Other nations from Europe to China are experimenting with a variety of such taxes and incentives.[29]

Finally, government subsidies for environmentally destructive activities like harvesting timber on public lands and supplying cheap water to western farmers should be eliminated. Secretary of the Interior Bruce Babbitt announced sweeping plans in early 1993 to raise grazing, timber, mining, and water use fees to market levels, reversing a "century of practices that have promoted development of the West at government expense." Although these initiatives have thus far been stymied by western senators and representatives, there is mounting pressure from free-market conservatives and taxpayer groups as well as from environmental liberals to eliminate these forms of corporate welfare. A "Green Scissors" coalition representing such disparate interests has identified potential savings of $39 billion over the next ten to fifteen years.[30]

Devolution to States and Communities

States vary greatly in their commitment to environmental protection and in their capacity to effectively implement policies, and there is recent evidence that some states have become increasingly lax in enforcing federal policies.[31] Nevertheless, as Barry Rabe argues in chapter 2, the long-term trend in most states is toward improved regulatory capabilities, and in many cases states are now in the forefront of innovation. In this light the National Academy of Public Administration has proposed selective devolution of environmental protection functions to qualified states so that the EPA can concentrate its attention on problems of genuinely regional, national, and international significance. For example, the states could be given much greater authority to set cleanup requirements for local Superfund sites and drinking-water protection, while the EPA would maintain surveillance over transboundary problems such as air and water pollution. The agency could practice "differential oversight" in these areas as well, allowing states with good performance records in implementing federal pollution laws greater flexibility than that afforded states that have not met federal standards.[32]

EPA is experimenting with selective devolution to states through its National Environmental Performance Partnership program and could do much more to improve federal-state relations. Greater trust and cooperation between levels of government could do much to enhance the effectiveness of policymaking and implementation.[33] Individual companies and communities might also negotiate comprehensive compliance agreements with the EPA that allow them to develop their own methods for meeting pollution prevention and reduction goals. For example, under EPA's Project XL program, companies that exceed federal and state pollution standards are allowed greater freedom to devise their own control strategies (see chap. 8). Although it is too soon to judge the success of these innovative programs, more decentralized approaches will be necessary to encourage sustainable development at all levels in the future.[34]

Collaborative Planning

Within the federal-state structure, there are enormous opportunities for improving environmental performance through new collaborative planning and decisionmaking processes. Collaborative planning involves a search for voluntary, consensual solutions to environmental problems through joint participation by federal, state, and local agencies; business and industry; environmental groups; other interested nongovernmental organizations; and citizens. Such processes can be used to address a wide range of problems such as preservation of endangered species, wetlands, and other natural resources; development of area-wide pollution prevention strategies; and siting of facilities to promote social and racial justice. In some cases collaborative methods can also be used to negotiate regulations with industry as an alternative to adversarial rule-making processes.[35]

One increasingly popular form of collaborative planning is the development of habitat conservation plans that protect endangered species while permitting some development in surrounding areas.[36] As of 1998 there were several hundred of these agreements that had been completed or were being negotiated (see chap. 14). By intervening before an ecosystem becomes so degraded that few options are left, this approach facilitates carefully planned trade-offs between environmental protection and economic growth and thus supports the goal of sustainable development. However, care must be taken to ensure that such agreements are enforced and that they are flexible enough to permit revision if new scientific information demonstrates their inadequacy.[37]

Environmental Research and Technology Development

Increased support for environmental science and policy research is essential if we are to deal effectively with the growing list of domestic and global environmental problems demanding attention. More precise and systematic knowledge is needed in many areas of science if we are to set environmental priorities on the basis of relative risks and benefits. Although support for environmental research has recovered from its low point in the Reagan administration, it remains a small fraction of the $80 billion federal R&D budget. Total federal environmental research runs to about $5 billion a year, of which about 10 percent finds its way to the EPA.[38] The rest is divided among twenty other federal agencies, dispersing its effect.

Much more of the R&D carried out in the government's research laboratories could be redirected toward environmental and energy problems. In 1994 the Clinton administration proposed a "green industrial policy" to promote the development and adoption of environmental technologies. Among other actions, the administration hoped to assist in the commercialization of new products and help promote sales of green technologies overseas. Congress has been cool to the idea of governmental promotion of environmental technologies, believing such activities are best left to the private sector. Nevertheless, there is considerable potential for increasing governmental or joint public-private funding of basic and applied research in areas such as electricity generation without distorting market competition.[39] As was pointed out recently by a committee of the National Research Council of the National Academy of Sciences, it is imperative that we develop alternatives to automobile transportation if we are to mitigate climate change and achieve sustainability in this critical sector.[40]

Sustainability Indicators

The concept of sustainable development itself has many meanings, and requires much more discussion and research than it has had so far in the United States. One suggested working definition is "improving the quality of human life while living within the carrying capacity of supporting ecosystems."[41] Whatever our exact definition, however, we need to begin to formulate concrete indicators by which to measure progress toward sustainability in different sectors. This work requires that we develop not only better measures of environmental quality per se—that is, the health of ecosystems and the limits to the stresses we can place upon them—but also improved gauges of progress in human activity to reduce our impacts on natural systems. For example, we need to focus on trends in energy consumption, greenhouse gas emissions, land use, waste generation, recycling and reuse of materials, agricultural practices, and driving habits. But broad social and cultural factors such as income inequality, population growth, educational patterns, political representation, and access to information can also be considered important indicators of sustainability.[42] Many governmental and nongovernmental organizations are working on such indicators, including the EPA and other agencies of the federal government as well as state and local bodies.[43]

Our traditional measures of economic welfare need to be modified in this light. Standard national accounting indexes that measure gross national product (GNP) or gross domestic product (GDP) in monetary terms fail to capture many facets of human and environmental well-being. For example, they count all expenditures for pollution control and cleanup as part of the output of goods and services but do not subtract the economic value of losses caused by environmental degradation and depletion of nonrenewable resources.[44] Increased pollution thus counts positively rather than negatively, while depreciation of environmental capital is ignored. As Vice President Gore put it, "For all practical purposes, GNP treats the rapid and reckless destruction of the environment as a good thing!"[45]

A number of economists and international agencies, including the World Bank, have been developing alternative measures of welfare that more accurately value environmental goods and services and overall quality of life. The United States does considerably less well on some of these scales than on conventional economic indexes. The Commerce Department has begun to use "satellite accounts" for assessing the depletion of natural and environmental resources in order to develop more accurate measures of net domestic product. Until we begin to think differently about basic economic indicators, we are unlikely to make genuine progress toward sustainable development.

Rethinking Environmental Politics

Broadening the definition of environmental policy to include economic sustainability and social justice presents great challenges and opportunities for political action. The monumental scope of the ecological problems now recognized is mind-boggling and calls for action on nearly every front. Insofar as the fundamental problems are long term and global, they are likely to command an increasing share of intellectual and financial resources for decades to come. The concept of sustainable development touches every aspect of human life, from individual lifestyles and tastes to the corporate strategies of multinationals. We are still in the early stages of conceptualizing many of the implications, but they undoubtedly carry far beyond our preoccupations of the past three decades with national regulation of specific types of pollutants or preservation of individual species and landscapes.

Environmental policy itself thus has to be rethought in "ecological" terms; that is, reconsidered in relation to the larger social, economic, political, and moral systems within which it is embedded. To be successful, environmentalists will be challenged to develop new skills and broaden their understanding of other human values. As Robert Paehlke suggests in chapter 4, there is great potential for integrating and balancing the "three Es"— environment, economy, and ethics. But alliances with civil rights, social justice, and community development groups may require greater tolerance of differences and, in many cases, more flexibility and modesty in advocating particular solutions.[46] A willingness to try less intrusive, less centralized approaches such as market incentives, voluntary collaborations, and citizen participation in defining sustainable development goals at the community level might lead to superior results in the future. At the same time, we need to become much more aware of our responsibilities to the global ecological system.

Governing the Future

It has been said that for the first time in evolutionary history human beings have achieved a greater measure of influence over the future of their planet than evolution itself. If this is so, we have no alternative but to decide what kind of future we want. One possibility is to continue on our present course of human development. A growing world consensus holds, however, that this course cannot be sustained without triggering catastrophic changes in the Earth's natural systems. A 1992 report of the National Academy of Sciences and the Royal Society of London opened with a dire warning: "If current predictions of population growth prove accurate and patterns of human activity on the planet remain unchanged, science and technology may not be able to prevent either irreversible degradation of the environment or continued poverty for much of the world."[47] We do not know whether changes in the planetary life support system, such as deterioration of the atmospheric ozone layer, are irreversible. Yet most environmental experts believe we have time to preserve our essential life support systems if we act with sufficient foresight in the next few decades.

Doing so will demand far more international cooperation and "governance" than we now have.[48] The challenges we face are ultimately human and political: meeting basic human needs, limiting population growth, restricting consumption of nonrenewable resources, building a sense of world community, and negotiating mutually beneficial agreements among nations. These goals can be achieved only with a much longer time horizon than we are accustomed to in democratic societies. Political leadership is therefore essential. Democracies in the twentieth century have proved capable of sustaining national and international efforts to defeat enemies in war and to contain them for decades in peacetime. Sustainable development will be the challenge of the twenty-first century.

Notes

The chapter epigraph quotes the "Vision Statement" from the report of the President's Council on Sustainable Development, *Sustainable America: A New Consensus for Prosperity, Opportunity, and a Healthy Environment for the Future* (Washington, D.C.: GPO, 1996), iv; and Lester R. Brown, "The Acceleration of History," in *State of the World 1996*, ed. Lester Brown et al. (Washington, D.C.: Worldwatch Institute, 1996), 3.

1. World Commission on Environment and Development, *Our Common Future* (New York: Oxford University Press, 1987). See also Norman J. Vig and Regina S. Axelrod, eds., *The Global Environment: Institutions, Law, and Policy* (Washington, D.C.: CQ Press, 1999).

2. See Regina S. Axelrod and Norman J. Vig, "The European Union as an Environmental Governance System," in Vig and Axelrod, *Global Environment*, 72–97; and Susan Baker, Maria Kousis, Dick Richardson, and Stephen Young, *The Politics of Sustainable Development: Theory, Policy and Practice within the European Union* (London: Routledge, 1997).

3. *Choosing a Sustainable Future: The Report of the National Commission on the Environment* (Washington, D.C.: Island Press, 1993), xi.

4. President's Council on Sustainable Development, *Sustainable America*, 1. See also *Partnerships to Progress: The Report of the President's Commission on Environmental Quality* (Washington, D.C.: President's Commission on Environmental Quality, January 1993); and Business Council for Sustainable Development, Stephen Schmidheiney, chair, *Changing Course: A Global Business Perspective on Development and Environment* (Cambridge, Mass.: MIT Press, 1992).

5. Robert L. Paarlberg, "Lapsed Leadership: U.S. International Environmental Policy Since Río," in Vig and Axelrod, *Global Environment*, 236–255.

6. National Academy of Public Administration, *Setting Priorities, Getting Results: A New Direction for EPA* (Washington, D.C.: NAPA, 1995); and NAPA, "Resolving the Paradox of Environmental Protection: An Agenda for EPA, Congress, and the States" (Washington, D.C.: NAPA, September 1997).

7. "Climate Change: 1998 Was Warmest Year on Record," *Greenwire*, January 12, 1999. According to this report, "The global mean temperature in 1998 was 58.1 degrees Fahrenheit, 1.2 degrees above the long-term average value of 56.9. This was the 20th consecutive year with a global mean temperature exceeding the long-term average."

8. Herman E. Ott, "The Kyoto Protocol: Unfinished Business," *Environment* 40 (July/August 1998): 16–20ff.; Margaret Kriz, "After Argentina," *National Journal*, December 5, 1998, 2848–2853.

9. John H. Cushman, Jr., "Clinton Seeks Tax Credits for Fuel Savings," *New York Times*, January 31, 1998, A11; and Allan Freedman, "Clinton's Global Warming Plan Meets Wall of Opposition," *Congressional Quarterly Weekly Report*, February 7, 1998, 320.

10. William K. Stevens, "One in Every 8 Plant Species Is Imperiled, a Survey Finds," *New York Times*, April 9, 1998.

11. Andrew Pollack, "U.S. Sidetracks Pact to Control Gene Splicing," *New York Times* [New York edition], February 25, 1999, 1, C4.

12. Margaret Kriz, "Aiming for the Green," *National Journal*, October 4, 1997, 1958–1960; Michael J. Bean, "Endangered Species, Endangered Act?" *Environment* 41 (January/February 1999): 12–18ff.; "Saving the Salmon," *Time*, March 29, 1999, 60–61.

13. *CQ Weekly* staff, "Congress Compiles a Modest Record in a Session Sidetracked by Scandal: Legislative Summary and Appropriations," *CQ Weekly*, November 14, 1998, 3086–3087. See also Margaret Kriz, "Fish and Fowl," *National Journal*, February 28, 1998, 450–453.

14. Chuck McCutcheon, "Can Richardson End the Nuclear Waste Wars?" *CQ Weekly*, October 17, 1998, 2807–2810; and Jonathan Weisman, "Waste Site Bill Passes Senate, Remains Vulnerable to Veto," *Congressional Quarterly Weekly Report*, April 19, 1997, 902–903. See also James Flynn et al., *One Hundred Centuries of Solitude: Redirecting America's High-Level Nuclear Waste Policy* (Boulder, Colo.: Westview, 1995).

15. Milton Russell, E. William Colglazier, and Bruce E. Tonn, "The U.S. Hazardous Waste Legacy," *Environment* 34 (July/August 1992): 12–14, 34–39.

16. See, for example, Allan Freedman, "With Bipartisan Deal Elusive, Superfund Dies," *Congressional Quarterly Weekly Report*, July 20, 1996, 2044; Charles Pope, "Future of Superfund Overhaul Looks Anything But Bright," *Congressional Quarterly Weekly*, March 14, 1998, 661; and *CQ Weekly* staff, "Congress Compiles a Modest Record," 3107.

17. U.S. EPA, "People, Places, and Partnerships: A Progress Report on Community-Based Environmental Protection" (Washington, D.C.: EPA, Office of the Administrator, July 1997); and U.S. EPA, *EPA Strategic Plan* (Washington, D.C.: EPA, Office of the Chief Financial Officer, September 1997). See also Daniel A. Mazmanian and Michael E. Kraft, eds. *Toward Sustainable Communities: Transition and Transformations in Environmental Policy* (Cambridge, Mass.: MIT Press, forthcoming 1999).

18. "Clinton-Gore Livability Agenda: Building Livable Communities for the 21st Century" (Washington, D.C.: The White House, Office of the Vice President, January 11, 1999); Charles Pope, "Suburban Sprawl and Government Turf," *CQ Weekly*, March 13,

1999, 586–590; and John H. Cushman, Jr., "Politicians of All Persuasions Rally Round Rival Bills to Protect Lands," *New York Times,* March 11, 1999, A19.

19. See Christopher H. Foreman, Jr., *The Promise and Peril of Environmental Justice* (Washington, D.C.: Brookings Institution, 1998).

20. Norman Myers, *Ultimate Security* (New York: Norton, 1993); and "Eco-Terrorism: Activists Step Up Actions Around the World," *Greenwire,* January 20, 1999.

21. *CQ Weekly* staff, "Congress Compiles a Modest Record," 3085–3086.

22. Daniel C. Esty, *Greening the GATT: Trade, Environment, and the Future* (Washington, D.C.: Institute for International Economics, 1994); and John J. Audley, *Green Politics and Global Trade: NAFTA and the Future of Environmental Politics* (Washington, D.C.: Georgetown University Press, 1997).

23. See also Daniel C. Esty, "Economic Integration and the Environment," in Vig and Axelrod, *Global Environment,* 190–209.

24. Joel S. Hirschhorn and Kirsten U. Oldenburg, *Prosperity without Pollution* (New York: Van Nostrand Reinhold, 1991); and Business Council for Sustainable Development, *Changing Course.*

25. Gary Bryner, "Congressional Decisions About Regulatory Reform: The 104th and 105th Congresses," in *Better Environmental Decisions: Strategies for Governments, Businesses, and Communities,* ed. Ken Sexton, Alfred A. Marcus, K. William Easter, and Timothy D. Burkhardt (Washington, D.C.: Island Press, 1999).

26. J. Clarence Davies, ed., *Comparing Environmental Risks: Tools for Setting Government Priorities* (Washington, D.C.: Resources for the Future, 1996); and NAPA, *Setting Priorities,* chap. 3.

27. Terry Davies, "Risk Assessment in Environmental Policy," *Center for Risk Management Newsletter,* Resources for the Future, winter 1998, 1–3.

28. See, for example, David Malin Roodman, "Harnessing the Market for the Environment," in *State of the World 1996,* ed. Brown et al., 168–187; and Robert Repetto, Roger C. Dower, Robin Jenkins, and Jacqueline Geoghegan, *Green Fees: How a Tax Shift Can Work for the Environment and the Economy* (Washington, D.C.: World Resources Institute, 1992).

29. Organisation for Economic Co-operation and Development, *Environmental Taxes in OECD Countries* (Paris: OECD, 1995); Timothy O'Riordan, *Ecotaxation* (London: Earthscan, 1997); and Robert A. Bohm, Chazhong Ge, Milton Russell, Jinnan Wang, and Jintian Yang, "Environmental Taxes: China's Bold Initiative," *Environment* 40 (September 1998): 10–13ff.

30. Jill Lancelot and Ralph De Gennaro, " 'Green Scissors' Snip $33 Billion," *New York Times,* January 31, 1995, A11.

31. John E. Cushman, Jr., "E.P.A. and States Found to be Lax on Pollution Law," *New York Times,* June 7, 1998, 1, 17.

32. NAPA, *Setting Priorities,* chap. 4.

33. Denise Scheberle, "Partners in Policymaking: Forging Effective Federal-State Relations," *Environment* 40 (December 1998): 14–20, 28–30.

34. President's Council on Sustainable Development, *Sustainable America,* chap. 4. See also DeWitt John, *Civic Environmentalism: Alternatives to Regulation in States and Communities* (Washington, D.C.: CQ Press, 1994); and Michael E. Kraft and Denise Scheberle, "Environmental Federalism at Decade's End: New Approaches and Strategies," *Publius: The Journal of Federalism* 28 (winter 1998): 131–146.

35. Edward P. Weber, "Successful Collaboration: Negotiating Effective Regulations," *Environment* 40 (November 1998): 10–15, 32–37; and Michael E. Kraft and Bruce N. Johnson, "Clean Water and the Promise of Collaborative Decision Making: The Case of the Fox-Wolf Basin in Wisconsin," in *Toward Sustainable Communities,* ed. Mazmanian and Kraft.

36. See Timothy Beatley, *Habitat Conservation Planning: Endangered Species and Urban Growth* (Austin: University of Texas Press, 1994); and Reed F. Noss and Allen Y.

Cooperrider, *Saving Nature's Legacy: Protecting and Restoring Biodiversity* (Washington, D.C.: Island Press, 1994).

37. See Fraser Shilling, "Do Habitat Conservation Plans Protect Endangered Species?" *Science,* June 13, 1997, 1662–1663; Jon R. Luoma, "Habitat Conservation Plans: Compromise or Capitulation?" *Audubon,* January/February 1998, 36–43; and Ted Williams, "The New Guardians," *Audubon,* January/February 1999, 34–39.

38. David Malakoff, "2000 Budget Plays Favorites," *Science,* February 5, 1999, 778–780. A useful Web site with links to information about federal environmental R&D is sponsored by the Committee for the National Institute for the Environment *(www. cnie.org/).*

39. See, for example, M. Granger Morgan and Susan F. Tierney, "Research Support for the Power Industry," *Issues in Science and Technology* 15 (fall 1998): 81–87.

40. Transportation Research Board and National Research Council, *Toward a Sustainable Future: Addressing the Long-Term Effects of Motor Vehicle Transportation on Climate and Ecology* (Washington, D.C.: National Academy Press, 1997). For a review of the report, see Malcolm Fergusson and Ian Skinner, "Greening Transportation," *Environment,* January/February 1999, 24–27.

41. World Conservation Union, *Caring For the Earth: A Strategy for Survival* (London: Mitchell Beasley, 1993), 211, as quoted in Alex Farrell and Maureen Hart, "What Does Sustainability Really Mean?" *Environment* 40 (November 1998): 4–9, 26–31. This article provides an excellent overview of the concept of sustainable development and efforts by various governments and organizations to develop sustainability indicators. See also Norman J. Vig, "Introduction: Governing the International Environment," in Vig and Axelrod, *Global Environment,* 5–10; and Lamont C. Hempel, "Conceptual and Analytical Challenges in Building Sustainable Communities," in Mazmanian and Kraft, *Toward Sustainable Communities.*

42. The United Nations Commission on Sustainable Development has identified 134 indicators of sustainability; see Farrell and Hart, "What Does Sustainability Really Mean?" 9.

43. Ibid.

44. See Robert Repetto, "Earth in the Balance Sheet: Incorporating Natural Resources in National Income Accounts," *Environment* 34 (September 1992): 12–20, 43–45; Herman E. Daly and John B. Cobb, Jr., *For the Common Good* (Boston: Beacon, 1989), 62–84; and Clifford Cobb, Ted Halstead, and Jonathan Rowe, "If the Economy Is Up, Why Is America Down?" *Atlantic Monthly,* October 1995, 59–78.

45. Al Gore, *Earth in the Balance: Ecology and the Human Spirit* (New York: Houghton Mifflin, 1992), 85.

46. See, for example, Martin Lewis, *Green Delusions: An Environmentalist Critique of Radical Environmentalism* (Durham, N.C.: Duke University Press, 1992); and Robert C. Paehlke, *Environmentalism and the Future of Progressive Politics* (New Haven, Conn.: Yale University Press, 1989).

47. Quoted in Lester Brown, "A New Era Unfolds," *State of the World 1993,* ed. Lester Brown et al. (New York: Norton, 1993), 3.

48. See Vig and Axelrod, *Global Environment.*

Appendix 1 Major Federal Laws on the Environment, 1969–1998

Legislation	Implementing Agency	Key Provisions
		Nixon Administration
National Environmental Policy Act of 1969, PL 91-190	All federal agencies	Declared a national policy to "encourage productive and enjoyable harmony between man and his environment"; required environmental impact statements; created Council on Environmental Quality.
Resources Recovery Act of 1970, PL 91-512	Health, Education and Welfare Department (later Environmental Protection Agency)	Set up a program of demonstration and construction grants for innovative solid waste management systems; provided technical and financial assistance to state and local agencies in developing resource recovery and waste disposal systems.
Clean Air Act Amendments of 1970, PL 91-604	Environmental Protection Agency (EPA)	Required administrator to set national primary and secondary air quality standards and certain emission limits; required states to develop implementation plans by specific dates; required reductions in automobile emissions.
Federal Water Pollution Control Act (Clean Water Act) Amendments of 1972, PL 92-500	EPA	Set national water quality goals; established pollutant discharge permit system; increased federal grants to states to construct waste treatment plants.
Federal Environmental Pesticides Control Act of 1972 (amended the Federal Insecticide, Fungicide, and Rodenticide Act of 1947 (FIFRA)), PL 92-516	EPA	Required registration of all pesticides in U.S. commerce; allowed administrator to cancel or suspend registration under specified circumstances.
Marine Protection Act of 1972, PL 92-532	EPA	Regulated dumping of waste materials into the oceans and coastal waters.

(Continued on next page)

Appendix 1 (*Continued*)

Legislation	Implementing Agency	Key Provisions
Coastal Zone Management Act of 1972, PL 92-583	Office of Coastal Zone Management, Commerce Department	Authorized federal grants to the states to develop coastal zone management plans under federal guidelines.
Endangered Species Act of 1973, PL 93-205	Fish and Wildlife Service, Interior Department	Broadened federal authority to protect all "threatened" as well as "endangered" species; authorized grant program to assist state programs; required coordination among all federal agencies.
Ford Administration		
Safe Drinking Water Act of 1974, PL 93-523	EPA	Authorized federal government to set standards to safeguard the quality of public drinking water supplies and to regulate state programs for protecting underground water sources.
Toxic Substances Control Act of 1976, PL 94-469	EPA	Authorized premarket testing of chemical substances; allowed EPA to ban or regulate the manufacture, sale, or use of any chemical presenting an "unreasonable risk of injury to health or environment"; prohibited most uses of polychlorinated biphenyl (PCBs).
Federal Land Policy and Management Act of 1976, PL 94-579	Bureau of Land Management, Interior Department	Gave Bureau of Land Management authority to manage public lands for long-term benefits; officially ended policy of conveying public lands into private ownership.
Resource Conservation and Recovery Act of 1976, PL 94-580	EPA	Required EPA to set regulations for hazardous waste treatment, storage, transportation, and disposal; provided assistance for state hazardous waste programs under federal guidelines.
National Forest Management Act of 1976, PL 94-588	U.S. Forest Service, Agriculture Department	Gave statutory permanence to national forest lands and set new standards for their management; restricted timber harvesting to protect soil and watersheds; limited clearcutting.

Carter Administration

Law	Agency	Description
Surface Mining Control and Reclamation Act of 1977, PL 95-87	Interior Department	Established environmental controls over strip mining; limited mining on farmland, alluvial valleys, and slopes; required restoration of land to original contours.
Clean Air Act Amendments of 1977, PL 95-95	EPA	Amended and extended Clean Air Act; postponed deadlines for compliance with auto emission and air quality standards; set new standards for "prevention of significant deterioration" in clean air areas.
Clean Water Act Amendments of 1977, PL 95-217	EPA	Extended deadlines for industry and cities to meet treatment standards; set national standards for industrial pretreatment of wastes; increased funding for sewage treatment construction grants and gave states flexibility in determining priorities.
Public Utility Regulatory Policies Act of 1978, PL 95-617	Energy Department, states	Provided for Energy Department and Federal Energy Regulatory Commission regulation of electric and natural gas utilities and crude oil transportation systems in order to promote energy conservation and efficiency; allowed small cogeneration and renewable energy projects to sell power to utilities.
Alaska National Interest Lands Conservation Act of 1980, PL 96-487	Interior Department, Agriculture Department	Protected 102 million acres of Alaskan land as national wilderness, wildlife refuges, and parks.
Comprehensive Environmental Response, Compensation, and Liability Act of 1980 (CERCLA), PL 96-510	EPA	Authorized federal government to respond to hazardous waste emergencies and to clean up chemical dump sites; created $1.6 billion "Superfund"; established liability for cleanup costs.

Reagan Administration

Law	Agency	Description
Nuclear Waste Policy Act of 1982, PL 97-425; Nuclear Waste Policy Amendments Act of 1987, PL 100-203	Energy Department	Established a national plan for the permanent disposal of high-level nuclear waste; authorized the Energy Department to site, obtain a license for, construct, and operate geologic repositories for spent fuel from commercial nuclear power plants. Amendments in 1987 specified Yucca Mountain, Nevada, as the sole national site to be studied.

(Continued on next page)

Appendix 1 (*Continued*)

Legislation	Implementing Agency	Key Provisions
Resource Conservation and Recovery Act Amendments of 1984, PL 98-616	EPA	Revised and strengthened EPA procedures for regulating hazardous waste facilities; authorized grants to states for solid and hazardous waste management; prohibited land disposal of certain hazardous liquid wastes; required states to consider recycling in comprehensive solid waste plans.
Food Security Act of Agriculture 1985 (the Farm Bill), PL 99-198. Renewed in 1990 and 1996, the latter as PL 104-127.	Agriculture Department	Limited federal program benefits for producers of commodities on highly erodible land or converted wetlands; established a conservation reserve program; authorized Agriculture Department technical assistance for subsurface water quality preservation; revised and extended the Soil and Water Conservation Act (1977) programs through the year 2008. The 1996 renewal of the farm bill authorized $56 billion over seven years for a variety of farm and forestry programs. These included an Environmental Quality Incentives Program to provide assistance and incentive payments to farmers, especially those facing serious threats to soil, water, grazing lands, wetlands, and wildlife habitat.
Safe Drinking Water Act of 1986, PL 99-339	EPA	Reauthorized the Safe Drinking Water Act of 1974; revised EPA safe drinking water programs, including grants to states for drinking water standards enforcement and groundwater protection programs; accelerated EPA schedule for setting standards for maximum contaminant levels of eighty-three toxic pollutants.
Superfund Amendments and Reauthorization Act of 1986 (SARA), PL 99-499	EPA	Provided $8.5 billion through 1991 to clean up the nation's most dangerous abandoned chemical waste dumps; set strict standards and timetables for cleaning up such sites; required that industry provide local communities with information on hazardous chemicals used or emitted.
Clean Water Act Amendments of 1987, PL 100-4	EPA	Amended the Federal Water Pollution Control Act of 1972; extended and revised EPA water pollution control programs, including grants to states for construction of wastewater treatment facilities and implementation of mandated nonpoint-source pollution management plans; expanded EPA enforcement authority; established a national estuary program.

Global Climate Protection Act of 1987, PL 100-204	State Department	Authorized the State Department to develop an approach to the problems of global climate change; created an intergovernmental task force to develop U.S. strategy for dealing with the threat posed by global warming.
Ocean Dumping Act of 1988, PL 100-688	EPA	Amended the Marine Protection, Research, and Sanctuaries Act of 1972 to end all ocean disposal of sewage sludge and industrial waste by December 31, 1991; revised EPA regulation of ocean dumping by establishing dumping fees, permit requirements, and civil penalties for violations.

Bush Administration

Oil Pollution Act of 1990, PL 101-380	Transportation Department, Commerce Department	Sharply increased liability limits for oil spill cleanup costs and damages; required double hulls on oil tankers and barges by 2015; required federal government to direct cleanups of major spills; mandated increased contingency planning and preparedness for spills; preserved states' rights to adopt more stringent liability laws and to create state oil spill compensation funds.
Pollution Prevention Act of 1990, PL 101-508	EPA	Established Office of Pollution Prevention in EPA to coordinate agency efforts at source reduction; created voluntary program to improve lighting efficiency; stated waste minimization was to be primary means of hazardous waste management; to promote voluntary industry reduction of hazardous waste, mandated source reduction and recycling report to accompany annual toxics release inventory under SARA (see above).
Clean Air Act Amendments of 1990, PL 101-549	EPA	Amended the Clean Air Act of 1970 by setting new requirements and deadlines of three to twenty years for major urban areas to meet federal clean air standards; imposed new, stricter emissions standards for motor vehicles and mandated cleaner fuels; required reduction in emission of sulfur dioxide and nitrogen oxides by power plants to limit acid deposition and created a market system of emission allowances; required regulation to set emission limits for all major sources of toxic or hazardous air pollutants and listed 189 chemicals to be regulated; prohibited the use of chlorofluorocarbons (CFCs) by the year 2000 and set phaseout of other ozone-depleting chemicals.

(Continued on next page)

Legislation	Implementing Agency	Key Provisions
Intermodal Surface Transportation Efficiency Act of 1991 (ISTEA, also called the Highway Bill), PL 102-240	Transportation Department	Authorized $151 billion over six years for transportation, including $31 billion for mass transit; required statewide and metropolitan long-term transportation planning; authorized states and communities to use transportation funds for public transit that reduces air pollution and energy use consistent with Clean Air Act of 1990; required community planners to analyze land use and energy implications of transportation projects they review.
Energy Policy Act of 1992, PL 102-486	Energy Department	Comprehensive energy act designed to reduce U.S. dependency on imported oil. Mandated restructuring of the electric utility industry to promote competition; encouraged energy conservation and efficiency; promoted renewable energy and alternative fuels for cars; eased licensing requirements for nuclear power plants; authorized extensive energy research and development.
The Omnibus Water Act of 1992, PL 102-575	Interior Department	Authorized completion of major water projects in the West; revised the Central Valley Project in California to allow transfer of water rights to urban areas and to encourage conservation through a tiered pricing system that allocates water more flexibly and efficency; mandated extensive wildlife and environmental protection, mitigation, and restoration programs.

Clinton Administration

Food Quality Protection Act of 1996, PL 104-170	EPA	A major revision of FIFRA. Adopted a new approach to regulating pesticides used on food, fiber, and other crops by requiring EPA to consider the diversity of ways in which both children and adults are exposed to such chemicals; created a uniform "reasonable risk" health standard for both raw and processed foods that replaced the 1958 Delaney Clause of the Food, Drug, and Cosmetic Act, which barred the sale of processed food containing even trace amounts of chemicals found to cause cancer; required EPA to take extra steps to protect children by establishing an additional tenfold margin of safety in setting acceptable risk standards.

| Safe Drinking Water Act Amendments of 1996, PL 104-182 | EPA | Granted local water systems greater flexibility to focus on the most serious public health risks; authorized $7.6 billion through 2003 for state-administered loan and grant funds to help localities with the cost of compliance; created a "right-to-know" provision requiring large water systems to provide their customers with annual reports on the safety of local water supplies, including information on contaminants found in drinking water and their health effects; made small water systems eligible for waivers from costly regulations. |
| Transportation Equity Act for the 21st Century (also called ISTEA II or TEA 21), PL 105-178 | Transportation Department | Sweeping transportation measure. Authorized a six-year, $218 billion program that increased by 40 percent spending to improve the nation's highways and mass transit systems; provided $41 billion for mass transit programs, with over $29 billion coming from the Highway Trust Fund; allocated $592 million for R&D on new highway technologies, including transportation-related environmental research; provided $148 million for a scenic byways program, $270 million for building and maintaining trails, and continued support for improvement of bicycle paths. |

Note: Like the 104th Congress (1995–1996), the 105th Congress (1997–1998) was unable to reach agreement on reauthorization of most major environmental laws, and the responsibility for forging a consensus will fall to the 106th Congress. Laws to be reauthorized include the Clean Water Act, CERCLA (Superfund), and the Endangered Species Act. Readers who would like an update on these developments should consult *CQ Weekly*, other professional news sources, or Congressional Quarterly's annual *Almanac*, which offers summaries of key legislation enacted by Congress, along with descriptions of the major issues and leading policy actors.

Appendix 2   Federal Spending on Natural Resources and the Environment, Selected Fiscal Years, 1980–1998 (in billions of dollars)

Budget item	1980	1984	1988	1992	1996	1998
Water resources	4.085 (7.611)	3.781 (5.598)	4.295 (5.608)	4.768 (5.359)	4.254 (4.339)	5.127 (5.026)
Conservation and land management	1.302 (2.426)	1.389 (2.056)	2.650 (3.460)	4.652 (5.229)	5.377 (5.484)	5.516 (5.408)
Recreational resources	1.642 (3.059)	1.453 (2.151)	1.647 (2.150)	2.690 (3.024)	2.851 (2.908)	3.857 (3.781)
Pollution control and abatement	4.672 (8.705)	4.037 (5.977)	4.932 (6.439)	6.605 (7.424)	6.430 (6.558)	7.197 (7.056)
Other natural resources	1.395 (2.599)	1.622 (2.401)	1.852 (2.418)	2.575 (2.894)	2.698 (2.752)	2.779 (2.725)
Total	13.096 (24.401)	12.282 (18.184)	15.376 (20.075)	21.290 (23.930)	21.610 (22.039)	24.476 (23.996)

Sources: Office of Management and Budget, *Historical Tables, Budget of the United States Government, Fiscal Year 1999* (Washington, D.C.: GPO, 1998); *Analytical Perspectives, Budget of the United States Government, Fiscal Year 1999* (Washington, D.C.: GPO, 1998); and *Budget of the United States Government, Fiscal Year 2000* (Washington, D.C.: GPO, 1999).

Note: The upper figure represents budget authority in nominal dollars. Actual budget outlays differ only slightly from these amounts. Figures for 1980 are provided to indicate pre-Reagan administration spending bases. The lower figure in parentheses represents budget authority in constant 1997 dollars. Figures for 1998 are deflated using an estimate of 2.0 percent. Other amounts are adjusted to 1997 dollars using the GDP implicit price deflators as calculated by the Bureau of Economic Analysis, Department of Commerce, and reported in the February 1998 *Economic Report of the President* (Washington, D.C.: GPO, 1998).

Appendix 3   Budgets of Selected Environmental and Natural Resource Agencies, 1975–1999 (in billions of dollars)

Agency	1975	1980	1985	1990	1995	1998
Environmental Protection Agency operating budget[b]	0.850 (2.270)	1.269 (2.364)	1.340 (1.918)	1.901 (2.283)	2.471 (2.577)	2.324 (2.278)
Interior Department total budget	3.818 (10.196)	4.678 (8.716)	5.016 (7.179)	6.690 (8.034)	7.542 (7.867)	8.198 (8.037)
Selected Agencies:						
Bureau of Land Management	0.400 (1.068)	0.919 (1.712)	0.800 (1.144)	1.226 (1.473)	1.180 (1.231)	1.257 (1.232)
Fish and Wildlife Service	0.207 (0.553)	0.435 (0.811)	0.586 (0.838)	1.133 (1.360)	1.278 (1.333)	1.366 (1.339)
National Park Service	0.416 (1.110)	0.531 (0.990)	1.005 (1.439)	1.275 (1.530)	1.453 (1.516)	1.891 (1.854)
Office of Surface Mining	NA	0.180 (0.334)	0.377 (0.540)	0.295 (0.354)	0.293 (0.306)	0.306 (0.300)
Forest Service	0.956 (2.552)	2.250 (4.192)	2.116 (3.029)	3.473 (4.171)	3.613 (3.769)	3.369 (3.303)
Army Corps of Engineers (civilian)	1.449 (3.869)	3.234 (6.025)	2.883 (4.126)	3.164 (3.800)	3.344 (3.488)	4.215 (4.132)

Sources: Office of Management and Budget, *Budget of the United States Government,* fiscal years 1977, 1982, 1987, 1992, 1997, 1998, 1999, 2000 (Washington, D.C.: U.S. GPO, 1976, 1981, 1986, 1991, 1996, 1997, 1998, 1999).

Note: The upper figure represents budget authority in nominal dollars. Actual budget outlays differ only slightly from these amounts. The lower figure in parentheses represents budget authority in constant 1997 dollars. The figure for 1998 is deflated using an estimate of 2.0 percent. Other amounts are adjusted to 1997 dollars using the GDP implicit price deflators as calculated by the Bureau of Economic Analysis, Department of Commerce, and reported in the February 1998 *Economic Report of the President* (Washington, D.C.: GPO, 1998).

[a] The EPA operating budget (which supplies funds for most of the agency's research, regulation, and enforcement programs) is the most meaningful figure. The other two major elements of the total EPA budget historically have been sewage treatment construction or water infrastructure grants (now called state and tribal assistance grants) and Superfund allocations, both of which are excluded from this table. The operating budget is defined here as the remaining amount. Readers should be advised that the EPA and the White House define the agency's operating budget differently. They do not exclude all of these amounts, and thus arrive at a higher figure. The president's FY 1999 budget reports an EPA operating budget of $3.6 billion. For background, the water infrastructure or state and tribal assistance grant authority (not adjusted for inflation) totaled $7.7 billion in 1975, $3.4 billion in 1980, $2.4 billion in 1985, $1.9 billion in 1990, and $1.9 billion in 1995. Spending for 1998 was $3.2 billion. Superfund authority in 1985 (there was no program in 1975 and 1980) was $0.61 billion, $1.5 billion in 1990, and $1.4 billion in 1995. Spending for Superfund was about $1.5 billion in 1998. The total EPA budget authority was about $7.0 billion for FY 1998. For consistency, all figures in the table are taken from the president's budgets for the respective years.

Appendix 4   Employees in Selected Federal Agencies and Departments, 1980, 1990, 1998[a]

Agency/department	1980	1990	1998 (Est.)
Environmental Protection Agency	12,891	16,513	17,862
Excluding Superfund-related employees[b]	NA	13,185	14,571
Bureau of Land Management	9,655	8,753	9,933
Fish and Wildlife Service	7,672	7,124	6,771
National Park Service	13,934	17,781	18,382
Office of Surface Mining	1,014	1,145	654
Forest Service	40,606	40,991	34,595
Army Corps of Engineers (civil functions)	32,757	28,272	24,832
U.S. Geological Survey	14,416	10,451	6,781
Soil Conservation Service (renamed Natural Resources Conservation Service)	15,856	15,482	10,319

Source: U.S. Senate Committee on Governmental Affairs, "Organization of Federal Executive Departments and Agencies," January 1, 1980, and January 1, 1990; and Office of Management and Budget, *Budget of the United States Government,* fiscal years 1982, 1992, and 1999 (Washington, D.C.: GPO, 1981, 1991, 1998).

[a] Personnel totals represent full-time equivalent employment, reflecting both permanent and temporary employees. Data for 1998 are estimates based on the FY 1999 proposed budget submitted to Congress by the Clinton administration in early 1998. Because of organizational changes within departments and agencies, the data presented here are not necessarily an accurate record of agency personnel growth or decline over time. The information is presented chiefly to provide an indicator of approximate agency size during different time periods.

[b] The Superfund program was created only in late 1980.

Index

Abelson, Philip, 222–223
Abortion, 91, 326, 331–332, 333
Acid rain, 14, 44–45, 106, 128
Adams, John H., 121
AEA. *See* American Electronics Association
Africa, 85, 326, 329, 330, 334, 335, 338. *See also* Developing nations; Tropical forests; *individual countries*
African Americans. *See* Environmental injustice; Racial and minority issues
Agenda 21, 344–345
Agency for Toxic Substances and Disease Registry, 243
Agenda setting, 8, 11–12, 99, 100. *See also* Public policy
Agriculture
  developing countries, 366
  genetically altered crops, 374
  livestock runoff issues, 41
  price supports, 207
  production, 334–335
  standards, 366
  subsidies, 337
  use of chemicals and fertilizers, 89, 92, 93, 205–206, 241, 336
  world agricultural crisis, 334
Ahuja, Gautam, 260
Air quality. *See also* Pollution and pollution control
  arsenic, 199
  asbestos, 154
  benzene, 156–157, 199
  cost-benefit analysis and cost-effectiveness, 194, 198
  cotton dust, 156–157
  EPA accomplishments, 171
  interstate issues, 44–45
  minority areas, 241
  monitoring and data, 20–21
  regulations, 20
  state programs, 42
Air Quality Management District (Los Angeles, Calif.), 202
Alabama, 41
Alaska, 12, 308
Alaska Lands Act (1980), 309
Alliance for Reasonable Regulation, 142n25
American Electronics Association (AEA), 274
American Forest and Paper Association, 275
American Industrial Health Council, 231n32
American Petroleum Institute, 156
Ames, Bruce, 222
Amsterdam (Netherlands), 88
Anderson, Robert, 66
Anderton, Douglas, 239
Angola, 329. *See also* Africa
Animal rights, 80
Antienvironmentalism. *See* Environmental issues
Antiquities Act (1906), 115
Appropriations process, 58–59, 124, 127, 132–135, 312
Arctic National Wildlife Refuge, 112, 308, 309
Argentina, 293
Arizona, 49, 314
Armey, Dick, 125
Army Corps of Engineers, U.S.
  budget issues, 19
  New Jersey wetlands action, 155

Refuse Act of 1899, 11
  structural policy approach, 310
  waterways management, 305
Arnold, Ron, 59
Arrhenius, Svante, 286
ASARCO Inc., 311
Asbestos, 154, 211
Asia, 330, 333–334, 335, 338, 339. *See also* Developing nations; Tropical forests; *individual countries*
Australia, 357
Automation, 89
Automobiles and automobile industry. *See also* Transportation
  corporate average fuel economy, 108
  environmental issues, 88, 89, 296
  gasoline taxes, 298–299
  off-road vehicles, 60
  reformulated gasoline, 356–357
  sport utility vehicles, 58, 296, 381
  subsidies, 297
  taxation, 381
  trade issues, 354–355

Babbitt, Bruce, 303, 319
  appointment of, 15
  biological resources survey, 23–24, 316
  Congress and, 61
  fees for grazing, timber, 110, 381
  National Biological Service, 374
  public opinion and, 112
  reform agenda, 109, 311
Banff National Park (Canada), 318, 321. *See also* Canada
Bangladesh, 335–336. *See also* Asia
Barrett, Robin, 66
Basel convention on hazardous wastes, 361
Baton Rouge (La.), 239. *See also* Louisiana
Bazelon, David, 147, 151
Beatley, Timothy, 319
Been, Vicki, 239
Benzene, 156–157
Berlin Mandate, 291, 292
Better America Bonds program, 113
Beverage containers, 38
BIA. *See* Bureau of Indian Affairs
Biodiversity, 23, 153, 315, 316, 374–375
Biodiversity treaty, 107, 110, 345
Blackmun, Harry, 160–161
Bliley, Thomas J., Jr., 98, 121
BLM. *See* Bureau of Land Management
Boehlert, Sherwood, 133, 142n20
Borden Chemicals and Plastics, 249
Boskin, Michael, 105, 106, 107
Boster, James, 83
Botswana, 85. *See also* Africa
Bowman, Karlyn, 57
Bramwell, Anna, 66
Brazil, 339, 356, 357. *See also* South America
Brennan, William, 157
Breyer, Stephen, 159, 160
Broeker, Wallace, 286–287
Bromley, D. Allan, 105, 106
Brown, Jerry, 108
Brown, Lester R., 333, 370

as court participants, 154, 156
decentralization, 32
environmental injustice, 247
environmental problems, 207, 216
environmental responsibilities, 4, 7, 10–11, 27, 50, 101, 151
Exxon *Valdez*, 152–153
resource management, 304–312
role of Congress, 100
shutdowns and gridlock, 135
strategies for environmental protection, 2
suits against, 148–150
support of state governments, 33, 42–43, 48
waste disposal, 45–46, 152
Government, state and local. *See also individual states*
air quality programs, 42
budget and spending issues, 26, 33, 41, 42, 43, 48
changes in, 33
conventional view of, 32
devolution to, 381–382
environmental issues, 2, 31*n*55, 44, 175–176, 249–250, 376
as EPA constituency, 168, 176, 183, 224
federal dependency, 33, 42–43, 48, 161
federal government agencies and, 149
federal regulatory standards, 41
inter- and intrastate issues, 40, 43, 44–46
National Environmental Performance Partnership System, 179–180
natural resource policies, 307, 314
as "new heroes" of American federalism, 33–36
Performance Partnership Grants, 180
permitting, 36, 318
pollution fees, 202
Project XL, 178
property rights laws, 49, 150, 157
ranking, activity and innovation, 35, 40
regulatory burdens, 223
role in environmental protection, 32, 33–34, 40–42, 48
rulemaking, 263
Safe Drinking Water Act Amendments, 137
Source Reduction Clearinghouse, 263
in the Southeast, 41
state support of local governments, 36
Superfund projects, 376
unfunded mandates, 132
water quality programs, 41
wetlands, 375
Grand Staircase–Escalante National Monument, 115
Grants, 42–43, 48, 180
Grassroots Environmental Effectiveness Network, 62
Grassroots environmental groups. *See* Interest groups
Gray, C. Boyden, 107
Great Lakes, 21, 43, 45
Greenhouse warming. *See* Climate
Greening. *See* Business and industry
Green Lights initiative, 267
Greenmoney Journal, 269
Green Party, 66–67
Greenpeace, 63, 71, 72, 235, 236, 263, 291, 358
Greenpeace International, 71
Gridlock, 122, 123–126, 127–130
Gulf of Mexico, 43

Habitat, 38, 93, 114. *See also* Endangered species
Habitat Conservation Plans (HCPs), 319
Hahn, Janice, 66
Hamilton, James, 246
Hansen, James, 287
Hardin, Garrett, 327–328
Harrison, Paul, 343
Hart, Stuart, 260, 261–262

Hartley, Jennifer, 83
Hastert, J. Dennis, 139
Hatch, Orrin, 161
Hays, Samuel, 9, 77
HCPs. *See* Habitat Conservation Plans
Headwaters Forest (Calif.), 114
Health issues
carcinogens, 214, 222, 226, 242
Clinton (Bill) administration reforms, 109–110, 114
as a core environmental value, 81–82
cost-benefit analysis and cost-effectiveness, 82, 86, 199, 214
cotton dust, 157
diet, 334, 336
drinking water contamination, 41
effects of environmental pollutants, 242–243
environmental politics and, 211
fine particles, 194
immunizations, 330, 344
minority and ethnic issues, 243, 253
OSHA regulations, 156–157
pesticides, 241
population, 329–330
right to know provisions, 226
risk assessment and management, 214, 216–217, 218, 219, 222–223
U.S. disease data collection, 237–238
Helvarg, David, 62
Herbicides. *See* Pesticides and herbicides
Heritage Foundation, 18, 129
Houston (Texas), 245. *See also* Texas
HR 9, 131–132

Idaho, 37, 318
Idea of Wilderness, The (Oelschlaeger), 80
IISD. *See* International Institute for Sustainable Development
Illinois, 45. *See also* Chicago
Impact statements, 25, 103. *See also* Environmental impact statements
Incentives. *See* Economic issues
India, 85, 327, 330–331, 333–334, 335, 357. *See also* Asia
Indiana, 45
Indonesia, 333–334, 335, 337, 339. *See also* Asia
Industry. *See* Business and industry
Inference guidelines, 215–216
INFORM, 263
Inglehart, Ronald, 78
Initiative and referendum, 33, 34–35, 62–63
Innovations in American Government Award Program, 267
Insurance issues, 152
Intel Corporation, 178, 179
Interagency Pollution Prevention Advisory Team (MN), 36
Interest groups. *See also* Environmental movement
advocacy explosion, 125
budget issues, 68, 69*t*
business groups, 60, 125, 150, 276, 290
coalitions, 61, 62, 129
confrontational tactics, 308–309
courts and, 148–150, 154, 158–160
election spending, 138
environmental issues, 2, 59, 62, 127, 234–237, 371–372
as EPA constituency, 168, 183
global activism, 72–73, 290–291
grass roots, 62–65, 319–320
issues, 63, 73–74
"Lite Greens," 58
litigation, 148, 159
lobbies and lobbying, 62–63, 68–73, 311